Social Media Marketing & SEO Mastery

7 Book In 1

Facebook, Instagram, WhatsApp, YouTube, Tik Tok Marketing Strategy & Blogging for Beginners

By: **Blake Preston & Brian Scott Fitzgerald**

Published By: **Fitzgerald Publishing Group**

© **Copyright Fitzgerald Published Group 2023 - All rights reserved.**

The content contained within this book may not be reproduced, duplicated, or transmitted without direct written permission from the author or the publisher.

Under no circumstances will any blame or legal responsibility be held against the publisher or author for any damages, reparation, or monetary loss due to the information contained within this book. Either directly or indirectly. You are responsible for your own choices, actions, and results.

Legal Notice:

This book is copyright protected, and this book is only for personal use. You cannot amend, distribute, sell, use, quote, or paraphrase any part of this book's content without the author's or publisher's consent.

Disclaimer Notice:

Please note that the information contained within this document is for educational and entertainment purposes only. All effort has been executed to present accurate, up-to-date, and reliable, complete information. No warranties of any kind are declared or implied. Readers acknowledge that the author does not render legal, financial, medical, or professional advice. The content within this book has been derived from various sources. Please consult a licensed professional before attempting any techniques outlined in this book.

By reading this document, the reader agrees that under no circumstances is the author responsible for any losses, direct or indirect, which are incurred as a result of the use of the information contained within this document, including, but not limited to, — errors, omissions, or inaccuracies.

How to Make Money: THE SERIES

I created a series of 20 (twenty) books on How to Make Money.

Feel free to read any of my books in the series, which can be found on my Author page on Amazon at:

You can visit this link or Scan this QR code to get access

https://www.amazon.com/author/brianscottfitzgerald.

Content

Your Free Gift 1

Book # 1: Social Media Marketing for Beginners 3

    Introduction 4

    Chapter 1: Social Media Marketing – An Overview 10

    Chapter 2: Reasons Why Social Media Marketing is Essential 14

    Chapter 3: Manage Social Media Marketing Campaigns Depending on Your Online Business 22

    Chapter 4: The Classic Way to Do Social Media Marketing and Why it is a Waste of Your Time 26

    Chapter 5: Steps to Quicker and Easier Modern SM Marketing 28

    Chapter 6: Niche Research and Targeting it the Right Way 30

    Chapter 7: Your Secret Social Media Marketing Weapon: Content Curation ... 33

    Chapter 8: Reverse Engineer Your Competitors' Top Content 36

    Chapter 9: Fine Tune Your Payload Content 39

    Chapter 10: Market Your List Right 42

    Chapter 11: Unlock the Power of Repurposed Content 46

    Chapter 12: Use Automatic Content Sharing 48

    Chapter 13: Scale Up Your Targeting 51

    Chapter 14: Sell to Your List Differently 53

    Chapter 15: Reinvest Your Profits the Right Way 58

    Conclusion 61

Book # 2: Social Media Marketing Blueprint 63

Introduction 64

Chapter 1: The Essentials of Social Media Marketing and Its Necessity for Your Business 68

Chapter 2: Differentiating Social Media Marketing from Digital Marketing 75

Chapter 3: The Five Cornerstones of Effective Social Media Marketing............................. 77

Chapter 4: Marketing Strategies Every Business Owner Should Know 85

Chapter 5: Case Studies: Brands That Have Mastered Social Media Marketing................. 89

Section Two: The Social Media Platforms 92

Chapter 6: Facebook—The King of social media 93

Chapter 7: Instagram—The Visual Storyteller 105

Chapter 8: Twitter (Now X)—The Pulse of Real-Time Engagement 108

Chapter 9: YouTube—The Power of Video Content 114

Chapter 10: Pinterest—Visual Discovery and Inspiration 118

Chapter 11: WhatsApp—The Personal Marketing Channel 120

Chapter 12: LinkedIn—The Professional Network 122

Chapter 13: Snapchat—The Ephemeral Content King 124

Chapter 14: Tumblr—The Underdog with a Punch 127

Book # 3: YouTube Secrets Hacks for Beginners 129

Introduction 130

Section 01: Understanding YouTube 132

Chapter 01: What You Need to Know Before Getting Started 134

Chapter 02: Why YouTube? 141

Section 02: Your YouTube Channel 146

Chapter 03: Determine Your Focus 148

Chapter 04: Understanding Your Audience 154

Chapter 05: Branding Your Channel 158

Section 03: Creating YouTube Videos 161

Chapter 06: Creating Quality Content 163

Chapter 07: Recording YouTube Videos 178

Chapter 08: Editing Videos 188

Section 04: Managing Your YouTube Channel 194

Chapter 09: Best Practices for Managing Your YouTube Channel 196

Chapter 10: Growing Your Community 202

Section 05: Monetize Your YouTube Channel 205

Chapter 11: YouTube Monetization Made Easy 207

Chapter 12: Creative Ways to Make Money on YouTube 209

Conclusion 213

Book # 4: SEO For Beginners 215

Introduction 216

Chapter 1: The Search Engines 219

Chapter 2: Google, Bing, and More 228

Chapter 3: The Meaning of Optimization 234

Chapter 4: Keywords Crash Course 240

Chapter 5: On-Page SEO 249

Chapter 6: Off-Page SEO 253

Chapter 7: Content Marketing For SEO 257

Chapter 8: SEO For Your Website 265

Chapter 9: White Hat Vs. Black Hat SEO 268

Chapter 10: SEO Analytics and Reporting 270

Chapter 11: Social Media Marketing and SEO 277

Chapter 12: SEO Tools And Software 281

Conclusion 283

SEO Terminologies That Are a Must-Know 284

Book # 5: Instagram Marketing for Beginners ... 287

Introduction ... 288

Section 1: Understanding Instagram ... 291

Chapter 1: What You Need to Know Before Getting Started ... 292

Chapter 2: What Motivates You ... 297

Section 2: Instagram Account ... 302

Chapter 3: First, You Need a Niche ... 303

Chapter 4: Do You Know Your Ideal Audience? ... 310

Chapter 5: Branding Your Instagram Account ... 315

Section 3: Creating Instagram Content ... 325

Chapter 6: The Content Plan ... 326

Chapter 7: Taking Great Pictures for Your Instagram Account ... 336

Chapter 8: Creating Awesome Videos for Instagram ... 345

Section 4: Managing Your Instagram Account ... 352

Chapter 9: The Best Practices on Managing an Instagram Account ... 353

Chapter 10: Gaining Followers ... 356

Chapter 11: Using Instagram for Business ... 358

Section 5: Monetizing Your Instagram ... 361

Chapter 12: Making Money with Instagram ... 362

Conclusion ... 364

Book # 6: TikTok & Twitch for Beginners ... 365

Introduction ... 366

Section 1: Understanding Social Media Algorithms ... 369

Chapter 1: Starting With the Roots: Everything You Need to Know About Algorithms ... 370

Chapter 2: Taking Advantage of Social Media Algorithms ... 377

Section 2: Starting Your Trend on Tiktok 384

    Chapter 3: Get to Know TikTok 385

    Chapter 4: Taking the First Steps 391

    Chapter 5: Getting More Views 400

    Chapter 6: The Blue Check Mark 407

    Chapter 7: Monetizing Your Content 411

Section 3: Dominating On Twitch 416

    Chapter 8: What's Up with Twitch? 417

    Chapter 9: Setting Up Your Studio 420

    Chapter 10: Make it Look Professional 428

    Chapter 11: And We Are LIVE! 436

    Chapter 12: Improving Your Stream and Getting More Viewers 442

    Chapter 13: Monetizing Your Content 447

Section 4: Growing Your Brand 453

    Chapter 14: Engaging with the Community 454

    Chapter 15: Connecting and Expanding 459

    Conclusion 464

Book # 7: Blogging for Beginners 465

    Introduction 466

Section I: Blogging Basics 469

    Chapter 1: Introduction To Blogging 470

    Chapter 2: To Get Started with Blogging 474

    Chapter 3: Your Passion Will Lead to A Successful Blog 478

    Chapter 4: How To Pick the Right Name Even as A Newbie 480

    Chapter 5: Hosting Your New Blog and Tools of The Trade You Must Know 483

Section II: Copywriting, Content Creation Hacks, And SEO 488

    Chapter 6: Content Creation Like A Pro 489

Chapter 7: SEO - Part I 495

Chapter 8: SEO - Part II - Ten Tips for Getting Ranked in Google 501

Chapter 9: How To Write Blog Posts That Go Viral 504

Section III: Publishing, Promotion, and Driving Traffic to Your Blog 508

Chapter 10: What To Do Once You've Hit Publish 509

Chapter 11: Best Social Media Channels to Promote Your Blog 514

Section IV: Blog Monetization 522

Chapter 12: Affiliate Marketing 523

Chapter 13: Selling Your Products 528

Chapter 14: Online Advertising to Market Your Blog And Sell On Overdrive 532

Conclusion 534

Thank You 535

Your Free Gift

Thank you for your purchase; I'm offering my readers the FREE PDF version of ChatGPT Prompts.

To get almost instant access, go to this website.

https://go.fitzgeraldpublishing.com/opt-in-page-smm-seo-7-in-1

Or use your phone to take a picture of this QR code, and it will take you to the Website for your Gift.

Inside the book, you will discover:

- **3000 Prompts** To help you make even more money online.
- **Save time:** You can search for new topics to create content on ChatGPT.
- **Expand knowledge:** Our Package of ChatGPT Prompts covers various topics, from science and technology to art and culture.

If you want to make even more money online, grab this free PDF.

Wait, that's not all; just for buying this book and getting the free PDF above, you can also earn another free Book.

You can use your phone to take a picture of this QR code.

Use the latest AI techniques to uncover online innovation's future. Take advantage! "Beyond ChatGPT and 50 New AI Tools: The Ultimate Guide to Discovering Cutting-Edge AI Tools Beyond ChatGPT" offers endless possibilities. Explore a variety of cutting-edge AI solutions to transform your work. Discover advanced AI tools beyond ChatGPT on this thrilling voyage.

Grab this free book if you want to make even more money online.

Book # 1

Social Media Marketing for Beginners

Unleashing the Power of Digital Marketing, Build a Strong Online Presence of Your Business

Introduction

Hi there, and welcome to endless possibilities with Social Media Marketing. My name is Blake Preston, and with the help of Brian Fitzgerald and Fitzgerald Publishing, I will teach you the reality of social media marketing, which will shift your view of this powerful platform. Discover easy ways to boost website traffic instantly. The idea that all you need is "viral content" is false. Creating content with a focus can increase website traffic.

Instead of waiting for overnight success, use proven strategies to develop your internet profile. Follow our advice to fascinate and move readers. Maximizing your site's potential increases traffic. Suppose a substantial percentage of website visitors buy in the future. People believe this, and I can help you achieve it even if it seems impossible.

Our new ideas might transform your online persona. Imagine using social media viral material to boost website traffic. These clever methods may help find the perfect clientele. Give up paper advertisements and go digital! You should anticipate viral content's consequences on your organization.

Learn how social traffic may quickly deliver successful transactions regardless of platform or credentials. Discover the truth behind these myths. Sad to say, most gurus and experts are wrong.

If you believe any of these views, you should not be surprised if you achieve little despite your best efforts and a substantial commitment of time, energy, and money. The world is new, exciting, and full of possibilities.

A metaphor may help your organization maximize social media. Consider your website traffic a cash flow. You may utilize this metaphor or viral content to explode your social media following. You may lose hope while you seek it.

The suitable mental model unlocks social media marketing's full potential. You can enjoy maximum convenience with our cutting-edge autopilot methods.

New "set it and forget it" methods are sweeping the world. These needs likely interest you. They picked the correct brand name. Discover the unique potential of social media marketing automation! Automation technologies make internet presence optimization easy. One-click can reach more individuals, stimulate their curiosity, and boost your chances of success. Switching from email alone simplifies ads. The secret to limitless riches is passive income. Planning may help you achieve your financial objectives.

Enjoy efficiency without sacrificing passion. Our tips and techniques might help you overcome any challenge. Stop striving for more and appreciate your achievements. We guarantee success

Introduction

with our unique processes. Refrain from settling for mediocrity when you can shine bright.

Each new concept and powerful brushstroke might make you look accomplished. I hope you are receptive to change as we happily and carefully assist you in developing and polishing your thinking.

Consider the significance of your message—set goals. Believe in your freedom of expression. An inverted pyramid will demonstrate social media marketing's attraction. Excellent funnel form. Use a metaphor to increase your social media following.

Turn social networking into cash. Consider the appeal of an inverted pyramid. Let this fantastic idea enter your mind; the world is your oyster. The new design centered on a large foundation. Only the pyramid's peak offers these tremendous views. Spread compelling information on the top four social networks to get fans. Use cutting-edge digital choices wherever feasible.

It would be nice to understand and notice your target audience. We will assist you in incorporating social media into your business. Famous social media networks Facebook, Twitter, YouTube, and Pinterest are fantastic. Millions of people worldwide are drawn to these digital titans' unmatched powers. You may meet new people, debate intriguing issues, and obtain endless creative ideas.

The astonishing figures on these four social media sites will wow you. Learn how these sites and others can draw massive crowds. Your success will increase after employing our unique tactics. The road to greatness and fame begins here. Your site will attract visitors and possibly sell if you succeed.

Since our concepts are ageless, they may be applied to different mediums. Asset enhancement allows subtle enhancements. With our help, you may customize them to your liking. Let your creativity and abilities shine. Make use of Instagram's versatility and marketing possibilities. Share our professional advice on social media to understand how these basic concepts may increase your Instagram presence.

Social media has a considerable reach. People may not click on internet content. Discover the legend's truth. Major networks offer unmatched coverage.

Sharing across platforms boosts content visibility. Discover the wonderful Facebook sharing secret. Some people who see your link in your friends' posts will click it.

Discover why increased Facebook "reach," or exposure, doesn't automatically mean more clicks. Fresh thinking that challenges traditional wisdom. Use a unique strategy to win. Change your mindset and recognize the future's potential. The first step in a new effective process is to enhance content exposure across all platforms. Flaunt your individualism; you must. Showcase your efforts. International expansion may boost your reputation.

Visitors to your site will be more engaged. Even if it's not the focus, a click-through is unmatched. You can profit from our skills and doors. Discover how our unique techniques may enhance your company and personal life. Come on for this fantastic experience with us as your dependable travel companion.

Discover internet visibility secrets. Knowing this is vital. Want to maximize it? Want more and better exposure? It may get fewer visitors. You read this book because you recognize it's more than it seems.

Consider getting intrigued by an advertisement. How recently did you click an ad without thinking? The ad may take many viewings to "get it," as many do. Take the marvelous throne. An intriguing commercial or ad may grab attention.

Social media success depends on memorable content. Increase your internet presence to attract people. Use social media to communicate and interact. Tell captivating stories to differentiate your business. Discover how to use social media to get thousands of visitors.

Popular headlines and photographs are essential, but they cannot guarantee success. It doesn't work that way, which is surprising. I've never felt uncomfortable writing and distributing great work that inspires action.

Maximize Your Internet Presence.

One-click may transfer your viewers to a thrilling new realm. Help others show their gratitude by visiting your YouTube channel, clicking "like" on Facebook, "following" you on Twitter, or "pinning" a post. Use this opportunity to rivet listeners! Enjoy the dialogue when site visitors subscribe or follow you.

The second level of current social media marketing funnels is an inverted pyramid. Building platform trust is crucial to success. Expertise is advised.

Our help can speed up your expert status. You may grow your consumer base and wow your target audience. It's too intriguing and well-meaning to write randomly. It's a masterpiece made to attract your audience. This particular material preserves your talent and individuality.

Use captivating images and content to market your business and stand out. Because of its uniqueness, consumers will remember your brand even if they don't click on your ad. Discover repetition's advantages. Your firm will gain visibility even if a tiny portion of your audience interacts with your social media postings.

You need to provide engaging material to maximize social media accounts. After grabbing their attention, use the "call to action" info. Use your email list to test it. Be memorable to your specialty. Email marketing firms should be joined. Take advantage of this unique chance to gain new consumers and fans. Sign up today to gain subscribers. Find fascinating social content with attractive prizes.

Learn what makes your product or service unique. Amazing freebies like booklets or software are always accepted. Freebies, webinars, and fun online presentations are available. Always prioritize recruiting exclusive group members. The epic "The Endgame" emphasizes forethought, competence, and tenacity. Your goal may be to attract people to click and buy your adverts. Give it your all.

Utilize this social media opportunity. Imagine being invited to an exclusive club. Imagine your previously dispersed online audience becoming loyal and enthusiastic—list membership peaks

Introduction

when the pyramid is turned upside down. Enjoy converting social media admirers into moneymakers.

In this surreal world, the impossible is common. The unlikely and strange are common in modern culture. In-person, the dazzling performance will be unforgettable. Amazing things await you beyond this door. Squeeze pages that promote mailing list signups can boost revenue. People offer you their email addresses because they trust and want to work with you. How to protect and strengthen love. Send them your best content, and stay in touch.

A new view on relationships that values transparency, thoughtfulness, and commitment. The spam-free era of direct touch has begun. Watch out for the guest who messes up your list as we bond.

Consider how your tone and words affect your audience. Words and actions can stir up trouble. Keeping your comments updated helps them understand. Imagine completely controlling your list's sales, engagements, and conversions.

Discover how seven-figure list marketers make money only from mailing lists. Using lists effectively is essential to success. Discover why selecting repeat customers carefully pays dividends. See your carefully chosen list of smash sales records. How well you utilize your list depends on its quality and attractiveness.

There are several ways to turn a large social media following into loyal clients. This meaningful unlocks social media marketing's full potential. Other social media marketing books provide several strategies. These books wrongly claim that a substantial social media following is enough by equating web ad clicks to monkeys' random actions—a safer way to cross this challenging region.

Find something that can boost your progress daily. Our advanced techniques can help you work faster. Why settle for mediocrity when you can excel? Make a complete 180 today for a brighter future. Many marketers might use some advice. Create something unique. Our method will amaze and change your viewpoint; you'll never make mistakes again.

The less-than-ideal truth must be learned. At this stage, many business owners quit. They send social media followers to a sleek landing page to promote their content. Unique material and rewards on squeeze pages keep people coming. Too much good may require addressing.

Unfortunately, marketing wastes many prospective subscribers. New email users must know the terrible truth: be prepared for anything. Want a unique vacation? Surviving the unexpected requires preparation. These people have boundless learning and advancement potential. It may take some employees time to acclimatize to our strict criteria. See these people grow in ways you wouldn't expect.

Look into their experiences—you may be shocked. See how their talent improves the item. Let me present the worst individuals who will astound you with their capacity to push limits and relax.

Learn the importance of a brief list. Why waste time with a vast roster when a lean, efficient team would do? Thin, profit-generating networks replace resource-hogging list squatters. If you choose quality above quantity, you can make more monthly.

Preventing list bouncers and improving service are smart. Welcome a population that registers for your email list for your tempting premium offer, downloads it, and leaves without opening it. You eliminated them well.

Effective Social Media Marketing

Advertising via social media might help you stand out more. Promoting your company with engaging content that strengthens connections with your audience is efficient. Social networking sites might completely revolutionize your company and bring you unimaginable prosperity. The speed with which beneficial relationships may be converted into outcomes is greatly enhanced by social networking. Spread the word using your email list.

Our state-of-the-art method of email list creation lets you lose on precision. I use selected social media content to craft artwork based on your promotion efforts. If you target the right people with your ads, you'll see a considerable increase in responses. Get the best social media marketing outcomes available.

Social Media Marketing: a Revolution

Step into a world where every piece of information, story, and photo that is proudly published online becomes a beacon, drawing in customers quickly. Discover the truth about digital and social media advertising. Which is more exciting? Unleash your tremendous might!

See how quickly things change in the digital realm. Join the hundreds of thousands of new social media users every day. Get to know individuals who share your passions and expand your knowledge. Use the many willing people who have tried your products to your advantage. The right strategies can help you capitalize on this invaluable resource and expand your business.

Learn how to make meaningful connections with others. Learn the transformative potential of one-on-one contact. Learn the potential benefits of close relationships. Learn the magic of connecting with others.

Learn more about the human connection captured by social media. Find out how to raise your online profile's visibility. It would be best if you rethought the way you approach content. Have faith in your methodical technique and give up on luck. Real connections with the audience are successful. Tell brand and personal tales to pique their interest. There is such a thing as resonance magic. Social media's influence is unprecedented. Get your message out there and create an encounter that will make people care about what you're doing and want to spread the word about it.

Take advantage of the Domino Effect!

Picture a fascinating pebble in your writing. Your material's power will slowly permeate social media, sparking a massive uptick in attention and discussion. As the flood of likes, comments, and shares sweeps over the web, it sounds like a symphony. Don't be surprised if your sway eventually extends beyond your devoted fan base to the general public. This excellent book contains game-changing strategies. Be astounded when your brand's message spreads from a trickle to a flood. Get ready for massive growth and remarkable achievement.

Unleash Creativity

Has the constant change in social media algorithms worn you down? Don't let defeat get you down. As a savvy marketer, you have earned the right to keep and expand your online presence. Please assist us in deciphering and utilizing the algorithms of social media. I help you overcome obstacles and succeed in the digital world by providing the necessary resources.

Make use of numbers and figures in your marketing strategy. Real relationships, genuine content, and open participation are the three pillars of effective digital engagement. Including these foundational elements will increase the likelihood of your message being heard and remembered. Capture attention and spark interest in your product. Step into the spotlight in a world ruled by algorithms. If your readers enjoy and trust your posts, no algorithm will be able to outrank you. Engage with customers and other business owners to expand your company.

A wonderful self-discovery experience.

This is a captivating tale unlike any other. A journey of profound self-discovery and exploration awaits you on every page. If you can crack its code, you'll get access to a wealth of information that will alter your life irrevocably.

Act authoritatively and clear the way. Marketing in the social media era is a must. Feel the revitalization of your brand like never before. Our fresh perspective will excite listeners and stimulate growth in the economy.

Think Creatively

Every product line has a unique history that contributes to its uniqueness. Make use of marketing on social media. Keeping an audience interested is essential while narrating a narrative. Benefit from the revitalization of your brand thanks to the vital connections made possible by social media.

The revolutionary changes in marketing will soon astound you. Help me usher in a new era of advertising by coming along on this incredible journey. Expect ground-breaking concepts, mind-blowing originality, and brilliant advertising. Things in marketing are going to heat up. This book unlocks the secrets of social media advertising's enormous potential.

Do you have the innovative resources, astute methods, and expert understanding to rule social media marketing? Get ready for an adventure that will alter how you approach marketing, making connections, and growing professionally. Buckle up because you're in for a ride of a lifetime. Be led by a revolutionary revolution.

CHAPTER 1

Social Media Marketing – An Overview

The Digital Revolution Awaits

Prepare for an exciting adventure into the Digital Revolution. Prepare for limitless possibilities and groundbreaking advances. Take advantage of the future. Embrace

Enter a domain where your tweets, posts, and stunning images transcend the fleeting digital universe. Each sentence becomes a masterpiece that captivates the public by turning ordinary words into exceptional expressions. It seamlessly guides thousands of eyes to your brand, messaging, and visionary goals. Enter social media marketing and be amazed by its revolutionary potential!

In the digital age, social media is powerful. Unleash the power of billions of users on Facebook, Twitter, Instagram, and Pinterest. You'll be amazed by the reach. The ultimate secret to unlocking social media's full power: a skill few have but holds the key to extraordinary success. While most people use social media, only a few know how to maximize its potential. Start a remarkable journey here.

Discover Social Media's Untapped Potential

Be fascinated by the stories of brands going viral overnight. Prepare to be amazed by postings with millions of shares. And prepare to be amazed when ordinary people become internet stars. This collection of stories will surprise you. Despite being genuine, these tales only touch the surface. Explore the immense ocean of potential beneath the surface. Prepare to dive into unlimited possibilities.

But let me explain. This is not about viral trends or short-term stardom. Discover how to build lasting relationships, create a captivating brand presence, and use social media to interact with your audience.

Launch Your Brand's Potential in a Revolutionary Marketing Era!

Enter the future of marketing, where billboards and TV ads are obsolete. Your target audience is captivated by internet platforms in today's fast-paced digital world. They effortlessly scroll through their feeds, avidly devouring content that matches their interests and passions. They engage with digital content that speaks to their hearts and minds, from fascinating films to thought-provoking posts. And what makes it great? Direct communication, meaningful dialogues, and a vibrant community around your great brand are possible.

Social Media Marketing – An Overview

Unleash your exceptional potential. Accept your immense power because it comes with a great responsibility. This incredible power comes a world of unlimited possibilities and a huge responsibility. In today's noisy digital environment, noise is everywhere. The internet is packed with posts, tweets, and videos in a 24/7 digital environment. Are you ready for the final test? Raising your voice in the noise ensures your message reaches and resonates with your audience.

"Social Media Marketing for Beginners" Will it help if you are fed up with being stuck and unclear about how to succeed? Look no further! "Social Media Marketing" is here to help.

This chapter will take you on a beautiful journey to understand social media marketing and provide an overview. Learn how to write articles people want to read again. You should deliberately choose material that will engage your followers like never before, not merely publish on your page. It's about more than contacting everyone. Learn that social media is about connecting with others, not simply following.

To succeed online, you must overcome your limiting beliefs and adopt the strategies that have made the most successful companies. Discover the intricate science and art of creating appealing content. Release your vital techniques to increase your voice and influence. Discover hidden gems that turn readers into brand evangelists. Expect an interactive, persuasive learning experience.

Discover life-changing journeys' endless possibilities. Your amazing adventures will enchant you. Once you make that daring move, you'll discover who you are and grow. Consider all the fascinating travel prospects. Imagine your brand having a more profound influence on your audience than visibility. Imagine a large, rapt audience listening to your every word. Imagine a company-changing marketing approach.

Prepare for a fascinating trip via deep comprehension, powerful strategies, and extensive information. This primer covers everything you need to master social media marketing. A fantastic voyage into social media advertising awaits! I feel like a revolution is happening!

Clear up social media advertising confusion. Explore the intriguing world of social media marketers, where every perspective and interpretation matters. The reading options will amaze you. Learn about social media marketing, where several disciplines form a unique online environment.

Content, navigation, or social media expert? Everyone has an online strategy. Some focus on the network, others on exciting content. Then, there are some with meaningful relationships. Your distinctive opinion, regardless of your side, will stand out online.

Use social media marketing's untapped potential to engage your target audience. Discover how I can explain this complicated environment to help you achieve. Use the changing digital world to grow your network, influence, and wealth. Join this exciting adventure to discover social media's advertising power.

Do you require additional explanation? Fully comprehended. Don't worry—it's typical. When I'm confused, I try to explain. By accident, I'm focusing on tiny aspects to boost traffic.

Discover why many internet marketers and company owners fail at social media advertising. Discover the incredible potential ahead. When something happens, it works. A good definition is essential to project success. Without it, obstacles may arise.

Limiting expectations opens many doors. If you fail, try again—victory against obstacles. Realizing your potential requires accuracy. The correct definition may alter your life. Align yourself precisely and clearly to succeed. Always choose the best while preparing for the future—experience how a detailed explanation may lead to success.

Victory Secrets in a Winning Definition!

Discover the amazing world of social media advertising and how it may benefit us. This revolutionary list marketing course will teach you how to monetize your social media following! Prepare for a trip where social media marketing revolves around fascinating content that builds lasting relationships. Prepare to see how content can build long-term audience relationships. Social media marketing is a versatile tool that personalizes interactions with your target audience through engaging content.

Make use of Strategic Advantages.

Can you fascinate certain groups and make genuine connections? Master communicating with your target audience and keeping those critical connections. Find a relationship that transcends words and alters you forever. Change your definition of love and commit forever. Make a relationship real. Only your mailing list needs your attention now. Discover the thrilling challenge of email list growth.

Be ready for the grand finish—everything has been built to it. Expand your network to maximize its possibilities. Create an engaged, contributing group. Social media marketing may generate new subscribers without any effort. Having a list changes everything. Prepare to be revolutionized by this remarkable gizmo. One item that will shape your social media activities.

Management of Expectations

Are you sick of life's disappointments? Now stop! The best answer is my words. A unique social media marketing strategy that will change how you communicate with your target audience through content and interaction. Give up paper advertisements and embrace digital marketing. Social media advertising is best learned from classic books like "How to Dominate Twitter." Learn how to keep visitors coming to your website.

Discover the terrible truth: counting makes you think more is better. While reasonable, this thinking may leave you feeling despondent as the day ends, significantly if traffic doesn't grow. Despite the success, more is needed. The breakthrough social media marketing method of using content to engage audiences. You want to win over your target audience with relevant, helpful, and exciting content.

This game will transform your life. Marathon running is a testament to tenacity. The sprint tests willpower and commitment to the limit. Drive yourself to new boundaries with each mile and enjoy the race. Not racing, but the tremendous experience every stride brings. Set ambitious goals immediately to succeed. Avoid being the following social media marketer who goes in unprepared and gets no visits. Explore their knowledge to discover extraordinary possibilities. Master their craft and see their revolutionary results. Their incredible talents will amaze you when they cast their spell.

Focusing on definition unlocks the capacity to control expectations. Surprises and thrills await you on the path to calm and fulfillment. Rather than typical, you'll stand out. Change your mindset and anticipate with joy to open many doors. Remember to underestimate the difficulty; be positive.

Since you understand social media marketing, I can focus on content-based relationship-building. Discover how to differentiate your brand. The thing that changes everything for you.

Relive real-world driving excitement. Moderate visitors get plenty of light from my modern infrastructure. Prepare for fantastic city culture and nightlife. Try real-world traffic! A distinctive, engaging, and convincing brand may boost your bottom line. Use a solid brand to attract and keep customers easily. Build a legacy. Active learning, not passive browsing. Find varied folks who love your product. Discover their insatiable curiosity. They want to know the planet's secrets. They're information junkies.

They want to know you and your character out of curiosity. They want to see your affluence and try your products. They want you to believe your cause is unstoppable. This collection of people is excellent. Develop a powerful brand to grow your business. With a big name, possibilities are endless, and I will help you gain an incomparable advantage.

Imagine achieving your goals with content marketing alone. Learn that such statements, although sincere, are false. Discover the exciting reality under the surface. The resolution illuminates inevitable consequences, but much remains unknown. Expect insight as we explore the character. Absolutely! You need engaging material to keep your audience. After joining your elite club, people anticipate and deserve outstanding value.

Learn branding best practices. See the significant shift when people subscribe to your list. Expect to enjoy their time with you. Expect regular, high-quality upgrades that enhance their lives without effort. Social media marketing may boost brand exposure at unprecedented speeds. Discover cutting-edge social media advertising! However, the excitement shows that many need help building credibility. Most of their findings could have been more accidental.

Our most significant hidden discovery will wow you. Discover how content-driven campaigns may improve audience engagement. The upcoming chapters will explain this equation's complex sections so you may understand it. Prepare for an intriguing trip through word meanings and shocking reality. Let this passage's beauty overwhelm you. Follow our detailed project definition.

Setting realistic objectives may help you avoid self-criticism. Never accept less than your due. Develop an attitude that lets you accomplish without self-criticism.

Chapter 2

Reasons Why Social Media Marketing is Essential

If you still need to figure out social media marketing's importance, let me give you eight persuasive reasons why it's essential to your online marketing plan. Discover the power of a balanced marketing plan. I understand the importance of both search engine marketing and outreach.

Add social media marketing to your online marketing plan to boost it. It's the missing component that completes your approach and increases brand value. It must be seamlessly interwoven into the composition, not just an afterthought or overshadowed by other considerations. Discover the power of social media marketing with these eight convincing reasons, just a taste of the many benefits your company, regardless of size, will get.

Learn about social media's unmatched power. Social media may boost your message directly and through virality by connecting people globally.

Create a captivating Facebook page to maximize its influence. Directly connecting with your target market has unmatched benefits. Make your page powerful! Discover your extraordinary potential as a select fraction of your loyal followers see your intriguing updates. Discover the truth: Facebook is actively reducing page organic reach.

The latest breakthrough: a fantastic method that effortlessly overcomes all difficulties. You may steer visitors to a more engaging experience on your page. Encourage them to like your page and discover the hidden gem in your page's settings—the ability to prioritize updates. By doing so, they'll never miss a beat and keep current on your engaging material.

A fascinating video lesson that seamlessly walks viewers through the process is the perfect way to engage and educate your audience. Release your imagination and enchant your audience with an animated gif. Discover the key to keeping ahead! Discover how to prioritize updates and always catch every beat. Unlock your settings' hidden potential and take control of social media.

Tell your friends and followers they may join the privileged group that gets your updates first. Remove the darkness and illuminate the way to perfect visibility! Discover how to grab attention and spark curiosity. Your material must be enticing to engage. Be confident and in charge. Discover the appeal of actual value that will attract your readers and get them to act on your website. Instructing others might boost your direct reach.

A revolutionary feature elevates your material! Imagine that people may easily share your content with their whole network if they love it. This could affect your reach and influence.

Prepare to see your content fly, spreading like wildfire over many walls. Unleash organic sharing and watch your content go viral! Facebook's social ties are robust. The possibilities are unlimited with friends who have friends.

Expect an astounding exponential impact. Discover the incredible power of genuine connections! Imagine having a few hundred likes on your page, but they're not ordinary likes. There are actual people with natural social groups. Prepare for the day when one of your postings goes viral, engulfing the internet. Prepare to be amazed!

Discover how social media combines habit and fascination in a compelling dance. Expect to be captivated by this digital world where scrolling, liking, and sharing are second nature. Join the seductive social media rhythm, where every click and swipe.

Discover the exciting world of social networking, where various demographics exhibit unique usage habits. Some may say that daily, weekly, or monthly participation has weakened, but the truth is that many people still use social media regularly. Discover the extraordinary morning practice that many follow.

Start your day with modern convenience. They grab their sleek phone or tablet before sunrise, eager to explore unlimited possibilities. They stay in touch with the newest news and updates with a swipe. Start the day with technology and stay informed. Discover how easily it becomes a daily practice. Unleash the power of engaging content to put your brand in front of millions of hungry eyes.

Captivating Target Audiences

Those elusive individuals crave content in many intriguing ways. Yes, my reader, these people have a particular taste for diverse information consumption. They desire content that speaks to their souls unimaginably, from exquisite writing to compelling graphics that paint a thousand stories.

Break free from a single content type and unleash social media marketing's power. Celebrate infinite creativity and captivate your audience with a variety of intriguing content. Social media marketing holds as many possibilities as the digital horizon. Be creative without limits! The possibilities are unlimited for intriguing films, breathtaking photographs, engaging links, thought-provoking blog articles, appealing text, and captivating audio recordings. Let your imagination soar and create memorable content! Explore a universe where platforms flourish in their formats.

Create appealing content on one platform and quickly translate it into captivating versions across numerous formats to increase your reach across multiple platforms.

Imagine carefully weaving words into an engaging blog post that resonates with your readers. Imagine sharing this literary gem on Facebook, where your words can fascinate and inspire a large audience. With innovation and social media, the possibilities are unlimited. So, release your inner wordsmith and watch your blog post fly on Facebook's limitless potential. Introduce a captivating image to make your blog content stand out.

Enhance your Facebook page with attractive photos! Watch an image teaser draw your viewers in and make them want to learn more. Visit my intriguing website to experience the power of a single click that opens up unlimited possibilities.

Share your graphic easily on Pinterest to maximize its potential. Make a slideshow movie from your blog post or article to attract readers. You may easily create and distribute your material on YouTube with simple steps. Add a compelling video to your blog post smoothly. Our revolutionary function unleashes social media power! Strip engaging samples from your articles or posts and distribute them on Twitter with a compelling link to the complete material. Increase audience engagement and reach like never before. Try it now and see the magic!

Discover this extraordinary system's flawless operation. You can easily reach diverse audiences across platforms by cleverly reworking and recycling your great content. Maximize reach and effect by seamlessly distributing compelling formats on each platform. This fantastic solution unleashes your limitless potential.

Unleash Social Media Segmentation!

Instagram is a mesmerizing universe where every photo tells a story with many tags. Twitter is a mesmerizing world of trending tweets and hashtags. Discover the incredible value of these tags. Increase your internet presence with tags!

Our advanced content categorization function makes organizing and classifying information easy. Use tags to find captivating content—the power of our cutting-edge segmentation technology.

Chihuahua puppies with hashtags designed for cuteness seekers. These hashtags, carefully picked to capture the essence of these lovely critters, contrast with libertarian political content hashtags. Use hashtags to navigate social media with precision. Social media networks' powerful segmentation capabilities and features let you reach your intended audience easily.

Discover the truth: massive audiences with precise targeting are helpful. Discover the potential of social media marketing's advanced segmentation! This game-changing tool lets you effortlessly contact highly targeted audiences across various platforms. Skip wasted attempts and say hello to a fascinated audience who cares about what you say. Unlock the power of segmentation techniques to generate a highly refined and qualified audience. Enjoy higher revenues with this fantastic offer. With this novel strategy, you may significantly improve your deal-closing odds.

Discover the extraordinary power of automation for sharing captivating content across various platforms. You may easily share your views, tales, and thought-provoking ideas with a large audience with a few clicks. Enjoy the efficiency and convenience of automatic content sharing instead of manual sharing. Automation lets you reach more people, save time, and thrive on every platform.

Stop manually exploring Facebook or Twitter and copying and pasting text from documents. No more hours are spent carefully scheduling postings. These groundbreaking tools make social media management easy and efficient. Maximize productivity and efficiency through automation. Our cutting-edge platform lets you easily organize and publish up to six posts, freeing time for other vital duties. Use our advanced technologies to simplify your social media approach. Automate posting instead of manually posting. Feel the future of content management now.

Facebook lets you connect with friends and family like never before. Spend months exploring the colorful and dynamic community to discover unlimited possibilities. Imagine easily maintaining an active Facebook account and sharing engaging posts six to ten times daily or more. Best part? You won't have to monitor it continually since you've fed it lots of intriguing content.

Experience the utmost convenience with our cutting-edge automation technologies. Their capacity to seamlessly manage big feeds makes your tasks easier and more efficient. Abandon manual labor and embrace automation. Format your work easily in Excel to maximize its value. Convert it to CSV and plug it into these powerful tools easily. Remove the burden of manually entering materials and introduce a game-changing solution that boosts productivity and impact. Experience the unmatched benefit of saving time and effortlessly expanding your reach.

Discover how mailing lists can enable a dynamic two-track marketing strategy. This creative method can help you maximize your brand's potential and reach more people. Increase your marketing and watch your business grow. Take advantage of this chance to transform your marketing approach. Use email lists to achieve unprecedented achievement.

A highly focused email list can boost your content-based audience connection marketing campaign on social media. Captivate your audience with precision and refinement to find success. Your brand's message should resonate with those who matter most. Improve your marketing strategy with a well-crafted mailing list. Many assume they are going to greatness after carefully crafting their list.

Unleash your potential and start your millionaire adventure! The new, groundbreaking idea of being wonderfully unorthodox. It's not simply wrong—a bold declaration that challenges the revolutionary answer linking your existing procedure and ultimate success—the missing step! Unlock the secret to success with fantastic efficiency and effortless growth. Don't miss this vital item.

Discover the tremendous benefits of joining our exclusive email list. Enjoy the fantastic thrill of receiving a professionally curated selection of intriguing content suited to your interests and preferences. Join our acclaimed community today to discover unlimited possibilities. Welcome to a unique mailing list. Introducing "general," a fantastic discussion that covers every possible topic. Bringing a unique perspective. Conversations that exceed expectations. Explore undiscovered places with endless possibilities. I'm here to explore public interest using the topic's appeal. Discover the exciting puzzle of differentiating actual buyers from curious souls seeking knowledge as they journey to see if they can trust you.

The perfect sales strategy: start with a complete general list, then quickly transfer to the highly wanted buyer's list. Upsell and grow your business!

Discover the keys to outstanding achievement. Unleash your potential and achieve greatness. Experience our proven approaches' transforming impact. Allow yourself to excel and exceed expectations. Find the solution to your question and explore our exclusive general list of affordable gems—no matter the price, little issues. I understand your main goal is to let people quickly identify as purchasers. That's why I created a simple, hassle-free method that makes it easy for everyone. Discover the secret power of a dollar, an essential money that often goes overlooked in daily life.

Please find out how buying our product makes the pain disappear. A game-changing strategy: they are painlessly removed from your general list when they enter your buyer's list. A clean list of buyers remains. That list is a treasure trove, my friend. Discover the best platform for captivating your audience with intriguing case studies and convincing them to invest in your fantastic affiliate programs or exclusive products. Increase your buyer's list and achieve unprecedented success.

The groundbreaking two-track marketing campaign! Experience the unmatched power that has changed lives and created incredible fortune. My friend, avoid a common pitfall. Do not believe that having an extensive mailing list ensures success. The revolutionary new strategy that challenges the status quo. Experience a paradigm change like nothing before. Discover the transforming power of your following essential action.

Strategic multi-platform marketing gives your brand organic repetition. Having your brand flawlessly integrated across platforms will capture your target audience and leave an indelible mark. Unleash exponential growth when your brand message resonates across channels, strengthening its presence and connecting with customers. Take advantage of multi-platform marketing and see results.

Imagine having your social media accounts linked across all four leading platforms. Imagine a consistent symphony that gives you several chances to fascinate your listeners. Every post, update, and interaction can leave a mark. Embrace consistency to attract innumerable followers. Set the setting, ripen the apple, and capture the spotlight. Discover the truth: you do. Discover the thrilling possibilities when your brand engages fans on Facebook and quickly moves to Twitter.

Discover visual cohesion's strength! Brands with graphical solid resemblance have a fascinating presence across platforms. Imagine your audience seamlessly interacting and connecting with your brand throughout the internet.

A unique familiarity is built through time, resulting in unmatched comfort. This exceptional comfort may inspire them to join your distinguished email list when you make a persuasive call to action. Establish accounts on all the top platforms and experience organic development effortlessly. Watch success unfold as you start building your online presence. Creating a brand that effortlessly captures people's hearts everywhere they go. Passionate fans of your specialty love our unmatched appeal.

Discover the magic of content re-purposing and save money like never before. With this clever method, you can optimize the value of your existing material and boost your savings. Remove wasteful costs and replace them with a more cost-effective way to transform your organization.

Never underestimate content creation costs. Discover the power of forming a team of highly qualified, talented, professional, and experienced people from English-speaking countries. Even with such a large group, unexpected problems may develop.

Discover the opportunity to save thousands annually. Discover the appeal of talented writers from India, Pakistan, and the Philippines. They may be more affordable than American rates, but consider the cumulative impact on your spending.

Explore the limitless potential of social media marketing! Imagine the joy of creating intriguing material that can be recycled into many engaging formats. Let your imagination shine and maximize your brand's messaging across platforms. You can captivate, inspire, and make a lasting effect on your audience. Create content and see your brand's story unfold in ways you never thought possible. Experience massive expense reductions with this new solution.

Hire a talented Indian writer to unleash global brilliance. Just $1,000 per month can guarantee a steady stream of high-quality, customized content. Enjoy the ease and reliability of constant content production while focusing on business growth. Tap into Indian writers' vast potential to unlock endless possibilities. At this crucial point, you can invest $1,000 in the acclaimed individual's knowledge to uncover abundant, unmatched content. You can also cleverly turn their content into intriguing films, gorgeous infographics, or thought-provoking tweets. The options are endless!

Our diagram-making talents will make your ideas look great. I can also convert your carefully created videos' voice-overs into high-quality sound files. Behold the ability to make spectacular slideshows with these exceptional elements effortlessly. Repurpose your content to maximize its impact! Imagine the potential when format-specific platforms host your painstakingly created creations.

Start captivating your audience like never before. Make your content sparkle! Imagine effortlessly sharing your fascinating presentations with the globe. Your presentations will gain exposure and interaction using Slideshare's power. Showcase your ideas, thoughts, and expertise in a spectacular manner that will wow your audience. Slideshare lets you share your creativity. Pinterest enables you to share stunning infographics to unleash visual storytelling quickly.

Show your goods' magic on Instagram. Ensure the feed has gorgeous and intriguing general product photos that will leave you wanting more. Explore beauty and inspiration on Instagram with us. Enjoy the extraordinary and satisfy your senses. Let the magic begin today by following us. Twitter lets you easily share your questions with the world, maximizing their potential. Enjoy communicating with a large audience, starting interesting conversations, and discovering fresh ideas. Take advantage of social media to elevate your questions. Twitter awaits curiosity.

YouTube lets you share your videos with the world. Sharing your content in any format on Facebook, the world's most popular social media platform, is straightforward. Explore the fascinating mechanics of this clever invention. One strategic investment unlocks content optimization and boosts your internet presence. You may easily repurpose and distribute premium content, increasing your chances of garnering valuable visitors and awareness. Repurposed material can improve your digital success.

Discover continuous creation with our unique approach. Say goodbye to static ideas and hello to limitless, fascinating content. Adopt ongoing innovation and watch your brand flourish. The trick is creating captivating pieces that captivate viewers worldwide. Discover the best way to maximize their potential and value. A dramatic shift in content strategy: no more cranking out articles for a few glances. Explore the extraordinary. The one-way ticket to poverty!

Transform your content into attractive formats to maximize its potential. Distribute your material efficiently across platforms optimized for each design to maximize its potential. These eight persuasive reasons will fire your social media marketing game! Fuel your excitement and success with these clear reasons. Take responsibility and conduct social media marketing right!

Discover how social media can transform customer feedback and engagement. Leverage dynamic channels that connect you directly to your audience to maximize brand potential. Social media can build a lively community where customers feel heard, respected, and involved. Use client input to improve your products and services and stay ahead of their requirements.

An innovative consumer feedback method! Stop waiting weeks or months for the organization to receive your critical thoughts. Our revolutionary company approach has changed client feedback and action. Real-time communication lets you see your thoughts' immediate impact. Join us on this exciting adventure as I connect customers and corporations to make your voice heard—and experience rapid response on social media. Discover the real power behind every like, share, remark, or retweet—your audience's feelings. Our unique real-time feedback method is the best tool for businesses to stay ahead! With this cutting-edge technology, you can adjust faster, answer concerns promptly, and open a world of creativity based on your audience's true desires. Stop guessing and start succeeding!

Social media also gives businesses an unmatched chance to engage with their customers. Authentic audience engagement unlocks power. From thoughtful responses to comments to fascinating live Q&A sessions, these meaningful interactions bring your brand to life and build trust. Engage with customers like never before. Our creative strategy builds brand loyalty and turns ordinary customers into brand advocates. See the fantastic impact as people enthusiastically promote your products and services.

Discover how social media may boost your website's SEO and organic visibility. Strategically use social media to promote your internet presence. Watch your website rank higher in search engines and grow naturally. Social media integration into your digital marketing plan unlocks unlimited opportunities for your brand. Don't

Discover the power of social media and its impact on SEO. Discover Google's game-changing power, which now prioritizes content that sparks social sharing and fascinating engagement. Social media can boost your content's potential. When your carefully prepared words are shared widely, they tell search engines that your material is valuable, reputable, and highly respected by users. Use this chance to make an impact and boost your internet visibility. Social sharing may make your content sparkle like never before.

Learn how a solid social media presence may quickly provide organic traffic to your website, increasing its visibility and rating. Content sharing unlocks your website's possibilities. Sharing valuable content creates a magical backlink, instantly enhancing your website authority. Enjoy watching your online visibility soar as your material becomes viral. Take advantage of this fantastic chance to boost your website's credibility and visibility. Let the world see how your content may increase your online success. Watch your website's search engine rating rise over time. However, by becoming a niche authority, you may engage and inspire your audience like never before.

For the next chapter, choose a social media marketing approach tailored to your internet business. I'll help you select a campaign that's effective and almost guaranteed to succeed. So buckle up for a voyage that will transform your internet profile! Join us at the place for excitement.

CHAPTER 3

Manage Social Media Marketing Campaigns Depending on Your Online Business

This chapter will captivate and test you. Prepare to focus on this chapter. The information may seem overwhelming, but it's vital to grasp. Discover why so many expert social media marketers fail. In other words, they're missing the boat by searching in the wrong area. This novel method of website and social media promotion is unique.

Let me show you the plan's apparent drawbacks. This eye-opening essay shows that the tried-and-true strategy fails in many areas, including social media marketing. Changing your perspective may help you perceive your project differently. Social media visitors are no longer the primary source. Step up your game and create plans for advertising each website or online business. Instead of a cookie-cutter approach, use your ingenuity to boost results.

Content is crucial to social media interactions. A cookie-cutter approach is only sometimes the best. Discover this absurd idea's massive scope. Preparing would be best since a content-based campaign exacerbates its negative consequences. Discover the truth: various businesses require different content and publishing strategies. Create and publish a masterpiece of social media content to match your website. Change, tweak, and personalize everything to create a seamless campaign your target audience will adore.

Excellent new website customizing possibilities are available. Discovering all the options will leave you spoiled for choice. A wealth of alternatives will inspire infinite investigation. Let your imagination go free to find your boundless possibilities. I differentiate publication, online retail (including drop shipping), email lists, and traffic sales websites here.

Discover the several business job possibilities. I'll simplify the endless options. I may divide the many businesses into four groups by looking at the ecosystem as a whole. Discover the intriguing details of these themes, each with its unique prerequisites. Focusing on certain qualities helps you achieve your goals. You may only get what you want if you think about it.

Social media marketers often fall into the trap of promoting blogs like drop shipping or e-commerce websites. Discover those that naturally convert social media followers into readers with intriguing content marketing. Check out how they balance selling and blogging like no one else. Their mastery of digital marketing will amaze you. This breakthrough answer will solve your issues overnight. Stop inefficient processes and encourage simplified operations. Learn about our groundbreaking idea that defies logic and challenges the status quo, made possible by cutting-edge technology. Expect to be surprised when you enter a world where common sense and the status quo are challenged. Enjoy solving riddles while exploring the mystery.

Discover that different methods require different materials. The first and most crucial step of your online marketing plan is developing and emphasizing your digital entity's unique value proposition—secrets to blog marketing success. Dive into our information ocean to find enlightenment. Discover the riches in our digital refuge, where the words you read will captivate your curious mind as they dance across the screen.

A vast material repository can satisfy your interest. Explore the power of collaborative invention as diverse individuals create captivating new content. Welcome to your publishing platform, where your words may reach readers worldwide. Our cutting-edge technology makes telling storytelling easy. Create a literary legacy and join the renowned. Do you have the courage to start a business? Stop searching—I have everything you need to create a successful dropshipping business. Please browse our vast selection of excellent items and order quickly. Stop waiting and leverage Shopify's full potential to join the thriving e-commerce community. Oberlo offers hundreds of high-quality Aliexpress goods.

Try our cutting-edge e-commerce platform to see how easy and profitable it is. Customers may order items with a few clicks, and our advanced technology will handle Aliexpress shipping. Best of all, you keep what's left! Use our easy and practical way to maximize revenues. Large retailers or one-person shops can use us. Congratulations on opening an online store! When your internet business is successful, you may reach customers worldwide. Display your beautiful products and offer a top-notch shopping experience with a few mouse clicks.

Our innovative publishing firm will permanently revolutionize your book view. Learn the stark difference between social media marketing and mailing lists to optimize income. Compare the practical approaches for your significant mailing list to those for your internet business. Watch concentrated marketing improve your business and yield extraordinary returns. Discover the benefits of customizing your content. Try a personalized technique and see what happens. Integrating all your information with your unique ways will change your life. When combined, these two forces provide limitless possibilities. Accept several methods and discover your excellent resource selection. Browse our various selections, carefully selected to match your needs. Try anything in our extensive collection. I have everything from high-tech devices to luxury couture.

After inspiring you to think imaginatively about the fantastic individuals who visit your website, let me show you the many intriguing content types you may use. Break free from mental constraints and experiment. Creative thinkers have the world at their fingertips. Learn how to use your various tools to produce unique content.

I am happy to provide our cutting-edge solution tailored to your organization. A vast selection of content types to boost your websites! Every kind of content has some appeal, but to create an effect, you need to specialize. Prepare for a thrilling advertising journey!

Audio clips—exciting new media! Our fantastic assortment will take you to music and sound, from moving songs to Slideshows—an intriguing new media. Enjoy a breathtaking visual experience.

Introduce you to infographics, an excellent medium. These stunning masterpieces are the perfect blend of some of our innovative diagrams! These artworks will amaze and enlighten.

This is the most comprehensive list of intriguing blog links that will take you somewhere fresh and thrilling every time you click. Introduce you to video, an excellent medium. A visual feast will transport you.

Links that go beyond mental connections change everything!

Seeing so many excellent social media marketers focus solely on link promotion, I feel sad and uneasy. Discover their ideal culmination. Absolutely! Links are essential for online presence. Put yourself in their shoes to understand their values and views. By imagining others' perspectives, we can obtain knowledge and compassion that can be utilized to bridge gaps and form friendships. Empathizing helps us appreciate our shared humanity and our distinctions.

One mouse click unleashes instant traffic. Diversifying content helps you develop a more substantial brand presence on your target site.

Audio, visuals, and graphs may persuade in many scenarios. Why use plain links when you can engage users with captivating content? In a world where we receive many links daily, standing out and providing information more engagingly and memorably is crucial. Success awaits those who keep their promises. To attract your target audience, use engaging content types. Contacting them personally will increase the likelihood of them clicking on your link.

Discover the sad fact that many get this wrong. Understand content strategy. Start with connections, then add different content kinds for engagement. Impress your audience by using all your skills. They know they're a day late and a dollar short. Discover the various benefits of avoiding certain activities. Discover derivative material's advantages. Putting it front and center hooks listeners immediately. Use natural links to create an intriguing tale. Your site's theme should guide your layout. A non-customized format won't meet your needs.

Develop a competitive edge by researching their intriguing world. Explore your competitors' domains and pay attention to their exciting content. Learn about their perfect presentation. Their kind gift of picture quotes opens up new inspiration and visual enjoyment. Take a deep breath and prepare for a visual and linguistic feast that inspires and uplifts you with each page. Their profound teachings and skillful delivery will motivate you. Find out the love diagrams. I provide a selection that defies chance. Learn everything you need to engage ideal consumers. The secret methods for contacting your target audience are disclosed.

Now is the time for daring, out-of-this-world ideas. This novel solution will revolutionize the game. I'll disclose a groundbreaking innovation that will wow you. Forget your problems and look forward to a bright future. This attempt is unique; it's a chance to understand why your competitors could be more active in adopting a comparable technique. Now is the moment to study others' ways. Decoding their shapes gives you a strategic advantage and new insights.

Giving your organization a unique identity may help you maximize its potential. Options expand significantly after this. Try several formats and approaches to discover the perfect fit for your firm.

Discover success via reverse engineering. Study your profession's early adopters' tactics. Only then will you be ready for the challenges ahead. Give your tasks to specialists to attain academic success without worry. Enjoy the simplicity of having consummate specialists execute your work. Use this opportunity to save time and improve results. Let them do your homework, and your academic experience will improve.

Recognize your numerous achievements and use them to achieve more. Allow your forward momentum to take you higher. Recognizing and developing your skills will provide you with endless possibilities. Keep up the excellent work, and you will amaze yourself. Find their hidden value and give an enticing offer to keep them wanting more. Find out if watching for what others miss works. Discover how to reach your potential and leave unfulfilling activities. Take an action that boosts your progress. Stop your money-losing initiatives and start a bright future.

Discover your answers. Make sure your carefully crafted content matches your company's needs. Your sharing techniques should also reflect your brand's attitude. Make reverse engineering transformative and discover its endless potential. Learn to comprehend complexities and find the fantastic journey ahead. Discover how even a little reverse engineering may boost your career. You can own the world if you work hard enough at reverse engineering.

CHAPTER 4

The Classic Way to Do Social Media Marketing and Why it is a Waste of Your Time

This session should start with a discussion of other social media marketers. Imagine seeing a handful of pennies on the ground and resisting the urge to pick them up.

However, it will knock you off balance. It will make you feel like you're receiving something when you're not, and you'll give in to your darkest desires.

Since humans choose the easiest choice, this is usual. They're hard to blame. However, telling you what happens will help you learn from your error and focus on doing things right.

Traditional Social Media Advertising Methods

How would one usually promote on social media? It's easy to find out. You should only "follow," "like," or "friend" those interested in your specialization on Instagram, Twitter, or Facebook.

After following several individuals, many may follow back. Only 20%–30% of 100 Twitter followers will follow you back.

This is when things become worse. Traditional social media marketers spam fans and friends. They'd bombard you with unrelated content and unfollow you. See the trend? Send likes, spam, and unfollow. I'd argue it's random, but "professional marketers" use many intricate systems to attain their goals.

This procedure was perfect till recently. Many Twitter users were drawn to this tactic. But no longer. This practice can get you banned from the service.

If you get traffic this way, it won't be good. Why? Targeting is impossible. No screening is done on your potential followers.

You started following them, so they followed. Shopping variety—where is it? Where will they shoot? The numbers game of speculating won't get you anywhere. No amount of effort pays off.

You may succeed with this selling strategy. That's not my point. My point is that opportunity, time, and effort expenses aren't worth the advantages. Quality work will benefit you.

People Desire Quality.

Social Media Marketing Revolution's success depends on helpful content. Work will speak for itself. Your content will pre-sell your brand. What you post online represents you. It represents the firm values you want people to associate with it.

The Sad Reality

The rules have changed, so "follow, get followed, spam, and unfollow" is still thriving for specific individuals but is usually frowned upon. Social media interactions determine excellent and negative feedback. Take Facebook as an example. Facebook used to have huge traffic potential—no more.

Keeping a huge Facebook following demands frequent involvement. With usual participation rates, success is anticipated. That's how bad things are. Therefore, I'm explaining why "classic social media marketing" is obsolete.

Variations That Failed

It would be improper for me not to tell you about failed social media marketing attempts. First off, hashtag searching is worthless. Marketers search for trending hashtags. They would post niche content with irrelevant hashtags.

This lets them "hitch a ride" on hashtag popularity. They know certain hashtags attract specific users. They're attempting to steal hashtag trend enthusiasts' attention.

Low-quality visits are inevitable. If your content is unrelated to consumers' wants, they won't click through. Even worse, someone may report you.

Influencer spamming has failed before and should be avoided. There are prominent persons in almost every industry. Watch this on Facebook or Twitter. Many niche Facebook and Twitter groups exist.

Regularly quoting these influencers in your work is only worthwhile if it provides value. Having a good reason to communicate with opinion leaders would be best. Getting their attention is only the start. Promoting your product only because you like it is a poor idea.

Your engagement label should emphasize what they did. If an influencer talked about the latest sports footwear fashions, I might utilize it to create a piece about how they affect large shoe and apparel manufacturers' profits.

I exclusively connect to high-quality, relevant stuff, so this influencer will be very interested in what I say. Do you get the nuances? Do you see my connection? I relate this to a foreign exchange influencer when talking about Bitcoin.

The person will get upset. Do you see the difference? Automatic publishing with marketing will succeed. You throw spaghetti against the wall and hope to get some sticks. If you schedule posts on Twitter, Facebook, Pinterest, etc., it's impossible to predict how many people will interact with them. It would be best if you grabbed readers' attention. Promote your social media profiles to qualified, established audiences.

Maximize your best work. If done well, automated social media posting may be beneficial. The shotgun approach to social media marketing may provide the same disappointing results as other marketers.

Chapter 5

Steps to Quicker and Easier Modern SM Marketing

In this chapter, I'll provide a high-level summary of the training's 10 Steps. This methodology is the result of several unsuccessful attempts. You may rest assured that I have heard of any "hot" or "groundbreaking" social media marketing techniques or strategies you may have encountered. That is something I have accomplished. This education is the total of our life's experiences.

What does not work, I also know. I'm aware that everyone's knowledge base, availability, and budget for a given job are unique. I am aware of the constraints. I can relate to the general public's skepticism about social media advertising. As a result, I developed a 10-step Program that social media marketers of various experience and financial levels can follow.

You can put this social media marketing strategy up to mostly run itself, making it one of the most effective options available. I'm about to outline the steps, so please understand me. Steps. Observing them is mandatory. There is no way around this. Just because I've used specific terms or am discussing general concepts doesn't mean you already know everything there is to know.

Please read this as a beginner learning social media marketing for the first time. Don't be shocked if the strategy I'm teaching you doesn't pan out if you don't have that attitude and are willing to skip stages. What gives? You breezed right past it. You were in a hurry. There were important details that you glossed over.

You'll need to take things slowly and carefully to get the most out of this software. Continuing only once you've mastered the current phase would be best. You probably need more time, but please do this properly. If you don't put forth the effort, you have only yourself to blame if things go wrong. So, do I have this straight? Okay.

For more efficient and effective social media marketing, consider these ten steps.

1. Finding and targeting specific niches
2. Methods of Organizing Existing Content
3. Competitors' best material can be reverse-engineered.
4. Develop optimized data for the payload
5. Effectively promoting your mailing list.
6. Explore the potential of cross-platform content repurposing
7. Optimized content distribution

8. Raising the Stakes of Targeting
9. Modify your approach to list sales.
10. Spend wisely what you've earned.

In total, there are ten measures. I know these sound simple. They look simple, but the devil is in the details.

CHAPTER 6

Niche Research and Targeting it the Right Way

Whenever I meet a social media marketer, they ask me how to increase traffic. Build up any old site and stop worrying about specialty research and consumer intelligence.

Let's cut to the chase and get to the "good stuff." That's the thinking I encounter frequently, and it's one of the main reasons so many people fail in this game.

Put it bluntly, you'll be chasing your tail until you figure out which tree you should be barking up. I apologize if I keep comparing things to dogs. These are the best. Most individuals are futilely squandering their time and energy on activities that contribute little to their bottom line.

Many of these, and probably all of them, may be easily avoided with little preliminary niche targeting. In other words, focus on your target market. Now that you have a detailed description of your ideal customer, you can set out to locate them on various social networking sites.

It may seem wild, and it certainly does sound odd. Still, people on social media sites are already discussing or displaying interest in whatever you promote, no matter how esoteric, obscure, or bizarre. As a marketer, you are responsible for identifying potential customers on these sites.

The first step is zero in on somebody you want to buy from your company. Unfortunately, very few marketers pay any attention to this. Social media marketing is seen as little more than a traffic generation exercise by these people. There you have it. That's what you're supposed to do. That settles the matter, period. Knowing exactly who you're writing for is crucial to your success.

This is only sometimes simple. Sometimes, you feel that "educated guesses" regarding your target audience are the best option. That fails to function in the vast majority of cases. Fortunately, there's a more straightforward method. The more time and resources you waste taking wild assumptions and shooting in the dark, the more you lose.

The problem may be solved quickly if you locate your rivals. Seriously. Locate them, please. And believe me, there will always be at least one rival on social media, no matter how obscure, obscure, or "unknown" your specialty may seem.

Find that company and hire them to undertake market and niche analysis. Look at your rivals' social media pages to see how they communicate with your target demographic.

Find out who they are pursuing by using deduction. Watch out for the people they intend to hurt. Check out how they divide themselves up. Said, focus on the hashtags that accompany their posts.

These hints should be sufficient to get you started. You'll have a head start this way. You aren't helpless and without any idea what to do. You can access some objective data that has been tried and tested instead.

Find Your Niche Market

Every company may be seen from one of two angles, and you must keep that in mind as you strategize. The wider your target audience, the more approaches you may use. Various specialty subsets are available for investigation.

You need to know how this operates because even if you think you have a well-defined niche, there are likely multiple sub-niches within that larger one. Possible distinct subsegments exist there.

You should know exactly what your specialty is, as well as the smaller niches that exist inside it. Once again, you can try reverse engineering your rivals' systems. Whatever the case may be, you must act now. This is the knowledge that you must get.

You may now visit YouTube, Facebook, Twitter, and Pinterest to find your niche market. Now, look at the size of the material and messaging spaces available on various sites, such as Facebook pages, groups, Google Plus communities, Twitter hashtags, Pinterest Pinboards, and current YouTube channels.

Check out these venues to determine if there is a sizable audience for your specialty. A red flag should go up if the material on a given platform isn't very relevant to your thing. There needs to be more interest. It may not be worthwhile due to the small amount of the audience.

On the other hand, you can see it as a good indication if you discover that other movies cover the same ground as your own. However, you will need to dig deeper into this issue. Think about how many rivals you have in your market.

There will be trouble if there appear to be many rivals vying for the same market share. If, however, you find that there is a great deal of information aimed at your niche but that a small number of sources create it, take this as a positive indicator.

Think about how engaged your intended viewers are. Take a look at the stuff that's being discussed about your specific field. How active is the community? Do folks talk about this stuff? Is the # trendy?

Please keep an eye out for these and other measures of effectiveness. Suppose you can make sense of these signals. In that case, you'll know with absolute certainty whether or not a particular platform is suitable for promoting your niche's interests or whether you should go elsewhere.

Specifics of Your Target Market:

Observing how your specialty is represented on other sites is essential for reverse engineering. Hashtags, classes, keywords, labels, and tagging schemes all fall within this category. Put them to use in the analysis I just outlined. Sub-niches exist in every market. Therefore, you'll want to create a sub-niche or unique selling proposition for your content to avoid being overwhelmed by the competition.

You're still capitalizing on a huge market, but you aren't dooming yourself by going up against established industry players. You will likely need to try a few until you locate a promising niche.

Chapter 7

Your Secret Social Media Marketing Weapon: Content Curation

Finding content is the next stage after deciding on a certain sub-niche to target and completing in-depth research into the social media platforms frequented by members of that sub-niche or niche segment.

There's good news and terrible news here. The good news is that you may expect significant financial savings. Unfortunately, you'll have to devote significantly more time and focus. There is just no denying it. You must maintain a high standard regarding the material you want to post on social media.

Your brand should be strengthened with every piece of content you publish. This is not up for discussion. You can't just pick stuff that relates to your niche.

That won't attract the correct kind of customers. It would be best if you had more than that to build the trust and authority required to turn the targeted, high-quality social media traffic you're getting into actual dollars.

A Definition of Content Curation.

I've already explained why content curating is so financially advantageous. You aren't going to use your original work, after all. Sharing the work of others on your social media profiles is what "content curation" is all about. As a result, everyone benefits.

You're effectively giving the content's creator free promotion by spreading links and summaries. Conversely, you increase your credibility by providing your followers highly targeted, specialized, value-added material in exchange for their attention.

There are triumphs for all those involved. Everyone, including the user, yourself, and the original content producer, benefits from this situation. This is how things are meant to operate. You win big since you don't have to spend nearly as much time or money creating brand-new material, giving you a significant financial advantage.

Writing your material or hiring a company in the United States or elsewhere to do it for you may rapidly become costly.

Curating content is a low-cost strategy for establishing your expertise in the eyes of your target audience. You are using someone else's work. You'll be able to win their trust while also entertaining them. Time is an issue here. Although you won't shell out any cash, you will invest some time.

As I've already indicated, being picky is essential in content curation. If consumers discover that you only curate and disseminate low-quality information that could be related to your niche, any goodwill you've built up for your brand will quickly evaporate. That won't do the trick. Not.

Use Effective Content Curation Techniques

Now that you know where your target audience spends their time online, you can boost your reputation by sharing material from reputable, authoritative sources on the social media channels where they spend the most time.

You'll be interspersing those resources with your unique posts. Incentives for subscribing to your mailing list are something you'll periodically remind your audience to check out. This is the proper strategy for winning.

If people follow you, they should expect nothing but the best from you. Whether or not you had a hand in creating that content, your followers will benefit from following your account anyway.

Specialized content is provided for them. You can earn their confidence over time by consistently providing people with high-quality content. They begin focusing on the content you've provided. People start paying attention to the materials you distribute, which motivates them to join your mailing list.

That's a crucial part. You add in some of your creative flair here and there. You establish a positive reputation by only delivering the material from third parties. You then combine this with your unique material on par with the rest of your transmission. When they've warmed up to your brand, they'll be ready to engage with your call-to-action material.

You encourage people to take advantage of the goodies you're offering. Whether your freebie is software, a brochure, discount vouchers, or a full-fledged book doesn't matter. You act unethically by asking for their email addresses in exchange for the reward. That's how you get people to sign up for your newsletter.

In addition, you encourage people who sign up for your mailing list to forward the messages you give them. You could ask them to share the email with their contacts. Perhaps you'd like it if they copied and pasted the content into their Facebook wall.

What I Like Most

One of content curation's finest features is how easily it can be automated. Seriously. This strategy for content marketing lends itself well to robotic execution. It's as simple as collecting the links to the external sources you're using in an Excel spreadsheet. Then, you change the

Create a comma-separated values (CSV) file that can be read by scheduling apps like Hootsuite and SocialOomph.

You won't need to key in every detail by hand. Planning doesn't have to be done manually. All of this is automatable in software. That's fantastic, right? You may boost your reputation while doing less actual labor. With that in mind, you must prioritize the quality of your content.

Paying Close Attention to Details Is Crucial

It would be best to fight the urge to acquire everything remotely connected to your specialty that comes up in simple keyword searches on Google or social media networks. That's a sure way to ruin your reputation. As a result of your efforts, your social

Watching your hard work and dedication to building your media brand go up in smoke would be terrible since the quality of the stuff you're collecting might vary considerably.

There might be stretches when you send nothing but the most insightful updates about your specialty, followed by periods where you send nothing but fluff. If you were a potential fan, what would you think? They may see your company as unprofessional or untrustworthy. Whatever the situation may be, you won't succeed in persuading consumers that your brand is dedicated to excellence.

Selecting material requires careful consideration. The items must be read in their entirety. Make sure it's fresh, up-to-date, and written effectively. Of course, this will take some time. The benefit is apparent: reduced financial outlay.

The material you provide is a reflection of your company. Therefore, it's vital to choose it carefully. Its quality will either elevate or diminish your company's reputation. Your option is open.

CHAPTER 8

Reverse Engineer Your Competitors' Top Content

I recommended incorporating some of your unique material into the mix in the last chapter. The question on your mind is, presumably, "How do I know which content to produce?"

I've already highlighted two approaches to this during the training. You may let your competitors do your homework for you by figuring things out on their own and engaging in various experiments, or you can try to figure things out on your own and engage in multiple experiments.

I trust you now see the most straightforward way forward. That goes without saying. Your original material ought to be just as good, if not better, than the content you are putting out. They won't bite if your followers suspect you're trying to trick them. You may need to remember they trust your company.

They like that you're keeping track of all this data and will likely continue monitoring your social media profiles, but you should expect more from them. They have no reason to sign up for your email list.

For what reason should they? The quality of your writing could be better. If they look at the quality of the third-party content you share and compare it to the unique content you make, they will immediately identify your flaws. Can you see where I'm going wrong?

If you want people to take your brand seriously, you need to put out quality material. Thankfully, it's simpler than you may have imagined. Just study how they did things backward.

Check out what has sold the best for them. How do you know that? Examine the content's social media metrics. How many "likes" do their best pieces typically receive? Is there a count for the number of "shares?" Is there anything else that may indicate this material's popularity?

Check out how many people have commented on the article. A backlink checker may determine how many other blogs or websites link to a particular content.

This is how you evaluate the overall efficacy of any piece of material before adopting it as a "template" for your work. I'm not advocating theft, but rather that you take what works and build upon it to create something even more significant.

It's important to zero down on successful strategies. By analyzing the most shared articles produced by your rivals, you may create content that is more likely to be successful. They're popular among the people you want to reach. You won't be throwing away time or resources speculating.

Reverse Engineer Your Competitors' Top Content

One of the most typical blunders made by those working in social media marketing. They fancy themselves experts in their field and think they know what will be "hot" regarding content. They produce a wide variety of works they consider to be outstanding but which ultimately fail to impress.

If you were to create a hundred pieces of that kind of original material, just ten would get any momentum at all in your area. It wastes too much money and time. Fortunately, there's a more effective strategy. The key is determining what makes your rivals' most popular content click.

Put that to use as a jumping-off point. You may tweak them and make your changes, or use them as-is to get a head start on something new. When you first get started, at least you're in the general vicinity. You aren't only stumbling about in the dark.

Study Your Victories

Monitor your analytics after you have begun curating and incorporating your unique material. The most popular pieces of your fabric should be highlighted for you.

You should pay special attention to the curated third-party material that generates the most retweets, Facebook shares, or other forms of social media interaction.

They touched a raw nerve on some level. They were a big hit with the people in the crowd. Seek out these well-received collections and develop your takes on them.

Similarly, a tiny fraction will be widely read and shared even if you produce a large quantity of unique material. Take note of those. Find it. When you've found a winning formula, replicate it. Maintain coherence and consistency in your approach to related topics and material.

The trick is to build on what is already successful. Get rid of the useless items. Focus on what you do well. Make New Versions of Your Best Content on Different Platforms

Now that you know what works in content, stop trying to figure it out yourself. It would be best to keep doing it, but you must also shift your focus elsewhere. Make a fork or a port to another system.

Take social media as an example: a certain kind of blog post does well everywhere. Determine its primary ideas and recurring patterns, then use that information to inspire a new blog entry. Find out if that helps.

You'll be onto something good if you can replicate that degree of success. This is not a random occurrence. This won't be a one-and-done occurrence. You've hit on something that resonates with the listeners.

Taking it to the next level is the next step. Make videos instead of merely writing about the topic on your site. Construct specialized charts. Develop some infographics.

Use the social media sites that cater to these media to disseminate these materials. You may use social media like Twitter and Facebook to spread links to your articles. Use YouTube to share your video content. Pinterest is the place to publish your diagrams and infographics.

Digging deeper, look at your most popular blog pieces and extract the most crucial questions to utilize as tweet prompts. Send out many tweets with the same message over a week. Drop them gradually rather than all at once. But if you ask the appropriate questions, you may get attention on Twitter. Use relevant hashtags with these.

The benefits of content curation include cost savings and an improved ability to focus on what you do best. You zero down on the working aspects and figure them out so that you can consistently crank out winning material.

This, of course, will not occur instantly. You must keep trying new things until you identify the topics that consistently resonate with your target demographic.

Chapter 9

Fine Tune Your Payload Content

As I've already indicated, the social signals of the excellent third-party materials you're collecting may serve as inspiration for your original content. When you go through your sources, you will repeatedly come across specific types of information that generate significant online discussion.

The objective signs indicate this material is of excellent quality and in high demand. You'll then be able to create your unique take on the material.

It can serve as a model for your work. One alternative is to start with a round of curation. You may set your social media accounts to post third-party material of a high standard automatically and with strong social signals.

The curating campaign lasts for a few weeks. You'll start to see a trend very quickly. Eventually, you'll notice that certain pieces of content receive significantly more attention than others. After that, you're free to create your variation.

Both strategies are used in the content selection process. The first option is what I do if I need folks to join my email list quickly. However, I'll continue with the second approach if I need to learn more about the niche or my target audience. There needs to be a correct response. It's easier to say without knowing further details.

The second approach is preferable since it allows you to tailor your unique content strategy to the performance of your social media profiles. It's important to remember that even if third-party information of high quality may contain many objective social signals, such signals may have been developed in various settings.

The first publisher did something you need to do. See how it benefits you? Still, if time is of the essence, the first approach is perfectly viable. However, the second approach is worthwhile if you have the time. Please start with the curation, give it time to run, and then look at the data. It would be best if you noticed a trend.

Popular content is typically concentrated around a few central ideas. Almost all of the content that did well on the internet for several of my campaigns revolved around a single question. That's how niche the requirements of your target audience might be.

Look at the content's click-through rate and engagement to see how well it's doing. This is where many social media marketers need help. They mistakenly believe that interaction is the critical factor. The value of engagement signals, such as the number of likes, shares, and comments, is negligible if readers don't go on to engage with the content by clicking through.

Keep in mind that, in the end, what you need is traffic. That's the whole point of all this effort on your part. It will do you no favor to avoid getting preoccupied with the number of retweets, likes, or comments your content receives. Click-through rates require constant monitoring.

There must be a connection between interest and action rate. You should pay greater attention to information if its click-through rate is high.

Pay Special Attention to Content That Gets Lots of Clicks and Engagement

After finding successful pieces of curated material, the next step is to examine them in great detail. Think about the issues that would be of interest to your target audience. Do they try to evoke feelings with the headline? Do they include question marks in the subheadings? Do they force the individual to follow along or present everything front and center?

Take care with the superficial details. People do indeed evaluate a book by its cover, which is valid with blog postings and articles. In what kind of format do these resources come? Do they have a broad vision? Do the pages have images in the header? Do they employ schematics? Precisely, what are they doing, you ask?

After you've thought through and settled on answers to all of these questions, you may go on to develop your content specification document. Use this as a model for your work.

Now check that you are relying on only some viral articles. It's possible that unexpected success with third-party material was just a fluke. That piece of fabric went viral for whatever reason, and the firm behind it could be lucky. That won't do you any good.

The success of several pieces of curated content should serve as a basis for your template. In this approach, you can rest assured that you will get some respectable outcomes even if you partially meet all the requirements.

Make Up Some Content for the Payload Based on the Above

Now that you have your outline, you can focus on developing unique content to attract and retain readers. You'll use this material to get individuals to sign up for your mailing list. They should avoid this, having gotten eager to sign up for your email list. This is the type of material that is most likely to be believed and spread.

How enthused are you? Do not get your hopes up, though. Many folks go in but sabotage themselves because the material they write for the payload reads like advertising. That's just blatant spam. That's not something anyone would entrust to you.

You're just attempting to play games and pull tricks. No way could work. Instead, the material should be helpful, like an informational commercial. You have a product to sell, but the value your customers receive must be substantial.

You have to balance on the edge of a cliff. There's a fine line between forcing information down people's throats and helping them out at no cost to yourself. A reasonable middle ground between the two is what you need to find.

Ultimately, it's all about ensuring the stuff you put out is valuable. Your content needs to be helpful to the individuals who read it. That's the way to establish trustworthiness. That's the way to get folks interested in signing up for your mailing list.

Remember that your list is meant to improve their daily life somehow. If the information you provide has no value, you will have difficulty making that impact. I'm hoping it's clear to you.

Chapter 10

Market Your List Right

After deciding on the material to be sent in the "payload," the following step is determining the kind of freebie necessary to get readers to join the mailing list.

The best-case scenario is that others recognize your worth. All they have to do is look at the material you publish and the critical insights they gain from your premium content. They get a taste of who you are and what you offer with this premium material and understand why it would benefit them to join your mailing list.

Things don't pan out like that, though. People still need encouragement to join your mailing list, even if you have the finest blog entries and articles on the web. Incentives play a crucial role in this regard.

You'll repackage pricey stuff that people would enjoy, but you'll make it available for free. You wrote a book on it, or you could create a reference guide, condense it into a pamphlet, or program it.

Whatever the situation, offering such valuable information for free will encourage individuals to sign up for your mailing list. In return, they receive a free copy of the offer for their email address.

A bribe of morality, if you will. You're using incentives to get individuals to join your mailing list. They typically wouldn't do it. The quality of your blog posts and articles makes no difference; very few people will bother to join your list. That's the way things are.

Determining an Appropriate Motivator

You'll agree that providing freebies in exchange for email addresses makes sense if you want to grow your mailing list. Often, people only need a little bit of encouragement. The average person requires a little sugar on the happening deal. They need an incentive to finally commit to joining your mailing list.

The next step is to decide what type of freebie you'll provide in exchange for email addresses. The good news is that you won't be starting from square one—no need to speculate wildly.

You may avoid blind fire by preparing correctly. If you analyze your best-performing original material, you should have all you need to create an attractive bonus.

Suppose you operate a gardening blog and find that your readers are particularly interested in articles on tomatoes (as seen by clicking the "share" button and other forms of engagement).

In that case, consider offering a free book on constructing a low-cost greenhouse for growing tomatoes as a giveaway. See how it benefits you?

Focus on the unique material that is performing the best. Please look at the questions they address and those they don't. This way, you may leverage your most shared articles as a springboard for incentive-based articles.

You tell your readers that there's more information available at this link if they want it, which they probably do because the material they're now perusing is incomplete. Your "squeeze page" may be found at that URL. The squeeze page promotes your freebie and explains why people should download it. The process is simple. All you're doing is selling access to the same premium content that links to your free stuff.

Since they do not provide such information, they direct readers elsewhere. They do admirably in establishing trustworthiness and authority. They do an excellent job of improving your readers' lives, but it's clear that they need certain information. They need to sign up to receive the supplementary resources. It doesn't cost you a dime. They won't be out any money, but they must join your mailing list.

This is the proper procedure for creating a mailing list. It needs to be well integrated with your paid material. It's not a good idea to come up with incentives or freebies that have nothing to do with the work you're doing at the moment. There is a high probability that you will fail. Adding value to your disseminating content is as simple as generating relevant incentive content. A sense of seclusion is also present.

Once your audience knows who you are and what your brand stands for, thanks to your content, you can offer them a bonus. People unfamiliar with your brand must be aware of this limited-time offer.

Always prioritize growing your mailing list in the content you create from scratch. Please emphasize the email list's importance before highlighting the incentive material's worth. This may seem backward, but if you stop to consider that they are subscribing to a mailing list, then it makes perfect sense.

You're trying to entice them with the gift you're offering. Nothing more than an email address entry field is intended. Utilize your unique material to promote the idea that readers can access this supplementary material. You shouldn't be surprised if they sign up for your list only to immediately unsubscribe when they realize they don't care about it.

You're in a precarious position once again. One goal is to generate interest in the freebie you're offering in return for an email address. In contrast, you want potential subscribers to appreciate why they should join your mailing list.

This is the correct strategy. Your email list should be prioritized in all of your unique material. Your original material should emphasize that people who join your mailing list will continue to acquire relevant information from you even after receiving the incentive.

People are less likely to sign up for your mailing list only to quickly unsubscribe when you promote it with material that has shown to be successful in the past. They appreciate the benefits the list may provide in their daily lives.

Then, you promote the access to premium features that members receive. It's a bonus, to put it another way. The item is secondary on the list. Please keep the list consistent with the incentives individuals receive for signing up for it.

You want to highlight the list first, so this is apparent. Still, the premium material (whether it's a free book, booklet, cheat sheet, pre-recorded video, or anything else) must be presented to incentivize visitors to purchase.

That's what it comes down to. Aside from the incentive, all of your unique material and, by implication, your website should encourage the viewer to realize the value of becoming a list member.

Many people who work in social media marketing need to realize this. They believe the key to success is in effectively advertising the reward. What happens, for instance, once you've convinced them to sign up for your list in return for the greenhouse guide? Nothing, you read it correctly.

Why? You made such a big deal out of the greenhouse guide that individuals signed up for the mailing list without knowing what they were getting in return. It's common for some of your subscribers to report your updates as spam.

Because they were preoccupied with acquiring the free book, they were surprised to find correspondence from your mailing list. Miscommunication on your website or blog causes this problem frequently.

You can't afford to act like this in the game. It was a concerted effort on your part to attract so many people from social media. You put in a lot of work and money to make your brand reputable. You need to include the target in promoting your email list.

The list must be sold before the incentive may be utilized to motivate buyers. This is the proper order of importance. Nothing else will work.

Maximize Your Squeeze Page's Shareability.

I've already emphasized how important it is to promote your email list through your content. Your squeeze page's content should be used to make additional sales pitches. However, well-designed squeeze pages are acceptable. That won't do the trick. Your squeeze page's design is crucial. After all, you've landed on a dedicated employment website.

You need to convince visitors of this page to sign up for your mailing list for reasons other than the reward. Although the incentive is the main focus of a squeeze page, you still need to make it apparent that visitors are signing up for your mailing list.

That being said, argue your point. For what possible reason should we follow your updates? Just what are the benefits of remaining on your email list? What use would it provide them?

Remember that "What's in it for me?" is continuously being asked. Your squeeze page has to provide a solid and convincing answer to that query. Your squeeze page's design has to be conducive to making that connection, and it also needs to be social media marketing friendly.

Your squeeze page might benefit from a Pinterest-friendly image. Consider including a YouTube-friendly video on your squeeze page.

The possibilities are practically endless. Your squeeze page must be optimized for sharing on social networks. Additionally, it needs to be effective in bringing in new employees.

Create an Appropriate Verification Page

Welcome new subscribers and thank them for joining your list. You must also forewarn them of the nature of the information they will get. Convince them that what they did was the appropriate thing to do. Please give them the impression that they've accomplished something great. In addition to obtaining the digital freebie you're offering, they'll be provided with helpful knowledge on a topic they're struggling with.

The list can be sold in this manner. To turn social media visitors into buyers, you need more than just a lot of hype and promotion of the premium. No way is it going to happen. The list needs to be sold. Having faith in the list is essential.

Chapter 11

Unlock the Power of Repurposed Content

I covered this in greater detail in an earlier chapter, but it bears repeating because of its significance. When you write anything new for your blog or website, you do it with the knowledge that your target audience will well receive it. You are aware of the high demand for this subject matter.

Not only are you selecting material based on your data, but you're also basing your selection on the social signals of your competitor's content, which you reverse-engineered. In other words, you're basing your work on successfully used information.

You aren't just making educated guesses and holding your breath, hoping that anything works. You have instead created a judgment based on what is practical. Congratulations. But it would be best if you did more than that. Once you see that this material is performing well in terms of clicks and social media interaction, the next step is to repurpose it for other uses. Transform them into new content and distribute them again on sites catering to those new forms.

If you see that a particular blog article generates many shares and hits, you could find it helpful to reformat it into a series of questions. This is easy to do because, at its core, all material is just questions and their answers. Though the information may not directly answer the reader's inquiries, it is designed to address their problems even if they are not immediately apparent. Questions might be posed in response to these worries.

Reduce your most impactful and successful content to a sequence of questions. Then, the article or blog post that addresses each query is linked. Combine these tweets with relevant hashtags to reach your target audience.

Using automation software for maximum exposure, you may swap out questions pointing to the same information. Switching up your hashtags increases the likelihood that individuals searching for various subsets of your specialty will see your tweet and click through.

Making presentations from your writing is another option. Numerous visual associations may be made with each item. Create a basic PowerPoint slideshow by considering relevant images to accompany each point in your text. Slideshare should be used to disseminate these PowerPoints. Your slideshows may also be turned into videos with the help of other technologies. You may upload your finished videos to YouTube like any other type of content.

Alternatively, you may transform the points you made in your blog article into visual guides called infographics. Infographics are simplified visual representations of written content like blog posts or news stories. Streamlining your arguments visually draws attention to what's most crucial to the reader. Use Pinterest to spread these infographics.

Finally, you should always choose a captivating header image while publishing content online. A lovely preview will appear when the link is opened on Facebook. It draws attention and motivates individuals to spread its message.

Many different types of content are available for use on Facebook. You may upload and share everything from links to movies, infographics, images, and audio files. After publishing content to your Facebook page, you should distribute the link to that post in groups specifically or broadly interested in your area of expertise.

This is the key to unleashing the potential of recycled materials. Playing the game in this manner necessitates devoting less effort to content creation and more to promotion. Getting your name out there is crucial. Even if your content is excellent, it won't help if no one knows it exists. Ten hours of promotion work should be done for every hour spent on content creation.

This is the proper way to grow your mailing list. Building a solid online identity in this way is essential. Start with impactful content, then make many variations and share them across various social media channels.

Chapter 12

Use Automatic Content Sharing

Another incentive to re-purpose your material is highlighted before we move into automated content distribution. Your audience members will likely become disinterested if you repeatedly cover the same ground.

People are hungry for fresh music. They want you to investigate their ancillary requirements. They would rather you refrain from repeating the same ideas repeatedly. That's the type of danger you face if all you do is keep offering folks more of what's already working.

You have discovered the successful content theme. You can see that there is a lot of interest in it. It's no secret that this gets a lot of views. Your need to return to the same topic is understandable. Please don't.

Keep your attention fixed on the most effective means of presenting that idea. Do it only a few times, but put greater emphasis on recycling. In this approach, readers will see that you are discussing topics of interest across several channels. There is a greater possibility that they will listen. The likelihood of their clicking through increases. They're more open to giving things away.

Keep this in mind while you consider other uses. Refrain from assuming that reading Chapter 11 is unnecessary. Not. You want as much of the stuff in your social media feeds to be as popular and engaging as possible.

It would be a tragedy if you figured out what works and stopped caring about anything but the text itself. Unfortunately, there is a limit to what can be accomplished with textual information. This leads me to the topic of automated content sharing. Your hands will be busy if you do this manually since you will be sharing a great deal of stuff; most of it will be from third parties and original and repurposed.

First of all, you have a lot of forms to fill out repeatedly because you will be covering various channels and publishing many different formats on those sites. Even if you have already signed up for these services, the submission process still entails filling out forms. Form completion is required while making a Facebook post.

Assuming you have little material to disseminate, this should be doable. However, you should automate your social media publishing if you want to increase your exposure by posting many times every day.

Unfortunately, it won't help much if you feed data into content publishing systems. The timing of your publication is crucial.

Use Automatic Content Sharing

You'd be surprised to learn that most people in your target demographic only log in to their social media accounts (including Facebook, Twitter, Pinterest, and YouTube) during a specific time window every day. You will only reach your core audience if you publish within that window.

It seems promising up to this point. Now, here's the rub: not all audiences are interested simultaneously. But how could you tell? Here is where trying out different things might help.

The first step is to disperse your daily content updates at irregular intervals. Try to spread information at least once an hour. Publish at the top of each hour using content automation technologies. Let things play out for a couple of weeks.

Examine the data once the test time has ended. For instance, Facebook Insights may reveal the peak viewing times for your page's content. With this knowledge in hand, you may adjust the schedule of your automated program to distribute your material during peak hours.

In the beta phase, you could release one piece of content every hour. That's 24 individual bits of material dispersed evenly during 24 hours. You discovered from Facebook Insight that your content is most prevalent between 8 AM and 5 PM. Then, you condense those twenty-four updates into the time frame of eight in the morning to five in the afternoon.

The clustered publication follows these steps. Any intervals of time outside that window can be disregarded. In this approach, you may increase the likelihood that your material will be seen by its intended audience.

Twitter/X-Special Remarks

Repeatedly posting during the best times of day is essential if you use Twitter for publishing. Facebook Insight has previously informed you that people see your posts at certain times. Your Twitter followers probably enjoy the same kind of content on other social networks that you do. Stay within that estimated time.

Here's what happened. The material should be scheduled to be tweeted many times throughout that time range using automated content publishing systems, and various hashtags should be used each time. You may target specific subsets of your specialized market using hashtags that reflect their interests.

Facebook-Specific Remarks

Be bold about re-posting previously published stuff on your Facebook page. Do not publish the same thing more than once. Successful material that has been republished should be sandwiched between pieces of high-quality, selected content.

More eyes will be drawn to your most valuable work in this approach. If they do, you'll have another opportunity to get them to sign up for your mailing list.

Remember that you are giving up traffic in exchange for sharing high-quality material created by others. Although your reputation grows, you cannot attract new email subscribers to your squeeze page. No way is it going to happen. Sharing your unique material increases readers' likelihood of clicking on your recruitment page.

This is why it's crucial to periodically republish your most popular content with other, similarly high-quality pieces of curated content.

Chapter 13

Scale Up Your Targeting

Hashtags can be used when posting to social media platforms like Facebook and Twitter. With Instagram, this is undeniably the case. Feel free to experiment with different labels and tags for your material, no matter the medium.

Numerous classifications exist for every specific field. Use them in your experiments. Check the social networking site you're sharing to see which tags generate the most likes or comments.

Of course, you will only discover the ideal hashtags after some time. There's no chance of it occurring. You can only learn this by extensive practice over an extended time frame.

However, a trend should show up in the data from these studies. You'd quickly learn that some hashtags are far more fruitful than others. A lot more people look at them. They are given far more focus. Moreover, they have significantly higher levels of interaction. Don't stray from those.

Try Out Different Methods Of Labelling Influencers In Your Niche

Researching hashtags on Twitter might lead you to influencers who are experts in that particular subject. These folks have an insatiable appetite for posting material on specific topics. Every time they make a post, they always utilize the same handful of hashtags. It appears that is their exclusive preoccupation.

Determine where these individuals are. Read what they have to say. How often are they being retweeted? Is there a lot of interest in what they're offering? Do many people interact with them? Are people reacting on Twitter? You should be able to tell at a glance which accounts have any weight in your field and which do not.

Please avoid getting caught up with the quantity of their fan base. Consider the ratio of their followers to the accounts they follow and the total amount of engagement they receive.

Suppose I discover Mike Smith to be a prominent poster in my niche because he appears to choose from the top ten hashtags for my specialty randomly. In that case, I may investigate the ratio of his followers to the accounts he follows. Mike Smith may be influential if 15,000 people follow him, but only follows one.

I mention this because I need to check how actively people respond to his articles before drawing firm conclusions. Do many people RT his updates? Is there a large amount of feedback? Is the 'love' button getting a lot of use? If his posts have these qualities, they're worth checking out and following.

When posting on Twitter, it is crucial to include notable users. In your article, you use the most effective hashtags you have. This will help them notice you. If you share information comparable to what these individuals like, they will be alerted that you do so.

Don't be shocked if they decide to promote your work to their followers after checking out your job. Talk to them. Get your concerns or ideas over to them. You should interact with them so extensively that they could share your guest articles (if they are bloggers) or talk about your work (if you are active on social media).

When you form a partnership with them, at the absolute least, they join your network of content distributors. Many of these can even land you interviews on popular industry websites.

Refrain from assuming that tagging is the only way to interact with influencers. That's not even the start of it. That's only the beginning of the story. There's so much more they can do to help you. You should constantly interact with them and make conversation.

This in no way necessitates a cheek-to-cheek greeting. It doesn't follow that you must always tell them "Amazing post" or "Great post" in response to their updates. My heart leaps at the thought. No way could work.

Not moving in that direction won't go far enough. It would be best if you gave it some effort. And this might come out as criticism at times. You may come out as unpleasant, but you need to get their attention by doing so. It would be best to convince them that you are an expert in this field and a reputable source of information.

That's how you earn their respect and attention. That's the type of interaction that is sure to make you respected. If you don't stand out, you'll blend in with the rest of the chorus. They need more motivation to include your interview or guest post. For what reason should they? You aren't contributing anything new or offering any perspectives that stand out.

Try Out Some Paid Promotions

Considering buying visitors after you've exhausted all other options, mainly free traffic generation strategies like social media marketing would be best. This may seem excessive, but hear me out.

Initially, you can't predict when your intended readers will see your content. You can only guess at their demographic make-up at first.

How many guys are there in comparison to females in your target demographic? What kinds of articles do men and women like from you? In what age ranges do they fall? When do they come?

I'm hoping you can put this into context. To perform preliminary audience intelligence, you must rely on unpaid traffic. After gaining this knowledge, you may now afford Facebook advertising and those of other platforms.

You will likely waste time and resources if you begin before this stage. Check the numbers first. Observe your audience's behavior closely. Remove any adverts that fit these descriptions.

Chapter 14

Sell to Your List Differently

You have successfully converted your social media followers into email subscribers. Feel proud of yourself. You've accomplished something most social media marketers require assistance or don't consider. This is an impressive feat.

It still needs to be simplified to make a mistake even now. Many list members never switch to another list. They consider themselves successful if they can convince enough readers of their blogs to join their mailing lists.

Yes, they are right on some level. You may expect a certain percentage of your list's subscribers to purchase from your affiliate links. Some people on your mailing list will likely purchase your unique works. Others may decide to shop at your virtual wares expo.

The issue, however, is that if you settle with this arrangement, you will be getting pennies on the dollar. In a sense, you are. Do you want to make the most of the time, effort, and resources you put into your business? Why wouldn't you desire the highest possible benefit from your efforts?

You'll need to market your mailing list uniquely to make the most out of your mailing list. There is just no denying it. Any alternative strategy would produce subpar outcomes at best and none at all. Consider these suggestions.

Change up the List of Items You Use

Subscribers may sign up after being inspired by your writing. They are well-versed in the topic at hand. They know what excellent work you produce. They get the points you're trying to make. For this reason, it is illogical for you to include duplicate items on your list.

People aren't stupid, so you may alter the title and rearrange certain things. That won't fool them for a second. They are wise that you give them information they have likely seen previously because of your recycling practices.

Do you believe that this form of training increases self-assurance? Do you think that this approach will result in increased trust being established? Naturally not. You'll need to come up with new material.

Can you describe the required material? First, you don't need us to tell you which posts are the most read on your site. Try these first.

Not in the sense of re-releasing them, though. I mean looking at them critically to identify any discrepancies. Is there anything you still need clarification on? Do the explanations you provided in those viral posts need to be clarified? These ideas should give you a good foundation for the targeted, high-quality material you want to distribute to your subscribers.

Remember that your updates' content is the main draw for your list of subscribers. Your squeeze page's CTA may have been a pricey download, but after your subscribers receive it, they have no reason to continue receiving your emails. Do you get what I'm saying?

Make the reward the revised material you give, and you will be doing yourself a tremendous service. In this way, you may encourage individuals to read your emails and other content regularly. They made your list, so reward them.

Don't let your guard down or allow yourself to get lazy. It's time for you to step into the spotlight. Everything that came before was only practice for this moment. It ends here. This is the point at which everything becomes concrete. And you have to deliver results.

Benefit from Paid Material

Sending out notices to your email list highlighting the material's uniqueness is a sure way to have it go viral. Where do you even begin? Make use of examples from the real world or social proof. These are the words of others who have followed your counsel or had the experiences you describe.

These tales have the power to captivate everybody who reads them. They'll get sucked into the story nonetheless. Your readers will find common ground with the folks giving their tales since they are genuine people. Your mailing list's performance will improve dramatically with such enticing material.

Why? The vast majority of your rivals are only reusing materials. They're taking back their most valuable assets because they know from experience that they work, but they also know that they need to set themselves apart. Taking the easy way out isn't good for their reputation as a company.

It would be best if you decided to alter your approach. This is how you get people to stick with your material over time. Remember that the emails you send out are your material while managing a mailing list.

Try, Try, Try to Make a Sale

The term "upsell" keeps popping into my head. Upselling is essential if you want your mailing list to generate revenue. You don't have to save the day anymore. There's no need to go crazy with this. You needn't put on an air of super-salesmanship.

Most individuals have some idea of how bothersome pushy salespeople can be. In all likelihood, you will resist. You can ignore them and stop receiving them by doing so. I certainly don't blame you. That is the typical reaction of consumers to aggressive salespeople.

What I mean by "upsell" is that you should provide material that draws attention to an issue and suggests a solution. To put it simply, that is upselling. You make individuals aware of the breadth of their problems and the depth of the answers available.

Sell to Your List Differently

Of course, there are plausible and even better answers to this problem, as there are in most situations. Your mission is to outline conventional solutions that are fine but might be better and to send out email updates that get people interested in finding a solution.

You are directing them toward the optimal answer to their predicament. Use a mailing list for social media advertising. Tell individuals that making picture quotations or video montages out of images is a fantastic answer to their demand for fresh material.

However, an even more ideal approach would be to automate the production of such resources, allowing users to click on photographs and instantly generate a movie. It's a huge time saver, and the finished product would be posted to their social media channels without any more work on their part.

That's the critical difference between adequate solutions and those that stand out better. This is the method of converting leads into subscribers. You are still adding value, answering their questions, and meeting their wants, but you are now presenting them with various alternatives.

They can try to solve the issue independently, as most people would, or they can try something else. When people click on that link to see "something else," that's when you make a sale of an affiliate product, a product of your design, or a service. It's preferable to upsell or upsell regardless of the approach taken.

I wish it were that simple to tell you. This is as easy as outlining several options and emphasizing the best choice. The most significant option, of course, is the one that gives you a cut of the profits from every sale.

It's more complex because there are more moving parts involved. I'll explain why. People join your email list for a variety of reasons. Some visitors are only interested in the freebie but need more initiative to opt out.

You can't seem to shake them. They won't even bother to read your emails. They need more time to read your email messages. You won't see any improvement from them. If there are enough "list squatters" on your email distribution list, your mailing list service will begin charging you extra money each month.

You must employ an open rate filter to remove these people from your list. Again, you'll only be able to reduce its population rather than wipe it out entirely.

Some users on your mailing list may have shown initial enthusiasm but have stopped opening your emails. Even if many people are interested in what you have to say and eagerly await your emails, they can't afford your premium offerings because of the high price tag.

Let me fill you in on a little secret right now. When someone complains that your product or service is "too expensive" or "too unaffordable," they're just trying to tell you that they're not convinced it's worth the cost.

You still have to filter them, though. Either they need more intrinsic motivation to succeed, or you must provide them with sufficient external incentives. Nonetheless, they have yet to make up their minds. Pushing them off the wall is the most incredible option.

In the eyes of a seasoned salesperson, there is no such thing as "unaffordable." There is no difference between selling a $10 product and a $1,000 product if you can talk to someone and convince them that they need to buy your product. You've successfully shifted their perspective from want to need. Therefore, they'll believe that thing.

Individuals put their requirements first. Frequently, their needs are put second to those of others. I hope you get this. I'm assuming you read this. It has nothing to do with the absolute cost of your affiliate product. Instead, you'll need to do some further qualifying or convincing.

This is why more is needed to rely on upselling. The following step, which I will detail below, must be taken.

Apply the Filtering Strategy Based on $1 Lists.

You need to divide your subscriber list into two categories: those who are merely curious and those who will make a purchase. These two communities couldn't be more unlike.

Email opens don't always indicate future purchases. As I noted before, your argument could have been presented better. You may need to provide them with the right qualifications.

To help you appropriately filter your list members, I'll show you a $1 list filtration strategy. Instead of trying to upsell them to more expensive goods (such as those costing $19.95, $34.95, or $349.50), you would set the price of everything on your general list at $1.

What I mean when I say "general list" is the list in which anyone who signs up for your mailing list is included. Your default set of items is here. Please use this broad checklist as a guide. This is the undifferentiated, massive crowd of people considering purchasing your product.

Upselling with $1 incentives allows customers to categorize themselves according to what drives them. Those individuals are enthusiastic enough to spend one dollar. That is to say, they agree with you about the worth of your material and are prepared to back it up monetarily.

Here's what happened. The gap between $1 and paying $100 is not significant. I discovered this the hard way.

When I started doing this, I foolishly assumed that only cheapskates would want to be on my dollar list. They are stingy people. I didn't think they'd go for the big-ticket stuff, at least in my thinking. Oh, how wrong I was!

If a person can mentally overcome the gap between 0 and 1, they can do the same between 1 and 100 with the right amount of exposure and information. This is not a conjecture or hypothesis. This happens right in front of my eyes all the time.

It is up to you to narrow down that long list. When advertising these $1 deals, you challenge potential customers to demonstrate whether or not they are only pretending to be interested. The system is designed to sort itself out. Use it.

People who join your general list likely care about receiving helpful information from you. That's why they exist. However, only a tiny percentage of them would pay for it. This "golden fraction" is what generates profit for you. Your buyer's list is the secret to your financial success.

Once more, a novel approach to list sales is required. This also pertains to your two distinct mailing list categories. Your standard audience receives unique content, including social proof, case studies, and upsell messaging. However, your customer base benefits from higher-value upsells and access to more in-depth content.

Again, if someone is ready to go from zero to one dollar, you can convince them to go from one dollar to one hundred, one thousand dollars, or any other quantity you choose. Keep in mind that the higher the value of the dollar, the lower the conversion rate.

It would be ideal if people separated themselves into groups according to how ready, willing, and eager they were to make a purchase. Since $1 is almost "friction-free," this technique for filtering lists is quite effective.

Chapter 15

Reinvest Your Profits the Right Way

You're now making a respectable sum of money monthly from social network traffic thanks to the $1 filtering process. The following action is to establish a company.

You may start thinking of what you're doing now as little more than a pastime. It's a pastime that pays well, but it's still a hobby. That might also be a trap. This can prevent you from reaching the heights of social media traffic success you would otherwise have.

How do you use the knowledge I've given you to build a successful company that will last? It's easy: just put your money back where it belongs.

After you've mastered the system, you may branch out into other areas. Find your market niche with the aid of this education. I have also provided the methods necessary to succeed by leveraging social media visitors. You can afford to dream on a grand scale when you've established a steady income stream from your expertise. Investigating similar niches in addition to your primary focus would be best.

This line of thought is relatively simple. If you've mastered your niche to the point that you're producing passive money every month, you may use your existing method to break into adjacent niches.

That's how you expand your company to new heights. You no longer rely on just one income source; you diversify your earnings from the one method you perfected.

You have mastered the art of social media marketing, from selecting the most relevant hashtags to using effective content presentation and mailing list promotion. Your system incorporates these and many others. It would be a pity to limit the use of that system to a narrow field.

Once you've mastered those, you can branch out into similar subjects. The most effective list marketers use many lists. It's one of several they run. And it means six- or even seven-figure salaries every year. Your success is inevitable if theirs is.

Spend more money on targeted clicks once you've determined what's practical.

Once you've figured out what kind of content marketing plan performs best on Facebook, you may invest in qualified leads. How? Use Facebook's "look-alike" feature to reach new individuals who share your audience's interests. This is the reason why Facebook rocks. This is also the cause of their legal troubles.

The moment you go onto Facebook, whether you want to believe it or accept it, it spies on you. It takes into account your preferences and comments, as well as those of your friends, to make educated guesses about your future actions and tastes. As such, it builds a profile of your interests based on the content you've indicated you enjoy.

Using Facebook's look-similar audience technology, you may identify new potential followers who share the same interests as your present followers but have yet to visit your page. Wow, that's some impressive gadgetry. Use this to your advantage. You may advertise in front of people more likely to be interested in your brand.

Increase Your Spending on Unique Material

Creating unique material is an option worth considering. You may take your business to the next level if it is already profitable by providing additional value to the people who follow your brand across various social media platforms and on your blog or website by creating unique content.

This means you can start banging out articles later. You can get somebody good at writing to do it for you. Thanks to worldwide outsourcing, websites like ozki.org can provide high-quality, unique content without breaking the bank. Superior content that keeps readers interested should stay within your bottom line.

Spend money on regularly updated content. This piece of advice naturally follows from the last one I made. If you want to spend more money on original material, you will also spend more on expanded content updates. More of what you create will be uniquely yours.

You can only do one with the other. Whatever the case, you must improve your content update frequency to provide more value.

In the early stages of implementing this framework, you will likely be interested in affiliate sales if you follow the instructions in this tutorial. You enroll in an affiliate program and then promote your affiliate link in regular email newsletters. You'll earn a commission when someone follows the link and purchases an item. Easy to understand and follow.

If you're serious about financial independence, you should abandon affiliate marketing. You do. You'll need to market your wares instead. The main reason you should do this is for control purposes. When reselling the work of others, you are at their squeeze pages, landing pages, and, ultimately, the product's mercy.

Okay, but what if their stuff stinks? What if their landing page only converts a small percentage of visitors? That's a bad break for you. That's what it comes down to. You should put your money into your creative works if you value financial independence.

You can always rely on outsourcing, which is excellent news. Professional content producers like ozki.org and others may assist you in creating unique, high-quality content for pennies on the dollar.

Create and Market Your Video Membership Courses to Sell

The primary issue with online goods sales is that you only make a sale once. The transaction is finalized when a customer selects the "buy" button, completes payment, and receives the download link. They have the item already. They are free to take, use, or discard it as they see fit.

However, this was a one-time deal. Getting regular monthly payments from kind individuals would be fantastic, wouldn't it? Wouldn't it be amazing if you had a steady stream of money coming in? And that's precisely what you get when you start charging for your online video courses.

If you run a gardening blog, you could create a video-based course in which you instruct others on how to grow a garden. A certain amount is automatically deducted from each member's PayPal or credit card every month. Nothing at all is required of you. And it keeps happening every month until they finally give up and cancel.

Intriguing, right? The videos only require one shoot, yet they continue to bring in cash month after month. That's cool. Income that doesn't need active effort is termed passive income.

The best part is that you are open to more than just video. It might be for any club or organization. You may provide them with access to images. You could grant them access to a set of files or some software.

They are paying for the privilege of downloading the content repeatedly each month. That's a crucial part. The end aim must be a steady stream of money. How to get the most out of your efforts. The less effort you put in, the more money the system rewards you.

This is not something you will be able to master immediately. It also only occurs slowly. Please put your time and effort into the preceding stages initially.

Conclusion

Many people need help with social media marketing. You'll be in trouble if you allow the urban legends around it. This lesson reveals a tried-and-true strategy for converting your online following into actual, tangible dollars.

I'm not saying it's simple, but it is possible to follow these instructions. Do what it says, try different things, and zero down on what works.

The goal is to adapt this knowledge to your situation to develop specific, doable strategies for generating genuine passive income. It would be best to continue once you've mastered the current level.

Now that you have access to all the resources you need remember that it won't do you any good to keep this knowledge to yourself. No way, no how, never, ever. They need action on your part. A sense of urgency is necessary to turn this information into action. The longer you think about it, the less likely your financial situation will improve.

Set a deadline for yourself. Set a precise date to get started. Begin at once as that time arrives. You don't have to save the world or smash a grand slam on your first try. Even a baby step in the right direction is better than none.

Why? Even the smallest of victories is cause for celebration. It would be best if you persisted in this. You need to proceed methodically. Nothing about your current mood or which side of the bed you woke up on is relevant. The most important thing is that you stay the course.

The key to success is dedication and single-mindedness. I hope and pray that you achieve enormous success. The training you just saw was beneficial.

Book # 2

Social Media Marketing Blueprint

The Ultimate Guide to Social Media Marketing for Business Growth through Organic & Advertisement - Facebook, Instagram, WhatsApp, YouTube, TikTok, and Pinterest Marketing Strategies

Introduction

Hi there, and welcome to endless possibilities with the Social Media Marketing Blueprint. My name is Blake Preston, and with the help of Brian Fitzgerald and Fitzgerald Publishing, I will teach you to exponentially grow your business and increase revenue this year without getting into debt or overworking yourself.

If that sounds like a bold promise that is too far-fetched, then I'm even more thrilled that you decided to purchase this book because I intend to show you how simple it can be to 10x your business growth this year using social media marketing.

Regardless of how far along you are in your business, whether you're a solopreneur, entrepreneur, or small business owner, I want to help make life and your finances a little easier by showing you strategies that will get you raving fans and repeat customers, and the power to control your financial destiny. It sounds too good to be true. Well, trust me, it isn't.

There is a goldmine up for grabs on the Internet, and I want to show you how to do it. Every chapter in this book is designed to fill you in on the secrets you need to know regarding social media. I know what you might think: "I'm too old, not educated enough, don't have capital funds to invest in sales and marketing," or perhaps you're going for the common trap of thinking it's too late to win with social media. None of these thoughts are true. I will be busting a few myths before we get into the heart of this book to help you avoid the self-sabotage that I see with so many businesses.

Increasing revenue through social media marketing efforts sounds far-fetched for many business owners. Some find it daunting, especially when they consider the big brands in their space that have amassed large followings and invest millions of dollars each year in marketing. When you feel like a grasshopper, it can seem impossible to compete against the giants of the land. But here's the thing - on social media, the grasshopper has a higher chance of winning real business than the giant.

Why Social Media Marketing (SMM)?

Because social media rules differ from traditional marketing, with that in mind, can you see the possibility of success as you take the driver's seat and start accelerating forward with the right social media strategy? The Internet is ripe and ready. Social media platforms have created communities of savvy, engaged people who can quickly become loyal followers, fans, prospects, and ultimately buying customers.

Introduction

All you need to do is understand the game of winning on social media. By reading this book, you increase the chances of blowing up your business growth in unimaginable ways. You are, in essence, taking a step toward more business growth, freedom, and financial prosperity simply because all the attention is on social media. Where there's attention, there's money to be made. Plenty of books on this subject, so why should you invest in this one? Simple. I aim to address a problem that only some have a solution.

The Big Problem

According to statistics from Social Media Examiner, 97% of small businesses use social media to attract new customers. Still, eighty-five percent are in the dark and need clarification on what tools to use or how to leverage it as an ROI-positive activity for their business effectively.

Even worse, most books focus only on tactics and setting up a social media account. They need the strategy that one would need to succeed. As we all know, social platforms are continually changing. It would be best to have a plan and a core understanding of the fundamentals to keep up with the changes. So, these books could be more straightforward for small business owners and new start-ups, but they quickly become outdated and never give the business owner practical, tangible steps that can be tracked and measured. That's where this book is different.

In This Book, You'll Learn:

- The fundamentals of social media marketing.
- The difference between digital marketing and social media marketing.
- Set the right goals and pick the channels to serve your small business needs and target audience.
- How to grow, optimize, and get more customers.
- The essential tools needed to succeed in social media marketing.
- How to create an effective social media marketing strategy.
- How to plan, complete, and schedule fantastic content that gets people hooked.
- How to leverage both paid and organic systems.
- How to successfully run social media marketing campaigns.

And so much more.

I will also share some hacks I've used in the last decade to take my businesses from zero to seven figures. Yes, you read that right. I started several small businesses from scratch and needed to gain a tech background or capital funding when I started. Worse still, I wanted my business to flourish in a competitive area where well-known brands existed for decades with nationwide branches. So, when I tell you social media marketing will be 10x your business, I say it from a place of experience and authority. In this book, I am spilling out all the secrets I've implemented to gain raving fans and repeat customers.

If you choose to apply all the strategies and hacks diligently, you will not only have increased brand awareness, but you'll also get more traffic to your website. Your search engine rankings will improve, and you will notice better conversion rates. More importantly (especially if you are in the people business), you will have better customer satisfaction and brand loyalty because when people feel like you care, they go all out to support your business and mission.

How Businesses Are Growing from With Social Media Marketing

More and more businesses are going from zero online sales to thousands, if not millions, in annual revenue. And this goes for start-ups selling simple merchandise to prominent venture capitalist-funded start-ups. For example, the founder of a newly established T-shirt company shared his story with me at a networking event. He is in a highly competitive space and, in 2018, struggled to make payroll. So, instead of giving up, he doubled down on social media marketing.

Social media was more like a to-do list in his endless list of business activities. Often, he felt like he had no time to use social media (something I can relate to). However, given the dire nature of his business finances and that he couldn't afford to pay for traditional print ads, he decided to focus on social media, at least for the last quarter of 2018. He devised a simple strategy that included organic and paid tactics following a blueprint like the one I will share in upcoming chapters. Within three months of doing this, he went from zero sales to $3,526.72. It's important to note that he used both paid and organic (you'll learn about both in this book), but here's the great news: his paid ads budget was only $30 per day. That's an initial return of 3x on his marketing investment. Today, that business is doing over $150,000 in annual revenue in online sales alone, and he has never been happier.

Another example worth learning about if you want to grasp how powerful social media can be for your business is the story of the Wish company. The Wish App (which I had just heard of a few months ago) has grown from zero to billions of dollars on the back of social media and, more specifically, Facebook. In 2010, former Google software engineer Peter Szulczweski (pronounced 'sell-chess-key) and Yahoo developer Danny Zhang founded the app that has turned into an eCommerce company that generates billions of dollars in annual revenue. When it started, it was a simple app where users could create wish lists of their favorite products. Then, they started monetizing using the pay-per-click model. As the business grew, Wish began to promote similar products to its users based on their existing wish lists. This created new opportunities that led to partnerships with some merchants who provided their products directly to the consumer via the Wish platform. Connecting third-party sellers to buyers through Wish.com was the best business model currently sustaining their growth. The entire business was built off their Facebook page and presence.

Szulczewski started Wish's parent company, Context Logic, in 2010 as an online advertising start-up that used machine learning, and it was meant to challenge Google AdWords. But then he quickly pivoted that to Wish, the app that allowed users to make wish lists of their favorite products. Wish used Context Logic's machine-learning expertise to create a more personalized shopping experience, and the rest, as they say, is start-up history. Wish has aggressively marketed itself solely on social media with astounding success. According to Sensor Tower, it was the second-biggest app advertiser on Facebook in the second quarter of 2017, the sixth top advertiser on Google, and the fourth top advertiser on Pinterest.

It would be best to make social media marketing grow your revenue. Wish App spends over $100 million (and growing) a year just on Facebook, and they are estimated to be worth between $4 - $8 billion, depending on which report you choose to read. The bottom line is they are making tons of money from social media marketing. At that time, intelligent start-ups were raising funds to invest in product development and other internally focused objectives. Today, brilliant start-ups are focused on raising funds to support sales and marketing activities.

The good news is you don't need to be a venture capitalist-funded start-up with millions of dollars to increase revenue through social media marketing. Even a small business like the T-shirt Company I shared earlier, or my local retail store can stand firm and have a competitive advantage on social media. That is the beauty of choosing to walk this path.

The Big Promise

My significant, bold promise to you is that if you stick with this book, read it to the end, and implement everything you learn, you will grow your revenue and improve the current state of your business. Your relationship with your customers and your return on investment will improve, and you will finally have a competitive advantage over the more prominent brands that have scared you in the past. By the time you're done, you will know exactly where to focus your energy on tracking and measuring your progress, and you will have the right tools to help you achieve it all. I want you to work smart, not just hard. That is what social media marketing will help you accomplish.

The fact is that people consume more advertisements online than in print media, radio, or television. For example, think of each time you Google something. What shows up at the top? What about when you watch something on YouTube? What shows up before your desired video starts playing? These are just a few examples of how dominant online media ads have become. As much as I don't want to be harsh, I'm convinced your business risks becoming irrelevant if you do not prioritize social media marketing. As a fellow business owner, I hope you take immediate action and ramp up your social media marketing efforts so that your business can have the highest chance of surviving in this digital economy.

Chapter 1

The Essentials of Social Media Marketing and Its Necessity for Your Business

Let's clarify that social media isn't just a fad. It is going to be around for a long time. With more than 4 billion people now connected to the Internet and our natural tendency to be social creatures, there's no way social media is just a trend. This means your business needs to have a social presence. Whether you run a local shop or a big national company, social media marketing must be integral to your business marketing strategy. But what exactly is social media marketing?

Social media marketing uses social media platforms to connect with your audience to build your brand, increase sales, and drive website traffic. Social media marketing empowers you to serve your clients and achieve customer satisfaction in ways that would otherwise be impossible or cost thousands of dollars each month. The ability to reach any of your clients and send them a follow-up message, a thank you video, or handle a concern from the comfort of your smartphone and for free is unparalleled.

Before social media, reaching your existing customers was an arduous task that required lots of planning and workforce. Today, you can provide world-class service and create happy customers 24/7 without increasing overhead. It's evident why you should be investing in social media, but if you still need to decide, let's dive into more reasons why you must make this a core business strategy.

Building Awareness

As a business owner, you continually try to reach new customers. Well, this is the only form of marketing that can grow your reach and place your brand in the eyes of potential prospects faster than leveraging social media. Why? Because the smartphone has become the new television. All the attention is on our phones, and many studies focus on smartphone addiction. I will show you some alarming statistics on this in just a bit, but if you want people to know your brand, social media marketing will help you make that happen.

Providing Support

Social platforms have successfully broken-down barriers between companies and their customers. They've leveled out the playing field. In today's world, when a customer of Virgin Airlines has an issue, instead of calling a customer service line, they will go on Twitter or Facebook to solve the problem, ask for assistance, or find information. Think of how much good you can do with this type of access.

You can hire a small team to serve and satisfy your customers. You only need to develop a system for tracking customer comments, questions, and complaints on social media. Then, create a reputation of being responsive, caring, and supportive through chosen social channels. This will build brand loyalty with your existing clients and attract new ones.

Growing Your Leads and Sales

Surprisingly, many people still need to see how being active and strategic on social media can lead to business revenue, so a quick story will emphasize this even more. Jenny has a yoga studio that could have done better. Yes, she did a little print advertising with the tiny budget she had when she first opened, and it got her some foot traffic, but as the months rolled on, things became stagnant.

She started putting posters advertising her classes on the noticeboards of the local library, grocery stores, and even her local university, but that needed to generate more numbers. Then, she decided it was time to be unconventional in her marketing and joined social media. Jenny started to share videos of her and a few friends doing some of the yoga techniques they most enjoyed.

She then started a regular Facebook live chat, sharing her thoughts on life, yoga, and energy. Jenny filled her Instagram feed with yoga poses in beautiful outdoor locations. It took a lot of time and effort just putting content out there, and not once did she ever sell or promote her yoga studio. I learned about her when a customer came to make a particular order for Jenny as a "token of appreciation" for the transformation Jenny had sparked in her life. The woman discovered Jenny on Instagram, followed some of the teachings and pieces of training Jenny was giving each week, and eventually decided to do live classes, which led to joining her program at the yoga studio. Six months later, the woman had become a brand advocate, claiming Jenny's yoga helped her reclaim her health.

While it may seem like her social media activities were growing her business, a little inspection shows Jenny has found a way to increase revenue. I have since become friends with Jenny because we are both local business owners leveraging social media. When I asked her about her current business results, she was kind enough to reveal that it was a hard grind. She committed to the process and focused on putting out valuable content.

Slowly, engagement and reach started growing. The more training material she put out, the more people commented and started giving her 5-star reviews. Then, requests began pouring. People asked where they could sign up, how to be part of her classes, where to buy excellent yoga equipment, etc. Today, she has a waiting list for one-to-one consultations and is a regular guest at events nationwide. That has created more income streams than she initially anticipated. Social media marketing does boost leads and sales.

Okay, now we are starting to understand the potential of making this business move, but where do we start? There are so many platforms out there. Which ones are the best for your business? Before discussing the ten most popular and valuable social media platforms, it's only fair to disclose that even this marketing activity has drawbacks. Getting into it with the right mindset and expectations would be best. Therefore, you must understand the pros and cons of leveraging social media as your core marketing strategy.

Reduced Marketing Costs

Social media marketing is pennies on the dollar compared to traditional marketing and advertising channels such as print, radio, and television. Even more encouraging is that you can do it with zero advertising budget. If you have some money, I encourage doing paid ads because that accelerates growth exponentially.

Increased traffic to Your Website or Local Store

Self-explanatory. The more people interact with you on social media, the more curious they become about your business, which means they will come to check you out. This is the case even if you have a brick-and-mortar business. A lady recently told me that she's been consuming my content on Instagram and testing out some of the designs I often suggest. Then, a few days ago, as she was driving by my store, she saw the name and immediately made the connection. She was so excited to see that my IG profile was an actual brick-and-mortar business, so she impulsively stopped, found parking, and walked back to the store to say how much she loved watching my weekly videos. More people knowing your brand on social equals more traffic.

Greater Access to International Markets

This is something only some of us ever think about. It's mainly because, in the past, you could only serve the people in your area if you had a local business. People are starting to think globally, thanks to the Internet and social media. Social media lets you connect with and serve clients in different states, countries, or continents. It just takes a little creativity and innovation. Later in the book, I will share how my friend and his wife have taken their linen business internationally, thanks to eCommerce platforms and social media.

Better Customer Engagement and Customer Satisfaction

This must be emphasized more. The more you can directly engage with your customers, the happier they will be, and the better your chances of receiving high ratings and reviews. When people know you are reliable and trustworthy and genuinely care about their problems and concerns, they will choose you over a big brand any day of the week because, more than ever, people want to purchase from companies they feel connected to.

Higher Ranking on Search Engines

Did you know that Google ranking considers how influential your social media presence is? The more activity you have on social media, the more people talk about your brand, and the higher your website and content will rank on Google and other search engines.

Data Mining

Data mining allows you to conduct market research to understand your customers better. Previously, only big companies could afford to do product and customer research. With social media, you can get the real-time data you need and immediate feedback from the people who matter most: your customers.

Now that you have a clue about the positives of making this business move, let's go over some of the cons:

Tarnished Brand Reputation

This is especially true if you pay attention to your account or deliver a poor online customer experience. An easy way to solve this is by actively engaging, posting, and monitoring all your social media accounts.

Quant-based metrics don't work on social because you can't attribute any single action or engagement with your content to a sale. Most traditional sales metrics will only work on social media if you state with certainty that posting on Instagram will lead to $100,000 in six months. The easiest way to solve this is by developing platform-specific KPIs, which will help you monitor the customer purchase journey.

With a well-defined, pre-meditated, and documented strategy, you will win. Especially if you need more consistency, even if you have a marketing budget for paid ads, you need a clear action plan, or the money will result in negative ROI for your business. An easy way to solve this is by ensuring you develop a social media marketing strategy. By reading this book, you will fortunately understand what you need to create your social media strategy today.

The pros and cons I have shared are by no means exhaustive. You can find many positives and negatives if you dig deeper, but in the end, the pros will always outshine the cons. Suppose you feel happy enough with the logic behind leveraging social media platforms as your core business strategy. In that case, you're ready to start learning about the leading platforms and how to start running ROI-positive campaigns. Let's explore the most popular social media that I recommend you consider joining and the number of users and engagement level each has.

FACEBOOK

Fast Stats: Facebook is the third most visited site in the world. As of 2019, Facebook had 2.45 billion monthly active users. Out of that mind-blowing number, 1.62 billion users visit Facebook daily.

The age range is between 18 - 65+, and 71% of American adults use Facebook. It is considered the king of social media, reaching 60.6% of Internet users globally. Users spend an average of 38 minutes daily on the platform—more stats on the section dedicated to Facebook.

INSTAGRAM

Fast Stats: There are currently over 31.8 million photos being uploaded on Instagram each day. Instagram is the second most downloaded free app in the App Store. One billion people use Instagram monthly, making it the second-ranked traditional social network for active users and fifth among all social platforms (non-traditional social media like WhatsApp and WeChat).

Five hundred million people use Instagram Stories daily. While Americans are the largest

Instagram audience, they are not the majority, with 89% of the users currently outside the U.S. and 37% of American adults using Instagram. However, remember that the network is far more popular with younger users. It also has an audience of 18 - 56+, but the highest range is 18-29 years. More on this when we get into the Instagram section.

TWITTER

Fast Stats: Over 294 million tweets are published on the platform daily. But you must remember that half of those tweets are by the government or political.

Twitter used to measure its user population by monthly active users, which they reported in Q1 of 2019 as 330 million. They are, however, shifting to focus on more valuable metrics, especially for business owners. By the end of Q3 of 2019, Twitter stated it had 145 million monetizable daily active users who see ads. If that number seems low, please remember that for most platforms, including Facebook and Snapchat, their data includes all daily active users, including those who don't see ads.

Americans comprise the largest group of Twitter users, taking up a 20% share. 44% of Americans aged 18-24 use Twitter, and according to the Pew Research Center, a vast majority of tweets come from a minority of users. U.S.-based Twitter users are younger, more educated, and higher income earners than the general U.S. population. According to Pew, 71% of Americans on Twitter read the news, and 42% use the platform to discuss politics. It might not seem worthwhile to have your business on this platform; however, considering that 2 billion videos are watched on Twitter daily, and 32% of people say they go on Twitter to watch videos, it makes sense to position yourself as a culturally relevant and inclusive brand that provides value on the platform. More on this later.

PINTEREST STATS

Fast Stats: There are over 242 million daily active users on Pinterest. 70% of Pinterest users are female, with men accounting for only 7% of total pins on the platform. 50% of pinners live outside the U.S. Millennials use Pinterest as much as Instagram.

In America, Pinterest outranks LinkedIn and Twitter. WhatsApp and Snapchat. It is the fourth most popular social media platform, with 250 million people using it monthly. Pinterest reaches 83% of American women aged 25-54 years, and user monitoring shows that Pinterest users are primarily using the platform to plan "life moments."

80% of Pinterest users are on mobile. 59% of millennials have discovered products on Pinterest, and 90% of weekly users report using it to make purchase decisions. Whether they purchase online or offline, immediately or later, Pinterest boards are becoming more of a shopping list than a simple mood board, and that's where the opportunity lies for your business.

LINKEDIN

Fast Stats: LinkedIn has 630 million users and 303 million monthly active users, with 177 million residing in the United States. Two new LinkedIn members join the platform each second, which makes this platform extremely attractive, especially if you're in the B2B space.

More than 70% of LinkedIn users are outside the U.S. It is considered the number one channel for B2B content marketing. 57% of active users are male, 43% are female, and 49% of LinkedIn users earn more than $75,000 in a year. Ninety million LinkedIn users are senior-level influencers, and 63 million are in decision-making positions. So, if you have a business that targets professionals, leveraging the tactics I will share could give you a more significant return on investment than any other marketing tactic you had planned this year.

YOUTUBE

Fast Stats: Data shows that YouTube gets 1.9 billion logged-in user visits each month, and every day, they watch a billion hours of video. 96% of Americans aged between 18-24 years use YouTube. According to Statista, 51% of American seniors over 75 are using YouTube. The platform is in 80 different languages, and according to Alexa, it is the second most visited website. YouTube reaches more Americans, especially between 18-34, than any other television network. 70% of millennial YouTube users say they used the site to learn how to do something new in the last year.

If you can create educational content (we'll talk about that shortly), you can quickly attract a tribe of loyal fans around your brand. One more thing to note is that people have watched 50,000 years of product review videos in the last two years alone. Whether they're window shopping or in the final stages of product comparison, consumers are turning to videos on YouTube to decide. YouTube also reports that people prefer watching a YouTube video to reading an instruction manual. The more information, education, and entertainment you can provide about your products and services on YouTube, the higher your chances of creating happy customers and new buyers.

TUMBLR

Fast Stats: This is a popular micro-blogging and social media platform among teens and young adults. There are 463 million blogs with 171.4 billion posts. The social platform ranks seventh globally, with more than 23 million active users in the United States. 21% of people aged between 18-29 use Tumblr actively. The average visit duration on the platform is 10 minutes and 25 seconds. Given that the biggest demographics on this platform are Millennials, learning the strategies I will share later in the book will be worthwhile if your business serves that age group.

SNAPCHAT

Fast Stats: The platform has 310 million monthly active users and 190 million daily users. 24% of Americans use Snapchat. There are 3 billion snaps created every day.

The average time a user spends on the platform is 30 minutes. 90% are between 13 and 24 years old, 39% are between 18 and 24, and 41% of American teens say Snapchat is their preferred social media platform.

Now that you understand the potential attention you can get on any of these platforms and the various audiences let's focus on what you need to do before launching your brand. I know some of those numbers were mind-blowing, and it's easy to get excited and try to reach the whole world. That would not be a wise decision. You need to contact a small pocket of those millions or billions of people on these platforms.

Remember, you will only go far with your social media marketing with a well-thought-out plan. Seeing small and big businesses winning on social media is not a fluke. A lot of time, effort, planning, and execution was involved. Roll up your sleeves, and let's get into the nitty-gritty of making this work for your business.

Chapter 2

Differentiating Social Media Marketing from Digital Marketing

If you want to eliminate the confusion many businesses owners experience when understanding the internet and how things work, getting this fundamental insight is essential. Digital marketing and social media marketing are not synonyms, like the internet is not social media. It's time to accurately define digital marketing and how social media ties into it.

Digital marketing is building awareness and promoting a brand, product, or service using digital channels. Here's the key idea: social media is a component of digital marketing. Digital marketing has been around for a long time. Television, radio, billboards, and print are all part of digital marketing, but we consider them offline channels as opposed to online channels, i.e., internet-based channels.

Online marketing has the following main categories: search engine marketing (which includes SEO and PPC), website marketing, email marketing, video marketing, and social media marketing.

Social media marketing refers to building awareness and promoting a brand product or service on social media platforms. Any digital channel, including television and radio (if it can be used to promote a product or service), can be considered a viable candidate for digital marketing. Social media marketing, however, is restricted to social media platforms.

This book focuses on social media marketing and will thus cover strategies that serve social media platforms. If you want to extend beyond social media platforms, you have other options like email marketing, search engine optimization, banner ads, affiliate marketing, etc., that are also online marketing activities. They require their study and understanding to implement them in your business. I recommend focusing on one marketing strategy until you see results. A digital marketing strategy may be broad enough to cover all these aspects. In his 2019 keynote, Neil Patel showed that most businesses invest their marketing budget on Google AdWords rather than social media.

Social media ranks third or fourth place, depending on the report, but as more and more small businesses get in the game, there will be an increase. So, while a digital marketing strategy would include Google AdWords, SEO, and all the other channels your business will need to reach desired objectives effectively, a social media marketing strategy will focus on how best your business can engage with social media users. It's about building a fanbase, getting your brand in front of them, and speaking to them in a way that resonates and causes them to take the desired action.

Why Focus On Social Media Marketing Strategy Instead Of A Digital Marketing Strategy?

Small business owners and entrepreneurs have a better advantage if they leverage social media than more prominent brands. An effective digital marketing strategy also requires tremendous time, energy, and resources, which most of us need when starting. So, while educating yourself on the difference between the two is essential, feel free to have your entire digital marketing strategy perfectly laid out before you act on the information in this book. You don't need to do anything except read this book and apply the process as presented.

Speed is your best friend. As a small business owner, you can make decisions and act fast. That's a significant advantage on social media, where things change overnight. Speed works in your favor when reaching your ideal customers, as nothing works more quickly and better than social media marketing for businesses. Running a campaign using any other channel would be a lengthy process, involve a lot of people, and feel out of your control. With social media marketing, you are always in control, and your customer base, aka your followers, is just a click away.

CHAPTER 3

The Five Cornerstones of Effective Social Media Marketing

When social media marketing started, it was more like a broadcasting activity that's "nice to do" for your business because it provided traffic to the website and hopefully generated some sales.

One of the entrepreneurs' and business owners' most significant mistakes is not treating social media marketing like a serious business strategy. For example, many businesses are not undertaking social listening to understand what customers say about their brand. However, this is not a one-off playground. It is just as severe and requires much thoughtfulness and planning as television ads, direct mail campaigns, or customer relationship management programs.

The question you should be asking now is: How can I think about social media strategically?

Intelligent businesses go above and beyond posting content to leverage the power of data platforms like Facebook have amassed in the last decade. They use this data to run highly targeted advertisements for specific audiences. Whether you've been active on social media for a while or are just getting started, there are many ways to leverage it for your business, and none of it is guesswork.

There's an art and science to winning on social media. The best way to run a successful social media marketing activity for your business is by understanding and implementing the five pillars of marketing. The five pillars are based on understanding the philosophical foundations needed to be successful on various platforms and the best social media tools available to meet your needs.

The five pillars of marketing are Strategy, Planning and Publishing, Listening and Engagement, Analytics and Reporting, and Advertising. For a business to achieve long-term success in social media marketing, all the pillars must be in place. Let's take a closer look at each one.

Strategy

What is a social media strategy? If you're a one-person show, this is a big-picture conversation you need to have with your marketing team or yourself. The process you create will guide all your actions and help you determine whether you succeed. The deeper and more carefully thought out you can get with your strategy, the better.

Keep things concise and easy to understand, and make sure it's attainable within the allocated time. I want to help you create your social media strategy as we go through this book, so open your Word doc or grab a pen and notepad as I walk you through the action steps of each of these five pillars.

STEP ONE: SETTING S.M.A.R.T GOALS FOR YOUR BUSINESS

We need to start with the end in mind. The easiest way is to define goals that align with your business objectives. S.M.A.R.T is an acronym for Specific, Measurable, Achievable, Realistic, and Timely. You must first identify your business goals and how you want social media to help you attain said goals. Connecting social media goals to business objectives is a considerable aspect of winning with social media marketing, but it won't happen by default.

Some businesses want to use social media for brand awareness, others for driving website traffic, and others for foot traffic and sales. That's why it's important to note the difference between KPIs and goals before you begin this exercise. To win with social media marketing, you need your big S.M.A.R.T. goal - the significant business objective and social media goals and KPIs.

What are social media KPIs? These are Key Performance Indicators, i.e., the metrics you will measure on social media to determine your progress toward achieving your goals. What are social media goals? These are specific numbers you want to hit for each KPI.

Do This Now:

Write down your primary business objective over the next 12 months. Make sure it is a S.M.A.R.T. goal. An example of this is that we want to sell 25% more running shoes to college-aged sports enthusiasts in the next 36 months.

Determine how social media can contribute to the main objective. Set social media goals that will help you achieve that business goal. For example, you might set a goal to increase your percentage of social media followers who are in college.

Now that you have your social media goals, it's time to establish the main KPIs you want to monitor closely. Decide whether you will select a corporate brand, a personal brand, or both accounts on the social media platforms you choose.

STEP TWO: CHOOSE YOUR SOCIAL NETWORKS INTENTIONALLY

As pleasant as it is to be on all the social platforms, you will run yourself ragged if you don't have a dedicated team working on it daily. Instead of being mediocre in your execution, focusing on one or two channels you feel best suited for your business is better. To determine which ones to go for, you must thoroughly understand your audience—more on this in an upcoming chapter.

If you need help figuring out where to begin, here are a few things you can do. First, research your competitor's social media profiles for their largest audience since you and your competitors are after the same audience. Where they have the highest engagement is where you should be, too. If you can find at least five of your competitors and check what they are doing on Twitter, LinkedIn, Pinterest, Facebook, etc., you will know which social media sites your audience is most active on.

Check metrics like the number of followers and engagement. Once you have this data, figure out the kind of content that works best. Are they doing videos or images? What tone of voice are they using? What seems to be performing best? Is the content focused on branding, motivational quotes, jokes, or other types of messages? With that information, you can move on to the next step.

If you already have a website or blog, you can easily track the traffic through the free Google Analytics Custom Report. That will enable you to see precisely which networks give you the most traffic. Where you see most traction is where you need to double down.

STEP THREE: DECIDE ON YOUR PREFERRED CONTENT

It's important to decide what your primary mode of communication will be right off the bat. The three best communication ways are video, voice, and written word. While it is essential to consider what you're naturally good at, remember to bear the consumer in mind. You want to create as little friction as possible for the person on the receiving end. So, think about the type of content (created and curated) that will attract your target audience.

Again, the more you understand your ideal audience persona, where they are on their journey, and what content will bring the most value, the easier it will be to complete this step. Remember, this isn't fixed. It's a dynamic process, and the type of content you create will morph as your audience grows and engages with your brand.

Do This Now:

List two to five social media platforms that are popular with your audience. Decide how many platforms you want to be on. Choose your primary type of content based on the platform and audience persona.

PLANNING AND PUBLISHING

Approximately three billion people are using social media, which keeps growing. It's safe to say that your future customers will be on social media, and the best you can do is have a consistent presence to increase the likelihood of discovery.

This involves knowing what you want to create, curate, and share with your audience. Planning the content, you share on your chosen social platforms is paramount to success. It would be best to have an editorial calendar to help you streamline this process. It would be best if you planned how often you would share content. Here are some best practices to adopt if you're just getting started.

- Facebook: 1 post a day; curate one every other day.
- Instagram: 2 posts a day, curate one a day.
- Twitter: 15 tweets a day, curate seven tweets per day.
- LinkedIn: 1 post a day; curate one every other day.
- Pinterest: 11 Pins daily, pin at least five Pins daily.

- Tumblr: 2 posts a day, blog one every other day.

There are tools you need to effectively plan and publish your content, many of which I will share at the end of this chapter. Don't feel you need everything on the list, especially if you're starting. Social media publishing doesn't have to be daunting, either. Set up a social media publishing plan to help you share your content in the best way possible and at the right time for your audience.

Remember that some news feeds (most) have a concise cycle - think Facebook and Twitter. In such cases, publishing more than once is good because many people will unlikely see it the first time. The important thing, however, is to plan your content instead of spontaneously. The more consistent and frequent you are, the higher your chances of success if you create quality content.

Regarding your social media strategy, you must capitalize on your strengths. I have seen many aspiring social media influencers fall flat on their lofty dreams because they needed to approach the concept with the proper planning and mindset.

A woman recently told me she quit her dream of becoming an Instagram influencer after three months because six weeks in, it became too arduous to publish lots of quality content daily. She attempted to use video as her primary medium for communication, but she lacked natural flair and charisma. Her videos could have done better because she didn't come across as an influencer in any way. A few weeks into it, even shooting the videos became a headache, and the rest, as they say, is social media history. Now, her social media channels look like a ghost town. All because she didn't take the time to do what you are doing now.

Do This Now:

Write down your topics of expertise. Write down in one sentence what your business is about. For example, if your business is a shoe store, start with - shoes. Then, create sub-topics around the various types of shoes you sell.

Find overlaps between your business, interests, and expertise and add this as an additional category to test with your audience. For example, if you have a shoe store and love cross-fit training, what topics can you create for this mash-up between training shoes and cross-fit? This can be a grand experiment, as it will help you see if your audience enjoys receiving educational content about sports and fitness.

Create a content plan that is tailor-made for each platform. For example, if Instagram and YouTube are your leading platforms, ensure a content plan that plays to each forum and engages different audiences. This sounds like a lot of work, but it will pay off because it will ensure your content is relevant for that audience type. What apps and software do you have access to for content creation?

LISTENING AND ENGAGEMENT

As more people learn about your business, it's crucial to develop the skill of keeping your pulse on what customers are saying. The more followers you have, the more the conversation will grow. People will comment, tag you in their social media posts, review your product or service, and message your discussions about your brand. If people talk about your business without tagging or letting you know, having the ability to surprise and engage them can generate new attention to your business. This is regardless of whether the conversation was positive or negative. I know many people emphasize only positive feedback, but I would like you to get into the habit of responding to all feedback, including the negatives. I suggest using social media listening and engagement tools to do this efficiently. Sure, doing it manually from each platform is possible, but do you have that much free time as a business owner? Several software products aggregate all your social media mentions and messages, including posts that didn't even tag your business.

Social media listening is also a great way to acquire new clients. Most people raise their eyebrows when I say this; it's so elaborate. Lead generation is a pain point for many of us, and while paid advertising will help (as you will learn later), it can be expensive. Understanding "social selling" helps a lot. What is social selling? It's when you use social listening apps to discover people looking for a product or service like yours directly. This is why monitoring customers unhappy with your competitor's products or services becomes vital.

Social media is brimming with complaints and requests for recommendations. It would be best if you had a tool like Boolean search to use this tactic to your advantage and find qualified leads. Write search queries describing what you're selling and phrases people will likely use when searching for it on social media. For example, "Can anyone recommend..." or "advice on...." You can also set up searches that help users unhappy with your competitor's product. Before you know it, your feed will be populated with leads you can contact.

How Hilton uses social listening to win customers. Hilton is one of the most famous hospitality brands in the world. They own seventeen brands worldwide, including over 6,000 hotels in 117 countries. With that many customers scattered worldwide, Hilton is challenged with providing the most convenient communication channels. On average, Hilton Hotels receives about 1,500 Twitter mentions every day. Most are related to special offers promoted by tourist companies, advertising news, and guests sharing pictures and tagging the location.

Often, people post about their positive experiences in Hilton. They show their cozy room or a beautiful view, publicly thank the staff for their services, or say how happy they are with their trip. These kinds of mentions don't require a response, but acknowledging positive experiences makes a brand seem more humane, genuine, and caring. Moreover, if your customer has some social media following, your responses will likely be noticed. That's why acknowledging your customer's positive mentions is always a good idea, and Hilton does it perfectly! But it's not all roses and peaches. As with any big brand, there are occasional complaints. And in hospitality, complaints from a client are significant. A disappointed guest should get an answer immediately because the longer it takes, the harsher they become with their critique.

The average response time for a brand on social media is 10 hours, while the average user will only wait 4 hours. On average, Hilton Hotel answers 3.3 tweets per hour, and the average time between a tweet and a response is 37.3 minutes (an analysis of 872 tweets conducted in 30 days). To put it simply, that is social listening at its best. Hilton's social media team reacts and engages in real-time, depending only on its workforce. Hilton combined their social customer support with a call center and in-app support through the Expion tool to make their customer service experience flawless. Their social team monitors all Twitter mentions around the clock and aims to engage with guests within 30 minutes of a tweet being sent. But it goes beyond reacting and responding to existing customers. Hilton used social listening across different platforms to gather valuable insights for their overall brand strategy. They ensure that guest experiences get turned into actionable insight. All guest comments become part of their reporting. What's even more exciting about the brand is "Hilton Suggests." Every marketer is fascinated by it. Why?

With the Hilton Suggests campaign, the brand is not only using social listening as a helping hand to inform its marketing strategy but also to react to someone else's social posts. The main idea behind this campaign is to help people without ulterior motives make a sale. Hilton Suggests a helpful concierge for everyone traveling to or around more than 115 cities worldwide. Launched in 2009, the Hilton Worldwide initiative is a collection of Hilton employees who volunteer their best local advice with the aim of surprising and delighting travelers on Twitter.

This unique service is based on something other than customers tweeting to @HiltonSuggests and asking for recommendations. Instead, the inquiries are found strictly through social listening for anyone planning a trip to one of the participating cities. The team created specific listening rules based on thorough research powered by social listening to find and reach travelers who might never expect to hear from Hilton.

By taking this first step and reaching out with highly relevant information, Hilton can promote their brand to people unaware of it or who have yet to consider staying with it. Hilton proves that social listening can help us improve our business activities and create something new, which would only happen with the power of social media.

I understand you need more resources or a workforce than a brand like Hilton does. Still, the fundamental idea is the same and can be applied to any business. Start small if you need more money to invest in a software product. Think of questions they might be asking within groups or on their feeds. Leverage hashtags and the search bar. Your lack of effort limits you, but if you learn to listen carefully to the conversations on social media, you will win.

Do This Now:

Do your homework on the various software products that enable you to monitor your social media accounts actively. Schedule a date and time (at least weekly) on your calendar to go through data to ensure you've responded to and served everyone who mentions your business.

Start actively social listening. Go on Facebook (or your desired platform) and use the search bar to type in queries you think your ideal audience might use to ask a question, complain about a competitor, etc. You can also invest some time following the conversation on your competitor's feed to monitor comments so you can genuinely help where appropriate - not with a sales pitch but with a helpful answer.

ANALYTICS AND MONTHLY REPORTING

Whether you're publishing content or engaging on social media, you need to track and monitor the performance of your efforts. Even if you're a small local shop and the only person working on your social media marketing, I still want you to get into the habit of tracking and analyzing the performance of your social media accounts. You need to know if you're making progress monthly or losing.

Most social media platforms provide great insights into business accounts. Start with the insights provided by the platforms. As you get used to analytics, you can opt for advanced software tools that offer in-depth reporting. If you use scheduling tools like Buffer and CoSchedule, then you're in luck because they also provide insights into how your content is performing.

Do This Now:

Familiarize yourself with the analytics tools you will be using to monitor and report on the performance of all your published content. That includes all content posted on each social media platform you choose to build your social presence.

Create a simple template for your reports (for each chosen social platform) so that you can monitor the progress against your chosen KPIs and goals each month.

ADVERTISING

This is the fifth pillar of social media marketing, and we need it if you want to reach your customers fast and make sales. Organic works if you do things right, but it will slowly burn. On social media platforms like Facebook, you need to pay to play. If you're serious about social media marketing, you must include a budget (depending on your current situation) to promote your posts and reach a bigger audience. Please don't jump into it unquestioningly, though. Take your time to understand the platform and figure out the content that performs best. Start small, setting a budget limit you can afford without feeling the pinch until you learn the ropes. The only way to know what works in social media advertising is through practice.

One of the main advantages of including this in your strategy is that you can specify to whom you want to show your content, creating a highly targeted audience based on demographics, interests, behaviors, location, and so much more. If you're going to grow fast and connect with your ideal customers, paid ads on social media are the best way.

This is an initial step toward streamlining social media marketing. With this, you now have documentation that can guide you as we get into the details of each social media platform. I promised to share a list of social media tools you need. Remember, things rapidly evolve and change online, so these are a handful of what's working now. The market may have newer, cheaper, or better options in a few months. So, don't limit yourself to this list.

THE ESSENTIAL TOOLS FOR EFFECTIVE SOCIAL MEDIA MARKETING

Before jumping into the next chapter, ensure your toolbox is complete. I recommend using the following types of tools or something similar.

Social Media Calendar - Having one central calendar where you can plan and execute your strategy makes it easy to see all your social media posts alongside your other projects. Consider using a spreadsheet-based calendar template, as I find these easiest to work with. Free tools like

GSuite have built-in Google Sheets, or you can create your own Excel spreadsheet. If you have a little budget and a team working with you on this, check out an app like Schedule.

Curation tools - You want to curate content to fill gaps in your calendar quickly. You could do this manually with the time and patience or use tools to automate this process. CoSchedule has a Chrome extension that makes this easy to do. If you're not a CoSchedule user, you can opt for Scoop: it, BuzzSumo, Feedly, Curata, and Quuu.

Analytics tools - The easiest and best place to start is with the analytics provided by social media platforms. I also encourage you to get Google Analytics. It's accessible and efficient enough until your business is ready for more robust (and expensive) tools like social bakers.

Scheduling tools are a must-have for busy entrepreneurs and small business owners. We wear so many hats, and social media platforms often require multiple postings at odd times of the day. Get software that will automate the publishing process to ensure consistency and the right frequency. CoSchedule can also do this, but if you're working with a small budget or no budget, check out Buffer, Meet Edgar, Hootsuite, Tailwind, AgoraPulse, and Sendible, to name a few.

CHAPTER 4

Marketing Strategies Every Business Owner Should Know

Succeeding as a business owner often comes down to how effective your marketing efforts are. It's about more than just the numbers or having the right KPIs. It requires greater depth and understanding of the various creative resources you can utilize to maximize return on investment from your campaigns consistently.

As a business owner, I try to choose the lowest marketing plan budget, but I am quickly learning that cheap is sometimes expensive. That means you can still break the bank with your marketing efforts. I've learned some cool ways of running high ROI-positive activities on social media that often involve a combination of other marketing strategies. That's what I want to share with you.

CONTENT MARKETING

According to the Content Marketing Institute, content marketing can be defined as a strategic marketing approach focused on creating and distributing valuable, relevant, and consistent content to attract and retain a clearly defined audience and, ultimately, to drive profitable customer action.

Instead of dry pitching your business, you would provide relevant and valuable content to your prospects and customers to help them solve their issues. There are three key reasons content marketing is suitable for your bottom line and your customers: it creates more loyal customers, it's affordable, and it is proven to increase sales.

Quality content will be an essential part of making social media marketing work for your business because at the heart of social media is engaging, relevant, and compelling content. People go on social media to discuss, share, or even debate topics that matter to them. You must ensure your brand becomes so exciting that someone will want to talk about it and share it with friends. You can't accomplish that with informational garbage or "infomercials," as most marketers do. The best way to succeed on social media is by creating engaging, relevant, high-quality content your audience will want to engage with.

CONTENT MARKETING CAN SURVIVE WITHOUT SOCIAL MEDIA, BUT NOT THE OTHER WAY AROUND

Social media is only popular with interesting, informative, and humorous content. Therefore, your business cannot achieve its social media marketing objectives if it ignores the foundations of effective content marketing. Taking the time to figure out how to deliver exciting content consistently is critical, so let's go over a few questions you need to ask yourself before moving on.

What niche do I want to be known for?

Example: Yoga Instructor

What challenges are my customers experiencing?

Example: Weight loss

What kind of content do they consume?

Example: Videos and Articles.

How can I create exciting yet consistent content to attract new customers and retain old ones?

Example: Weekly YouTube videos with one new training showing them how to do a cardio yoga routine at home. At the end of the day, what business results do I want to achieve for all my hard work?

Example: More client sign-ups for my 3-month in-studio yoga program so I can have full classes and more revenue. How will I know my content marketing is working?

Example: I will do monthly reporting to measure how many new clients and how many recent sales are coming in since executing my content strategy and social media marketing strategy.

EMAIL MARKETING

Email marketing is another common marketing strategy many business owners and entrepreneurs use to grow. Combined with social media marketing, it can work wonders for your business. As I recommended undertaking social media and content marketing, please consider combining email and social media marketing.

HOW IT WORKS:

Depending on your needs, budget, and preferences, you sign up for an account with an email software provider such as MailChimp, Aweber, Klaviyo, Drip, or ConvertKit. Create custom messages to a group (often called a list) of subscribers. Your job is to get people to subscribe to your email list, after which they regularly receive your communication. Having permission to drop a message in someone's inbox is such a powerful way to build relationships and credibility. You can send educational, entertaining, and promotional messages advertising a particular product or service.

Forget about what you might hear internet marketers say - email marketing is not dead. It is one of the most effective marketing methods because it enables you to gather information about a potential customer and serve their needs before asking them to buy. According to a McKinsey report, email is almost forty times more effective than Facebook and Twitter when helping your business acquire new customers. Whether you're an eCommerce business selling products online or a retail store looking to increase traffic to your website, email marketing campaigns can help.

With email, I can offer that extra personal touch to my clients. I organize my audience into segmented lists based on interest, purchase behavior, etc. Besides, I realize that by marketing on social media, I am attracting people who love what I do but need more time to purchase. When these people join my email list, I can continue nurturing the relationship and providing value so that my brand comes to mind when they feel ready.

By using email combined with your social media marketing, you'll be able to grow your audience without paying for other advertising channels. Remember that although social media platforms have a lot of attention and traffic, you don't own or control any of it. Facebook or Instagram could decide to take away all your followers at any point, and there's nothing you can do about it. Your email list is different. It's called owned traffic, and rightfully so. The people on your list are your people; you control what they receive, how, and when. If you keep providing value and remain relevant to your list, they will always respond whenever you reach out.

It took me a while to realize the importance of adding email marketing to my digital marketing strategy. At first, I was only doing social media marketing, and although it worked well for me, adding the email aspect truly changed my business results. Once my social media engagement was healthy and steady traffic was coming to my website, I created a gift for anyone joining my mailing list. Soon enough, I was having people sign up 24/7. Some who were not yet interested in buying from me stayed on my active reader list for weeks (sometimes months).

I had a very active participant, Emily, who always opened every email I sent but has yet to purchase. Six months after joining my list, she sent me an email one day saying she was planning a surprise party for her new boyfriend and would like my advice and complete service to make sure his birthday was extra special. That's when I realized the power of combining social media and email marketing.

Today, I have taken it a step further. Not only am I driving social media traffic to my list-building efforts, but I am also collecting emails from first-time clients who come to my shop. If they still need to be added to my list, I invite them to do a quick sign-up in exchange for a gift that changes depending on the season. Sometimes, it's a valuable digital gift (like an exclusive video tutorial I've created). Other times, it's a seasonal physical product at my shop that I'm giving away. That way, my offline buyers end up on an exclusive list where I can continue to nurture them into repeat buyers. The possibilities are endless once you apply a little creativity.

SEARCH ENGINE OPTIMIZATION

SEO, or Search Engine Optimization, is getting traffic from organic or natural search results on search engines. That includes Google, Bing, and Yahoo. This is a great analogy to help you understand what SEO was shared by Search Engine Land in the following story. Imagine you're a librarian, but not just an ordinary librarian. You're a librarian for every book in the world. People depend on you each day to find the exact book they need. To efficiently serve these people, you need a system. You need to know what's inside each book and how the books relate to each other. Your system would need to take in a lot of information and spit out the best answer for the patrons. This is a challenging job. Search engines like Google, Bing, and Yahoo are the librarians of the internet. Their systems collect information about every page on the web to help people find what they are looking for. Each search engine has its algorithm. An algorithm helps turn all the information stored in the system into helpful search results for the end consumer. If you own a website, search results matter. If your pages have high rankings - that helps more people find you. The key to a higher order is ensuring your website has the right ingredients search engines need for their algorithms. The process of doing this for your website is known as search engine optimization.

Whenever someone goes on a search engine to seek information, your business can serve that person if you've positioned your brand properly with relevant content. The search engine allows the person to come to your website to obtain that information at no cost. This can quickly become income-generating if you've done your SEO right. What main ingredients can you start working on to implement this marketing strategy? Let me share a few.

Ingredient #1: Words. The words you choose determine whether people will find you. For example, if I type in cheap designer handbags, the search engine will show me the most relevant results that match my search query. Keep this in mind when you're creating a copy for your web pages.

Ingredient #2: Titles. Each page on your website has a title usually attached to the code the algorithm reads. This title helps the algorithm determine what kind of content your page has. Based on that summary, it will choose where to show your page. If you don't do an excellent job with your titles, you may end up on the wrong search queries and get no traction, or worse still, you may not show up anywhere.

Ingredient #3: Links. It is imperative to link the pages within your website and use backlinks (external sites linking back to you). When many websites link back to you, the algorithms find your website more desirable.

Ingredient #4: Reputation. The more fresh, consistent, and high-value content you produce for your website, the better the experience will be for your users. The algorithms will perceive it as a reputable site and rank it higher.

These are just a few things you must learn about search engine optimization. One more thing I must tell you is that doing SEO is a long-term game. Don't expect to see results within a week or a month. In today's world, experts are saying it takes at least twelve months to see any traction in your SEO efforts. And that's when you're doing everything right. So, while I encourage you to educate yourself on this marketing strategy further, stick with social media marketing if you want to see a positive ROI fast. Later, invest in SEO once your business is profitable. Now that you know the various marketing strategies you can deploy to grow your business, let's move on to the next chapter.

Do This Now:

Decide which other marketing strategies you want to combine with your social media marketing. My top recommendation is content marketing. If you choose to leverage content or email marketing, plan that out effectively so they can support everything you do on social media.

CHAPTER 5

Case Studies: Brands That Have Mastered Social Media Marketing

I always find it helpful to share real-world examples of businesses succeeding through social media marketing. Getting inspired and motivated so you can persevere and make your marketing work is essential. Some of the methods these businesses have used are so simple that anyone can emulate and experiment with them.

WENDY'S:

Wendy's is an American international fast-food restaurant chain founded by Dave Thomas. They use fresh, never frozen, beef on their hamburgers. They also use social media marketing to grow their brand and enhance customer satisfaction. Wendy's Twitter account is sarcastic and funny, with lots of fan interaction and input. One important thing they do on Twitter that boosts their interaction and helps them classify as one of the best social media brands is to stay on top of current events. "Perfect play calling in action," they tweeted on September 24th after one football game. This tweet got 15.6k likes, 2036 retweets, and 201 comments. Talk about social media engagement!

There's always something going on in the world, sports or other. Before you post on your social media accounts, scroll through your feed to figure out what's in the news that your brand can piggyback on. Once you have a handle on what everyone is talking about, put your spin on it and make sure it's a topic that aligns with your brand.

Wendy's also has an excellent Facebook Page that has framed itself to deal with two essential things: Customer service and seasonal posts. This is something you can start doing immediately in your business. Facebook is a great place to provide customer service through Messenger and respond to comments. Regarding seasonal posts, find creative, entertaining ways to produce content themed around whatever holiday is approaching.

CUPSHE:

Cupshe is a swimsuit brand that focuses almost exclusively on social media marketing and, more specifically, user-generated content in its Instagram strategy.

They let their followers know how to be featured - by tagging @cupshe in their photos. Cupshe has made its social media accounts about sharing pictures and posts that customers have created. It works incredibly well because it leverages social media and content marketing uniquely. Instead of the brand having to plan and design everything, the customers get to do it for them, making a more compelling social strategy. Why? Because user-generated content helps to engage and build a community around a brand. People are always happy and excited to share photos of their products if they think the business might see and respond positively. I have started asking my customers to tag me in a picture, and my social mentions have grown dramatically. Consider emulating this as it is simple and easy to implement.

How Makaro Is Increasing Jewelry Sales with Facebook Dynamic Ads.

Makaro is an Austrian jewelry brand founded by Hanna and Matthias to create beautiful, sustainably made jewelry at accessible prices. The business enjoyed a 3x increase in sales since starting its social media marketing. They invested explicitly in Facebook and Instagram marketing, and thanks to a carefully planned campaign, they turned tried and tested Facebook and Instagram content into ad creative that struck the perfect tone with their target audiences. The marketing campaign ran for six weeks, achieving a 3x increase in sales, a 4.6x increase in view content events, and a 3.6x increase in add-to-cart events.

Makaro's primary goal was to increase online sales, but Hanna and Matthias also wanted to strengthen brand awareness in European German-speaking countries. They needed to create a conversion campaign with ad creative that would appeal directly to their target audience's tastes, needs, and values.

Hanna and Matthias hired an agency (Freiheit Media) to help with their social media marketing. For their campaign, Hanna and Matthias first used Facebook Insights to identify the brand's best-performing organic content on Facebook and Instagram. Then, they tested different ad creative variations among different audiences to understand what motivated people the most.

Equipped with this knowledge, Makaro, and Freiheit Media created ads based on the most popular content, using compelling copy, text overlays to call out product features, and hard-to-resist incentives like free shipping. They used photo and video ads as well as ads in the carousel, collection, and Instant Experience format. Women aged 25 and older living in Germany, Austria, and Switzerland interested in jewelry and fashion accessories were served the ads. The team expanded the audience further by creating a look-alike audience of people who had previously made purchases and friends who liked the Makaro Facebook Page. Ad delivery was optimized for purchase events (that means the ads were shown to people who were most likely to take the desired action).

The other clever thing they did was retarget the people who visited the website and added a product to their shopping cart but still needed to complete the purchase. Makaro and Freiheit Media carefully monitored ad performance with Facebook analytics throughout the campaign and scaled back any ads that didn't perform well.

By meticulously planning and testing ad creative to ensure it was relevant to its audience, Makaro successfully attracted potential customers and encouraged them to act. If you're already excited to jump in and run a similar campaign for your business but wondering what tools to use, you're in luck. I want to share with you why I think this campaign worked and the specific tools you can use:

Case Studies: Brands That Have Mastered Social Media Marketing

They combined content marketing with social media marketing. They created and published high-value content for a specific audience, posted it organically, and monitored performance long before starting the paid campaign.

They leveraged Facebook Insights to determine their audience's wants and, more importantly, the best-performing organic content. With that knowledge, they created ads that were bound to work. They used retargeting efforts.

They created lookalike audiences from customers who had already purchased as well as people friends of people who were already followers.

There are other little things that they sprinkled in that made a massive difference in the overall results, but let's talk about the different tools. These are all available to you when you choose to run a paid Facebook and Instagram campaign.

They used Dynamic ads, Carousel, Collection, and Instant Experience. In the next section, you will learn more about these tools and how to use them best.

Section Two

The Social Media Platforms

Chapter 6

Facebook—The King of social media

Facebook is the king of social media in today's world. It is the cheapest tool available to get attention from the right audience. It is currently the most underpriced advertising platform. That's not an exaggeration.

Did you know that as of 2019, 93% of social media advertisers use Facebook ads? Entire companies have been built off Facebook marketing (like Wish), so you want to pay close attention to this section even if you think your audience will be off the platform. I hear that a lot. So, let me disqualify that thought (even if you're in the B2B space) with some motivating statistics. Here are some more facts and data points about the platform that you should know to help inform your marketing efforts.

The average engagement rate for Facebook posts is 3.6%. Feel free to use this as a benchmark for your engagement rate if you're starting. Anything lower means you need to improve your creatives and audience targeting. 60% of Americans who watch digital videos do so on Facebook. 42% of marketers report that Facebook is critical or essential to their business. While it is becoming a crowded marketplace, you can only afford to sit it out if the odds are relatively high that your competition is already there.

87.1% of U.S. marketers will use Facebook marketing this year, according to estimates from eMarketer.

There are over 90 million small businesses currently using Facebook. Still, many only leverage free tools like groups, messenger, and Facebook Pages. Only 24.6% of Facebook Pages use paid media. The average price for an ad decreased by 4% in Q2 2019. That's excellent news because it means we get slightly more bang for our buck.

Marketing is by no means simple. With limited resources, it gets even trickier. That's why you must learn valuable hacks and equip yourself with the right tools. Facebook cares a lot about the members of their community and is, in fact, their number one priority. But let's face it; they also want to be a profitable business. This means they need to make the environment conducive for businesses.

As a business owner, your primary concern should be, "How do I get my ideal audience to know that I have an offer or solution that is valuable for them? How do I stand out?" Before you can adequately answer these questions, you must understand two things - Intent and Context.

HOW FACEBOOK FOR BUSINESS WORKS:

Facebook is a marketing tool, not a sales tool. For example, Google is about sales. People go on Google intending to buy. Only some people go to Facebook to buy. There is no direct intent to purchase. That doesn't mean a transaction won't take because of an ad or engaging content a user sees on their feed. Still, their intention for being on the platform is socializing.

Facebook helps us to know who is on the platform and their current behaviour and preferences. This is the real power that Facebook has compared to something like Google because, in general, we tend to know what someone wants based on their search query, but we don't know who they are. The power of targeting a particular audience is one of the great benefits of using Facebook marketing. It is essential to bear these subtle differences in mind. What you must stop or avoid doing if you want social media marketing to work for you on Facebook:

STOP POSTING BORING CONTENT

Facebook wants people to remain engaged and active within their platform. If you publish boring stuff, Facebook has no choice but to hide your content. In the last few years, Facebook has dramatically cut down organic reach, making it difficult to reach your audience when starting. Part of this change is because people have been posting content that puts people off.

Boring or low-value content will only do well on the platform if you share it organically or throw some money at it. The good news about Facebook for business is that you can make it work regardless of your ad budget or expertise. You can always start small and grow as your business revenue grows. The bad news is Facebook has become a "pay to play" platform, which means you won't get very far with organic reach. I will share how you can leverage organic and paid strategies to grow your business.

STOP FOCUSING ON VANITY METRICS

As small business owners and early start-ups, our pockets don't run as deep as some big corporations' competing for attention on social media. That's why I urge you to stop fussing over likes and followers count on your social media platforms, especially Facebook. It would be best to focus on what makes a difference to your bottom line, not something that gives you an ego boost. Meaningful metrics include CTR (click-through rates), video views, comments, and messages.

DON'T BE PURELY FOCUSED ON PROMOTING AND SELLING YOUR PRODUCTS

As I mentioned, there is no buying intent on Facebook. It is a platform based on interest primarily built for connection, community building, and meaningful conversations. So, steer clear of pushing products in users' faces on Facebook. People have become savvy enough to know when they are being sold versus when a brand genuinely tries to make a connection.

Today's Facebook user wants to connect with a business with relevant and relatable content, not a sales pitch or infomercials. Approach your Facebook Page with the mindset of building a community or gathering your tribe. An excellent way to avoid being too promotional is to vary your posts. Include posts from other sources that align with your brand. Curate and create fantastic content that sparks conversation.

FACEBOOK ORGANIC REACH:

What is organic reach? Organic reach is the number of people seeing your content without paid distribution. It includes people who are shown your posts and your Facebook page.

Is organic reach dead? As Facebook matured, Mark Zuckerberg has tweaked and changed the platform. In Zuckerberg's words, "Recently, we've gotten feedback from our community that public content - posts from businesses, brands, and media - is crowding out the personal moments that lead us to connect more." Zuckerberg wants Facebook to be better geared to curate content that builds meaningful relationships. With that, the platform changed, leading to a massive decline and what marketers called the "death of organic."

Depending on where you get your statistics, it is reported that organic reach is now between 2% - 6%. There are better viable options for building awareness or generating leads. That doesn't mean it's dead and gone. The key to winning if you can only afford to do organic Facebook marketing is to understand the changes that have taken place with the Organic Reach algorithms and then craft a plan that works to your advantage.

Facebook is waging war against low-quality content, which means with a bit of creativity and goodwill, you can still find avenues that yield positive results.

ORGANIC FACEBOOK STRATEGIES FOR YOUR BUSINESS

Get to know what your audience is looking for. You need to understand what your audience cares about and then reconcile it with your brand and offers. Find topics that are meaningful and craft something that's both relevant and shareworthy. The more targeted you are, the better off you'll be. I'm serious!

Focus on quality, not quantity. So many business owners and entrepreneurs approach Facebook for business with the mindset of spamming and making as much noise as possible to get attention. That is a clear route to failure. You need to focus on quality over quantity. If you can handle quantity and quality, then go for it, but until that happens, it's better to put out one high-quality content a week than mediocre ones every day.

The more you post for the sake of posting, the worse things will be, especially with the new changes. For example, Buffer conducted some tests between 2016 and 2017, whereby they significantly dropped the number of posts they were putting out each day. By mid-2017, they were posting half the number of posts, and yet, oddly enough, this shift helped them increase their Organic Reach. They went from getting an O.R. (Organic Reach) of approximately 70K to 170K. That's a 100K Reach spike that can be directly related to the frequency they posted on their business page. As Organic Reach increased, so did their engagement. This isn't a fluke; it's the new state of Facebook organic marketing.

Natively publish more videos. Video posts get more shares than any other post type, so if you're starting, I encourage you to incorporate video into your marketing strategy. The average video share count is about 98.5 shares. Remember, you only have a few seconds to capture viewer attention, so make sure it's sharp, educational, and entertaining. Keep your videos short. Two minutes or shorter is what experts suggest. Make it look professional and authentic. Create movement in the first two to three seconds to grab the attention of people who have autoplay. There are three categories of videos to create.

CATEGORY # 1: WHY

Create at least three videos answering questions and sharing your mission, vision, and the story behind your brand. Answer questions such as: Why did you start this business? What's your company's vision/mission? What's the backstory that led to the launch of the business? Why does your business exist?

CATEGORY #2: HOW-TO

Create at least three videos that show your audience how to do something. For example, as a flower shop, my portfolio of how-to videos includes walking my audience through the process we use to set up a flower arrangement for a corporate event. The set-up costs $1500, so I help people understand why we charge such prices and the magic behind it. According to current data, 50% of videos on YouTube are how-to videos, so you can see why this would be a good investment.

CATEGORY #3: WHAT

So far, we have not asked for anything or made any offer, and that's how it should be. It would help build trust with your Facebook audience before asking for money. Ensure you've added enough value through the first two categories before making videos for this category. This is where you call them to action. Your job with these types of videos is to highlight the problem or challenge and the solution you offer to that problem or challenge. Then, you can call them to action by asking them to buy, sign up, book a call, etc. Talk about what the business does and the benefits your audience will get from choosing to do business with you.

Use organic post targeting. Did you know that Facebook allows you to target your posts? It's not just limited to paid ads. This feature is handy as organic reach continues to decrease. You can serve your post to relevant customers based on gender, age, education, location, and interest. Here's how:

First, enable the targeting feature on your Facebook page. Do this through your page settings tab under "General."

Second, choose one or more target categories. To do this right, I encourage you to spend some time on your Facebook Insights so you can understand a bit more about your audience before setting parameters. You can also restrict who gets to see your post under "Audience Restrictions."

Third, experiment with at least three targeted posts using different parameters. That way, you can test how your content performs for different audiences. For example, when I first applied this strategy, I entered my Audience Insights and found the websites and pages my visitors liked.

Then, I took the top four and targeted fans of my page using the "interests" option. When I checked my results, I realized my organic content did better when I targeted that core audience.

Fourth, analyze your results. Go to Facebook Insights to see if the organically targeted post performed better. In my case, I found a 3% increase in reach and engagement on the posts I organically targeted.

Add integrations and customization to your page. There are many new apps that you can integrate with your Facebook page to increase the usability of your page and amplify your marketing efforts. Consider customizing with email capture forms, podcasts, quizzes, apps to run contests, etc.

Extend outside the Facebook platform. If you have a following on Instagram, Twitter, YouTube, or any other medium, consider promoting your Facebook page and give them a compelling reason to follow you on Facebook. For example, if you have a sizeable audience on Pinterest, you can invite them to join you for a weekly Facebook Live, where you share some insider secrets that could benefit them. You can also leave a link to your Facebook page in the bio of your other social accounts or the latest video that people have engaged with a lot.

Create invite-only groups for your most engaged audience members. I keep saying it, but it's worth reiterating that Facebook is about building communities. That's why you should consider having your group. Create a tightly-knit community where your members can safely connect, discuss, and share. The best addition to your organic Facebook marketing arsenal is starting your group. However, if it feels too daunting, join a highly engaged and relevant group that serves your business goals. One of the great benefits of starting or joining a group is using it for social listening and engaging with potential brand advocates.

Collaborate with other Facebook Pages in your niche. This is something only some small business owners easily accept. Still, it can be a great strategy to grow your brand quickly. If you look at the Facebook pages of media websites like Huffington Post and Elite Daily, you'll notice they share a similar audience, and both have huge followings. But here's the thing: although they could be "competitors," they share each other's blog posts on Facebook regularly. That collaboration boosts views for both Facebook pages while providing fantastic content they didn't need to create. I call this intelligent social media marketing.

If you have a collaborative mindset and want to try this, I recommend doing an outreach campaign to manageable and manageable pages. In other words, get yourself an influencer outreach strategy. But you want to make sure you reach out to the right influencers. Only aim high enough if your page has zero authority. A few things you want to consider before choosing your list of people to partner with are: How much reach and engagement do they have? Is your target influencer the right fit for your brand? Will that audience be a good match for your products or services? How much authority do they have? They need to be able to inspire action among their audience. What's your leverage? You must have enough value to offer if you want others to partner.

PAID FACEBOOK STRATEGIES FOR YOUR BUSINESS

This is a broad topic that could be its book because Facebook advertising has a lot of areas to cover. However, I want to give you the fundamentals that you can implement to see instant results. No trick or secret recipe will provide you with instant success with Facebook ads. It's all about testing. While there is no one-size-fits-all template, there are some common mistakes too many businesses make with their advertisements that are detrimental to the company. So let me share a few that you must avoid.

MISTAKE#1: GOING AFTER THE WRONG AUDIENCE

Facebook advertising is unique, mainly because of its superior targeting features. Even if you're working with a small budget, you can still reach out to specific audiences. The sheer size of Facebook's user base can be a disadvantage, especially when picking an audience. Do not try to target everybody with your ads. This is a huge mistake many first-time advertisers make. The excitement of generating lots of engagement and a ton of clicks can be alluring, but will it lead to business results? It's only beneficial to get people to engage with your ad if they can gain access to or benefit from your product or service.

Solution:

Your ads should only be seen by people who benefit the most from that ad. So, how can you ensure you do this right? Use Audience Insights to gauge your defined client persona's interests and typical demographics. Conduct a customer survey to understand better your buyers and their demographics, such as job position, gender, age, location, etc.

MISTAKE#2: BEING TOO BROAD OR TOO NARROW WITH YOUR COLD AUDIENCE CHOICE

This is another mistake small business owners tend to make. Once you've done enough research and decided which set of audience to go for, Facebook usually shows you the number of people you can reach with your ad campaign. Pay attention to this and ensure your chosen size aligns with your budget. Most people need to be narrower or narrower with their cold audience. This is a huge mistake. Instead, find a sweet spot.

Solution:

Ask yourself some high-powered questions to decide whether the potential reach Facebook is showing you makes sense. Here are three questions. Will you benefit by reaching out to 1 million people? Do you think many people will be interested in your product or service?

How big is your market? If you feel too broad, narrow it down by adjusting your demographics and interests. Stay high, too; Facebook may not deliver the ads. To have a strong return on your investment, I encourage you to balance the quality of your audience, size, and the price you're paying to reach them. I've gone after a target audience of as low as 50,000, and it worked very well for me because I was focused on achieving a specific audience within a small radius of my business. It would be best if you started by going after an audience of between 100,000 - 800,000, depending on the nature of your business. Test and see, but keep those three questions in mind and try to discover your optimal audience size.

MISTAKE #3: USING THE WRONG CREATIVE.

Execution is critical, and often, we strive to get something done even if it could be better. That's a great strength in the business world, but I've learned from running Facebook ads that paying close attention to the creative details can be the difference between a high-converting ad and a total flop. Using an image just for the sake of it can quickly backfire on you and result in underperformance.

Facebook ads are very visual. If users stop scrolling and look at your ad, the first element they will notice is the image and how interesting it is. If the creative is appealing to your target audience and communicates the right message, you can avoid losing their attention and valuable clicks. According to research by David Ogilvy, images hold precedence over text because they are viewed and absorbed faster than text.

Solution:

Carefully choose an image or images (depending on the type of ad) that connects to the "why" behind your ad. It should be relevant to your offer, compelling, and with minimal text. I recommend using a free graphic designer like Canva to enhance and customize your images.

MISTAKE #4: TWEAKING OR PAUSING THE AD TOO EARLY.

Instant gratification is the poison of social media marketing. If you want to run successful ad campaigns, you need patience. It is easy to get impatient, especially as money goes out but no sales. It might feel like you're losing money in the beginning. That's one of the main reasons small business owners stay away from paid ads. They want to see instant results, and when that doesn't happen, they either start messing with the ad or pause it.

Solution:

Get your mind right before hitting publish on that campaign. It would be best to be comfortable with your ad spend, and you must know how much you can spend to gain a single customer. For example, suppose you sell a product for $30 that costs you $12 to manufacture, package, and ship. Then, you can spend up to $18 to acquire a customer because that would be a break-even point. While it's not profitable initially, the more you optimize Facebook ads, the better results you will see until you finally start making a profit. You need data to be analyzed and evaluated to determine what works. I've found an ideal minimum number of 2,000 people in my business. With that, I can decide if the ad performance is good, if I am heading in the right direction, or if something is going wrong. Then, I decide whether to tweak or pause my campaign.

TYPES OF FACEBOOK ADS

These are the various ad types you can choose to implement on Facebook.

Image ads

These are the fastest and best ways to get started with Facebook advertising. You can boost an existing post from your Facebook page or create one within the Ads Manager account. Image ads are simple, but take your time making them and ensure they are compelling and relevant to your target audience.

Carousel ads

A carousel ad allows you to use up to 10 images or videos to showcase your product or service. It's been one of my favorite ad types for my flower business. You can use it to highlight the different benefits of one or several products or use all the photos to create one large panorama image.

Video ads

These are hot on Facebook as more people consume videos on the platform. Organically, video posts get way more engagement than standard posts, so naturally, a video ad will also perform well. Video ads can run in News Feed and Stories or appear as in-stream ads in longer Facebook videos. You need to be compelling and grab your audience's attention within the first few seconds. Keep the videos short. A good rule of thumb is a 60-second video ad. If you're camera shy or need more time to invest in video equipment, use GIFs or other animations to capture attention or explain your offer.

Video poll ads

This mobile-only Facebook ad format incorporates an interactive component with video polls. It's a relatively new ad type, but early data shows that these ads can significantly increase brand awareness, perhaps even more than regular video ads.

Slideshow ads

Slideshow ads offer an easy way to create short video ads from a collection of still photos, text, or existing video clips. You can choose stock photos available on Ads Manager if you don't have images. What makes slideshow ads compelling is that they have an eye-catching motion, just like a video, but use five times less bandwidth. That means that even if your audience has a slow Internet connection, they can still enjoy the ad. It's an easy, low-impact way to draw attention.

Collection ads

These are exclusive to mobile devices and allow you to showcase five products that customers can click to buy. Collection ads pair well with Instant Experiences, enabling people to buy your products without leaving Facebook. If you're an eCommerce vendor, this is worth testing because people can shop fast and easily while on the go, even if they need a better Internet connection.

Instant Experience ads

Previously called Canvas, these full-screen ad formats load 15 times faster than a mobile website outside Facebook. With Instant Experience ads, you can link additional Instant Experiences so your audience can access even more of your content on mobile.

Lead ads

Lead ads are only available for mobile devices because they're designed to make it easy for people to give you their contact information. These ads are compelling for local businesses, but I've seen them work for digital companies. With a lead ad, you can collect newsletter subscriptions, sign someone up for an appointment, test out a product, or allow people to request more information so you can follow up with a call. They are a powerful and effective way to feed your sales pipeline, qualify, and follow up on leads.

Dynamic ads

Dynamic ads allow you to promote targeted products to the customers who are most likely to be interested in your offer. For example, if you have an eCommerce store and someone visits your store, adds a few items to their shopping cart, and then abandons the purchase, you can retarget them with dynamic ads, and they will see the products they chose on their Facebook feed. Amazon does a fantastic job with this "reminder" ad; now you can too. Make sure to do it tastefully and don't come off as pushy or creepy - no one likes a stalker!

Messenger ads

Facebook Messenger ads are placed within the Messenger tool. All you need to do is choose Messenger as the desired placement. You can also run "click-to-Messenger" ads in the Facebook feed. These ads feature a CTA (call to action) button that opens a Messenger conversation with your Facebook Page so that people can communicate with you or your team.

Stories ads

Stories ads are full-screen vertical video format ads, allowing you to maximize real estate without expecting viewers to turn their screens. I know what you might think: "Why does that matter?" According to Scientific American, 72% of millennials won't rotate their phones to watch widescreen videos. If your business serves that audience group, it's worth testing with Stories ads. These ads are highly effective. A Facebook-commissioned Ipsos survey showed that more than half of the participants said they made more online purchases because of Stories ads.

Stories augmented reality ads

Augmented reality still needs to be mainstream in our society, but Facebook is already taking the lead as it grows in popularity. Expanded reality ads use features like filters and animations to allow people to interact with your brand. This is a new ad style (even for a giant like Facebook), but 63% of U.S. Internet users say they have already tried an AR brand experience.

Playable ads

This is yet another new ad format that incorporates interactivity. You create a game experience that encouraging people to interact with your creative content and brand. Given how much people love playing games online, this ad type might become a high performer for businesses. Only time will tell.

PAID FACEBOOK ADS STRATEGIES

Set up a conversion funnel. When running Facebook ads, ensure you have a back-end plan driving that decision. It would be best if you began with the end in mind. Our end goal is lead generation that results in revenue and happy customers, so we need to set up a funnel that takes our cold audience through discovery, consideration, and purchase.

If you stood at the mall entrance and asked every person walking in to buy you a bouquet, they'd probably give you a weird look and walk away. However, if you stood at the entrance of the same mall with beautiful flowers and asked every person walking in if they would like to receive your flower as a gift, chances are a good number would accept. A handful would be so grateful and stop to discuss why you offer such beautiful flowers for free. The people chatting with you are more likely to share their interests and needs, which would quickly lead to new sales.

I've tried this second option and know how effective it can be. But it only works if you're willing to build a relationship first. On Facebook, a conversion funnel represents a similar experience, but the best part is you can customize it to develop different relationships with a target audience. Some people are ready to buy from you, others might be interested during the holidays, and others may need proof that your stuff is the best. It gets hard to cater to all these different needs in person when you have limited resources, but online, it's easy. It would be best to have a funnel that attracts, converts, closes, and delights your customers. A well-defined conversion funnel is a must. It will enhance all your social media marketing efforts. Think of it as building touchpoints for your future customers.

Use the Facebook Pixel

A Facebook Pixel is a small code that can significantly impact your ad campaign. Once you place the code on your website, it allows you to track conversions and remarket to people who visit your site and those who abandon the cart. It also enables you to create lookalike audiences easily.

When you're just starting, I advise you to avoid engaging in advanced and sophisticated strategies like retargeting, but install your Pixel now. That way, you'll have tracking and remarketing data ready to go when you master the basics and start scaling and optimizing your ads. It is also an excellent way to monitor the performance of your conversion funnel.

Track and Monitor Performance

You can monitor your campaigns' performance in Facebook Ads Manager. When you find a winning ad, put more money into that and pull back on those that aren't. Running several ads with small audiences and small budgets is best when starting out. Once you determine what works best and find at least one winning ad, double down on that primary campaign until you get some results. Then, you can get into more advanced strategies with more variables and larger audiences. You can also re-allocate money from your underperformers to top performers, even if they're on another social network.

Drive a direct sale.

This is a quick and fast way to start driving in some revenue. Remember, Facebook is not built as a sales tool, so this strategy will work best for a brand that's already well known. This strategy will work if your business or brand is known and your price point is relatively low. I encourage you to target people who have already considered buying your product. Consider testing offers, product recommendations, or reminders to complete a purchase.

Convert a proven piece of content into a video ad.

Assuming you have decided to combine content and social media marketing, this strategy will work exceptionally well, even if you're unknown. It's one of the first campaigns I put money into while learning the ropes of social media marketing. The best way to do this is to identify your best-performing content (whatever got the most traffic or engagement). Then, I want you to convert that content into a short video and run it as an ad. If you're worried about production costs or the technical side, don't be. Here are some social media video tools to lighten the burden of producing engaging videos.

Animoto. It's free for 14 days; plans start from $26/month.

Biteable. Without a camera, you can create complete videos, including actual footage. It's free, but I encourage you to get the premium plan for $99 per year as a business.

Go Animate. You can create custom characters using the character creators. In other words, you can make a digital version of yourself, your target customers, or any creative concept you want to bring to life. It's free for 14 days, and plans start at $39/month.

Spark Video by Adobe. It's free to use and comes with video templates that guide you through creating a compelling video in minutes.

Segment Your Audience

First, you need a buyer persona identified. Then, it would be best if you mapped out their journey or what I refer to as the conversion funnel. The first "seed" you build is a cold audience. But once you make them aware of your brand, you start having what's known as a warm audience. This is where you need to get more innovative with your offers. Consider segmenting your audience further instead of fitting everyone into one bucket. The recommended customer segmentation includes past blog readers, engaged blog readers, landing page visitors, shopping cart abandoners, repeat customers, and lukewarm leads. All these people represent your buyer personas at different stages of the purchase journey, which means a different advertising approach and targeted offers. Each business will have unique customer segments, so you must learn about yours. That way, you can create increasingly relevant ads and offers that will convert better.

HOW TO MAKE IT WORK FOR YOU

Follow these steps to implement Facebook marketing in your business correctly.

Create a realistic buyer persona.

Refine your audience persona to ensure you have a natural person, not just some abstract person. Get into your buyer's mind and confirm you know that person to their bones to match their expectations and use the correct language. Revisit things like age, location, job title, challenges, pain points, and, more importantly, when and how they use Facebook. More importantly, you need to understand how your buyer personas identify themselves. That requires a serious time investment, but I promise you, the hours you spend on customer development will be well spent.

Once you know who uses the platform and how it maps back to your product or service, go to Facebook Audience Insights. Use this tool to drill down all the details you can find about your potential customers. Search for Facebook usage, language, relationship status, past purchase activity, etc.

Set the right KPIs that align with your primary social media marketing and business objectives. It's time to get tactical and set Facebook KPIs that you will measure to know if you're headed in the right direction. Focus on things that will impact your bottom line, such as leads, conversions on your website, or improving customer service. Get even more detail with these broader KPIs, for example, 100 new leaders in the next ninety days. All your efforts on Facebook should support those KPIs. That includes both organic and paid campaigns.

Install the Conversion Tracking Pixel

Head to the Pixels page in Facebook Ads Manager and click Actions. Then click View Code and copy-paste that Pixel code between the <head> tags on each web page or your website template to install it on your site. You can also use Google Tag Manager to place the Pixel. Add a specific conversion tracking code, such as purchases or lead conversions. With a Facebook Pixel, you can track up to nine different custom events, and yes, all you need to install is that one pixel. For more details, I have included the Facebook Pixel setup on the resource page.

Combine content marketing with Facebook ads.

The best way (in my experience) to turn cold leads into warm leads on Facebook is by combining content marketing and ads. Instead of going straight for the sale, start slowly, connect, build a relationship, and share valuable content with your audience. Start by sharing your post on Facebook. If you have team members, friends, or family willing to help, ask them to share and like the post. Then, boost that post with a paid ad to reach a wider audience. If you want to get serious, instead of increasing the post, go into your Facebook Ads Manager and set up a campaign, then use that single Facebook Page post across multiple ad campaigns so that all the social proof (likes and shares) will show under a single ad.

CHAPTER 7

Instagram—The Visual Storyteller

Instagram marketing is rising and is projected to keep growing this year. This social network is too popular to ignore whether your business deals in physical products, digital products, or services, even if you're strictly a local store. Don't believe me? Here are more facts and data points about the platform to help inform your marketing efforts.

11% of U.S. social media users shop on Instagram. Earlier in the buying cycle, people use Instagram to research products and services. 62% of people say they have become more interested in a brand or product after seeing it in Stories. Two hundred million Instagram users visit at least one business profile daily. The sooner you get your business on the platform, the sooner you can enjoy some of that attention.

Mistakes small business owners are making that you must avoid:

MISTAKE #1: NEVER COMMENTING ON OTHER POSTS

Remember that Instagram is a social platform. That means you need to engage and connect with the members of the Instagram community. Publishing content is only half the equation if you want to do well. Your prospective and existing followers are posting content, too, and if you ignore this, it will seem like you're just using the platform for self-promotion.

Solution:

Take a few minutes daily to comment and engage with the images you see in your newsfeed. If you're building your Instagram business account, allocate more than a few minutes for social engagement and go into the accounts of your followers, influencers, and other people in your niche to engage with them.

MISTAKE#2: FAILING TO RESPOND TO COMMENTS ON YOUR POSTS

This one annoys the heck out of me. Whenever I find a post with comments from people, and the brand doesn't acknowledge or respond to those comments, I immediately get turned off by that brand. You work hard to create and publish this content - but for what?

Isn't the whole point of social media marketing to connect, build relationships, and turn those relationships into business results?

Solution:

Make sure your brand is manageable for social engagement. Whether you have one or one hundred comments on your post, please pay attention to them. Always acknowledge anyone who takes the time to show interest in what you say and thank them for being present and engaged. It makes your brand seem relatable, friendly, and more down-to-earth. More importantly, it shows you're a good person. In today's marketplace, people want to buy from good people.

MISTAKE #3: BEING IMPERSONAL

As business owners, we are often led to believe that positioning ourselves like Coca-Cola or Nike will make us seem like a big deal, and people will want to follow our brand. Trying to filter out your personality and being serious (adopting a corporate voice) so that you can be what you think people expect from a company is a better way to win with social media marketing.

Unless you have a lot (and I mean a lot) of marketing budget and are willing to put in the resources, time, and human resources it has taken these companies to build a connection, positioning yourself as an impersonal "corporate" brand will hurt your chances of fast growth.

Solution:

Leverage your unique personality. Instagram is a social spot, and the more human you can be, the more your tribe will quickly recognize and flock to you.

MISTAKE #4: OVERDOING IT WITH HASHTAGS

Yes, hashtags are great; you need them to gain visibility, but please do what is necessary. I saw a post recently with one sentence in the copy and thirty hashtags. It came across as exploitative and spammy.

Solution:

Be mindful of the hashtags you use. Ensure they elevate your brand and are relevant to the content and your ideal audience. Choose a number that is a little when deciding on how many hashtags to put on a post.

ORGANIC INSTAGRAM STRATEGIES FOR YOUR BUSINESS

Create product teasers that smoothly urge people to buy. As a small business owner, Instagram is a great place to advertise your products or services. And if you do it tastefully, you will satisfy users. Product teasers are a great way to tell a story and talk about your product without being pushy.

Last Christmas, I posted a teaser after watching Starbucks do the same. And I offered a holiday discount with my post, where I showed some of the exclusive (personalized) creations we had created for our pre-order list. That post received thousands of likes and comments, and I even got 10 DMs asking for a quote. I got two orders from that post, so I used that content piece to run paid ads, creating a snowball effect on our Christmas sales.

When you tease people with a beautiful story and imagery or video about products they are interested in and don't push them into buying anything, they're more likely to pull the trigger and buy something. If not, they'll at least engage with it by liking, commenting, or sharing it with a friend.

Instagram Stories

Instagram Stories are great for generating leads.

They are only live for 24 hours, but stories can be saved and reused later.

Learn from your competitors.

Even if they are your competitors, you should still use their accounts. Your competitors' social media accounts can be a great learning tool. Analyze what they are doing, what's getting the most traction, their frequency of posting, and how they've positioned themselves on the platform. Use it for inspiration and emulate what you see working.

Paid Instagram Strategies for Your Business

Only run paid ads on the content already performing well on the platform. Use Instagram story ads to build a warm audience and retarget the friendly list. Test different creatives to see which ones work best for your target audience. Make your ad as authentic as possible to fit into the platform seamlessly. People don't like clicking on infomercials, so avoid those on Instagram.

HOW TO MAKE IT WORK FOR YOU

Refine your Instagram audience persona. Get a content plan created that aligns with the needs and best practices of the platform. Consider leveraging Instagram influencers, primarily if you sell products. Organically test your creatives and products before doubling down on paid ads.

CHAPTER 8

Twitter (Now X)—The Pulse of Real-Time Engagement

Twitter is a great platform to increase your business's online reach. The average Twitter user follows five companies, and 80% of all Twitter users have mentioned a brand in a tweet. In a survey of over 1,000 users, Twitter found that 51% used their platform daily. On average, these users followed around 21 small to medium-sized businesses, and 30% regularly saw tweets from the companies they followed while browsing. That's a lot of brand exposure. One of the best things about Twitter is that it has a lot of flexibility to start conversations with peers, influencers, and potential business prospects on a whim.

Here are more facts and data points about the platform to help inform your marketing efforts. Twitter users spend 26% more time with ads than social media users. Regular Twitter users following a new small to medium-sized business on the platform are likelier to shop on the brand's website. Twitter ad engagement is up 23%, and the CPE (cost per engagement) is down 12%. Twitter ads with video are 50% cheaper in cost-per-engagement, so you need to invest in that if you're doing paid ads.

It's worth noting that Twitter doesn't just help grow your customer base through word-of-mouth marketing but also a platform that enables you to meet and speak to your customers right where they are. There are a few critical mistakes to avoid when attempting to do this.

MISTAKE #1: TOO MUCH SELF-PROMOTION

As with other social media platforms, being too self-focused will hurt your brand, especially on Twitter. If you only promote your business and continuously mention yourself, it will rub your audience the wrong way.

Solution:

Mix things up and strategically publish content that you've created, as well as content you curate. In your created content, promote your business with content that leads to conversions, purely value-adding, and brand-building.

MISTAKE #2: USING TWITTER MASS FOLLOWER TRICKS

One of the biggest mistakes business owners are making, which can lead to penalties by the platform admins, is following users aggressively in the hope of getting more followers. Twitter admins frown upon this and could easily suspend your account. Besides, it seems desperate and unappealing if you're following people to get a large following.

Solution:

Follow people with purpose. Don't follow more than 100 people a day. Regularly do a Twitter cleanse to unfollow people who aren't right for you or those you feel aren't responsive enough. By using a tool like unfollowspy.com, you can see people you are following who aren't following you, making it easy to cut them off.

MISTAKE #3: GOING IN BLINDLY WITHOUT A STRATEGIC PLAN

With a plan, you'll drown in the ocean of tweets and need help knowing if progress is occurring. Most people post randomly on Twitter and wait till they come across something exciting or until it's convenient. Like Facebook, Instagram, LinkedIn, and the other major platforms, consistency and clarity of purpose are necessary for success.

Solution:

Map your specific Twitter KPIs to move you closer to your overall goals. You can include KPIs like increasing the number of followers, increasing engagement, driving traffic to your website or landing page, etc. Make a one-pager specifically for Twitter that describes your target audience on this platform, the hashtags you'll be using, the types of tweets you'll post, and frequency.

ORGANIC TWITTER STRATEGIES FOR YOUR BUSINESS

Start by building your community. If you're starting, there's no need to follow every other person you come across on Twitter. Instead, follow those already part of your business community or people you believe you can benefit. Make a list of your customer base, current prospects, relevant influencers, friends, colleagues, related businesses, competitors, and those who provide you with exciting and valuable information. Follow a handful of the people on that list daily until it is complete.

Next, engage with them. If you want people to mention your brand and have meaningful conversations, you must do much more than follow them and tweet about your brand. Be active, add value to your content, like or re-tweet other people's tweets. You can tweet about your new product, customer feedback, something motivational, etc.

Leverage Twitter Chats

A Twitter chat is where users meet at a pre-determined time to discuss a particular topic using a designated hashtag. Buffer calls it a business networking event without a dress code.

Twitter chats are so effective for business owners mainly because the people who participate in them are the ones who enjoy engaging on the social network. People taking part in Twitter chats don't just do it to distribute and consume content. They are using Twitter to interact. These are the users who are going to reply to your tweets, retweet your content, and help amplify your message.

To get started, join a Twitter chat in your industry to get a taste of what it's like, and if you enjoy it, consider starting your chat. The best place to discover Twitter chats is Tweetreports.com because they share a list of all the available Twitter chats daily. You can get tools like Tweetchat, which helps you quickly interact and reply to Tweets. Once your Twitter account is connected to Tweetchat, you can easily keep up with the fast-paced nature of Twitter chats as it updates in real time. You can also use Tweet-deck, owned by Twitter, to accomplish the same thing as Tweetchat.

Use Twitter Video

Twitter might not be the first platform you think of for video marketing, but it works exceptionally well as an organic strategy. Use Twitter's native video feature to record up to 140 seconds and upload the video directly to your Twitter stream. Use video to break new stories, offer a behind-the-scenes look, evoke emotion, or give extra life to your post.

Respond when someone tweets you. A lot of small business owners take their followers for granted. Doing your best to respond in some way when a user tweets or mentions you can go a long way in creating a positive brand image. It increases the chance that the person will continue to engage with you in the future, and any new prospective followers will feel encouraged to follow you when they see your brand is responsive and caring.

Follow conversations on specific hashtags and dedicate time daily to engage proactively with other Twitter users. A discussion on Twitter is like having a face-to-face meeting with your customers. Use the most relevant hashtags for your business to initiate the chat so people can get used to seeing you as responsive and friendly.

Use Direct Messages

Give your potential customers the ability to contact you directly. It's a great way to encourage conversations and make connections. Check your settings to ensure you can receive Direct Messages from anyone, even people who don't follow you. Then, monitor your inbox so you can follow through on incoming messages. You can also send messages to your followers with valuable content or an irresistible offer.

Keep your Tweets brief.

That sounds wild, considering Twitter already has a character limit. According to several surveys, tweets between 80-100 characters are more likely to be concise, full of value, and elicit retweets. Users will have enough room to add their thoughts and hashtags while referring to you briefly. This is a great way to encourage users to share your content.

Ask for retweets and offer an incentive.

Some brands will offer a discount or a giveaway if users retweet a specific tweet. This can be an excellent hack for an organic campaign to go viral. Just be sure to offer something valuable and relevant.

Use Twitter cards to maximize exposure.

Twitter Cards are a great way to provide extra information about your content to Twitter so you can maximize the potential of any tweet shared. Adding Twitter Cards serves two purposes.

First, they make the tweet from your website stand out in the news feed. Second, you get in-depth analytics of the engagement you receive from your tweets with Twitter Cards from your website. You can create a summary card, a photo card, a gallery card, an app card, a player card, a product card, or a lead generation card, depending on the nature of your business and what you want to promote.

Summary Cards work well for articles, blog posts, and other informational pages on your website. You can use the summary card to pull a thumbnail, title, and description from the page, or you can use the summary card to pull a large image, title, and report from the page. An App card will let you show viewers a link to your app based on the device they've used to view the tweet. iOS and Android users see details about the app specific to their device.

A Player card allows you to play videos from your website directly on Twitter, like when you share a tweet of a YouTube video. You must install a code for Twitter Cards to work efficiently on your website. Sometimes, you will need approval from Twitter before you can use the Player Card on your website. Twitter provides a lot of helpful tutorials to set these cards up, and on the resource page, I have linked a video that can help.

TYPES OF TWITTER ADS:

Promoted Tweet

Promoted Tweets are ordinary Tweets purchased by advertisers who want to reach a wider group of users or spark engagement from their existing followers. A promoted Tweet can appear at the top of relevant search results, in search results for a Promoted Trend, on your timeline, on user profiles that fit the targeting credentials, and on official Twitter clients.

Promoted Trend

A Promoted Trend is a 24-hour high-impact takeover of the Trends list on Twitter. They are usually displayed at the first or second slots of the "Trends for you" section in a user's timeline and "Explore" tab. Promoted Trends are similar to any other trending topic; users can interact and engage with them similarly. The only difference is that a Promoted Trend is purchased by an advertiser and marked as "promoted."

Promoted Account

A Promoted Account suggests a Twitter account that people don't currently follow and may find interesting.

They help introduce a wider variety of accounts people may enjoy. They are usually displayed in multiple locations, including a user's timeline, "Who to Follow" section, and search results. This might be a suitable ad type to expand your account's reach and grow your audience. They are best for boosting follower growth and engagement or amplifying your message on and off Twitter.

PAID TWITTER STRATEGIES FOR YOUR BUSINESS

Avoid selling right away and focus on brand awareness first.

Choose the awareness, consideration, and conversion strategy because it works best. When advertising to Twitter users who have yet to visit your website, start with a soft sell and high-quality content instead of asking them to purchase immediately. Offer an eBook, a webinar, or a free trial and warm people into your funnel first.

Use Twitter Cards

Twitter cards are helpful for both organic and paid ads. We've already talked about organic Twitter cards, but you can also use instant unlock and conversational cards for your paid campaign. You could also promote a Website Card to get people to click on your website. Consider a lead generation card to get information directly from the platform. The best part about using this card in your campaign is that you won't have to worry about potentially losing leads or making people leave the platform because this card allows the user to give you their information on the tweet.

Be precise with your Targeting.

Target the right audience in your ad campaign. Twitter offers aspects that may or may not be relevant to your specific goals, so study your options and determine the best targeting specs for your audience persona. You can target by location, interest, behavior, followed accounts (such as your competitors), events, and more.

Create High-Quality Visuals and Multimedia

You need to invest in multimedia, GIFs, and high-resolution imagery if you want your ads to pop. Users love attractive images, so don't just slap on any image. Take the time to pick visuals that help sell your main message and ensure the image is share-worthy.

Use Power Words in Your Ads

Using powerful words and superlatives in your copy can increase clicks and engagement on your tweet. For example, instead of saying, "Increase your followers on Twitter," you could say, "Learn the best way to increase your followers on Twitter fast." Make your copy as appealing as possible while providing value.

Use Contrasting Colors

The human eye is attracted to anything with contrast, so it shouldn't be surprising that your ad might capture more attention if you use colors that contrast. A study by Usability Tools showed that highly contrasting CTAs had a 75% higher click-through rate than low contrast CTAs. As you choose your images and CTA buttons, keep this in mind.

Create "Question-based ads."

Twitter is a great place to encourage conversations, and if you research enough personal and business brands, you'll see a lot of engagement stems from questions. Ask your users a question in your promoted Tweet, which will compel them to engage with your ad and create a sense of connection instead of advertising.

Run separate ad campaigns for mobile and desktop targeting. This is especially important on this platform. Mobile is fundamentally different than desktop, and user behavior and purchase intent also tend to differ, so I encourage you to split-test the campaigns. That way, you will learn the nuanced user behaviors for each.

Match Your Bid to Targeting Size.

If you target a specific audience on Twitter with your campaign, increasing your bid might be a good idea because the more detailed, the more expensive it gets. For example, suppose you're a local business that wants to target a specific geographical region. In that case, you may need to bid more to win the same number of auctions as advertisers targeting a less specific audience.

Keep refreshing your creatives.

The lifespan of any content on Twitter is very short. Things happen fast, and if you don't keep refreshing your creatives, it will be hard to serve as many impressions as you'd like.

Create a retargeting ad campaign.

Take advantage of your ad's attention and remarket to the people who visit your landing page but don't convert. Make sure to exclude past converters when you do this. Remarketing is a powerful way to nurture that relationship and avoid being pushy. Use content that adds more value and increased brand awareness. If you already have an email list, you can upload this list to Twitter to target them with specific offers.

HOW TO MAKE IT WORK FOR YOU

- Set the right objectives and decide on a budget if you will invest in paid advertising.
- Polish your profile and make sure it's aligned with your brand message.
- Create a content strategy for Twitter and determine the type of content you will create for free and paid plans.
- Engage on Twitter, join Twitter chats, respond to tweets, ask for retweets, and start your Twitter chat.
- Create high-quality images, videos, and multimedia assets.
- Retarget the warm audience from the first cold ad with more relevant brand-building content to nurture that relationship further.

CHAPTER 9

YouTube—The Power of Video Content

YouTube is the world's second-largest search engine (behind parent company Google) and can be an asset for your business regardless of industry. Competition is fierce on this platform, as over 500 hours of video are being uploaded every minute. Gaining tangible business results will be easy with a strategy that includes your audience research, content strategy plan, CTAs, posting frequency, and how to form partnerships and create backlinks to your products or services.

This is one of the platforms that will only work if you combine content marketing with your social media strategy. Everything is about the content you create and the value you provide on each video. Even though I said it's fiercely competitive, you need to understand that most of the content being uploaded needs to be done by businesses. Only a tiny percentage of small businesses are seriously doing video marketing, which is why this is the best time to invest.

Here are more facts and data points about the platform to help inform your marketing efforts. YouTube mobile ads receive 83% viewer attention, which is excellent because your chances of getting your brand known are high. The average viewing session, which keeps going up year by year, is 40 minutes. That's the most elevated viewing session of any platform, which implies if you publish great content, your tribe will watch it even if it's long.

In today's mobile-first society, over 60% of people prefer video platforms to live television, so even if you have the money to pay for traditional media channels, I encourage you to consider leveraging the power of YouTube.

ORGANIC YOUTUBE STRATEGIES FOR YOUR BUSINESS

Create a consistent publishing schedule. People will follow your business and become subscribers if you inform them of how frequently you publish and then deliver that promise. So, you can't just produce videos when convenient. As with all other social media activities, consistency will give you the momentum needed to help you grow.

Create a Netflix Effect

By this, I mean creating a series of content that people can binge-watch. Since you are taking the time to organize and plan out your content, I encourage you to also think about creating content that feeds into more content so that people can stay hooked on your channel. The more top of mind you are, the higher your chances that people will respond to your CTAs.

Make Your Videos Personalized.

The more personalized your video is, the better it will perform. For example, if you are a local bakery, I encourage you to target some of your videos to individuals in your local area. Give an anecdote or mention something only people around your neighborhood would know. That video may not go viral globally, but you will notice a high engagement with the right audience.

Build Relationships Within the YouTube Platform

Engage with content from other channels, find peers and competitors, and be active members of those pods where you see much activity. The more you can participate, help people, and genuinely chime in on conversations, the more people will want to associate with you.

Reply to Comments

This is something I recommend for every platform. If you actively publish on YouTube, why ignore the comments people leave after consuming your content? Even if it's one comment, acknowledge and appreciate their engagement.

TYPES OF ADS FOR YOUTUBE

These ad formats are known to perform best on the platform. TrueView, Discovery, True-View In-Stream, and Bumper Ads. TrueView Discovery - this ad appears next to related YouTube videos on YouTube search results or the YouTube desktop and mobile homepage. You only pay when a viewer clicks on your ad and watches your video. This is a great ad format to reach specific people browsing or searching for videos in those moments of discovery.

TrueView In-Stream - this ad immediately immerses viewers in your content. After 5 seconds, they can keep watching or hit the skip button. The best part about this ad format is you pay when a viewer watches 30 seconds (or the whole video if shorter) or if the viewer interacts with your ad. This ad format is best when you want your video ad to appear before, during, or after other videos on YouTube.

Bumper Ads - this ad is 6 seconds or shorter and plays before, during, or after another video. The best part about this ad format is that viewers cannot skip it. You have six seconds of uninterrupted attention to make your potential subscribers discover your excellent channel. For this ad format, you pay per CPM (each time your ad is served 1,000 times). If you know you've got a short, powerful, and memorable message and want to reach a broader audience with a hook that will have them running to your channel, I highly recommend testing this ad format.

PAID ADS STRATEGIES FOR YOUTUBE BUSINESS

Leverage your best-performing content first. This goes back to using content marketing and paid advertising. Publish a few content pieces and monitor the best performers. When you spot one organically performing well, invest a small budget to reach a broader audience. Build an ad that incorporates clips or concepts from your best-performing video.

Use Advanced Targeting

YouTube allows great flexibility to take control over who sees your ads. Starting with demographic targeting (and the info from your audience persona document), you can layer on affinity audiences (to target people interested in a particular topic), custom affinity audiences, and in-market audiences. For example, if you were selling yoga lessons for a specific location, it would make sense to advertise in that region to the demographics of your typical clients who are already interested in yoga.

Incorporate Interactive Elements.

YouTube gives you interactive elements that can deepen your viewer's engagement with your video. Did you know you can link your shopping cart with a TrueView video ad? It's a great way to drive tangible results and produce new business. Use cards for a few seconds to tease something (another video or playlist). If you are using the TrueView In-Stream ad, you can have a companion banner with a clickable thumbnail. This is a great way to guide viewers to "watch more" or "subscribe." Whatever you choose to use, make sure it's not too distracting or overly done.

Set up Video Remarketing.

This is one of the most effective ways to utilize YouTube ads. It works exceptionally well because the audience that sees your ad has already expressed interest in your business by visiting your website. People who visit your site, landing page, or other social networks can be tracked and remarketed with the right offer. And it's a lot easier to get those people to act on your request than people who've never heard of your business.

Optimizing Your Skippable Ads.

In Skippable ads, you must ensure your "view rate" is high. That means you must create a headline that grabs attention, a description that hooks people, and an eye-catching thumbnail.

You want to ensure your CTR (click-through rate) is high regarding non-skippable ads. Having an engaging video that hooks people in the first three seconds is vital. Your video content must be good enough and relevant to the target audience that is seeing your video.

HOW TO MAKE IT WORK FOR YOU

Set up your channel correctly with suitable artwork to help people understand your brand, how they will benefit from subscribing, and how often they can expect to hear from you.

Do your research and find content in your space that is already popular but has yet to be popular so you can create something better and reach the same audience. Create an effective content plan that will enable you to publish consistently. Have clear CTAs on all your videos, making sure to do what is necessary when asking the audience to watch more videos, subscribe, or visit your website. If you're selling a product, do something unique, entertaining, and engaging to show how reliable and original your product is.

Create unique, eye-catching thumbnails, and work on your titles, descriptions, and keywords for each video you publish. Mix up your content to keep your tribe interested and engaged and to grow your subscribers. Depending on your topic, consider combining product reviews, tutorials, and motivational and entertaining videos.

Create playlists that make it easier for new and existing subscribers to navigate your channel and even binge-watch the topics they most resonate with. You can also create a trailer that walks people through your layout and the areas you cover in your content.

Instead of focusing on viral videos, create series-based content to create that Netflix effect that encourages binge-watching. Then, recommend a relevant video and links to what you want people to watch. Set aside the proper budget that will be good enough revenue to create a positive ROI if you choose to do paid ads. Ensure your funnel is optimized and congruent with the video ad you create.

Chapter 10

Pinterest—Visual Discovery and Inspiration

Pinterest may not be as large as Facebook, but it's an important social platform with very profitable demographics. The platform offers an excellent opportunity to reach new potential customers in affordable and even freeways. Half of U.S. millennials use Pinterest, not just young people saving ideas and wish lists.

Women between the ages of 25 and 54 are active on the platform and make online and offline purchase decisions directly by interacting with brands on the forum. The best part is users are very open-minded. You don't need to be a well-known brand to gain new customers. 97% of Pinterest searches are unbranded. Pinterest serves 2 billion searches every month, which means that 1.94 billion are unbranded searches. In other words, there's plenty of room for your business to be introduced to your potential customers.

Here are more facts and data points about the platform to help inform your marketing efforts. Pinterest users click through to shopping sites way more than Facebook, Snapchat, or Twitter users. The platform drives 33% more traffic than Facebook, 71% more than Snapchat, and 200% more than Twitter. Pinterest users spend 29% more while shopping than non-users and are 39% more likely to be active retail shoppers compared to people who don't use Pinterest.

According to a study by Analytic Partners, Pinterest averages a $4.30 gross return for every $1 spent on ads. According to Pinterest's internal analysis, pins that feature life moments experience a 22% lift in sales and a 10x lift in awareness. Pinterest users are more motivated to buy, with 50% claiming they often buy something after seeing a Promoted Pin. 35% of Pinterest users make more than $75,000 annually, meaning the audience has enough disposable income to buy your products or services.

ORGANIC MARKETING STRATEGIES TO ADD TO YOUR MARKETING PLAN.

Create Pins that lead to valuable resources. The Pinterest algorithm has been upgraded so it can favor high-value content. That means putting up a beautiful image that doesn't direct to something useful for the user will not benefit your business, so consider creating a blog or downloadable resources.

Use keywords in your pin descriptions and board names. Selecting the right keywords and hashtags lets you quickly discover yourself on Pinterest and Google.

Join a Group Board so you can get as much exposure as possible. Group boards are boards that have more than one contributor. It's a great way to increase reach and have hundreds or hundreds of thousands of people discover your content, even with no following.

Apply to get Rich Pins. These pins contain extra information that makes them stand out on the Pinterest feed. With Rich Pins, you get bold titles that grab attention and increase the likelihood of getting clicks. You need to apply to get them, and it does talk a little backend work, but it's a great way to encourage engagement and direct sales.

Types of Pinterest Ads

Promoted Pins are Those saved to your profile that you'd like to boost with paid aids. Promoted App Pins are like Promoted Pins but include a download button that links users directly to the App Store. Promoted Videos are short-form videos that are around 30-90 seconds long. Videos play automatically, a great way to introduce your product to a new user.

Paid Ads Strategies for Your Business

Use text overlay to add content to your images. Incorporate a CTA (call to action) button in the picture. It will encourage users to click on your image to drive conversions. Offer Buyable Pins so that users browsing through Pinterest can see your product and the price and even purchase it with a few clicks on their mobile device. Create shopping recommendations for your users underneath each Pin. It's an excellent placement for your ads, and if you use high-quality images that appeal to your audience, you'll notice high engagement and conversions.

Create attractive boards that you know your audience will love. Amplify the quality of your visual content and consider doing more than just regular images. Create charts, advice guides, and infographics that are visually stunning.

HOW TO MAKE IT WORK FOR YOU

Refine your Pinterest business profile by including a relevant branded description that points to a link and highlights what followers should expect. Optimize your Pins using relevant keywords and hashtags so you can begin to enjoy some free SEO juice. Try to combine both niche and industry hashtags. Create high-quality content focused on offering solutions. If you sell services or products, consider creating articles and resources that solve a problem for your ideal client or the benefits of what your business offers.

Integrate Pinterest into your website. I especially encourage this if your niche is very aesthetically pleasing. Use Pinterest's widget builder to create a customizable copy-and-paste feed on-site so you can enable more social following. Create visually stunning theme boards. I recommend focusing on content that helps you build your brand instead of selling products.

Chapter 11

WhatsApp—The Personal Marketing Channel

WhatsApp marketing is increasingly becoming a common practice for small business owners, and with good reason. WhatsApp was created in 2009 by Jan Koum and Brian Acton (both former Yahoo employees), and Facebook acquired it in 2014 for a sweet $19 billion.

WhatsApp is currently used in 109 countries and is growing. 70% of WhatsApp users are on the app daily. Over 100 million voice calls and 55 million video calls are made on WhatsApp daily. The app is available in 53 languages.

As a small business owner, WhatsApp is more than just an excellent marketing tool; it can lead to actual business revenue. The app is free, and it allows you to communicate directly with your customers. You can use it to poll your customers, organize meetings or in-person meet-ups, and share catalogs, videos, content, brochures, etc. It's also great for sending out reminders and follow-up messages. If you want your business to have a personalized feel that doesn't cost extra, WhatsApp is your marketing tool.

WHATSAPP MARKETING STRATEGIES FOR YOUR BUSINESS

Create a brand persona to chat with users. This will help you bring in new and existing customers. It will also help build buzz around your business. Offer discrete advice and services to high-value customers.

You can offer your top customers updates on new arrivals, launches, and business events before sharing them with the public. You can also allow your customers to have direct access and ask for advice from the privacy of the messenger service. It's a great way to create a VIP feeling within your business.

Create a WhatsApp group.

WhatsApp enables you to create groups of up to 256 members. You can create a focus group for your product or service or a weekly mastermind. You can also start a "collective chat" to get to know people's public opinions on specific topics or even your products.

Host a Contest Through WhatsApp.

You can decide on a duration when the contest is running (a week, a month, etc.) and ask your customers to join the group/text you to participate.

Use Multimedia and Rich Texts.

To attract and keep the attention of your WhatsApp tribe, consider using italics, bold texts where appropriate, emojis, GIFs, images, and links. The most important thing is to keep it relevant, so don't overdo it.

Create and Share High-Value Content.

As personal and casual as WhatsApp may seem, you must maintain brand consistency and genuinely share value. Don't spam people with irrelevant or overly promotional content. It's not meant to be used as a broadcasting or infomercial platform. WhatsApp is for interacting and giving a personalized effect. Post content that will be valuable to the receiver.

Create a Follow-Up Sequence for Customer Acquisition.

If you do your follow-ups on WhatsApp instead of direct phone calls, you will get a 40% lift in your response rate. In today's hectic world, people are not interested in being ambushed by an unknown number, but they are more likely to respond to a personal message. Create a scripted sequence of letters you can send to prospects interested in your offer but have yet to close the deal.

Depending on your niche, this will differ, so get creative and think from your customer's perspective. For example, if you've sent a quotation to your potential customer but have yet to hear from him, you could call him again, send a follow-up mail using formal language, or send a short message on WhatsApp asking about the status. Chances are you'll get a faster response using WhatsApp in this creative way.

Use it to perform a service that offers convenience.

Depending on the nature of your business, you could use the platform to direct clients to book or receive courier services. For example, you could do flower delivery, cake booking, or even food orders. Let your imagination run a little wild as you consider the nature of your business and how you can provide a personalized service to enhance the appeal of your business to new prospects.

Chapter 12

LinkedIn—The Professional Network

LinkedIn is a potent B2B tool that can boost your revenue immediately if you know what you're doing. If you're not in the B2B space and want to know if this will apply to you, I encourage you to try it. LinkedIn used to be a job/career platform for networking and recruiting, but in 2019, it became one of the rising trends on social media. They want to become a content platform, which means a lot of new opportunities and attention now exist, and you can take advantage of this shift.

The platform enables you to run paid ads as well. Still, given that they are the most expensive ad platform (not worthwhile for a new or small local business), I encourage you to focus on the organic strategies until you get some results before venturing into paid ads. Did you know that in 2019, 80% of B2B leads generated on social media came from LinkedIn?

Here are more facts and data points about the platform to help inform your marketing efforts. InMail has a 300% higher response rate than email. 50% of B2B web traffic originating from social media comes from LinkedIn. 91% of executives rate LinkedIn as their first choice for professionally relevant content. 45% of LinkedIn users are in upper management levels. 94% of B2B marketers on social media use LinkedIn to publish content. 49% of LinkedIn users earn more than $75,000 a year.

If these statistics inspire you to dig deeper into the platform and make it work for your business, below are strategies to test out.

LINKEDIN STRATEGIES FOR YOUR BUSINESS

Build a professional and personal brand. Polish your personal profile and company page. That will ensure your company looks legitimate and authoritative. Build a LinkedIn funnel that lets you take a cold connection into your world and turn it into a buying customer.

Publish articles consistently on your topic of expertise on the native publishing platform. Once you publish a new post, send private messages to relevant connections with a personalized note. Create customized scripts that you can send out to new contacts to initiate rapport. Remember, LinkedIn is professional, so be thoughtful with your hands. Invest in a LinkedIn premium or sales navigator so you can send more Emails to the right individuals if your business deals with high-level decision-makers.

Follow your competitors to gain insight into what they're offering, whom they serve, and what they're sharing. That can help you determine which niches within your market are underserved and where growth opportunities exist. Create a company showcase page to segment your products for specific audiences.

Use advanced search to identify the people you are targeting for a chance to connect with executives and decision-makers easily. It's advantageous if you're in a business that usually makes it tough to reach such people. Remember to save and track your searches. Join or start a group for your niche market that will enable you to get in front of your ideal customer. Be active in the group and share your expertise. Invest in sponsored ads if your budget allows.

HOW TO MAKE IT WORK FOR YOU

Create a clear and compelling pitch on your company page and personal profile. Publish relevant and high-quality content regularly. Create and publish videos natively for maximum organic reach. Become a groupie. Pinpoint the LinkedIn groups your target decision-maker would likely be a part of. Aim for a group with less than 5,000 members. Participate in numerous discussions and always focus on how you can help your targeted prospects.

Create personalized scripts for connecting with cold leads and initiating them into your well-thought-out funnel. Give away as much high-value content as possible, such as free white papers, eBooks, and advice within the community and groups. Combine automation with personal input on LinkedIn. Use relevant tools to help you reach more people, but at the same time, infuse that personal touch as soon as you make a connection so you can address more needs, solve more problems, and attract new business.

CHAPTER 13

Snapchat—The Ephemeral Content King

Snapchat differs from other social platforms, intimidating even seasoned social media marketers. But don't let this stop you because this platform does provide new opportunities and ways to connect with your target audience. The most important thing about Snapchat is that you will do well if your business serves its core audience.

Only some small business owners should invest in Snapchat (especially if your target demographic is purely middle-aged to older adults). Still, I encourage you to educate yourself enough to figure out if your target audience hangs out on the platform. If Millennials are included in your target audience, you should be on Snapchat.

Here are some facts to help inform your marketing efforts. There are more than 10 billion daily video views on Snapchat. 76% of Snapchat users spend an average of 30 minutes daily in the app. 25% of Snapchat users are under 25, and 37% fall in the eight to 24-year-old category. 12% of 35 to 54-year-olds are currently using Snapchat.

TYPES OF SNAPCHAT CONTENT YOU CAN CREATE

- Images - the best are in portrait format.

- Snaps - these are images or videos that are sent privately and only to specific users. They expire and disappear after a time.

- Regular videos - the time limit on these videos is ten seconds.

- Stories - these are images or videos that are shared with your followers. They are great for mass broadcasting.

MARKETING STRATEGIES FOR YOUR BUSINESS

Post your story often. Anything you post on Snapchat disappears after 24 hours, so you must be proactive to stay relevant. Posting content about three or four times per day is ideal because it will help keep your engagement high and prevent your followers from getting drained by your content.

Give a Behind-the-Scenes Look

It can be a great way to attract new users and engage existing ones. Consider showcasing your business's raw and honest story and the people you work with if you have a team. Connect with influencers and let them do a Takeover. Snapchat takeovers are among the most effective marketing strategies on the platform. This is especially true if you work with someone influential to your fans. Allow that person to take over your account for a day and create meaningful, fun content around them. Only script the entire project a little because you want the message to be authentic and genuine.

Take advantage of Snapchat features. There are so many filters, stickers, and editing options, such as drawing tools, text add-ins, emojis, and so on, that you can use to make your content stand out. Feel free to test and get a bit silly and wild with your content on Snapchat because the nature of the platform is to be goofy and humorous.

Create a Sponsored Lens.

People love using Snapchat filters and lenses because they can be fun. As a business owner, you can create a sponsored filter, which is excellent for brand awareness and engagement. The only problem with this strategy is its cost, so working with a small budget may be better.

Offer Coupons and Discounts

A tried-and-true tactic that works exceptionally well on Snapchat is giving coupons. There are countless ways to do this right, and the style you use to offer up your coupons and promotions depends on your brand style and the nature of your business. For example, you could offer a voucher in exchange for users sending you Snaps. Or you could offer a 20% discount for a limited time when someone spends a certain amount on your product. Coupon codes and deals are great for motivating real engagement and driving sales. They are also trackable, which is super important. You want to know if your social media efforts are becoming business results.

Feature User-Generated Content

Ask your existing customers and followers to send you pictures and videos of them interacting with your brand or using your products for a unique feature. Use this content on your Snapchat story. If you run a contest or giveaway, you can also use that opportunity to create user-generated content that you can use on Snapchat to create engagement and brand awareness.

HOW TO MAKE IT WORK FOR YOU

- Create a Snapchat account for your business and make the profile image captivating.

- Develop a content strategy that is relevant to the audience that is most active on the platform.

- Consistently and regularly publish content. Aim for no less than three times a day.

- Connect with influencers in your niche that have an active audience. Let them do Takeovers.

- Create urgency when running campaigns or offering coupons and discounts.

- Test content in private messages first to measure engagement so you can easily monitor what works.

Track, measure, and monitor data as best as you can. Yes, Snapchat isn't easy to measure, but you can manually keep track of your views and, over time, compare it against your total number of followers. You can also track the number of followers and sales for discounts (or coupons).

Chapter 14

Tumblr—The Underdog with a Punch

Tumblr is for you if you want to spread brand awareness through a platform that is often not mentioned in trending news despite its continued rapid growth. This is a unique social platform that's combined with microblogging. Tumblr's traffic is growing at 74% annually and has over 300 million monthly unique visitors. Talk about an untapped goldmine.

Here are a few other facts that might inspire you to act—43% of Internet users between 18 and 24 use Tumblr. Most Tumblr users from the United States of America are college-aged, so if your business serves that demographic, I encourage you to jump in. Tumblr's reach among the U.S. population is projected to be 8.8% in 2020. The platform is the 51st most visited website in the world. Brands like Starbucks, Pepsi, Nestle, Covergirl, Tide, Ivory, Spotify, Toyota, and many more are now advertising on the platform, meaning rapid growth is happening.

You could reach more than 800 million visitors using Tumblr's sponsored posts, thanks partly to Yahoo's buying Tumblr in 2012.

If you feel ready to jump on the Tumblr bandwagon and your business serves the demographic that enjoys being active on the platform, here are ideas that will help.

MARKETING STRATEGIES FOR YOUR BUSINESS

Familiarize yourself with the language of the platform. The nature of the demographics you will find on Tumblr does require you to be able to speak their language. Tumblr maintains an underground appeal to many niche markets, so be thoughtful about your words.

Customize your content plan and your content to match the tone of voice. Create niche-specific long-form content. Most people assume that short-range will perform better because it's a young demographic. The truth is that long-range will outperform short content. You must ensure it's high value, entertaining, and hyper-focused.

Curate content from all over the web that revolves around one specific interest or topic relevant to both your business and ideal audience. Follow your fans and share their content on Tumblr. Doing this shows them that you're listening and appreciate what they say.

Invest in visually appealing imagery, GIFS, animations, and high-quality videos around your niche. Install Disqus on Tumblr to open a commenting feature with which anyone (even non-users) can interact. For those who find your content and enjoy it but don't have a Tumblr account, it can be tough to engage with you because the usual activities within the platform are to "like" or "reblog" content. By adding Disqus, anyone can engage with you, and you'll be able to track replies and moderate comments.

People can also vote for the best words so they rise to the top, encouraging positive engagement. Use tags to boost your content. Labels explain and categorize your content, making it easier for people to find it. Consider using between 7 and 12 tags so you can show up in as many searches as possible. Choose the right time to post to get more reach with your content. The best time for this young crowd is before school starts (before 7 a.m.), at lunchtime, and before dinnertime.

HOW TO MAKE IT WORK FOR YOU:

Create a content plan that includes curated and created content. Refine your audience and make sure you learn the language of this demographic.

Create long-form content that is niche-specific and SEO-optimized. Use tags with your content so you can get easily discovered. Add Disqus to ensure you can engage with users and non-users of Tumblr.

Create fresh images, GIFs, videos, and animations that appeal to a younger demographic and keep them entertained so they can share it. Test post timings to determine the best times to put out your content.

Book # 3

YouTube Secrets Hacks for Beginners

A Complete Guide for Making Money with Video Content and Become a YouTube Influencer with Strategic Content and Monetization Techniques

Introduction

Hi there, and welcome to endless possibilities with YouTube Social Media Marketing. My name is Blake Preston, and with the help of Brian Fitzgerald and Fitzgerald Publishing, I will teach you to exponentially grow your business and increase revenue using YouTube.

YouTube dominates the vast, ever-changing internet video landscape. YouTube has transformed the video business from its 2005 founding as a site to post personal videos to its status as the world's second-largest search engine and a vital tool for corporations, artists, and influencers.

Consider the effect's astonishing magnitude. YouTube has about two billion unique, logged-in users monthly. YouTube viewership exceeds 1 billion hours daily. Among these staggering figures is an opportunity to do what you care about, express what you think, promote what you offer, or tell a story that matters.

This book aims to be your YouTube trip buddy and the complete guide. This book is for everyone interested in YouTube, whether they're aspiring video creators, companies looking to build their audience, or curious about the medium.

Consider Why YouTube is Revolutionary:

YouTube isn't only for kids and techies. It attracts all ages, backgrounds, and nations. This implies that even specialized content may be interesting.

Others who use YouTube as a creative outlet make money on it. This book teaches you how to monetize your content using ads, sponsorships, and more.

Personal Growth and Education YouTube has endless knowledge on every topic. This makes it a great teaching tool. When you start generating YouTube videos, you join a community of creators with different perspectives.

On any road, challenges are expected. The site's magnitude may intimidate some users. How can you be heard in the noise? How do you ensure your work reaches the right audience? How do you navigate YouTube's features?

Why You Should Read This Book.

We discuss YouTube's numerous aspects in the first chapter. This section offers project history and operations, which is crucial before starting.

Introduction

Section 2 focuses on the foundation. Like a structure, your YouTube channel needs a solid foundation, which involves researching your audience and creating a unique personality. Use this section as a map to stay on track.

Section 3 covers YouTube's mainstay: video creation. From the definition of outstanding content through filming and editing, this part covers making your content stand out.

Successful channel management is covered in Section 4. Learn these ways to boost content visibility, engagement, and conversions.

Section 5 concludes with commercialization. Following one's passion and gaining money aren't mutually incompatible. Follow the procedures in this section to optimize YouTube profits.

This handbook is also a guide, resource, and incentive. As we go into YouTube, remember that every YouTuber, from the most successful to the newest, started with the same goal: to share something. This voyage's limits are unknown if you're well-equipped.

Enjoy your YouTube experience. Start this journey with me.

SECTION 01

Understanding YouTube

In this age of immediate information and ever-changing social media landscapes, YouTube has become a staple of internet media. It combines TV, cinema, and the internet so everyone can voice their ideas. To truly utilize YouTube, one must first understand its intricate design.

YouTube: A Future, Present, and Past Time Machine

Let's revisit February 2005. Ex-PayPal employees Chad Hurley, Steve Chen, and Jawed Karim created YouTube. They laid the groundwork for a digital empire without knowing it.

"Me at the Zoo," uploaded by Jawed Karim in 2004, is considered YouTube's first video. It was brief—18 seconds of Karim discussing elephant trunks. This marked a new era of information delivery.

Today, YouTube has changed drastically. After Google bought it in November 2006, it soared from obscurity to global fame. YouTube receives billions of views daily and posts over 500 hours of video each minute, indicating its unparalleled influence on modern business, entertainment, and society.

YouTube's future seems brighter. YouTube's viewership and content diversity will likely expand as internet access and digital device use spread worldwide and younger, more acclimated generations become vital customers.

Video Development for YouTube

YouTube's variety and quality have grown over time. Once dominated by raw, unedited content, the site hosts feature films, documentaries, debate shows, and music videos.

The creative community has grown from amateurs sharing home videos to professionals with studios. YouTube is a top destination for short videos, serials, and documentaries.

The Future of YouTube

YouTube goes beyond keeping up with technology. With VR180 (which enables producers to record VR films with standard cameras) and YouTube Shorts (which competes with short videos), the platform is continually evolving.

Advanced analytics tools and AI are coming to enhance user experience and ad environments. As traditional TV and internet streaming merge, YouTube will be crucial.

Using YouTube to Network

YouTube is essential to social media discussions. Video makes YouTube more immersive and entertaining than text or photos.

The video's comment section allows debates and comments. Like, share, and subscribe enable users to engage with material and writers. YouTube is social because of this uploader-viewer interaction.

YouTube for Search Engines

YouTube is the second-largest search engine behind Google, yet this needs to be addressed. This distinguishes the platform for creators, companies, educators, and marketers.

When trying to "learn how" or "find out about," individuals prefer videos over text. We'll cover YouTube's search algorithm later, but for now, know that bringing suitable videos to the right viewers is crucial.

YouTube Search System

Anyone who wants to be seen on YouTube must learn its search tools. YouTube's algorithm is secret; however, a few factors impact a video's search ranking.

How well the video's title, description, and substance match the user's search is "relevant." Videos with more views, comments, and shares rank higher in search results. Video Length: Longer videos perform higher on YouTube's search results. The software also considers watching and searching histories.

Important Additional Information

A video's exposure and success depend on several things beyond the original search. The suggested video's sidebar boosts video visibility. Getting mentioned here can boost page views. Titles and thumbnails create first impressions. Attractive images and clear titles can increase click-through rates.

Investigation of YouTube is Activity #1.

Apply the fundamentals in a practical exercise. YouTube for downtime. Find what interests you. The most notable results—how are their names, photos, and descriptions? Participate systemically. Comment on a video, share it, or see some recommendations. Examine a popular channel in your profession. In what respects are they successful? Write this down.

This activity will familiarize you with the site and give input for future material.

Here's how to navigate YouTube's massive ecosystem. But this is only the start. Later chapters will teach you how to navigate this terrain and be noticed.

Chapter 01

What You Need to Know Before Getting Started

Suppose you will invest the next few months and years in establishing your brand on the YouTube platform. In that case, it makes sense to learn a little about the platform's origins and what makes it so unique. For example, did you know YouTube started as a dating platform? Few people know this, but co-founder Steven Chen said it was initially designed for dating so people could upload videos of themselves talking about their dream partner.

In this chapter, we will cover a bit of YouTube's history, present, and future, as well as why it's a social platform search engine. We will also get technical by introducing you to the robust YouTube algorithm so you can create your channel and content with the understanding necessary to help your videos perform well.

YouTube is a unique social networking platform for this simple reason. It's both a social networking channel and a search engine. So, it falls into the social media category, yet it's also far grander if you think about it. But how did it become this big giant? Indeed, it's not just because the Internet giant Google owns it. Right, you are! This is why it's best to start with an overview of YouTube's past, present, and future to align yourself with this ever-growing social and search engine platform.

YouTube: The Past, The Present, And The Future

Few people know this, but YouTube came due to a combined effort from three former PayPal employees. Chad Hurley, Steven Chen, and Jawed Karim believed that ordinary people would enjoy sharing personal homemade videos. So, they created the first website version of what we know today in early February 2005. The beta version was launched in May 2005 and already started attracting 30,000 visitors daily. Yes, that was a massive number at the time. By its official launch in December 2005, the platform had over two million video views daily. By January 2006, those numbers had increased to more than 25 million views. A few months later (March 2006), the platform had over 25 million uploaded videos, with over 20,000 uploaded daily. Even back then, these were huge numbers. The platform has shown no signs of slowing down since its launch.

Regarding funding, the founders got their first actual funding in November 2005 from Sequoia Capital, which invested more than $3 million. Of course, with the massive growth I just shared, it wasn't too long before popularity took over, and Google decided it was time to take their lion's share. In November 2006, Google bought YouTube for a cool $1.65 billion. Yes, that was a B (billion), not a million.

Fast forward years of successful growth, more popularity, and many stardom case studies from YouTube creators who gained fame and fortune, YouTube has yet to show any signs of slowing down. But their early days were rather humble. In the early days, YouTube was very "homely" and raw. You'd find hilarious pranks, videos showing interesting locations, crazy stunts, and neighborhood entertainment. There were only square videos available at that time. But with time, the platform matured and expanded to include political debates, unfiltered war footage, musical performances, instructional videos, and lots more comedy and entertainment. In 2007, YouTube partnered with CNN to create an opportunity for ordinary citizens to interact with potential United States presidential candidates, exponentially increasing the platform's engagement.

Video Progress on YouTube

As I mentioned, the first video ever published was titled **"Me at The Zoo."** Since then, YouTube has gone from zero to 1 billion views in under a decade. According to Statista, YouTube currently has 2 billion users worldwide and is growing. (Statista, 2019). It, therefore, stands to be the most prominent social network - even more significant than Facebook.

Many still consider it the most accessible platform to share video content with a broad audience. Setting up a channel and getting started is fast and straightforward, as you'll learn in an upcoming section. With a good strategy, you can be unknown today and reach millions of views worldwide by the end of the week.

You can easily reach people of any age group today on YouTube because research shows that young and older people using the Internet also watch videos on YouTube. Since most people prefer to consume visual content, the growth of YouTube and your ability to succeed are unlimited. But what about in the future? What are some of the predictions being made?

The Future of YouTube

Video is still expected to remain front and center in our society. It has become the most effective strategy anyone can use to connect with an audience. You don't even need fancy equipment or a professional studio to do so.

Many smartphone users find engaging video content challenging to resist, which will continue to be the case. Why? Because according to recent data, 85% of Internet users in the U.S. watch video content. And in 2021, the average person is expected to spend 100 minutes daily watching online videos! That's a 19% increase since 2019.

While it's hard for anyone to accurately prophecy where any of these social networking platforms will be in another decade, there is enough reason to assume YouTube will only go for a while. There's a strong chance that today's YouTubers will become tomorrow's moguls. The Internet and the digital economy are still in their infancy. We know the best is yet to come, and those who learn to ride this wave with YouTube might continue to experience tremendous success regardless of the new adaptations the platform brings about.

Consider people like PewDiePie (Felix Kjellberg). He is arguably the most famous YouTuber on the planet, generating billions of views from his channel. With all the fame and money he's acquired over the years, it's unlikely he would sizzle out quickly. In fact, according to an interview with The Guardian Magazine a while back, PewDiePie hinted that he's contemplating expanding into creating a multi-channel network at some point. There's a good chance many of these YouTubers who have become influencers are more likely to seek out television stardom or even develop their networks. Imagine any future you'd like, and I can assure you YouTube can become a vehicle for that accomplishment.

As for the platform itself, given that its parent company is Internet Goliath Google, it will continue to evolve, adapt, and invest in further growth within the forum.

When the platform launched, it only had square videos and no advertising opportunities. Over the years, it has evolved and expanded to include a very robust advertising system. The video formats have also been growing. It's wise for every YouTuber to keep up with these ever-changing video requirements. As an overview, YouTube allows you to upload sizes ranging from 240p to 2160p(4K).

- 240p: 426x240 pixels
- 360p: 640x360 pixels
- 480p: 854x480 pixels
- 720p: 1280x720 pixels
- 1080p: 1920x1080 pixels
- 1440p: 2560x1440 pixels
- 2160p: 3840x2160 pixels

If you're learning his stuff, you can upload a video as tiny as 426X240 pixels or go as large as 3840X2160 pixels. But dimension is one of many things you need to get right. You must also consider video size, length, and aspect ratio, especially now that they have added new features such as vertical video stories.

We will dive deeper into the different video sizes available, whether you're running ads or posting organically for your channel, so stay tuned for those fresh updates and features in an upcoming chapter. For now, realize that it will be essential to use the recommended video size and keep refreshing yourself on the latest changes. Why?

If you want to attract more views and profit, use the correct YouTube video size. Failure to do so will result in low-quality content, repelling the audience you're looking to attract. Therefore, please regularly visit the Content Creator Academy webpage, which has all things YouTube-related.

YouTube As A Social Media Platform

Do you know why YouTube is considered a social media platform? To answer that effectively, let's clarify an online social network. An online social network is a platform where you and other like-minded people can connect. You can build relationships, exchange and share information, etc. YouTube is a platform that enables you to do all that and so much more. Not only can you build new connections, but you can also learn from new people who are halfway across the world from you. When a social network is done right, it becomes a thriving ecosystem where content creators, brands, and users benefit from actively engaging on the platform. I'd say YouTube has done a fantastic job creating such an environment.

One of the critical factors to consider when labeling YouTube as a social media platform comes from this simple word - community.

There is a massive community on YouTube of people producing, sharing, and consuming content. The platform's most active and engaged people feel part of something more significant, as they belong. These people support each other, hang out together, and share common values. That, my friend, is called community building. It may not be a community in the traditional offline sense of the word where everyone is physically next to each other, but it is, nonetheless.

Because YouTube is a social media platform, more is needed to occasionally post videos and pray to the traffic gods that your channel will attract people. Focusing solely on data and getting views on your video could be better. The approach should be the same as any other social networking site. It would be best to focus on connecting with and interacting with the people you wish to have as part of your YouTube community. We will talk more in-depth about how to do this, but it is essentially about posting quality videos with content your ideal audience will find valuable. Like other social channels, you can send out friend requests, ask people to subscribe to your channel and engage in live chats, especially when you do live streaming. More on that later.

The other thing I love about YouTube is that you can create honest conversations around your video content. Since most people spend a lot of time watching videos on the platform, if you engage and interact with community members by asking questions on the comments and making sure you reply to all the comments people make, you can demonstrate to your new audience that you care. And they, in turn, will follow and consume what you offer. The more value and engagement you bring to this social network, the more success you will experience, especially as a business owner.

YouTube As a Search Engine Platform

A while back, Google (the parent company that owns YouTube) released a resource that answers many of the questions we all ask when we decide to set up a YouTube channel. Namely, how exactly does YouTube work?

While I'm sure they didn't spill all their secrets, they have given us enough knowledge to leverage to our advantage. In a later chapter, I will discuss the YouTube algorithm and hacks to help you rank higher on their search engine. But to get the most out of that conversation, you must understand that YouTube is a search engine like Google, Yahoo, etc. There's a tremendous amount of organic traffic to be enjoyed within YouTube's platform because many people use that search bar. Besides that fact, we also have the added benefit of being favored highly by Google when they rank content on the homepage. Videos from YouTube consistently rank high on a Google search page, and I don't know if you noticed, but Google added a new tab specifically titled "video." So, when doing the regular search, people are still being served video results for their queries. Let me put this practically for you so you can understand the power of this.

Suppose your potential client is looking for a service you can offer. They head over to Google and type in their query. Millions of results show up in the form of regular articles. But they see a tab "video" and click on that because, let's face it, most people prefer to watch than read. Videos are more saturated than text-based solutions. Since you're smart, you have a video explainer showing them exactly how to solve their need and how you do it fast and affordable. What are the chances of getting that cold lead and converting a customer? I'd say high. You don't need a big audience or a huge channel. What you need is to understand how to leverage YouTube.

How YouTube Search Works

The search ranking system on YouTube is fantastic because it sorts through over 500 hours of content uploaded every minute. Then, it finds the most relevant results for the search query given by the end-user. Thanks to Google's information, we know you need to focus on three main elements: quality, relevance, and engagement.

Quality:

That refers to how authoritative your channel and content are for the target audience. YouTube wants expert, traditional, and trustworthy content for its community members. That's why I always recommend starting narrow with a specific topic. It's much easier to prove that your channel is worth being promoted when you focus on delivering quality content on what you know well. The more you can provide that, the better your videos will perform.

Relevance:

YouTube's algorithm is still a mystery, even for expert hackers. But what we all know for sure is that being relevant is a critical factor for channel growth. There are many indicators the algorithms look for to determine whether something is relevant to an audience or not, some of which include the video content itself (though not 100% perfect), title, description, and tags.

Engagement:

The last thing I want us to discuss here that the algorithm cares about is video engagement. Watch time is especially critical for the algorithm because it uses that as a key indicator of whether to continue promoting your content. The more people watch and stay on the platform thanks to your video, the more they will promote your stuff to a bigger audience.

Other Factors That Are a Must-Know

In the earlier report, YouTube shared that they care a lot about promoting authoritative content from reliable sources. But only when it is appropriate. So, when it comes to scientific, political, medical information, or breaking news, they will promote the most credible channels and personalities on the platform.

The critical thing to take away from this is to build credibility. You do not have to be Oprah or CNBC, but you do need to demonstrate to the algorithm that your content can be trusted. This is especially true if you are dealing with educational type of content. This may apply less to entertainment or music channels because what matters most in such cases is popularity, freshness, and relevancy, which we already discussed.

Recommended videos

This is exciting because it offers us an opportunity to do well immediately. Have you ever noticed the "recommended" icon when watching content on YouTube? You can usually see it in your dashboard's "Up Next" section. This is YouTube's way of suggesting what you should consume next. The algorithm factors in many things before making that recommendation, including the channels you're subscribed to, your watch history, the time of day, etc. Getting your video to appear on this recommended list will significantly accelerate your channel growth. I even have hacks that will increase your chances of appearing on that suggestions list.

Before we can move on, I'd also like to emphasize that YouTube does factor in personalization when determining what to show a user. If you've noticed how many times recommended videos show up based on your recent activity, this will make sense. As a YouTube user, your interface gets populated by more things you've watched, liked, and interacted with. Flip perspective for a bit and think like a creator. The more you can create content that a user interacts with, the more of your stuff YouTube will serve them. Therefore, it is imperative to create content with your ideal consumer in mind. You want to create content you feel confident they will want to click on, watch, and like. That's your golden ticket to the success you desire on this platform.

Want to Get More Technical About How the YouTube Algorithm Works?

If what I just shared needs to be more sophisticated for you, I've got something that will satisfy the tech geek in you. There's a research paper published by Google engineers Paul Covington, Jay Adams, and Emre Sargin. They break down the signals they use to rank videos for YouTube recommendations. If you can recall, recommendations are a huge deal when getting more people to know about your channel. In the paper, they talk about the following:

1. Click-through rate. That refers to the likelihood of someone clicking on your video after seeing it.
2. Watch time. That refers to the total time viewers spend watching your videos.
3. How many videos the user has watched from your channel?
4. Recently, the user watched a video about the same topic.
5. What the user has searched for in the past.
6. The users previously watched videos.
7. The user's demographic information and location.

Want to read the entire research paper (Deep Neural Networks for YouTube Recommendations)? Check out the resource section for links.

Activity #1: Exploring YouTube

Now, it's time to start taking some action. Before getting into the next chapter, it's good to familiarize yourself with this platform through the lens of the new insights and lessons learned. So here's what you're going to do.

Open an incognito webpage, sign into your personal YouTube if you have one, and start browsing. First, begin by entering the homepage and playing around with the search bar at the top. Type in a query around your topic of expertise or whatever your channel will be about. Observe how many search results come up. Notice which top channels are being promoted and look at their titles, video length, number of views, year of publication, and quality of the content. You should also check the sidebar menu and notice what YouTube recommends. Browse the platform from the eyes of a consumer, your potential subscriber.

Before moving on, the last activity is to type in the same search query on the main Google search tab and then hover over "videos." Notice how many videos you encountered on YouTube show up here. What you learn from exploring YouTube through this new lens will equip you as you move forward.

Chapter 02

Why YouTube?

By now, it should be evident that YouTube is on fire. Billions of users log in every month to consume content. There are also as many content creators or YouTubers in the backend, pushing out hundreds of content every minute of the day. The amount of activity taking place on this platform can feel quite overwhelming. The fact that you can find almost any topic on any genre can make one wonder why they should even consider setting up a channel. Everything is already there.

Yes and no. There's a lot of content on any topic you might have in mind. Still, the reality is you are a unique individual. Even if you start a channel with a common issue, as long as you remain true to yourself, it won't be like any other channel because no one can imitate you. That is what makes YouTube unique. There's enough room for every content creator. Your only obstacle is figuring out how to be more of yourself so your content stands out.

The question you need to ask isn't why I should invest my time, resources, and energy on YouTube when over 500 hours of video are uploaded every minute. Instead, it should be a question directed at your self-expression as a unique human being. Meaning - what am I highly passionate about that I can also become an authoritative voice for?

Most people who start a channel do so out of sheer passion and an urge to share their message, but that's not the only reason to become a YouTuber. You could also do it because you want to become famous like the Kardashians or to generate income. There shouldn't be a wrong or right reason, but there should be a big enough reason.

Always start by identifying your "why" for creating a successful channel because you will need the fuel when the going gets tough. So here are some of the reasons I know of for starting a YouTube channel:

- For Passion, to express yourself to the world.
- For money.
- For fame.

For Passion

If you want to use this platform to express yourself and share your passions with the world, you're not alone. Many of the channels that have successfully grown to millions of followers were created by YouTubers who had a power they wanted to share with an audience. To do the same, the first thing you must do is identify what your passions and talents are.

What's real and proven about creating a passion-based YouTube channel is that you can go right. Passion always drives success. In the world of content creation, knowing how long and how much effort is required to grow a thriving channel, your passion is the fuel that will keep you going until things start to snowball. Consider this for a moment. Have you ever been given a task or project you disliked or didn't care about? Can you recall how laborious and lengthy the process was? Perhaps you procrastinated, quit, then un-quit several times over, and it was an experience you couldn't wait to finish.

Now, think about when you got to work on a project you love. How enjoyable was that experience? You probably skipped meals, worked overtime including weekends, and even forgo your weekend Netflix Binge-watching just because of how immersed you were. Your YouTube content creation and channel management should resemble the second example. How do you do this? Let me share a simple process to help you identify a topic you are passionate about. Once you pin that down and it feels right, every other choice will revolve around that passion.

How to Discover Your Passion and Turn It Into Video Content for YouTube.

Open your Google Docs or Word document, and let's carry out an exercise to help you identify your passion. Remember, this exercise should be fun. Don't overthink things. Write anything and everything that comes to mind because there is no right or wrong. If nothing comes, make something up.

Ask yourself this question - What do I love doing and talking about? Example answer: I love running in nature, cooking, traveling, reading comic books, painting, hiking, and writing poetry.

Answer this question - I can spend hours reading, researching, thinking, and learning about...X...[fill in your blank]. Example answer: I can spend hours reading, researching, thinking, learning about comic books, and creating characters.

Write down all the activities you've enjoyed. Go back as far as you can and list everything down. Example answer: Selling lemonade when I was nine, drawing manga as a teen, playing piano, cooking, painting with watercolors, juggling, writing comedy, etc. Anything and everything you've enjoyed doing should go on this list, whether you did it a year ago or ten years ago.

Write down all your strengths, skills, and any work experience you've had. Make sure these are practical. For example, answer social media manager, sales representative, party planner, florist, etc.

What are some of your personality traits that people say they like about you? Three qualities that people have mentioned make you unique. They must be positive traits; if you don't know, text a few friends now and ask them to share with you. Example answer: Funny, resilient, and confident.

Pick and choose, and then put in some research time. Pick the top three topics or activities that stand out from your list and order them in priority. The one with the most electrifying energy is the one you should start researching most.

Researching in this context means heading to the YouTube search bar and typing in the chosen topics. See what comes up. How much content has been created around your passion? Are people engaging, commenting, and liking existing content? What quality is the content? Which titles are performing best? Click on the channels with the content you're passionate about and notice how that channel is set up. I recommend getting a Google Chrome extension like VidIQ or Keywords Everywhere if you'd like to see exact metrics and volume searches. These are great for helping you figure out what keywords and content are performing well at high volume and low competition.

The purpose of doing research is to ensure you're going after an interest that has an existing and engaged audience. Most people say YouTube needs to be more saturated, and there is still time to start a channel. I'm afraid I strongly must disagree. Now is the best time to start your track, and you can grow it even faster than the rest of us because you get to ride the wave of success we've already created.

By finding channels posting on the topic you're passionate about, you can get ideas of content topics that work. You also get to see the mistakes they are making or the gaps still need to be filled. You will also feel what the audience cares about and what they want to see more of. So, if you find competition around your topic, get excited because you're on the right path, and I will show you strategies to leverage this competition.

Now that you've identified your passion and validated that there's an audience for that topic, it's time to start thinking of content you can post. If you still need to identify what you love, don't worry. Here are some more questions that will help.

1. If you could be remembered for three things after you're gone from this life, what would you want those three to be?
2. What would you do with your time if money wasn't an issue and you had financial freedom?
3. What is one thing your friends and family usually come to you to ask for advice or a recommendation? Make sure it's something you also enjoy helping them out with.

For Money

Some people start their YouTube channel because they hear of the many YouTubers making a full-time income and traveling the world. There are also countless stories of content creators who have started a side hustle of YouTube content creation and generated more passive income than their primary job salary.

For example, I have a friend who was employed as a customer service rep in a furniture company. He decided to test his ability to succeed on YouTube and generate passive income by teaching arts and crafts, DIY sessions, and promoting unique furniture pieces. His channel now earns him about $15k in passive income each month, more than his salary at the store. So, if you've been wondering how to make a side income or even want to be a full-time YouTuber traveling the world and creating fantastic content about the cool places you're exploring, this can be a great way to fund that lifestyle.

Many consider YouTube to be the king of the side hustle. Why? Here are some reasons worth knowing if you want to increase your income. YouTube monetization is very consistent and can be very lucrative if you have the right strategy. In a later section, we will talk about different monetization methods. For now, realize that as a content creator on YouTube, you will have the opportunity to generate income on your channel.

They're recurring and evergreen income possibilities on YouTube. What do I mean by this? You can create a video this week and, three years from now, still make money from it. I noticed some similarities after interviewing many YouTubers and plotting my success on the platform. A key one that stands out is that video creation has been happening for years. Years ago, no one knew us when we started making the videos. If we were lucky, video views ranged from a few hundred to a few thousand, but we kept creating awesome videos.

I can tell you there was no income coming in for any of us. I certainly never made a dime. But I kept persisting. After a few years, I noticed my growth started to gain momentum, and then slowly, a few thousand views turned into a few hundred thousand. By then, the subscriber count was decent enough, and each video's earnings increased. Ultimately, a good, steady income becomes a reality. I've heard this from almost every fellow creator I've interviewed, with just a few exceptions. All this to say, you can do it, but you need to play the long game. And the best part about YouTube is the more mature your channel becomes. The better you'll be rewarded by your older content if you didn't take shortcuts initially.

Suppose you're looking for a side hustle or want a lifestyle funded entirely by your content creation. In that case, YouTube is excellent for helping you accomplish this. And as I shared with you, I know many people who earn more from their YouTube than their 9 to 5.

For Fame

Want to become YouTube famous? It's not too late, but you need to be prepared to put in the work. Being a YouTube favorite has become a real thing. It is considered just as substantial as being a rock star. Of course, it's more challenging than it used to be, but it's still possible.

If you want to become a social media influencer or grow a brand, YouTube is a great platform to help you create fame. Nowadays, some famous YouTubers have the same special treatment as TV celebrities. Have you noticed? I have seen comedians, musicians, and other entertainers jumpstart their careers by being "discovered" on YouTube. Even Justin Beiber first started on YouTube. So, whether you want to grow a personal or company brand or become a well-known social media celebrity, YouTube can make that happen.

But before you get too excited, let's ensure you set realistic expectations. You may think YouTube will make you a celebrity overnight. There was a time when it could happen, but given how mature the platform has become, it will take a lot more strategic thinking and effort.

When YouTube first started, platform tools like the video response tool could be leveraged to gain a new audience's attention. You could piggyback on the rise and success of a YouTube star just by directly engaging in their hit videos using the video-response tool. This option no longer exists.

There's also the opportunity to collaborate with other successful YouTubers. That could help you get in front of a vast audience and go from zero to famous in a day, but unfortunately, a lot of work goes into creating these collaborations nowadays.

There must be a real-world connection. The more prominent stars are increasingly difficult to access if one is just getting started. Besides, even if someone has a big audience, they can still subscribe to your channel. And then, of course, there is the growing issue of creating high-quality videos with graphics, excellent studio lighting, scenery, etc. Top creators already have the financing, resources, and support from the partner program and other sponsorships, but when you're just starting, all you have is a webcam in your bedroom or living room. It will take a while before people start to respect and admire what you do. But if you keep persisting, it is possible.

Activity #2: Finding Your Motivation

It's time to implement what you've just learned in this chapter. If you want to become successful with your YouTube endeavor, you need to know what drives you. What is causing you to start this channel? What's your big "WHY" for this? The bigger the way, the more likely you are to persist and succeed. To do this, here are some questions to answer.

1. What is my goal for this YouTube channel?
2. Why am I choosing that goal as my primary goal?
3. How far am I willing to stretch to make the goal a reality?
4. What is my vision for myself if I consider where I want to be two years from now?
5. What is the vision for the channel? I.e., what do I want it to represent?
6. Why is the success of this channel so vital to me now?
7. How will my life change when I hit the goals I have set for this YouTube channel?

SECTION 02

Your YouTube Channel

Your channel is your shop in YouTube's rising economy. It's when individuals learn about you and your brand's benefits. Whether you want to educate, entertain, inspire, or all three, how you build and manage your channel may make or break it. Let's begin creating a meaningful channel.

Focus Attention

Find your channel's specialty before filming or designing a great logo. Without your YouTube channel's basement, the building may fall.

Find your market by picking a niche. Content producers often use "niche" as a buzzword. It denotes a small yet significant market segment. Discovering your YouTube specialty is like finding the sweet spot where your hobbies and audience demands meet.

A target market may help you focus. It enables personalization, audience analysis, and sticking out in a crowded medium. Encouraging individuals to watch specialty channels helps them meet others with similar interests.

The way to find your target market. Ask yourself: What matters? Which talks or activities keep you interested in hours? Checking Competition: Anyone Else Making This Content? Does this target anyone? Use YouTube's suggested searches and Google Trends. Identifying Need: Do you know your market's information gaps? Perhaps you found your way in.

Competency Assessment

What Are You Contributing? Target Market Characterization: Identify your ideal reader. Consider their demographics to create appealing content. A/B and Iterative Improvement First, make some videos, then observe how people react. Don't be afraid to change. Stay focused on your specialty. Building audience trust demands consistent, high-quality content.

Knowing Your Audience

You've chosen an audience for your work. Knowing your audience is as vital as learning your topic. Despite appearances, studying rivals might help you understand your target market. Your niche's successful channels will have done the work for you. Their articles, audience engagement rates, and comments may teach you a lot.

Shortlist the top channels for your profession. Use these recommendations to proceed. Check its contents: Think the scope is what? How are their videos structured? They update material how often?

Check their involvement: Which videos got the most reactions? This may reveal your target market's priorities. Join the comment feedback loop. Viewers often propose changes or additional content. This info is helpful.

Naming and Branding Your Channel

Building a channel brand requires more than a logo and name. Your audience's feelings, thoughts, and actions are in reaction to your content and their group identity.

Make your video stand out from the crowd online. Uniformity builds audience trust and devotion. Community: Brands can make viewers feel like they belong. The Basics of YouTube Channel Creation Your channel name should represent your videos' tone and be memorable.

Your logo and banner symbolize your brand. Consider utilizing fonts, colors, and pictures that match your writing style. Channel summary: Summary of what to expect. Search engine optimization keywords can also be added naturally. Channel Promo: Like your network's teaser. A captivating video that summarizes your persona and work in minutes.

YouTube allows you to customize your channel's homepage to highlight your content. You may organize and prioritize audience content using playlists, highlighted videos, and other channel sections.

In conclusion, your YouTube channel represents your passion, dedication, and goal of providing value to your audience. Establishing a channel identity, understanding its audience, and providing content that connects will help you attract and retain viewers. We'll study content development science to keep your channel full of relevant, entertaining videos.

Chapter 03

Determine Your Focus

As we gain momentum on this quest to become a highly successful income-producing YouTuber, it's time to turn your focus on delivering value. What can you bring to the platform that will cause others to pay attention, engage with your content, and become loyal subscribers? To help you answer that question effectively and efficiently, we will break down how you can pick or decide on a niche. I'll also share with you the best types of niches that are performing well. But before we get to that, perhaps you're wondering why picking a niche is essential.

I've been in heated conversations with intelligent business owners who wondered the same thing. Creatives need help understanding that marketing to everyone means you're marketing to no one. Recently, I was introduced to a life and health coach who was in the process of starting his YouTube channel. He wants to become an authority on the platform and attract hot leads that can easily convert into paying customers, and he wants that to happen fast. When I asked what his niche would be, he hesitated and said, "I want to help billions of people, so I don't want to limit myself by being so narrow with a niche topic."

That, my friend, is the recipe for YouTube's failure, especially now that it has matured. The best-performing channels are super niched. And you know why? Because when you focus on one vertical, you become known as the industry leader, the credible resource, and the go-to person for that topic. When new potential subscribers and future buyers come across your content and immediately understand the problem you can solve for them, they are more likely to stick around, engage, connect, and convert. When you focus on one niche, you have clarity, and people love clarity.

It also makes your channel more memorable. Can you imagine how Coca-Cola would be if they had started advertising soft drinks, shoes, and food years ago? Building the fortified brand we've all grown accustomed to would have been extra hard. Everyone sees that red label on a soft drink or Santa holding a bottle, and we immediately think - Coca-Cola.

You don't have deep pockets and years of branding budget to waste, so please save yourself by focusing on a niche. Bring as much clarity and simplicity to your new audience as possible so they quickly associate you with the result you offer.

Picking A Niche

How, then, does one determine a niche for their new channel? In the case of the life and health coach I mentioned above, he could talk about mindset, lifestyle, working out, healthy eating, nutrition, and the list goes on and on. While he can always create content around any of these significant categories once his channel gains momentum, it is best to focus on one vertical when just starting. But which one first?

You may need help determining your niche or have too many options. Regardless, we can still help you figure out the perfect place. To start, go back to the answers from previous chapters. The exercises you've been doing so far are a foundation for this exercise because now you understand more about yourself and why you want this channel. Now, it's time to dive deeper. We need to find that sweet spot between gained knowledge about ourselves and what we know about our ideal audience. In other words, the overlap between what you love (what you're passionate about) and what your ideal audience wants is the sweet spot for your content. That becomes your niche topic.

Steps to Selecting Your Niche

Review Your Strengths and Skills

The first step is detailing how you've been most helpful to others throughout your career. Suppose you're coming out of college and think about what friends usually come to you for help with. Again, I want you to write the answers down. What skills have you developed? What leading roles and responsibilities have you had? What primary benefits did you deliver in the parts you've had? What successes have you had? Make sure to be super specific here.

Map Out Your Ideal Audience and What They Need.

It's imperative to identify what your ideal audience considers valuable and what needs they have that you can fulfill. You must create a detailed audience persona profile to help you figure out this puzzle piece. Here are some of the questions to answer for that persona profile.

- •Whom would you love to work with?
- What shared values do you have with this person?
- What makes them unique?
- Why does this person come to YouTube? What are they looking to experience?
- What are their goals and ambitions?
- What are their current challenges and worries?
- What is their purchase behavior? For example, they research online but like to buy offline.
- What is a pain or problem or lack they are experiencing as it relates to what your channel can offer?

Research to See if There's a Demand for Your Identified Topic.

Now that you've found that sweet spot between what you love and what your audience needs, it's time to head over to YouTube and see how much demand there is for your topic. We do this to ensure people want to watch your content type.

To conduct this research effectively, you need to write down keywords from your chosen topic or some titles you would make a video about. Then, type in that title or those keywords on the YouTube search to see what comes up. If there are a ton of results (millions of results), then I suggest getting more specific with that title. If there are zero results, no one may be looking for that type of content. What I recommend is to create content that is somewhere in between those two extremes.

Do Some Due Diligence for Income-Earning Potential.

Even though a topic is popular, it may be different for you, especially if you want to get rich. Many niches do well on the platform but earn the content creator little money. So, if you're going to make a lot of money through your channel, check to see income-earning potential. Find out if a company would be willing or likely to sponsor you to use their products or whether you can create a side business alongside your channel. Monetization is worth thinking about before settling on a niche. Sponsorship is very lucrative, but you need a good strategy; otherwise, it won't work.

Your channel must be aligned with the income avenue you wish to leverage most. For example, if you want to be paid by brands, research the brands that seem to be paying fellow YouTubers to create content. Most good creators always let their audience know when doing sponsored content, so that's a great way of getting some companies' names within your niche. If you're interested in sponsorship, make sure you have some offers to give your audience as they learn to trust you. Having this plan from the start ensures you'll make all the right choices, including niche picking.

Best Types of YouTube Niches

Not every niche can be monetized. The most popular ones work well; some are way easier than others. Here's a list of the most popular and easy-to-monetize niches.

- **How-to Tutorials**

This is the most popular and best niche on YouTube. Based on my experience, most people on this platform want to learn something. And since we all, at some point, need to know something, starting a channel that teaches "how-to" for your skill, talent, or passion seems like a great idea. It can also become very lucrative. Answering "how to..." questions can quickly build your audience and generate clients for your brand or business. Whether it's how to tie your unique shoelaces, how to clean your carpets, how to make specific floral arrangements for a particular occasion, how to get rid of a stain, or whatever else you do, you can quickly gather tens of thousands of not millions of views over time.

- **Animals**

Cute animals have been trending on YouTube since the beginning, and the trend hasn't slowed down. This niche is still popular, and given how trendy cat videos have become, you can consider getting into this niche if you love animals. That doesn't mean everyone with cats should start a YouTube channel.

Make sure it aligns with your brand and the objective of the channel. For example, a bakery should avoid getting into this niche! A vet should consider having a channel around cute animals. You can create content with animals doing funny things and center it on humor and entertainment. If you're more of an educational type, consider making videos on animal training, pet product reviews, and animal care.

- **Lifestyle**

Lifestyle has become one of the more popular niches on the platform. It's mainly because a lifestyle vlogger needs to fit neatly into a particular niche. So, their content can be wildly varied and carry differing undertones. Some lifestyle vloggers rely heavily on humor, sarcasm, drama, or gossip, giving their content an edge that people seem to love. Another thing about lifestyle vlogging is that it's incredibly personal. People usually disclose a lot of personal information about themselves, so if you lead a private life, there may be a better type of content for you.

- **Food**

Cooking and all things food-related are massive on YouTube. So, if you love cooking, eating, and critiquing food, you can create a successful channel with a vast audience. Show off amazing recipes, share some of the gadgets and tools you use in the kitchen, and you can't go wrong. Foodies are abundant on YouTube.

- **Gaming**

The most famous YouTubers are gamers. Correct me if I'm wrong, but some of these individuals have become real-world celebrities. PewDiePie, Jack Septiceye, Markiplier, and SSSniperWolf are just a few names that have gained global recognition. Why? Because these individuals have dominated YouTube. They are making tons of money doing what they love the most - gaming. You could be the same, but you must be fresh and different.

- **Makeup**

One of the most popular YouTube niches is makeup, so this is a great starting point if you're in the beauty space. And before you assume I am only talking about women's makeup, I'd like to point out that you could do well with men's makeup. Yes, you read me right. Even men want tutorials on how to do their makeup! Be forewarned, though; competition is fierce in this niche, but the audience is enormous and engaged.

- **Fashion**

Fashion is another popular niche on YouTube; you can approach it from various angles, even if you're not a designer. You can review clothing items, share styling tips, or start your fashion line if you're talented. This is one of the best and most accessible niches to get sponsors or even do affiliate marketing, which we will delve into later.

- **Tech review**

As we become a more tech-driven society, more and more people are coming to YouTube to watch tutorials or reviews on the latest tech and software products. Whether it's apps and software or physical hardware, you will have an audience if you can create engaging and valuable content. Are you good at helping others learn how to operate, assemble, or choose the right tech for their needs?

You can focus on workplace and productivity tech, home tech, or even small tech gadgets we carry daily. Your only limitation is your need for imagination and creativity.

- **Sports**

Are you a sports fanatic or maybe a former pro or amateur athlete? Then YouTube has an audience that would love your content. I have seen everything from sports vloggers to amateur reporters following around their favorite sports teams and sharing a different perspective with their audience than what professional journalists would share. And all these types of content do well. You don't have to be an officially appointed ambassador to create excellent content and keep your audience updated with the latest news. All you need is passion. Just be careful not to show copyrighted materials because that would lead to many unpleasant experiences with the authorities.

- **Photography**

Another popular niche is photography. Many budding photographers look to YouTube for sound advice on how to take better shots. You can offer tutorials on photography and the equipment you use. This can be an excellent channel for affiliate marketing opportunities.

- **Travel**

Who likes a great travel channel? Some of the sexiest YouTube channels I've come across are travel channels with great storytelling infused into them. A vast and starving audience is waiting for you if you love to travel the world and have fantastic stories to share. People love escaping reality or that horrid cubicle with a good travel video. It inspires, motivates, and uplifts travel enthusiasts. The best part is that many full-time YouTubers are digital nomads traveling the world and finding creative ways to cover their expenses to continue building their channel. If you dream of traveling the world, YouTube could be your golden ticket to seeing some of our planet's best-hidden gems and the wealthiest cultures.

- **Music**

Do you have a passion for music? Do you compose, sing, DJ, review, or teach others how to play an instrument? YouTube is an excellent platform for launching yourself. Some of the most viewed videos are music videos, and the best part is that you can go into any music genre, and you'll still get a decent audience size. I also know some channels that do commentaries on music news, give advice, report on the latest news from their favorite musicians, or even teach others how to play a particular instrument. Your options are endless regarding content types, and there's a healthy audience to support you.

- **ASMR**

ASMR, or Autonomous Sensory Meridian Response, has grown in recent years. It's all about the experience - using soothing sounds and imagery to relax viewers. ASMR content creators are all about taking their audience on a transformative journey through their sense organs.

And there you have it: the top niches on YouTube that are popular and easier to monetize. These niches already have audiences looking for content daily, so if you pick one, you are in luck. There's a ready-made audience for you, thanks to the work of your peers who launched before you. All you must do is develop the right plan to attract some of those engaged people to your channel.

Activity #3: Time To Choose

As you might have realized by now, each chapter must close with an implementation step. After going through the different exercises and discovering the top-performing niches, it's time to pick your niche.

Review your notes and come up with the top three niches that excite you the most. If you already know precisely the one to go for. But I encourage you to have more than one that you can start experimenting with for at least six weeks before settling on one. This is because I have seen many of my students get bored a few weeks into their content creation and give up on growing their channel.

Listen, you'll need to consistently create unique content for the next many years if you want to succeed at this. Therefore, you need to pick a niche that you are confident won't become a bore or burden 50 videos into it. That's why I suggest having more than one - but limited to three - different verticals and then creating content on each for a short while to see which one still excites you after a few weeks. It also allows you to see the audience response to test if one of them attracts more eyeballs and subscribers.

Pro tip:

When you make your choice, be sure to pick complementary niches. For example, Lifestyle vlogging and photography can align well. If, after a few weeks, you realize lifestyle isn't for you, then it's lovely to focus on photography only. Now it's your turn. What niche will you choose?

Chapter 04

Understanding Your Audience

There are a lot of unhelpful myths surrounding the existing YouTube audience. It will serve you well to read and understand this chapter carefully, as it will impact your content strategy and channel growth moving forward.

Most people assume YouTube is for young single male personas or that only the younger demographics are active users. This is not accurate. According to a study conducted by Google and Nielsen, the average YouTube viewer is just as likely to be female as male. Young single Millenials being the only audience is also a myth because the same research said YouTube users have more potential to have kids than non-users.

Another report, by Cast from Clay, shared U.S. statistics about YouTube users and revealed data that proved men and women use YouTube equally. There's a robust usage of the platform across all age groups, so this isn't just a younger demographic platform like TikTok and others. You will find a healthy and active audience of 65-75-year-olds. Granted, they use the platform in different proportions than the 15-30-year-olds. Still, they are actively engaged nonetheless. The data from Cast from Clay shows 96% of users aged between 18 - 24 years, 95% of users aged between 25 - 34 years old, 90% of users aged between 35 - 44 years old, 85% of users aged between 45 - 54 years old, 79% of users aged between 55 - 64 years old, 66% aged between 65 - 75 years old and 51% users aged 75 and over. Keep in mind these statistics reflect US users only. What we can take away from this is that all kinds of YouTube users range from teenagers to retired. Even in the United Kingdom, the statistics remain steady, showing YouTube has a stronghold in every age group and demographic.

How does knowing these different types of YouTube viewers benefit you?

It's straightforward. You can have any channel you desire, and your ideal audience will be ready to embrace your brand. Remember, you can only become a video influencer with one to influence. Well, I have just proven to you that on YouTube, you can become an influencer at any age, for any demographic. The most important thing is to determine what audience your content will serve and then focus on understanding what your people want. It's not enough to create a persona based on shallow things like gender, location, age, and job title. You need to know your audience more deeply so they can immediately resonate with your channel.

Understanding Your Competition

If you're a beginner, this part will help you quickly determine what works and doesn't in your niche. It will also show you best practices, industry standards, and some benchmarks you can

Understanding Your Audience

use to create a fantastic channel. Even if you've set up your channel, I still encourage you to consider this book section. It's where you can learn how to check existing and trending channels in your niche. The goal isn't to copy your competition but to learn from them and improve their work. That way, your young channel can shave off some mistakes and learning curves they had to go through. Let's walk through how to do this now.

Creating A Benchmark for Your Channel

Make sure to fire up your Google Doc or Word document to create your custom benchmark in this process. Make sure to document this as much as possible.

Step one: Find the Best-Performing Channels in Your Niche.

I recommend gathering the top five to ten preferred channels where you know your audience is hanging out. Need help finding your competition? Here's a simple exercise.

Do in-depth market research online to determine who is discussing the same topic or selling the same products and services you want. By now, you should have the primary keyword or niche topic you'll focus on. Put that keyword or key phrase on the main Google search bar to see what comes up. You'll see a list of websites and ads ranking for it, and if you click on the "video" tabs, you will see all the videos ranking on Google. This is great because it already shows you the channels competing with you. Record everything on your Google sheet and click the channels of these videos whenever one resonates with you so you can see how they've set up their entire YouTube channel.

You can also go to a software called Ubersuggest and type in each keyword. You'll get a downloadable report of all the websites ranking for that topic. Take the names of those sites and head over to the YouTube search bar to see what kind of content they have on their channel. If you realize some high-ranking websites need a better YouTube channel, that's great because that's the opportunity you need to seize. If you find a great channel with lots of engagement and high-quality content, add that to your list of competitors. You can also do the same thing on other social media channels like Twitter and Instagram, especially if your topic is popular on these other networks. Use hashtags to find the most engaged accounts and spy on their YouTube channels. Your goal is to have a comprehensive list of five to ten competitors. Then, move on to the next step.

Step Two: Take Note of The Following Metrics For all the Identified Competitive YouTube Channels.

- The Total Number of Subscribers on the Channel.
- Subscribers Change.
- The Total Number of Videos on the Entire Channel.
- Videos Change.
- Videos Table.
- Views Total.

- Views Change.
- View Subscriber Rate.
- Average Views Per Video.
- Engagement Rate.
- Average Engagement Per Video.
- Middle Favorites Per Video.
- Average Likes Per Video.
- Average Dislikes Per Video.
- Moderate Comments Per Video.

Granted, this will be a lot of manual work, especially if your competitors have created lots of video content on their channels. So, if you'd like some help with this process, consider using software such as SocialBlade, a free online tool that can help you track YouTube statistics more effortlessly. In the resources section, you will find all the tools I've recommended throughout this book.

Once you've gathered all this data, it's time to decide which benchmarks you will set for your channel. Allow that to influence the KPIs you'll put in the coming months. How will you know if your channel is doing well?

The data collected from channels in your niche can help you determine what a good audience engagement should be. You can continue using analytics to track growth month over month. The YouTube analytics dashboard will find many of those basic data sets. However, if you'd like something more robust to help you with analytics, consider investing in tools such as Tubular Intelligence, which allows you to see what's trending on YouTube and how your videos perform. You can also get BuzzSumo, which is quite popular nowadays and has a YouTube Analyzer. This tool can help you find the right keywords, get a list of the most popular videos for your niche, analyze specific videos, or keep an eye on competitor channels.

Find my Audience Tool

This is a new tool by "Think With Google" that I've played around with and found extremely useful. It will help you get an overview of where your audience might be hanging out on YouTube, which channels they are likely watching, and what they plan to buy.

Once on the site

(https://www.thinkwithgoogle.com/feature/findmyaudience), you can begin by taking a tour. A "Take a tour" tab in the top right corner walks you through how the site works. I recommend signing in with your Gmail so you can save the detailed information you gather. For example, I typed in "In-market" for my audience preference, then chose the sports and fitness categories.

I learned three YouTube audiences are researching or planning to purchase sports and fitness-related products or services. The three groups are fitness products and services, outdoor recreational equipment, and sporting goods. When I clicked on fitness products and services, I found the top YouTube channels people shopping for fitness products and services are likely to be watching. Jeff Nippard (2.14M), Body Project (1M+), Sydney Cummings (706K), and Muscle & Strength (816K) are the channel names that popped up.

The tool also revealed some of the top products and services most relevant to my audience, including Activewear, video games, etc. This is valuable information for someone setting up their fitness channel, wouldn't you agree?

Now, you can access the same so that your channel can reach the right audience with the right message and offers based on their preferences.

Activity #4: The Channels on Your Chosen Niche

It's time to implement all that we've learned. In this activity, you will complete researching between five to ten competitor channels using the tools I suggested.

Identify what makes these channels popular. Identify some gaps, if any, or think of what you could do differently and better. Read as many comments as possible to see how the channel interacts with its audience. This is also an excellent opportunity to gain content ideas because you will find questions, concerns, or even requests from the community that you can leverage on your channel.

Record as many of the detailed metrics I shared earlier as you can. If you do it manually, then do the best you can. Otherwise, use tools like Social Blade, BuzzSumo, and Tubular Intelligence. Once you've done this extensive research, start looking for the gaps in content and brainstorm how to improve on what you've seen out there. Document every idea, no matter how trivial it may seem. These notes will come in handy as we get into strategy and implementation.

Chapter 05

Branding Your Channel

It's time to get to the fun and creative part of setting up your channel. Now that you know what your channel will be about and whom you'll be creating content for, we need to make the different graphics, artwork, and other necessary pieces so that your channel can instantly attract potential subscribers. That's where branding comes in.

Why You Need to Brand

You'll find different definitions of a brand in today's digital world. I want to keep things simple, so here's how we will approach this branding concept.

Branding is about taking your best aspects and recreating them online so that people can have a real sense of who you are and what you stand for the moment they land on your YouTube channel. It's a lot harder to make a great first impression online, so by giving your channel an identity that's true to you, there's a higher chance you'll bridge that gap better and use technology to reinforce relationships rather than hinder them.

Branding has become extremely important on YouTube because you need to stand out and attract the proper attention from the right people. Social media has also become dominated by alluring aesthetics. Like it or not, if your channel doesn't look appealing to the audience you wish to attract, it will be tough to gain momentum. Most importantly, I emphasize branding a lot on YouTube because it is a social platform built around the concept of community at the end of the day and sharing knowledge and ideas. That means there's a strong need for a sense of belonging for the people hanging out there. Your branding does wonders when it comes to creating a signpost with your core identity written all over it, and that helps your "tribe" recognize and connect with you.

How do You go About Establishing Your Brand?

That must be completed on time. It is a natural growth process that will improve as you create content and interact with community members. However, a few key questions will enable us to start the journey of branding your YouTube channel. Ask yourself the following:

- Who am I, and how do I want to be known on YouTube? For example, a speaker, digital marketer, life coach, etc.
- What kind of voice do I want to build on YouTube? For example, funky, laid back, humorous, formal, etc.
- What kind of vocabulary, personality, and verbiage will I use? For example, think of Gary Vee. His language and vocabulary are very distinct. You want to figure out what yours is.

- What emotions, experiences, and benefits do you want your tribe to have from consuming your content?
- What colors and designs will you be using to stand out?

These are just a few questions you must answer as you build your brand. In this chapter, I will walk you through the key elements and how to set each up. Follow along, and your channel will be ready for launch by this end.

Setting Up Your New YouTube Channel

If you already have a channel, you may skip this section if you like, but I still encourage you to go through it. To get started, you must first sign up for a Gmail account. If you already have a Google account, head to youtube.com and click the Sign In button in the top right corner.

If you create the account for the first time, you will be asked to choose whether to make a channel for yourself or a business once you sign up. You will have the option of creating a personal brand or business brand, depending on your objective.

You will need to fill out the details, such as your name the name you want to use for the channel, and then choose to verify the account. Later, you can add a channel manager if you've set up a business channel. To prove your channel, you must give a mobile number where a text or voice message will be sent with a code. Once the code is entered and accepted, YouTube will let you upload videos longer than 15 minutes, add custom thumbnails, do Livestream, and so much more. So please make sure you do this as fast as possible.

Once done, you can head to your channel dashboard and see a blank canvas to add your creativity and personality. This is where the fun begins. If you have other social media profiles or websites you'd like to add to the main dashboard, you can add them here. For now, the most essential step is adding the artwork and graphics to personalize your channel and make it more appealing to your ideal audience.

Channel Images

Let's pick out the main image elements for your channel. Even if you're not a design expert, you can still create incredible images without spending a fortune or hiring expensive graphics designers. Tools such as Canva, PicMonkey, Word Swagg, and Picktochart are just a few of the tools you need to add to your toolbox. These software products are either free or low-cost and require little to no experience in graphics design. My preferred is, of course, Canva, which has a free and pro version. With Canva, you can design epic-looking images in seconds, from your channel art and logo to your thumbnails.

Hire a professional to create your graphics. You can hire a professional to create your channel art with a small budget. Websites such as 99designs are great for outsourcing, but you can also go to Upwork or Fiverr and hire someone for as little as $5 if you know exactly what you want.

Once you have the main channel image, it's time to brand your new channel. Here's how:

Sign into your YouTube studio, and from the left menu, select Customization. Use the tabs to customize your channel by changing the profile picture, banner image, and video watermark. This is also where you'll have the ability to change the layout.

For the profile picture, YouTube recommends uploading a JPG, GIF, BMP, or PNG file of 800X800 px. It can be square or round and renders at 98X98 px. Don't use animated GIFs for this.

For the banner image, you need a minimum dimension of 2048 X 1152 px, with an aspect ratio of 16:9. The file size must be 6MB or smaller. If you go with the minimum recommended dimensions, ensure the area for text and logos is 1235 X 338 px. Larger images may get cropped on specific devices because the banner comes across differently depending on whether it is viewed on desktop, mobile, or TV displays.

For basic channel info, you also can personalize what is displayed by adding or removing the information you want to be shared with the public. You must create a brand account if you want a different name from your Google Account. This would be different from your personal Google Account, making it easier to give other people (team members) access to your YouTube channel without sharing your Google Account details. It's also great if you know you'll want to have multiple channels in one account. I highly recommend getting a Brand Account for influencers because of its flexibility. The best part is you can call your channel whatever name you like.

Channel Layout

You can customize your channel so that new viewers and potential subscribers can see your channel trailers, certain featured sections, or a featured video when they first land on your homepage. Channel trailers are great because they offer the new visitor a preview of your channel and what you're all about. It's a great way to make a positive first impression and connect with your audience. Setting up a trailer video is easy. Just select Customization and then "Layout." Once you see "Video spotlight," click ADD and select the video you want to make the trailer. Hit publish, and you'll have your very own trailer. Making a great video trailer is essential, so keep reading to learn how to create an epic video that leaves your audience wanting more.

If you want to avoid having a trailer for the homepage, you could also feature a particular video. Some YouTubers place their most-watched video as the first thing a new visitor sees so they can immediately receive value and see why everyone else has subscribed to that channel. So don't feel pressured to create a trailer; even a high-value content piece will work just as well.

Activity #5: Create Your Channel

Now that you have all the essential elements of setting up your channel, it's time to implement what you've learned. Before you get into the next chapter, decide what kind of channel you want to set up and then get to work coming up with the design, image profile, and logo if necessary. Then, head over to YouTube and create your channel. Feel free to explore the different menus in YouTube Studio and read their community guidelines. Section four of this book will cover more on navigating YouTube Studio, but I want you to start immediately. Create your channel now.

SECTION 03

Creating YouTube Videos

YouTube is a large ecosystem, and although building a solid channel and learning the site is crucial, videos make it tick. Here are detailed YouTube video creation tactics people can't stop discussing.

As every successful YouTuber would tell you, quality beats quantity. But how can we measure quality? Unique ideas or new spins on familiar themes stand out in a sea of information. Your material is more relevant when it meets readers' current needs. Videos that garner comments, likes, and shares do better. Ask questions, survey, and debate.

Different Video Formats.

You can pick from several content types:

- Increase your expertise with lessons and guides.
- Authors share their lives and opinions through vlogs.
- Conversations with influential or topic matter experts.
- Critiques of media, entertainment, and products.
- Real-time spectator interaction during live streams.
- Documentaries are in-depth.

YouTube video streaming/recording: Make sure everything is in order before recording. The primary gear is better to start with. For beginners, a smartphone usually works. Later, you can improve your camera, microphone, and lighting. Keep the space peaceful and well-lit. Consider the setting—it must be unaffected. Even if you don't memorize lines, a good script will keep your video on track.

Editing makes content more engaging and polished. Cut, trim, and splice film to learn video editing. Remove errors and unnecessary material. These assist viewers in keeping on track as the video switches scenes or topics. Transitions and visuals: Exercise caution. Title animation, remarks, and relevant graphics are essential, but overuse can distract.

Speak clearly. The background music should match the subject, but it should keep your speech intact.

Regular uploads show subscribers your reliability. How often do you post, but what, how, and how well? Schedule uploads weekly, bimonthly, or monthly you may manage. Brand your videos using recognizable opening and closing sequences, imagery, and color schemes.

Avoid abrupt changes in tone or presentation.

Teamwork expands your channel's reach. Find content providers with similar audiences—collaborations featuring guest appearances on each channel. Working collaboratively on a project lets both authors use their expertise.

YouTube videos demand creativity, technical expertise, and brand cohesion. Know your audience, provide them value, and improve. Remember that each video we view will teach you something new. Feedback, analytics, and trends will guide improvements. However, your narrative is crucial. If you deliver well, people will listen.

Chapter 06

Creating Quality Content

This section of our book focuses on creating fantastic content to get you views and subscribers. For creatives, this is the most exciting part of their YouTube channel management. But why invest time in learning how to create quality content?

- Your content will stand out more if the quality is better than your competitors.
- Quality content is usually so packed with value that a new audience can't help but want more of what you're creating, which will lead to more subscribers.
- With great content comes the potential of going viral.
- Quality content will serve you for years to come.

We call it evergreen content only because once you create it, the number of views, engagement, and potential business grows over time. I have a video that's three years old and still brings in new business inquiries.

What Exactly Is Quality Content?

As stated, quality refers to the experience of the user. You can have lots of bells and whistles on your video, but if the users have a poor experience, then it won't matter. That content will be considered a flop. Quality includes all the technical aspects of video, including audio quality, visual quality, editing quality, and the quality of the shared script or content. For example, consider whether the video will be HD or 4K. Then, ask yourself, are the colors right? Is the lighting proper? Is it sharp and crisp? Is the audio good? Was it edited in a way that makes sense and tells a story? These are a few examples of objective quality, and the best part is that they are measurable and easy to control on your part.

However, we also need to think about subjective quality. We care about these as human beings, which will directly influence your channels' growth. It includes making it relevant, interesting, and engaging to the end-user.

According to a Google report, "when people choose what to watch, relating to their passions is 1.6X more important than whether the content has high production quality." I'm sharing this to inform you that objective and subjective quality matter. And while the objective is easy to measure and control, the emotional quality will ultimately determine how well your channel does in the long run.

We want to ensure you have the best chance of winning the hearts and attention of your potential subscribers. The best way to do that is to combine the technical aspects of video production with world-class content that resonates with the targeted audience. It would be best if you come across as relatable, and the stuff you put out should be focused on providing value in some way, shape, or form—more on how to do that in the unfolding chapters.

The Different Kinds of Video Content

Growing your YouTube channel can be manageable and straightforward. You need to know which types of content people love to watch and create more of those types. Here are the top ones.

- How-to and Tutorials
- Behind-the-scenes video content.
- Interview and Q&A
- Pranks
- Vlog
- Product reviews
- 360
- User-generated content
- Webinar
- Presentation
- Livestream

• How-to and Tutorials

Most famous YouTubers you might know have gotten that rise to stardom through this content category. Millennials are exceptional at creating this type of video content. It performs well because people love watching videos, and they love watching actionable insights. Some YouTubers have gone from zero to earning over $50 million by creating excellent tutorials.

I love this type of content because you're not limited by anything, and you can be as creative as you want. You can't go wrong if you understand your audience's values and create lots and lots of free content around it. It can be tutorials on anything under the sun. This is the age of information, and people love to learn. Ensure the tutorials are high quality to help, not make a sale!

• Behind-the-scenes video content

These types of videos are great for companies and solopreneurs. They are firmly rooted in raw storytelling for branding purposes. What do I mean by that? It's about revealing what you stand for and the culture you're building as a team or organization, and it pulls back the curtain on your brand to allow customers and potential buyers to forge a connection with it. It goes from being an impersonal operation to actual human beings with emotions, frustrations, ambitions, and personalities. If you have a remote team, get creative about how to record and edit funny behind-the-scenes content. If you fly solo, you can show a behind-the-scenes or sneak peek video about an upcoming project. A great example of this type of content can be found on Mind Valley Academy or Vistaprint.

- **Interview and Q&A**

These types of video content are great for authority building. Suppose you can get influences, experts, or even celebrities to come and answer your questions. In that case, you'll start attracting the attention of those who resonate with that information. This video content lets you connect with and align your brand with inspiring people and thought leaders. It also helps you look more trustworthy since you're hanging out with and getting answers from a respected voice.

A good interview requires planning, but don't make it appear too polished and scripted. It should be natural and intimate so potential subscribers can fully immerse themselves in that experience and feel like they know you and your guest better. As the interviewer, you need to ask powerful questions, direct the interview in the best direction, and make it as meaningful as possible for the user. I love interviews because you can create lots of evergreen content without running out of ideas or topics. You can even give exclusive access to your audience by tapping into well-known influencers and celebrities. There's a lot of power in leveraging this if you know how to do it right. A great example is Lewis Howes's "School of Greatness."

- **Pranks**

A huge and hungry audience awaits you on YouTube if you enjoy pulling off pranks. These types of video content are primarily for entertainment. As the creator, you would prank a friend or stranger and capture it on film. Of course, you must ensure the pranks are subtle enough to avoid offending anyone. What you're looking for is to make people laugh and disrupt their day or their thought patterns. Some people have been extreme and created a lot of controversies, and it has worked. Still, I strongly urge you to avoid that because, based on what I've seen, people enjoy funny pranks, not offensive or extreme pranks.

- **Vlog**

These are video blogs. They are usually raw and require minimal cost production. All you need is a unique brand voice and a personality that resonates with your target audience. Most vlogs are off-the-cuff and unpolished. All you need is a smartphone or webcam as equipment. I encourage you to have a script or bullet point to ensure your content is concise and well-thought-out. As a video influencer, you could do daily vlogs sharing your day at work. Think of this as documenting your journey. Share whatever you're in the trenches trying to build with the community, and you'll start to see a tribe joining you on the ride. I suggest checking out Gary Vaynerchuck's "Daily Vee" for inspiration on this type of video content.

- **Product Reviews**

This type of video content is like how-to content. It's meant to be insightful and focused on helping, not selling a product. Consumers flock to YouTube every minute of the hour, looking for help along their purchase journey. They want to know which product is best, how it works, and whether it will be good value for their money. A product review can help answer all those questions. However, I recommend doing product reviews once you've established credibility and trust with your audience because they need to trust you before following your advice—affiliate marketing partners up very well with product review videos. But again, you will need to walk that fine line of helping your audience make the right decision, not just selling them something because you're making money. By the way, you don't need to talk about products in your niche. For example, if you're a personal trainer, you could talk about the best running shoes or home workout equipment - even if they aren't directly related to you. Bringing that service and customer-focused value to an audience can cause someone to trust you and even hire your personal training services. Think creatively about which products you review and intend to bring value.

- **360 or VR content**

360-degree videos are our latest alternatives as we move closer to a complete virtual experience. Yes, we still have a long way to go, but people dig 360 content as it is immersive and puts the users in the center of the action, allowing them to pan around the room with their smart device. In other words, this type of content focuses more on bringing the end-user an immersive and exciting experience. Don't think you need to be fancy or have a huge company to make these videos work for you. Experiment and see if it matches your brand and personality.

- **User-generated content**

This type of video content will work once you have a growing customer base. If you have a business, find creative ways to get previous or existing customers to create social content. Something sharable that sells for you. User-generated content has become massive on social media. It's a great way to get free testimonials, demonstrate your credibility, and gather new leads because people love to see social proof. Most social media users say that UGC is the most authentic type of content, and they want to see more of it. So whether you're just starting and need time to build a customer list or already have people who can create this for you, come up with a plan and incentive to make people want to record short videos about how great your brand is—wondering how to get started? Consider running a contest on YouTube and other social media platforms. Encourage people to send over videos of themselves using your product. Or you can start a campaign for your brand and products and create a trending hashtag, then ask people to use it as much as possible.

- **Webinar**

Did you know you could host webinars on Google Hangout? It's simple and easy to navigate. This type of video content is precious for an audience that loves to learn. It can exponentially grow your YouTube channel because you can offer and share webinars on your channel. Just make sure it's educative and actionable information. Since the pandemic in 2020, we've seen a massive spike in virtual webinars, so now people are accustomed to learning online. If you don't want to use Google Hangouts, you can do Zoom webinars and then upload the recording to your YouTube channel. Think of webinars as a free live event. This is an opportunity for your potential subscribers to learn something valuable from you and begin the purchase journey. It can be a solo webinar or a roundtable panel discussion with several gurus in your niche.

- **Presentations**

Have you ever heard of Ted Talks? Of course you have! These are a form of presentation content; as you know, they perform well on YouTube. A presentation type of video content (even if it's not a Ted Talk) can work well because it combines the excitement of a live event with a virtual webinar's practicality to create something compelling and shareable. You could be on the other side of the planet watching a presentation from someone you could have never met. Of course, if you want to do Ted Talks, you can do that too, but there's a long process of making that happen. If you will leverage this video content, please start by giving as many presentations as possible at different locations. The size of the audience doesn't matter. Ensure the presentation is excellent, and you capture the whole thing on video.

- **Livestreaming**

The last type of video content we will discuss is Live streaming, which was added a few years ago. Since then, there has been increasing demand across all social platforms, including YouTube. People love interacting in a Livestream, and it is expected to become a $70.5 billion industry by 2021. YouTube allows you to participate and enjoy a portion of that success. The best part about live streaming is that you can do it in any category, niche, and subject matter. Places such as cooking, self-improvement, motivational speeches, DIY arts and crafts, makeup routines, dance choreography, workout routines, yoga, meditation, etc. can all perform great on the Live stream.

Why does this work so well? It comes down to the fact that people love the suspense of Live video. They can't resist the urge to tune in because they don't want to miss out on getting new gossip, learning something new, or connecting with someone they admire.

Studies have shown that live streams generate up to 10 times more engagement than regular videos. Neil Patel said that live video broadcasts receive 600% more engagement than regular posts. So what are you waiting for?

You can be completely unknown today, but if you create great content, you can become a YouTube superstar using any content type in no time.

Why You Need a Solid Video Content Strategy

Creating a well-thought-out video content strategy is necessary if you want long-term success. Here's the thing. Building brand authority or a robust library that keeps drawing in traffic will take time. That's okay. Instead of fussing about the daunting work ahead of you, focus on creating a simple and easy-to-execute system you can follow. Ensure your plan is flexible because you'll need to adjust as you grow.

Why do you need to come up with a clear strategy? Because if you don't, you'll end up disheartened and feeling like you're not progressing. That will likely cause you to give up too soon. It will also be hard to measure and monitor your growth if everything is random. Posting a content idea that comes to you occasionally will not bring you the change you need. Trust me on that. And more importantly, I want to help ensure you always stay focused on content ideas. The more precise and well-planned your strategy, the easier it is to keep producing even after a dry spell.

So, how do we go about creating your strategy? I borrowed insights from Think with Google, who share many relevant ideas on winning big on YouTube. They interview and run case studies on some of the biggest brands in the world. Think Johnson & Johnson, Nike, and even Marvel Movies. It's only wise to listen to their advice on building fantastic content on our YouTube channels. We may need more resources or money to create at the level of these giant corporations. Still, we can implement the same principles driving their success. A simple framework I have learned from studying those case studies is to Create, Collaborate, and curate.

The 3 C's for A Simple And Efficient Content Strategy

Create

Your strategy should include a detailed brainstorm of the titles, keywords, lessons, or subject matter your videos will cover over a certain period. We can call this a video content plan. For this section of your strategy, you will need to research the top-performing content in your niche market and then make a list of what you will create.

Depending on your preference, you can have a monthly or 90-day content plan. I recommend starting with a 30-day content plan to stay calm. Then, decide whether you'll batch these videos together so you can shoot once or twice a week. If you're bold and committed to being on camera a lot, you can also shoot, edit, and publish on the same day. I recommend giving yourself enough leeway for emergencies, equipment glitches, and editing time.

If you plan to release one new video daily, the above options work well. If you remove more than one video daily, you must batch your video recordings to allow ample editing and personalization time. Remember, the quantity must not compromise the quality of your video content.

Collaborate

Creating strategic partnerships is the best way to build up your library and grow your brand on YouTube. A section on your content strategy should exist for collaborations with peers and other YouTube influencers. The great benefit of partnering up with others in your space is your channel's increased exposure.

Make sure, however, that the agreement is mutually beneficial. I recommend creating an outreach campaign once you've hit your first 1K subscribers. And when you do, begin with those most likely to agree to this partnership. For example, asking someone with 3 million subscribers to collaborate when you only have 1K followers may yield negative results. You need to pay them handsomely to ensure these categories of YouTubers are out of reach at first. But if you started reaching out to influencers with 5K - 30K subscribers, they will likely want to work with you if you can prove how valuable the experience will be.

When you collaborate, you co-create the video content and then cross-post on each other's channels for maximum exposure. Not only will you be adding to your library, but you'll also bring value to a new audience that didn't know you existed.

For example, there's a YouTuber with a channel on physics experiments and how to apply them to everyday life. She collaborated with a guy with a channel for testing and reviewing tech gear. Their collaboration involved using physics to see whether the iPhone 11 Pro could withstand a massive hit without breaking. The video was entertaining and cool to watch, plus we learned a lot about Vacuum and how powerful nature is. Even the iPhone isn't built to withstand the powers of Mother Nature. I share this simple example to show you what's possible with collaborations. You can find the video on both channels and now, the tech-savvy geeks who didn't know about the physics channel got a chance to subscribe and follow "Physics Girl." That's the power of a good collaboration.

Curate

The last C we want to add to your content strategy involves curating content. This isn't content you create. Instead, it comes from existing customers, subscribers, and loyal fans who want to praise you and your brand. That's why this part of your content comes when the channels begin to mature because it's likely you're starting from scratch, and that's okay. Just know that you can do this type of content at some point, and it'll boost your credibility and authority. Fans and customers love sharing their experiences, stories, and opinions. Getting this type of content will be easy, especially if you're regularly running contests and giveaways. Think of it to invite your audience to help you tell your story on YouTube.

A content strategy doesn't need to be perfect, but you must have one. With these three different areas, you also want to know what metrics and measurements of growth you'll be going after. As a beginner, here's a simple template I encourage you to follow.

- Write down the big and little goals that lead up to that big one.
- Write down who the content is for.
- Write down the influencers your audience follows on YouTube.
- Please write down the experience you want the audience to have and how the content should impact them.
- Write down your expected milestones and principal return on investment (ROI).

How To Plan with Your Content

The more thought you put into your video content before hitting that record button, the better the quality and performance. Whether you're doing a technical how-to or a daily vlog, it's essential to plan. How much planning you do is entirely up to you. Some people want to script out every word. Others need a vague idea of the main message they want to pass on before shooting. There's no wrong or right here. Your personality and experience with being on camera influence how you plan your video content. Still, I will share a few best practices below.

Remember that the first place to start, as stated earlier, is with a documented content plan. It can be two weeks, thirty days, sixty days, or even a ninety-day plan. If you're one of those who cannot start thinking too far ahead, then opt for a weekly program. Sit with your journal or a Google document and plan the video content topic, title, and key points you'll create over the specified period. You can also use a content calendar for this. If you approach your content planning from the perspective of creating a viral video or a single piece of content that will make you an overnight sensation, then you will fail. Those short-term rewards have nothing to do with growing your channel or brand. Instead, focus on creating consistent content that will engage your audience. The sweet spot to hit is that point of intersection between what your brand stands for and what your audience cares about.

Researching content topics

If you have an existing customer base or a following on another social media platform, you can create a questionnaire asking your current fans what they'd love to learn from you. Social media users are very interested in sharing opinions and offering suggestions. If you don't have any followers, look at your competitors and peers. Subscribe to their channel on YouTube to see what's working and where the gaps are. Please read all the comments on their most engaged posts. These are all great places to get new title ideas and topics.

Once the research is done, it's time to get specific and decide on the types of keywords you'll focus on. You'll need more informational keywords if your channel is more educational and informative. But if the content focuses on selling, you'll need more transactional keywords integrated into your video content, title, descriptions, and tags.

A content plan should be integrated with your calendar using software like Asana, Buffer, etc. You can also create your own using a spreadsheet. All you need to have in the columns is the publish date, title/description, status (in progress, completed, delayed), type of content, and main keywords.

How To Structure the Video Content - A Simple Template

- Map out the first 15 seconds.
- Outline the key points.
- Use the proven formula H.I.C.C (Hook Intro Content Call-to-action)

Hook

The hook is the thing that will grab attention and get people to watch the video. Include it at the beginning of your video within that 15-second window so people don't click away.

Intro

The intro helps the audience understand what you'll cover, why they should listen to you or care, and a bit about yourself as the host.

Content

This is the meat of your video. All the value goes into this section, and it should take up the most time because you will be giving people what you promised at the beginning of the video.

For example, if you're a personal trainer, this part would be the workout to tighten your abs.

Call-to-action

Always have a call to action at the end of each video. Summarize what the video was about, especially if it was informational or educational, and then ask them to act. Even if it was purely an entertainment video, you could still add a call to action by asking your audience to subscribe, like, share, or comment on the video.

Keep your video structure super simple by following the above form until you get the hang of things. Then you can get a bit fancier.

Collaborating With Other Creators in Your Niche

As I said before, a strong content strategy always has a section for collaborations. The smart YouTubers understand the importance of leveraging this tactic. Still, you should know there are some advantages and disadvantages to using this method.

Pros:

- Collaborations are free, so it's a great way to tap into an existing audience without spending money.
- It exposes you to a new audience, benefiting a young channel.
- It enables you to create more content.
- The quality of content improves because you always learn so much from these types of partnerships, especially if done with someone who has been around a lot longer than you.
- It's a powerful way to establish connections and build genuine relationships with people who share your passion and desire to serve an audience. Some of these collaborations may turn into new lucrative opportunities.

Cons:

While I don't believe in disadvantages when creating collaboration because every experience has something to teach us (even those that don't work out), I can share a few things to become aware of.

- It will require a lot of upfront energy to get these relationships started. You are 100% responsible for getting their attention and making them interested in your offer.
- It would be best if you did many follow-ups when going after your list of potential collaborators.
- You might experience lots of rejection, and that's okay. Learn to handle these situations.

When doing collaborations, make sure you give and serve first. Don't be overly self-promotional. Most importantly, be authentic. If you are fully confirmed, you will only resonate with a new audience and have them interested in checking out your channel, so don't try to "fake it" or "fit in." This will ensure you get the most out of that experience.

I also encourage you to go into it open-minded and focused on having fun. It doesn't matter how many people end up subscribing. Learn to take your mind off metrics and data and be a passionate creator. That will make the influencer you're working with also appreciate the experience, as they will see you care more about serving the audience than getting subscribers, which might lead to more collaborative opportunities.

How To Make Sure You Never Run Out of Great Ideas

You'll hear many content creators talk about going through a "dry spell," and at some point, you might find yourself experiencing the same. So, let's talk about how to handle these situations. The worst thing to do is force yourself to get on camera when you feel completely drained of value and inspiration.

I usually encourage clients to take a day or a week away from the spotlight and reset. Sometimes, the pressure becomes too much and causes our creative juices to stagnate. However, my advice only works if you already have enough content in the pipeline to allow you that "off-time." I encourage you to batch your content creation and schedule it beforehand. At a minimum, one week early. Some people prefer to design it a month in advance. Whichever frequency you choose, ensure you have enough ready-to-go content so you're not rushing or banging your head against the wall because it's Monday morning, and you have nothing to post. To help ensure you have enough ideas, here are some best practices.

- Once a week, sit with a Google doc and write down all the titles you want to create content for.

- Always carry a pen and notepad or train your Siri to be alert when ideas come to you while running errands, working out, driving, etc. Some of the best ideas come to us when we least expect them.

- Download an app such as Evernote to help you capture screenshots, save, and bookmark links that inspire you as you browse the Internet.

You might come across an article or video that stirs up your creative juices, and there's nothing worse than trying to find that link (days later) in your long browser history.

A Simple Formula to Get Over 100 Video Content Ideas in Less Than 20min.

• Content Topic Generators

These are your most accessible source of inspiration and content ideas. You could have content for a month in less than twenty minutes. The list of content generators continues to grow, so keep checking for new ones. How it works is that these software apps use the most popular title formulas and fill in the blanks with your specific terms and keywords. Check out

1. Portent Content Idea Generator
2. ContentIdeator
3. Content Strategy Helper
4. Hubspot's Topic Generator

• Buzzsumo

Head over to Buzzsumo and type in the keyword you want to discuss. You'll see a breakdown of all the most famous content based on social shares. It's a great way to know what people love, and when you find articles that are doing well, a video version will likely perform well. With their free version, you're limited to a few searches, but it should be enough to get your juices flowing, and you can see what's done well in the recent weeks, months, even a year ago.

- **Ubersuggest**

This tool gives you a lot more than content ideas. It also shares keyword ideas and tells you which content is doing well based on search volume. It's a great way to see the top-ranking sites and the range, making them rank so high that you can leverage those titles.

- **Answer The Public**

This tool helps you find all the common questions about the keyword you type in. In just a few seconds, you can have abundant content ideas and similar keywords organized in an easy-to-read diagram that you can easily download. The tool offers keyword alternatives like comparisons, prepositions, and related phrases.

- **Quora**

Quora is a trendy Q&A platform that has gained much traction recently. Head to the forum and type in the keywords or topics you want to be an authority on. Then, look at all the questions asked in your niche and pick the ones people are most interested in. You can tell by the number of followers and the number of upvotes for the top responses.

Once you find a hot question, shoot a video with your best answer. Be as educational, informative, and helpful as possible in that video. Try to be comprehensive with your reply so that when people click to watch the video, they can immediately see the value you bring and hopefully subscribe. But you still need to finish.

Once you've published the video, return to Quora's original question. Answer it with a few words explaining your thoughts and letting people know you've shot a video with a more detailed answer. You can link the video here to drive traffic directly to your YouTube video. I recommend keeping a spreadsheet with the list of questions and a direct link so it's easy to find them again once you've shot the video. It also helps you track performance because you can check once a month to see if people responded and voted you up. It's impossible with Quora to run out of ideas because you don't need to come up with any. Just find questions you can best answer on video.

Aside from Quora and Answer the Public, you can also check forums like Yahoo, Reddit, or specific industry forums where your audience most likely hangs out. You want to find questions, problems, complaints, or inquiries that people bounce back and forth in these forums.

- **Online Groups**

These include Facebook groups, LinkedIn, Twitter Chats, Instagram Pods, etc. People get together to discuss interesting topics or even complain about products or services that might

belong to your competitors. Look for groups that only allow a few articles to be shared to avoid spammy ones. The best groups or pods have lots of questions and answers.

- **Industry Publications and Blog Comment Sections**

Most people must realize what a goldmine it can be to spend half an hour going through your favorite publication's comment section. Suppose you're a personal trainer or dietician wanting to create unique content. By browsing big online blogs such as Bulletproof and other health publications, you will likely come across many great ideas from their readers. Sometimes, readers will even ask questions or raise concerns over something that needs to be covered. Those are the gaps your video content should fill. The demand is there, and your content can be the solution.

- **YouTubers You Follow**

I already asked you in an earlier chapter to list your top competitors. These are the people who are already crushing it in your niche. You need to be subscribed to their channels to learn and get inspired by them. One of your competitors created content six months ago that's now a little dated, or they may only share a brief overview of the topic. Still, you can go deeper and create something even better. That's your ticket to growth and value-adding.

- **Social Media Influencers You Follow**

With this hack, you want to research all your top social media profiles to see whom you follow or who follows you and shares great content. Look at what they engage with and see if there are any topics you can add to your content planner.

- **Webinars**

Most people don't think about this when first getting started, but given how popular webinars have become, it's a great place to get content ideas. Check out popular websites in your niche. Research the top influencers in your industry who usually do webinars and follow them to see topics they keep running webinars on. The most popular webinar titles would also be great for video content.

- **HARO (Help A Reporter Out)**

Helping a reporter out is a great place to see trending topics, and it can be an opportunity for your brand to be featured. When you share your expertise on the platform, a reporter can pick up your story and share it with the world, giving you free publicity. But I am sharing this platform with you because by being on it, you get a glimpse of what people are looking for in terms of topics and stories.

- **Google**

If your keywords are correct, Google can show you trends (go to Google Trends) or related searches from the search bar. By clicking on the tabs labeled "Video," you can also see the top-ranking videos in your niche, indicating what area to focus on. Google also added a section called "People also ask," - which is great for finding more questions about your topic or keyword. All these are great spots for coming up with fresh and relevant content.

- **Self-help magazines**

There's a reason why magazines like Men's Health and Cosmo are so popular. These magazines tend to have highly clickable titles. They know how to give people what they want. I have a friend who first opened my eyes to this little trick. Now I use it all the time. Whenever I am in a store, I look for the magazine section to browse some of these popular magazines quickly. You can do the same. Just take a quick snapshot of the titles most resonating with you and add your industry's words.

- **Amazon**

Amazon is another excellent hack because it is an endless ocean of content. You can create many "how-to" content or answer questions left in the comment section of books, apparel, or whatever else your niche focuses on. Since there's a book written on almost every topic under the sun, consider browsing authors in your industry and look for bestsellers. Then, open to read the table of contents for title ideas. If you want to hit a vein of gold, go through the comments people leave and compile them into more content ideas. Although this might take a little longer than twenty minutes, it'll be worth your time, and you will end up with ideas that last a year.

Do You Need a Script? Yes Or No?

While it would be easier to give a yes or no answer... the honest answer is - it depends. As the content creator, you can determine what's wrong or suitable for you. This scenario has no one-size-fits-all because some people swear by script writing and teleprompters. In contrast, others would rather die than script out their content. You can start with either and see which fits best. Still, suppose you're a complete newbie. In that case, I encourage you to practice scripting or, at the very least, create bullet points and prompters to assist you as you build confidence in front of the camera.

If you already know scriptwriting is not for you because you've tried it for a while and it didn't pan out, no matter what you did, please skip over to the activity section of this chapter. But a script will be the best way to go if you're unsure and feel your confidence still needs to be improved. It can be as simple as having a bullet point on a sheet of paper dangling next to your camera, where you can easily read the main points. Or get a teleprompter and write out a killer video script. Remember, this isn't a movie screenplay. You're creating something for a social network, so the flow of it will have to be different. Here is a guideline to follow:

Get the Essential Elements Right.

As we said before, you have a fifteen-second window on YouTube to grab the attention of your potential subscribers. If you miss that window, the user will likely click away, and we don't want that. So, prioritize the hook and flow of the content.

Create a basic model for your script that can be explained in 1min. Break down the main points so you can easily communicate your message without losing the viewer. People need to understand your concept quickly.

Make sure the audio is of excellent quality. Audio matters a lot! If you add background music, ensure it doesn't overpower or disrupt your voice. Don't you hate it when you can't hear what the guy says in his cooking video because of the loud music? Don't do that to your audience.

Have a strong point of view.

Your YouTube channel is supposed to show what your brand stands for. Having a clear point of view and confidently expressing it is essential. People who struggle to share their opinions boldly rarely do well on this platform. Since we've gone through exercises in earlier chapters to determine your channel's identity and your target audience, be sure to speak your opinion authentically and confidently about the topic you cover.

Pacing.

When writing out the script, be sure to pace yourself accordingly. Add only a few filler words or create awkward silence in your content. Let it flow naturally like you're sitting with a friend in Starbucks having coffee. And please don't be like those late-night infomercials guys who barely breathe between sentences. Take your time to meet a specific deadline. Pace yourself and keep a steady tempo that is true to your personality.

Include lots of emotional words and triggers.

Do you know why a video prank of a teenage daughter scaring her mom performs better than a reporter talking about inflation? Simple. Emotional content will always get more views because people can relate to it more.

Be clear, concise, and conversational.

Whether you create a detailed script or an outline, it's crucial to be conversational and concise. To help ensure you do this, I suggest you avoid writing lengthy sentences when writing. Videos don't require too many words because onscreen visuals accompany them, so you don't have to worry about using significant, complex sentences. If anything, stick to terminology and penalties that a 6th grader can easily follow.

Example template to follow:

Introduction. The first fifteen seconds of your video make or break your chances of winning a potential subscriber, so make your introduction short, sweet, and attention-grabbing. Introduce yourself and the topic at the beginning of the script, and please remember to add a strong hook.

When scripting this part, ensure the first few lines contain the hook to keep people tuned. Follow it up with a clear breakdown of what the audience will learn by the end of the video. Example: Are you freaking out because it's just a few weeks to your wedding day, and you still haven't shed those extra pounds for your big day? Fear not, because, by the end of this video, you'll know precisely how to drop at least ten pounds in the next five days without ever hitting the gym! I'm Jenny, and for the past fifteen years, I've been helping couples look hot for their big day and that special honeymoon week. Let's get you lean and ready to enjoy your special day now!

Main Content and Ask an engaging question.

Once the intro is done, script out the main content. This is the meat of the video. I often like to include questions to keep the viewer's attention. Something simple that gives a yes or no answer should do it, and it's a great way to encourage people to comment. In this section, script out word for word what you're going to teach. Returning to the example I just shared, scripting this section would require Jenny to write exactly how the viewer will shed those ten pounds within five days. What are the steps? What secret hacks or ingredients should the viewer know about?

That is also where a story would come in handy. Suppose Jenny has experienced this process of transformation. In that case, she can talk about how she did it and shed that weight before her special day. Perhaps one of her clients has an incredible transformation story that could be interjected here with a few before and after snapshots. Storytelling will keep the viewer glued to the screen and give them a glimpse of how powerful this solution is.

When scripting your content, be conversational, don't use big words, and make it short and punchy. The more concise you are, the easier it will be to edit the video and the more engaging it will be for the viewer.

Summary and call to action

In this last part, as you bring the video to an end, I suggest you do a quick recap of all the good stuff they learned. That is especially important if you're teaching something. Otherwise, summarise the main idea and tie it back to your main objective if there's a specific action step like downloading something, signing up for an event or program, etc. When you have softer CTAs, you can sprinkle them throughout the video, such as "Before we jump into the main secrets I want to share, let me remind you to hit the subscribe button so you never miss another cool video like this one." Ultimately, you can also say, "If you liked this video, give it a thumbs up and share it with a friend."

Activity #6: Create And Schedule Your Content

Now that you've learned how to plan your content and where to find great ideas, it's time for action. Create a list of the video titles you will shoot over the next 90 days. Get your content calendar out and start brainstorming and researching using the various hacks you learned in this chapter. By the end of this exercise (before starting the next chapter), you should have ninety potential video titles mapped out on your content planner. Schedule a time to create, edit, and publish each content on a calendar. Don't worry if you just got a panic attack when I mentioned video editing. Yes, it can be a daunting process, but the next chapter two chapters are designed to ensure you have an easy and fun time. Let's put some ideas on our planner and prep ourselves for success.

Pro Tip:

If you want to stay focused and on-point with your content planning, fill out this simple statement and let it direct your focus on content ideas. Keep this statement in mind, print it, and stick it where you can see it often so you always stay relevant and interesting to your ideal audience.

Complete the following:

The video content I produce helps my brand accomplish ...[name goal]... and ...[name goal].... by providing ...[adjective]... and ...[adjective]... content that makes...[name emotion].... feel...me emotion]... or...[name benefit]... so that they can... [Name benefit]...

Chapter 07

Recording YouTube Videos

Recording your video should be as easy as switching on the camera and pressing the red button. Well, that's true, but a lot more goes into recording. Lots of things must be prepped beforehand. It's known as the pre-recording phase. Many items must also occur once you're done recording (the post-production phase). The pre- and post-recording stages affect the video's overall result, so take advantage of this and the upcoming chapters. This chapter will focus on what you need to know and do to be camera-ready and produce amazing videos. So, before you hit that record button, let's cover some best practices and the type of equipment you'll need to make your YouTube channel successful.

The Only Equipment You Need to Get Started

Video production can be costly; I won't lie. Some YouTubers have invested tens of thousands in having the recording studios, equipment, and crew you see on their channels. I created this book with the simple intention of helping the beginner who may or may not have a budget available yet still wants to create something beautiful. If that's you, this chapter will ease some of your concerns. Whether you can afford to spend a few thousand, hundreds, or zero dollars on equipment, I'm here to show you how to be camera-ready. The essential gear you need includes:

- A camera that can shoot in HD
- Good lighting
- Great Audio
- Video editing software
- Camera stabilizer or mounter

Whether you're broke or have some money to invest, these five things are fundamental to recording your video. I will break down some options for those serious about getting the right equipment, but there are some simple workarounds even if you still need to afford a dime.

Need More Money to Spend? Read This.

If you have no money to invest in equipment, consider using your smartphone camera or the webcam from your laptop. Most of the smartphones come with incredible video quality. The minimum quality standard you need to go for with a camera should be 1080p. Ensure you also have a laptop with free editing software like iMovie (for Mac users).

Of course, you will need to mount the recording gear somewhere, so get creative. If you can't afford a stabilizer like a tripod, stack some books or boxes on a desk near a window to get that natural lighting. You can always use the phone or laptop's built-in audio system when it comes to the audio.

This is going to produce something other than top-notch quality. However, you can still shoot decent videos if you play around with an excellent background and use editing and filters. For free graphics editing, you can use Canva, which is perfect for producing attention-grabbing thumbnails.

Got Some Money to Invest? Read This.

Here are eight (8) essential things to consider if you can invest money into your equipment setup.

The Camera.

Get a camera that shoots in 4K. Since it will be the most critical piece of equipment, please invest to the best of your ability. If you have no limitations with your budget, then the sky is the limit. Your options are plenty. Quality camcorders or webcams (if you're using a laptop to shoot) are great for beginners. Still, if you can afford to spend more, I suggest you buy a DSLR camera. How do you decide what to purchase? Think about your budget and the type of content you'll be creating.

Camcorders are designed to record videos. Hence, they are the easiest to operate, light to carry around, and can handle almost any shooting scenario, whether vlogging on the go or in your basement studio. A good recommendation for this would be the Sony HDRCX405, which costs about $198. What's great about it aside from the pocket-friendly price is that it is full HD with an image stabilization feature, which reduces shaking and blurring when shooting handheld. It can shoot 1080p videos at 60fps and is equipped with a Carl Zeiss zoom lens with 27x true optical zoom for lossless magnification and excellent overall video quality. It also allows you to record in MP4, which makes web uploads super-fast and convenient.

I recommend the Logitech C920 HD Pro for webcams, which goes for about $89.99 and shoots full HD 1080p and 720p. If you're a gamer, this will be a perfect fit because the camcorder uses its processor to encode videos instead of relying greatly on your computer power. That means it won't slow down your computer, which is excellent.

DSLRs are the most favored and highly recommended cameras for YouTubers across all niches. I use that, too, and I'm happy with the quality. I love these cameras because of their adaptability in low-light situations and the polished video recording quality they provide. But trust me, this is for someone willing to invest more money. There are many great options, whether you prefer Sony or Canon, but I will share my two favorite options: Canon Cameras. The first is the Canon 70D, and the second is the Canon EOS Rebel T5i. Both are amazing, so do your research, and based on your budget and content needs, pick one.

The Microphone

There's no way around this. You must invest in a lapel or an omnichannel microphone for excellent audio. Great audio only happens sometimes. Even the best cameras need a little help regarding audio quality.

The microphone you choose can be cheap. You can get a Lavalier mic, which picks up less background noise and is pocket-friendly. You can do something decent starting from as little as $30 on Amazon. If you want to invest a little more, here are some great options.

Get a USB microphone. These mics have become popular with YouTubers because of their ease of use and sound quality. They are also affordable. If you want to go this route, consider getting the Logitech Clear Chat H390 for around $39.99. It's super easy to use and provides a clear, crisp sound. You could also go for Audio-Technica AT2020USB Plus, which costs $149. What's great about this is that it allows self-monitoring through its built-in headphone jack with volume control. It offers mix control so you can blend your microphone with pre-recorded audio.

Go for shotgun microphones if you're serious about becoming a heavy hitter. You'll need to have deeper pockets for these types of microphones. They work great with a small professional camera and have shock mounts that help reduce the noise coming from mechanical vibrations around the mic. These microphones are known for capturing crisp sounds and vocals, even if you're recording outdoors. If your pocket allows, I recommend going for Rode Microphones VideoMic Pro R, which sells for about $299. It's a handy version that's perfect for your DSLR or camcorder. It has a super-cardioid polar pattern system and is powered by 9V batteries, so you can use it for up to 70 hours.

The last option I want to give you is a lavalier mic, aka lapel mic, which is the easiest route. All you need to do is discretely clip it onto your clothes or belt. It comes in a set with a transmitter to which the lapel and receiver connect, allowing sound to be picked up even from great distances. If you're a speaker, you've seen these at conferences. I recommend the RODELink Digital Wireless System, which costs $399, so you'll need a big budget. The benefits make it worthwhile because it works even from a hundred meters away and offers the ability to select the best signal to deliver audio as reliable as cable connections.

Lighting

Natural sunlight is, of course, one of the best lights you can have for your video. Still, you're not at a loss if nature isn't working in your favor as you begin this journey of YouTube stardom. If you can invest in good lighting, even a tiny space in the basement can produce a high-quality video. Lighting greatly influences your setup's mood and brightness, so here are some options to ensure you look professional.

The first recommendation is getting a softbox. It can emulate the natural soft lighting from a window. If you want to go with something subtle, this would be the ideal choice, and the best part is the Flashpoint SoftBox goes for only $49.95. It comes with a 70W fluorescent light unit and an AC plug that's easy to use. You can use this kit indoors with camcorders and digital cameras.

The second recommendation is a ring light. Ring lights are super popular with vloggers. When its ring shape emits light around you, it eliminates shadows from every direction, making you look more attractive in front of the camera. So next time you see those doll-like beauty vloggers - don't envy them; appreciate their creativity and lighting system! If you'd like a similar setup, experiment with Flashpoint 19 Kit. It uses 80W power that doesn't emit too much heat, so you could even have it closer to you, especially if you plan on doing close-up shots.

I would like to make one last recommendation if you need something lightweight that can be mounted on the camera. It's the iKan iLED-MA Micro Flood Light, which costs about $29.99. It can emit a dimmable wide 120-degree beam of bright 5000K+ Daylight with 21 1.2-watt LEDs. It comes with a MicroUSB cable for charging and a shoe mount fixed to a back holder so you can position it vertically or horizontally once it's on your camera.

The Tripod Or Stabilizer

You can opt for a tripod or a gimbal stabilizer, depending on how you shoot your videos. They both accomplish the vital task of keeping your image steady, which increases production quality. Most beginners opt for a tripod, so I'd recommend you start there too. Most of them are under $100 on Amazon, and they work well, especially if your camera is light enough. If you need something sturdy and more durable, a few options will keep the bank, including the iKan E-Image EG01A2, for only $169. This tripod can handle most DSLRs and camcorders and holds up to 11lbs. The extension of this tripod is over 5 feet, making it easy to shoot from exciting vantage points. The best part is that it can collapse to 33 inches and weighs only 10lbs, making it ideal for travel.

I recommend the iKan FLY X3-Plus Gimbal Stabilizer gimbal stabilizer, which goes for $69.99 and is perfect for content creators continually shooting on the move. Let's face it: no matter how steady your hands are, handheld shooting will produce shaky and jarring videos. This gimbal is fantastic because it has a 3-axis stabilizer system with brushless motors to smoothen your camera movements. It also has a battery life that can last up to 5 hours! Talk about good value.

Video editing software

Post-production is just as important when aiming for high-quality video, so you must invest in some editing software. If you have a Mac computer, of course, you've got the free iMovie that comes with it (Windows Movie Maker for PC users). Still, you may want to consider other products in the market.

There's software that comes highly recommended by many of my peers, and it has a free version that a beginner can use to test out. It's called Hitfilm Express. It has professional-grade VFX tools. They claim it's perfect for beginners, gamers, or any creative who needs a budget. It might be worth checking out.

Adobe Premiere Elements 18 is an alternative many videographers promote. Of course, you need a budget for this and some skills, so give yourself time to learn how to use it best. If you'd like something easier to work with, I recommend Camtasia, which will cost about $199. It's easy to navigate and versatile. The learning curve is short, so if you're not too crazy about graphics and editing, that should sort you out. Need more software options? Keep reading this book as I cover more alternatives in an upcoming chapter.

For those who want to get fancy, add the following equipment.

Digital Recorder

If this is your first time hearing the term "digital recorder," don't worry. You're not alone. We've all had to learn what it is and why we need it. Usually, only the pros get this type of fancy equipment because they want to elevate that sound quality. At first, I hesitated to invest in it, but after using it for a few years, I can't believe it took me so long to get it. A digital recorder is helpful because it transforms any environment into a studio-like effect. This will be a worthwhile investment if you like crisp, high-quality sound. I especially recommend it if you'll be doing many interviews. A great one to start with is a Zoom H4N pro. It's handy, easy to carry around, and lasts a while.

Teleprompter

Another fancy piece of equipment you could get is a teleprompter to help you flow better with your script. It will ensure your message is on point and save you hours of filming and editing. Nowadays, various varieties can work with a camera or a smartphone. Amazon should have plenty of options, but you can always check out Caddie Buddy, which is pocket-friendly and functional.

Get a studio backdrop.

The last fancy piece of equipment you can get is a studio background. If you plan an indoor setup with minimum movement, consider getting a green screen or whatever studio backdrop fits your budget. Some of these can be quite costly, ranging thousands of dollars, so research first. When I'm shooting, I just opt for a natural background in my home with a bookcase in the set showing some of the awards I've received over the years. Nothing fancy. For my personality and audience, it works. But suppose you want to go for something flashy. In that case, you can check out this inexpensive backdrop I found on Amazon for $58 called Slow Dolphin Fabric Video Studio Backdrop Kit.

One recommendation I can make here is to create a large banner with your branding. Depending on the size, it could be anything from $100-$500, but when designed well, it can be a great way to reinforce your brand and make you look super professional.

Best Practices for Recording Your Videos

• Make sure your video has a purpose.

Don't just shoot a video because you heard the topic is trendy or because you promised your audience to post daily/weekly. Each piece of content should be planned on time. It should also serve a purpose. So, ask yourself, "What does this video want to accomplish? Is it views back to my website? New subscribers? More comments, likes, and shares? I encourage you to get laser-focused on one specific target.

- **Make the video valuable and relevant.**

Your video needs to add some value to your audience and potential subscribers. Whether you're a comedian, gamer, vlogger, stylist, personal trainer, or coach, ensure the content is relevant and valuable. If you're an entertainer, entertain and leave the viewer renewed and amused.

- **Do what it takes to have great audio.**

You might need more money to invest in expensive equipment, but you can still produce good-quality audio. If people can't hear you well, it doesn't matter how many filters and post-production software you use.

- **Always have a teaser at the beginning of the video.**

Any video content you create should always have a tease at the beginning, promising a specific result if someone watches the video all the way through.

- **Have a call-to-action at the end of each video.**

Many YouTubers shy away from this because they are afraid of seeming pushy, but the only way people will turn into fans, customers, and subscribers is if you ask them to act. Always ask them to do something if they received value at the end of the video and enjoyed watching your content. It can be as simple as subscribing or leaving a comment for you. You can also ask the viewer to like, share, or DM. Or you take it a step further and can ask them to head to your website to download something for free.

- **Lighting is crucial if you want people to view more of your videos.**

If people can't see or hear you clearly, you won't retain their attention for long. So, having the right light is equally important as investing in good sound quality. I shared lots of alternatives for lighting equipment earlier. Even if you can't invest in any, you can still create something that looks good if you stand in front of a large window. As you can see, the more natural sunlight falls on your face, the better the image quality.

#1 Tip for All Beginners

The best advice I could give you is to shoot one video daily. It's the first tip for all beginners who want to thrive on YouTube. If you ask any seasoned content creator, they will insist that you train yourself to create at least one piece of content daily. Why? There are several reasons.

The first thing this will do is raise your confidence and ability to shoot great videos. The more you practice using your equipment experimenting with different angles, lighting, sound, and content topics, the easier it becomes and the more natural you appear on camera. The second reason you want to shoot a video each day is to enable you to re-watch yourself and quickly pick up the mistakes you tend to make. Check your body language and posture. Notice how well you get into the flow and tempo of your script.

One last reason is that shooting videos daily ensures you have lots of content available, increasing your posting frequency. The more you can create a consistent publishing schedule whereby potential subscribers realize they can receive fresh, relevant content from you daily, twice, or three times a week, the more likely they are to subscribe and keep checking your channel for the latest stuff. It will build that connection and sense of community with your audience quickly. With all that said, consider challenging yourself to attempt to create a video each day for the next 30 days. There are many "Video Challenges" and contests on social media groups today that you can join. Even without joining a group challenge, if you are serious about becoming a YouTube superstar, you can commit to yourself, block out time on your calendar over the next 30 days, and begin.

Shooting Techniques for Beginners

Whether you use a smartphone, camcorder, or a DLSR camera to shoot your videos, here are some tips that will give you that professional look even if you're a total amateur.

Tip #1: Always shoot landscape.

By landscape, I mean horizontally instead of vertically. That is especially important to remember when using your smartphone.

Tip #2: Use the overlay grid if you have it on your device and observe the Rule of thirds.

The Rule of thirds is something all pro videographers know. It's about placing your head slightly higher than the frame to give yourself visual breathing and walking space when facing the sides. Using a grid will guide you and help you position yourself correctly to maintain eye level with your audience. Otherwise, you will come across as looking awkward. The viewers will struggle to maintain eye contact as they watch you.

Tip# 3: Create stability for your camera.

You can invest in a tripod, or if doing a home video, you could get creative and stack books to help your camera remain still. The more still your image, the better the quality will be. Avoid shaky filming unless you want to come across as a complete amateur and give your viewers a nauseating feeling. Investing in stabilizers and a good tripod is necessary if you're doing an outdoor recording with many movements.

This creative bonus tip will make you look like a pro. If you're shooting at home or in a home office, get a flat surface like a table and stack it with books. Place your laptop on top of the stack, and if you're shooting from your smartphone, place the phone on the computer for extra support and stability. You'll be amazed by how good the shot will be.

Tip #4: Time your shots.

I've seen several pro videographers sharing these hacks, and ever since I started implementing them, my videos have improved significantly. You time your shots by ensuring no sudden movement or change of scenery for about 10 seconds between each shot. That means you need to record with that in mind. You can have a different scene every five to ten seconds but only go as long to retain the viewer's attention. Remember, your videos will look way more professional when creating your outline or storyboard.

Tip #5: Keep a simple background.

It might be tempting to be fancy and outlandish with your background, but simple tends to produce a better quality-looking video. If you're shooting from home, remove as much clutter as possible. I also recommend shooting in front of a plain white background. Please avoid doors or windows where people could unexpectedly pop up and ruin the shot. If any elements appear in your camera, ensure they add to your story and do not distract viewers from your content.

Tip#6: Be intentional with your lighting.

This must be one of the biggest secrets for getting that professional look and feel. If you have a budget, invest in the different types of lights you'll need to achieve your desired look. If you're on a budget and can only work with natural sunlight and a few lamps, then get creative. Experiment with different angles and light setups to make your equipment work for your space.

Tip #7: Experiment with different angles.

I want you to create extra creative shots to produce exciting video content when shooting different scenes. It also ensures you have some backup or safety content in case you need to edit out some parts of the video. As much as possible, get some shots above and below your main recording vantage point. You don't need to have several cameras. Hit pause, move to a different angle, and hit record following the script or outline.

Tip #8: Keep the editing in mind during filming.

You need to know where you will make cuts, add filters, change scenes, etc. If you have this in mind while shooting, it will make the filming and editing process faster.

Set And Follow a Realistic Schedule

One thing you should know is most of the time; you're going to be completely off with your timing. I cannot emphasize the importance of setting the right expectations for yourself and creating a schedule you will stick to. Many YouTubers fail and give up because they could have done a better job creating a plan they could stick to. Most of them underestimated how long it would take to go through all the different shooting phases. Unfortunately, that led to stagnation, procrastination, and eventually defeat.

To help you avoid falling into that trap, we need to give you direction and a strict schedule that you must commit to. I can only offer guidance when it comes to creating your plan.

It would be best if you customized it to suit your needs. Depending on your lifestyle, whether you're currently working on other projects or a job, raising a family, etc., your schedule will match your case. If you're working full-time and need to start this after working hours, your shooting schedule recording space and editing need to be that. Maybe you can shoot daily after work, then edit and prepare them for publishing over the weekends. If you're flexible enough to shoot during the day and edit in the evenings, build your schedule around that. Regardless of your choice, understand that you must set a definite time for scripting, recording, editing, and publishing the content.

Pre-production tips:

Make sure you block out time for research, scripting, and even storyboarding if you're going in that direction. Plan out the different shots and scenes that you wish to have. I'd recommend making a shot list and ensuring you have the location or setup space needed for the photos and the necessary gear.

How long will a single shoot take? That will vary from person to person. If you have experience being on camera and know how to use your equipment, you can do it quickly. But often, it takes much longer than any of us anticipate. So whatever estimate you give yourself, permit at least 60 - 90 minutes longer.

To help minimize the time it takes, I encourage you to keep time limits on yourself. For example, set a five-minute timer to do all the technical setup. Also, give each scene a time limit and allow yourself to reshoot a scene twice before moving on to the following prominent location. That way, you won't have to recreate the whole thing.

Post-production tips:

So far, we've focused most of the content on shooting. We need to address post-production as well. Review your script, storyboard, or outline, depending on your work. This is important to ensure you filmed everything. Start the editing process. If you're editing yourself, you need software like iMovie, Camtasia, or another solution. You need to upload the different pieces of your video to the software and organize them in their proper order so you can decide what to keep and what to discard.

If you have enough coverage, picking and choosing the perfect ones would be easier, making this process faster. If you only shot once and there were many mistakes, give yourself time and patience. Such cases will require much refinement to get the video ready for publication.

What elements can you add to the video? You can use photos, b-rolls, interviews, titles, sound effects, transitions, intro and outro, music, and your logo.

Create thumbnails.

Use Canva or your preferred graphics creator software to create a compelling thumbnail for your video. Make sure it's attention-grabbing and helps the viewer know what the video will be about. In an upcoming chapter, we'll discuss how to create epic thumbnails.

Watch your video at least once before publishing. Make sure you watch the video at least once with a friend or family member to get some feedback. If you want something else, manage it to keep the flow and quality intact.

Once you feel it's ready, export it and upload it to YouTube. Depending on your experience level, this entire post-production process could take an hour, a few hours, or several days. When just starting, allow yourself a full day of post-production for each video if you want good quality. With lots of practice, that duration will significantly decrease.

If you decide to batch post-production, shoot videos daily, edit them on the weekend, and ensure you have enough videos ready for the upcoming week.

Implementation Activity #7: You Have to Do It

It's time for you to act and record your first videos. Your challenge in this section is to commit to a thirty-day video challenge. Keep yourself accountable and choose the setup and equipment most accessible to you. Every day, you will shoot a ten-minute video that's valuable and relevant to the viewer.

You can choose to post-produce one by one or batch them up. But make sure the recording happens daily. By the end of thirty days, you should have thirty videos of ten minutes each. Please make sure they are of high quality technically and that they deliver in terms of content value.

Chapter 08

Editing Videos

Video editing is an integral part of creating awesome YouTube videos. It can be as simple as removing unwanted footage, creating a flow, or as complex as adding effects, graphics, music, and giving a video a particular angle. Depending on your editing goals, you can spend a few minutes to several days or weeks. I always suggest setting simple goals and striving for progress instead of perfection for beginners. If you want your videos to look like a Marvel production in the first few months of editing, then be ready to invest a ton of time.

My best advice is to understand the basics and allow yourself to grow with your skills as you continue to shoot more videos. In this chapter, I will teach you the main elements, share the tools I recommend, and walk you through adding music to your videos. Let's get started.

Understanding the Basic Elements of Video Editing

Before sharing the main elements you need to consider when editing, let's clarify some jargon you'll often hear during this process.

- **Crop Factor**

The crop factor is a number that represents the ratio of a sensor's imaging area to that of a full-frame sensor. It's usually 1.3-20.

- **Aspect Ratio**

The relation between the width and height of your video is the Aspect ratio. The most common are 4:3 (This is the standard-definition video), 16:9(standard high-definition video), and 1.85:1(used for most U.S. theatrical showings since the 1960s). If there's one thing you'll need to remember, it's 16:9, as you'll use that one the most.

- **Close Up**

You'll often hear this term: shots that frame the subject tightly. For example, a close-up would fill the entire screen with your face if you were shooting in front of the camera.

- **B-roll**

This is additional footage meant to either smooth out an incongruent scene or provide more details for the story. Suppose you're talking about cooking ingredients and want to shift into a new location where you start demonstrating. You could add a still image of the elements you'll use to create a seamless transition from your talking head to you standing behind the kitchen counter, ready to cook.

- **Jump Cut.**

These cuts should only be used if you want to come across as an amateur. They are abrupt changes between sequential clips and often make the subject too jumpy from one scene to the next, disruptive for the viewer.

- **J-Cut**

Not to be confused with the other term; this is when you place the audio from the next shot before the video.

- **Resolution**

Resolution is the actual number of horizontal and vertical pixels your video contains. The most common are SD 640x480, HD 1280x720 & HD 1920x1080.

- **Shot List**

This is a checklist of all the shots you want to include in the production. Shot lists help you avoid wasting time and money and ensure you plan.

- **The Rule of Thirds**

The Rule of Thirds is a helpful grid used when shooting to make your video production aesthetically pleasing. To do it properly, separate the screen into nine sections. The Rule of Thirds suggests that points of interest line up with the intersections on the grid.

- Tilts are vertical movements made with your camera that are fixed.
- Pans are fixed horizontal movements made with your camera. Think of them as the opposite of tilts.

You are getting the pacing of the story right. Every video has a certain pace and tempo to it. Some scenes might need to be slowed down; others might need to speed up, etc. When creating your video, make some breathing room for your viewers to digest the essential parts of your video. That might include changing the speed in certain sections but ensuring a smooth and gradual transition to avoid confusing the viewer.

- **Adding the proper transitions and special effects**

We already mentioned this earlier. Adding special effects during editing, such as titles, transitions, and text effects, is a great way to make your videos look professional, but only if you know what you're doing. If in doubt, don't add fancy effects. The more natural your video is (without too many abrupt transitions and confusing impact), the better it will look.

- **Choosing the right sound and music**

That can include sound effects, audio background music, or anything else you think will make the video more impactful. Music usually adds a great atmosphere and increases that emotional connection, especially when done right. However, ensure the piece is non-intrusive and doesn't repel the viewer or obscure critical audio cues.

Understanding the technical and subjective things that cause people and YouTube algorithms to perceive your video as sound quality is essential.

A good video communicates a specific message. If it's an educational, inspirational, motivational, informational, or entertaining video, the viewer will come out on the other side having received that particular benefit. Therefore, a good video must add lots of value.

- **High quality**

Producing a high-quality video is as simple as following all the instructions outlined in this book. They include no shaky imagery, proper lighting and sound, avoiding noisy backgrounds, working on the script or outline, etc.

- **Clean and professional-looking editing**

This is another vital thing to remember when going through your post-production process. Keep things clean and simple. Only choose the best footage and eliminate what doesn't need to be there. Use elements like filters, music, sound effects, and transitions tastefully. Let everything on that video help you tell the story and pass on an easy-to-understand message.

- **Ideal length of content.**

A good quality video isn't too long and tedious or too short and unhelpful. You must pick your ideal length and ensure it's as long as necessary to accomplish the video's purpose. We talked about giving each video a specific purpose to fulfill. Let that be the guiding star when determining your videos' length.

- **Attention-grabbing thumbnail and intro**

Most people will never click on a video if the thumbnail isn't enticing. Do you know that about 20% of people who click on your video will exit after the first ten to fifteen seconds if you could better retain their attention? Even worse, these people are likelier to give your video a thumbs down within that first fifteen-second period. Therefore, you must ensure a strong intro and graphics that draw people in.

Once someone sees your awesome thumbnail and clicks to view it, you need a killer intro that immediately teases why they should watch to the end. Set expectations right and make them feel personalized. That builds a connection that ultimately creates trust and that sense of "this guy/girl knows what they're doing."

- **Branded intro and outro footage**

Add an intro and outro footage that aligns with your brand. This branded content gives new and existing viewers an impression of who you are and why they should continue hanging out on your channel. It makes you memorable, especially if you do it right. Given how many videos are uploaded each minute of the hour, and most viewers watch hundreds of videos across different channels, adding this branded content to your video will make it pop. It will increase the viewer's chances of recalling your brand the next time they come across your range on YouTube or elsewhere on the Internet.

Video Editing Tools That Every YouTuber Must Know

Now, let's talk more about editing tools that can help simplify post-production.

• **Adobe Premier Elements**

Adobe Premier has been an industry leader for a long time. It does cost a significant amount to get the software going for about $79.99. Now, there was a time when it was the ultimate; however, with recent advancements, many new players offer the same or even better at a fraction of their price.

It is still an excellent option for beginners and has many guided tutorials to make the learning curve swift. Its simple interface and suggested edits will get you going in no time.

• **Adobe Premier Pro**

As the name suggests, this software goes pro and offers you some of the best functionality you can find today. One of its best features is the Lumetri Color tool, which features color adjustment and manipulation close to what you'd get in Photoshop. It also has a multi-cam feature, allowing you to work with unlimited camera angles. The interface is easy to use, even for a beginner, and comes with a monthly fee of under $20.

• **Apple iMovie for Mac users.**

Suppose you are a Mac user and wish to refrain from investing in third-party software. In that case, you can create cool-looking videos with Apple's free editing software, which offers various transitions, sound effects, etc. You can easily do a montage, standard cut, J-cut, wipes, and almost every other editing effect. It's free and easy to use once you get the hang of it.

• **Apple Final Cut Pro X**

If you love iMovie and feel ready to go all the way, this software might be the one for you. This software comes with all the bells and whistles and can even superimpose 3D titles over your videos. It has a hefty price tag and could be a more straightforward interface. Still, you want to be a serious contender and produce incredible professional videos. In that case, you can transition from iMovie to Final Cut Pro for a one-time payment of $ 299.

• **Filmora from Wondershare**

Filmora is Wondershare's standard, high-quality, and easy-to-use video editing software. You can upgrade to unlock more sophisticated features. Still, I suggest starting with this one because the design is intuitive. It has filters, overlays, motion elements, transitions, and much more - basically, everything you need as a beginner. I love Filmora because all it takes is an easy drag and drop. Thanks to their easy mode feature, you can choose themes, select free royalty music, and end up with a fun, polished video. And compared to some of the prices I just shared, this one is pretty good because it starts at $59.99 for a lifetime license or $39.99 for a year.

• **Pinnacle Studio 21**

Pinnacle Studio 21 is another excellent and easy-to-use software with a drag-and-drop feature.

It's intuitive, has a short learning curve, and has effects like 360-degree and stop-motion, making it stand out. It has top-of-the-line rendering speed and goes for a one-time payment of $129.95.

- **Lumen5**

While Lumen5 is more of an editing tool than software, I am still adding it here because of its increased popularity. It's great for creating fun, shareable videos and can even turn your blog content into video. So, if you have an existing blog, this is an excellent option. You can create as many videos as you want with their free version for 480p videos. If you're going to edit in 1080p HD, you must invest $50 monthly.

Adding Music to Your Videos

Background music can elevate your video and help build a stronger connection with your audience, but you can't just throw in any song. You need to become aware of copyright restrictions and opt for royalty-free music. You should also choose a theme that supports the unfolding story or message of the video. You're wondering where to find great music.

YouTube offers some music options, and some software comes in-built with sound effects and free royalty music, but I recommend you research online. Go to sites like Epidemic Sound or Royalty-free Music to find stock music you can use.

Adding music to a video using Mac:

Once in the iMovie interface, you should see the Audio tab under the main menu bar within your new project. A drop-down menu will appear, allowing you to go into iTunes, Sound Effects, or GarageBand. In most cases, you must select iTunes and see a list of all your files. Then, it would be best if you dragged it down to the project timeline. If you need to trim the song, use the handles at the beginning and end.

Adding music to a video using Windows:

Double-click a video file to open it, and you'll see it opens in Movies & TV. Instead of that option, right-click the file and select Open With > Photos. You'll see a toolbar; click Edit & Create, then select Create a video with text. You'll then see Photos's editor screen and a Music button should be in the top toolbar. Click that and set your Music. After choosing the file, drag your selected clip down to the storyboard at the bottom of the screen. And when you play, you should hear music in the background.

Adding music online: Visit addaudiotovideo.com, and you can add music to your video without downloading any software. It's fast and straightforward. Once on the site, click Browse under "Select video file" to choose the video. Next, you want to choose the audio file by clicking Browse. Once you've selected both audio and video, click on Upload and give it a few minutes. Once it's ready, you'll see a " Completed " message and a download link.

YouTube Music: If you'd like to use YouTube's Audio library once you upload the video, click on the Editor and look for the audio row. You'll see a list of tracks you can listen to, and once you find what you like, add it to your video. If you'd like to adjust which part of the audio is played during your clip, click the Position Audio button and drag the song's leading and trailing edges to change their position.

Activity #8: Start Honing Your Skill

The videos you've started creating from the last chapter now experience your art. Your assignment is to begin implementing all the editing techniques, hacks, and guidance you've received in this chapter.

Remember, this is a skill that takes time and practice. As with all things, it will get easier. I suggest you allocate time specifically for editing your videos, whether you do one at a time or batch a few of them together. You can opt for free software or invest in one of the many examples I've shared throughout this book.

Your assignment is to open your editing software, upload your first YouTube video, and start editing. See if you can add a few transitions, a title, and background music to create an attractive flow with your video. Don't get too fancy. Please keep it simple. Once it's ready, please give it to a trusted friend or family member to watch for some helpful feedback.

SECTION 04

Managing Your YouTube Channel

YouTube channel management goes beyond uploading videos. Optimization, involvement, analysis, and adaptation continue. We discuss the complexities of channel management and offer tips for simplifying your plan, increasing audience engagement, and assuring long-term success.

YouTube Channel Success Tips

Sound management may help your channel succeed. Make appealing titles, descriptions, and tags that match the content. Write descriptively, using terminology naturally. Tags will classify your movie, so choose wisely.

An intriguing thumbnail may boost click-through rates significantly. It must look good and convey the video's message. High-quality videos should always be uploaded. YouTube supports several file kinds, but the most significant user experience is with high-quality videos.

Videos in relevant playlists help visitors browse and stay longer on your channel. Comments let you connect with readers and establish a community. Answer questions, acknowledge remarks, and lead group conversations to keep the mood light.

YouTube's analytic tools can help you evaluate your channel. Look at demographics to know your audience. Increase core audience engagement by making content more relevant. Watch time and retention measure viewer involvement. Information with low retention may need to be changed or made more intriguing.

Knowing where your traffic comes from—organic searches, suggestions, or other sites—can help you improve your marketing. Likes, shares, comments, and subscriptions indicate involvement. These show popularity and affect YouTube's recommendation systems.

YouTube SEO increases platform visibility like website SEO. Find relevant keywords for your essay and organically incorporate them. To improve SEO, include keywords in the first few lines of your video's description.

Making your content accessible with subtitles/closed captions provides more indexable content. Join the Discussion Now! YouTube rewards discussion-generating videos. Discussions on videos, especially immediately after upload, may improve their popularity.

Nobody views your YouTube channel alone. Off-site interactions may grow your community and viewership. Share your films on Twitter, Instagram, and Facebook. Create social media-specific content to promote your products.

Collaboration with other YouTubers may generate something extraordinary. This may expose your channel to more people. Join niche forums, groups, and communities off-platform. Join arguments and provide helpful content.

YouTube and the internet are constantly evolving. Follow YouTube's algorithm, feature, and policy developments. Trends: Following current events and viral challenges can inspire material and increase reach. Regularly solicit viewer feedback. It engages listeners and offers advice.

YouTube channel management is constantly evolving. You must understand the platform, know your audience, and be flexible enough to adapt to market changes. The proper channel management approaches focus on building a loyal, engaged audience around your content rather than chasing views. Even as you grow, sincerity is crucial. Your voice will distinguish you in YouTube's vast globe.

CHAPTER 09

Best Practices for Managing Your YouTube Channel

One thing about YouTube you need to remember is that it's both a search engine and a social networking platform. So, while it's essential to implement everything you've learned so far, I also want you to be deliberate with certain aspects of search engine optimization, as that will enable your videos to perform well longer.

Brian Dean of Backlinko is a specialist in search engine optimization, and you can learn a lot by subscribing to his YouTube channel. But let's touch on the key things I've learned from the best SEO guys in the marketplace.

Creating Video Titles, Descriptions, And Tags

Assuming you have a comprehensive list of the keywords you wish to rank for in any video, the title, description, and tags are where you need to sprinkle those pre-determined keywords strategically.

YouTube Video Title has a limit of 100 characters, so you need to use this space to build curiosity, create an emotional response for the viewer, and still add your keyword. Aim to place the main keyword at the start of the title as much as possible or at least within the first 70 characters so that it's viewable in the search results.

YouTube Video Description has a limit of 5,000 characters, so you've got plenty of space here to communicate your message and add relevant keywords. The first three lines are the only visible part of the description, so I recommend having your primary keyword here. You must also describe and sell the viewer into watching the video here. Remember to include the relevant URL you'd like people to visit after watching your video.

Throughout the description area, I'd aim to sprinkle the primary keyword about three times and other secondary ones to support your SEO.

YouTube Video Tags can be up to 30 characters, and you can add up to 500 characters in the tag section. Add the primary keyword, any words that describe the video's content, brand-related or channel-specific tags, and any LSI (Latent Semantic Indexing) keywords you might have.

YouTube Thumbnails

It would be best to have thumbnails that attract the viewer to get potential subscribers to click on your videos. Thumbnails are also the first thing searchers will encounter on Google and YouTube search results. The first thing you need to know is the ideal size. Google recommends 1280 by 720 Pixels with a minimum width of 640 Pixels and an aspect ratio of 16:9. It should also be formatted as a JPG, PNG, or GIF for the best results. Make sure the file size is at most 2MB for easy upload.

Remember to use attention-grabbing texts, fonts, colors, and images when creating your thumbnails, but do what is necessary. Ensure the thumbnail is relevant to the content people will find once they click and that it's congruent with your brand identity.

If you're working with a graphics designer, they'll take care of these technical aspects, but if you're going solo, I suggest using Canva. They are free graphics design software that requires little to no experience and even have pre-made templates. You can also purchase their royalty-free images for $1, and they offer a pro version that unlocks even more features. Another tool that can help you create awesome thumbnails is Spark by Adobe. Check out these online tools to find the one that suits your objective.

Uploading Videos

Uploading videos to YouTube is as easy as signing into YouTube Studio and clicking Create > Upload Video. Once you've selected the video you've finished editing and processing, YouTube will take over and do its thing until it is ready for publishing. The video file format recommended is MOV, MPEG4, MP4, AVI, WMV, MPEG-PS, FLV, 3GPP, WebM, DNxHR, ProRes, CineForm, or HEVC (h265).

If you want to upload a video longer than 15 minutes, you must go through a quick verification process where they will send you a security code through your cellphone. Once your channel is verified, you can upload up to 12 hours or 128GB.

You can upload up to 15 videos at a time using your computer. And don't worry if you accidentally close the upload page. The video is usually saved in drafts until you finish choosing the settings.

If you want to upload high-dynamic range (HDR) videos, you can do it directly to the platform. Viewers can watch HDR videos with compatible devices or stream HDR videos using Chromecast Ultra to an HDR TV. If the viewers don't have a compatible device, they will see the video as a standard dynamic range (SDR). Although HDR videos can't be edited with YouTube Web editor once the video is uploaded, YouTube will automatically convert HDR video to SDR.

Once the video renders and completes processing, you can add basic info, including an SEO-friendly title, description, and tags, and upload your thumbnail. You can also choose more advanced settings and how you want to monetize if you're eligible. We'll be talking more about monetization options in the last section. If you're happy with the settings and preview of your video, it's time to share it with the world.

Creating A Trailer Video

The trailer or welcome video can be one of your most fun activities. It doesn't need to be an expensive production. But it will require lots of creativity and time investment. I've seen some epic trailers (check out the Slow Mo Guys Channel Trailer to see what I mean). You can start from scratch or get a template from online platforms like Biteable to simplify the process.

The actual process of a welcome video is super easy. Like any other video content, you must create, edit, upload, and hit publish on your channel. The only difference is that you want to head to the "Customize Channel" section with a trailer video and upload the video from there. Once uploaded, you can add SEO-friendly data like tags, descriptions, etc. The last thing you will need to do is set the video as the YouTube channel trailer by clicking "For new Visitors." That way, anyone who lands on your channel for the first time will always see that video.

Some best practices for the trailer video:

Keep the video brief and concise (under 30 seconds is ideal). Think of it like those epic movie trailers, and share all the necessary information about your channel. Your viewers should feel like they understand what you're all about and how they'll benefit by subscribing, but it should still leave them hungry to learn more.

The best trailers have a great story, implement their brand identity through the music, fonts, colors, etc., and always incorporate a call to action.

Categorizing Your Videos into Playlists

YouTube playlists are similar or related videos on a particular subject. You can create a playlist using your videos or curate other people's videos to get people to binge-watch and stay on your channel. It will help with the discoverability of your rut and increase watch time, which, as we know, will help rank your videos higher on search.

Go to Video Manager > Playlist to create a playlist, then select New Playlist. Give your playlist a name and click Create. You can also create playlists as you navigate YouTube. This is especially important if you're curating videos. When you find a video you'd like to curate, click the plus icon to add it to an existing playlist or create a new one. You can make your playlist public, unlisted, or private, depending on your preferences. It's also possible to optimize your playlist for search by editing the title and description with a specific keyword and a compelling explanation telling people why they should watch.

Pro Tip:

If you want your playlists to stand out, consider adding an intro welcoming the viewer and offering tips or letting the audience know what they can expect by going through each video on the playlist. This can work exceptionally well if you're creating an educational video series.

Creating YouTube Stories

If you're a fan of watching YouTube from your smartphone, you already know about YouTube Stories. Previously known as YouTube Reels, these are like Instagram or Snapchat Stories. They can only be viewed on the mobile App. Viewers access them either from the channels or Watch pages of their subscriptions.

YouTube stories aim to increase that bond and connection with your community. It needs to be done in a very informal and casual way. You need to make sure it's a regular activity so people can get used to interacting with you directly.

You can add an image or video to a YouTube Story. To add a photo, tap the capture button like when taking a regular print. Suppose you want to record a video; press and hold the capture button until you're done recording. Stories videos can only be 15 seconds long, so make sure it's short and sweet. Plenty of editing tools are available to add elements that will help make your content more appealing. You can also edit aspects of your recording and even delete an existing video or image from your story. Tap the story and play segments to navigate to the video or photo. Look for the three-dot menu and tap Delete.

Applying SEO

Now, let's talk about ranking factors and how to apply SEO to your videos. Throughout this book, we've discussed the importance of using keywords strategically. As I shared earlier, Google says ranking factors are important—relevancy, interest, etc. You will agree with me; there must be more that we can do to stand out.

Given that over five hundred hours of video are uploaded each minute, we need many more tools and techniques to ensure our videos get promoted by the algorithm. Here are a handful to add to your toolbox. You already know the basics, i.e., Keywords, title optimization, description, tags, and producing high-quality video, so let's talk about new ones.

- **Watch Time**

Watch time is a huge ranking factor for YouTube. It's the time a viewer spends on your video before clicking away. The longer a session, the more the algorithm will favor your content.

- **User Experience and Engagement Level**

That includes how much people comment, like, dislike, share, and subscribe after watching your content. Videos with higher engagement will be ranked higher.

- **View Count**

Getting many views on your video matters. Putting more pictures equals a higher ranking, especially if you've optimized your keyword.

- **Closed Captions & Subtitles**

Adding closed captions to your videos benefits you in multiple ways. The main two are: 1) you get crawled by search engines faster, which can give you a significant SEO boost, and 2) you open your content to a broader audience. People who are not natives of your spoken language can easily understand you, increasing the chances of more engagement and subscription to your channel.

Mastering The Use of YouTube Analytics

Your channel will only grow successfully by combining front-end creative efforts with back-end tracking and monitoring. YouTube has an in-built analytics system to track the right metrics and build your dream business. To get started, you must sign in to your creator studio and find your way to the main menu's analytics Tab. You'll see the last 28 days by default, but you can customize it to suit your needs.

If you enjoy data crunching, YouTube allows you to export datasets as Excel or CSV. However, most of us let the system do the manual work. All we need to monitor and track, especially at the beginning, are:

- Watch time reports
- Interaction reports
- Revenue reports

With watch time, you want to answer questions such as, how long are people watching my videos, and how many views do I have in the chosen timeframe? Is it the same as last month? Who is watching my videos? Where are my viewers located? What are some sources of my traffic? What percentage of my views come from mobile, desktop, or elsewhere?

Interaction reports will show you things like subscribers, likes, dislikes, comments, and sharing. You can see how many new people subscribed and how many unsubscribed. You can see how your audience feels about your content and whether they resonate with your message. Monitoring comments is also important because it gives you a sense of how active and engaged people are. Remember to be responsive but don't get sucked into the world of troll hunting or toxic people.

When it comes to revenue reports, this is all about the monetization of your money. You've been waiting to hear about it because your money will be recorded here. The following section will discuss monetization and how to do it right. For now, recognize that this is where you will come to monitor your revenue within a given period, including your paid ads on YouTube, Ads other companies are paying to display on your videos, and other income streams like YouTube Super Chat. The main thing to track here is the estimated income from all Google-sold ads and the projected revenue from AdSense and DoubleClick ads.

Promoting Your Channel on Other Social Platforms

It's essential to think outside the box to grow your channel. It would be best if you were discovered, and your channel needs to escape obscurity. Everything this book outlines will enable you to set the proper foundation for that, but you must continue. Social platforms like Facebook, Instagram, TikTok, and LinkedIn have so much traffic. With some creativity, you can get more views on your video. How? By driving that traffic toward your YouTube channel. You don't need to get in front of YouTuber users only. You can also leverage organic and paid strategies to promote your channel on other social platforms.

For example, you can write articles on high-traffic sites like LinkedIn or Medium and embed a video or link back to your YouTube for free. But of course, you could take it further with a little paid ads budget. Do this by creating an epic video ad for Facebook or Instagram that drives traffic back to your YouTube channel for the whole experience. Once you look at your YouTube analytics and determine the location and audience type that best engages with your track, invest a little money and run a highly targeted ad on Facebook to bring in more of the same people. Please refer to the resource section to learn more and expand your traffic source strategies.

Continuously Learning from Others

As you can tell, this book is only the beginning. Something easy to follow to help you gain some momentum. The journey is long, and there's much to learn, so make sure you continue educating yourself as the platform evolves and new hacks emerge. One way to stay up to date and discover the best and latest hacks is by following and initiating friendships with fellow YouTube creators. You can join meetups either locally or virtually. You can also attend events like VidCon or Social Media Marketing World. I have included links in the resource section to learn more about these opportunities.

Activity #9: Start Tinkering Around

This chapter shared lots of technical knowledge that will only work if you apply it to daily activities. If you have not worked on previous exercises, now is the time to do that. Once you have that video ready to share with the world, make sure also to include the things you've learned in this chapter, including:

- Creating your thumbnail.
- Uploading your video to YouTube.
- Customizing and optimizing the video titles, descriptions, tags, and any other effects you wish to have, such as music, captions, and subtitles.
- Follow a YouTube creator from whom you want to learn more as you grow your channel.

CHAPTER 10

Growing Your Community

YouTube is all about community engagement. If you're unwilling to spend time and effort building a connection with your tribe, you won't do well on this platform. Having read this far, I'm confident you want to grow a channel that serves your tribe and makes you money. To hit both targets, we need to understand some strategies that will enable us to draw in more eyeballs.

Sources Of Traffic

Do you know how your video can be discovered on YouTube? I've mentioned several throughout this book, but it's worth listing them here.

- YouTube search
- YouTube advertising
- External websites
- Browse Features
- Suggested videos
- A particular playlist or channel page.

You need to figure this out as your channel grows so you can refine your SEO efforts and invest in the right strategies.

Using The Audience Tab

Did you know YouTube Analytics offers an inside glance into your audience's behavior, location, and preferences? This tab shows you where most of your viewers are located, the language they speak, what they love watching most, and their age group. You need to be signed in to your YouTube Studio to see this. From the left menu, select Analytics > Audience. That will open information on gender, age, when your viewers are on YouTube, and other videos your audience watched. Use this data to inform your content strategy.

Engaging Your Audience

As a YouTuber creator, your job is only done once you interact and engage with your audience. A few things that work well for engaging my audience include initiating engagement myself. That means I don't just post and wait for something to happen. Instead, I go and find content that's meaningful to me, and I like, comment, and share that content. I also reply to every comment and intend to do that until it becomes too much for me to handle.

I've set aside twenty minutes weekly to visit the channels of people who have liked or engaged with my content. I do the same on their channel, which creates impressive rewards later. Consider asking questions that benefit your community and encourage them to interact. The bottom line is you need to give more than you ask of your community. If you observe highly engaged channels from YouTubers like Gary Vaynerchuck or Neil Patel, you'll see they always give, give, and give before making any ask.

Pro Tip:

If you're serious about showing your community that you care, take a screenshot of a comment left on your video or a video title shared by someone you want to promote. Create a video out of that featuring their content. It will cause the person to respond immediately and even share your video.

YouTube Community Tab

This is a feature YouTube designed to promote community interaction. It's meant to help you interact even more with your people beyond creating and publishing videos. You will have the ability to post polls, text-based posts, and images.

This feature is meant to give your channel a different edge and to get even more personal. You can also promote older videos or products and merchandise. However, ensure you balance the promotion and the value-adding interactions. It is an incredible way to excite people about something you're doing. It could be the launch of a new product, an announcement of a free webinar, or training.

I have used the Poll feature to get ideas of what to include in my online course to make it more valuable. My friend Jeremy uses it to give behind-the-scene sneak peek of his latest documentary shoots, which excites people. The most important thing is to come from a place of adding value. Give people a reason to interact and follow your updates using the Community Tab feature.

Maximize The Use of Live Streaming

What is Live Streaming? It's being able to record and broadcast in real-time simultaneously. YouTube has become famous for live streams, and it is the perfect way to retain or draw in a new audience. You will need to educate yourself on the best equipment for live streaming, but YouTube enables you to go live from your smartphone or tablet, a camera, or a computer. Once you get the kit sorted, it takes one button click.

Before attempting to go live, verify your channel (www.youtube.com/verify). If doing it from a computer, you must sign into your dashboard and click Create > Go Live. Open the YouTube app from your mobile, click the camcorder icon on the top right, and then tap Go Live. If it's the first time to livestream, you must wait for 24 hours to activate your account. Also, note that you must hit your first milestone of 1,000 subscribers before live streaming from your mobile.

When it comes to the recording, you can either do it through a webcam, mobile cam, or encoder streaming. The easiest option is the camera on your laptop, but if you want a more professional look and have the competency, you can always get an encoder because the quality will be better.

To ensure you produce the best live streams, have your thumbnail image, an SEO-friendly title, and description ready. If you're ready to record from your desktop, click the camcorder icon once you're in your dashboard >Go Live > Webcam. Add a title and privacy settings, click More Options to add the description, turn live chat on/off, promote something, and more. Click Next. YouTube will automatically take a webcam thumbnail photo, but don't worry; you can upload the thumbnail we created later. Select Go Live, and that's it! Once you're done, you can select End Stream.

A Checklist for Optimization

Here's the beauty of live streaming - it's live. There are no do-overs or edits. So before you begin to broadcast, take the following steps.

- Check the audio to ensure the sound is optimal and that people can hear you.
  - Adjust your lighting to ensure the audience can see you.
  - Keep the devices plugged into a power source. You wouldn't want to run out of power halfway into your rant!
  - Test your connection speed to avoid low-quality streaming. You can run a speed test with speedtest.net. What we are aiming for is about 10MB of data per minute.
  - Turn off interruptions and ensure nothing inappropriate or confidential is in the backdrop.
  - Have a bottle or glass of water next to you. I also recommend tissues or anything else you might need if you get a scratchy throat, cough, or sneeze.

When it comes to live streaming, timing is everything. There's no perfect time per se, but based on your YouTube analytics, you can make an educated guess based on your audience interactions and behavior. If most of your audience is global, you want to pick a time that works in multiple time zones.

Pro Tip:

As your audience grows, you can consider running polls for people to vote the best time for the live streaming, and once you have a winner, schedule it in advance. Give people time to add it to their agenda and set reminders.

Activity #10: What Moves You?

Before we hit the last section of this book, it's time to start engaging with your potential audience. You may not have any subscribers yet (aside from friends and family), but you can still create that momentum for engagement. If your published videos have received many comments, shares, and likes, you can find channels worth interacting with. Leave a comment, like, and share it. Repost it using your Community Tab, as you learned in this chapter. Demonstrate that you are here to build an active community. It all begins with you.

Section 05

Monetize Your YouTube Channel

YouTube exploration goes beyond video creation and management. The chance helps many artists generate money. Monetizing your YouTube channel may transform your pastime into a business. Here are several ways to generate cash from your track and be reimbursed.

YouTube Income: The Easy Way First, learn YouTube monetization basics to make money with your videos. The YouTube Partner Program (YPP) is its primary revenue source. You can apply for YPP with 1,000 subscribers and 4,000 watch hours in the last year. Advertising can start when your movies are approved.

YouTube has display advertising, non-skippable video commercials, skippable video ads, and bumper ads. Understand potential revenue sources by learning about them. You can limit ads to the film's beginning, middle, or end. Keep the watching experience enjoyable by finding a balance.

YouTube Income Without Ads. Besides standard ads, there are other techniques to boost channel profits. Promote your items and affiliate links in your movies. Each referral link sale earns you a commission.

A firm pays you to market their products or services in sponsored content videos actively. To be honest with readers, label such content "sponsored." If you have a loyal fanbase, selling branded t-shirts, mugs, and posters is a good idea. Your channel's premium subscribers should receive a badge, emoji, or additional content. Viewers may pay to have their comments "pinned" to the top of the chat window in your live broadcasts using "Super Chats."

YouTube Moneymaking: YouTube's monetization rules maintain content quality and community standards. Video material must comply with YouTube's advertising restrictions. Content that's contentious or offensive may not sell.

Avoid unlicensed use of protected works. Copyright strikes may limit monetization. Be transparent about paid promotions and other relationships to maintain audience trust and platform compliance.

They are diversifying income sources. Online services like YouTube are dynamic, so don't put all your money in one basket. Creatives receive direct audience funding via Patreon. You might offer premium materials or other incentives as recompense.

Presenting paid seminars or lessons online may be an option if you have vast knowledge. Private consultations: Offer expert guidance and counsel.

Money Management and Investments. Financial management becomes more critical as your channel grows and income rises. Record all income and expenses regularly. Consider your income tax. To be safe, consult a tax specialist. You may invest income in the channel to improve it. New technologies, visuals, marketing tactics, or staff may be needed.

YouTube channel monetization is an art and science. Understanding the platform's technical needs is vital, but success comes from being authentic, consistent, and valuable to your audience. Monetization should increase content quality and trustworthiness. It would be best to prioritize trust and transparency with your followers as you negotiate the YouTube revenue market. YouTube channels are valuable for the relationships they build, not for their revenue.

Chapter 11

YouTube Monetization Made Easy

For many readers, these last two chapters contain the answers to critical questions that led them to purchase the book. If you have been wondering how to make money on YouTube or what kind of money you could make, this is where you'll get your answers. How much money do YouTubers make? Some make zero, while others make millions in annual revenue. The range is vast because it depends on how well the channel performs.

How Much Can One Earn on YouTube?

The best way to approach this question is to start from what we know YouTube pays out. We know that Google pays 68% of their AdSense revenue. Some quick mathematics will show that if an advertiser pays $100, Google will pay $68 to the publisher. An advertiser's rates will vary between $0.10 to $0.30 per view, but let's go with an average of $0.18 to make calculations easier. So, on average, your channel can receive $18 for every 1,000 ad views ($3-$5 per 1000 video views).

While these simple numbers can help you estimate what you can expect, realize the first dollar will be the hardest to earn. Building up to that momentum will require tremendous effort, but the more subscribers you have, the more people will click on your ads. The more that happens, the more money you will make from

Google AdSense and other opportunities. So the correct answer is - you can earn as much money as you want. It all depends on your effort and strategy. If you're in a niche that quickly gathers crowds, like celebrity gossip or gaming, you'll likely start earning money sooner, but still don't expect it to be within the first couple of videos. In the first phase of your YouTube growth, you want to focus on building a reputation instead of income. Then, as you get real traffic and engagement, you'll see the revenue growth from a few dollars each other to hundreds and, ultimately, thousands of dollars each month.

The Simplest Way to Earn Money From YouTube

The simplest way to earn money from YouTube is to join the YouTube Partner Program (YPP). You will need an audience before becoming part of this program and making money. Your content must be epic to attract an audience that engages with your content and subscribes to your channel. Everything discussed in this book is designed to help you attract, build, and monetize your audience. Once you have momentum and see constant growth, I recommend applying for the YouTube Partner Program.

To qualify for YPP, you must be in good standing with YouTube. Your content should be considered high quality. You also need 4,000 public watch hours within the last 12-month period. Lastly, you will need to hit that target of 1000 subscribers. These basic requirements are vital before your qualification can be accepted. Once you cross this threshold, you'll be taken through creating an AdSense account and a few other simple logistics. The YouTube team will review and approve you for monetization. Besides streaming ads, you can earn through channel membership and Super Chat as long as you meet their criteria.

Activity #11: Become A YouTube Partner

This activity will require time, so I recommend adding it to your planner or setting a timer so you can return to the designated time to complete it. Once the channel grows in the coming months, and you cross that threshold of 4,000 watch hours within 12 months and 1,000 subscribers, please submit your application for the YPP monetization opportunity.

CHAPTER 12

Creative Ways to Make Money on YouTube

Now that you've established a great YouTube channel that is steadily growing, it's time to focus on making money. Combining several revenue-generating strategies might be the right approach if you want to start seeing income from all your hard work. Instead of depending on earning directly from YouTube (YPP), which requires a specific number of subscribers and strict watch time regulations, you can leverage other moneymaking options such as affiliate marketing, sponsorships, etc. Let's go over the main ones now.

Become An Affiliate

Affiliate marketing is one of the easiest and most lucrative ways to earn an income on your channel. The best part is that you can use a small audience. In recent years, brands have sought micro-influencers and social media channels with decent-sized following and lots of engagement to help promote their products.

Franck is an excellent example of this. A software company approached him about a month ago and gave him a very enticing offer. Franck was provided the free software for six months and would earn a percentage for every person who signed up and purchased through the affiliate link they gave him. The best part is that Franck has 2400 subscribers! It's only been a few weeks, and he's reported that a portion of his audience has signed up for the free trial, and some have paid. Income is already coming in, and soon, he will be making a projected $7k in passive income.

Affiliate marketing is simple. You have a product you believe in and a link to send people. Whenever people buy, you get a small commission. Monthly sales can earn anything from a couple hundred to several thousand if it's a well-priced product. I know YouTubers who also run affiliate products from Amazon and ClickBank. These are massive affiliate platforms that anyone can join. But I suggest doing this once you have an active audience.

Become An Influencer

Influencer marketing is all the rage. Stay-at-home moms, artists, beauty specialists, and high school students have all turned their love for selfies into income-earning opportunities. What is an influencer, and can you become one on YouTube? An influencer is a person who can affect the purchasing decisions of others because they are perceived as an authority in that given niche. Influencers have strong relationships with their audience, making them powerful. An influencer is not a celebrity and doesn't need to be a Kardashian with millions of followers. The size of their following depends on their niche or topic. Brands are always keen to work with influencers of all sizes.

If you can build a reputation as someone knowledgeable and an expert in your topic through your YouTube content, you can become an influencer. As a result, you can get paid partnerships, collaborations, and sponsorships with the brands that align with your channel. There are various types of influencers, including mega-influencers (think Kardashians). These are often celebrities like movie stars, musicians, athletes, etc. To join this rank, you must have at least 1 million followers. Macro-influencers are a step down from the mega-influencers. These are usually up-and-coming B-grade celebrities or super successful self-made online experts. You'll need at least 40,000 followers on YouTube to join this rank. Micro-influencers are the first significant milestone I would set for you. This category of influencers are ordinary people who have gained respect and recognition for their knowledge.

You can create a relationship with your subscribers; over time, they will see you as someone worth following and turning to for advice. In this category, it's not about the number of followers. It's absolutely about the relationship and engagement level. So a micro-influencer can have between 1000 – and 40,000 followers on YouTube. Franck is an excellent example of how a brand perceived him as a micro-influencer and offered him the chance to collaborate through affiliate marketing. The same thing can happen to you. As an influencer, the most important thing to remember is to maintain your integrity and promote brands you genuinely believe in.

Once you are an influencer, companies will offer you deals and opportunities to make money because they need your audience. Be intentional about the ones you say yes to because your audience is more valuable than any money a company offers. Always think long-term and think about what's best for your audience.

What kind of income can you make from influencer partnerships?

Depending on the size of your audience and the budget of the company or business you work with, you can earn a few hundred bucks to shoot one video or thousands of dollars to run a specific campaign over an agreed-upon timeframe. Influencer marketing requires planning, strategy, and a solid business plan to get paid what you're worth.

Sell Products and Merchandise of Your Brand

Another fantastic way to earn money as a YouTuber content creator is to create your merchandise. These can be T-shirts with your brand, coffee mugs, calendars, art, paintings, comics, recipes, or whatever else you can create for your niche. The best part about this is that you get to keep 100% of the profit. Use platforms like Shopify and Amazon to set up shop quickly, then leverage your growing audience to drive traffic to your online store.

Crowdfund Your YouTube Project

If you're not looking to support your YouTube career with ads, affiliate marketing, and selling merch, you could go the crowdfunding route. Some have found it highly successful. Unlike ads, you are giving your audience more of what they want. The focus here is content and engagement. Check out a channel like Hasfit, which mainly grew and still focuses on crowdfunding. You can crowdfund your channel through websites like Patreon or use the YouTube Sponsor Button, a newly established feature that lets your fans support your channel in exchange for some "perks" you give.

Fan Funding

As the word states, this is a way for your fans and subscribers to tip and support your hard work. The more great content you produce, the more likely you will build fans who love and appreciate all the effort and dedication you put in to serve them. If you want to create an easy way for people to "tip" you, then consider checking out a site like ko-fi.com, enabling you to receive tips or donations. You can also create a simple PayPal button that people can use to "buy you coffee" if they love your content and channel. Remember to make it easy for people to give you their cash by placing links under each video's description.

Social Media Marketing on YouTube

Social media marketing uses platforms to connect with an audience to market your products. If you get the right strategy, you can use social media marketing to grow your YouTube channel and sell products or services. The system can be both paid and organic marketing efforts, but I suggest using some paid social media advertising if you want to see results fast.

You can make money on YouTube using social media marketing by running ads on Instagram and Facebook that drive traffic back to your channel. You could also create a social media campaign offering a free lead magnet that leads to people sharing their data with you. Once you have that data, you can send people to your YouTube channel to promote whatever product or service you wish to sell, or they can be served ads through your YPP. If you'd like to learn more about social media marketing, a deep and vast topic, I suggest getting one of my other guides.

Applying YouTube to Your Existing Business

The benefits of integrating YouTube into your business marketing and development strategies are too numerous to mention. Let's start with the fact that your Search Engine Optimization efforts will exponentially pay off when you leverage video marketing. As the second-largest search engine on the Internet, having your videos rank high on Google will drive more traffic to your website. You will also develop an instant connection with your audience. Existing customers and prospects will feel more connected to your brand when you use videos to educate, inspire, and showcase your products.

We know content marketing is here to stay because today's consumer prefers to learn about a product, feature, or brand through sharable, informative content instead of traditional dry ads. By creating great videos, you're serving your potential customers' needs far better than your competitors, who might still be focused on conventional ads. Video marketing makes it easy for anyone with any budget to succeed because it's no longer about throwing money at ads to manipulate people into purchasing. People want to feel valued, and with video, you can show your audience that you care and that your product or service is the best solution. I cannot think of a better way to market to an existing or new audience than through video content and a great YouTube channel.

YouTube Advertising

YouTube ads are great for attracting customers or new subscribers to your channel if you have the budget. Introduce your brand or business using YouTube ads, and your track will grow exponentially. But it would be best to do more than throw money into this. Ensure you have a solid plan with clear objectives before spending a dime. YouTube isn't as inexpensive as Facebook and Instagram because it's a mature platform, so the learning curve necessary to pull off a great campaign is steep. Luckily, they have many resources, educational content, and even a certification process to empower you to use their powerful advertising features. You can go from knowing absolutely nothing about Google ads to setting up a successful ad campaign in no time with as little as $10 per day.

There are several options when it comes to ads. You can create skippable in-stream ads, non-skippable in-stream ads (including bumper ads), video discovery ads, and non-video ads (the overlays and banners).

To advertise on YouTube, you must upload a video and set it to Public or Unlisted. Then, sign into your Google Ads account and select New Campaign. Choose your goal (sales, website traffic, brand awareness, reach, or brand consideration. Please define your campaign parameters and budget, target your audience, and enter your link to hit the create campaign. And that's it! Your ad is live and ready to bring you a new audience.

Use storytelling and emotion to connect with your audience to get the most out of your campaigns. Have an appropriate call to action and consider using the correct type of ad for the specific goal. For example, if sales were your main objective, I recommend setting up a TrueView for an action campaign. That will allow multiple clickable elements so viewers can click and act before the video ends.

Sticking to the recommended length and video formats is also a good idea. Skippable ads should be a minimum of 12 seconds and a maximum of 3 minutes (you can have a max of 60 seconds on YouTube, kids). Non-skippable ads are 15 seconds (In Singapore, Mexico, India, Malaysia, and EMEA, they allow 20 seconds), and bumper ads are 6 seconds.

For discovery ads, YouTube recommends having AVI, ASF, QuickTime, Windows Media, MP4, or MPEG file format. The video codec should be H.264, MPEG-2, or MPEG-4. The audio codec should be AAC-LC or MP3. The aspect ratio should be 16:9 or 4:3; the frame rate most recommended is 30 FPS.

Activity #12: Optimization

You've made it to the last activity for this book. Here, it's all about optimization. So far, you've learned how to turn your growing channel into an income-generating machine. Take time to decide how to earn money and set up the necessary processes. If you're getting into influencer marketing, get a book and learn how to pitch, sell, and win deals with brands. You'll need to learn how to market yourself so that brands find you appealing.

Suppose you're getting into affiliate marketing or creating and selling your products; that will require some action steps to plot and implement. Use this time to figure out how to act on those activities that generate your money. You must also keep tweaking, iterating, and improving your channel's SEO. Monitor and track everything as you publish new content so your psychic can become a profitable YouTube business.

Conclusion

You have made it to the end of this book. We've given you lots of material and assignments to work with, so feel free. Each section of this book was placed in the order you must follow as a beginner.

The monetization section came last with good reason. A mistake many new YouTubers make is to focus on monetization too early in the game. As you put down this book, your main work is implementing the first three sections to the best of your ability. If you can get that done, monetization will be a natural by-product, and you will succeed.

You will only get very far if you develop the mindset, discipline, persistence, and consistency necessary for this journey. Again, let me remind you that your WHY must be more significant than your obstacles and the insecurities and doubts that will pop up along this journey. Your passion and desire to share your message, build a community, and serve others will determine how far you can go as a YouTuber.

The YouTube platform is one of the most powerful vehicles in 2021, where you can be, do, give, and share whatever you believe in. Done right, it will open opportunities and rewards beyond your wildest dreams. Many have started with an idea, built a brand over time, and turned a sad story into a YouTube empire. You have the potential to do the same. All you need is a plan. Each chapter of this book has given you guidelines and procedures, from setting up the channel to researching content, finding your brand's identity, and posting your first video.

You have learned hacks that will save you time and energy when editing and putting out professional-looking videos, even shooting from a basement. What you need now is a serious commitment to your dream. If you are ready to be a successful YouTuber, it's time to put in the effort and reap the benefits of having thousands or millions of people watching your content, taking your advice, and buying things from you. Whatever your end goal might be - a lifestyle of travel, sharing your passion with the world, becoming famous, earning a six-figure income, boosting your local business, or any other objective, the first step is to implement the lessons this book offers.

BOOK # 4

SEO For Beginners

How to Get to the Top of Google, Bing, and More Through Search Engine Optimization

Introduction

Does SEO work? Can anyone start from scratch without prior knowledge and still drive a ton of traffic that turns into business without spending a dollar on advertising?

The short and sweet answer is yes. However, that will only happen in 2023 and beyond if you invest time learning and practicing proven strategies and tactics.

You're in the right place if you're here to learn more about using SEO for your blog, website, or eCommerce to drive traffic and gain new business. Congratulations on being smart enough to realize that you can still win in today's competitive online marketplace by maximizing your knowledge and skills in applying SEO. The beauty of SEO is that it works exceptionally well for traditional and digital businesses.

You are now reading through the initial pages of a resource that will prove valuable to you, whether you've already been through some SEO or are a complete beginner wondering where to focus. This topic is often overwhelming, and I know many business owners who shrug at the thought of dealing with their website SEO. Instead, they prefer to hire SEO experts who charge a fortune but need more transparency or results regarding growth.

I should know this pattern because I was once one of those business owners who felt scammed and manipulated after a poor experience with an SEO agency.

When I decided to build an online presence supporting my business, I naturally did what most of my friends at the time were doing. I hired someone to make my website and consult on SEO practices and how to set up my blog. Once my website was up, I focused more on blogging to drive traffic and grow an audience until social media caught my attention. I spent the next several years in the trenches figuring out how to leverage platforms such as YouTube and Instagram for business. I have books on gaining followers and new customers through these social media channels, which you can also check out if you want to go down that path.

As my social media marketing grew, I wanted to ensure I wasn't losing out on free traffic and authority building on Google and other search engines. So, I decided it was time to invest in SEO. The trouble is, I was overwhelmed by the confusion most teachers of the subject portrayed. I was also a little lazy, and I underestimated both the value derived from this strategy and the work needed to learn the skills of applying proper SEO. After dabbling a little on a few SEO websites and binge-watching YouTube channels that got me nowhere, I decided to hire an agency.

Hiring an expert would save me time and enable me to bring in more sales faster. That would

Introduction

probably work if the SEO expert knew what they were doing. Six months into my agency contract, I realized this was a bust, so I counted my losses and walked away with less money in my pocket and a deflated spirit. That was when a thought occurred to me. Why not learn this thing for real this time?

My business was in a good place, and I had a decent following on my social media that kept my pipeline flowing so I could dedicate time and energy to getting this right.

Most of my friends thought it made no sense given that I already had traffic from my social media marketing, but the truth is, few things are more potent than proper SEO. Aside from the fact that it costs zero to get yourself in front of a prospect, we also know that high rankings on big giants like Google build brand authority and create an evergreen effect of potential customers as they keep finding you on search. It was a no-brainer for me, and this time, I committed and went all in, and the results of my learning, practicing, and experimenting have grown one of my businesses to seven figures. This book gives you the blueprint of what works, how to do it, and why.

My traffic has been growing steadily each year, no matter what changes occur with algorithms, and I am consistently getting over a million visits a month. 40% of those visitors are all from SEO, meaning I only invest about 60% in advertising and social media marketing. The good news is these results are not exclusive to me. Any industry can get fantastic results by implementing SEO in their business. I've worked with many small business owners who have experienced traffic and revenue growth by following what you're about to learn.

Over the chapters, I will walk you through a deeper understanding of SEO, keyword research, on-page and technical SEO, content marketing, and link building. But I am doing it in a digestible way so that you don't get as overwhelmed and frustrated as I was when I first studied this.

And even if you decide to get a team or an agency to take care of your SEO in the future, I want you to be knowledgeable enough to know what to track, what questions to ask, and how to measure success. A key aspect of why I felt scammed by the SEO agency was that I was flying blind. An expert can only prove good enough to help your business if you're safe enough on this topic. So, I encourage you to read and practice everything you learn in this book, even if you plan on delegating and outsourcing. Everyone must understand SEO basics in a world where Google dominates and digital is the new economy.

By learning these proven strategies, hacks, and tactics, you'll increase your confidence and knowledge of how SEO will build your brand authority and bring in new customers. You'll also learn to implement on-page SEO and ensure your website ranks high. I will share the tools and software you need to have in your toolbox, and perhaps most important is that you'll learn how to communicate effectively to your prospect because by doing keyword research and learning to "speak" in the language that your potential customer is already using, people will naturally gravitate toward you and your products or services making sales a natural byproduct of this process.

Failure to learn these things means you'll waste a ton of time and miss opportunities to make sales using this free strategy. If all you do is depend on social media marketing and advertising, your profits and revenue will always be a fraction of what they could be. Worse still, if you decide to hire a team before you gain enough understanding of SEO, there's a good chance you'll end up like me with less money in the bank and no results to show for it. If you want to avoid this pitfall, this book is the key. SEO for business does not have to be complicated; with the proper blueprint, you can navigate this world of search engines. With that said, let's help you succeed and get the traffic you deserve.

CHAPTER 1

The Search Engines

Do you know what SEO is and why it's vital for your business?

Most people think SEO, an acronym for Search Engine Optimization, is only for specific industries or niches. I've heard many people say that SEO wouldn't work in their market or that it's unnecessary. Some are under the false belief that it's only for big companies to invest in because it takes a lot of money to win online. None of these ideas are true. Yes, it might take some niches longer to rank than others, but SEO is for every business owner and can work for any industry.

How do I know this? Because research shows that 93% of online experiences start with an online search. And that's for more than just the obvious Google search. We are now accustomed to using all kinds of search engines throughout the day, whether booking flights, hotels, or looking for a great eatery around us. We are all using search engines, and so is your ideal customer. The best part is by the time you're done consuming this blueprint; you will only need to spend a little money before figuring out how to unlock SEO and leverage it as a critical marketing channel for traffic and sales.

Before dissecting search engines, let's review why SEO is so important.

Importance Of SEO

SEO is optimizing your content for search engines so the system can recognize your brand as the best option for a specific term or keyword. SEO is like a never-sleep salesman working for you when done right. Consider the contrast with paid ads. Sure, it works well as long as ads run and you're spending money on Facebook, Instagram, Linked In, or Adwords, but as soon as you stop spending money, the traffic stops. With SEO, you'll get that traffic from all over the world 24/7 without spending a dime on ads. So, not only does SEO grow and drive traffic to your website, but the return on investment can also be huge. It's also great for building authority and brand awareness, which builds trust. The other reason SEO is necessary in 2023 and beyond is that your competition is already doing it. Do you want to stay caught up?

What Are Search Engines?

I like to think of search engines as massive answering machines. Think about this for a minute... The internet is a whole of content (webpages, images, videos, PDFs, and so much more). It's almost like a giant virtual library. We'd have a manageable mess with some form of organization and the ability to pull out the best information required at any given moment. All that information would be of no use to any of us. I would type in "Italian restaurant near me," and I'd get billions of results, most of which have nothing to do with what I need because of lack of organization and systematization. For me to get an answer that is accurate, timely, and ideally suited for my location, there has to be an invisible librarian sorting all the information and dishing out only what's requested by me (the user) to satisfy my question. That's where search engines come into play. The search engine discovers, understands, and organizes all available content through a process known as crawling and indexing.

According to Wikipedia, a search engine is a software system designed to systematically carry out web searches for particular information specified in a textual web search query. The web results are generally presented in a line of results commonly referred to as SERPs. We'll talk about those shortly. Before we do, let's talk about the top search engines you should become aware of so you can consciously choose your battleground.

The top five must-know are Google, Bing, Yahoo, Baidu, and Yandex. There are others, such as Yippy and Duckduck go, but these are smaller than traffic. But Google is the most popular, covering over 90% of the global market. So, if you invest time learning Search Engine Optimization, focus on seriously understanding and making Google fall in love with your brand. Although we will discuss various search engines, this book will focus mainly on Google. If you can nail that, you can determine the others.

Types Of Searches

If you want to be loved by search engines like Google, your focus should be on serving the users who come to get answers and solutions to their problems. That means you need to invest time thinking about your user's experience, why they have jumped on their desktop or smartphone (aka the intention), and learn about the three main types of searches most of us are making.

Think With Google US is an excellent site you need to bookmark immediately because they release a ton of helpful information that will enable you to keep your SEO game in top shape. They continue to do a lot of research about the users who go on their search and why. Expert researchers have identified the main ones as navigational, informational, and transactional search queries.

Navigational search query

This type of search is done to find a particular website or webpage. For example, you might type in "Facebook," "Grant Cardone," "Target," or "JC Penny" into the search bar instead of entering the URL into the browser. That's a simple example of a navigational search query. The user is clear about whom or what they want, and you need to own that search term to show up. You will only be relevant to the user if you appear at the bottom of the page results.

You can only target or optimize this type of search query if you're the owner of the brand the user is searching for. So, as you think about competitors or peers, attempting to outrank them organically with this type of query is futile.

The best thing you can do is to ensure you dominate your brand's navigational query. When you or anyone searches for your name, your site should appear at the top of the page, and your content should ideally take up all of page one results. Your website should always populate the top with your brand name, location, products, services, blog contact, and other relevant information.

Pro tip:

If you want to step up and own your navigational query, consider buying branded keywords even if you're already ranking organically. These types of keywords tend to drive both clicks and conversions. That way, your profits will increase because you own the whole page results and show up for sponsored content.

Informational search query

Informational search queries occur when a user wants to know something. According to Wikipedia, an informational search query covers broad topics such as sports, trucks, Miami, etc. In other words, issues that might have thousands of relevant results. Users who enter an informational search query on a search engine seek information. They are likely seeking something other than a specific site, as previously discussed with navigational search queries. Instead, they want an answer, a solution, or to learn how to do something.

The best part is you can target this search query to work to your advantage. But it's important to realize that monetizing this type of content is the hardest of the three. High-quality SEO content that genuinely provides valuable information relevant to the query is your saving grace. You still won't monetize it immediately, but it can start that process of taking people through a funnel. Content such as long-form blog posts, videos, eBooks, Infographics, and guides are among the top-rated informational assets you need to invest in to leverage this search query.

A great example of this type of content is Wikipedia. It could be better, but it does demonstrate the concept well because it's purely information-based. That's why it consistently ranks on the first page for about half of all searches. Granted, they also do excellent link-building, which we'll be addressing in a later chapter, but for the most part, their success comes from this focus on consistently producing informative content.

Now, if an average site like Wikipedia can build such a reputation and do well on this search query, imagine what you could do if you committed to producing ten times better content than your niche market provides. Brian Dean of Backlinko and Neil Patel are great examples of how easily a single individual can grow in brand, authority, and sales through leveraging informational search queries.

A few things you should start doing include:

- Creating high-value blog posts that are generally long-form.
- Creating detailed report guides and hosting them on your website.
- Shooting how-to videos that are relevant to your business.
- Designing awesome infographics, presentations, etc.

The important thing is to leverage content to position yourself as trustworthy and the best source of information—more on this when we talk about content creation.

Transactional search query

A transactional search query has the intent of completing a purchase. It's based on buying a product or making an order. A user will often go to the search bar with a specific brand or product name such as "iPhone 11", or sometimes it can be a bit more generic, e.g., "coffee maker." You can also find what's referred to as vertical searches in this category whereby the user types in a specific industry like "three-star hotels in Los Angeles" or "fine dining restaurants in Manhattan."

Sometimes, the user might include terms such as "best deal," "purchase," "buy," or "book." Regardless of their varying times, we can infer that the user is ready and willing to pull out their credit card and order something soon.

Regarding the sales process, these would be the people further down the purchase journey and fall at the conversion level in your business funnel.

Most local searches are usually transactional as well. For example, if you visit Colorado and type "Best wine shop in Colorado," you likely want to purchase. Therefore, these search queries are precious and worth investing resources and effort to rank on page one when a user types something related to your offer.

If you have the solution (product or service) for this type of search query, you can target users through the following means:

#1. Add relevant and valuable information to the pages containing your products or services. These pages should be jam-packed with specific things such as featured products, color availability, size, material, and other essential items to help the user make an informed decision. Add features and pricing options to this transactional page and the guarantee policy if you provide a service.

#2. Ensure your page has the proper CTA (Call to action) to boost conversions.

#3. When creating the page copy, optimize the title and image alt tags, and sprinkle in the relevant keywords for your product or service.

Your chances of ranking transactional pages on search engines like Google depend significantly on how thorough and informative your product and service listings appear. And since we want Google to love you, invest in appropriate content optimized to help your audience make more informed purchasing decisions.

Pro tip:

Consider investing in PPC as well as optimizing your listings page. PPC (pay-per-click) ads work well with transactional search queries because the intent is already high. When someone lands on your website through a PPC transactional search query, they are 50% more likely to purchase an organic visitor. Why? Because these ads usually appear at the top of transactional searches, making it easier for users to click and take action if it's a proper fit.

This can be an excellent way to drive traffic even on products Amazon already ranks high for. Organically, it might be hard to rank on page one if you're a new website with product listings already found on Amazon, eBay, and these more significant eCommerce sites. But with some creativity and PPC, you could still appear at the top of page one and get those transactional search queries landing on your website.

Understanding SERPs

Search Engine Results Pages (SERPS) appear on a search engine when a user makes any search query. These pages are usually numbered; especially on Google, page one is the most important. The top search result page usually includes organic search results, paid Google Ads results, featured snippets, knowledge graphs, and video results. Since our book focuses mainly on Google SEO, most of what you will learn here can be applied to all others.

Google now has dozens of SERP features on page one, but the two most important categories are paid results and organic results.

Naturally, paid results come from the PPC model of Google Ads. The highest bidder with the most relevant ad usually wins the spot at the top. Organic results are earned. That means you can only rank high if Google's algorithm determines your content as the best and most relevant for a given search. In other words, if Google loves you, they will rank you.

Understanding SERPs is vital because it helps you optimize your website. Nowadays, more is needed to show up on page one. It would be best to show up as close to the top as possible. With the new SERP features that Google has added, you can be on page one but appear so low on the page that people hardly click on your site. A solution to this is to learn how to leverage link-building.

Another thing you want to consider with SERPs is that when there are many SERP features (especially the Featured Snippet), you'll likely experience more "no-click" searches. No-click searches are when a user Googles something and gets an answer immediately. For example, type in "How to post an Instagram Story," and you immediately get the four steps that walk you through sharing your Story.

Why would you click on any other link after that? Therefore, these types of SERP features lead to fewer clicks on any of the links on page one. The solution is to focus on keywords that have few SERP features. So, what determines a typical Google SERP?

#1. Organic Search Results

Google's complex algorithm uses over two hundred ranking signals to determine which content should go on page one. We are still determining the exact workings of the Google algorithm, but there are a few publicly confirmed factors, which you'll learn in Chapter 2.

#2. Paid Search Results

Paid search is marked with a small "Ad" icon in the top left corner of their snippet. According to Rank Ranger, ads appear on 51.61% of page one SERPs either at the top, side, or bottom of the page. While avoiding keywords with lots of ads is a good idea, given what you've learned about transactional search queries, I suggest you create content where people bid on the exact keywords. It shows these keywords are valuable and possess a high transactional intent. You will get fewer clicks because you'll compete with organic and paid content, but the clicks you get should be worth the effort.

#3. Featured Snippet

A Featured Snippet is usually pulled from a webpage or video. Ahrefs did a study and suggested that about 12% of all SERPs have a Featured Snippet. These include FAQs, Bulleted Lists, Numbered Lists, Tables, and Video Featured Snippets. Returning to the earlier example where a featured Snippet came in response to the query "how to post on Instagram Stories," you don't need to click on the link attached to the answer because you get the 4-step process right there. However, you see which link source the answer came from, which is still good. So, Google always credits their source of information for Featured Snippets.

Featured Snippets almost always show up at the very top of the SERPs, and that can be a bad thing as it will push organic results further down the page. However, if you crack the code of getting your content featured, this is an incredible opportunity because your content will be at the top of the page. It becomes unmissable, and that leads to a super-high organic clickthrough rate.

#4. Direct Answer Box

Similar to a Featured Snippet, a direct answer box gives you an immediate answer to your question. But the critical difference is it won't credit any particular source. For example, when I type in, "When was Instagram launched?" I got a direct answer – on 6 October 2010. These answers are considered public domain.

#5. Local Packs

Local Packs show up when it's a local search query such as "Italian restaurant near me" or "Starbucks coffee Boston." Sometimes, they appear when Google feels that a "normal" search needs a few local results, depending on your type. For example, if you search for "Electrician" or "Dentist," Google assumes you require someone nearby.

#6. People Also Ask

Recently added, this feature is often in the middle of the SERP. When you click on the question, it expands with an answer. I like to use this section to develop great content ideas for my social media and podcast since these are my audience's common questions.

#7. Google Image Results

You've seen images of your search populate the results based on what you typed. For example, if you order "Tony Robbins" or " Red Ferrari," you'll get many images corresponding to your search. Google recently switched things up and created a whole tab dedicated to Images.

#8. Video Results

These results are becoming extremely popular and appear in a pack of three with a carousel option to view more. Most of the videos that show up (88%) are pulled from YouTube, so if you're growing your YouTube channel as well, this is a bonus. You can also access only Video results by clicking on the video tab.

#9. Twitter Results

These results show up when you type a specific keyword or navigational search query. Google pulls the latest tweets from a particular Twitter account. For example, if I type in Tony Robbins, it shows his Twitter account with links to the last three tweets.

#10. Knowledge Graph and Knowledge Panel

Knowledge Graphs and panels show up on the right side of organic results. They give you statistics and information about a company or an influential person. Most of this data is sourced from sites like Wikipedia and Crunchbase.

#11. Google Shopping

Google shopping is, at times, referred to as Product Listing Ads, and these only appear for specific products. They appear at the very top of the page (even above traditional ads). Even though most Google Shopping Results are ads, you can also find a few selected organic results.

#12. Top Stories

These search results show up for trending keywords and whatever Google has certified as newsworthy. To show up in the Top Stories section, your site needs to be Google News approved.

How Search Engines Work

To understand how these answer machines, known as search engines, work, we need to dive deeper into some of the terms mentioned earlier, namely crawling and indexing. We will also add a third term here, known as ranking. Before you can rank, your content must be found, which is critical to winning with SEO. Since more than 90% of all search activity takes place on Google, we'll decipher (as best as possible) this process of being discovered and ranked on Google. After all, if you win on Google SEO, you'll likely succeed with every other smaller search engine.

Search Engine Crawling

This is the discovery process. The search engine will send out a team of robots known as spiders or crawlers to find new and updated content. This means more than text-based content on a web page. It can also be video, PDF, Infographics, and so on. All these different formats are discoverable by links. The Google crawler will start by fetching a few web pages, then following the links on those web pages to discover even more URLs, and continue doing this link shopping to add it to Caffeine. No, it's not coffee-related! Caffeine is the name given to a massive database of discovered URLs. These URLs will be retried when a user types the search box seeking information matching that particular URL's content. So, the main work is to do some matchmaking between the searcher and the best URL. Caffeine is also referred to as an index.

Search Engine Index

What is a search engine index? It is a database where the information that the crawlers deem good enough (based on their pre-determined criteria) gets processed and stored.

Search Engine Ranking

Ranking refers to the ordering of search results. Or stated the organization of the effects a user will see after asking a question or requesting information from the search engine. This organization of results is based on relevancy. When you type in a search, you will receive the highest-ranking answer that Google believes is most relevant. When ranking your content, this is where the fun begins because understanding how to play this game with Google will ensure you show up on the user's dashboard as the preferred result. When giving crawlers access to your site, you can block them from accessing part of your site if, for some reason, you don't want the entire website to be indexed.

If you want your site to show up in the SERPs, you need to ensure it is getting crawled and indexed. A good starting point is to assess your current status. Are any of your sites getting crawled? One way to check is to type your URL on Ubersuggest.com or head to Google and type "site: yourdomain.com" into the search bar. This will yield the results that Google has in its index.

Another thing you can do if you want more accurate results is to sign up for a free Google Search Console account. This robust tool allows you to submit sitemaps for your site and monitor how many advanced pages rank on Google's index. It also shows you the top-performing ones that need help and so much more.

What to do if your site isn't appearing on search results:

If your website isn't showing up on search results, you could give it time to populate and for the crawlers to finish doing their thing. But if you still need help seeing any sign of existing online after several days, ensure your site is linked to an external website. Sometimes, nothing shows up because you're not linked to any external website, which Google values a lot. You can also consider restructuring your page hierarchy and navigation. If it's too complicated and cluttered, the crawlers might need help to crawl effectively, hurting your rankings. On a more technical note, if Google has penalized your site for spammy behavior or if some basic code is installed that directs the crawlers to block indexing, you'll have trouble showing up on any search. A Google search console can help you figure out where the problem is so you can quickly fix it.

I want to note here that telling the crawlers which page to avoid is okay. Sometimes, it's just as important as telling them which pages are most important for indexing. Duplicate URLs, test pages, select promo pages, or old URLs with subpar content should be hidden from indexing. To do this, use robots.txt.

What Is Robots.Txt?

These are files located in the root directory of your website (yourdomain.com/robots.txt) that tell the spiders which parts of your site search engines should and shouldn't be crawled. You can also give specific directives of the speed at which they should crawl your site. When a Googlebot finds robots.txt files, it will follow the parameters and suggestions. If it encounters an error while accessing the site's robots.txt file, it won't crawl the site anymore. However, if it cannot find a robots.txt file for a site, it will crawl the site using standard protocols.

While most bots follow this protocol of robots.txt files for the proper purpose, some bad apples (hackers and people with bad intentions) will use it to access private content. So, I suggest NoIndex the pages containing sensitive and personal information. Gate them behind a login form instead of having them live in your robots.txt file.

Crawl Budget Optimization

This term and process should be well known if you intend to have a site with lots of information (think tens of thousands of URLs). But even if you have a couple of hundred links in there, it's still good to block crawlers from accessing content that isn't relevant.

CHAPTER 2

Google, Bing, and More

Most of your efforts need to go into Google SEO if you want to win online. However, you shouldn't limit yourself to one search engine as other smaller ones can drive some high-quality traffic to your site. If you are going to do SEO right, it's worth exploring more than just Google, and in this chapter, we cover the top five so you can leverage other potential traffic sources as you grow your business.

#1. Google

This Photo by Unknown Author is licensed under CC BY-SA

There's no denying this is the giant regarding search engine market share. Between Google search and YouTube, there's a lot of traffic to capture, whether you do organic or paid. With great opportunity comes great competition as well. Everyone and their mother are competing for traffic on Google. Even more challenging is that many of the recent changes Google made, such as adding Featured Snippets (we talked about this in the last chapter), links are being pushed further down the page.

The story of Google is beautiful to learn for any business owner and investor. What started as a research project in 1996 turned out to be a company worth billions of dollars and growing. The founders Sergey Brin and Larry Page wanted to sell their engine in 1999 to Excite for $750,000, which was rejected, and the rest is business success history. I almost feel bad for the guys who left them, given how massive Google's parent company, Alphabet, is today. In case you're wondering, Google is the third U.S. tech company worth $1 trillion!

Not only does Google power its search results, but it also provides search results for smaller engines such as Ask.com. Organic traffic is tough competition, and it's only getting fiercer. While it can be overwhelming to keep up with all the ranking factors and Google SEO jargon found on SEO experts' websites, sticking to what you learn in this book should help you see results and growth in your traffic.

How Google Search Works

Google is the most complex search engine to date. Hundreds (some claim thousands) of factors are considered before the search engine determines what should go where. We may not know all these factors, but we don't have to win with SEO. The most important thing to understand is the intention behind this search engine. The foundation Google was built on is one of scientific research and academia. Google has stated its mission of organizing the world's information to make it universally accessible and helpful. So, what Google cares about is understanding the nuances of human language and intent and answering questions such as "What results most accurately answer the searcher's query?"

Google needs to do an impeccable job collecting all new data, organizing it, and storing it so that it's fast and efficient in delivering a specific content piece to the right person at the right time. That's no small feat, considering that Google processes over two trillion searches within a year.

In 1998, while Google founders were still at Stanford, they released a paper entitled "The PageRank Citation Ranking: Bringing Order to the Web," which describes a method for rating web pages objectively and mechanically. In academia, where this idea was adopted, academic papers are often ranked by the number of citations received. The higher that number, the more authoritative the report would be considered. Larry Page and Sergey Brin wanted to apply that same grading system to the web's information. On Google, backlinks are used as the proxy for votes.

Link building on Google matters

The more links a page receives, the more authoritative it's seen on that particular topic. Before you get too excited and buy fake links, it's good to know that not all links are equal. In upcoming chapters, we'll dive deeper into this, but for now, realize that Google factors in the quality of the association, meaning who is doing the linking. So, for example, if CNN or Forbes link to your website, that will be seen as a high-quality link. But if you have 100 unknown and fake blogs linking to your page, it will have a more minor impact than that single link from Forbes. It might hurt your Domain authority and rankings.

Google also takes into account relevance. That means if you sell shoes, links from other sites that talk about fashion and things related to shoes would be worth more than a site that talks about dog food.

This doesn't mean that all you have to do is get someone in your niche to link back to you, and you're done. These initial factors are over a decade old, and the algorithm has become even more sophisticated.

RankBrain

A technology Google has been working on to help search engines handle the massive increase in volume without losing accuracy is called the RankBrian. I consider this the secret sauce of Google as it uses artificial intelligence. The more information it processes, the better it gets as it continues to understand new user search queries and the right kind of information to display. RankBrian helps analyze and understand the connection between links (citations) and words (content and queries). In other words, Google uses your past and regular activity to piece together what you need when you ask a question.

For example, suppose you type in "pet food". Think about it for a moment. What kind of pet are we talking about here? A dog? A cat? A parrot? Google would now do its best to figure out precisely what you're looking for by piecing together the puzzle based on several factors. Suppose you've been searching on Google for things related to your new pet in the last few weeks. Maybe you searched for the best veterinarian in your city for cats. You could also search for personalized cat collars and where to buy one near you. You may follow someone on Twitter or Instagram who offers tips for cat grooming, and you may have watched a YouTube tutorial on the best diet for your cat. See? By piecing everything together, Google knows what type of "pet food" to show you, even without explicitly typing the word cat.

Some people find that a bit too creepy, but in some ways, RankBrain is only there to make your Google experience more personalized and fast at solving your problem.

Organic and paid ads on Google are complicated and require further study to rank higher organically and get great results with your PPC. Keep reading each chapter as we fill in that knowledge gap for you so you can make Google fall in love with your website.

#2. Microsoft Bing

This Photo by Unknown Author is licensed under CC BY-

Bing is a Microsoft-owned and operated search engine. Previously MSN, it has gained significant market share over the years as it grew and also took on a deal to power Yahoo, then added AOL in 2016. These additions have helped them become a serious contender, raking in 33% of all U.S. searches.

Microsoft Bing shares a similar look and feel to Google, but one thing that stands out is that it offers a rewards program. When you search or shop on the engine, you get points that can be redeemed as gift cards, non-profit donations, and much more. Pretty cool, right?

Microsoft Bing may not be as massive as Google, but the U.S. and U.K. markets show deep respect for this search engine. Their algorithms aren't as sophisticated as Google's, but sometimes, that is a good thing because it makes predicting and optimizing easier. Organically ranking on this is pretty straightforward once you study the system. Although the traffic is lower than Google's, their ads also increase in value and effectiveness. You can go further with less ad spend here. **To** learn more about Microsoft Bing, check out the resource section.

#3. Yahoo

Although I find this search engine too noisy and messy, Yahoo is still worth exploring. It has a little over 3% of the global market share. As mentioned, Microsoft Bing powers it so that you would get the same results.

#4. Yandex

This Photo by Unknown Author is licensed under CC BY-SA.

Russian-based search engine Yandex started as a project developed by two Russians in 1990 under the company Arkadia. The purpose behind it was to aid in the classification of patents. Of course, that has evolved over the years. Adapted in 1993, Yandex means Yet Another Indexer. They probably weren't that interested in expressing creativity with their naming.

Yandex went public on the New York Stock Exchange in 2011 with an IPO of $1.3 billion. At the time, that was a big deal. Only Google had scored a more significant IPO. Since then, Yandex has continued to hold steady in the Russian market and powers over half of all search engines.

The traffic on Yandex might be less than big giant Google, but so is the organic and paid competition. Compared to Facebook, Google, and Bing, the cost per click tends to be lower. So, paid ads are a good investment, but organic traffic can be cumbersome to crack because of certain elements that make it a little challenging for outsiders to use. So, if you're in Russia, this is ideal. If not, it's a little less perfect but still worth exploring.

#5. Baidu

This Photo by Unknown Author is licensed under CC BY-SA.

Baidu is a Chinese-based search engine founded in 2000. It has dominated over 82% of the market share (compared to Google, with a rate of 0.61%) in China. Of course, outside of China, Baidu could be more influential. It's a great option if you are looking to reach and work with the Chinese market, as there are over 3.3 billion daily searches. Remember to study how to best communicate on this search engine because it's completely different from Google SEO. This market's visuals, vocabulary, and customs must be intentionally created with a thorough understanding of the Chinese market. Google Translate doesn't help you win over customers and drive traffic. You need to invest in getting someone who speaks the language and understands the marketing culture (2 years of high school Mandarin won't cut it).

The algorithm is one of the simpler ones to understand, and their paid system is a breeze compared to the complexities of Google advertising. I want to note here that International SEO is quite different from what we are accustomed to, so invest in more education before jumping into this one.

#6. DuckDuckGo

DuckDuckGo is an American-based search engine that prides itself on being a private search engine that allows you to be anonymous while browsing the Internet. Google is notorious for tracking your behavior and storing all your data and browsing history. DuckDuckGo is gaining popularity as people want to escape the manipulation of the filter bubble. That's not to say there are no ads because the company makes money through ads. The main difference is that the ads must be personalized since they don't have your data. So, if you were shopping for shoes on Amazon, you would avoid getting bombarded by subsequent shoe ads from Amazon as you keep using the search engine.

This search engine interface is clean and straightforward for anyone to use because it offers only one search page. By 2023, DuckDuckGo continues to grow with over 80 million daily direct searches. It's gaining steam in the market, and as people seek more privacy, there's a good chance this search engine will continue to grow.

#7. Amazon

Most people need to realize this, but Amazon is a search engine—the most significant e-commerce search engine in the market. More than 50% of product searches are on Amazon, making it a huge contender, especially regarding online sales and search queries. Amazon used to be just a product listing, but today, given that over 500 million products are listed on Amazon.com, there's a strong need to learn SEO, even if all you have is an Amazon store.

We must realize that Amazon's algorithm differs from the previously discussed search engines, especially Google because it's built on a revenue model. Jeff Bezos, the founder of Amazon, launched it in 1994 after reading that the web was growing at 2,300%. He decided to list the top products that were most likely to sell online and settled for books because of their low cost and high demand. Even as the company grows, Amazon focuses more on showing users the product they are most likely to buy at the best price possible.

This search engine isn't about answering the questions asked. Instead, it's about ranking products based on their propensity to sell. The algorithm and ranking factors will not be related to what we know about Google SEO. Their algorithm is designed, first and foremost, to sell as many products as possible through its online platform. The core ranking pillars are conversion rate, keyword relevancy, and customer satisfaction. So that means you need to consider things such as price optimization, product listings and descriptions, image optimization, relevant keywords, and customer reviews, among other things.

To make Amazon SEO work for you, invest time learning the algorithm and focus on increasing the conversion rate, choosing the most relevant keywords, and building solid reviews. I also encourage you to invest in PPC on Amazon and drive external traffic, as that supports organic performance, especially for new products. If you'd like to learn more, check out the recommended guide on my resource page.

CHAPTER 3

The Meaning of Optimization

There's a common joke amongst SEO experts that goes like this. If you ever need to hide a dead body, place it on the second page of Google. It's funny and might even make you chuckle, but when you understand the importance of ranking on page one, you'll see the underlying anecdote within that joke. Think for a moment here. When did you last search for an answer on Google pages two, three, four, or five? Be honest.

I often get the same results whenever I ask this question in a live audience. One hundred percent of the people openly say they never go past page one. If they can't find what they want on page one, they'll usually change the search phrase or seek answers elsewhere (sometimes a different search engine). Rarely has a single individual who says they scroll down and then hit the following three pages. Why is that?

It's simple. Over the years, Google has demonstrated that it is consistent, accurate, and fast at giving us exactly what we need when we query. It has also trained us to believe that the best answers are the ones that rank the highest and most definitely only what shows up on page one to save us time and effort. So why would we click beyond "the best option." That's why optimization is vital for SEO. After all, it's in the name itself (Search Engine Optimization).

As you've learned so far, all search engines are different. The most popular ones, like DuckDuckGo, Yandex, and Baidu, are great and easy to understand because they run on basic algorithms. On the other hand, Google is the mother of search engines, and it runs on highly complex and mysterious algorithms. If you can optimize and rank high in a complex and highly competitive environment like Google, you will easily win on the other search engines.

Why is everyone optimizing

There are so many reasons why optimizing your website matters. The main one is that it drives more traffic. With more traffic, you will ultimately generate more revenue. Another primary reason for optimizing is that you will keep generating leads even if no ads are running. Over 62% of consumers say they go to search engines first to learn more about a new business, product, or service, and about 41% visit the official business website when they feel ready to buy. So, if understanding and nailing the buyer's journey is essential to you, then optimizing for SEO is a must.

Even if driving traffic for revenue isn't your primary concern, optimizing your site should still matter because nothing boosts your credibility and authority better than ranking high on Google. When users see your brand and pictures populating Google or when they search a particular key phrase, and the first page is filled with your content, it increases your perceived value and expertise. That's why brands like HubSpot and Moz or personal brands like Grant Cardone and Neil Patel have invested much in search engine optimization and online branding. They know that as Google continues to push them to the users as authoritative sites, their perceived value in the marketplace increases. You can enjoy the same benefits.

The History Of SEO

Only some people realize that SEO has existed far longer than we think. Although sites like Google and Yahoo took to the scene from the mid to late 90s, an early form of SEO existed as far back as 1991 when Tim Berners-Lee launched the world's first website. Soon after, as more and more websites launched, the need for structure and accessibility increased tremendously. Search platforms like Excite (the company that turned Google down on their offer of purchasing at $750,000) emerged and started cataloging and organizing information. That was back in 1993. In this primitive stage of SEO, it was easy for marketers to take advantage and use keyword stuffing, spammy backlinks, and excessive tagging to generate high rankings in searches. The caveman-like years of SEO went on for years because even major algorithm updates required several months to complete. However, a shift started happening as Google took form and gained stable ground in the early 2000s.

SEO in the early to mid-2000s.

Google emerged as the leading player and continued to improve the relevancy and value of results, which created a more personalized experience for the user. The era of the early 2000 updates and developments in algorithm functionality, especially on Google, forced marketers to change strategy somewhat. The focus shifted to generating inbound links to increase search exposure. As Google continued to promote and build a foundation for a more personalized and user-focused web, we saw the launch of features like Google's Universal Search, which offered more engaging content media in search, including news, images, and video. Most people consider this the middle ages of SEO, where real-time updates from Google News, Twitter, and newly indexed content become a trend and highly desirable experience. We still needed to catch up to the search engine experience we know today when 2008 hit. Google made yet another shift, which helped lay the foundation for a more captivating and personalized web experience. They launched Google Suggest, which significantly improved usability and offered more relevant content by displaying suggested search options based on a user's historical data. This was the rise of Google Trends, Google Analytics, and keyword research tools.

SEO Changes Between 2010 and 2012

One of the most significant shifts in the history of SEO took place between 2010 and 2012, when we finally became enlightened enough to focus on quality. Marketers and brands everywhere were forced to re-evaluate how they approached SEO and the user experience. Google enforced stricter regulations on keywords, content quality, and over-optimization. Yes, there is such a thing as over-optimizing your website. Anyone who failed to comply with the new regulations had their name dragged through the mud to set an example (ask sites like J.C Penney). We also saw the launch of more features like Google's Knowledge Graph in SERPs, and local results were listed directly in SERPs for easier access. Right around this era was the launch of Google+ and the +1 button, which significantly boosted content visibility for a while. Social media was also rising, and YouTube was gaining fast momentum. For marketers, this meant it was time to learn how to develop valuable and shareable content that was user-friendly. These trends led to the dawn of the information age, which is still strong.

Present times:

Since 2013, we've been experiencing the most modern version of SEO. There's lots of personalization, and users are used to a fast-paced, engaging web experience that shows no signs of slowing down. Google continues to take market share regarding SEO, especially since purchasing YouTube, which has become a massive search engine. Other smaller players have tried their best to keep up with their algorithms. Unfortunately, the struggle between personalization and privacy continues to brew. Brands like Google leverage user data to develop their digital presence by personalizing results based on history, location, and device. Marketers usually need help getting their hands on this data, so we've learned to have a more creative approach to generate engagement through content optimization. You'll learn more about that in chapter seven.

You need to know now that creating relevant content that's mobile-friendly and catered to local search is vital if you want to win with SEO. The most significant opportunity to increase authority and rank high is to create segmented content optimized for the device and the user's intent. That means you must know your audience well and understand their needs at different points of their buyer's journey. The more you can personalize your content and create something high-quality and valuable for the end consumer, the better results you'll see.

Search Engine Position

Search engine positioning is a subset of optimization that involves tweaking and improving specific pages to achieve higher rankings. This would contrast working on the entire site or performing technical SEO improvements for the whole area. According to Backlinko, the top three results of the best-performing pages on page one usually get the lion's share of organic links. And if you move up just one spot, your click-through rate can increase by 30%. But we must remember that it's no longer just about being among Google's top ten blue links. Thanks to SERP Features, the ten blue links are usually further down the page than before. People love utilizing SERP Features. Therefore, it's not just about moving up a spot; it's also about maximizing your SERP real estate. You'll quickly see the organic results you want if you can rank multiple times on the same page or get a rich snip.

How to implement search engine positioning:

#1: Tweak and re-optimize your existing content.

The first thing to do is ensure your current pages are 100% optimized for SEO. Check what pages rank on Google's first (even the second) page. If Google deems you relevant, that's a clear sign you need to perform a search engine positioning. It would be best if you made some On-Page SEO, which we'll dive into in chapter five. You'll also need to make some UX improvements to ensure you're mobile-friendly and valuable. Your content needs to be updated or more straightforward to navigate on the page. Then, you want to ensure that it's fixed and that you update old content. You also want to add subheadings and use large fonts where appropriate to make it easier to navigate and read.

Where to access the correct pages:

Head over to your Search Console and log in to access your website's "Performance" section. Sort the "Queries" by position. You aim to find keywords with an average of about eight, as those will be the priority.

#2. Add some internal links

Another essential thing to do is add internal links on authority pages. Then, have those links point to pages that need a rankings bump. If you still need to learn the pages with the most authority, tools like Ahrefs and Ubersuggest can help you identify them. Another tip to apply here is to use rich anchor text when doing the internal linking so that Google can know that your page is about the specific keyword you want to rank for. For example, if your page is about "Oven Baked Chicken," then make sure that's the descriptive term you use to link to that page.

#3. Optimize for Organic Click-Through Rate

All SEO experts don't necessarily follow this hack because some claim it doesn't work. Here's what I know for sure. Google only cares about showing users the best and most relevant content that matches their query as perfectly as possible. And, of course, they use things like backlinks, social shares, quality of content, and so much more to figure out which content to place at the top of page one. More and more experiments have been conducted by marketers that prove that Google also uses your site's click-through rate to determine where to rank you. So, how do you ethically get more clicks to your page? Brian Dean of Backlinko has a simple method that has yielded great results for me. Check Google ads in the topic you want to rank for to see the most compelling keywords. Add these keywords to your intended headline and description in a cohesive manner. If you can't find any relevant keywords on Google ads, focus on incorporating power words into your headline and description. Terms such as easy, quick, fast, step-by-step, works quickly, etc., tend to draw attention and attract organic clicks.

I tried this simple tactic on an existing page, and I saw an uplift in my ranking, where I went from twelfth position to tenth. Keep in mind I only updated my headline and description.

The Difference Between SEO and SEM

SEO and SEM are sometimes interchanged by so-called experts, which shouldn't be the case because it confuses us. So, I want to clarify the difference (yes, they are not synonyms) before jumping into more technical SEO concepts.

What is SEO? As we've already discussed, search engine optimization is the process (some call it an art) of ranking high on a search engine, especially Google. The higher your website appears, the better for you because that's evergreen organic traffic that will ultimately drive your brand's revenue and authority.

SEO focuses on On-Page SEO, Off-Page SEO, Technical SEO, and User Interaction Signals.

What is SEM? Search engine marketing is concerned with SEO, plus there's an additional element of PPC (Pay-per-click) because it's increasing visibility and driving traffic using paid and organic methods.

SEM focuses on Bidding, Quality score, Ad copy, Ad Groups, and account management, as well as everything I mentioned under SEO.

So, we can safely state that SEM is a broader marketing strategy encompassing organic (SEO) and paid (PPC) strategies and tactics to accomplish one objective: More traffic and visibility for your website.

On Google, your website can show up on organic and paid search (you can show up multiple times on the same page), which is excellent when you need to see more traffic fast. One key difference between SEO and SEM is speed. SEO must be timely. It takes time, especially if you have a new site with few backlinks and no authority. Ahrefs suggests it should take an average of 2 years to rank on Google's first page if you're new to the game. If you check most of the top-ranking pages for your niche, you'll find most of them are at least three years old.

Of course, if you're committed to massive action and executing the best practices outlined in this book, you'll likely see results sooner.

In contrast, SEM happens pretty quickly. You can run an ad to your website in the morning and start seeing traffic pouring in and getting conversions before dinner time. The return on your investment will depend on how good the ad is, which must be timely and require a lot of experimentation. But here's the thing with PPC. Your website traffic goes to zero as soon as you stop running ads. On the other hand, if you have SEO, especially if you rank high on Google, you're set.

Is SEO cheaper than SEM since you're not spending money on ads?

Most people assume SEO is free. But it's not. Not even close. To rank #1 on Google organically requires time, money, and effort to invest upfront. Often, you will need help to write epic content that stands out. Even if you decide to write it yourself because you feel it's worth 20 hours instead of hiring a writer, you will still need a tool like Ahrefs or Ubersuggest to help you with proper keyword research. You'll likely need a graphics designer, illustrator, or video editor to help you create multimedia that makes your content pop when people click so Google can rank you highest. The good news is that all this investment is a one-time thing. Once you type, you don't need to invest much money to maintain your high ranking.

The bottom line is when it comes to cost, both SEO and SEM have price tags attached to them, and they do require upfront cash. With SEM, you see results faster but must keep pumping in money to see traffic. With SEO, the results take longer, but once you're in the top three, you can enjoy the rewards for a long time without doing much else. Both have pros and cons, so it depends on your current objectives.

As a good rule of thumb and if budget allows, I often encourage new websites to launch with

SEO and PPC. That only applies if you have a consistent ad budget. Set aside a regular monthly budget that you can play with until you figure out what combination of keyword targeting, ad copy, and landing pages works best. That's not something you can determine in a few days.

Remember, Google ads are no joke. It's a very complex and mature system, so you need to take some of Google's free training and learn as you experiment with your ads. It's a process, and the learning curve is enormous, especially if this is your first time. But if you enjoy learning new things and tweaking landing pages, this shall be a fun experience. That said, ensure you don't just stick to a single website URL. With PPC, you need targeted landing pages to run A/B tests to determine the best performers. Invest in software like ClickFunnels or LeadPages that create accessible landing pages to track and modify. Otherwise, you might need to depend on a developer, and we all know how expensive and draining that can be.

That said, focusing on SEM may be wrong for you now. If you have a minimal budget, focus 100% on SEO and implement everything you learn in this book. Understand that it might take several months to years to enjoy the full benefits of your hard work. But if the alternative is to run one week's worth of ads, I say stick to organic SEO and master that game. The results will be worthwhile.

Focus on ranking for informational keywords. In the next chapter, we dive deep into keywords and the best places to find the keywords that will make Google love your website.

CHAPTER 4

Keywords Crash Course

It's time to roll up your sleeves because we're getting into the heart of what it takes to see your site ranking on Google. Many components help your site rank, but the starting point is keywords. As a newbie, the topic of keyword research can feel daunting, but by the end of this chapter, you'll have a compact strategy and the right tools to help you figure out what people are searching for, which keywords to optimize your content for so you can rank and so much more. First things first.

What are SEO Keywords?

People type These key phrases or terms into a search engine for a particular answer. Although we refer to the term keyword, understand that it doesn't need a single word. The best SEO keywords to go after will be multiple words or phrases. Why? Because we never go to Google and type in a single word. I wonder how weird it would be to type "Italian" in the search box. I need to find a way to get accurate results that satisfy my query. I need to type in "Italian restaurants near me" or "Italian restaurant recommendations," Now we're off to the races! These two are examples of keyword phrases. The best one to go after for your keyword strategy is focusing on keyword phrases with a particular intent.

Why is this important for your SEO?

Some people assume that keywords are now insignificant in 2023. Those people are wrong! In fact, in Google's "How Search Works" report, they stated the following. "*The most basic signal that information is relevant is when a webpage contains the same keywords as your search query. If those keywords appear on the page or in the headings or body of the text, the information is more likely to be relevant.*"

The most advanced search engine in the world still uses old-school methods like searching for keywords on your page.

By sprinkling the right words and phrases people search for, your website can rank high on page one of Google. The higher your rank, the more traffic you drive to your website. Step one of any SEO blueprint will always be finding the right keywords that match your business objectives. Once you figure out the right keywords, you'll need to make a task list that includes mapping your site architecture, planning product and category pages, writing epic blog posts, creating awesome YouTube videos, and optimizing landing and sales pages. But let's not get ahead of ourselves here. First, we must find keywords and match them with our business objectives.

If you want keywords that yield satisfying results, you need clarity on what success looks like.

Do you know what goals these keywords should achieve?

In other words, what is the purpose of the keyword you're going after? Should it sell your product or service (transactional keywords will work best), should it feed different sections of your sales funnels, build awareness of your site, products, or services so everyone knows you (think Nike or Coca-Cola), or do you want all that organic traffic because you plan to remarket to those people through ads?

Once you have that clarity, match it with your customer's journey. Understand that all your customers start at the same point, i.e., they all have a problem that causes them to go online. The end of that journey is usually when they find their solution and either transact or become a lead to get more information. These are real people with emotions; the best way to create this match between your content and the user is to understand their problems. As such, I tend to follow this simple process:

- •**First is researching the keywords.**

That's where I research and build my keyword list. I usually use Ubersuggest and will walk you through how I've been doing it.

- **Second is researching the target audience.**

That's where I invest time online, getting to know more about my ideal customer. I use Wikipedia, Reddit, Forums, Facebook, LinkedIn Groups, etc. I do a lot of intensive work going into various platforms to develop a complete persona document showing my customer's motivations, frustrations, and goals. That way, I can ensure the chosen keywords will serve their needs.

- **Third is understanding the metrics.**

At this point, I want to understand search volume and things like seasonal trends, average monthly searches, cost per click, and SEO difficulty. Here, I look for terms with low SEO difficulty and a high cost per click.

- **Fourth is matching buyer journey with SEO keywords.**

That's when I bring out my persona document and keyword list and shortlist or narrow down which keywords will work to meet my desired objectives. By mapping out different touchpoints that my persona will need to go through with specific keywords and content, I can see how my SEO efforts will be rewarded. A tool like Ubersuggest is perfect for helping with this type of mapping because you can see which keywords are best for transactional purposes and which should be informational.

- **Fifth is keyword refinement.**

The last step here is to narrow down and refine the list of keywords. So, go back to your business objectives, then look at your competition ranking to see if the keywords you want to go for are worthwhile. The last thing to do is to group your final keywords. Consider grouping topics or the same themes. If you have an excellent tool helping you with this, you can check out what your competition is already ranking for and how they've grouped their keywords on their top pages—no need to reinvent the wheel here.

According to Ahrefs, you can rank for up to 600 keywords. That's a lot! So, don't limit yourself, and the best part is that as you build domain authority through link building and other efforts, you will start ranking for more and more keywords. Ahrefs also reported that for a new website looking to see some quick wins, focusing on low-volume keywords (about 1K monthly search volume) can be a good strategy as it's easier to rank.

Bonus Tip:

If you go for multiple low-volume keywords, you can start driving massive traffic within a few months. Ahref estimates low-volume keywords take about 121 days to rank, whereas high volume takes over 365 days. Imagine focusing on 200 low-volume keywords of 1k monthly searches and doing the implementation process right. Well, at the end of 121 days, you'd be getting approximately 200,000. It's alright for a newbie with a new website.

Free Keyword Research Tools

#1. Google Suggest

Although this isn't a tool, it's a neat hack that can get you lots of long-tail keywords based on what Google knows users are typing. First, type a word or two in your Google search bar and let it autocomplete. For example, When I start typing the phrase "Italian restaurant," it auto-suggests "Italian restaurant near me" and other relevant suggestions. It's easier to rank for that four-word term than the two-word term if you're an Italian restaurant owner.

#2. Google AdWords

Google has a keyword planner that gives you access to search volume and competition for any keyword. It's free to use once you sign up for an account, and you can utilize it without running a live PPC campaign.

#3. SeedKeywords.com

This neat SEO tool is free to use and lets you find creative keywords that people type. How? It allows you to ask customers, colleagues, or clients how they would search for something on Google. For example, how would you find an SEO expert online to help you with your new website? By leveraging your existing customer base and followers, you can get many answers you wouldn't have thought of or found on standard tools.

#4. AnswerThePublic.com

On this platform, you can type in any topic or keyword, and it will provide many results with what your target audience asks about your case online.

#5. Amazon.com

Most people need to realize what a goldmine Amazon is for Keyword research, and the best part is that it's free. Of course, if you're an eCommerce store, then this is a must! But even if you deal with services such as consulting and coaching, you can still learn a lot by visiting Amazon. For eCommerce, the process is pretty straightforward. Head over to the search bar and type your product name. Amazon will start auto-filling suggestions for you. Take note of any relevant terms that come up.

#6. WordStream Free Keyword Tool

I recently discovered this free tool, which works well to get search volume data. It allows you to filter down your results based on industry and location. It's powered by Google Ads, which makes it easy to identify niche keywords that are performing well so you can incorporate them into your content and ad campaigns. If you're happy with the results, you can have the data emailed to your inbox.

#7. Ubersuggest

Neil Patel's SEO keyword tool started as free but now includes a paid version. You have three free daily searches, after which you need to upgrade. The free version lets you see search volume, SEO difficulty (how easy or hard it would be to rank for the term), paid difficulty, and cost per click. It also gives you keyword ideas and content ideas, and for an upgrade, you can even get a full report of how many people click on organic vs. paid results on Google. There's even data on the searcher's age range, which is pretty cool.

#8. SEMrush and Ahrefs

These are popular and highly praised SEO tools that many SEO experts rely on to rank on Google. SEMrush is a robust tool that covers various aspects of SEO, not just keyword research. It offers a seven-day free trial. Ahrefs is used by prominent SEO experts like Brian Dean of Backlinko, but it comes with quite a price tag each month of a couple of hundred dollars. The good news is you can test drive it for seven days for only $7.

Best Practices for Researching Keywords

- **Focus on long-tail keywords**

These are usually 4+ word terms that searchers use in Google and other search engines. They tend to have a lower keyword difficulty than a single word or even a three-word term. Utilize Google Suggest to help you come up with long-tail keywords. For example, if I go to Google and type in "how to make ravioli," I get many valuable suggestions from Google to autocomplete, including "How to make ravioli without a pasta machine." If I wanted to rank for ravioli pasta, that would be a better strategy than going after a single keyword.

- **Don't just stop at search volume; check for trends as well**

When you start doing your keyword research, it can be easy to settle for keywords that show high search volume, but unfortunately, that can sometimes lead to a blind spot. You might pay for a keyword fading out, meaning no one will search for your term in a few months. And since search volume cannot tell you how popular the keyword is, I suggest running your chosen keywords or at least the main topic through Google Trends. If you see it rising in popularity, it will be worth all that effort to make it rank on page one.

- **Align your content with user intent**

Google's main priority is to satisfy search intent, so this one is a big deal. Learn to ride this wave, and you'll enjoy lots of traffic. How do you do this? Go back to the three types of search intent we discussed earlier in this book, i.e., informational, transactional, and navigational. Keep these in mind as you start working out your content creation and the keywords you'll go after. For example, if you want to rank for the keyword "low-carbs keto-friendly protein bars," you must realize that the intent here differs from "What is a keto diet?"

The critical point here is to create purposeful content that matches the user's intent. More on that when we talk about creating epic content.

Researching Keywords

Keyword research will make or break your SEO campaigns. They are that important in this game. The right keywords will make you money and build brand authority. The wrong ones will hurt you. There are various ways to approach keyword research. You can do it manually and follow a more traditional path or use paid tools to help you with this process. Using a tool like Google Keyword Planner is a more conventional route. You'll see examples of how to do it that way, but I'm also going to share an example of using a tool like Ubersuggest, which makes the process less daunting and takes out the guesswork.

Regardless, you must invest time and effort to find the right keywords.

If you want an incredible hack for researching and finding keywords, I have an all-in-one tool that can help - BuzzSumo. You can type in a topic, keyword, or competitor's site on the platform and get a list of the top-performing content. It's great for digging up SEO keywords and killing the guesswork of what phrases to focus on. The free version will give you primary access, and if you enjoy using it, you can sign up for the more robust features they offer, which will even help with social media marketing.

Now that you have a tool follow these steps for your keyword research.

Step one: Build a keyword list.

You will need a massive list of all the keywords you could use for your SEO campaign. Don't worry so much about competition or the cost per click. It would be best to have volume, so fire up your Google Sheets and head over to Google Keyword Planner, Ubersuggest, or both. We talked about both of these tools earlier. Google Keyword Planner is designed for Google ads, but it's also great for SEO research. I like that it's free as long as I have an active Google Ads account. You don't need to run campaigns to use this tool. Create an account and find the tab on your left titled "Keyword Planner." Enter the keyword related to your business in the "Find new keywords" field, and Google will spit out a ton of data. Only try to take some things, as some might have nothing to do with your business. Pick the keywords remotely related to your company and add them to your Google Sheets Keyword List.

The process will be the same if you use a paid tool like SEMRush or Ubersuggest. A tool like SEMRush lets you see what your competitors are already ranking for, saving you guesswork and time. If you have an existing audience to survey, consider searching in other places I've mentioned, such as Google Suggest, BuzzSumo, and SeedKeywords.

The most important thing to remember here is that you need to dig like a miner looking for gold regarding keywords. Gather as many as you can, and only then do you move to the next step.

Step Two: Identifying low-competition keywords.

Your list should be at least several hundred, even if you serve a small niche. Out of these, you will identify the ones that could be more competitive. You can use the paid version of Ubersuggest to get this data or test a free tool like MozBar for Chrome that shows you keyword competition inside the search results. It can offer you a page's Page Authority (PA) and the Domain Authority (DA). Given that every niche is different, experience will help you determine what's "low competition" in your industry. A good rule of thumb is to go for lower DA and PA. If you go for a tool like Ubersuggest, you'll get a full report of how competitive and even how hard it would be to rank for the specific keyword. This would be called keyword difficulty scores. But so that you know, Keyword Difficulty Scores are based on backlinks. So, it's good to look at that but pick the right keywords.

Step Three: Monthly Search Volume.

You need to know how many people are searching for the keywords you want to rank for. After all, what's the point in organizing if no one is searching for your keywords? You should see the average monthly searches if you return to the Google Keyword Planner, Ubersuggest, or whatever tool you used to gather the keywords. How do you determine what search volume is right to go after?

Again, there's no binary answer here. Given how different every industry is, it all depends. A B2B niche might have a monthly search volume of 25K, which would be considered high. On the other hand, an industry in B2C with the same 25K monthly search volume (like the fitness industry) would be regarded as too low. Once you know how big your industry is and what substantial search volumes look like, opt for a keyword that's considered relatively strong.

Step Four: Check for Earning Potential.

A business must make money; otherwise, it will be a business for a while. Ensure the keywords you research and pick have earning potential. Many keywords across all industries get lots of search volume and have almost no competition, but the value equals zero dollars exchanged for money. If you want an expensive hobby, go for it. But for the rest of us who have bills to pay, all this SEO effort needs to produce a good enough return on investment.

If you want to figure out whether a keyword can make you money, the Google Keyword Planner shows you "Top of page bid" so you can see how much it would cost to place your ad and get a click at the top of Google's first page. If it's a high cost, you know it's a strong keyword with high commercial intent. That's a good thing.

Another thing you need to consider is how well the chosen keyword fits your product or service offering. In other words, does it have a buyer's intent? Would that be a keyword that customers type in the search, and does it somehow relate to or tie into what you sell? For example, if you're a dentist, a keyword or phrase that goes something like "flossing tips for teens," "how to keep my teeth white," or "best toothpaste for whitening teeth" may not directly sell your services. Why? Because there's no direct intent to purchase anything. This person wants information. But the person searching is still part of your demographic, and they have shown interest in teeth maintenance and having healthy, beautiful teeth. So, if you can have excellent content for these queries, you can quickly drive traffic and leads.

Step Five: Estimate Organic Click Through Rate.

Now that you've done most of the legwork, it's time to get an estimate of actual numbers. You indeed get a lot of traffic if you rank on page one of Google, but how much traffic? Since Google uses millions of Featured Snippets to answer your query without clicking links, search volume doesn't tell you about the clicks to your site. That's why we need a little logical thinking here. Look at the SERPs first. Type your keyword and observe what happens. If you get a lot of stuff on the first page, i.e., Featured Snippets with videos, images, ads, etc. A good chunk of users will likely never click on organic results. That's not to say it's a wrong keyword. Just make sure to think it through before shortlisting it on your final keyword list.

If you're fortunate enough to have a tool like Ahrefs, then you can get that data under "Clicks," which tells you exactly how many people click on a particular keyword and how much of that was paid vs. organic. It's yet to be an exact science, but it will give you a good feel of which keywords to keep and which to shelve.

Step Six: Identify The Trending Keywords.

As you narrow down the list to the top ones that you'll go after, I also encourage you to tag the trending keywords. You can ride the wave of the right ones by determining whether a keyword is trending up or down. Google Trends is your ally. With it, you'll see precisely how each keyword performed over the last five years. You want to spot the ones that are stable or trending upwards. If you find a keyword going down, I wouldn't recommend investing the time and effort to rank for it.

Using Keywords

Research from SEOprofiler shows that over 95% of people only look at the first page of search results, and 50% of clicks go to the top three links. That's a hard truth for anyone looking to drive traffic to their site through a search engine. Keywords, as we have said, are the fundamental step to have you enjoying the fruits of showing up at the top or leading you to your demise.

So far, you've learned how to do your keyword research, and if you followed the steps outlined above, you now have a Google Spreadsheet with lots of keywords and your top, narrowed down, and intentionally picked keywords. What do you do with these? That's what I want to show you next.

- **First, you need to optimize for Page Titles.**

This is considered technical SEO, so consider yourself in the trenches of becoming an SEO expert. The page title describes the main subject of your page. You'll see it as the first line of a search result. It lets Google and searchers know what the page is about. This would be the post's headline if it's a blog post.

When writing your SEO keywords, try to place the term, phrase, or word at the start of the page title as much as possible. It makes the page appear more relevant and avoids getting cut off in mobile SERPs.

Pro Tip:

Get Yoast SEO (a WordPress plugin) to help you optimize your page and posts.

- **Second is to use it on your Meta Descriptions**

Under the main headline (usually blue on Google), you will see a description commonly referred to as a meta description. The main reason to add the keywords in a way that describes your content is to help searchers decide whether to click to see the full range. It also helps Google determine how relevant your content is, but don't mind that too much. Focus on using the right keyword and clearly describing what's in it for the searcher if they click on your website.

- **Third is URLs.**

If you want to turn off your visitors, skip this advice. URLs that run on endlessness with weird characters and strings of meaningless numbers are a big no-no for both searchers and crawling spiders. It would be best to have a URL that hints at the page's content. That helps Google connect your headline and content, and it's excellent for searchers. By integrating the primary keyword in the URL, you can describe what someone can expect, and searchers find that more appealing.

For example, which one are you more compelled to click on now? //yourdomain.com/lkjhytnamdoy29812nfg568202n165899 OR //yourdomain.com/seo-made-simple

- **The fourth way is to use it on as many subheads as your content flow allows.**

In chapter seven, we'll discuss creating SEO-friendly content, but let me remind you that subheadings are vital. They make your content easy to skim, and crawlers love finding the right keywords. Just make sure you do everything correctly.

- **The fifth place to use your keywords is in the body of the content.**

Keyword usage or overstuffing will help your SEO. Proper use will amplify your SEO. So, think of the user (your audience) when sprinkling in the keywords. It should flow and feel natural.

More on that later.

- **Sixth is tagging images with your keyword**

Most newbies must remember to label their photos before and after uploading, which wastes SEO opportunities. Google constantly indexes images. Did you know that? Make sure the file name is accurately labeled, and feel free to include LSI keywords where it makes sense. Remember to add the relevant keywords in the image title and the alt text. Regarding the alt text, don't just type in the keyword. Make it descriptive so that even people with disabilities can access your content.

A working example of how I do my keyword research using Ubersuggest.

Once in the Ubersuggest dashboard, you can type in a competitor's domain or the topic you want to rank for. On the left-hand side, it shows you a tab, "Keyword Ideas," which gives you lots of excellent information, such as the volume, cost per click, SEO difficulty, and paid problem. Unlike Google Keyword Planner, this one shows us what's popular and what people spend money on. That makes it easier for us to determine the money makers. You'll see all the websites currently ranked for that exact keyword on the right-hand side of the keyword ideas report. You'll notice each top site's estimated visits, the domain authority score, and social shares.

If you need to dig deeper to gather more keywords, consider going into Wikipedia, Quora, Amazon, or Google Keyword Planner, depending on your niche. Once you have a long enough list, it's time to focus on getting insights about your customers.

For this, you can combine Ubersuggest and Facebook Audience Insights. On Ubersuggest, under the "Keyword Ideas" tab, you'll see "Related," "Questions," and "Prepositions." The data could help you know what people are asking and searching for. Take the most appealing keywords and test whether these ideas are trending. If you find them doing well on Google Trends, that's a good signal that you should consider moving forward with that keyword.

Underneath the "Keyword Ideas" tab, you will also see "Content Ideas," which will be extremely useful when creating content. But it's also good to check it now because it helps you see the most popular articles on your chosen keyword and how many backlinks and visits the article gets from Google. With that, you can reach the final stages of finding the overlap between what your customer cares about and the keywords you want to rank for. Narrow down your list using the tactics I shared earlier, and you'll be off to the races with confidence that your keywords are the right ones.

Regarding Facebook Audience Insights, you'll need to create a Facebook Fan Page, set up your ads manager, and add a pixel to your website (check out Facebook's instructions for this), which is quick and easy. Once you connect your website with Facebook, they'll track your account's activity and give you information about the people visiting your site so you can know details such as interests. These are great for helping you get into the mind of your customer. Over time, data will add up, and you'll better understand which keywords to focus on most. But it's time to move on to the following big chunks of search engine optimization.

Chapter 5

On-Page SEO

All search engines have one thing in common. They want their users to be happy when they visit a website. They know that as long as a user is satisfied, growth and all the good things accompanying it will continue. Google has become a global giant on the back of this principle of being accurate, reliable, fast, and capable of offering the best responses to a user's query.

That said, the only way Google would know how happy your site makes users is based on how engaged a searcher is when they land on your webpage. How long do they hang around and invest time reading your content? That is where on-page SEO comes in. This chapter offers a crash course to make your optimization easier.

What Is On-page SEO?

On-page SEO is optimizing particular web pages so search engines, especially Google, can rank that specific page higher. Some experts might call this on-site SEO. As discussed in the previous chapter, it includes optimizing title tags, content, URLs, and more. An excellent way to look at this from a fifty-foot view, so you stay calm, is that on-page SEO has three big chunks. Namely, Content, HTML, and Architecture. It's our job to break them into digestible chunks so you can immediately execute them.

Content - is extremely important because, with excellent content, everything else you do will matter. Google and other search engines exist to serve users. Your content should help these search engines meet that end. Within scope, you need to become aware of things like Keyword research, user intent, customer persona, buyer's journey, the quality of your content, and how fresh and up-to-date that content is.

HTML - you must consider title tags, meta description, schema, and subheadings.

Architecture - the main focus is UX experience for users, link building, and proper organization so that it's easy for crawlers to understand your page. It's also about having a mobile-friendly site because most searches are on mobile. If you can focus on getting these things right, you will win with SEO. Let's break them down further and discuss the ranking factors.

On-Page SEO Factors

Although we started mentioning the main factors in the previous chapter, there's still much to learn if you want your on-page SEO to yield results. In addition to the page title tags, subheads, URLs, images, and body content I mentioned, you need to optimize your content for search intent. You must check page loading speed, bounce rate and dwell time, click-through rate, and user experience.

Time to get practical:

- **Optimize page speed**

If your page takes too long to load, you'll kill your conversion rates and ultimately lose traffic and ranking. Research shows that for every additional 0.5 it takes to load your site, you significantly increase the number of people who abandon it.

Use tools like Google PageSpeed Insights to check your current page and receive insights on improving. You can also use Ubersuggest's site audit tool to show you the loading time for both mobiles and desktops. The tool additionally gives you the speed index, time to interact, first contentful Paint, estimated Input Latency, somewhat meaningful Paint, and first CPU Idle.

If your site is slow, there are many ways to increase site speed, including using search engine content delivery networks. That costs a lot of money, so before opting for that paid solution, consider checking your plugins and deleting those that suck your speed.

- **Use the targeted keyword in the first one hundred words.**

Yes, it has to be at the beginning of your content. Preferably in the first paragraph between the first 100-150 words. That helps Google understand what your page is about.

- **The blog post title should always be in H1**

The H1 tag is like a mini title tag that helps Google understand the page's structure. If you have a WordPress site, the blog post title is automatically H1, but if you're working with any other platform, I recommend double-checking to ensure this is the default. Remember, only one H1 title tag is needed if you're working with HTML5.

- **Make your subheadings H2.**

You don't need to make all subheadings the H2 tag, but I recommend that at least a couple of them be tagged H2. There needs to be objective evidence from Google that this helps your content rank, but this is a best practice based on our understanding of content architecture and how crawlers work.

- **Keyword sprinkling**

When optimizing your page, I suggest using a frequency of between five and ten. Stay moderate with keyword stuffing because the content is for humans at the end of the day, and the keywords are for the crawlers. They only need a little to get the hint and determine the core topic. Most experts recommend between six and twelve times. If it flows naturally, repeat the primary keyword as you see fit.

- **URLs optimization**

URLs have become even more critical. URLs now appear above the title tag on mobile and desktop SERPs, so here's how to optimize for this new change. Keep the URL short, and include the main keyword in every URL.

- **HTTPS and SSL**

Most experts say having a secure site helps you rank better. From what I've seen, Google actively issues a warning sign when people land on a website that's not secure, so I encourage you to get an SSL certificate immediately. If you will work so hard to build a site that ranks, why risk getting this red flag? I suggest activating either HTTPS (a secure version of HTTP) or SSL (Secure Socket Layer) protocol. If you have a new site, ask your domain registrar or web hosting service to add it to your purchase. Otherwise, it's a process if you are trying to move an old site.

There's a variety of options depending on your needs. Single Domain only works with one Domain. It won't, however, serve for subdomains in case you plan on creating that. As the name suggests, Multi-Domain works for multiple standalone domains but won't work for these individual sites' subdomains. The wildcard is another option you have, and this one will cover subdomains as well, so it's highly recommended for someone with an eCommerce store and a website. Extended comes with the bonus of showing in the green address bar, but you should know that setting it up requires some extra work.

- **Description tags and title tags**

According to Google, Title tags still help determine your ranking. That's why we insist on having your keyword as close to the beginning of the title as possible. Sometimes, this may not be possible, and that's okay. Just bear in mind that the closer it is, the better. The ideal length is between 50 and 60 characters, so Google doesn't cut it off. Moz has a preview tool to help you see how your title tags will appear in the search engine.

I also want you to use modifiers like "fast," "best," "review," or "cheat sheet," as that can help you rank for longtail versions of your target keyword.

Regarding meta description, stick to 160 characters, focusing on using synonyms or LSI (latent semantic indexing) to describe the content.

A simple formula for your meta description:

Even though Google can override meta descriptions with their snippet, they still recommend writing your own. Why? Because we tend to see a boost in organic click-through rate when the meta description is compelling. Here's a template adapted from Backlinko that you can copy to ease this process:

This is a (give an overview). Learn how to get (name particular benefit) from this (content description).

Example. This is a step-by-step guide to a successful keto diet. Learn how to shed body fat fast and get your six-pack abs in time for summer with this comprehensive seven-day course.

- **User experience**

The last thing I want to mention for on-page optimization is that it's all about the user experience. Your website should be human-focused. So, you need to present your content and designs in a manner that appeals to people. Make sure duplicate content is No-Indexed for the crawlers and the content on the page is easy on the eyes and well developed. Keywords should not appear spammy, and your content should serve a purpose. Focus on adding value to the user who clicks on your webpage—have you ever heard of Brian Clark? He's a name worth Googling. He founded the now-famous Copyblogger.com platform. Once upon a time, it was just a simple blog. Today, it's a seven-million-dollar digital company, and how did he do it? By producing the best content with a clear SEO strategy. You can do the same as long as you remember that Google relies on you to deliver valuable content that users will be excited about.

Internal Linking

That would be considered internal linking when you hyperlink a word or phrase and link it back to a page or post hosted within your Domain. In contrast, we also have external linking (links that go out to other pages on other domains). Internal linking helps Google understand your site better, and it helps build page authority when used strategically. It will help your audience navigate your site better and receive more value on a topic they're already interested in.

To use internal linking to boost your ranking, always use keyword-rich anchor text. What do I mean by this? If I am writing about the Keto dict and how to start correctly (a Keto Guide), I can hyperlink the words "simple keto recipes for breakfast" and point it to a new page titled "keto recipes for breakfast meals that keep you in ketosis." The line between nailing this and getting penalized by Google is relatively thin, so I encourage you to only link to important pages. To determine which pages, get a tool like Moz Pro or Ahrefs and type in your Domain. Let the device show you the pages that have the most link authority. These are the pages you need to link to through keyword-rich anchor texts. Going back to the example of the page "Keto recipes for breakfast meals that keep you in ketosis," I would only use that in my newly created Keto Guide to boost this since I know that that other page has high link authority.

Where do you put your internal links? The higher up your page, the better. It works well because it gives people something to click on, leading to more time spent on your site. If you can link to multiple pages, use different anchor texts to avoid confusing the crawlers. Also, double-check to ensure these links all do-follow links so you can have PageRank.

It would be best to use internal linking to organize and build up your site's architecture, connect orphan pages to fresh new pages to continue getting indexed, and use it to drive authority from your homepage to your blog posts.

Bonus tip:

Google Search Console has a nifty " links " feature that shows all internal links' states and where they point.

Chapter 6

Off-Page SEO

Off-page SEO is the next big puzzle necessary to help you rank high on Google.

What Is Off-page SEO?

It's all the activities necessary to improve your search engine rankings that take place outside of your website. Think about it for a minute. On-page is about site structure, content creation, keyword research, site speed, and so on—basically, things you do on the pages you want to rank. Off-site is what you do outside of those pages (outside of your website) with the same intention of increasing your rankings. So, what kinds of activities would this include? Most people assume link building is what off-page SEO is about, but that's just a single aspect. With a bit of strategy, things like guest blogging, commenting on other blogs, and social networking can all be tactics for off-page SEO.

Why off-page SEO matters:

Building backlinks is at the heart of all your off-page SEO efforts, and this is important to search engines like Google because they view this as a signal that indicates you have high-quality content. Therefore, a site with many valuable backlinks will usually rank better than one without. Please pay attention to my word choice here. I specifically said, "valuable backlinks." All backlinks are not made equal, and mature search engines like Google are smart enough to know this. Let's educate you on the types of links you want and some mistakes you must avoid when doing your link-building strategy.

What to know before you start link building

There are three main types of backlinks: Natural links, manually built links, and self-created links. As the names suggest, natural links are editorially given without any action on your part. This would happen if another blogger in your niche found your content excellent and added a link to their article or video that points back to your site. These are great, but not that easy to come by, and you need control over when this would happen.

Manually created links are all based on your efforts. If you hustle and work with a good strategy, you can make deliberate links (*don't worry, I will share hacks for this later on*). Last but not least, self-created links also require your initiative. You're getting a forum, a press release, an online directory, or even adding a signature when you comment on other blogs online, leading back to your site. This one is usually frowned upon because it's considered black hat SEO, so I would tread cautiously.

You can build backlinks and contribute to your SEO rankings through these three approaches. But do you recall I said not all links are made equal? That's because search engines like Google generally look for specific indicators to determine how valuable a link is. They check the linking site's popularity, trustworthiness, and authority. Relevancy is also essential, i.e., how does your site relate to that external website, and is the linked topic relevant or related to your page? They check the anchor text used on the linking site and how fresh the link is. That's why you need to do some initial prep work and develop a link-building strategy to get only the suitable backlinks.

Best Practices For Backlink Building

• Start with the pages that are optimized for SEO. That means you've done your internal link building, content optimization, and page layout as specified in previous chapters. An excellent way to ensure your design is set correctly is to have silo pages that connect to your category pages and supporting pages/posts. By organizing your site like this, each link will pass SEO juice to the other interconnected pages.

• Make sure your on-page SEO is on point. Implementing everything discussed in the previous chapter before building backlinks would be best because they all come together to give you a greater reward. For example, if your keyword is lacking, Google won't know what to rank you for. So, all your backlinking efforts will be in vain. To avoid this, make sure your on-page SEO and technical SEO are optimized.

- **Create useful Infographics**

If you have the budget, I encourage you to create infographics hosted on your site that can be embedded into other sites. Neil Patel reported that his infographics generate 35.7% more backlinks than standard blog posts. These infographics need to be visually appealing and rich in value. Statistics from your industry, data, and other intriguing findings work exceptionally well but feel free to get creative with the content.

Suppose you need to find a way to hire a graphic designer. In that case, you can create something beautiful in Canva or check out gifographic, which uses the infographic model while featuring GIFs to make it more interactive.

- **Guest post strategically**

The best way to succeed with this tactic is to keep the long view and prepare to guest post at least five times a week for a minimum of a year. Those who have seen the best results are often in the B2B space, but you can try your hand at this even if you're in the B2C space. However, random guest posts will yield little results and won't help build domain authority or ranking on Google. To do it right, devise a long-term plan and build relationships with suitable sites.

- **Leverage social media**

The more active you are on social media, the better. You can drive traffic to your site, improve your rankings, and build brand authority by being social and engaging. Most people don't see the connection between SEO and social media, so in Chapter 11, we will discuss how to bridge the two to make it work. The main thing to do now is to check your social media profiles and ensure they all link to the site you want to rank for.

Other Off-Page Factors

- **Brand searches and mentions**

Even seasoned SEOs often overlook this tactic, yet Google has openly stated they care about promoting legitimate brands. The more of a brand you build, the higher authority you'll receive. As a new website, you won't have any mentions or people searching for your brand, so first, you must build this up. Then, you can use a tool like Google Search Console to monitor performance over the next year. The report will show you Clicks and Impressions. The Impressions tell you how many people have searched for your brand name over time. If you have an existing website, you can do that now to see where you stand and what to improve over the next few months.

If you want a great hack to help grow your brand search, leverage YouTube. Given that it's a massive search engine (Google Search + YouTube = over 90% market domination), using videos can help you get in front of many people. And as more people interact with and talk about your brand online, Google will pick that up. I noticed with YouTube (which is why I wrote a book on YouTube marketing) that when people get used to receiving value from your videos, they will search for your brand on Google.

You can also set up brand tracking using tools like Mention.com or an alert feature on Google and BuzzSumo so that you can follow up each time someone tags or talks about you in any way. That interaction sends signals to Google that your brand is a big deal.

- **NAP citations**

Name, Address, and Phone citations, collectively NAP citations, impact your off-page SEO. Moz reports that they affect local businesses the most and can help boost your ranking.

One neat trick to help you find the best places to add citations is to use a tool like Whitespark or Ahref's Link Intersection tool. It will look for websites that link to multiple competitors but not you. That helps you know what your competitors have that you don't and the best place to push for those citations. As I said, this is perfect for local SEO, and if you want to dive deeper, check out the recommended extra resource on how to crack local SEO.

Off-Page SEO Techniques

#1. Do an outreach campaign to collaborate with more prominent brands in your space.

That will require some upfront work, and you need to have some legit value to offer. However, it can be gratifying and help you develop relationships that continue to drive traffic for years to come. You can create a piece of high-value content or offer your product or service in some way to the brand that you want to collaborate with. In return, they can do a brand mention and backlink. For example, if you're a marketer, you can reach out to a brand with many social media followers and blog readers and offer to create an infographic. Make sure it's a value that they will appreciate. If they say yes, they might add your logo and give you a mention as they promote it to their audience. It can't be improved for a new website or someone building online authority. That becomes a huge credibility booster.

#2. Get Positive Reviews

If you run a local business, this is a no-brainer. But even if you're entirely online, getting positive reviews and ratings will help because that signals to Google that you are an authentic and trustworthy brand that people love. If people love you, Google will love you too. If you're in a space where reviews aren't irrelevant, consider going after awards. It shows Google how other experts feel about your website. You can get recommendations from professional societies, media, etc. This shows strong evidence of a positive reputation and positively impacts your E-A-T in the eyes of Google.

#3. Get Interviewed

Podcasts are a great way to gain exposure and boost your off-page SEO. If you can't get into a podcast, consider being interviewed on other websites. But I highly recommend podcasts, especially those with many listeners and monthly downloads. But don't just scour the Internet for any podcast show. Focus on the ones that relate in some way to your niche and your product or service to create that congruency with the backlinks and mentions.

#4. Press Release

A little good PR done the right way can help boost your SEO. Great Press Releases can lead to brand mentions and backlinks. Just make sure you have something newsworthy to share.

CHAPTER 7

Content Marketing For SEO

One of my favorite SEO components is content marketing, which this section will focus on. I want to ensure you know how to crank out content like the pros, even if you're a one-person/woman show.

Do you know what content marketing is or why it's vital for SEO?

A definition I like when explaining content marketing comes from Content Marketing Institute (you should bookmark their website), which goes like this. "Content marketing is a strategic approach focused on creating and distributing valuable, relevant, and consistent content to attract and retain a clearly-defined audience - and ultimately, to drive profitable customer action."

Pay close attention to some key ideas, such as valuable, relevant, and consistent. Why? Suppose you commit to something other than consistently producing content that you know is relevant and useful to your ideal target audience. In that case, you won't do content marketing right and fail at SEO. So, how do you become consistent? You need to start with a process that enables you to be consistent. Content marketing is gaining more interest among our population. With over a billion blogs published online, there's enough proof that content marketing works, and people want more.

But what makes content marketing for business owners important? We know it creates better brand awareness and builds authority and trust as you educate your audience. That ultimately drives lead generation because the more people know, like, and trust you, the easier it becomes to do business with you. Content marketing converts six times better for those who do it well than other marketing channels. And since we know that 27% of U.S. users are using ad blockers, content marketing is a great option to attract more of that audience that would otherwise never see your brand through paid ads. While all these statistics help me to know and make a solid case, let me share why I got into content marketing for SEO.

After establishing a decent following on the social media platforms relevant to me and my ideal customer persona, I returned to content marketing for SEO because I realized that my less-than-deep pockets wouldn't make a dent in competing against some of the more prominent brands in my location. But by adopting content marketing as the backbone of my marketing, I could go up against anyone and still win. I also realized something else. The bridge that could connect social media and SEO was none other than content marketing.

By prioritizing content marketing, I can leverage social media to boost my search ranking. It has become the perfect solution for me, and I currently see three times higher quality leads than my paid search advertising methods. When it comes to winning with SEO, take your content marketing seriously. Commit to a consistent plan and borrow the framework I share in this chapter, and you'll do well.

How to make the most of your content

If you want to maximize the ROI of your content, you need to begin with a good content strategy. A content strategy will help you streamline your workflow by defining the topics to be created, writing style, formats, design, and promotion beforehand. What makes this work is that you find that overlap between what your audience wants to read, listen to, or watch in your niche and the keywords you wish your website to rank for. Then, with some creativity and planning, map out the actual topics. Once you know what you want to create, decide what category or types of SEO content you'll make. They can include product pages, blog articles, guides, videos, infographics, slideshows, and more.

If you want to get the most out of the content you create, begin with a plan. Develop a content strategy. Here are a few things to consider.

- **You need to define your goals.**

The overall business goals should be clearly outlined by now, and you should also have your keyword goals nearby. Notice the dominant theme in your plans. Is it more sales? Do you want to monetize your blog? Are you looking to build brand awareness or nurture your existing prospects and clients? Whatever the main goals are, your content should be adopted to help you achieve those goals. For example, if you're an eCommerce primarily focused on driving product sales, your primary focus is creating informative product pages optimized for search and conversions. The keywords chosen should have strong commercial intent. You can also have a secondary focus on producing blog content that educates your audience and demonstrates when and how to use your products. Using tactics like internal linking, you can lead people to the product page from the blog post. See where I'm going with this?

So, consider your niche and map out the best type of content and how to align it with keywords and business objectives. As you do this, pay attention to what your audience cares about for a minute. Remember, if you create content that search engines love, but your audience doesn't resonate with, you won't win because people need to engage with your content. No one will find you if you create content your audience loves, but it must be optimized for search. It still needs to be the right approach. That balance is fundamental to your success.

- **Create an editorial calendar**

You need a calendar that helps you schedule your content to create consistency. Make it a regular schedule, mainly if you're producing blog posts. Use Google Calendar, Outlook, or even a third-party software like CoSchedule to help you set up a calendar you and your team can work on. If you're a solopreneur, Asana is excellent to help pace your content creation and publication. How far out should you plan? Unless you're a big team with lots of workflows and time needed, something sustainable, like two weeks ahead. Besides, the Internet changes so much that you want to save time planning for the next year if all your content is evergreen.

- **Set up analysis, tracking, and monitoring**

If you want your SEO to work, you must monitor performance regularly. Tools like Ahrefs and Moz can help you track and watch all kinds of metrics because they have plenty of bells and whistles. But even Google Search Console is a great starting point. Here, you can measure your site's performance and traffic. It will help you see how your on-page SEO is going. Still, you want to understand everything, including off-page SEO. In that case, you'll need a paid tool like SEMRush or Ubersuggest to keep track of other vital factors like social media engagement (which does affect your ranking), among other things.

The best part about having a content strategy is that you document all your tactics and efforts, which helps you figure out what works and what doesn't. As you find what works, focus on doing more of what works.

Writing for SEO

SEO writing is a perfect marriage made in heaven where valuable content targeted to your customers gets combined with on-page SEO techniques, which you learned in a previous chapter. The result is simple. People find your content appealing, keep coming back to your site, share the content, and Google algorithms love you because they can easily understand and index the content. That naturally builds your authority with Google and enables you to rank high. If you want to develop this skill of SEO writing, here are the various aspects to develop. We already discussed some of these, but I want you to know how the different SEO components align to create a well-oiled machine.

- **Headline**

"On average," David Ogilvy said, "five times as many people read the headlines as read the body copy. When you have written your headline, you have spent eighty cents out of your dollar". Think about that whenever you choose your headline, even if you only do organic content marketing. Regarding SEO, writing the headline is extremely important because it needs to grab attention and prompt the user to click and read further. Copywriters charge lots of money for this service because they've practiced and written thousands of headlines. So, don't worry if, at first, your headlines suck. The more you practice, the better you will become. Remember to use your primary keyword when crafting your headline as early as possible. I also encourage you to use a good like CoSchedule's Headline Analyzer to help you create fantastic titles.

Tip:

According to a survey done by Conversion XL, using a headline with numbers will increase your chances of appealing to both the Google algorithm and your target audience. I found a report that said 3 out of 5 post headlines on Lifehack's website (which is well-known) use numbers. Websites like Inc Magazine, Business Weekly, and Mashable regularly use numbers for their headlines.

Example headlines:

Ten steps to losing belly fat before summer.

There are 20 ways to make money from your couch with a laptop only and no prior experience.

- **Content**

The entire game of SEO lies in your ability to produce content people want. Think about it for a moment. We all go to a search engine because we want something. We are either looking to learn more about a product or need information about a place, service, or topic.

It would be best to keep this in mind when crafting your content. Aside from appealing to humans, you also need to know that search engines love fresh content. So, ranking on search is an inevitable by-product when you do your part right. What I've learned when it comes to creating SEO-friendly content is that keyword stuffing is a no-go that will only harm your site. Longtail keywords are the best, and whatever keyword you choose, make sure it flows within the content and reads smoothly. A standard length for a blog post should be 1000 words, and whether you create an article or a video, make sure it's rich in value. The only way to make it prosperous is to understand your audience so you can solve specific problems you feel confident they care about. Usually, I break down my written content into an introduction with a hook, the main body, and a conclusion. I include my longtail and related keywords in the subheadings and throughout the content as appropriate. In other words, when I'm done writing, I read it and ask myself whether I would enjoy reading that content if I bumped into it on the Internet.

- **Keyword Frequency**

Piggybacking on what we just discussed, let's emphasize the importance of deliberately using any chosen keyword a specific number of times. Why? If you come across as spammy, Google will penalize your content. Brian Dean says the only way to tell if your repetition of keywords is super or spammy is to measure that frequency against your content's overall length. A keyword density greater than 5.5% could make you guilty of keyword stuffing, and Google could penalize your page.

I recommend activating Yoast within your WordPress backend so that you can see how your SEO will rank based on the quality of content and keywords for that particular post.

- **Meta Description**

We previously described what meta descriptions are and some best practices for them. Since we know that Google uses meta description on your page as a snippet when people type keywords relevant to your page, writing out this copy before publishing the content is crucial. What shows up on that snippet copy will determine whether you get clicks. If you ranked #2 or #5 on page one with a fantastic headline title and a highly appealing meta description, you would get abundant traffic to your page even though you're not ranking first. This is why meta descriptions matter. Stick to creating between 150-160 characters to appear fully on Google search. A tool like Yoast can help you stay within the green zone when writing this copy, but you can also get the All-In-One SEO pack plugin if that's your preference. They both do an excellent job with this.

Tip:

When it comes to writing fantastic meta descriptions, remember what your keyword intent was and make sure to communicate that. Be concise, and let the reader know what your page is about and how they will benefit by clicking on your link. Never use duplicate meta descriptions, and do not stuff keywords here. One is more than enough.

- **Site Speed**

Site speed matters regarding SEO writing because people today want instant gratification. If the headline is great and a user clicks, but the page loads quickly, the chances of abandoning your site are extremely high. Although this has nothing to do with writing, it will impact how well your site performs and ranks.

Tip:

If you already have a website and notice load time takes too long, consider deleting old plugins and unnecessary data. You should also check if your image file size is optimum and use the right plugins to help compress photos. Speeding up your site's load time will improve your conversions by up to 7%.

Learn Semantic SEO

Search engines have evolved tremendously in the last decade, going from clunky things that only work if keywords are stuffed on a piece of content to extremely intuitive algorithms that determine what you mean when you type. This is commonly referred to as semantic search. Plainly stated, it is an information retrieval process used by almost all modern search engines that give you relevant results based on search queries instead of the conventional way of keyword matching. Why should this matter to you? Because users often type in their questions in language, you may only sometimes predict, and it's common for them to use words different than your targeted keyword even though they want what you have to offer.

Let me ask you. Have you ever fired up your desktop, opened up Google, and then stared at the search bar, wondering how to frame your question or what words to use to get the desired results? It happens a lot to me, so other users must often experience the same. The best they can do is type in what they think might be the best articulation of their query. Now that we've entered the era of voice, semantic search is becoming even more common as people ask Siri, Alexa, and Google Assistant to find answers based on a long-winded conversational style question. The number of ways to express a problem or search for something continues to increase, so more than traditional keywords will be needed to cut it moving forward. That's why understanding semantic search is super beneficial. So, when a user searches for Apple, Google must know whether the user wants to learn about the fruit or the company.

Context becomes super essential when it comes to semantics and the meaning of words. Since 40% of English words are polysemous (more than two meanings), you can see why semantics have become an essential SEO element.

Over the last decade, Google has done an incredible job of understanding lexical hierarchy, entity relationships, personal interests, and trends. It uses the data from your online activities to determine what you mean. So, if you're a computer programmer and type in "Python," it would understand you mean the programming language, not the snake. Google's ability to temporarily adjust search results based on dynamically changing search intent is fascinating. For example, as Coronavirus grew in popularity in 2020 (even though it's a term that had been around long before that), Google's SERP quickly adjusted to match the new demands and offer the most relevant and up-to-date information.

Similar things occur during global events like Christmas, World Cup, or even big sales like Black Friday. These events' intent is dynamic, and Google knows how to adjust accordingly to provide the most relevant results. But how does it all work?

It comes down to these critical aspects: the hummingbird algorithm, which was introduced in 2013, RankBrain, Bert, and Knowledge Graph.

Google's Knowledge Graph was released in 2012 and helped kickstart the era of semantic search. There are two main methods of feeding it. The first is structured data, and the second is entity extraction from text. Therefore, natural language and the ability to understand context became paramount, and that's where Hummingbird and the rest of the updates come into play.

Before Hummingbird, Google relied almost 100% on keywords. That all changed when they developed this smart little birdy to analyze the entire content piece and understand the context, similar to how a human would.

RankBrain is Google's solution to solving a problem that even Latent Semantic Indexing (LSI) cannot solve because it's powered by superior technologies that enable it to understand the meaning of unfamiliar words and phrases. Through the use of highly sophisticated machine learning algorithms, RankBrain can understand both familiar and unfamiliar terms.

BERT is short for Bidirectional Encoder Representations from Transformers. Yes, it's a mouthful and sounds super complicated. It has affected approximately 10% of all search queries since the end of 2022 and is considered the latest upgrade for semantic search. The most important thing to know about BERT is that it is the solution for understanding long and complex queries. It strives to deal with ambiguity and better understand the context when a user types a complex sentence.

Best Practices for Semantic Search Engine Optimization

Some of these technologies are so advanced and sophisticated that it's hard to pinpoint one specific thing you can do to make it work in your favor. For example, BERT is excellent to know about, even though you can't optimize your content in any way for it. But I do encourage you to publish "topically relevant" content. That means, instead of just writing an article about the paleo diet and then moving on to intermittent fasting, it's better to go in-depth with paleo. Write a complete guide and long-form posts covering everything possible around paleo. What am I saying here? Instead of putting all your energy into keywords, target a specific topic.

Another thing you can do, albeit it might be a bit technical, is to use HTML5 because that gives you the most semantic elements to work with for your website. That makes it easier for the crawlers to recognize navigation blocks, headers, footers, tables, and videos. You can also use schema markup or structured data, which is a common framework for the web. Head over to Schema.org vocabulary, where you'll find hundreds of options that you can use to markup your content in a way that's easy for Google to understand.

One last tip I will give you is to maximize your internal and external linking strategy. Remember to use natural anchor text to help Google figure out what your content might be about even before processing it.

Rich And Featured Snippets

There was a time when all you needed to focus on was being part of the ten blue links on page one of Google, and you'd have a ton of traffic. Those days are long gone. Nowadays, besides working hard to rank first organically, you must contend with Featured Snippets. These snippets appear at the top of the page, becoming a critical aspect of SEO. You may have also heard of rich snippets that confuse a newbie. These snippets have lots of information depending on your niche and the information you provide, including images, URLs, and maybe even a carousel. Rich snippets tend to have a higher click-through rate than regular snippets, which usually have no photos.

Featured Snippets are there to answer user's questions instantly. That's why more and more people call them "answer boxes." The good news is that if you can get featured, you'll experience a lot more traffic because you'll likely rank twice on the same page. The three types of featured snippets you can aim for are paragraphs (give the answer in text form only or with an image as well), lists (answers in the form of a list), and tables (provide the solution in the form of a table). According to Getstat, the most popular featured snippet is "paragraph" snippets covering 81.95%. The paragraph snippet usually adds a URL, exposing the site being sourced for information.

You might ask yourself, How do I get a featured snippet?" We know that over ninety-nine percent of featured snippets already rank in the top ten of Google. The better you optimize, the higher your chances of getting featured. It's essential to go for content that big sites like Wikipedia.org still need to grab, as the competition would be hard to beat. And if you're creating content in finance, mathematics, health, and DIY processes, getting featured will be more straightforward. The better your page ranks and the more authoritative your site, the higher your chances of being featured at the top, e even if you don't rank #1.

Use LSI Keywords

The topic of Latent Semantic Indexing (LSI) is widely controversial even today. Some experts claim you need to learn and use it, while Google openly states that it doesn't use it. What is LSI? It's a technology developed in the 1980s, even before the creation of the World Wide Web as a natural language processing technique for large documents. Knowing how it works is far too complicated unless you understand mathematical concepts (which I don't), so let's not bother ourselves with such things. Instead, let's focus on best practices.

Given that LSI was created to index document collections and used to be a patented technology until 2008, owned by Bell Communications Research Inc., it's safe to say Google doesn't rely on LSI as much as most people think, mainly because of RankBrain. We also know Google has indexed synonyms and other meanings since early 2003, so overusing LSI is optional. However, I still encourage you to use synonyms and related words in your content. Google has become wise when it comes to understanding context and overall topics on any given page. Using cars and automobiles in the same article can tell your intention. Therefore, the best thing you can do is to find words and phrases that are naturally related. For example, if you write an article for your flower shop, you want to add roses, orchids, flower set-up, wedding set-up, bouquet arrangement, and all other related words that a user might type. If you specialize in specific flowers, include those in your content.

An excellent place to find synonyms of phrases you can use is to type in the desired keyword and watch for any autocomplete suggestions. You should also check the bottom of the page for "searches related to X" (your chosen keyword). You can also use an LSI keyword tool, and last but not least, use common sense.

Tip:

Check out knowledge bases like Wikidata.org and Wikipedia, which often have many related terms. If you go into Google's knowledge graph, you can also figure out what words to add to your content by reverse-engineering the results you get. This is especially useful for niches with Knowledge Graphs and Featured Snippets. What I strongly urge you to avoid is getting too sucked into LSI. Instead, recognize that search engines are working hard to become more human-centric. They want to understand how humans communicate and deliver results based on that, so semantically related words, phrases, and entities are far better long-term than chasing after a technology like LSI, which is bound to be obsolete anyway due to its current limitations.

Chapter 8

SEO For Your Website

Before you can apply search engine optimization, you need a website that is well-designed and beautifully structured. That's where web design and web architecture come into play. Web development is a massive umbrella that encompasses web design.

What Is Web Design?

The process of creating a website that includes the webpage layout, content production, and graphic designing. The primary markup language used to design a website is HTML. Web designers use HTML to code all the elements on the site (Headers, buttons, footer, images, etc.), and CSS is used to style those elements (for example, changing the font or making the header blue).

Another critical aspect to consider when designing your site is architecture. Keep things as simple as possible to make it easy for users and crawlers to navigate your site. Why? It would be best to optimize your website's architecture so search engine spiders can find and index all the pages you want. And if you have essential pages several clicks away from your homepage, they'll likely need to be indexed. Link authority flows around your website when the site's architecture is good, improving Google rankings.

There are two ways to build out your site. You can use flat architecture or deep architecture. As the names suggest, flat is the easier one and what I most recommend. In this case, you'd have up to four clicks to reach any of the essential pages on your site. Deep architecture, on the other hand, can have up to ten clicks. Having fewer steps and linking all the main category pages to your homepage will maximize your juice, especially if you have backlinks from authority sites. That's not to say that you cannot have multiple pages. You only need to use your category pages wisely. This is especially true for large websites such as eCommerce sites, which often require many pages.

Is SEO Ideal for Web Design?

Web design and SEO must work hand in hand if you want to win this game. A good web designer should already factor in that you care about SEO, and they should integrate many of the things discussed, such as using the correct HTML, using flat architecture, etc., as they design and create your website. If the web designer makes you the most beautiful-looking website but makes it too difficult for the crawlers to navigate and index your site, you won't succeed. You need a website that's both human-centric with a pleasant user experience and search-engine friendly.

Applying SEO On The Web

These are the best practices for applying SEO to your website. We previously mentioned some of the best techniques, such as creating robots.txt files, working on your site speed to increase loading time, and using title tags and links with rich anchor texts. If you need to, re-read those topics to see how to apply them to your website. Aside from that, you can also use the following.

- **Build Site maps**

Create a sitemap for your website to help search engines find, crawl, and index your website's content faster. You will need a normal XML sitemap that links to different pages on your website, a video sitemap that helps Google understand the videos on your website, and an image Sitemap that points to all the images hosted on your site. If appropriate, you should also get a news sitemap if your website has been approved for Google News. Using WordPress, you can easily create your XML sitemap within the Yoast SEO plugin, which will update automatically. You can also use other plugins like Google XML sitemaps, which do the same job. If you are among those not using a WordPress backend, use a third-party tool like XML-Sitemaps.com to generate a file you can use as your sitemap. You'll need to submit the sitemap to Google, so head over to your Google Search Console and look for the tab on the left-hand side. Sitemaps are great for helping you find problems with indexing. Once it's up and running, you can see what's being indexed and what isn't. Then, you can decide what pages to work on to get them indexed and which to remove entirely.

Google and Bing allow up to 50MB sitemaps, so stay within that range. You could also use a Video Schema instead for video sitemaps.

- **Avoid duplicate content**

Duplicate content harms your SEO. It can be word-for-word identical or even rewritten to appear different, but given everything you've learned about Hummingbird and RankBrain, it should be evident that Google will figure you out. Google loves fresh, unique content, so if you want more organic traffic and indexed pages, you'll check that no duplicate content (including meta descriptions) exists on your website.

If you're building an eCommerce site, it's easy to fall into this trap because you might end up having the same content on different URLs. This is not a good thing. To avoid getting penalized, ensure all the product content is on a single page. Be mindful of your site's architecture to avoid creating duplicate content that confuses the crawlers. How do you quickly fix this?

With 301 redirects. You could delete the unnecessary pages if that works for you. Otherwise, use a 301 to redirect them back to the original. What's vital here is that Google crawlers must understand which page is the "original" one. When the crawling spider comes across your duplicate content with a 301, it will stop and only index the original content, which will help your ranking.

What if you have similar content?

Since Google can often view similar content as duplicate, instead of blocking the pages, use a canonical tag, which tells the search engine that you have a bunch of similar content. The page with the canonical tag is original; the rest should be ignored.

If you want to know whether your website has duplicate pages, you can use tools such as Siteliner, which scans your website and tells you where the exact content might be.

Bonus tip:

I suggest combining duplicate content into something epic when fixing it. This is applicable if the content is similar. Combining them lets you create something in-depth and unique, which might help you get indexed and ranked better.

Chapter 9

White Hat Vs. Black Hat SEO

The strategies used to help your site rank high on a search engine can often be divided into two - black and white hat SEO. While building your SEO, you must know whether you're following a black-hat or white-hat SEO strategy. Why does this matter? Sooner rather than later, there will be consequences, and most of the time, black hat SEO never ends well. Even big names in SEO, like Neil Patel, share horror stories of how he got banned by Google for using black hat SEO strategies. Although it worked for a little while and made some money, the whole thing could have been more short-lived. So, I will share tactics known to work for both of these strategies, but be careful if you choose to go black. Before sharing those hacks, let's talk about the main difference between the two. What is white hat SEO and black hat SEO?

White Hat SEO

White hate SEO strategy is focused on optimizing for both humans and search engines. It's about following the guidelines and best practices that lead to long-term success on search engines.

What would white SEO focus on?

That would include creating quality content, optimizing for mobile, creating a great user experience, doing keyword research effectively, using a schema, and doing effective link building. It's also about creating unique and relevant page titles and well-labeled images.

As we said at the start of this book, there's no quick win or instant gratification in search engine optimization unless you tread in dangerous waters and want to enter black hat land.

Black Hat SEO

Black hat SEO is concerned about ranking fast on Google at whatever cost. The only thing this strategy focuses on is winning the crawling spiders over and getting to rank your website high in the shortest timeframe possible. Usually, that involves breaking many rules and doing fishy stuff. Neil Patel shares how he used to buy WordPress Themes to rank high for the keyword "Webhosting" even though he doesn't deal with web hosting. This is an excellent example of black hat SEO. Sure, he made money through affiliate marketing, but ultimately, Google caught up and banned him.

So, what are some black hat SEO tactics?

They include keyword stuffing, hidden texts or links, cloaking, sneaky redirects, link manipulation, doorway pages, content automation, article spinning, rich snippet markup spam, pages with malicious behavior such as phishing, viruses, trojans, and other malware, creating pages, subdomains or domains with duplicate content.

Choosing Between The Two

Let's remember one thing before we discard all black-hat SEO as evil. It works! In truth, while there are some shady, unlawful aspects of black hat, the fundamental understanding you need to have is that black hat is merely a good strategy gone wrong. It's only an unhealthy exaggeration of a white hat. If you choose a great topic and keyword to focus on, that's great. Sprinkle it in moderation across your content and have it in all the right places, and we call you a white hat SEO strategist. But take that too far, and you've landed in the camp of black hat SEO strategies. As you choose which path to follow, consider this and understand that it's not about demonizing black-hat SEO. There are several lessons to learn from black hat SEO.

For example, you know the importance of backlinks. We've talked about internal and external links, and you learned the importance of a link-building strategy that enables you to get backlinks from authority sites. Black hat SEO plays on backlinks and PBNs because these strategists know links are decisive in ranking high on Google. Black hat SEOs will usually go about their linking strategy in a less reputable way by using things like Private Blog Networks (PBNs). And does it work? Most of the time, it works, but only for a short time. If Google catches you, then it's game over. And so, you always fear that any moment could be your last. On the other hand, if you can honestly build backlinks through real testimonials and relationships or by including your website on third-party directories that have authority, you can still accomplish the same success. This time, however, you live without the fear of the Google Police.

Another example I can give you is keyword stuffing. With Black hat SEOs, reading their content is annoying. Take this example I found from an article posted years ago.

<u>Types of Firepit:</u>

"Firepits can create a beautiful ambiance for your backyard. Firepits can be created in just about every area of your home. However, backyard firepits are the most common. No matter what climate you live in, your home will be able to benefit from a firepit."

That's just the introduction. Who would want to read the rest? And that is why keyword stuffing is a big no-no. However, keyword usage is a huge factor in ranking, so we need to invest time in proper keyword research. Instead of stuffing, white hat SEO focuses on just sprinkling keywords throughout the human-centric content.

The last tip to consider is who is creating your content. Black hat SEOs are notorious for content automation and using robots to make content because they want to produce volume. Not only do I find this distasteful, but it also goes against everything search engines are built for. They are made to be virtual libraries, and it doesn't help when an unintelligible robot who only cares about stuffing keywords creates and publishes content on your website. There was a time when Google wasn't mature enough to pick this trick up, but today, you couldn't get away with it even if you tried. So, if you want to benefit from this tactic, consider that it's centered on consistently putting out a lot of content.

Chapter 10

SEO Analytics and Reporting

As a beginner, getting started with SEO can feel overwhelming. And even once you get things moving, this part of the journey where you need to start analyzing, interpreting, and creating your reports can feel as daunting as pulling your teeth.

As much as I understand how much you would prefer not to engage in this activity, rest assured it's just as important as everything else you've learned up to this point. So, please keep an open mind and trust this process instead of resisting it. Don't quit on winning your SEO just yet because I intend to simplify this process of analyzing and reporting.

A client recently asked me if it would be okay to set up her SEO and skip over the analysis and reporting since she's only doing SEO for her small local business. She learned only some of the nuances of interpreting data when not reporting to a boss. Unfortunately, this is the wrong mindset. It's not about writing to a boss or client. It's about understanding whether your efforts are paying off.

Is it Necessary to Analyze?

Yes. Regardless of why you've started doing SEO, you must measure, track, analyze, and report all your findings. You can't improve what you don't count. And if you're going to invest at least twelve to eighteen months, pouring your resources and energy into this, why wouldn't you want to track and analyze what's working and what's not so you can maximize your return on investment?

To me, it's a no-brainer. We must all learn to love this part of SEO, even if logic and data analysis isn't core strength. I wouldn't say I love going to the gym and getting my trainer to work out my muscles till I'm sore. I don't enjoy the fifty push-ups regiment I'm currently on. Yet, I've learned to enjoy the process and appreciate why it needs to happen. So, I willingly and committedly do it. This can be approached similarly if you prefer something other than data. I want to outline the simple way of approaching your data analysis, but before we do that, let's talk about some mistakes you must avoid with your analysis and reporting.

Mistake #1: Tracking for the sake of tracking

You should only do it if you're tracking with a plan and purpose. It might sound significant to track complicated custom events accurately, but you need to know what you're doing with that data and how it will help you reach your overall goals. What's the point?

Mistake #2: Getting insights from insignificant samples

You'll need an accurate sample size to understand what's happening with your SEO. More than thirty visits are required for any campaign anywhere on the Internet to determine anything statistically speaking. Thus, if you want objective analysis, work until you have a healthy sample.

Mistake #3: Not knowing what the data you're tracking represents

Specific metrics are included by default in many reports, and we assume they are valuable mainly because we need to understand what they represent fully. Take, for example, the average time on a page. If you found that your average time on the page is only 11 seconds, you may assume it could have been better. But what if I told you that might not be the case? If you know how this metric is calculated, you would react differently. What do I mean? The average time on the page is based on timestamps between GA hits. So, any bounced session is calculated as zero seconds long. On top of that, this particular metric doesn't consider inactivity, which skews the data a lot, especially since most of us tend to have several opened inactive tabs. Therefore, how can we honestly give weight to this metric?

Analyzing Data

Now that you know some of the mistakes to avoid, let's go over some best practices.

#1. Organic Traffic

The number one thing you must track and measure is your organic traffic. Why? Unless you're crazy, traffic is the reason for playing the SEO game. The more traffic you can get from search engines, the better. Hence, if you do not see organic traffic, SEO isn't working for you, and something needs to change.

To find and measure your organic traffic, log in to Google Analytics > Audience > Overview > Add Segment > Organic Traffic. Set the date range to the last 90 days.

#2. Keyword Rankings

You'll need to track your rankings, but remember this is less impactful than tracking your organic traffic. We follow orders to check if our site is trending in the right direction. By monitoring rankings, especially when building links, you'll see which campaigns help you build site authority. It can also be helpful when trying to diagnose a sudden increase or decrease in organic traffic. For example, if you notice a 10% bump in organic traffic to your site, keyword rankings can help you determine which web pages were behind that lift.

You'll find that rankings keep shifting, and that's okay. If you're tracking hundreds at once, get a tool like SEMRush to help simplify the process.

#3. Content Analysis

Content is king when it comes to winning with SEO. It's essential to monitor and keep track of the best performers so you can create more of what works. Make sure your content is unique and no duplicate content is indexed.

Use GA (Google Analytics) to find the most popular pages on your website and check the content on those pages. Be consistent with content production and follow your content strategy. I recommend having a spreadsheet or Google sheet to help you track your top performers.

#4. Page speed analysis

The loading speed is critical to track because you'll notice it directly impacts the conversion rate. A fast-loading page with an excellent user experience will increase your website authority and rankings. Regularly check your site speed through the PageSpeed Insights tool offered by Google.

SEO Metrics

Tracking metrics like backlinks and rankings can be overwhelming, even if you have the right tools. Often, there are more important metrics to focus on to determine your SEO efforts' success. We already mentioned organic traffic and the importance of seeing quantifiable proof month by month. Keyword rankings are another critical metric to track, enabling you to see whether your chosen keywords suit your brand. Let's touch on a few more essential metrics.

- **Organic landing page metrics**

Instead of relying on the overall website metrics, you must monitor and track organic sessions and goal metrics for specific landing pages, especially those critical to your brand. By doing this, you can identify the pages that have above-average conversion rates but low rankings so you can know where to focus more of your efforts. To determine your best performers, go to GA (Google Analytics) and find "Behavior"> "Site Content"> "Landing Pages." Apply the organic segment filter by organic sessions only. Then, you can track sessions, goal completions, conversion, bounce rate, and more for each landing page.

- **Organic conversions**

Once organic traffic comes in, you must determine the traffic quality. You'll need to set up your "Goal" or conversion events in GA (Google Analytics) to do this. It can be making a purchase, email sign-up, phone call, or phone submission, depending on your business objective.

- **Organic CTR (click-through rate)**

The organic click-through rate measures engagement while the user is still on the SERP. It gives you an indication of how relevant and appealing your content is to your audience. You will find this CTR within Google Search Console within your "Performance" report.

- **New backlinks and referring domains**

A study conducted by Backlinko, where they analyzed 1 million Google search results, found a strong correlation between rankings and the number of referring domains. Therefore, this is a metric you'll need to track as your site matures.

- **Local Visibility**

This one is a must if you have a local business or want to rank high locally. You will need to track specific metrics, including Google Maps Ranking, Google My Business Insights, and Session Location.

- **Mobile traffic and rankings**

Google switched to mobile-first indexing a while back, which means being mobile-responsive is more crucial than ever. Research indicates that 60% of all searches now come from mobile searches. To track and measure your traffic and rankings, head over to Google Analytics "Audience"> "Mobile"> "Overview". Scroll down to see mobile traffic vs. desktop traffic.

- **New vs. returning visitors**

To find out how well your site is doing and whether people are coming back, check on Google Analytics under "Audience"> "Behavior"> "New vs. Returning."

SEO Reporting

An SEO report is a document that provides an overview of how a website is performing on search engines. There's no right or wrong way of doing this. You can make it any length and create one as regularly as you like. What I don't wish to do is merely produce a data dump that does nothing to boost or give guidance on the direction you should take to improve your SEO game.

The main focus of your report should be domain metrics, organic traffic, and rankings. There are three things your information should convey. First is your progress (how many visits are you getting each month, and is it growing?). It would be best if you also had insights and recommendations. Based on what you see with the data, create some commentary on what could be done to make things even better. Below, I am sharing the main things to have on your report, regardless of how often you create it.

- **SEO Health**

With this first data documentation, you want to find any technical problems and errors that might affect your visibility. Google Analytics will let you know where these errors might be. You can also record how many pages have been indexed and the total number of links, among other things.

- **Mobile-friendliness**

Take note of how responsive your site is. Google Analytics will let you know how much traffic you receive from mobile vs. desktop and whether your mobile compatibility is on point. Document your mobile page speed to figure out how to optimize with time.

- **Ranking Progress**

Here, you will record the data of where your website and specific landing pages are ranking so you can keep tabs on any potential drop-offs or a sudden spike to higher rankings. Aside from page rankings, you can also report on what keywords are doing well. Include the keyword you're targeting, its landing page, current ranking status, search volume, and any changes in the position since your last reporting.

- **Organic Traffic**

Here, you're recording the pages driving the most traffic organically so you can understand which content is most relevant and appealing.

- **Backlink Health**

All links are not made equal. It would be best to record the backlinks pointing to your site, especially those boosting traffic and authority. Document the number of backlinks you have, the number of referring domains, and how many backlinks your competitors have.

- **Social Progress**

You can also include in your report how successful your content is on social media networks. See what traffic you get from Facebook, Instagram, Twitter, LinkedIn, etc. Of course, that means you need to be active and have a following on these networks.

- **Leads/Sales**

If you run an eCommerce or have created a lead generation campaign, you must map and record the conversions from SERPs to sales.

Now that you understand what to include in your report, remember that your information must be accessible for anyone to understand. This is especially important if you have a business partner or hire an SEO expert to take over further down the line. They need to know what you've done quickly and the return on investment the effort yielded. Depending on your budget, you'll need help from Google Analytics and a tool like Ahrefs or Ubersuggest to create an excellent report.

Here's a template you can borrow and adapt for quickly creating your report using PowerPoint or Google Slides. Each number given indicates a new slide.

#1. Title of report

Include the date, month, and year of the report, as well as your website URL.

#2. Summary of the report

Here, you will summarize the essential items in the campaign you're going after and any significant wins.

#3. SEO Health Overview

Include a snapshot of your website's health. If there are any technical problems and errors that might affect your visibility on search engines, include them here. You can get this data through whichever tool you use (Google Analytics, Ahrefs, or Ubersuggest).

#4. URLs Crawled

Here, you will go into more in-depth details of your SEO health by breaking down the number of URLs crawled.

#5. SEO Health Progress

This slide should help you add commentary based on previous slides and findings, and you can even do a side-by-side comparison to prior months. Discuss HTML tags, content, links, page speed, etc.

#6. Backlinks Profile Overview

Show all the backlinks that point to your website and the organic traffic they generate. Again, you can find all these data points using the tools above. Screenshots are great to add here as well.

#7. Backlinks Profile

This slide should include the number of backlinks you earned for the particular date range you report. If this is a monthly report, it should show data for the whole month, how much traffic those new links are bringing in, and if any have been lost. Highlight the links with the most quality traffic or any critical websites with high domain authority.

#8. Organic Search

This slide helps you tell whether your SEO is working and where your primary traffic is coming from. Add the screenshot from the data reporting you'll find on your chosen tool, and remember to include traffic and keywords. Add the actual monthly figures in the text box for easy referencing.

#9. Organic Keywords

Keywords are an essential part of search visibility. Include these in your report—showcase organic rankings and how these have changed from previous months. Check for keywords bringing in the most traffic and their landing pages, and highlight these here because they are your big wins. They are proof that your efforts are paying off.

#10. Ranking Visibility

I recommend adding small graphs that show trends of visibility, average position, and traffic for the specific keywords you're tracking. If you show up on SERP Features, include that in this slide.

#11. Ranking Insights

On this slide, you want to add your commentary to the SERP feature results and whether you see an opportunity to rank or not. If you notice that specific tracked keywords can rank easily, yet your website doesn't show up, what could be done to make this happen? If, for example, you notice an increase in keywords appearing in the Image pack, it might be a good idea to produce more high-quality images and prioritize image optimization.

#12. Ranking Progress

On this slide, you'll want the total number of ranking keywords, the amount of organic traffic generated by those keywords, and the URL that ranks for these terms. Even if traffic isn't going up, this data can tell you if the website is moving in the right or wrong direction. You can leave some of your keywords, especially if you're tracking hundreds of keywords. Just focus on the top ten or twenty that are most crucial.

#13. What's Next?

The last thing I recommend you include in the report is what's next. By this, I mean writing out a simple execution plan for the coming month outlining how you will implement the necessary changes to keep improving your SEO. Is there something that needs fixing? Do you need to refresh certain content pieces? Writing these out will help you focus on the activities that will produce the highest return and keep you moving in the right direction.

Bonus tip:

Focus on the areas that matter most to you. If, for example, you care more about local SEO, then your report should be focused on organic traffic to specific locations so you can highlight the geographical areas bringing in the most traffic.

If, on the other hand, you care about producing super high-quality content for your brand-building campaign, then drilling down on the content pages that generate the most backlinks should be the priority. See what I mean? Personalize your reporting based on your macro and micro goals.

Chapter 11

Social Media Marketing and SEO

Have you ever wondered if there's a connection between social media and SEO?

Well, there is, and in this chapter, I want to show you how to use these highly trafficked channels to drive leads to your business and grow your revenue. But first, what is social media marketing?

Social media marketing uses social media platforms to connect with your audience and build your tribe so you can bring them into your marketing ecosystem and ultimately offer them something valuable. I have several books to help you create a following from scratch on many of the extensive social networks. You can find a list of those books in the recommended resources section. Still, even if you don't grab one of those copies, I want to show you how to leverage your social media to drive traffic to your website and boost your SEO ranking and authority. To make social media and SEO work for you, a carefully thought-out plan for your social media must overlay your SEO strategy.

The Relationship Between Social Media And SEO:

The relationship can be symbiotic if set up right, and that's what I recommend. And the starting point is always going to be content marketing. If you consistently produce great content, people will quickly discover you on social media, ultimately driving traffic back to your site.

Does social media impact SEO? Yes, it does. You gain brand exposure when you share content across social platforms such as Facebook, Twitter, Instagram, and Pinterest. Over time, especially as people engage with your content, it adds up to build influence, which the search engine recognizes. It helps boost your local search engine optimization, enhances your brand reputation, and offers extensive content distribution. As more people share your content, search engines like Google see this as a signal that people love your website, and that causes them to love and respect it. Don't get me wrong; this doesn't mean it helps you with link building. Instead, it indirectly helps you with search ranking. When it comes to the best-ranking pages on SERP, you'll notice that they tend to be the pages with lots of social shares. If you get mentioned regularly on social media with people tagging you or recommending your brand, that also positively impacts search rankings. And, of course, if you have a healthy following, that will move traffic because when you offer them a good enough incentive, they will click from the social network to your landing page, which drives traffic, leads, and sales. That's why it's essential to have helpful content on your website. Whether you create blog posts, mini-guides, podcasts, or infographics, the more value you can bring to social media and grow an audience there, the easier it will be to boost your SEO.

Facebook

Facebook is still king on social media, with over 1.4 billion daily active users. Almost half of those people access the platform through mobile, so if you were still on the fence about making your site mobile responsive, let this be a reminder.

You can use this massive audience to build links through social shares, create enticing content that drives people back to your site, and so much more. The more people share your content on Facebook, the better for your SEO, as that provides a positive social signal to Google and drives traffic to your page. But how would this work? Suppose you create content, post it on Facebook, and people start sharing your content. By default, their friends will notice and click on the share, leading to a website visit where they can further engage with your content. You will have accomplished several things: link building, boosting visibility, getting higher click-through rates, and increasing traffic to that page. And because people intentionally clicked on that page, they are more likely to spend more time on-site, assuming you've done everything discussed in this book, such as being mobile responsive and having a fast-loading time. That is a simple example of applying SEO to Facebook and any other social network you choose.

Another way to leverage Facebook is by optimizing it with the exact keywords you want to rank for on Google. By optimizing your Facebook business page, you can improve visibility within Facebook when people search for your topic. Although that doesn't directly impact your SEO, it indirectly affects it because as more relevant people find your content on Facebook, they will end up on your website and spend more time engaging with it since it's what they searched for. That decreases your bounce rate and shows Google your content is considered valuable.

Instagram

Instagram is becoming a massive player in the social sphere, with 1 billion monthly active users. The latest stats show that, on average, people are spending 53 minutes per day on the app. Many engaged users are waiting to see your content, so here are simple tricks to boost your SEO using this platform.

First, you can optimize your Instagram profile by making it public, using an easily recognizable and searchable username that matches your brand (use your business name), and, most importantly, include a trackable link in your bio that drives traffic directly to the page you want to rank high on Google. When it comes to keywords, I encourage you to leverage the power of hashtags on Instagram. Make sure each post has relevant hashtags, and as much as possible, use the keywords you want to rank for on that particular topic as your leading hashtags. Most users will find your content through a hashtag, so the more strategic you are with the hashtags you choose, the bigger the win.

One last thing I want to mention is the Alt text feature that Instagram offers for their photos. Although it's designed to help visually impaired users enjoy content on Instagram, you can use this for SEO purposes by including the correct Alt text for each post. As we discussed, optimizing images for your on-page SEO requires adding keywords to help users and search engines identify that photo. I recommend using the exact text as the photos on your website to help create that connection for the algorithms. That way, your photos have a higher chance of showing up on SERPs when users search for that topic via voice or text.

Bonus tips:

Consider using the primary keyword you want your brand to rank for in the display name and the @username. You can also grab some secondary keywords and synonyms and apply them to your central bio as you describe what your business does. For example, if your keyword is "bakery," you can use terms like baked goods, cupcakes, fresh bread, etc.

Twitter

This social network is a powerful tool for populating Google, especially with a brand name or a business. Whether you have no search presence or wish to displace harmful content, using Twitter to build your SEO is an excellent hack that few newbies think about. So that's why I want to show you how to utilize it immediately.

First, you'll need to create attention-grabbing carousels. Google loves to display these. Search for any big brand (e.g., Whole Foods) and notice what appears in the search. The best part is you can be a small brand to show up like them under your brand name keyword. You also don't need a verified Twitter account to get a carousel. The process of getting it is simple. Tweet frequently and build enough engagement with other Twitter users. The more other users interact with your tweets (which you post consistently), the quicker you'll see that result on your brand keyword.

If you still need to get a Twitter account or any following, focus on getting a few hundred followers and investing time interacting with other Twitter accounts. Notice what works with your Twitter audience and encourage them to interact with you. Whenever you post something that gets lots of retweets (RT), likes, and replies, do more of that. Consider using memes, pics, and videos corresponding with your brand and the topics you wish to promote. Humorous riffs around current events also perform well but tread lightly. Do not stain your brand to go viral, as it will harm your SEO long-term. Instead, focus on actively engaging and providing value.

Bonus Tip:

If you'd like to rank for a single tweet, you can embed your Twitter page or a particular tweet onto your post or webpage, indirectly impacting your SEO and making it likely to appear on the search.

TikTok

TikTok grew almost overnight in 2020 and became one of the most downloaded apps. The audience might now be senior, but there's a lot of SEO juice to enjoy, especially if your products or services match the demographics that hang out on this social platform. I've noticed with TikTok that it works best when focusing on longtail keywords. And if you can use the keywords you're also looking to rank for in Google, that's a double win because you'll be hitting the right target. As more right users find your content, please encourage them to visit your website. Track the link and note the content pieces that drive the most traffic to your site. That will enable you to create content that gets people to click on your landing page and boost your SEO. The bottom line is that your SEO keyword research and creativity can help you leverage TikTok in ways previously unknown to newbies.

Best Practices for Social Media And SEO

Publish high-quality content.

As I said, it all starts with content marketing. However, if you choose between the two, I want you to focus on quality rather than quantity. The more you understand your ideal audience and work through the process outlined in this book, the easier it will be to produce great content.

Make your content shareable.

Include sharing widgets on your blog and have social share buttons within the content itself. Place compelling calls to action so your readers feel like sharing as they interact with your content. Use appealing visuals in your content and create an attractive layout, mainly if you're producing long-form content.

Be active and engaged on social media.

If you don't engage with people on social media and build real connections, posting content will not get you any SEO benefits. People go on social to socialize, not to be sold to or manipulated. Therefore, only leverage the networks you enjoy investing time in to go into the community and make real connections. Start a conversion around a topic you care about, even if it's not your main brand topic. Join a conversion and give real value by sharing your advice, and you'll see how quickly people will start flocking to your profile to learn more about you. The social media game is one of give, give, and then ask. You will see much SEO juice flowing if you're willing to put in the effort and nurture that engagement.

Chapter 12

SEO Tools And Software

Here is your complete list of useful SEO tools that are a must-know.

#1. Google Search Console

Google Search Console is a free all-in-one SEO tool that you need to have. It will help you understand your site's SEO performance in clicks, impressions, CTR, and average positions on an individual keyword level - ultimately helping you plan a growth strategy. You can also submit a sitemap, gain insights into your backlinks and internal links, and so much more.

#2. Bing Webmaster Tools

This free tool can give you many insights into your site's performance, including performance issues and where to improve. It also offers the SEO Analyzer, which offers best practice recommendations.

#3. Creaming Frog SEO Spider

This SEO tool allows you to crawl up to 500 URLs with a free account. You can find broken links, audit redirects, and analyze metadata. It can also help you discover duplicate content and easily export your findings on a spreadsheet.

#4. Rank Math

Rank Math covers everything from optimizing page titles and meta descriptions and monitoring 404 to creating XML sitemaps and identifying content opportunities. These are all essential for excellent on-page SEO.

#5. Yoast SEO

Yoast comes with a free and paid version, and it's essential for a beginner if you want your on-page SEO to be more manageable. It gives you complete control over your site's optimization for specific keywords.

#6. Google My Business

For free local SEO, you need this tool set up and active. If you have a physical store, use GMB (Google My Business) to claim your business listing so you can show up in Google Maps, Knowledge Panel, and in the Local Pack.

#7. Google Analytics

GA (Google Analytics) is another free tool you must have because it offers incredible insights and helps you with SEO reporting. You can analyze metrics like unique visitors, organic traffic, and conversions. You can also get detailed user data such as demographics and device usage to know how much your traffic comes from desktop and mobile.

#8. Google Data Studio

This tool is excellent for effective reporting. It's got a friendly dashboard that allows you to utilize multiple sources and even merge some of your data if needed. You can easily create an engaging report that shows real-time data, historical comparisons, and more. The best part is that it's free to use.

#9. SEMRush

This is one of the best tools for tracking, keyword research, and reporting. You can do keyword research, audit your site, check your website's traffic, and more. This is a one-stop shop for all your SEO needs, and if your budget can allow it (prices start from $99), consider investing in it.

#10. Moz

Moz is considered one of the best SEO tools in the market. It caters to webpage performance, local listing audits, keyword research, link building, analysis, and more. The free version is limited, so if you have the budget, give the Moz Pro version ($99 for a standard, which is enough for beginners) a test drive, as it can be your one-stop shop for all your SEO needs.

#11. Ahrefs

Ahrefs is one of my favorite tools to invest in. I suggest you get this all-in-one SEO toolset as soon as your pocket allows. All successful marketers swear by this software, and with good reason. It helps you optimize your website's SEO, analyze your competitors so you can see what's working for them, and use it to inspire your growth. Ahrefs also shows you top-performing content and assists in keyword research, so you save time with your SEO and content strategy. You can also track your ranking progress and so much more. It's not free, but you can do a free trial for only $7.

#12. Ubersuggest

The last tool I want you to add to your toolbox is Neil Patel's Ubersuggest. There's a free version and a paid upgrade. The free one gets you primary access and helps you gain insights into your SEO health and basic keyword research. If you want to dive deeper and get this tool's full suite of SEO, you'll need the paid version. In this book, I've given lots of examples of how you can use this tool as a standalone or in combination with Google, so you have plenty of examples of how I use this to generate keyword ideas, spy on my competition, and get insights into the strategies that are working for others so I can adapt, improve and gain an edge when it comes to my SEO.

Conclusion

We've covered a lot of ground with the SEO strategies, hacks, and tools you can now access. SEO is not an instant gratification marketing channel; it takes A LOT of work. But the fact is that it's going to be around for a while, and when done right, it can become an evergreen source of traffic for your business.

When someone Googles your business or brand name, what will they find? If your ideal customer is searching for a product or service you offer, will they be able to find you on SERPs? With a basic understanding of where to begin and how to strategically approach your SEO, keeping your business in mind with potential and existing customers will be manageable.

You now have all the basics for leveraging SEO in your business. You've learned what SEO is, how search engines work, and the difference between SEO and SEM, which most need help understanding. I also walked you through technical concepts like black hat SEO, white hat SEO, on-page SEO, and off-page SEO. Finally, we made the connection between social media web development and how they all need to build your SEO game so you can continue to grow in domain authority and user experience.

In 2023, SEO is still considered one of the most effective ways to build brand equity and drive high-quality traffic to your website and landing pages. According to a Forbes article, a survey conducted a few years ago revealed that 84% of Millennials said they don't like advertising, and many don't trust it. This generation of consumers is more resistant to conventional marketing methods, and they seem to be put off by things like cold calling, paid advertising, and even email spam. With an SEO strategy, you can build a strong connection and demonstrate your authenticity as a brand, leading them through a sales process more naturally.

Therefore, it's okay to have but necessary if you want your brand or business to grow in visibility, credibility, and revenue generation. The only caveat is that you must maintain the right mindset through this process. If you keep the proper perspective and move with purpose (focused on serving humans, not the algorithms), you are destined to reap great rewards and win in the game of search engine optimization.

SEO Terminologies That Are a Must-Know

Above the Fold

This refers to content that appears on a website before the user scrolls.

Algorithm

It is a complex computer program used by search engines to retrieve data and deliver results for a query.

Analytics

It refers to the science of collecting, organizing, analyzing, and interpreting data to take future actions on what has or hasn't worked based on historical findings.

Anchor text

It is a clickable word (or words) that point to a link. This anchor text is intended to provide contextual information to both the reader and the search engines about what the website or landing page being linked to is about.

Black hat

It refers to search engine optimization practices that violate Google's quality guidelines.

Bounce rate

It is the percentage of website visitors who leave without visiting another page on that website.

Canonical URL

An HTML code element that specifies a preferred website URL when multiple URLs have the same or similar content. The purpose of this is to reduce duplicate content.

Click-through rate

The rate in percentage at which users click on an organic search result. To calculate this, divide the total number of organic clicks by the total number of impressions, then multiply by 100

Conversion

This is when a user completes a desired action, such as purchasing, downloading premium content, completing a form, or subscribing to a newsletter.

Crawling

It gathers information using a crawler from the billions of public web pages to update, add, sort, and organize web pages in a search engine's index.

Crawl budget

It is the total number of URLs search engines can and want to crawl on a website during a specific time.

Data

Refers to all the complex numbers representing real customers needed to make informed decisions about SEO strategies and tactics.

De-index

This is when Google removes a website or webpage either temporarily or permanently from search results.

Featured snippets

These organic answer boxes appear at the top of SERPs for specific queries.

Google My Business Listing

It is a free listing available to all local businesses.

Intent

Within the context of SEO, intent means what users want or expect to get when they type their query into the search bar.

Local pack

A local pack is usually a three-local business listing that appears for local-intent searches.

Organic

This refers to earned placements in search results as opposed to paid advertisements.

Query

These are the words that a user types into the search bar.

Ranking

Ordering search results by relevance to the query.

Search engine

It refers to an information retrieval program or database that searches for items to match a request made by the user.

SERP

It is an acronym for Search Engine Results Page. These would be the pages that show up as results after searching.

Traffic

It refers to visits to a website.

URL

It is a shorthand name that stands for – Uniform Resource Locators. These are the addresses for individual pieces of content on the web.

White hat

It is the opposite of the black hat and refers to search engine optimization practices that comply with Google's quality guidelines.

Book # 5

Instagram Marketing for Beginners

A Complete Guide on How to Make Money with Instagram and Grow Your Business in No Time

Introduction

Most people associate Instagram with luxurious photos in exotic locations, cute animals, or what people eat tonight. When I think of Instagram, I see an untapped opportunity - a gold mine that anyone can leverage to gain fame, influence, and success. If you've picked up this book intending to become an Instagram influencer, social media marketer, or grow your brand, you're in the right place.

While Instagram is a top-rated social media platform for smartphone addicts, it has also proven to be an excellent investment for savvy marketers and business owners. It took a while for me to realize this. Once I realized I could grow my business even more by leveraging this platform, I decided to study, experiment with, and build my brand on the forum. So far, it has yielded outstanding results. You picked up this book because you want to do something similar for a personal or business brand. It could be different from the brand you want to help build. Both employees and entrepreneurs can benefit from the strategies contained in this Instagram playbook.

The intention here is to share all the secrets I've learned so that you can avoid making some of the mistakes newer marketers are making. Mistakes I made when I set up my account.

Instagram has so much potential, but it requires a good plan. You need to know the steps to follow from an average account posting pretty pictures randomly to an epic business account that generates revenue.

Unfortunately, there's a lot of misinformation and overwhelm around Instagram marketing. When you're just starting, it's hard to know what those initial steps should be and where to focus your time, energy, and resources.

You will fail badly if you attempt to copy mega influencers who have invested over a decade on the platform. The other thing to note is that your ambition and desire to grow a following fast is noble, but it won't happen in the first month you launch. By going through this book and implementing all that you'll learn, your following will grow, but your focus must shift from acquiring a large following to attracting an audience that resonates and connects with what you have to offer. A mistake many people make is to focus on getting that blue tick or becoming mega-influencers. That's the wrong approach.

The best way to succeed on Instagram is to establish yourself as someone worth following. You must build your reputation and allow people to see you're authentic, trustworthy, and caring about your tribe.

Introduction

Considering that over 62% of Instagram users say they've become more interested in a brand or product after seeing it in Stories and at least 80% of users follow a business, it's vital to establish your brand the right way.

So, let's start by eliminating some common mistakes that usually cause brands to fail on the platform.

#1: Avoid starting your Instagram journey without a clear goal and strategy.

This should be Instagram 101, yet most influencers and start-ups often need to catch up. It would be best if you started with a strategy to have a solid foundation. Without clear goals, targets, and a plan, you might end up wasting opportunities and losing morale because you don't see traction fast enough, and like most people, you'll conclude that Instagram doesn't work.

Don't worry if you're already concerned about strategy because this playbook gives you a walkthrough of creating one now.

#2: Avoid using a personal and private account

By having a private or personal account, you will have access to only a few of the beautiful features of Instagram. You'll also lose followers because most new followers steer clear of an Instagram profile with the "Private" icon.

#3. Focusing on quantity instead of quality is another mistake that must be avoided.

You'll find many reminders throughout this book emphasizing the importance of quality and serving your audience. That is by design. You see, after hustling on Instagram for a few years, I finally started generating income from my efforts. I can recall the first time I made $10,000 monthly from my Instagram campaign. The shift I had made a few months earlier was simple, yet it led to this tremendous income growth. What was the change? I stopped focusing on posting for volume and discarded the idea of buying followers so my account could look like it had a considerable following. Instead, I focused all my energy on producing helpful and inspiring content.

You can still post several times a day. What I want you to realize is that quality should never be compromised for the sake of quantity.

#4: Avoid the temptation of buying followers

This option sounds appealing to any ambitious entrepreneur or influencer starting from zero. I almost fell for it as well. However, after observing how some of my friends grew after purchasing thousands of followers for a few bucks, I realized I needed a different approach. Ultimately, this will have to be a personal decision. Getting real followers who love your content is worth more than any perception millions of bought followers could give your account.

#5: Do not misuse hashtags

It will mess with your brand credibility and stunt your growth. The last thing I want to mention before we jump into the first section of this playbook is that hashtags are valuable. Please treat them with respect. Be strategic about which hashtags you choose to use. Don't spam your content with trending hashtags because some guru said you could get free traffic. Although Instagram allows up to 30 hashtags per post, please fill up your captions and keep your brand's vision clear with a few hashtags.

We will talk more about this in a later chapter. For now, I want you to understand that Instagram is a platform that works best when authenticity and quality take the lead, so choose your hashtags wisely.

Most people assume all it takes to succeed on Instagram is to post attractive images, but the fact is, this is a serious business. You should treat Instagram as a real business if you want it to give you a good investment return. So, before we get started, let's make each other a promise. Suppose you commit to this journey and treat Instagram marketing with the same level of dedication and persistence that you would any business development project. In that case, I promise to give you all the tools, hacks, and strategies you need to succeed.

SECTION 1

Understanding Instagram

Chapter 1

What You Need to Know Before Getting Started

Instagram has over 1 billion monthly users, and over 500 million use Instagram Stories daily. Did you know that? Those are huge numbers for a simple image-sharing social network. The best part is that you can find both a male and female audience hanging out on Instagram, so whether you're serving a small niche of men or a sizeable stay-at-home mom audience, you can generate healthy attention on this platform. If those facts haven't excited you, here are some recent statistics about Instagram for business and user behavior.

- A third of the most viewed Stories on Instagram are from businesses.

- At least 63% of Instagram users login to the platform once per day, and 42% do it multiple times. Your content can receive great engagement if you know your audience and the best times to post.

- Two hundred million Instagram users visit at least one business profile daily. By setting up your profile correctly, your business might be the one they see next.

- For brands looking to serve the U.S. audience, Instagram is a goldmine, with 11% of American users reporting that their top reason for using the platform is to shop or find new products. The buyer cycle tends to be earlier in the purchase journey, so keep that in mind as you plan your campaigns.

- U.S. marketers love spending their budget on influencer marketing, especially on this platform. 69% have a budget to invest in Instagram influencers. That's a more significant figure than YouTube influencer marketing opportunities.

- Brands pay (on average) between $100 - $2,085 for influencers to post on the feed or Instagram Stories. So, if you're an influencer, get excited because we'll talk more about this income-earning opportunity.

If you are starting to see the opportunity, I'm glad. Instagram and social media could be the key to unlocking your dream lifestyle. Before you roll up your sleeves and start mining for the gold that awaits you, I'd like to give you an overview of the power of social media and why it is such a powerful vehicle for sales and marketing.

A Better Understanding of social media

You must understand human psychology to understand social media and win on Instagram. We are social creatures. It is in our DNA to come together, share, exchange, and build connections through social gatherings. Modern science has proven the importance and benefit, both mentally and physically, of encouraging social relationships. Since the advent of the Internet, we have taken this innate desire from our years as cave people and turned it into a daily habit via technology and smartphones. Social media platforms aren't just trendy; they have become a new way of life.

Thanks to social media, we can meet new people and keep in touch with friends and family living far and near. We can connect with like-minded individuals who share our values and beliefs, regardless of location. We can freely express our opinions about any topic (recall how crazy the last U.S. presidential elections were on the Internet, and you'll understand the power of social media). I could continue naming how impactful social media is in our modern world, but you get it. The best part is that businesses of all sizes, including startups, have realized this truth, too. Savvy entrepreneurs have entered the scene across major social networks, including YouTube, Facebook, Instagram, Twitter, LinkedIn, and others intending to leverage these platforms.

Never has it been more accessible for a self-made individual in any industry to build a brand, share a message, and impact the lives of millions of people. And you can do it, too, regardless of budget, experience, age, ethnicity, or location. What I love about social media is that you have the power to impact others, express your authentic truth, and make some good money in the process.

The journey and history of social media have been extended. On the resource page, I have listed an article that might be an exciting read for those interested in learning about the early years of social media. We focus on Instagram in this book, but I encourage you to get some of my other books, such as my last book on how to make money on YouTube, if you want to master more than one social media platform.

The History And Growth Of Instagram

Selfies have become an obsessive and addictive behavior in our society, but who can blame these half-naked boys and girls who like to show off their perfect images on Instagram? After all, we have always had a soft spot for pictures. Even before we became civilized, we were drawing paintings on the walls. So clearly, visual elements are very appealing to us. Before October 2010, when Instagram was launched, sharing pictures took a lot of work. Instagram emerged to change how we connect and share through visual content. By 2012, Facebook took the leap and bought the image-sharing app, and since then, it has been growing in popularity and style.

The founders of Instagram intended to create an app that would make a connection and cheer people up. So, for example, if you had a friend on the other side of the world freezing in the cold of winter and dreaming of a beautiful summer sunset, you could take a snapshot of your environment and instantly send it to your friend. Kevin Systrom was the guy who started working on what would become Instagram as we know it today. Kevin had no formal training but learned how to code during his spare time (weekends and after work). After meeting Mike Kreiger, the side project turned into Instagram.

The first attempt was made solely by Systrom, called Burbn, which didn't succeed as he had hoped. By the time Kreiger came on board, Burbn was mainly used to share photos. People loved sharing coffee pics, dog pics, bathroom selfies, and so on. After much research, they decided to transform Burbn into Scotch (true story! And yes, they enjoyed naming their projects after alcohol). Unfortunately, scotch was full of bugs, and the after-taste effects weren't that pleasant, so the founders kept tinkering until Instagram was finally launched in October 2010. The Instagram app grew by twenty-five thousand users on that first launch day.

Within three months, they hit one million users, and the rest, as they say, is success history since, as you know, Mark Zuckerberg bought Instagram for $1 billion in April 2012. The fascinating thing about Instagram is that its simplicity and ability to make an ordinary picture look extraordinary is the secret sauce behind its success. Lean into this innate desire for attractive visual elements, and you will build a decent audience on Instagram to meet your objectives.

People use Instagram to connect, get inspired, and share their feelings. They've recently started relying on Instagram to connect with new brands and discover new products from their favorite brands. I've also observed that Instagram users love using the app to escape their daily mundane or perhaps stressful realities. That's why you'll find crazy engagement and interaction in particular niches, especially travel. However, in an upcoming chapter, we will discuss niches and how to drive engagement. Now that you understand Instagram's history, user psychology, and the app's intention, let's talk about how it works.

How Instagram Works

Instagram is free to set up an account and use. It works on all iPhones, iPads, Android devices, and tablets from Samsung, Google, and others. Although it can be accessed from a desktop or laptop, it is designed to be a mobile app. As I said, this is one of the most popular social networks for teens and adults. You can take a standard pic, apply filters, adjust brightness, color overlay, and other technical things. You can also create short videos to post on your Feed, IGTV, or Instagram Stories, which we will discuss at length.

The first step you need to take is to download the app to your smartphone and sign up so you can easily follow along as each chapter unfolds new strategies to implement. Once you've signed up, you will get a personal account, which can later be adjusted to a business or creative performance. If you have a Facebook account, I encourage you to link them once you're done with the sign-up. That will enable you to take advantage of Instagram's recent cross-messaging feature. You will then need to fill in your bio information, add a profile picture, and customize a few other things we will delve into in a little while.

Each time you open the app on your phone, you'll automatically refresh your main feed, and the algorithm will populate your screen with content from the accounts you've shown interest in. A menu bar with the Home, Explore, Reels, Instagram Shop, and Profile tabs should be at the bottom of the app to help you navigate your account.

At the top right-hand, you will have access to the camera (camera icon), direct messages (through the messages icon), and activity where you can see likes and comments. Now, you can use that same button at the top of the Home tab to create a post, a story, or a reel. From your personal profile feed, you'll see in the top right-hand corner a plus + sign that allows you to create a post, a story, a story highlight, a video, a reel, or a guide.

There's also a collapsed menu that expands when you click the three parallel bars icon. You will find Settings, Archive, Insights, your activity, QR Code, Saved, Close Friends, and Discover people here. Speaking of the algorithm populating your feed, let's share what's known about the Instagram algorithm.

The Instagram Algorithm

At first, you will be encouraged to follow accounts so the algorithm can learn what you care about. It will also continue to monitor your activity in the background to figure out what content you're engaging with. In a while, you will only start seeing fresh content from the accounts you most engage with. That is the same experience all users have on the platform. Therefore, what we know for sure based on observation and what the Instagram team has shared is that the algorithm will prioritize which content to show first based on the assumed relationship. What do I mean?

An illustration will explain better. Suppose you are a friend, and you always comment on their posts, or they keep tagging you in their content. Likely, you'll always see what they post because Instagram will populate your feed with more of their content. It assumes this engagement implies that you're categorizing this account as "friends and family." Theoretically, the more you interact with an account, even if you hate it and post hate comments, the more you will see their content on your feed.

Now flip this around and think about your audience. The more they interact with and engage with your content whenever you post, the more likely they will keep seeing it on their feed. The algorithm uses signals such as:

- Direct messages
- People searched for
- Hashtags used

These activities signal to the algorithm that users want to interact more with the account they frequently engage in. Based on that behavior pattern, the algorithm populates the feed with more content from those accounts.

We also know from the Instagram team that, aside from relationships, they focus on timeliness, interest, frequency, usage, and following to determine what content to rank on the user's feed. Let's break down each of these a little more.

• **Timeliness** - It simply means that Instagram wants to show fresh content. So, something from last week might not appear on a user's feed because it's perceived as outdated. Each time a user logs back into their feed, Instagram wants to show them the latest and best content posted since their last visit. Which leads to our next micro-signal.

• **Frequency** - When it comes to frequency, it's about showing the user as much of the best and most relevant content as possible. The algorithm tries to show the newly logged-in user the best of what they've missed since their last visit. So, if your user logs in daily or even several times a day and you only post once a week, you might end up losing that connection because Instagram won't have anything fresh to show, and that will lead to lower engagement.

- **Interest -** This implies that the order in which a user will see content on their feed is determined by what the algorithm believes will be most significant to the person. So, the more relevant and exciting content to a particular user, the higher it will rank on the feed. The algorithm uses photo recognition technologies, hashtags, and the copy on the post to categorize and organize it.

- **Following -** This implies that the algorithm sorts through all the accounts a user follows to determine what to show them when the app is opened. The more accounts a user follows, the higher the competition because the algorithm can only select a few accounts. It will fall back on the main criteria of relationship, i.e., friends, family, and favorite charges.

- **Usage -** The algorithm will monitor the time spent on the app. Some people log in multiple times a day for short periods. Others like to binge-scroll through the feed for long sessions each day. Depending on the particular use case, the algorithm will prioritize and order the content from the highest priority to enhance user experience. Therefore, if your content isn't appealing and relevant enough based on the algorithm's criteria, your content may never show up on your followers' feeds. Therefore, getting into this Instagram game is paramount to providing quality content. Your posts must be precise enough for the algorithm to interpret appropriately. They must be targeted to the right audience and interesting enough for the end-user.

How To Leverage The Algorithm And Instagram Features To Grow Your Brand And Business.

By learning how the algorithm prioritizes content, you can create an advantage for yourself because you can commit to producing content that you feel confident about. And then, it's up to you to put some effort and creativity so that your followers can engage with you more so that Instagram can categorize your account as a high priority. How do you do this? There are many ways to build that relationship, and you will learn hacks and content types as the book unfolds. Examples include creating video messages and initiating video calls for your followers.

Creating fun Stories and making it interactive by adding a question sticker. You can also share longer edited videos with IGTV. A remarkable feature many business owners use nowadays is the QR code. It's a great way to bridge the online and offline worlds, especially if you already have an offline business. For example, if you're a bakery, someone can come in for some fresh bread, and before leaving, you could ask them to scan the QR code that leads to your Instagram Page. Or you can easily send it over as a text either to their number or email address. It's a great way to get more followers, likes, direct messages, and even sales because you can send them promos after they're gone.

Want Your Very Own QR Code?

It used to be that you'd have to create your QR code from Google or hire someone to do it for you. However, an update that just happened recently by Instagram makes your ability to have a QR code super easy. Open up your Instagram app and head over to your main profile feed. The menu icon (three parallel lines) is in the upper right-hand corner. Click on that to open up a list of options, including your in-built QR code.

I love this new feature because you can customize your QR code's look and background feel by taking a selfie that Instagram automatically attaches. You can also share the QR code from the app to WhatsApp, Messages, Email, Facebook, LinkedIn, and more.

CHAPTER 2

What Motivates You

Instagram is one of the best social platforms to grow your brand and make sales, even if you're a beginner in online marketing. But let's get something straight: it will still be a hustle. It would be best to put in tremendous effort to generate enough momentum for your account. That's why you must connect with your motive for starting this path. If you need clarity on why you're doing this and what motivates you, the lack of engagement and growth bound to occur in the early phases of your journey will cause you to give up too soon.

You will often see reports from small and large brands showing how fast they grew on a social network or how crazy their return on investment was for a particular social media campaign. It's easy to assume the same will happen to you. I'm sorry to burst your bubble. It won't.

You won't go from zero to Instagram famous in a few weeks or months. If that's why you picked up this book, you must find that kind of "get rich quick" mentality elsewhere. The reality of doing business is that you rarely have that stroke of luck and experience business miracles. The general rule of thumb is the slow grind and build-up to what will eventually become a huge success. So, buckle up and anchor yourself in the thing that motivates you. Some people are motivated by their business goals. Others care about changing their lifestyles or becoming social media influencers. Whatever your "WHY" might be, connect with it and keep yourself grounded.

Why Use Instagram?

Another question you'll need to answer is why you're choosing to grow your Instagram channel. Why not YouTube or LinkedIn? Give yourself a clear answer to this. I can share with you why I started using Instagram to market my business, and I also have reasons given to me by peers and students of my online courses.

Instagram is simple and easy to use. Compared to other channels, the simplicity and aesthetics of the platforms are very appealing to end-users. That leads me to my second point. Instagram has severe engagement levels. Compared to other channels such as Facebook and Twitter, you can be a brand-new account and still get an audience discovering and liking your content. For a solopreneur or start-up, this kind of organic engagement is priceless.

Instagram is known for nurturing and launching influencers successfully. Suppose you dream of becoming a social media influencer. In that case, Instagram is one of the best places to build your audience. Brands already know and budget for influencer marketing in 2021, and audiences engage more with influencers they know, like, and trust. Making a lucrative career on Instagram is highly probable, even if you're a stay-at-home mom or a struggling artist, and that will lead to tremendous financial freedom.

Partnering with influencers is more accessible on Instagram for business owners. The flip side of that influencer marketing concept is that as business owners and thought leaders, we can quickly get our account in front of a new and engaged audience without breaking the bank. There are different levels of influencers, each with its own pricing options. You could spend zero money, a few hundred dollars, or several thousand, depending on your budget and the relationships you build. The influencer can promote your brand, products, or services to increase sales. More on influencers and influencer marketing later.

You can make money directly from Instagram. As a business owner, revenue is significant to me. Instagram is very appealing because, through product placements, we can add tags to products in our photos with links that include product descriptions, prices, and the ability to "shop now." That means a user can go from Instagram to your online store in seconds, leading to sales. The best part is over seventy percent of users report they enjoy purchasing products through social media. So, what are you waiting for? Start planning how to engage people and drive traffic to your checkout page.

Instagram Goal Setting

Goal setting will be familiar if you've invested enough time online or in personal development programs. With a target to aim for, measuring progress or even attaining success is more accessible. Think of it like this... If you get into your car and start driving west, you could go forever because "west" could take you anywhere. Eventually, you'll run out of gas, the car will break down, or you'll get tired and give up without any sense of satisfaction.

To experience the fulfillment and success we crave, goal setting is essential in our personal and professional lives. This isn't a session on individual achievement and satisfaction, however, so if you're still confused about why you need goals, I suggest getting a book from a guru like Jack Canfield, Brian Tracy, John Assaraf, or one of those online gurus who teach that stuff. Setting the right goals for our Instagram success and brand growth will enable us to track progress, monitor development, and determine what works and what doesn't. It will give us a sense of direction and a focusing point, which is essential in the noisy social media world. It will also enable us to discipline ourselves and avoid falling for the shiny object syndrome that usually distracts many social media marketers.

If you need to learn how to set your social media goals, here's something simple you can follow.

First, I want you to determine and align your social media goals with your business goals. For example, your business goal might be to increase brand awareness. In that case, a great social media goal can be to increase organic reach. Coschedule created a fantastic guideline you can use as a reference. For the sake of convenience, I am sharing their basic outline below.

Increasing online sales (Business Objective) can align with tracking conversions from social referrals.

Boosting brand loyalty (Business Objective) can align with tracking the number of new subscribers from Instagram. Increasing revenue from new products launched (Business Objective) can align with tracking conversions from Product Campaigns on Instagram. This is, of course, just a guideline if you already have a business.

The second thing you need to do is set your S.M.A.R.T (Specific Measurable Aspirational Relevant Timely) goals. How do you do this on Instagram? By clearly defining what you want to achieve within a specified timeframe. For example, if you're a personal trainer looking to use Instagram to acquire new clients, then a great S.M.A.R.T. goal would be to convert ten appointments within 30 days by posting once a day on Instagram feed and three times a day on Stories with a clear call-to-action. My paid ads budget is $10 per day, which runs a campaign leading to my landing page with the "book free session now" button. The more detailed your goal, the better. If you're more interested in growing followers, then your first goal should reflect that.

The third thing to do before you complete setting your goals for Instagram is to clarify what kind of a goal you will focus on to meet that overall business objective. Here's why. Marketing is deep. You can either create a campaign for branding or selling, but you can rarely hit both properly. Unfortunately, few people understand the difference between branding and selling, so most social media content comes across as spammy.

To help you stand out for all the right reasons, I encourage you to have a healthy mix of branding and selling content on your Instagram feed. Your social media strategy should include both aspects because people will interact with your account at different points of their buying journey. It would be best to have branding and selling to thrive, so get creative with this.

Since you're in the early stages of business development on Instagram, you should have a primary business objective with a social media goal that aligns with that objective. Then, you should further break down that social media objective into milestones. So, going back to the personal trainer example. He should break down the goal of selling ten appointments further (especially if he's just started building up his Instagram account) into smaller milestones. He could break it down to how many followers he will need and what level of engagement he will be looking for before moving that audience into asking them to check out his landing page and book a session. Then, he could do branding and conversion goals, all for that same overall objective and getting ten new client appointments.

Remember, branding should be done consistently. It should be focused on giving. Goals for branding include increasing follower count, reach, likes, shares, comments, mentions, DMs, and saves. Most of this happens organically and over a long period. It will require daily posts, lots of research, and figuring out what your audience wants and where they are so you can engage with them and pull them into your world. If, for example, you want to grow your account to 100,000 followers in twelve months, that is a branding goal. There are action steps you need to take to make that happen. On Instagram, we value a lot the level of engagement. The more people comment, reply to Stories with a chat, direct message you, and heart your stuff, the more you'll know you're growing.

Regarding conversions that lead to sales, the best approach is soft selling. Direct (hard selling) only works on social media, especially Instagram. People want to be kept from being sold.

They want to be served. So, for example, instead of the personal trainer focusing on a hard sell, asking people to book a private session, he can post customer success stories with happy clients who've successfully gone through his program. If he targets people looking to lose weight fast, he could post a video with his client, who lost weight in time for her wedding. That will drive more engagement and create awareness around his particular program. It subtly suggests to the user that they should click on his bio to access the same magical program if they wish to experience similar results. Therefore, I encourage you to approach Instagram through this lens of adding value first. Think of growing a community and serving your audience instead of selling your products or services.

If you want to become an Instagram influencer and get brands to pay you lots of money for a shout-out, establish that credibility as someone who serves and provides exceptional content and value. In the user's eyes, the product you promote and encourage people to buy should be an add-on, not the main reason for creating your content. If you can achieve this high level of content creation, conversions and sales will become an easy game on Instagram.

What Are The Common Goals For Influencers And Business Owners On Instagram?

Increasing product sales, raising brand awareness, growing followers, driving traffic to a landing page or website, customer service, and customer satisfaction. You can also have the goal of list-building or identifying and building relationships with key influencers in your niche.

You must commit before your Instagram account can yield the desired goals and results. Your ability to consistently show up and put out great content without losing enthusiasm will go a long way toward attaining your desires. So, before we jump into the technicalities of setting up your account and growing it correctly, let's talk about getting your mind right.

Sticking To What You Believe In

Let me emphasize that you determine your growth and success on Instagram if it needs clarification. The platform is straightforward, and your ability to communicate your message and attract your audience is standard because it's an open playing field. The difference between you and every other business owner or influencer is the mindset you're operating on. That becomes the determining factor of whether you will rise and succeed or drown and fail. Therefore, getting your mind right is just as important as learning what to post, when to post, and hacks for generating engagement - do you agree?

After being online for over a decade, I realize success, fame, and fortune don't just come by luck or accident. Some certain qualities and practices lead people to their dream lifestyles.

Have you ever heard of the saying "success leaves clues"? Observing and learning from incredibly successful mentors, I noticed certain commonalities.

Every successful person I know in the online world possesses a certain mindset, approaches their work in a specific way, and is driven by their WHY. They didn't just jump into social media for the sake of it. Those who are influencers know why they want to become successful social media influencers. Business owners looking to grow successful social media channels have clarity on why this is important to them. I want you to have that same level of transparency.

The other common trait is that all successful individuals only talk about, teach, and promote what they believe in. It's not fake or hyperbole. They don't just accept partnerships or paid gigs to make a dollar. Instagram's best influencers only work with companies, products, and brands they genuinely believe in. The best business owners only post content and share the knowledge they've had experience in and are super passionate about. That leads to my big key takeaway for you. Stick to your truth and only share what you know and believe in.

If the content you create comes from that authentic place of passion, talent, and skill, you will stay grounded, energized, and in love with content creation because you'll do something you deeply care about. And because this is something you would do anyway, the hardships of growing your account won't wear you down. It will be easy to persevere and stick with your channel until your goals are attained. That is the path to success and whatever fame you wish to reap from Instagram. It won't be easy, and it's unlikely to happen overnight. But if you still feel this is your time to become Instagram famous after reading this last section, then move on to the next chapter because you're ready to go big.

Section 2

Instagram Account

Chapter 3

First, You Need a Niche

Whenever choosing a niche comes up, I always receive mixed reactions. Some people get it immediately, while others assume I am suggesting they limit their creativity. There was a time when social media was young and unsaturated with noisemakers. Anyone with a good brand and powerful message could stand out immediately. Those days are gone.

Social media is reaching maturity, and when networks like Instagram begin to boast the numbers currently reported (over 1 billion users), it's time to take a different approach. The riches are in the niches. You need to figure out your niche to build something substantial on Instagram or any sizeable social network.

Why Niching Down Is So Important.

I bet you're asking yourself why it's important to niche down. It's a great question, and you'll often hear varying answers. Some experts claim niching down is essential because it helps clarify your message and brand identity. That's true. Others will tell you that niching down enables you to quickly establish yourself as an authority in a specific topic, which will grow your following faster. That is also true. For me, the whole concept of niching down has become fundamental because of the shift in user behavior.

In recent years, we have seen a rise, stabilization, and a drop in social media usage in more extensive networks. Please don't misunderstand; I am not saying there are no people on Facebook, Twitter, Instagram, and all these extensive social networks. Data proves that the numbers are still staggering. But despite boasting huge numbers, the drop continues, and users are starting to slow down and refrain from engaging too much on these large networks. Instead, they prefer smaller and more personalized social gathering spaces where direct contact with like-minded people feels easier. As a result, marketing on social media is taking on a new look, and those who are winning are the business owners and influencers focused on a specific niche.

When you niche down, you're not permanently cutting yourself off from other areas of interest you might have. Instead, you are laser-focused on a single topic or area of expertise that acts as a beacon for like-minded individuals who care about that same subject. By niching down your odds of standing out, reaching your target audience, and generating higher engagement significantly increase. Whether you're an entrepreneur or influencer, that alone can shave down the journey of becoming successful on Instagram.

Many successful Instagrammers have shared stories of how they got started. Their content was all over the place. They attempted to succeed by drawing in a broad audience, but it didn't pan out. But after picking a niche and drilling down to that subject matter, things started shifting as they saw their tribe forming. It makes for a very effective marketing strategy.

Some people will immediately read the first few paragraphs and know what niche to go to if that's you; congratulations! I struggled for several months before figuring out what could become my niche because I had so many passions and different skills. I worked in several industries and loved business, personal development, DIY, and guitar playing. As you can imagine, I needed help to focus on one niche for Instagram. If you're multi-talented and multi-passionate, then don't worry. You're not alone. This chapter will provide a guideline to help you hone in and narrow down your focus.

Instagram Niches

There are thousands of niches on Instagram, and I'm sure the numbers will keep growing. That means whatever niche you choose, there's likely to be a ready-built audience and some competition. Trust me, you want competition; I will explain why later. If you're starting your Instagram account to generate sales, you want to ensure the niche is profitable. But don't pick a niche just because it's a money-maker! Here are some of the popular niches:

- **Lifestyle**

The lifestyle niche is about showcasing how incredible and inspiring your life is. It's about sharing your opinions, ideas, and truth. People love listening to amazing stories and envisioning themselves as part of them. If you have something that could wow your followers, make people wish they were in your shoes, or motivate them to think outside the box, then this niche might be for you.

- **Food and cooking**

Who doesn't love good food? Food will always be a massive part of our lives regardless of how advanced we become as civilized people. That's why Instagram favors the food niche a lot. Cooking continues to gain popularity on the platform as people share recipes, cooking tips, tutorials, and more. If your love is in food, no matter how unknown your type of cuisine, you can build a tribe around your topic as long as it's good food and great content.

- **Business**

This might be your niche if you love the world of start-ups, small businesses, and entrepreneurship. Thanks to the Internet, so many business opportunities can lead to income. If money-making is a passion, you could also create an account sharing ideas, tips, and motivation so your followers can make money and gain financial freedom.

- **Fashion**

Fashion niches are booming on Instagram, and with good reason. Brands of all sizes invest a significant amount of money on the platform, and users flock to these alluring accounts to get inspired, entertained, and even educated on how they should look. People care about their appearance and even more, so they want to know what celebrities wear. If you're passionate about fashion or have experience in this industry, this might be worth your time as a ready audience is waiting to see what you can offer.

- **Beauty**

More popular than fashion on Instagram is beauty. Over 96% of all beauty brands have invested in a strong Instagram presence. It's likely because many teenagers and women love interacting with beauty products on Instagram. Users want to see tutorials, beauty tips, product reviews, and whatever else you can cook up. Creativity and authenticity are going to be critical here. The more unique your content, the better it will perform.

- **Health and Fitness**

Many people have prioritized health and well-being, especially since the 2020 pandemic. So, it shouldn't be surprising that the health and fitness niche is profitable. It can be a subset of fitness or purely focused on nutrition. You can grow and monetize your expertise with creativity and hard work, regardless of your preference.

- **Animals**

People on Instagram love pets. Some accounts dedicated to animals (including pets) have become so popular they outshine human celebrities. So, if you're passionate about any creature, it's probable that you can grow a decent following and fan base around your non-human friend.

- **Memes**

Instagram is full of memes. They are entertaining, quick to create, and the perfect viral content recipe. If you naturally have a talent for making your friends laugh or want to curate memes across the web, this might be a great niche on Instagram.

- **Travel**

Travel is huge on Instagram. Some of these accounts have massive followings, and all they do is post breathtaking pictures of a place you've never even heard of and probably can't afford to travel to. That's perhaps why people follow these accounts. It gives them a sense of adventure, aspiration, and escapism from their little cubicle. These types of accounts bring the world's best to the travel enthusiast. If you love to travel or dream of traveling full-time, starting an understanding of your own is a great idea. Share your travel pictures, experiences, and love for our planet with the Instagram community, and they will reward you with lots of engagement.

- **Motivational quotes**

Another super popular niche that anyone can start is motivational. If you're a fan of collecting inspiring and motivational quotes from the greats, then, by all means, go for it. Some accounts on Instagram have gathered together crazy followings by posting beautiful quotes that make people feel good. It's like a fast espresso shot for personal development addicts.

- **Crafts and DIY**

Have you always had a knack for fixing things yourself? Do people call you when they need a homemade remedy of some kind? Then, consider creating an account where you share your passion and skills. DIY accounts are pretty awesome and garner decent followings. Building things with your hands and sharing them with your tribe isn't just rewarding. It's also a great way to monetize your account.

If you've gone through this list and felt utterly out of place because none of it resonates with what you want to create on Instagram, don't despair just yet. While I encourage you to pick a niche with a large enough audience, I know that specific niches have small followings yet still need to work. So, if none of the above felt hot enough, check out a few examples on Instagram accounts that are doing well, even though they serve a tiny audience.

Famous Instagram Accounts In Various Niches

If you usually geek out on topics and hobbies that leave your family confused, these accounts should encourage you to go after your kind of people and make your Instagram account a success story.

- **Vegan and plant-based food**

Food is a massive category on Instagram, but veganism isn't. Yet, one can create a healthy audience and get Instagram famous from this niche. A great example is Kate Jenkins, who has an account dedicated to vegan recipes that are easy to make. She gets a decent engagement with every post.

Another great example is dietician Catherine, who shares easy vegan recipes, as the handle suggests. With 300K followers and posts getting upwards of 4,000 likes each, Catherine is an excellent example of how a small niche can pay off big time. https://elisedarma.com/blog/tiny-niches-instagram

He's a cute dog-turned-entrepreneur. I didn't make up that title. I snagged it from Jiffpom, who has become an influencer on Instagram with over 10 million followers. He has even won awards and gets featured on media outlets such as Fox News. If you've got a cute pet that can entertain your audience, why not niche down to that?

- **Disney**

I bet you didn't see that one coming! Yes, Disney themed Instagram account is a real niche. It's tiny but will still make you money and get you followers. For example, Kait Killebrew has an account focused purely on Disney. Instead of a regular travel account, she only talks about the Disney world. She's got over 5K followers, and sure, that doesn't make her a mega influencer, but it does give her enough influence to get paid sponsorship gigs.

Brands that sell products related to Disney now want to work with Kait because they know her audience is ideal, hyper-engaged, and loyal to that kind of lifestyle. It might seem wild to think such a tiny niche is worth pursuing, but the results don't lie.

- **Search Engine Optimization (SEO)**

All businesses want to appear on the first page of Google. If your superpower and skill show others how to do this, why not create an account around SEO? You probably won't have crazy numbers as this is a smaller niche, but you can still do extraordinary in terms of engagement and income. For example, @conqueryourcontent focuses on all things SEO-related. She has a following of over 2K, which makes her a micro-influencer. According to the SEO experts, the small following brings her high-quality leads, and she's consistently generating new projects each month from her Instagram marketing.

Whether you already have an account, now is the time to build that proper foundation. Let the examples and categories I've shared inspire you to choose the niche you will successfully work on over the coming months and years. To help you do it the right way, follow the steps below.

How To Choose Your Niche The Right Way

Step #1: Begin with your passions, talents, and skills.

As I said, you will be doing this for a long time. Before that account can generate influence and revenue for you, there will be a lot of time, resources, and energy investment on your end, so it makes sense to do what you already enjoy.

That's why you must identify your strengths, passions, and interests. Make this process impactful by going through the following questions with me. You can write the answers on a Google document or a notepad—list as many as you can think of.

- What topic do you most enjoy talking about with friends and family? You could go on for hours if they'd let you.
- How do you like to spend your free time?
- What hobbies have you had since childhood?
- What did you want to do when you were 9? How about selling lemonade or creating comic characters?
- What topics do you enjoy learning? Look at the blogs, magazines, and social media accounts you follow.
- What skills have you trained on that you're good at?
- Is there something people love to get your advice on? It could be make-up tips, movie recommendations, or anything else.

Step #2: Do competitive research.

Once you identify what you're interested in posting, do a little research on Instagram to see what similar accounts are doing and their audience's response. Since you will share similar audiences, this is a great way to figure out what works and what doesn't. It also helps you identify potential brands you might work with once your brand is established if you're an influencer. At this point, you intend to find popular accounts and the best hashtags on Instagram for your content. You can also use a site like all-hashtags.com to find the best hashtags for your topic. For example, I typed "Leadership" on the site and got 30 of the best hashtags.

Influencer tip:

If you already know a specific brand you want to work with further down the road, research the influencers they currently use. Follow these influencers and note the campaigns they create, the hashtags, and the type of content they put out. Learn as much as you can and do your best to create content geared toward that brand's interests and mission.

Step #3: Find the gaps

The next important step as you move toward defining your niche is to find gaps that you can fill in terms of content. Is there a topic you feel needs to get the attention it deserves? For example, if you want a vegan recipe account, you can focus more on organic cruelty-free products because no one is doing that. That can be a great way to create a name for yourself within a broader category.

Step #4: Research what your ideal audience cares about

Remember that list of passions, talents, and skills? It's time to match it up with an audience. This will help you shortlist the best niche faster than any other step. It's also one of the most crucial steps you can take because it focuses on serving your future audience. Of course, if you have no audience or customer base, this exercise will require more research and some gut guidance. What it comes down to is answering a few questions. Namely:

- What problem or challenge is my ideal client facing?
- What desire or aspiration does my ideal client have?
- What values do we share in common?
- What type of content do they most care about?

If you start from zero and have no access to an existing audience, consider visiting forums and sites like Quora to see what people are discussing around your topic. It would be best to explore Google Trends, BuzzSumo, and Ubersuggest to uncover the search terms people are typing in related to their pain points and the social media content that's doing well on the Internet. If you need to know who your audience is or what's happening with them, the next chapter will guide you by finding your ideal audience and creating persona documents to help with your marketing campaigns.

This exercise aims to find an overlap between what you enjoy talking about and what your future followers care about. That point of intersection should be 70% of your content ideas and determine your page's theme.

Step #5: Make it beautiful

Instagram is all about attractive pictures, and your feed should have a look and feel appealing to your ideal audience. That doesn't mean going overboard and exaggerating or doing anything out of integrity with your personality (no need to get half-naked or show us your butt!). What it means is regardless of your niche, you need to choose a grand color scheme, font, filters, and mood boards that will create an appeal for your audience. I don't care if your account is on health insurance or home repairs; think out of the box and visit beauty blogs, lifestyle blogs, and other Instagram accounts with that wow factor. See what you can learn from them and apply what you learn to your topic.

Step #6: Determine whether you can make money with your niche.

Unless you're doing this as a non-profit, this step should be done before proceeding to the next chapter. I assume you've narrowed your list to one or two topic areas due to the previous actions. It's a good idea to check out the income-earning potential of each niche topic so you can see which one will yield a higher return on investment for all your hard work. ClickBank is a great place to find answers, but you can also go to Amazon if that feels more comfortable. ClickBank is my top recommendation because you can find almost every niche and category one might think of. There are different offers for these categories, and the more products you see for a particular topic, the more confident you can be that it's a profitable niche. If you find nothing, then there's no monetizable crowd. You can build an audience around that topic, but earning money from it will be challenging.

Step #7: Decide and stick with your niche

At this point, based on all your research and reflection, you need to decide if you'll move forward with your niche idea. Here's the deal: you must make this decision. And once you make that decision, you must stick with it long enough to see results. Now, that doesn't mean that every post should be on soufflés if that's your thing, but it does mean that a new follower should have the experience and immediately make the connection that you specialize in making great soufflés. So, your brand identity over time should become more accessible to connect with new and existing audiences as they interact with your content. Instagram influencers need to create consistency and stick to a niche to make a good living out of it.

Following these steps gives you a solid idea of your account's niche. This narrowed focus will enable you to build a name for yourself and experience growth quicker than trying to speak to everyone on Instagram. But there is one more important thing you need to invest time in before creating fantastic content that draws in followers. Head over to the next chapter to see what I mean.

Chapter 4

Do You Know Your Ideal Audience?

You've probably heard that Instagram is one of the most popular social networks on the planet. It's ranked 6th in the world, with 1 billion users only surpassed by Facebook (2.6 billion), YouTube (2.0 billion), WhatsApp (1.6 billion), Messenger 1.3 billion), and WeChat (1.1 billion). The best part is that Instagram has a vast global audience. But having an international audience means you can serve only some people on the platform. So before starting our content strategy for Instagram, we need to investigate the behavior of the users to figure out what your ideal audience likes to experience on the platform so that your content can move in that direction. You have chosen your niche and already know what problems, aspirations, and topics your audience finds exciting, but how do you align that with content creation? By getting into the mind of your ideal fan. First, when browsing the platform, You must understand who they are and their psychological state.

Instagram Users Statistics You Should Know

We all behave and set different expectations for the various platforms we hang out on. MY MINDSET IS DIFFERENT when I am on YouTube than when I am on TikTok or Instagram. The same is true for your ideal audience, so it's essential to understand how users behave on Instagram and what content is most appealing to them.

Here are some valuable stats that you should know from 2020.

- Five hundred million daily active users are accessing the app globally.

- People spend an average of 28 minutes a day on the Instagram app. Users under 25 spend even more time on the app, with data showing the younger demographic spending 32 minutes while those over 25 spend 24 minutes.

- The most popular countries with the highest usage include the United States (120 million), India (80 million), Brazil (77 million), Indonesia (63 million), and Russia (44 million). Five hundred million daily active users are accessing the app globally.

- 22.02% of the world's 4.54 billion active Internet users access Instagram monthly.

- In the United States, 75% of people aged 18 - 24 use Instagram, followed by 57% between 25 - 30 years old.

- Globally, gender use is pretty even, with 50.9% female and 49.1% male users.

- In the United States, adult users are 43% women and 31% men.

- Brands typically look to brands with 50,000 to 100,000 followers to promote their products. This number, however, can be less depending on niche and industry.
- According to the 2020 data, the best time to post on Instagram is between 10:00 pm and 2:pm Central Daylight Time. The best days are Wednesday at 11:00 a.m. and Friday between 10:00 a.m. to 11:00 a.m.
- Instagram images get an average of 23% more engagement than Facebook.
- Posts with videos receive 38% more engagement than photos.
- 70% of users look up brands on Instagram.
- 79% of users search Instagram for information on a product or service.
- 80% of users follow at least one brand on Instagram.
- One-third of Instagram users have purchased through the platform on mobile.
- 70% of consumers want to see brands they like and follow taking a stand on social issues that matter to them. Of those, 65% want the brands to take that stand on social media.
- The average engagement rate for branded posts is 4.3%.
- Having at least one hashtag can increase engagement by up to 12.6%.
- Longer hashtags get more results. The debate is still on, but the magic number is 11 hashtags for each post if you want optimum results.
- Four hundred million users watch Instagram Stories daily.
- 46% of Instagram Stories users like funny and entertaining content.
- Brand Stories have an 85% completion rate.

Should You Pay Attention and Leverage Your Instagram Competitors?

The simple answer is yes and no. If you have the right intention and strategy, these accounts can become a great source of information, inspiration, and lead generation. No, if you're from a lack of mentality and only want to copy others.

Instagram has plenty of people to turn into followers, so you should never feel intimidated by the fact that you will find influencers and profile accounts already established in your chosen niche. I encourage you to see this as a good thing. Think about it. Finding an account with an already established audience of people who would also benefit from your content makes it easier for you to grow your account as long as you do it the ethical way.

You can grow your Instagram account by networking, following, engaging with, and establishing relationships with influencers in your space. Find authority content and choose the most important statements that resonate with you and show signs of an engaged audience. I suggest making a list of 10 charges and researching the following:

- What is their follower count?
- How often do they post?

- What engagement do they get on average?
- What theme can you identify from their feed?
- How often do they post Instagram Stories and IGTV?
- What hashtags are they using the most? What's the number count of hashtags used on each post?
- What is their branding like? For example, observe their tone of voice, colors, fonts, filters, messaging, etc.
- What do they like posting about? Are there any gaps in the type of content they are posting that you can post on your feed?

The purpose of your competitor analysis is to learn as much as you can from your competition so that you can deploy the following tips.

#1. Consider doing an outreach campaign to all the accounts that resonate with you and propose a collaboration.

#2. Comment, like, share, save, repost, follow, and even create content mentioning the content you like from a competitor. Then tag them. And when you comment on a photo or video, make it thoughtful and valuable to the community so other users can also experience your personality.

#3. Consider offering to manage their account for free so you can promote your content. The owner will likely accept your proposal if you pick the correct statements with a decent following, high engagement, and no corresponding blog or website. Although this strategy will involve more effort, it also opens you up to an already established audience, meaning you can exponentially grow your following within days or weeks.

#4. If you run some paid ads, I encourage you to find a competitor with a healthy audience size and run ads against them. If you use this approach, polish up your Instagram profile and bio to create resonance so they can immediately feel a connection with you. For example, if the competitor is local, consider adding your city name to your profile.

Bonus tip:

If you want to dig your heels in with an organic strategy that doesn't cost a dime, here's an incredible hack. Follow 100 of your top competitors' followers. After you follow someone, browse through their feed and find between one and three posts you can read and comment on. Make that comment thoughtful, and don't be afraid to use some emojis and your unique personality. It will take some upfront investment of time and energy, but I can assure you at least a 34% follow-up result just by applying this simple hack.

Targeting Your Audience

Everything hinges on our ability to determine who your content will be created for accurately. Suppose we need to improve on producing content that engages a specific group of people from the one billion Instagram users. In that case, monetizing your account will be next to impossible. The statistics I have shared in this chapter prove that many active users are already hanging out on the platform daily. Unfortunately, they will still engage with and buy from your brand. So, how do we play to ensure the odds are in your favor? By investing a ton of time defining your target audience and continually carrying out tests to learn more about your tribe.

The first thing you should do is implement proven tactics that get this done. Suppose you need an existing customer base, business data to go by, or followers from other social media platforms to leverage; what then?

Start where you are with what you know. Ask yourself the following questions:

- Who is my product or service designed for?
- What is my ideal audience looking for?
- What conversation is taking place on my competitor's account that can give me a glimpse of what my ideal audience wants more?

Use a tool like Phalanx Influencer Auditor to provide you with insights such as demographics, brand mentions, follower locations, and engagement levels. That will enable you to see missing audience segments you still need to catch up on, the type of content your people might like, and the most active follower locations for your product or service.

The next thing you want to do is monitor your Instagram analytics as you publish and interact with your community. Instagram can tell you a lot about your target audience, especially if you have a business account. If you need to learn how to switch to a business account, I will demonstrate it in an upcoming section. Once you've been operating under the correct type of account for a while, data will populate your Instagram insights, which can be accessed by going to the "Insights" tab > "Audience." You'll learn more about your existing followers and their location, gender, age range, etc. Add this information to the document you've been filling in so far, and you'll have a healthy understanding of what your target audience looks like.

Once you have an idea of your target audience, it's time to reach out. All the data you've gathered will only mean a thing if you put it to good use by creating content specific to that user group and engaging them within the community. For instance, you could start by identifying those hot hashtags your ideal audience frequently uses. These hashtags should be included in your post where appropriate. You should also invest some time daily clicking on those hashtags to find top-performing content so you can comment, like, and interact with others who have commented. Get your voice heard and share your opinion where you find trendy conversations in your niche. That can help you get noticed by all the right people. A neat trick is to sign up for a social listening tool that allows you to receive notifications of topics getting a lot of attention on social media.

Another thing you can do is connect with the right influencers in your space. Create irresistible incentives for the influencers that serve your ideal audience. You can find these influencers through hashtag research, as mentioned before, or by using platforms like Influencer. Co. The only way this will yield positive results is if you plan on the offer for the partnership. Do you have a great product or service you can give out for the influencer to review? Can you partner up for a giveaway contest or have them do a take-over of your Instagram for a set period? You need to figure out what will be appealing to the influencer. When starting, stick to micro-influencers, as they will likely find your offer valuable. They are also easier to reach.

Suppose you have created a must-have, organic, homemade skincare product that works to heal acne. But it would be best if you had an Instagram following. Using the tips you've learned, you come across a beauty influencer who reviews organic make-up for sensitive skin. She's only got 20,000 followers and has high engagement. This would be a perfect influencer for you to tap into because her audience would likely find your homemade organic skin acne healer very appealing. All you'd need is to make the influencer an offer she cannot refuse—something that benefits her and her audience way more than it helps you.

Get creative and think of how to apply this to your niche.

Chapter 5

Branding Your Instagram Account

If you don't have an Instagram account, now is the time to do it. I will walk you through the simple process, and you can always reference the Instagram help center for any snags or new updates. Even if you have an Instagram account, I suggest going through this entire chapter. You can always pick up tricks and ideas on how to improve.

Creating An Account

The first thing you need to do is download the app from the App Store or Google Play Store, depending on your smartphone. Once installed, tap the Instagram icon to open and click the "Sign Up"/ "Create Account" button to create a new account. Use your email address or phone number and tap "Next." If you prefer using Facebook, then you have the option to sign up with your Facebook account. You'll then be prompted to log into your Facebook account if you're currently logged out. If you register with an email or phone number, create a username and password, fill out your profile info, and tap Next.

The default setting for all Instagram users is a personal account. We want to use it to build our brand and market our business, so we have to switch it to a business account and connect it to a Facebook business page. To link to your Facebook accounts and share posts directly from Instagram to Facebook, you need to go to your profile and tap the menu icon. Then click the little cogwheel for "Settings" > "Account" > Linked Accounts > Facebook. Enter your Facebook Login details and pick the page you want to be associated with this account.

If you're wondering how to switch from a personal account to a business account, it's super easy. Go to your profile and tap the menu in the upper right corner. Then go to "Settings" > "Account" > "Switch to Professional Account" > "Business." Here, you must add details such as business category (which should be chosen based on your niche) and contact information. Once information is filled in, then tap "Done."

Personal Versus Business Account

Do you know the difference between a personal and business account, or why we insist on switching to a business account?

Let's start with the fact that only with a business account will you be able to receive analytics from Instagram telling you more about your audience. That will enable you to know which posts are performing best, which viewers came through your chosen hashtags, and how many of the accounts being reached are currently following you. You can also get insights into your audience demographics.

A business account will give you access to a lot more premium features, such as the ability to add the "swipe up" feature once you get to 10,000 or more followers, and you also get a "contact" button so that people can call or email you directly from Instagram. With the launch of the Instagram shop and Reels, having a business account has never been more essential because only with a business account do you get the chance to show up on the Explore page through your reels. And, of course, having an in-built Instagram shop makes it easy for a follower to purchase something from you.

Tips For Setting Up Your Profile

Anyone can set up an Instagram profile within a few minutes, but setting one up that attracts new followers requires a lot of careful consideration. I am sharing best practices for correctly setting up your Instagram profile.

Tip #1: Make sure you've switched to a business profile

We've already discussed the benefits of setting up your account as a business profile. You want anyone worldwide to view your excellent feed and your posts to have a wider reach so anyone who resonates with your profile can instantly follow you. This is among the most important things you can do when setting up your profile.

Tip #2: Use an appropriate image that authentically expresses you and your brand

If your brand is centered around you, i.e., a personal brand, I encourage you to use an accurate picture of yourself. Look at accounts such as Marie Forleo, Gary Vaynerchuck, and Tai Lopez for great examples of ordinary folks who have built successful Instagram accounts. More people resonate with them because they come across as approachable and genuine. You want the same perception with your brand. However, if you choose the corporate route, learn from accounts such as Hubspot, Buffer, and CoSchedule. Use a simple logo and ensure it aligns with your main website and the brand identity. You might modify your primary logo to fit better with the platform's dimensions but keep the original look consistent.

Tip #3: Choose the correct username and Instagram name

Picking a name that's memorable, searchable, and aligns with your brand identity is more challenging than one might think. Be mindful of the word you settle for, especially if you're going for a username different from your real name or company name.

You have up to thirty characters for your handle; no symbols or spaces should exist. This is the name people will use when they mention you in a comment or if they want to tag you in something, so choose wisely. If you can't find something simple and creative, you can always use your name instead of combining it with your specialty, e.g., Suzie, who specializes in vegan cuisine recipes, can call herself Suze_veganlife or Vegan_Suzie. To edit your @username, go to the profile page > "Edit Profile." Click on the text or space next to the person icon and enter the desired username.

You can change the Instagram name as often as you like to test out different titles that communicate what your audience will resonate with. However, I don't recommend regularly changing your username because you'd have to change all the places you added or linked to this username. Otherwise, people will get a "broken link" or error page when they click on your old links.

Tip #4: Make your bio informative and engaging

Your bio on Instagram is the description at the top of your profile. It's what new visitors will see when they first encounter your profile. Depending on the first impression that your words make, a user is more likely to browse through your feed, engage with your account, and ultimately follow you, or they will click away. The copy on this bio is, therefore, critical. You only have 150 characters to tell people what you're about and why they should follow you. That's a little space to express yourself fully, so you need a lot of creativity to make this work.

The best way to approach this is to think from the perspective of your potential follower. They land on your profile either because they found your post through a hashtag they follow or some other reason. What should your bio profile say to make this person more interested in adding you to their feed? What's in it for them? Why should they care about your account? How will you improve their world and make them feel better?

As you come up with your ideas, don't be afraid to add your personality and play around with relevant emojis so people can "feel" the tone of your brand identity. An example I like is from Oreo's Instagram account. On their profile, they write, " See the world through our OREO Wonderfilled lens." You can also check out Nike. They regularly tweak their bio, but I especially like " Spotlighting athlete and 👟 (Sport shoe icon) stories."

Tip #5: Make the most of your clickable link.

You've got one chance to direct people to your website or offer, so save the link on your bio. That link is one of the most valuable real estate spaces for driving traffic to your unique product or service. To keep things super simple, you can use a standard link from your landing page and regularly update it with the latest offers. Savvy Instagrammers use tools like Tailwind to take things further and create a connection with multiple items. Regardless of your option, track that link to gain data about the users clicking to learn more about your brand.

Tip #6: Create an attractive grid on your feed

Why is this important? Well, think about it. When we discover a new account, we check out the profile pic bio and instantly scroll down to browse the feed. If our eyes and emotions resonate with what we see, it's an instant attraction, and we are likely to engage with and follow that account. If the feed repels us, it doesn't matter how much we liked the profile pic and bio; we'll likely click away without becoming followers.

I have often encountered a post while browsing a hashtag that matters to me and clicked through to check out more from the account. Once there, I become disinterested in the history because the rest of the feed needs to speak to me. Most Instagrammers need to realize how many followers they might lose because they need to invest time thinking through their grid layout.

It's almost like cooking and serving the best ingredients on an unappetizing plate. No one will want to eat that food. So, consider this exercise as important as creating great content and writing good copy for your bio. To ensure you set yourself up for success, craft a pattern following the existing rows of threes that Instagram offers. Your content can repeat in multiples of three, six, nine, twelve, or whatever you like, and it will always look like there's an overarching pattern that will create a sense of symmetry and consistency. For example, I've followed this pattern on one of my Instagram accounts by switching between white and colored backgrounds. So, post #1 is a white background, post #2 is a colored background, post #3 is a white background, post #4 is a white background, post #5 is a colored background, and so on. You could also go a different route if you sell a specific product by making every third post an image of that product. For example, if you sell puppy accessories, every third post could be an accessory. That would eventually create that sense of consistency on your grid.

Advanced tip:

If you're comfortable with color coordination, use color scheme coordination by pairing similar tones and colors on your grid. Just make sure the transition is seamless. It's perfect for feeds focusing more on selfies and human portraits as the main subject.

How To Brand On Instagram

Branding is a vast topic, so we will focus on the main technical things you need to know and implement for our beginner's journey. After all, it will take a lot of work to stand out in the ocean of fellow Instagrammers if people cannot immediately identify what you stand for and what makes you unique. So, when you think about branding, approach it from the standpoint of evoking a specific emotion and perception. It's about creating an experience for your followers and potential followers. So, what experience do you want to have, and how do you want people to remember you? Are you fun? Clean and minimalist? Youthful and rebellious? Serious and formal?

Branding is all about storytelling, trust-building, and perception. It must be timely, and it will take time to happen. Every post moves you along this journey, so you must clarify your vision for your Instagram page and the mission or reason for creating it. Always anchor yourself in these critical foundational elements as you determine what brand you're building. Another thing you want to think about is the tonality and personality that you want people to experience. A comical feed and a severe or impersonal tone would be awkward. That lack of congruency in your branding would unconsciously throw people off. The same is true for the colors and fonts.

The colors, font, and imagery you use should paint this picture to a user in seconds. Most people begin this journey of branding by creating a mood board. You can do this on software like InVision for free.

The next thing you need is to decide on brand colors. Instagram is a 100% visual-based app emphasizing aesthetics, so have fun here. Be true to yourself and find color combinations that enable you to express who you are while remaining relevant to your brand's message and offer. Different colors and shades have a different impact on the consumer. Some are perceived as calming or youthful, while others appear bold, rebellious, or gothic. This step might take anywhere from a couple of hours to several days. But try not to overthink it. A helpful resource that can guide you in choosing the right color for your Instagram brand is Colors. Cafe. They even have an inspiring Instagram account that posts color palettes with each color code listed to speed up your decision-making process. You can also check out Pantone on Instagram, where they share many fantastic ideas on mixing and matching colors.

Once you've decided on a color, it's time to find the correct font. Although the captions use a standard font on Instagram, your posts will require text occasionally unless you only specialize in selfies. This part of your branding is critical for a motivational account with quotes. The font you use instantly tells a story and reveals your personality. One thing I want to point out before encouraging you to pick a font is to be mindful of the font type because while some are extremely cute, they can be challenging to see or read on the Instagram feed. This is a mobile-first app, so everything needs to be ideal for the small screen.

Serif, Sans serif, Display, and Modern are the best and easiest to read on mobile. Serif fonts supposedly represent tradition, respectability, and discernment. San serifs are modern, objective, modern, and associated with innovation. Current fonts are considered stylish and robust. Display fonts are often associated with friendliness, amusement, and expressiveness. To help you figure out what fonts you should use, consider using a design app like Canva, which has an enormous font library to play with. They even have ready-made templates and font pairings. You can also follow the "We Love Branding" Instagram account for inspiration.

At this point, you already have your target audience honed in, as we discussed in the last chapter. Since you know who you will be creating content for, it's essential to do a quick assessment to see if the branding specs you're going for align with your target audience. In other words, are the colors, fonts, mood boards, and so on something they would find attractive?

Examples of accounts that are crushing it with their branding:

Example #1: BulletProof

They are a coffee and nutrition supplement company. They have three things going for them regarding branding – a minimalistic yet striking color scheme + simple images, + uniform quote tiles to break up their feed. The picture on the left was taken three years ago, so you can see while this is a great branding example, the growth still takes consistency and time.

← **bulletproof** ⋮

1,753 Posts   **325K** Followers   **577** Following

Bulletproof®
Fuel your journey with Bulletproof. Our approach to nutrition helps transform the way you feel.
linktr.ee/bulletproof

[View Shop]

[**Follow**] [Message] [Email] [⌄]

Highlights

Example #2: Starface

It is an up-and-coming skincare brand that makes unique acne stickers with stars. That fits perfectly with their bright yellow aesthetics, which is easy to see on your feed. Their theme is consistent while posting testimonials, memes, and more. Bright and colorful is what they're sticking to, and it is working, given their 335K followers and counting.

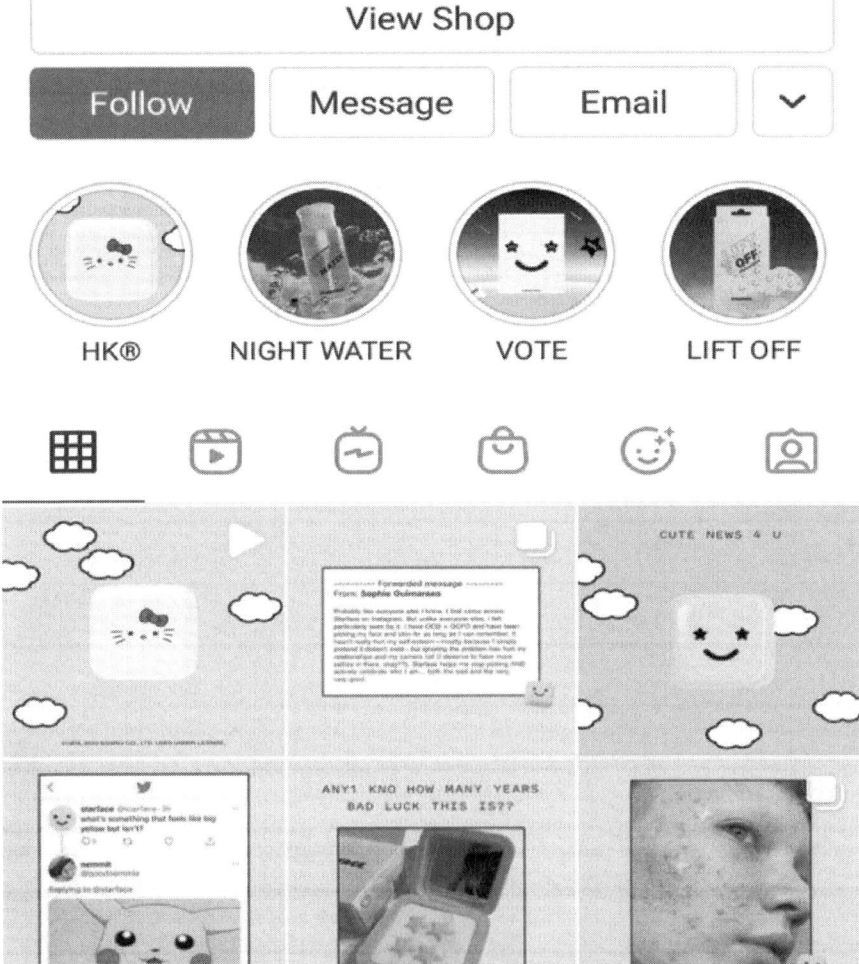

Branding Your Instagram Account

Example #3: Studiodiy

With over 400,000 followers, this account knows how to build an Instagram brand. It's colorful, whimsical, and feels like you're having a party. The feed is bold and fun, but don't be fooled; these guys have intentionally created this mood of "life is a party" by carefully curating their feed for maximum impact. The account uses various colors, but they disperse them thoughtfully to ensure no two side-by-side images look the same. If you observe the feed, you'll notice a running rainbow theme, which makes the aesthetics of the meal a great delight for the eyes as you scroll the posts. If you want this same bursting of-color effect, choose one or two bold primary colors and balance this out with a few pastel shades.

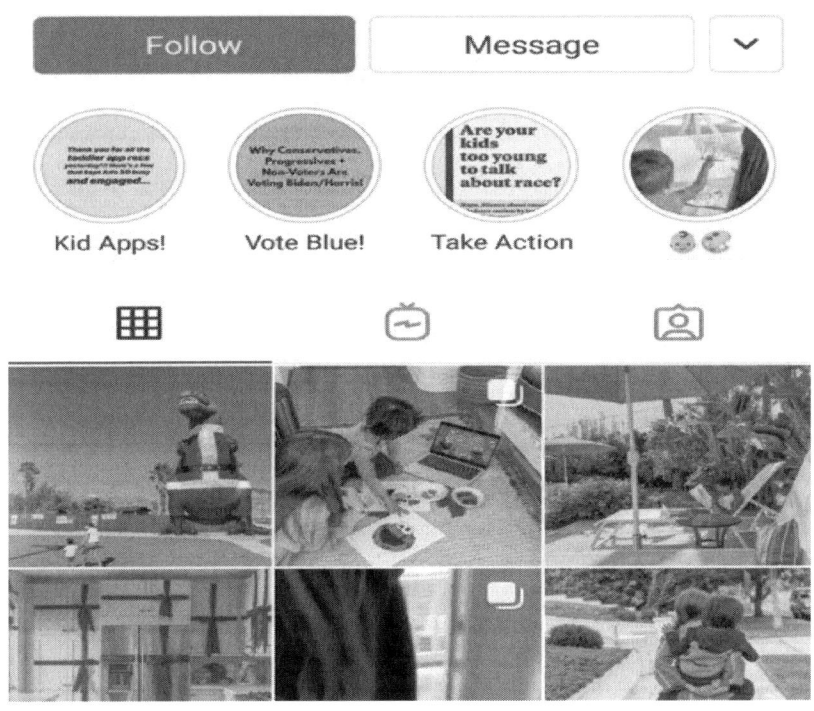

Before we move, here's a simple step-by-step to follow as you build your brand based on everything we've covered thus far.

Step #1: Begin with the end in mind. Set your objectives for Instagram.

Step #2: Narrow your focus and choose a style pattern or theme for your feed.

Step #3: Identify your ideal audience and determine their concerns.

Step #4: Create a killer profile and bio that speaks to them.

Step #5: Decide your feed's color scheme, font, and mood board.

Step #6: Identify your brand's tone and personality.

Step #7: Create excellent content.

Section 3

Creating Instagram Content

Chapter 6

The Content Plan

As you saw in the previous chapter, creating excellent content is fundamental to building a successful brand on Instagram. This is where we will cover everything you need to know to create engaging posts and videos. The bottom line is that you need to start with the ideas you've gathered after going through previous audience research exercises, competitor research, and determining your passion. The content should be aligned with your vision, mission, and the theme of your feed.

When we discussed theme or style patterns, we emphasized the colors you'd use and the filters you'd like to apply to your images. It's time to add another component: the type of content you will post.

Your niche will direct you on the type of posts to go for. Then, feel free to get creative when creating that harmonious and consistent feel. Your visual appeal and style should reflect your brand's identity. Once you nail that down, creating a content plan is time.

The goals you set at the beginning of this book should inform the content you will create and publish. It would be best to consider how much time will be assigned to content creation and publication. Unless you are fortunate enough to have a big team, you'll be doing all of this on your own until such a time that you're able to outsource. Please consider your current lifestyle, obligations, and whether this will be a full-time thing or a side hustle that you'll work on during weekends and late at night.

Take a moment to get honest about how much time you can commit to content creation each week. Then, mark it in your calendar to block out that time and get it done. We'll discuss the different types of posts you can create and the best-performing content on Instagram for some inspiration.

Sticking To Your Niche

Here's a mistake many newbies make. Once they publish a few posts, they start getting distracted by what they see on other accounts and start copying that, expecting it to get them results faster. Have you ever been to an account that felt overwhelming when you scrolled through the feed? That happens as a result of trying to appeal to everyone. The worst part about mixing up your themes on the spread is confusing your potential followers because they must identify what you stand for. And if your tribe cannot quickly identify you, they won't be sticking around long enough to become fans or customers.

Just because you see a cute puppy post getting lots of likes and attention on your feed doesn't mean you should switch to posting puppy pics when it has nothing to do with your brand.

The lesson here is on brand consistency. You already did the hard work of finding your niche, researching and creating a content theme, and planning for the type of content you'll be publishing. Stay consistent with your plan even if you don't see the results you expect. There is no such thing as an overnight success, so be patient with your project and stick to your niche.

Check What Others Are Doing.

From time to time, it's beneficial to check on your peers or influencers in your niche to see how they are growing their accounts. This can be used to get inspiration for your content and a hack for engaging with their followers, who might also be interested in what you offer. Invest some time each month to review the top ten people in your space and use social listening tools to inform you of their best-performing content. Then, analyze it to figure out what's working and what the audience wants to see more of, and challenge yourself to create something ten times better than what they have.

Getting Inspiration

Piggybacking on getting content inspiration from those in your niche, you should also gather inspiration for your content to remain fresh, relevant, and appealing to the Instagram audience. Here are a few places I find inspiration when planning out my content.

Google Alerts

This is an easy way to receive alerts from Google based on the terms you choose to monitor. By creating a sign on a specific topic, you'll receive email notifications on all the exciting and top-performing content across the web.

BuzzSumo

BuzzSumo software is preferred for learning what's popular across social channels. It's a personal favorite, and the main reason is that I can easily find the most shared content across all social networks on my chosen topic here. I can even plug in a competitor's website and determine their top-performing content. Once I find the top performers, I click to dig through the comments because I often find lots of inspiration on what to create next.

Pinterest Boards

Given how visual Pinterest is, it can be a great source of inspiration for your Instagram content. Pinterest is great for curating content. Find a group board on your niche topic where you can find links and infographics. You can custom-make your board and collect exciting articles. These articles are great for discovering what people want to see or learn more about.

Imgur

Only a few know this platform, but it's an excellent place for getting visual content inspiration. Imgur showcases the most popular images on the web. This is perfect for an Instagrammer, especially if you're looking for memes, quotes, or humor.

Remembering to remain on brand and stick to your theme as you gather these ideas is the most important thing to remember. Just because something makes you laugh or swoon doesn't mean it should be added to your content plan. Remember, inspiration comes from anyone and anywhere at any time. Always be on the lookout for ideas, stories, and insights that you feel will benefit your growing audience.

Instagram Posts

Now that you have inspiration on what to post and a plan that aligns with your theme and vision, let's talk about the different types of posts that perform well. Currently, Instagram allows images, videos, and carousels on the feed. But that doesn't limit what you can create within the context of an image, video, or carousel. Here are some popular content types.

#1: Motivation

This type of content can include videos of you inspiring and encouraging your audience or motivational quotes. Instagram users love getting encouragement from people with shared values and a powerful message. Some accounts have hundreds of thousands of followers, so if you're into speaking or have a powerful message to share, consider creating this form of positive content.

#2: Behind the scenes

This type of content gives your followers that exclusive inside look that makes them feel like they know you. This is your chance to show a more human and personal aspect of your brand. It's a great way to create genuine authenticity and connection, whether you're a personal brand or a large business.

#3: "How to" photos & videos

This type of content should be actionable and educational. How-to content is precious, and it performs well on Instagram. Whether you want to show your audience how to bake cookies, make a cocktail, or put on makeup the right way for different occasions, this content will attract the right tribe to you. You could also create a series of images showing your audience how to use a new feature of your software app.

#4: Giveaway

This type of content is usually part of a more extensive campaign. It is great for generating buzz and attracting potential followers and fans on Instagram. Why? Because people love free stuff! A giveaway post or video practically invites people to participate in something you've created so they can win something. It works because it encourages social sharing and is a fast way to grow your following. Just make sure you have a good plan behind it and that you give away something valuable to the audience while remaining relevant to your brand. For example, a golf brand should not give away an iPhone! Instead, something related to golf should be the main prize. See what I mean?

#5: Influencer takeover

You can partner with an influence in your niche and have them take over and post content and Instagram Stories for a set time. It will attract a new audience, exposing your account to their audience. It also creates an excellent variety on your feed. This content is great for growing your followers and fan base if you can access influencers.

#6: Posts featuring influencers

This type of post can either be created by you or by the influencer you are featuring. It works exceptionally well for eCommerce brands because if you can get someone influential to strut your product, you can show your followers how great it is. Even if you post an image or video mentioning the influencer using your products, users love seeing well-known names endorsing your brand.

#7: User-generated images and videos

This type of post is among the best-performing content regarding conversion. Although you don't create the content, you can incentivize people to make this type of content and share it with you so you can repost it on your feed. People are always more concerned about how your product or service can improve their lives, so this content produces excellent engagement. If you already have an existing customer base, this is content you can get immediately to boost your marketing campaign. Give the previous or existing customers an irresistible offer so they can create posts and tag you or use a particular hashtag so you can have this content easily accessible in one place, ready for curation and reposting.

Focus On Your Theme And Visual Style

In alignment with your content plan and sticking to your niche, it's also important to consistently maintain a theme that quickly reminds people of what you stand for. We already talked about the importance of creating a coherent look and feel. This could be as simple as the color you use, how you crop the borders, the layout of the patterns, or a combination of some of these. Having that consistency trains new and potential followers in your unique style and helps them know what to expect from you. It makes it easier for them to spot your content on their feed, increasing the chances of engagement. Let's share some examples of what a great visual style should look like and some examples of popular Instagram themes so you can stay focused.

- **Clean Background**

This theme is excellent for foodies or anyone who wants to emphasize details without distraction. By using this theme, your audience will be drawn more to the photo's main subject. Lots of food bloggers use this theme on their feeds. Getting a space with an all-white backdrop and good lighting is recommended to make it work for you. This will cut down your editing time tremendously, and of course, you can use an editing app for the final touches.

- **Bright Whites**

This is a hugely popular theme, especially for photographers and designers. It's fresh, clean, and bright, making the feed harmonious and pop out details. To create this theme, you must take most of your pictures in a bright white space with natural light. You can also use an editing app to help you get that bright, clean look. Then, arrange photos with pops of color in a balanced way to even out the color balance in your feed.

- **Alternating Borders**

This type of theme is quite popular on Instagram and easy to create. All you need to do is edit your photo in an app first. You can use Apps like InShot and A Color Story to frame your pictures.

- **Color Contrasts**

If you love bold splashes or contrasting colors, why not turn that into a theme? Yes, I know the norm is usually a single color, tone, or hue on a photo, but sometimes being bold can pay off. Check out @colormecourtney to see what I mean. Her feed is bold and full of vibrant energy. If you'd like something similar, then all you need to do is invest in an editing app to help you turn on the volume of all the radiant hues you'll have. And, of course, make sure to take pictures where you can find a lot of contrasting colors. As you publish your post, be mindful of the arrangement so you can balance out the visuals. A good rule of thumb is to switch up the placement of colors and to avoid blobs of one color dominating the feed. Go for that magical rainbow effect, and you will wow your audience.

Instagram Captions

Tell me if you've had this experience recently. You notice a post from your favorite celebrity and click on it to check out the full post. Then you realize the base (usually a selfie) has gathered thousands of likes and attention. Yet, the celebrity didn't even post a single caption. It was just a cute or sexy-looking selfie of themselves and their dog.

You may assume your posts will attract just as much attention even if you don't say a word in your captions. You'd be dead wrong! Sure, if it's a half-naked picture of you with lots of right hashtags, you might get lucky and receive some attention, i.e., reach, but if you want engagement and conversion, you'll have to do better than just a half-naked selfie and twenty hashtags.

What you need are potent captions. These are written copy carefully crafted to help you take your audience from curious and interested to seriously engaged in what you want them to know about your brand.

That celebrity who can get away with using zero captions on their post probably has millions of followers. So, getting a couple of thousand likes is feasible. Until you get to the point where people are so obsessed with your brand that they want to know what shake you had for breakfast, stick to creating posts with meaningful captions.

How do you create excellent Instagram captions?

Since Instagram is a highly visual platform, you don't have to become a copywriting expert. You can use a few words. People are on this platform to feast with their eyes, and reading is a low priority, so short and sweet will serve you better than long-winded rants.

The purpose of an Instagram caption is to tell more of the story behind your image or video post. Whether you do that in one catchy sentence or a few paragraphs, what matters is the message comes across clearly. Suppose the image or video is about a sale or event. In that case, your captions should give clear explanations and instructions on how to participate and where.

If your post is about your business, share why this impacts your audience, who was involved in that particular post, and maybe even celebrate team members if applicable.

Best Practices For Writing Instagram Captions:

- **Focus on adding value, not the length of the caption.**

There is no right or wrong length for your Instagram captions. Some accounts have long copies and still get high engagement. At the same time, others use a single sentence yet also have higher engagement rates. What matters is the value of the words written. Use that real estate to offer tips and share tricks or industry hacks. If you're talking about your business, ensure it is customer-centric and not self-promotional as much as possible. If you share a backstory, add relevant and appealing details to your audience. The more you think about user experience, the easier it will be to create something people want to hear, save, and share with their friends.

- **Write like a human for a fellow human.**

A mistake I see with some accounts is that they try to be formal and unnatural, which is easy to spot. It comes across as fake, especially when the tone of the copy doesn't align with the theme and images on the feed. On Instagram, you want to be as friendly and approachable as possible. Think of it like texting your friend. How would you communicate a message to them? That same authentic and natural flair is what you need to add to your Instagram captions. If you don't usually use big, formal words when you speak to friends, don't do that on your Instagram feed.

- **Use a hook.**

The first sentence of your captions should have an impact on the readers. This is what they will see before clicking on the more icon. Make it appealing, and you'll see better engagement.

- **Storytelling is the secret sauce for success.**

Personality and storytelling in your captions will cause people to engage with you more. Feel free to express your truth and spice things up with your Vocabulary. If you check out accounts such as @HDFMAGAZINE, you will get a taste of what authentic expression looks like on Instagram. This brand is consistent with its theme, type of posts, and captions on each piece. They post extended captions and still get fantastic engagement and interactions from their followers because they know how to use descriptive, emotional phrases and anecdotes in their captions.

- **Give each post caption a purpose and intention.**

There should be a specific reason for writing your captions. That reason should align with your overall business objectives and the image or video's objective, which we addressed earlier. Therefore, you will know the purpose of the captions and encourage your followers to take appropriate action. You can add a call to action or ask questions so your audience can enter a contest, shop for a specific product, ask questions for engagement and live interactions, visit your website, or follow your account.

There's no end to the actions you can request from your audience if it's congruent with the image or video. Examples of activities to add to your captions. "Click the link in the bio," "Leave me a comment below with your answer," and "Tag a friend who needs to hear/read/see/win this today."

- **Use emojis generously**

Emojis on your Instagram captions add that extra flavor that animates your captions. It makes you look lighthearted and full of personality. You can also use emojis at the end of a sentence as a bookend or to break up a long-winded copy. Given the fun nature of the platform, you could even substitute certain words with relevant emojis. For example, instead of writing the word "books," you can use 📚.

The only thing to be mindful of is the amount of emojis you use. Please don't overdo it; make sure whichever you use aligns with your voice. If you're looking for some inspiration on emojis that call attention to a call-to-action, here's what I like to use: 💧 ✋ 📌 🎯 🔗

Examples of Instagram captions to inspire you:

- **Funny Instagram Captions.**
  - Namast'ay in bed.
  - We need to find out what's tighter: Our jeans or company culture.
  - Friday… My second favorite F word.
  - I'm just a girl standing before a salad, asking it to be a cupcake.

- **Business Instagram Captions.**

At [your company name], our best asset is our people.

Big things often have small beginnings. [Your Business Name] 's story began right here in this basement.

- **Sassy Instagram Captions**
  - I have 99 problems, but an excellent marketing team isn't one.
  - It's not called being bossy. It's called having leadership skills.
  - I'm an acquired taste. If you don't like me, acquire some taste.

Take a moment now to think about the captions you'll create for your first posts. Are you going to come across as funny? Inspirational? Serious? Sassy? Controversial?

Hashtags Galore

Although Twitter was the first platform to adopt hashtags in 2009, the first hashtag's origin in 2007 is credited to Nate Ridder. He used #sandiegoonfire in his social messages to inform people about the wildfires his local area was experiencing at the time. Fast forward to 2021, and hashtags dominate many social platforms, especially Instagram. I'm sure you know and use particular hashtags, and you've heard marketers encouraging Instagrammers to use hashtags to increase reach. But do you know the real purpose of using a hashtag?

Hashtags are meant to help us group similar content. That makes it easier for the right person to find the right content at the right time with the least effort. Another of looking at it is through the lens of like attracts like. People with similar interests will flock together around a topic they resonate with. Your brand should create content that enables your tribe (people interested in your case) to learn more about your product, campaign, and the informative content you have.

We help the algorithm sort our content on Instagram and deliver it to the right people through the hashtag system. Currently, the most popular hashtags on Instagram are #picoftheday, #photooftheday, #love, #fashion, #beautiful, #instagood, #happy, #cute, #tbt, #like4like, #followme, #selfie, #me, #summer, #friends, #repost, #nature, #girl, #fun, #style, #food, #instalike, #family, #travel, #life, #beauty, #nofilter, #amazing, #instamood, #instagram, #photography, #fitness, #smile, #instadaily, #art

How To Create Your Branded Hashtag

This option is only favorable once you've grown a decent size following. The more people engage with you and become familiar with your brand, the more likely they will use your hashtag. Creating giveaways and contests is also great because people can add a specific campaign hashtag to participate. The bigger your brand becomes on social media, the more people will start using your hashtag, making it easier to do social listening.

When you decide on a hashtag for your brand, make sure it's brief and unique. It should evoke a specific emotional reaction that you've deliberately chosen. Whether offline or online, creating a hashtag specific to that event is a good idea if you run events. Feel free to incorporate a bit of humor and cleverness if it aligns with your brand and topic. I've seen some big flops whereby brands went too far and either needed to research the hashtag better or remember to consider whether there was a hidden meaning behind their chosen hashtag that would come across as unappealing. The most important thing is to know your audience and how they perceive your business so you can use the right tone when you come up with something catchy. Regardless of how sassy your brand is, be thoughtful about the hashtags you create and think about long-term association and perceived reputation. I love seeing branded hashtags like #ShareACoke or #justdoit, so once you have an active audience, consider creating your own branded hashtag.

Best Practices For Choosing Hashtags

I recommend creating a healthy mix of popular and super-niched hashtags to boost your account growth. For example, #love is enormous, with 1.9 billion posts. Getting your content noticed with that hashtag will be a considerable challenge. So, the best thing you can do is combine that hashtag with others that have less volume and competition. A great way to determine what to pair it with is to use a hashtag generator tool such as All Hashtag or Hashtagify. You can also do keyword research using Google or Ubersuggest. Longtail hashtags perform better as long as you know this is a phrase the user is typing. In addition to using the popular keyword mentions, you could also add #loveisintheair, #lovestory, #lovepuppies, #lovelife, #lovinglife, #lovethis, #lovenature, or another combination that better suits your content.

Aside from using a handful of popular hashtags, you can also use trending hashtags, but again, make sure it's relevant. For example, if it's a summer sale, then #summer and #sale will work best. Use the appropriate hashtag if you have something unique to offer for a special occasion or create content specific to a holiday. For example, use #valentinesday in February and #Christmas in December as these hashtags trend during those particular months.

Pro tip:

To get the most out of this hashtag strategy, follow a hashtag and location tag linked to your niche and interact with the participants. For example, if you're an up-and-coming Instagram influencer, you can find events for social media marketing or small business networking events for digital marketing.

Planning Your Posts

Instagram is a highly visual platform with plenty of competition, so you need to plan your content correctly to set yourself up to succeed. So, the next vital step is to map out the kind of content you will create on a calendar or template over the next 90 days. If you're more artistic or enjoy mood boards, now is the time to create one. If you want Excel or Google spreadsheet, use that to curate and map out the categories, topics, and type of post you will make.

Here's what you need on your spreadsheet: Date of publication, Time, Content file name or link (if it's an uploaded video), the link that'll be added to the bio section, Image caption, Hashtags, Goal/Campaign. Create a new page on your spreadsheet for Instagram Stories so you can monitor this separately.

Decide how much content will be created and how much will be curated, then gather the necessary content and start filling in your planner. Since this is a new account and you're still learning the ropes, allow yourself to be flexible with the content type of content. You might start assuming your audience will be attracted to your account mainly for bite-sized educational content but then quickly realize the best-performing posts are beautiful, aesthetically focused, or maybe user-focused scope. Watch your content performance from month to month to determine how to adjust and what content to create more of. Some key things to look for include the number of new followers you're gaining from one month to the next and the number of people liking, commenting, and saving your content.

Another thing you want to include as you plan the content is some variety. Images alone won't cut it in 2021. You need to experiment with videos and other excellent graphics as well. Remember to maintain a consistent visual theme even when testing video. As mentioned earlier, please consider the colors, filters, fonts, and style patterns.

Tools For Planning And Scheduling Your Posts

You can use planning and scheduling tools to make this process more manageable. You can create a spreadsheet for visual planning, as I just mentioned, for free, or get a tool such as Later, Asana, Trello, or any other productivity tool with the content calendar feature. The most recommended scheduling tools include Buffer, HubSpot, Later, Meet Edgar, and Sked. Although most tools only allow you to post a single image, you can go for software like Sked, which lets you post Stories and Carousels if you have a bit of a budget.

Instagram Guides

Instagram launched a new format for sharing curated, scrollable content called Instagram Guides, and they are quickly gaining popularity. It's a new way of putting out helpful recommendations and tips. Although it started as a way for Instagram to allow people in healthcare and other wellness advocates to provide resources during the COVID-19 pandemic, it's now available to all users.

You can access this feature by tapping the plus icon on the top right of your profile page and selecting "Guide" at the bottom of the list. Three formats will pop up once you click on them, i.e., places, products, and posts.

- Places recommend places in your city and beyond.
- Products recommend your favorite products.
- It is super handy for Instagram influencers and affiliate marketers.
- Posts recommend the posts you have created or saved.

As you can see, there's a tremendous opportunity for you as a creator to add value and build authority with your audience. For example, a post guide can create a thread of Instagram posts you previously made or saved with a custom headline and extra commentary. Use this to enhance your story-telling strategy. You can also offer helpful advice or guidance. If you open an Instagram Shop, you can use the Products option to curate your best offers.

How to use Instagram Guides to grow your brand and business. This is a potent tool for doing value-first marketing. Whether you are an Instagram Influencer or a small business owner, think creatively about serving your potential customers and new followers. What kind of content, advice, or guidance would benefit them that can also lead to business for you?

For example, if you're the owner or manager of a restaurant or café, creating Guides for "Places" is excellent for sharing location-based recommendations such as city guides, where to eat, etc. You can also curate your posts with the latest menu or chef recommendations. In other words, you are only limited by your creativity and willingness to put in the effort to create the guides.

For eCommerce stores, having a Product guide can enable you to showcase your bestsellers and get people to buy more than ever.

To access an Instagram Guide, go to your profile or a user's profile page and select the new Guides icon from the feed tab. By clicking on that icon, you will see all the guides created by the account owner. You can also easily share them to your Instagram Stories by tapping on the paper plane icon at the top right-hand corner of the screen.

CHAPTER 7

Taking Great Pictures for Your Instagram Account

Let's focus on the technical aspects of creating a successful brand on Instagram. As stated several times, this is a visual-first platform. It makes sense to give you some hacks on how to make your photos pop on the feed. If you're in an industry that photographs well, such as beauty, food, and travel, you'll have an easier time creating excellent content if you get the right equipment. We'll talk about what equipment you can use on a budget shortly. But what if you're in a niche that doesn't photograph well? What if your topic is dull and lacks that aesthetic appeal?

All is not lost. I've come across creative accounts from niches most consider dull, such as personal injury, life insurance, and investment banking, and I could go on and on. One thing I've noticed about "boring brands" that succeed well on Instagram is their approach. Most of these accounts don't try to be something they are not. Instead, they go with the flow and create an aesthetically pleasing feed to amass a large following. Their images are relevant to their main idea but focus on something other than selling their product or service. Instead, they want to grow a solid online presence with a large following.

For example, I found a beautiful motivational feed with stunning nature pics and motivational quotes on life lessons. I loved the account so much that I followed that account. Soon after, I got a welcome message followed by a video from the account owner, who, it turns out, is a lawyer. He curates quotes, takes beautiful nature pics to draw attention, and builds relationships. Of course, his conversion may be lower than that of a food blogger. Still, given that he has 300K followers, I'm confident he can convert enough clients for his personal injury services. That's a classic example of how much creativity can serve you on Instagram. So, regardless of your niche, you can succeed on Instagram. It begins with taking great pictures.

What Special Equipment Takes Great Pictures for Instagram?

You don't need a special camera to take an Instagram-worthy picture that will grow your channel. Some Instagrammers have become influencers and amassed huge followings with images from an iPhone. In contrast, others have invested thousands of dollars in equipment and a stunning studio setup. There is no right or wrong. Start where you are with the tools at hand.

The most important thing about your picture is the editing and the intention behind the photo. However, I will share a small list of things you can invest in if your budget allows it.

#1. A camera you know well enough.

While upgrading your tech and investing in expensive cameras is excellent, starting with what you know is better. You can use a smartphone, a mirrorless camera, or a DLSR.

Mirrorless cameras are smaller, lightweight, and have more modern features. DSLRs are heavier and more prominent in size, with longer battery life and better autofocus systems.

A smartphone can also do the trick, especially if you're working with the latest iPhones or Android mobiles. Smartphones like iPhone 11 Pro, Google Pixel 4, and Samsung S20 are great choices if you want to stick to mobile photography. It also simplifies the editing and posting, especially after learning the latest software to turn your images from good to extraordinary. You can also get an iPhone Lens to enhance the image. Consider getting the Moment lenses, which give you a wide-angle or telephoto effect. This is great for Instagram Stories as well. The most important thing is learning to use all the features on your smartphone. There's a lot of information on YouTube that can show you how to take the best pictures from your smartphone. TechSpot has a great article, which I will link to on the resource page, that shares tips for taking great pictures using a smartphone.

If you want a great mirrorless camera, consider getting the Sony a6100. It has a fantastic screen for shooting with live view and does 11 frames per second RAW shooting and 4K video. It also has eye-detection autofocus. The best part for a beginner is with the a6100; you can take photos high up or low to the ground without laying on the ground, thanks to its tilting LCD screen on the back. The screen flips over the top, making selfies and vlogging super easy. Another thing to mention is that the camera is Wi-Fi included, which every beginner needs to make image exporting faster. If you have an Android phone, this camera has NFC built-in to transfer photos with a tap, so if you have the budget and can afford to invest about $848, this is a great entry point.

Do you prefer Canon instead? How about experimenting with Canon Rebel T3i, which also has excellent features, including a screen that swivels around, making selfies super easy?

For a DSLR camera, I recommend the Canon T6i, which has a flip and touch screen. It comes with a 242 Megapixel CMOS (APS-C) sensor, ISO 100-12800 (expandable to H:25600), and the EOS Full HD Movie mode helps capture brilliant results in MP4 format. You can also check out Canon 80D and M50, which have dual-pixel autofocus. Why is that important? If you often shoot in live view, a DSLR camera with dual-pixel autofocus will serve you best. The T6i doesn't come with dual-pixel autofocus. Still, it does have built-in Wi-Fi, so you can easily edit and upload to Instagram.

#2. Great lighting equipment

The best lighting is always going to be natural sunlight. So, if you have no budget to invest in lighting equipment but live in a sunny location, you have everything you need for that perfect Instagram shot. However, if your budget allows you to invest in some lighting equipment, consider getting some ring lights, which usually vary in price. You can get some for as low as $20 or a softbox if you have the money. I started with a Neewer 700W Professional Photography 24" X24"/60X60cm softbox with an E27 Socket Light Lighting Kit. And it goes for around $90, but it's well worth the price.

#3. Tripod

You will need a tripod to hold your camera (especially when doing selfies or Instagram Live). No one likes shaky images or videos, so this is a great way to ensure your pictures look professional. Depending on your camera, you can get a tripod that holds explicitly your device in place. You don't have to spend a ton of money on this. An essential 60-inch tripod will do the work just fine.

#4. Remote

If you do this solo, an inexpensive remote that pairs with your chosen camera wirelessly and can be used within 10 feet is an excellent investment. It will save you lots of running back and forth or using timers.

#5. A blank canvas and reflective surface

This is optional but nice to have. Depending on whether you're a business doing mainly product images or a personal brand taking selfies and face-to-camera video recordings, you may want to invest in a blank canvas and a reflective surface for better quality production. I highly recommend using a cheap foam board for a reflective surface, which works as great as fancy professional studio equipment. To get the most out of your reflector, light your setup with the primary light source, and then use the reflector to bounce any light back into the shadowy areas.

You can also get creative with blank canvas options and improvise with a foam board again or even a plain white wall if you're going for that traditional look.

Other extras include a memory card, which is handy if you get a camera. I also suggest you get a camera strap and sleeve. These will protect you and the camera, especially If you're an active photographer. If you invest in a camera, one final tip is to get a great lens and perhaps even a secondary battery to ensure you're always prepared. Educate yourself on the various lens options available at a price point you can afford and pair well with your camera choice. And that's it! Nothing too complicated, and you could even get started with a smartphone until your account gains enough momentum.

Capturing Moments

Getting that right can be daunting if you're an active photographer and want to make your feed all about action moments of people on the move. So how do you do it either for yourself or a friend?

Well, there are several options to consider. If you invested in a remote control for your camera, you could always set down the camera in the right spot and take the picture. Or, if you're doing a mid-action shot, you could either set a timer or record it as a video and then pause and screenshot that particular moment you want to capture.

The main thing to note is that action pics can seem imperfect and out of this world. What matters is the intention and story behind the picture. So, if you're celebrating completing a marathon, taking pictures of clients having fun with your products, or wearing your swag outdoors, focus less on making it perfect and more on capturing the right light. Lighting is what it comes down to when it comes to capturing moments. Consider doing action pictures during sunrise or sunset, as that is the best time. This is, of course, mainly for photographers who are focused on outdoor images and content. But what if you want to focus on still photos at home? What's a good setup that's easy to create?

A Setup For Taking Still Photos:

Whether you use your phone or a camera to take still photos, here are some tips to help you take still pictures like a pro.

Go for bright

The best still pics are taken indoors with great natural light or outside in daylight. You just can't beat the clarity and crispness of colors that come with using great natural light. Good light is the foundation of a great photo, so take the time to study the device you'll be using.

Pro tip:

Light from the front is always going to be the most flattering. Light from the side makes your subject look more three-dimensional, highlights texture, and creates a moody effect; subjects lit from the back look dreamy and glowy.

- **Pick the right time for your photoshoot.**

Nature has its own Instagram filter known as the golden hour by photographers. Every photo looks more stunning when the sun is low on the horizon. If you can plan your shoot at this time, then, by all means, take advantage. But even if you can't, understand your limitations and what can work in your favor. For example, a midday shoot with plenty of clouds can work if you know what you're doing.

- **Follow the rule of thirds**

When taking a still picture, the rule of thirds is one of the most well-known composition principles. It divides an image into a 3x3 grid and aligns the subject or object in the photo along the grid lines to create balance. Some smartphones have an in-built grid to visually help you check your settings to see what's available. Turn on the gridlines for your phone camera to practice this before shooting.

- **Choose a different perspective**

The normal tendency is to take a picture from your phone or camera at eye level. But if you want to create a fresh viewpoint on your photos, I encourage you to experiment with different angles. Consider taking above or below shots. You could even take low-to-the-ground pictures without crouching or lying on the floor if you have a great camera.

- **Draw the viewer's eye**

This is something I learned from a professional photographer. He taught me the concept of "leading lines." These are lines that run through an image that draws the eye and adds a sense of depth. You can use this technique to add motion or purpose to your photo. Roads, buildings, and natural elements such as waves, trees, and waterfalls help create this effect, so always watch for the possibility of adding this to your photo when shooting. Another way to add depth is by including layers or using objects in the background and the foreground.

With that basic understanding of the principles of good photography, I would like to share some of the subjects and themes that perform well on Instagram.

#1. Symmetry – Anything symmetrical will always be pleasing to the eye. Whether taking a picture in nature or an artificial product, focus on creating balance, and you can't go wrong.

#2. Vibrant colors – Many tremendous Instagram profiles go against the trend and produce content with rich, bold, and bright colors. If you can capture this high energy and vibrancy in a still picture (don't worry, there are editing tools to give you that extra punch), even a mundane picture can look stunning.

#3. Patterns Our brains love patterns, so if you can capture beautiful designs in your pictures, you can do well. Look around you in nature and architecture to find ways that you can share with your audience.

#4. Captivating background: A still picture of a stunning location will almost always look gorgeous. This is an easy one to do, whether it's for a product or a selfie. Find or create an epic background to transform your picture's final look.

#5. Detail shots

Still, pictures can become attention-grabbing on your feed if you focus sharply on an unexpected or interesting detail. I find these photos very calming and cleansing to the eye, especially after scrolling through a noisy feed. Instagram has editing tools like vignettes or tile shit, which enhance details and specific areas of a photo. If you want a nice still shot with this level of fact, I recommend taking it in close range so the quality remains intact.

Once you decide which setup and direction work for your photoshoot, experiment with some of these ideas and let your creativity guide you into that perfect shot.

Using Filters In Your Pictures

I mentioned the use of filters such as Vignette, and if you're new to this, you might be wondering what filters are and why we need them. Remember the earlier anecdote about the sun having a natural filter when it's low on the horizon, making everything look more beautiful? If you test it out today by going out and taking a photo just before sunset and then again during the evening, you'll see what I mean. There's an added effect that makes the whole experience stunning. Instagram and other editing software tools have the same ability to "unnaturally" adjust and modify the look and feel of your photo. Instagram comes with in-built filters that you can use to manipulate your photo's final look before publishing. A harmonious effect is created by using one to three of the same filters throughout your feed. All the big accounts you follow, especially from beauty celebrities and fashionistas, have this in common. They all use certain filters consistently. Even the food blogger that makes you swoon each time a new post shows up is most likely using a carefully picked-out filter. As part of creating a brand identity and a consistent experience, it's your turn to choose a filter you can start testing for your feed.

The top and most popular filters on Instagram if you wish to use something other than an external app are Clarendon, Gingham, and Juno.

Clarendon brightens, highlights, and enhances your photo with one tap. It intensifies shadows and makes colors pop, making it multi-purpose, so it's not surprising that it's the number one choice for many Instagrammers.

Gingham has a vintage feel and brightens warm hues, making an image appear rich and authentic. Juno adds saturation, warmth, and a bit of punch to colors, making it a great all-purpose filter.

Aside from these filters, you also have Lark, Valencia, Mayfair, Rise, Amaro, Earlybird, Aden, and X-Pro II filter ranking as top filters to use on Instagram. The most important thing to remember is that you can use these filters and pick only a few on your feed. If you want to see big brands using filters exceptionally well, I encourage you to check out Lululemon, Sephora, and HubSpot. These may be outside your niche, but they will inspire you to choose your filters.

Decide whether you're going for a warm & rustic feel, clean & crisp, or dark and moody feed. That will guide you and help you rule out many filters to focus on the ones that match your feed's mood. Remember to check with your brand identity and make sure the choices align and help represent you well. The main intention here is to connect your audience to a particular emotion. Please note that you'll also have the option of adding filters for Instagram Stories. We'll discuss that when sharing hacks to crush it with Instagram Stories. So, even if you want to play around with multiple filters, you can do so on your Stories. If you want something more than what Instagram offers by default, you can download apps to help with your photo editing.

Photo Editing Apps To Make Your Pictures Stunning:

Do you need to add some visual flair and effects that go beyond the basics of Instagram? Although I think Instagram already provides tons of helpful functionality, here are apps that can help you do the trick even if you have no photography or graphics background.

VSCO for Android and iOS

Over 200 million Instagram posts feature the #VSCO, which tells me this is a super popular photo editing tool. This tool gives you about ten free pre-set filters to enhance your photo. You also get many other tools to manipulate contrast, saturation, intensity, etc. You can also crop your picture on the app. If you want more robust features, you can always upgrade to open up over 200 filters and other features.

A Color Story for Android and iOS

The app specializes in making colors pop in your photos. It's simple to use and has 20 free editing tools, including filters, effects, and pre-sets designed by professional photographers and influencers.

Adobe Lightroom Photo Editor for Android and iOS

Adobe products have powerful capabilities, and this photo editor is no exception. You can edit raw images and turn your mobile shots into high-quality, professional-looking photos that look like they were shot on film. The app allows you to manipulate hues, saturation, exposure, shadows, and more. It also comes with pre-set filters that are great for those who want to avoid getting into the nitty-gritty of editing.

Snapseed for Android and iOS

This app is handy for professional or amateur photographers. It allows you to work on JPG and RAW files with as much detail as you like and goes beyond the standard touch-ups we want to use. Yes, it comes with pre-sets, but what's great about this app is the severe photo editing skills you can do, thanks to the 29 tools and features that come with the app. You can even remove elements (including people) from your photo or adjust the geometry of buildings. And all that with incredible precision and quality.

Instagram Layout for Android and iOS

This layout from the Instagram app is free and allows you to compile up to nine photos in various combinations. It makes it easy to design and layout, especially if you want to create collages. You can add filters and other personalized elements to share on Instagram quickly.

Lipix app for Android and iOS

It is another excellent photo collage and editor that combines up to nine photos into a single frame. You can personalize and customize it with stickers and texts and easily share it on Instagram.

Canva

Canva is a trendy graphics designing software with free and pro versions. Even without design skills, this web-based software will help you create amazing photos with many filters and pre-made templates. They also have a mobile app for Insta Stories that lets you quickly create content for your Instagram Stories, just like the pros.

Saving Drafts

Once you've created your awesome picture, you may not want to publish it for whatever reason. During those times, you can take advantage of Instagram's draft functionality, which allows you to save the post and publish it later. Tap the camera icon at the top of your screen to create the post, then take or upload your photo and click Next. You can add effects, filters, a caption, or your location here. To save this post without publishing, go back to the filtering and editing step, then tap the back arrow in the top left corner > Save Draft. After editing the post and adding captions, location, etc., you can only save it as a draft. In other words, it must be ready for publication before you can save it as a draft. If you want to access your posts, tap the camera icon again, then find Library or Gallery, and you should be able to see them.

If you want to tidy up your drafts section and discard unnecessary posts, go back to the drafts section, tap Select All, and then tap the edit button. Tap the saved posts you want to delete and hit the discard posts button.

Posting And Sharing From Mobile And Desktop

We already know Instagram is a mobile-first app. Most of its features have been built to take a picture from your mobile phone, upload it, or instantly publish it to your feed. The process is pretty straightforward. It guides you through editing, adding captions, tagging people, adding your location, and even posting on other connected platforms such as your Facebook page. Once you hit publish, the post appears on your feed.

While this is fast and convenient, many creators, including myself, have been looking for ways to post from a desktop. Learning simple tricks to upload edited pictures from your desktop can save time and energy using more advanced tools and equipment. Here's how you can do it.

Here is a quick hack for posting from your desktop:

For this example, I am using a Mac desktop because it's what I use. First, you need to log into your Instagram account through Google Chrome. Once in your account, click "View" on the top-most ribbon of your computer screen (where your clock is) for a drop-down menu. Then, go to Developer > Developer Tools. A sidebar should open on your screen, showing you the code of the Instagram webpage. From there, click on the "Toggle device bar," which is an icon that shows a phone and a more significant device (next to "Elements"). Next, you should notice a little ribbon on the right part of your screen (next to the developer sidebar) with a drop-down menu set to "Responsive." Click on that and change the setting to your preference – like iPhone X. You should see the Instagram layout change to match your selected location, with the camera + icon at the bottom of the Instagram screen to upload a post. If this does not appear automatically, try refreshing your page. You can operate the Instagram page as usual. You're all set.

That's a fast way that costs you no money. Still, if you want to find alternatives, you can always sign up for third-party tools like Hootsuite, Later, CoSchedule, and Buffer, which all perform the same task.

Curating And Reposting Content From Other Instagram Accounts:

You can easily curate content from other accounts. You only need the account owner's written permission and an app or the weblink. I will walk you through it shortly. To get permission, consider leaving a message in the comment box or sending a direct message with your request. I also encourage you to tag and mention the source of your content whenever you repost something.

You have various options, most accessible for programming excellent content. Sometimes, you might need to download an app from your Google Play or Apple Store.

#1. DownloadGram

The first option is to use this web link to download high-resolution copies of Instagram photos and videos to repost on your account. I like this option because you don't need to download any additional app to make it work. Just follow these simple steps.

First, open your Instagram and find the photo or video you want to repost, then tap the ••• icon in the post's upper right-hand corner. Click "Copy Share URL."

Second, paste the URL into the DownloadGram, which can be accessed through your mobile internet browser at www.downloadgram.com, then tap "Download." Scroll to the bottom of the homepage and click "Download Image," you'll be directed to a new webpage with the content ready to download. Tap the download icon, then "Save Image."

Third, head over to your Instagram and upload as you would a standard image. It should be automatically stored in your camera images, so follow the typical editing steps, adding tags, captions, etc., before reposting.

#2. Taking Screenshots

You can also repost by photographing a photo you like on Instagram. For iOS, you must simultaneously press the home and lock buttons until the screen flashes. For Android, simultaneously press the sleep/wake and volume down buttons until the screen flashes.

Then head over to your Instagram and tap the camera + icon. Resize the photo and edit it to fit the Instagram size. In this case, I also encourage you to tag and include the username of the original creator.

#3. Repost for Instagram for iOS and Android

This free app integrates directly with Instagram and lets you curate and share content from your mobile device. To use it, download the app. Then open Instagram, tap the ••• icon on the upper right corner, and choose "Copy Share URL."

Open Repost and then return to your Instagram to find your desired image. Copy the specific post URL you'd like to share to your clipboard. Then, head back to repost, where the copied post should automatically appear on the homepage. Tap the arrow on the right-hand side of the post. This is where you do it if you want to edit or make adjustments. Once you're happy with the image, tap "Repost." Then tap "Copy to Instagram," where you can add a filter and edit the post. Remember to edit the post captions before sharing your repost.

CHAPTER 8

Creating Awesome Videos for Instagram

Just because you shoot videos for YouTube or Facebook doesn't mean you can automatically upload them on Instagram. The platform is designed for something other than long-form content, and since we know it's a visual-based image-first platform, experimenting with videos is an excellent idea if we add a bit of flair that aligns with the platforms' demands. In this book section, we will walk through the process of creating or even repurposing videos that attract and drive engagement to your profile.

There are several ways you can experiment with videos. First, you can upload the video on your feed as you do a regular still image. There is a limit on the size and length, which we'll discuss shortly. The second option is to publish Instagram Stories, which have become extremely popular. The third option is to create Instagram reels. Last, it is to build your own IG TV library. Let's start with the most popular choice – Instagram Stories.

Instagram Stories

What is Instagram Story? An Instagram story is a photo or video you create and share, which is visible to your followers and the users you follow. Instagram Stories are unique in that they disappear after 24hrs, just like with Snapchat. It is published separately from your feeds' gallery, although you can highlight them in your account's "Highlights" section.

To create an Instagram Story, open your Instagram app, and click your profile picture at the screen's bottom right. Then click the big plus + icon at the top right corner of the screen, which will open up a drop-down menu where you can select the "Story" option (the second option from the top under Create New). You can also start a Story by clicking on the +icon that appears right next to your image while viewing the "Home" dashboard.

You can share an existing image or video by swiping up, which will take you to your phone's camera. If you want to create something in the moment, you can choose the "Lens" icon, which lets you do several things:

- Create – this is the first option you'll see. It enables you to type text on a plain background without a photo.

- Layout – this option lets you take several different pictures to make a collage (up to six, depending on your chosen design). You can also upload images from your camera.

- Live – this option lets you broadcast live on the Instagram platform. Similar to Facebook Live, your friends and followers can interact with you. Once your broadcast is over, you can allow it to run its course and disappear, save it, or publish it on Instagram Stories, which can be accessed for an additional 24hrs.

- Standard – this option lets you capture a still image (tap once) or record a video (press and hold it down).

- Boomerang – this option films looping GIFs up to three seconds long. These are simple, fun, and get lots of attention.

- Superzoom is a video recording lens that zooms in closer and closer on your subject. Different filters produce various effects, such as fire, heart, and fun. These can be fun to play with.

- Hands-free – this option works like a timer on a camera. Use it when you want it to film for you, but make sure the subject is ready and your phone is set somewhere stable, like on a tripod.

- Reels – this option lets you take short videos you clip together. You can add music and filters.

How To View Instagram Stories

Instagram Stories appear at the top of your screen on the mobile app. They are positioned so that users have to see these first, which means they get a ton of engagement. That's why doing more Instagram Stories can help you grow your followers fast. To view someone's Instagram story, open your app and tap the home icon on the bottom left-hand corner of your screen. Once there, you'll see a series of circular icons along the top, each representing the active Stories posted by the users you follow. Tap on the circular icon to view a user's Story. A single Instagram Story can contain numerous individual photos and videos strung together in the order they were posted, starting with the newest. Swipe left or right to navigate between Stories from different users. If you're viewing an ad, swiping up will allow you to head to the link the user wants you to consider.

The Best Content For Instagram Stories

#1. Product explainer or demo

You don't need the sexiest or simplest product to make this work. With creativity and personality, you can create short, quirky videos demonstrating your product. Instagram is the perfect format for showing potential customers how your product is used and its benefits. Create a video segmented into 15-second clips to walk users through your product or even a service you offer and show them how their lives can improve. If humor is your thing, add a few doses of that.

#2. Give shout-outs to other businesses or influencers

This is a great way to passively nurture relationships with users that matter most to your brand. You can create Stories on a product you use that you'd love to partner with or praise an influencer for their latest review if you want to promote that influencer to your audience so you can eventually build a mutually beneficial connection. You can also create shout-outs for specific customers (with their permission). This will encourage them to promote your account because everyone likes to be praised on social media.

#3. Preview your blogs or Vlogs

If you are currently blogging on your website or Vlogging on YouTube, this is a great way to give your content more exposure. You can help Instagram users discover your excellent content for the first time. I've seen Google do this on their feed, previewing an article on their Instagram Story. At the end of the Story, Google prompts you to swipe up with your finger where you're sent over to the link with the full blog post.

#4. Share a day-in-the-life-of

I have seen many Instagrammers do this at some point during their journey. They document for an entire day how they spend their day, where they work, what it's like to be an Instagrammer, and so on. People love watching these types of stories. You'll need to plan it and figure out how to segment this and the different aspects of your day you can share. It can be fun and create a strong connection with your audience.

#5. Promote an event

You can create a series promoting an upcoming event you're hosting online or offline. You can also enable a conference or seminar you will attend even if you're not the host. People love seeing where you're going and the incredible people you meet. This is also beneficial because adding the event hashtags allows event attendees to discover your stories, giving your profile more exposure and new followers. Remember to add the event name and official hashtag when promoting an event.

Tricks And Hacks For Your Instagram Stories

- **Add your brand colors and fonts to your Stories**

There are a ton of fun fonts, and it's great to play around with different colors and fonts. But if you want to train your audience to recognize your brand, focusing more on using the fonts and brands you chose earlier in this book is vital. You must download the app Over mobile to have customized fonts. Once you download, AirDrop your fonts.OFT file into your mobile device. Follow the simple instructions, and once it's done, you can incorporate brand fonts into your Stories.

- **Turn Live Photos into Boomerangs**

You can turn a live photo into a Boomerang, but the live image must be taken within 24 hours. To do this, open Instagram Stories, swipe up, and pick a live photo from your camera roll. Once you find the image you want, press firmly on the screen for a few seconds until the word "Boomerang" appears briefly. And that's it! You just made a new Boomerang that you can share.

- **Copy a Photo from your Camera Roll**

By hitting the "Copy" option from an image in your camera roll and adding it to an Instagram

Story you're creating, you can add an extra photo or GIF as long as you're using the "Create" option of your Instagram Stories. It makes you post funkier, so have fun with this.

- **Track Best Performers**

Keeping track of the content getting you the most engagement is essential, especially reshares. Unfortunately, you won't find this data in the regular insights section. Instead, you need to tap the ellipsis in the top right corner of a post to pull up a menu with the option to "View Story Reshares." This will show you all the current posts that are being reshared. If you don't see anything, then it's likely that none is being reshared. This particular hack is handy when promoting an event or a sale because it helps you get user-generated content and shows how people react.

IGTV

Since its launch in 2018, IGTV (Instagram TV) has gained momentum and popularity among creators. At first, it only supported vertical videos, but today, it can help vertical and horizontal videos that are up to ten minutes long for regular accounts. Certified accounts (with the blue tick) get even more playtime on IGTV.

As a beginner, you can use those ten minutes to create incredible content to boost your engagement levels, especially with the proper content planning. IGTV videos can also be previewed from your main profile feed, making it easy for new or existing followers to watch them. You'll have to turn on the toggle that enables this functionality before publishing the video on IGTV. You and your audience can watch IGTV videos in the Instagram app, standalone IGTV app, or by clicking the IGTV icon accessible on the explore/discovery page. You can also click the IGTV button on your or someone else's Instagram profile. When you post a new IGTV video, your followers will be notified in the native Instagram app.

How to set up your IGTV

If you have an Instagram account, you can immediately start your Instagram TV because the feature is now fully integrated into their central platform. To upload an IGTV video, which can be a maximum of fifteen minutes long, open the Instagram app and tap the search icon (which looks like a magnifying glass) at the bottom of your screen. This will bring you to the discovery page, where you will see the IGTV icon next to the shop icon. Click on the IGTV icon, bringing you to a new area dedicated explicitly to IGTV content. You will see a Plus + icon in the upper right-hand corner, which, when clicked, will open up your video library. Choose the video you wish to upload, then click "Next." Here, you can add a cover by uploading a pre-made one from your gallery or simply sticking with the default that the app generates automatically. Click "Next" and add a title and description. This is also where you can switch on the ability to post a preview on your feed and profile. You could also make it visible on Facebook if you've linked your accounts.

If the video is part of a series of content, you're creating IGTV, which allows you to group them into a series that people can watch chronologically. This is wonderful for educational content and how-to tutorials. Once you're ready to publish, click post and give it a few minutes for the video to be distributed on the platform.

The best file format on IGTV is always MP4, with a video length of between 1 minute and 15 minutes. The maximum size you can upload if your account qualifies is 1 hour. Go for a vertical aspect ratio of 9:16 or a horizontal aspect ratio of 16:9. The minimum recommended resolution is 720 pixels and a minimum frame rate of 30 frames per second. The best cover photo size is a ratio of 1:1.55 or 420 px by 654 px. Regarding file size for videos that are 10 minutes or less, Instagram recommends a maximum of 650MB. The maximum file size for videos up to 60 minutes long should always be at most 3.6GB.

Types of content that perform well on IGTV

- **Tutorial Videos**

How-to videos covering various topics in your niche can build engagement. For example, if you're a fitness influencer, you could create a series focused on home-based workouts without equipment.

- **Educational content**

You can create fun, colorful educational content teaching your audience about something relevant to them. Take inspiration from Bulletproof's IGTV. They make videos explaining their ingredients, how they source them, and some of the more technical terms used in their products. Even if you're not a big supplement company like Bulletproof, you can still create something engaging using well-designed slideshows to educate your audience.

- **Showcase and behind-the-scenes content**

A great inspiration you can see for showcasing real estate is with Rob Report. They regularly publish videos showcasing incredible listings. You can give people a full home tour if you're in real estate. You could also give people a behind-the-scenes look if you work in a studio or have something working in the background that your audience usually doesn't get to see.

The most important thing to remember is to create content that suits your brand and enriches your audience's lives. Go deeper with your content, get creative, and focus on adding value.

Tips To Make Your IGTV Successful

- **Focus on quality**

Although you must create lots of content consistently, it's better to create good quality and engaging content than massive volumes of meaningless content. Play the long game and let your audience learn to trust your rate and the effort you put into these videos. That will drive more engagement as your account grows.

- **Design clear custom covers**

Invest some time in creating customized custom clear covers that communicate the main message. The optimum cover size, as mentioned earlier, is 420 by 654 pixels. Use a tool such as Canva, with pre-made templates and appropriately sized graphics that you can easily plug and play with.

- **Add a link to your IGTV video**

Instagram has added many new features since 2010, but URLs still need to be improved for us as there are only a few places to add a link unless you have many followers. Fortunately, IGTV allows you to insert a clickable link in the video description. You can link to a website, a freebie, or your shop, so take advantage of this feature.

Recording Videos

Recording your videos on Instagram is pretty straightforward. Open up your Instagram app and head over to the top left corner of the screen, where you should see the Camera + icon. To upload a video from your phone's library, select the video you'd like to share. If you want to record on the go, tap the camera icon above your phone's library and hold on to the circular record icon. Lift your finger to stop recording.

Like taking great pictures, you need to focus on having great lighting to record quality videos. Focus on one subject as much as possible, and keep the shot steady. Consider using a tripod or stacks of books. Instagram now accepts both vertical and horizontal videos. Still, I always encourage landscape for beginners, except for Instagram Stories Videos.

Before you post

Now that you have your video ready to share with the world add a bit of flair through editing to make it pop. There are a few handy apps that you can use, even if you're a complete amateur.

Boomerang

The boomerang feature comes built on the app and allows you to create bite-sized videos, almost like GIFs. It can be a quick, fun way to create a video on the go.

A Color Story

This app works for both iOS and Android and is all about filters. There are over three hundred filters, both free and paid. It quickly enhances the color and aesthetics of your videos and saves your edits as filters so you can apply the same look to the other videos.

Animoto

This app works with iOS and Android and focuses on creating epic slideshows. This is the way to go to combine several photos or videos. The free version works when creating videos of up to ten minutes.

Inshot

This video editing app is considered one of the best. It trims clips, changes footage speed, adds filters and texts, zooms in and out, and even lets you incorporate your music. The interface is super simple to use. Almost anyone can quickly turn their video into something that stands out on Instagram.

Livestreaming on Instagram

You can do up to one hour of live video broadcasting on Instagram. Once the broadcast is done, you can share the replay on your IGTV or put it on Live Archive to share later. To go live, tap the camera icon in the top left of your feed and scroll to Live at the bottom of the screen. Then tap the record icon. If you have viewers joining live, you should see the number count at the top of the screen.

Your viewers can interact with you during the broadcast. All comments appear at the bottom of the screen, and if you want to add your comment, Instagram has that feature included; tap the "Comment" icon. If you'd like to Pin a particular word, such as a link for your call-to-action, tap that comment and then tap "Pin Comment" so that all viewers can see it more easily. At the end of the Livestreaming, remember to tap "End" in the top right corner and then tap the download icon in the top left if you want to save it to your camera roll or share it on IGTV.

Reels

Reels are a new way to create and discover short, entertaining videos on Instagram. You can record and edit 15-second multi-clip videos with audio effects and more and then share them with your followers and the entire Instagram community because they appear on the Explore page. For business accounts, reels are a fantastic new way to be discovered by new users.

If you use original sounds and hashtags, you might go viral if people like the effects on your reel. Users also can use your audio when they select "Use Audio" from your reel. You can post your reel on your regular profile feed, where it will remain visible, or create a Story reel that will disappear after 24hrs.

Since this is one of the newer features Instagram added at the end of 2020, I expect they will give content creators with great reels much more reach to promote this feature, so get creative and start making your reels. To make your first reel, click on the "movie reel" icon that now shows up at the bottom of the screen. Here, you will have various editing tools, including Audio, AR effects, Timer and countdown, Align, and Speed.

AR Effects - you get many effects to choose from created by both Instagram and creators worldwide. Audio - opens up a music library. You can choose from one of the pre-existing tracks or use your original audio here. Align - line up objects from your previous clip before recording your following clip. That way, you can have a seamless transition.

Timer and Countdown - set a timer to record any of your clips hands-free. If Instagram loves your reel, they can tag it with a "Featured" label, driving massive attention across the platform and making it an incredible way to get more traffic to your profile and brand.

Section 4

Managing Your Instagram Account

CHAPTER 9

The Best Practices on Managing an Instagram Account

Now that your account is up and running, your job is to maintain it until you have enough momentum to create a snowball effect. Have you ever heard of Instagrammers who speak of overnight success with their accounts? Chances are, they were consistent for a prolonged period, and then one day, all that effort snowballed into spectacular results. So, once you're up and running, the main focus is to create structures that enable you to keep attracting new customers.

To do this, you need a tool that can help you analyze your success, learn more about your audience, and repeat more of what's working. While many social listening tools provide all this data for you, e.g., Iconosquare and Socialbakers, feel free to begin small if you need more money.

Develop A Daily To-Do List

Whether you're doing this full-time or as a side hustle after work, you need a daily list of things that must be done to ensure the growth of your account and brand. Always have a content calendar to work from so you can know what content to create and publish. I encourage you to have days scheduled for content creation and other days for community engagement. If you're using scheduling tools such as Buffer or Later to push out content, this will save you time so that you can invest it elsewhere, such as creating more content or editing your videos.

Make sure to make your daily to-do list possible to accomplish. A list of three things done daily and efficiently will yield better results than having too much to do, leading to procrastination. For example, you can have a daily task of investing 30 minutes exploring accounts and posting the same hashtags you use so you can develop that connection. You can also create one piece of content daily. However you choose to organize yourself, make sure it's manageable and can be done based on your time commitment. Reflect on your current lifestyle before determining your daily list.

Analyzing Your Instagram

You'll have to track and measure everything to grow your brand and account. That's the only way to know what works and what doesn't. Luckily, Instagram already offers that data for each post under your "Insights" tab. Go to your main profile dashboard for three tabs (Promotions Insights Contact). By clicking on Insights, you can instantly navigate between a summary or in-depth view of your account to see performance, content interactions, and followers. You can see the last seven days and the breakdown of the content you shared on the IGTV and Stories feed.

Suppose you're working on a campaign with a specific objective. In that case, I suggest you do some A/B testing to figure out what works best so you can adjust your strategy. A few things to remember when running A/B tests is that you must choose a single element to test. So that can be an image, caption, hashtag, etc. Only try one thing at a time. Create a variation based on the same content except for that single element being tested, and then track and analyze each post's results. The one that performs best is what you should create more of. If you want to experiment further and optimize, you can take the winning content, adjust another element, and test to find a new winner. Rinse and repeat this formula. Have a spreadsheet where all this data is collected if you want optimum results.

Dealing With Haters

Let's not kid ourselves; you will bump into many more haters as your brand and Instagram accounts grow with raving fans. The trolls of the Internet are plentiful and eagerly awaiting your debut. Many people have more courage to hate people while hiding behind a computer and fake usernames. So be forewarned; the success that awaits you will also bring some unpleasant trolls who enjoy criticizing and hating on all your hard work. Finding a mean comment on your feed can sometimes feel very discouraging, so how do you deal with this?

#1: Remember these are just insecure bullies

Even in school, the people who like to hurt others usually project their hurt and insecurities. Think of trolls the same way. That someone consumed your content and took the time to leave a mean comment means you must have had some impact on them. But their insecurities made them unable to express themselves correctly, so you triggered a nerve. That hater shows you how much they wish they had or could do what you just demonstrated. Keep that in mind the next time you find a mean comment, and instead of lashing out, keep scrolling and attending to your fans.

#2: Let your raving fans deal with haters.

If you already have an engaged community with active followers who love your content, hand over your trolls to your tribe and watch them eat them alive. I have seen this often with people like Gary Vee or Grant Cardone, who often get haters. What do they do? They turn it around to their community and ask for their input. The reaction is usually massive as their fans attack the troll and almost bury him in defense of their beloved guru. You may still need to have that much influence, but it's something to look forward to.

#3: Give kindness instead

If you are spiritual or religious, this should make sense. Kindness given to someone who doesn't deserve it can be very liberating to the one who gives. It's not always easy, but if you can find it in you to reply with a kind word, I encourage you to do so. Don't fake or force it. It needs to come from a place of authentic kindness and compassion. Develop the understanding that human beings are inherently good. Some of us are just raised poorly, or we've just endured way too many bad days.

How to avoid getting banned and what to do if you get shadowbanned by Instagram. As you grow your account, you need help with your content reach for various reasons. Instagram is constantly changing its algorithm, so it is essential to keep reviewing its terms and new updates. You should be fine if you avoid doing things that could get you banned, such as overusing hashtags, buying followers, and using bots. If, however, you still think your content needs to be getting as much reach as it deserves, Instagram is shadowbanning your content. Although they don't openly admit to doing this, they did release a report stating that some business accounts reported the issue and recommend focusing on putting out great content instead of hashtag stuffing. According to Instagram, the best way to grow and get your content seen by more people who don't follow you is to create something thoughtful and appealing to the Instagram community. It's not about trying to manipulate the system.

With that said, if you want to be sure that Instagram isn't shadowbanning you, here's a simple test. Post content with a single hashtag that is rarely used. Don't go for something with millions of followers because you won't know if your content is banned or hidden by competition. Once posted, get five people who don't follow you to search for the hashtag. If none of them see your post in those results, you've likely been shadowbanned.

As I just mentioned, you can get banned because of the tactics you've been using to grow the account. Instagram frowns on tools that shortcut your growth, such as bots, so review what you're currently using. If you are using anything Instagram considers spammy, stop it immediately. The other reason could be that you must use hashtags or broken hashtags irrelevant to your topic. Users could also report your account as spammy or inappropriate several times. This might lead to Instagram deactivating your account or shadowbanning you. That's why I have been insisting on targeting an audience that is narrow enough so that you can be confident they care about your content and topics.

One last tip I can give you is to regularly review the list of banned hashtags to ensure your use aligns with Instagram's terms of use. The best way to determine which hashtags are forbidden is to go to the "Explore" tab and search for the hashtag. If nothing appears, it's likely banned either temporarily or forever. You can also check Instagram's hashtag page, which posts new updates. Examples of prohibited hashtags that you must never use include #assday #curvygirls #petitie #alone #bikinibody #date #dating #humpday #killingit #kissing #mustfollow #pornfood #singlelife #stranger #shit #teens #thighs #undies etc.

Tools For Managing Your Account

Some tools you will need to manage your account have already been mentioned. A tool like Instagram Insights, which comes in as long as you have a business account, is excellent. If you prefer a third-party tool that's easy to use, you can opt for Later, Hootsuite, or Buffer, all of which have both free and paid versions. If, however, you'd like to explore more analytical tools, consider getting Iconosquare (specializes in social monitoring), Crowdfire (specializes in content curation), Pixlee (for social reports), Union Metrics (for hashtags analytics, Socialbakers (for competitive analysis) especially if you want to compare how your account is doing relative to peers in the same niche.

Chapter 10

Gaining Followers

Gaining followers is the key to getting the most out of your Instagram and reaching your business objectives. If you don't get attention and convert that attention into followers, fans, and buyers, all this effort is in vain. Instagram is a social platform where you must show people you are an actual human who enjoys engaging with others. It would be best if you remained active outside set posting times. You also need to follow other people if you want others to follow you. Nowadays, it's not enough to post content and use hashtags, so here are the various ways to get real people who care about and engage with your brand.

Like and comment on top accounts.

This is one of the most effective ways to build engagement on your account and have new people discover your brand. It requires time investment because you need to find and interact with accounts that you believe your users also interact with. Apply everything you've learned so far, and getting to know which accounts to interact with will be pretty straightforward. For example, if there's a hashtag that your users typically search for, you can visit it daily to find the top-ranked posts and leave a comment on the content that most resonates with you. That can lead the account owner and the other users to come to your account and like your content. It's a natural way of creating reciprocity and could lead to new followers, mainly if you target the right hashtags.

Respond to comments

This should be common sense, but common sense is only sometimes common practice. Always respond to all the comments on your post. The more people see you engaging with users who take the time to comment on your posts, the more likely they are to engage with you because they see you genuinely care about socializing. I know it's easy to find big brands with lots of comments that they never respond to, but don't use that as a standard policy for your brand if you want to gain followers. Human-to-human social interaction is what Instagram is all about. Until you become too big with too many followers to respond to, take time daily to reply in the comments section.

Reply to Direct Messages

Besides responding to people when they leave a comment, you should also reply to any DM (direct messages) that land on your Instagram inbox. Although the public doesn't see this interaction, it can help you grow your brand credibility. Another neat trick is to initiate communication via direct messages. Regularly inform people on your Stories or Feed that you usually offer goodies via direct messages. That will encourage people to want to follow and interact with you in this personalized way.

User-generated Content

Existing customers and fans create this type of content. They can develop shout-outs for you or short videos demonstrating or explaining how they've used and benefited from your product or service. This type of content is phenomenal because it sells for you. People love to be assured that purchasing your product is risk-free and will improve their lives. The more of this content you can push out to the platform, the more likely you are to attract potential buyers who will follow and interact more keenly with your brand.

Run a contest on Instagram.

Giveaways and contests are huge on Instagram and can be a great source of follower acquisition. Plan it right and make the criteria for participating by tagging a friend. You're likely to see a spike in your follower count. Just ensure the reward is exciting enough for the existing and potential followers you wish to attract.

Collaborating with Influencers

This is a strategy I used years ago, and it grew my account overnight. I know I'm just one of many who have experienced success with leveraging influencers. The trick is to build a strong relationship with the right influencer. Work with the right influencer and develop a mutually beneficial strategy. Getting that exposure to their audience will increase the number of followers who choose to continue consuming your content. The most important thing is to create high-value content and build a real connection with the influencer and their audience.

Get the blue tick, aka a verified badge.

Getting verified by Instagram can help you gain more followers because when people see that blue tick next to your name, it automatically makes them assume you're a big deal. People always love to follow important-looking accounts. Although anyone can request the badge, there are specific requirements Instagram demands. I suggest reading their terms before making the request.

If you qualify, open your Instagram app and tap your profile picture in the bottom right to go to your profile. Click on the three parallel bars in the top right, then tap Settings. Tap Account, then tap Request Verification. You must provide your details, including your full name and some form of identification. This verification badge will exponentially increase the number of followers because you'll be considered authoritative and newsworthy. However, it would be best if you attempted to request it once you get 5,000 followers.

Promote your account

It's time to think outside the Instagram box so you can bring more followers to your brand. Consider leveraging social networks like Facebook, YouTube, Twitter, Pinterest, and LinkedIn to drive traffic to your Instagram profile. You can also include your Instagram icon in the footer of your emails or as part of your signature and ask people to connect with you there. If you have a blog or website, consider embedding your Instagram feed to entice that audience to join you on Instagram. Free plugins like Smash Balloon make it easy to add a widget, even if you need to be tech-savvy. Be creative with this and how you cross-promote and repurpose your content across the web.

CHAPTER 11

Using Instagram for Business

With an Instagram business account, you not only have access to audience insight, but you can also conduct a lot of business to generate sales. Instagram just integrated the "Instagram Shop" tab across the platform, making it easier and faster for your followers to turn into buying customers. You can access the shop from the main profile feed by clicking on your profile picture. It's one of the primary three tabs next to Promotions and Insights. Here, you can tag products in your posts or stories, showcase your products in a customizable way, create your very own storefront, and even get insights about how your shop is performing.

Here are some helpful tips to ensure you get the most from your business account.

Take advantage of the new features.

Add a Shop to your Instagram profile and include contact information, category, and some calls to action so that users can know about your offer, how to get it, and how to connect with you.

Create Instagram Guides

Depending on the niche you serve, you can create motivational guides using posts product guides to showcase your best offers (make sure they are the ones included in your Instagram Shop), and you can even create guides for your city to offer helpful recommendations if you've got a brick-and-mortar business.

Link your shop to your Instagram Story.

This new feature lets you link to your shop with every Instagram story you create. Whether you sell a product or service, doing business has always been challenging.

Build anticipation and offer exclusive deals through your Instagram Stories and Instagram Live broadcasts.

This is a great way to get your audience excited about something new. It's also a nice reward for your new followers. Do you have a lead magnet that can lead to the latest product? Why not offer it exclusively to all new followers within a given timeframe? Create teaser photos and Stories, letting people know how they can receive your freebie and get their hands on your latest offer.

Run Instagram Ads

Instagram ads are sponsored content that allows you to reach a broader audience by paying

Facebook (the parent company). They are currently among the cheapest forms of online advertising. Yet, the return on investment can be huge if you have a strong paid ads strategy. I like Instagram ads because you don't need a big budget.

With Instagram Stories ads, you could spend less than $5 a day and get a lot of traffic to your profile or landing page. All Instagram ads have a "Sponsored" tag on them. You can run Story ads, Photo ads, Video ads, Carousel ads, Collection ads, Explore ads, IGTV ads, and Instagram Shopping ads. Each ad type works differently depending on your business goals. The most important thing to know is what objective you are aiming for and how much you are willing to spend.

Should You Hire A Social Media Manager Or Work With An Agency?

Most people assume social media marketing for business is as easy as social media for personal use. Unfortunately, this is far from the truth. Marketing a brand online requires discipline, planning, and significant knowledge of the best practices and trends. That is where a social media manager comes in. They gather metrics on page performance, engagement, and followers, set goals, focus on branding and brand awareness, create posting schedules, curate content that is attuned to your brand image, optimize content for search engines, design advertising campaigns, select posts to boost; runs ads interact with followers and so much more.

Outsourcing your social media has pros and cons, whether you get a freelancer or an agency. The best part about having someone assist you with growing your account is that you can focus your energy on more important things. Some social media managers and agencies charge a premium for their services, so hire someone who works with your budget and delivers quality.

Pros of hiring a social media manager

#1. You'll save time and avoid the overwhelm and frustration many business owners experience when growing their online presence.

#2. You can leverage the experience and knowledge the social media manager has.

#3. You will finally get someone competent to create a social media strategy that aligns with your business goals.

Cons of hiring a social media manager

#1. Hiring a social media can range from $400 to thousands per month, depending on the person. That means you need to have an allocated budget for this.

#2. A social media manager usually needs to gain more knowledge about your niche or the topic you want to specialize in, so you must train them to represent you well.

Pros of hiring an agency

#1. They will have the most advanced tools that enhance your ability to quickly grow and monetize your audience.

#2. They come as a complete team, so you will have varying skill sets working toward your desired goal.

#3. You will get a higher level of reporting and analytics due to the agency's process.

#4. They bring vast experience and learnings from testing strategies across many clients, leading to rapid strategy innovation and less trial and error.

Cons of hiring an agency

#1. Costs are usually higher.

#2. Response time is often slower, especially regarding community management, as the resource is usually only partially dedicated to one account.

#3. Quality control and sticking to your brand voice and identity can become issues, so you must develop a good process.

#4. The agency might need more specific industry knowledge, which might harm your brand perception and authoritativeness.

#5. Given the high turnover rate of agencies, it's likely that you will need more control over your account because you may be assigned different account managers as people quit and new hires come in. That might create consistency and a need for clarity for your Instagram.

Analyze the results

Whether you do it yourself or outsource some help, always remember to keep track of your progress using the right tools.

Section 5

Monetizing Your Instagram

Chapter 12

Making Money with Instagram

This chapter will discuss how you can turn raving followers and fans into buying customers to continue growing your brand and reaching your financial goals. If you started your Instagram account to make money, here are the easiest ways to earn an income on Instagram.

Become an Instagram Influencer

You can join the ranks of highly successful and well-paid Instagram influencers by becoming an authoritative figure in your chosen niche. Companies of all sizes will pay you to promote their products and services. You can make as much money as you want; the best part is you'll do something you love. The most important thing is first to build a hyper-engaged audience and earn their trust so you can influence their purchase behavior.

Affiliate marketing

This is the easiest and most common way to make money on Instagram. Affiliate marketing is about promoting someone's product through a link and receiving a small commission fee for every successful transaction. You can join one of the more enormous affiliate opportunities, such as ClickBank and Amazon Affiliates, or partner with small businesses with products you believe in. If you're in personal development or weight loss, you can affiliate hundreds of products from names like Bob Proctor, Tony Robbins, etc.

Sell products and services.

These include physical products and services like vintage baseball cards or in-house massage services. But that's not all. You can also sell digital products and online services that you create. Think about eBooks, Online courses, Virtual coaching, etc. The best part is with such services, you get to keep 100% of the profit.

Become a consultant

As you grow a decent-sized audience, you can start offering social media consulting services or even become an Instagram expert, showing others how to grow their accounts fast. I recommend you always show people or consult based on your experiences. So, if you're a trained personal trainer, you can offer online and offline consultation services. If you've grown your following from zero to 10,000, then yes, provide social media consultations. But always ensure you've mastered it before hanging your hat as a consultant.

Sell your photos

Selling art, photos, and other visual-based elements has become a massive trend on Instagram. If you've got talent and people love your photos, why not give them the option of purchasing for print or offline use?

I have a friend with 20,000 followers; she only posts photos of her sketches. Recently, she started offering personalized portraits for a fee, and people have been ordering like crazy. Currently, there's a three-month waitlist for pre-orders. This has taken years to build, but I can assure you the business is blowing up faster than she can handle. Her product is highly personalized and high-quality, so she's charging premium prices. Still, people flock to her DM daily with requests—all this to say that it doesn't matter how simple your skill might be. You could take breathtaking nature pics or draw the best Manga characters. Instagram is perfect for showcasing your talents and converting followers into buying customers.

Conclusion

You've made it to the end; congratulations on your solid commitment to mastering Instagram marketing. We've covered a lot of ground, and you are all set to survive and thrive in the social media jungle. It may seem like a lot to take in at once, so please don't read this as entertainment. Instead, please review each chapter and the action steps suggested, then work on each step before moving to the next.

You now better understand how Instagram works, how to choose your niche, and how to identify your ideal audience. I also showed you the basics of brand building, setting up your account correctly, and finding the right hashtags.

Remember that with Instagram, you need to master the fundamentals before getting fancy. So, improve your pictures, videos, and captions before reaching for the more advanced and fancy solutions to growing engagement.

After years of being on Instagram, I can assure you it will be a continuous hustle, but the rewards are worthwhile. This platform requires constant experimentation and reinvention because capturing users' attention as they scroll through their feeds takes a lot. The fresher and more alluring your content is, the easier it will be to grow and scale your account.

The relationships you build with influencers and your followers are the results you should aim for. With that outcome, you will follow all the rewards you wish to receive, so focus on that objective. And when setbacks catch you off-guard or things get tough, especially in the first year, don't allow yourself to despair. We've all gone through these hardships.

Although this book guides you through the fundamentals and makes you aware of the blindspots that usually trip people up, it doesn't eliminate all obstacles from your path. The path of entrepreneurship is riddled with hindrances - that's just part of the game. However, you hold in your hand a step-by-step blueprint that will make that journey more bearable and success inevitable if you put in the work.

Now that you know exactly what it takes to turn your Instagram page into a money-making machine and a powerful tool to help you achieve all your goals, it's time to take action and make your dreams a reality.

Book # 6

TikTok & Twitch for Beginners

A Complete Guide for Making Money with Shorts Videos, Master Influencer Marketing, and Unlock Millions of Views for Your Business

Introduction

Social media platforms have become the new norm for our society. Every smartphone has several apps installed where the consumer can connect, interact, and consume social content and trending news with friends, family, and total strangers who resonate. Some apps come and go in a matter of months. Others always need more traction. A few, however, seem to have some magical formula that propels them seemingly overnight to stardom. From humble beginnings to billions of users, we've seen a handful of apps like Instagram become household names, and in recent years, two platforms have followed suit. I'm talking about TikTok and Twitch. These platforms have grown so much (in a relatively short time) that it's impossible to ignore the opportunities they contain.

Most people used to hear "TikTok" and think about the hit pop single by Kesha, but for the teens of our current society, TikTok has an entirely different meaning. As one of the fastest-growing social media platforms, it is now considered a subculture for Gen Z. Most people love TikTok because it's like a one-stop shop for entertainment. It's a place where being raw, spontaneous, and different are fully embraced. I like the app because it takes creativity to a whole new level. You don't just create short, expressive videos. There's the bonus of editing and adding emojis, stickers, music, and more to the videos!

For anyone looking to create a passive income and build a solid personal or company brand, these platforms are too good to pass up for those who enjoy being on social media. You probably already knew that, so you picked up this book. Unfortunately, everyone else knows it, too, so people are storming these platforms trying to make it work. I don't know if you realize, but knowing what to do and how to do it are different. Many gamers, aspiring social media influencers, small business owners, and artists know they should be on TikTok and Twitch. Still, they need help with practical implementation. Where do you begin? How do you grow your audience and brand? What kind of content works best? How do you eventually monetize your efforts? These are the questions this book attempts to answer in simple, digestible vocabulary that anyone can grasp.

If you've been looking for a simple guide that can teach you everything you need to know about TikTok and Twitch so you can build your online business and create passive income through these platforms, you're in the right place.

What this book is not:

If you're looking for a get-rich-quick formula or a magic bullet that will shortcut the effort required to succeed on social media, this book is not for you. You're also not in the right place if you only care about a cookie-cutter system enabling you to spam different platforms with the same content. For example, if you're lazy and all you want is to create the same content on Twitch and TikTok with the expectation that they will both work to grow your followers, then I'm sorry to disappoint. That's not what we are about here.

The ideas and hacks shared in this book are proven. They've produced incredible results for many people, but only because these people put in the work.

So, before you discredit this book's content, ensure you do the required work. While it seems that influencers in your niche have an easier time as they explode their following/subscriber count, it takes hard work, consistency, and perseverance to get the results you dream about.

Why I wrote this book:

The steps you're about to learn have helped thousands of other fellow entrepreneurs and me over the years. People who started from scratch with zero followers have thousands (some tens of thousands) of followers and subscribers just because they are committed to the same guidelines you will receive. They now generate active and passive income thanks to their choice to establish a presence on these platforms. Some have dominated both Twitch and TikTok. Others only chose one and succeeded mainly because it was the right thing to do for their niche market. You'll learn later why you don't need to dominate both accounts to reach your objectives.

Why invest in TikTok and Twitch:

Both these platforms are fun, laid back, and brimming with an active audience. There's so much potential for success. It's one of the most underpriced ways to gain attention and spread awareness about your product, service, or passions. These platforms are also increasing. Check out these statistics.

The TikTok app was launched in 2016, and by February 2019, TikTok reached its first billion downloads. In a mere eight months, the app gained half a billion more. By April 2020, the video app had been downloaded more than two billion times globally and still needs to show signs of decline.

TikTok users spend an average of fifty-two minutes per day on the app. It is available in 155 countries in 75 languages, meaning it covers a considerable part of the global population. Influencers consider this platform the third-best platform for influencer marketing, right behind Instagram and YouTube, respectively. 41% of the audience is between 16 and 24 years old, with nine out of ten users logging into the app multiple times daily. If that is your audience range, TikTok should be a no-brainer. But even if you only serve adults, here's an interesting fact (especially if your audience is in the United States). 26.5 out of the 500 million monthly active users are from the United States of America. Although most are teens, a growing number of adults (currently at 14.3 million) continue to engage on the platform.

On the other hand, Twitch has gotten a massive boost thanks to the 2020 pandemic. According to Stream Elements and Arsenal.gg, there was a 50% increase in watch time between March and April 2020. In the US, Twitch viewers are currently 41.5 million and growing. Although gaming is the core of Twitch, other categories are spiking, especially since it gives entertainers and performers a platform to connect with their audience and monetization opportunities. Music and Performing Arts nearly quadrupled its viewership from April 2019 to April 2020, so it's worth exploring and testing this platform even if you're not a gamer.

The great promise to you:

While this isn't going to be a one-size-fits-all solution or a get-rich-quick scheme, I know you have the potential to crush it on TikTok and Twitch. By the end of this book, you will clearly understand how to do it, even if you're entirely new to social media. You will learn hacks to help you grow with and without a marketing budget.

Consider where you are right now. Are you hitting your goals yet? Have you seen success with the tactics you've applied so far? Have you become frustrated with the more mature platforms like Facebook and YouTube, which have high competition and low organic yield? If you know something's got to change, then why debate this new investment? Jumping into TikTok and Twitch now is like having the opportunity to jump into Facebook when organic traffic was still a thing. Please save your precious time to grow something profitable on these platforms while it's still relatively easy. Learn everything from this book, implement religiously, and trust in the process because success is inevitable for the one who perseveres in doing the right thing. Let's jump in.

SECTION 1

Understanding Social Media Algorithms

CHAPTER 1

Starting With the Roots: Everything You Need to Know About Algorithms

To succeed and sustain success on any social media platform, there's an essential term you need to learn and understand: Algorithm. Social media algorithms are what all social media platforms operate on these days. Most people shoot blanks when they hear the phrase social media algorithm. It's a mysterious puzzle that only a few seem to understand. Given how frequently the algorithms change, your content's health and reach depend mainly on your ability to grasp the founding principles behind algorithms. The good news is this chapter is written to guide you through this understanding so you can take advantage and exponentially grow your reach within TikTok.

Let's Talk About Social Media Algorithms

Before understanding how the algorithms work, let's define this term. According to Merriam-Webster, an algorithm is a step-by-step procedure for solving a problem or accomplishing some end. Tech Terms offers a definition that brings it closer to our understanding and usage of this term by defining it as a set of instructions designed to perform a specific task. This can be a simple process, such as multiplying two numbers, or a complex operation, such as playing a compressed video file. When it comes to social media, algorithms are used as the set of rules that operate in the background to sort out all the different posts to shape and match the preferences of their end-user. The basic premise is to provide the most enjoyable and personalized experience for the user in an automated and systematic way.

While programmers working on these social media platforms do their best to create efficient algorithms, there is always constant iteration of the system to ensure they continue to perform optimally and evolve their functionality. As such, we keep seeing new versions and algorithm upgrades, often disrupting our posted content's reach and visibility. While programmers might believe they are doing the right thing to keep changing up the algorithm, for those of us who are marketing and trying to grow our following, some of these changes can devastate our marketing efforts. Ask anyone who used to do their marketing on Facebook in 2012 how things used to be back then, and you'll see what I mean. But such is the nature of social media. It evolves, and so must we. TikTok and Twitch algorithms are highly favorable to any newcomer, hence the importance of jumping in to ride this organic wave.

Why is it a Big Deal?

Before algorithms became the norm for social media platforms, social networks displayed posts in reverse chronological order. So, a user would see the newest post from those they followed. In fact, on Twitter, you can still experience this if you choose to set your feed in chronological order. After the introduction of algorithms, things started shifting. That's because the algorithm was now responsible for sorting and sifting through available content.

Based on your preference as the user, it would show you only the most relevant ones and sometimes omit entirely what it rendered irrelevant. YouTube does a great job demonstrating how algorithms work. If you sign into your account today, you'll see recommended videos, your history, and any new releases from the accounts you most interact with. The algorithm digs into your behavior through categories, tags, and keywords. That same mode of operation is present on both TikTok and Twitch.

Why are they so important, and are they even necessary?

Learning about algorithms for the different channels you wish to dominate is essential because they directly impact your visibility, channel growth, and, ultimately, your income-earning possibilities. This matters because if your content is being served to your followers and any new potential followers, you won't grow, and your engagement rate will also drop.

Let me illustrate. A client shared his frustration before working with me. He had hired an agency to help him grow his following, and they did a great job taking his account from a few thousand followers to 30K within a few months. Unfortunately, his engagement rate dropped from 3% to 0.5%, and ultimately, he realized people still needed to see his content. What was the problem here? The agency might have done an excellent job getting the young influencer new followers, but they needed to understand how to play nice with the algorithm.

Consequently, it punished the account by cutting off reach and showing content to fewer people despite their increased posting frequency. All that could have been avoided if they had learned the ropes. That's what you're learning here, so hopefully, you will experience a different frustration.

Learning the Ropes: How Algorithm Works?

The result of an algorithm at work seems straightforward, but there are many complexities to learn about under the hood. It involves machine learning and data science. Don't worry; you're not about to die of boredom if these technical topics have no interest to you. There will be no problematic jargon or technical explanation. This is a crash course on algorithms for people who consider themselves tech-illiterate.

Since we established that an algorithm's end goal is to deliver the most relevant content to the end user, the only knowledge you need to have now is around the set of rules or the criteria that the algorithm is fed. Some social networks are more open to discussing how they set their algorithms, while others like to keep all of us in the dark. My gut feeling tells me there are fundamental principles applicable to all social networks, best practices that we can assume out the gates will apply to both TikTok and Twitch.

- **Relevancy**

Is your content relevant to your followers? The algorithm is more likely to recommend it to the user if it is. How will it tell? It will base this decision on the user's history and preferences. For example, if you have a follower who often interacts with fashion content and posts an image about fast fashion, that user is more likely to be fed that post.

- **High-quality content**

What determines high quality? The reaction and engagement of your audience. If there's a lot of activity on your content (likes, shares, comments, and reshares), the algorithms will read this as a signal that it should inform more people about your post.

- **Recency**

This signal is focused on your content being "fresh." The social networks want to feed their community the newest, freshest, and hottest posts to keep them engaged and thrilled. Human beings love novelty, and algorithms have been programmed to feed this addiction of getting something new each time. So, if you're not posting fresh content regularly, it will be hard to have the kind of reach you desire.

Now, let's look deeper into how the TikTok Algorithm works.

On TikTok, the user's preference determines the "For You" feed (the main discovery feed you land on when you log in). That means I will see a different meal from you depending on the people I follow, where I often interact, and the categories I am interested in.

Categories and interests are chosen when you first join TikTok as the platform tries to learn more about your preferences.

TikTok says, "The system recommends content by ranking videos based on a combination of factors - starting from interests you express as a new user and adjusting for things you indicate you're not interested in."

Recommendations are based on the following:

#1: User interactions

That includes videos a user likes or shares, accounts they follow, comments they post, and content.

#2: Video information

The video information used includes captions, sound, and hashtags.

#3: Device and account settings

That includes language preference, country setting, and device type. These factors are included to optimize performance but carry the least weight compared to the previous two elements.

It's also worth mentioning that the algorithm notes whether a user finishes watching a longer video. Users who watch a longer video from start to finish are more likely to receive similar content, even outside their country setting.

How Twitch Recommends Videos

People who have been active on Twitch can profess to the massive shift that has taken place in

Starting With the Roots: Everything You Need to Know About Algorithms

recent years as the guys behind the scenes tried to make the platform easier to navigate. Twitch is rather complicated and only works with a few algorithmic rules. What's more, is that we are dealing with live-streaming videos. That makes understanding the algorithm and getting more reach way more complicated.

It used to be impossible to find the content you wanted the instant you liked it. All that has changed and continues to change thanks to machine learning. Their Twitch algorithm focuses on specific indicators, the most important of which is live concurrent chatters. This means the algorithm will be triggered if you can have at least two active people chatting while you're live streaming. The other thing that matters is the category you choose. Your chosen type must align with the kind of content you create so that there is resonance as people join your stream. The better your content and the more accurately you categorize it, the higher the chances the algorithm will read your account as share-worthy.

Determining exactly how the TikTok and Twitch algorithms work will require firsthand experimentation and listening to what these networks say about their platform. Sure, that implies a lot of trial and error, but the fact is, all social media marketing is an ongoing process of experimentation, which means trial and error is part of the game.

The Different Social Media Algorithms You Need to be Aware Of

In 2021, there are over 3 billion users worldwide across various social media platforms. The best social networks must handle much traffic and activity, so they all run on algorithms. Without systematic order, these platforms would have no way of sorting content, keeping their audience's attention, or selling advertising space to eager marketers. Even if you don't plan on running ads across various social media channels, it's worth understanding how different networks work.

Let's talk about the four major ones:

Facebook

Facebook's mission is to bring people together. They care about meaningful conversations and interactions between friends, family, and brands. To do this, they created an algorithm to intensify the importance of viewership of local familial, friendly posts rather than sales-looking business-type posts.

Paid content, however, is set up differently but still revolves around consumer response, engagement, and relevance to the subject matter. Another aspect of their algorithm that only some realize is that Facebook sorts out spam content. So, it's about more than just creating user-friendly content. It's also about adding value to your account and maintaining integrity. There are four prioritized ranking signals you should know about.

Quality content - Facebook wants you to share relevant, helpful, and visually appealing content. So, if you want your content to rank better, go for high-quality images and create high-definition videos or graphics animation that can improve your quality score to land more views on the newsfeed.

Positive engagement - Facebook's algorithm constantly searches for the most interactive content. You will gain more attention and reach if more people engage in your posts. These positive signals include likes, comments, replies, mentions, and shares.

Power of community - The next important factor is growing an active audience. The algorithm considers how often your followers interact with your brand's posts. You don't need a big audience, but a real one where people express genuine interest in your publication.

Collaborative conversations - I'm sure you've seen a rise in quizzes, polls, jokes, and other types of content that trigger conversations. Some accounts intentionally start controversial conversations to provoke their audience into engagement. If it's within your brand's integrity, feel free to be a conversation starter because the more people interact with your brand, the more the algorithm will push out your stuff to new people who don't know you.

Anytime people leave long-form comments links or reshare your thought-provoking posts, the algorithm reads that positive signal and expands your reach. A fair warning here. Don't just create conversations for the sake of going viral or to get clicks. That kind of success will be short-lived.

Instagram

It's only natural that we also include the Instagram algorithm behind Facebook since they share similarities, given that the same parent company owns them. You may think of Instagram as the baby sister (a very vain baby sister who is really into aesthetics and perfect-looking selfies). The algorithm here also focuses on engagement and interaction, but subtle differences are worth noting.

Current trends - Instagram's algorithm is crazy about "the hottest new posts." Anything about a week old is "too old" on this platform. The fresher your content, the better reach you'll have.

Relationship interaction - Signals like being tagged in a video or photo, getting a mention, or engaging with someone in a direct message are what the Instagram algorithm uses to determine where to rank your content on the person's feed. The more often you engage with your followers, the more likely they will see your new content.

Individual interest - We must recognize the emphasis Instagram gives on personalizing our feed. They don't want to show me MMA posts if I already expressed interest in music and fashion. So, the algorithm looks at my past behavior to predict what content to place on my feed. If I interact mainly with business accounts, media forms, certain hashtags, or specific personal accounts, my content will come from those sources. Hence, you need to be more active and engaged on your brand account if you want to show up on your followers and a new audience's feeds.

Real accounts with verifiable followings. The idea of buying fake followers so that your account can look prominent caught fire very quickly. Why? Because too many of us love shortcuts. Pay for fake followers and bots to build yourself into an influencer, and everyone will believe you're a big shot, right? Wrong! No one believes you're a big shot when you have 50K followers and only two likes on all your posts. What's more, the algorithm can detect an account that's stacked with fake engagement signals. Instead of wasting money buying followers, please read this and

Starting With the Roots: Everything You Need to Know About Algorithms

my Instagram marketing book and work to grow a genuine and authentic audience around your brand.

Twitter

Twitter likes to prioritize content that is focused on the latest hot news around the world. The algorithm is hot for anything hot this minute. Other signals affect the algorithm, including the relationship between users, but ultimately, fresh hot content consistently ranks up. Here are some indications you need to know.

Rich Media - If your tweet contains images, polls, videos, or GIFs that are relevant to the tweet, you're likely to see a more extensive reach. People also engage more with these forms of media, so make sure you use the correct file size and make the text match the media content.

Receny - On Twitter, trending topics are always prioritized on the feeds. And if you post something that gets immediate engagement, the algorithm sees that as essential and pushes for more reach.

Hashtag

Twitter differs significantly from most other social networks because of its "text message" style and small character limit. For this reason, hashtags are a big deal. The hashtags organize tweets into searchable keyword categories. Then, the algorithm picks the hashtags with high search volume and pushes more of the content within that hashtag.

Relationship with your followers. Like other platforms, Twitter values the interaction between you and your followers. Your relevancy score increases if your fans comment and retweet your content. It also means you get priority on their feed.

YouTube

YouTube is both a social network and a search engine, so it's worth learning a thing or two about how they rank content. The platform continues to evolve and mature, and they are tightening down on clickbait videos that provide little value to their consumer. Here are some signals you should know if you want to start uploading your videos from TikTok or Twitch to YouTube.

Authentic and original content - YouTube doesn't like spammy, repurposed content. The algorithm will only favor you if you're committed to creating something original and valuable to your growing audience.

Keywords - Before posting a video, research keywords to include the correct terms your audience will search for. The algorithm will determine which video to recommend in a viewer's search query based on your video's title, description, etc.

Channel Authority - The YouTube algorithm will rank you based on viewing time, shares, thumbs-ups, linking your channel to a website, and high-resolution thumbnails on all your videos. That, in turn, gives you a specific channel quality score that positively or negatively impacts your reach. The higher your score, the better, so if you'd like to master YouTube channel building, I encourage you to check out my other published book on YouTube marketing.

Key Strategies to Keep You Going

Focus on sharing engaging content that reaches your target audience.

The only way to signal to any algorithm that you are worth being ranked at the top of people's feeds is to create content your audience understands and loves. If the material is not attractive, no engagement will occur. Make sure you invest some time doing market and audience research. A user's psychology on TikTok differs from that of the same user on YouTube or Instagram. Ensure you get these subtle nuances and dish out content that reaches them where they are in the manner they prefer. What am I trying to say? Know your audience; you will beat the algorithms across any social network.

Post fresh content frequently, but get to know the right amount for each platform. Social media platforms could be more quiet. Posting one piece of content a month will get you nowhere, regardless of how good your content is. It would be best if you had consistency and frequency. And you also need to understand the nature of the beast you will be handling. We'll talk specifics on TikTok and Twitch and what experts recommend later in the book. But a good rule of thumb on most social networks, especially Instagram and Facebook, is to post between 1-2 times daily. However, if you're on Twitter, you should do that once per hour or once every three hours. Why? The nature of Twitter is to give a short lifespan (about 18 minutes) to each tweet so content can remain fresh and hot. Experts recommend posting 15 times daily on Twitter, once daily on LinkedIn and Facebook, and twice daily on Instagram.

It's also important to remember the most active timings for your audience. Depending on their location, they might be involved in the morning, afternoon, or early evening. That might be while you're working or sleeping (if you have an international audience), so you'll need the help of a scheduling system like Buffer or Hootsuite to ensure you post frequently and at optimal times. Here are some standard recommended timings to experiment with on the leading social platforms:

Facebook: The best time is between 1.00 PM and 3.00 PM on Tuesdays and Fridays.

Twitter: The best time is between 1:00 PM and 3:00 PM, Mondays, Tuesdays, Wednesdays, and Thursdays.

LinkedIn: All day long on Tuesdays, Wednesdays, and Thursdays.

Use captions to drive more attention and engagement. This strategy is especially effective on Instagram. Most people invest time and resources in capturing that perfect image but then waste it all by adding a single sentence or word and a lot of hashtags. What a waste of precious real estate. Your audience and the algorithm will benefit if you invest time to create thoughtful comments that help you tell the story, inspire, or reflect on the chosen image, GIF, video, or graphic. When the audience is happy, the algorithm is comfortable, making you happy as more and more people are served your beautiful posts.

CHAPTER 2

Taking Advantage of Social Media Algorithms

By 2022, social media users exponentially grew, with 490 million new users joining various social networks. That's about 13% of annualized growth or roughly 15.5 new users every second! As it stands, 53% of the global population uses social media (4.20 billion), which will continue to grow, especially during the pandemic season. It's safe to say you are using social media already. That could be why you got curious about building your brand and marketing yourself because you realized the great opportunity social media possesses. Current data shows your hunch is spot on and worth going all in and pursuing your existing social media objectives. But one thing to remember is that creating a presence on multiple social networks is worth considering.

The typical user has an account on more than eight social networks and spends an average of 2.5 hours daily using social media. Now, let's assume this person sleeps about 8 hours per day. That would mean about 16% of their waking time goes to social media. Doesn't it make sense to interact with that person as much as possible? As a marketer, you want to ensure that wherever they invest those 2.5 hours of their day, your content will engage them. That brings me to my first suggestion. If you have interests or hobbies you would love to share with the world (cooking, gaming, working out, arts & crafts, wine tasting, etc.), consider sharing these across more than one social network. Let's examine how the extensive social networks have distributed audience attention.

Social media active user data based on publicly available data up to January 2023

- Facebook has 2.7 billion monthly active users.
- YouTube has 2 billion monthly active users.
- Facebook Messenger has around 1.3 billion monthly active users.
- WhatsApp has around 2 billion monthly active users.
- WeChat has around 1.2 billion monthly active users.
- Instagram has 1.221 billion monthly active users.
- TikTok has 689 million monthly active users.
- Quora has around 300 million monthly active users.
- Pinterest has 442 million monthly active users.
- Telegram has 500 million monthly active users.

- Snapchat has 489 million monthly active users.

Given this data, can we set up a TikTok and YouTube/Instagram/WeChat account to complete your marketing activities?

Answering the Big Question:

Can I Earn Through Social Media Platforms?

The answer to this question is controversial. Some say it's too risky or impossible unless you have a website and deep pockets. Every business is complex, so let's not use that as an excuse for discarding the idea. In a Forbes article, TikTok revealed their top seven highest-earning stars who made severe money the previous year. Topping that list was Addison Rae Easterling, who earned a whopping $5 million in 2019. Many experts estimate that TikTok creators are on the trajectory of making one million dollars a post very soon, but of course, all of that is speculation.

We cannot accurately state how much TikTokers are getting paid for sponsorship opportunities, but we know people like Loren Gray, Baby Ariel, and Zach King are at the top of the TikTok Rich list. Content creators don't habitually add price tags to their sponsored posts or announce their partnerships' value, especially not on this platform. Still, there is no denying that earning a ton of cash is possible for anyone who can build a large enough audience and get the attention of brands with big budgets.

Still on edge about making that passive income a reality?

Anyone with the right mindset, message, and work ethic can make social media work for them. But to learn how to earn on social media, you must understand some basics. For example, do you even know what the process looks like?

Social media monetization involves creating a systematic process that generates revenue from your ever-growing audience. That entails having a strong social media account and an engaged and growing audience. Audience targeting and nurturing determine whether you succeed with your monetization efforts. If you know what people you want and what you will offer them that they will find valuable, you're in a much better position to tailor your product or service to their needs and generate revenue. Excellent social media monetization is centered on a win-win philosophy. Given the statistics I just shared of billions of users online, you deserve to connect with, serve, and get rewarded by an audience who sees value in your brand.

Three Main Ways to Make Money Through Social Media Platforms

Depending on the platform you choose to be on, there can be various ways to generate passive income, including affiliate marketing, becoming a consultant, and selling informational products. But for TikTok, let's focus on the three best strategies that are proven to work.

#1: Influencer marketing

Every social platform has influencers. Companies often approach these influencers to promote their products, services, or the brand itself in hopes of generating sales. TikTok is doing a great job of creating and growing an environment for massive influencer marketing opportunities.

Working with influencers is an excellent strategy for companies seeking brand exposure and engagement.

First, instead of analyzing the app and its audiences for weeks or months to determine what content will be interesting, these more prominent companies prefer to work with an influencer with a decent following, videos with high engagement, and a visible track record of reaching the TikTok audience. It's also a great way to limit the time and resources needed to create videos because they can get the influencer to create quality content. So, this can be an excellent opportunity for you, but you will need to have an audience and demonstrate your ability to create great content.

#2: Sponsored content

Sponsored content is premium content that a sponsor will pay you to create and distribute on your social media account. Sponsored content is an ad, but it usually doesn't feel like it because it naturally fits the environment. For example, if you're a gamer and a gaming company hires you to sponsor their brand and a particular video game, that would qualify as a sponsored ad. It would feel accessible for your viewers because you already create content around video games in the same genre. Sponsored ads are great; companies love them because they add to the user experience instead of disrupting it.

It makes the brand feel trustworthy and credible because it places it alongside other things your viewers will enjoy, and you, as the account owner, are responsible for the execution of the content. This type of content is mutually beneficial because you get funded, and the brand gets access to your audience, who could turn into buying customers. The mechanics of this are simple, and if you do an excellent job of sharing sponsored content, you can earn a great income from it. Take the example of Loren Gray, who earned $2.6 million after landing a major Revlon deal where she created content for the company's TikTok account and Revlon-sponsored posts for hers.

#3: Selling your own branded merchandise.

Another passive income opportunity is selling your line of products. These can be as simple as T-shirts and coffee mugs to entire makeup line products, all of which have proven very profitable on TikTok. However, you must have a wildly popular account with lots of engagement. You should approach selling products the same way you would any other business venture. Do your research, be wise, and ensure you're profitable as early in the game as possible.

Helping Hand from Your Audience

Before you can hope to generate any passive income or sponsorship and partnership opportunities, you must focus on building a healthy audience. Your audience is the key to your success. That means you need to understand who you are creating content for and what they most resonate with on TikTok. If you don't invest the time to find that sweet spot, you'll unwittingly land on the wrong side of the TikTok algorithm.

There's only one rule of thumb to consider when it comes to growing an audience: Choose an audience you care about.

The content you create to attract these people to your account must be of high value and volume. One content randomly created cannot help you grow an audience. This process must be systematic and require effort, so you must care about what you're doing and the people you're doing it for. Otherwise, you'll want to quit a few months in. If you care about your audience, you'll be motivated to continue to create content even if no money comes in. And as this audience grows and falls in love with all you do for them, opportunities will start to present themselves.

I encourage you to list all the potential audiences you care about that you can see yourself helping for the next few years with no return.

Can't settle on just one audience?

If you realize you want to talk to more than one audience, that's okay. Pick one to get started with. For example, if you're into gaming and want to attract different segments of video-loving people, go first with the one closest to your current situation. The broader audience can come in later once you've gained momentum with this more niche audience that resembles you.

Avoid this mistake:

Don't build an audience of people who don't want to or can't afford to buy a product. For example, if you're a beauty makeup artist and want to become famous on TikTok, the best audience would be young ladies who love makeup. The worst audience would be creating an audience of minimalists or a young male audience who follows you just because you're pretty and make cool dance videos.

So, how do you know if you're building the right audience?

First, you must consider what your audience cares about and what they'd be willing to spend money on. There's no need to build an audience of extreme sports teenagers if your passion is playing video games. Similarly, if you create an audience of gamers, trying to sell them sports merchandise is not the best idea. That's why you must understand the audience profile as much as possible. Invest some time in researching basic demographic and psychographic information. Fire up a Google doc and start creating your audience personas. Let's start with demographics.

- Age
- Location
- Gender
- Income
- Education level
- Ethnicity
- Status

Figure out the demographics that are important to you. For example, if your audience is college students, marital status and children shouldn't matter to you. If you're selling makeup up, the gender should matter. This aims to define your ideal persona so you can create a strong content strategy they'll be interested in. Once you have all the details, move to psychographics. Psychographics is about figuring out what your audience thinks and believes.

- Why do they want to learn about your niche?
- How do they like to learn/be entertained (depending on your channel's offer)?
- What common questions do they have about your niche?
- How knowledgeable are they about your niche?
- How important is your niche to them? Do they approach it as a hobby or part of their job?

As you answer these questions, do your best to think from your audience's perspective. Do it right, and you'll be ready for the next phase, i.e., Positioning.

How to position yourself for success on TikTok and Twitch

Positioning is how you present yourself to your audience to make sure your audience associates your account or brand with a particular aspect of what you already know they value. This comes only after you know and understand your target audience. Your job should be to position yourself to a specific segment or group of people by creating content in a way that they want, but no one else is providing.

For instance, the gaming niche has many subcategories, such as reviews, walkthroughs, game news, etc. So, the best approach as a beginner looking to build an audience and, ultimately, a brand is to choose one of those subcategories to be the central theme of your account. If you're only doing walkthroughs, you can either go specific and only focus on a particular game (e.g., Tomb Raider) or do walkthroughs for various games in the same genre. Note that the former might be limiting in the long run because you might run out of content too soon.

The bottom line is that you want people to immediately associate your account with something specific. That's the easiest way for you to imprint yourself and stay top of mind. And just as a side note, you don't need to be excellent at playing the game. In a recent Google Consumer Survey, viewers often cited the "reactions" and "commentary" of the YouTube creator as a significant attraction factor for this kind of content. One respondent said, "It's a shared experience with a favorite creator."

An excellent example of this is Conan O'Brien's Clueless Gamer series. It's worth mentioning that he sucks at playing. But his commentary, observations, and reactions are just epic! He adds much value to the experience and offers a great laugh, so his audience keeps growing and returning for more. So, if you're worried you're not that good at playing, think again. You'll be fine if you've targeted the right people and added value through your personality. If you still need help finding your position, check out the positioning matrix I've added for convenience at this chapter's end.

Do you Have a Business? Boost it on Social Media Platforms!

If you have an existing business, social media is a powerful tool to leverage. The advantages are too numerous to mention here, but let's start with the main ones.

Building brand authority and credibility.

You appear more credible when people see your brand active on social media, especially when replying to customers and posting original content. Interacting with your fans and customers demonstrates that you care about serving and satisfying your customers, and that promotes brand loyalty and causes people to want to talk about your brand more.

The plus side of having people talking about your brand and making mentions on social media is that it helps you beat the algorithms. Not only does word spread about your brand, but it also enables you to avoid suffering the rage of ever-changing algorithms.

New growth opportunities

Social media is one of the best places to find growth opportunities. A lot can happen when your brand is visible and thriving online. You'll find people reviewing your products, tagging you, and creating user-generated content, all for free. You'll also find volunteers who want to become your brand's ambassador and other companies pitching partnership ideas because they recognize your brand and audience's strength. The possibilities are endless when you leverage social media and have a great product or brand.

More inbound traffic

If you're off social media, your inbound traffic is likely limited to people already familiar with your brand. Without running direct ads on your site, getting substantial traffic will take much work. So, building a solid social media presence is imperative if you have a website (whether you have a brick-and-mortar business or an eCommerce store). Each social media profile you add to your marketing strategy is a gateway to your website. Each post is another opportunity to acquire new prospects who could become customers. So, even if you only have TikTok content, think of how to start syndicating that fresh content to as many other platforms as possible - if it matches your target audience.

Brand Evangelist

Having your own brand/product evangelist can boost your revenue. Social media is a great place to gather enthusiastic and vocal people who love what you offer and spread great stories about using your product or experiencing your service. By nature, these super fans tend to create more super fans. By creating an online environment on social media where these individuals can receive special treatment (fun interaction, product testing, etc.), you'll develop evangelists who will draw in more attention, leading to revenue and opportunities.

Regardless of where you boost your business, do it wisely because it makes all the difference. Go where your ideal audience hangs out.

Positioning Matrix Simple Plot

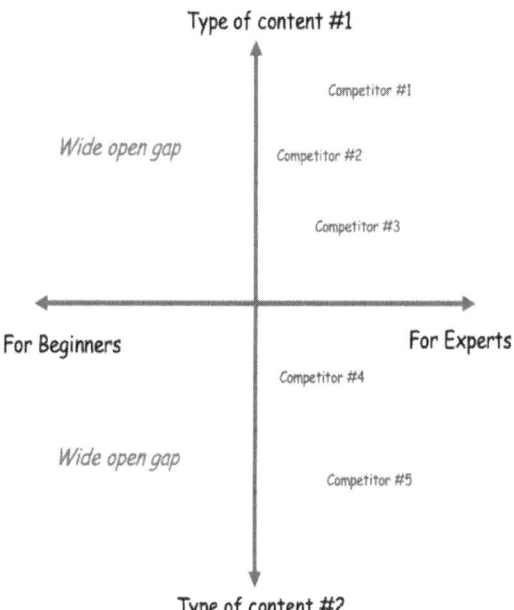

Step One. Identify differentiators.

Have a brainstorming session where you come up with everything your audience might find valuable. Make sure to complete this. Just think of what your audience may like or dislike. Write everything down on the same Google Doc that contains client persona information.

Common differentiators are Easy vs. Hard, Beginner vs. Professional, Brief vs. Step-by-Step, Short vs. Long.

Step Two. Identify your competitors.

Competition in the marketplace is good because it means there's a need/demand for what you have to offer. Identifying the top contenders in your niche will be easy. You can do some hashtag searches on the social media platform on which you want to establish your presence and use Google and Ubersuggest to see who is dominating online to learn from them. Try to find 5-10 competitors.

Step Three. Plot your competitors.

Now that you know your top competitors pick two of the differentiators you identified in step one and create a fundamental matrix with those differentiators as the axis labels.

Next, please review the competitors' list and determine how they fit on this scale. Plot each of them and notice where the gaps are. The aim is to find at least one significant gap you could fill. That becomes your ideal positioning spot.

What happens if there are no apparent gaps? It's easy. Pick a new set of two differentiators and repeat this process.

SECTION 2

Starting Your Trend on Tiktok

CHAPTER 3

Get to Know TikTok

What is TikTok?

TikTok is a short-form video-sharing app allowing users to create and share 15-second videos on any topic. The kids love the app, but there's much to learn for most people over 25 years. Initially, the platform was called musicl.ly until 2017, when it merged into TikTok. This Chinese-owned app (Douyin in China) bought Musical.ly and integrated the two into a single platform (at least in the international market) called TikTok. By 2020, TikTok had become the world's most popular new social media platform. A mix of music, lip sync videos, and micro-video content, TikTok is extremely popular with Gen Z (32% of all TikTok's active users are teenagers). TikTok is home to many lip-synching videos. However, it stands out and continues gaining popularity with its act-out memes backed by music and other sound clips, which get endlessly reproduced and remixed among its young users. Countless tunes (pop, rap, R&B, electro, and DJ tracks) serve as background music for the 15-second video clips.

TikTok is unique because it still needs to be dominated by celebrities or even micro-celebrities. Instead, the feed is often saturated by everyday users (amateurs) doing something cute, funny, or clever with a tacit acknowledgment that "yes, I am making a fool of myself, and I hope the internet finds it funny" underlying much of the content. Most of the content on TikTok is weird, addictive, and unique to the platform. Whether it's from Will Smith or some unknown teenager, many of the best-performing videos would probably not do well on any other social platform. Yet, on TikTok, it just works!

Key questions to ask yourself before launching into TikTok

Although TikTok's growth is enticing, not everyone should be on TikTok right now. So here are a few questions to answer to help you determine whether this app is right for you to build your brand:

#1: Is your target audience younger than 35 years old? If yes, this would be a great social media platform. As you saw in the statistics, most users are Gen Zers and younger Millenials. It might change significantly, but for now, this is where the kids like to hang out.

#2: Do you have visually appealing and demonstrative content?

#3: Are you an artist, musician, or gamer?

#4: Is your brand's identity leaning more toward fun casual with a "cool kid" vibe?

If the answers you come up with validate that getting into this platform is correct, go all in!

Talking About Algorithms

There have been many rumors and speculations about the TikTok algorithm, which makes the platform sound complex and challenging to dominate. All that is about to change because not too long ago, TikTok headquarters finally opened up about it, and you're about to learn the facts as learned from the experts!

First up, let's talk about how TikTok determines what shows up on your "For You" feed and, for that matter, what will show up for your audience. According to the platform, when you upload a video, the For You algorithm shows it first to a small subset of users. These people may or may not be existing followers of your account, but TikTok shows it to them based on their past behavior. If they respond favorably (sharing the video, watching it in full, etc.), TikTok offers it to more people with similar interests. That same process repeats itself, and if the positive feedback loop continues long enough, the video could go viral. Of course, the opposite is also true. If the first sub-segment doesn't show enjoyment, the content is delivered to fewer users, limiting the video's potential reach.

The For You is the best place to find new content. That's where you want to end up more often than not. According to TikTok, "The system recommends content by ranking videos based on a combination of factors - starting from interests you express as a new user and adjusting for things you indicate you're not interested in, too."

I bet you're wondering what these "factors" are. Here's what we know for sure:

- User interactions

    User interactions refer to the videos you like and share. It's also the accounts you follow, the comments you post, and the content you create for your account.

- Video information

    Video information includes details like the hashtags you use, captions, sounds, etc.

- Device and account settings

That refers to country setting, the device you're using, and language preference.

The TikTok recommendation system will weigh all the factors mentioned above to ensure each For You page is unique to the user based on their level of interest. TikTok also explains that they have strong and weak signals that help them determine where to rank content.

Strong signals include how long a viewer watched the video, whether the person shared it, and if they followed the creator who uploaded the video after watching it. If someone cares about your video from beginning to end, the algorithm uses that as a solid indicator to show more of your content. And even if you're not in the same country, your content is more likely to appear on their For You page. Weak signals include language preference, the device being used, and whether the consumer and creator are in the exact geographical location. There are also a few negative indicators that TikTok looks for, including whether a user taps "Not Interested" or if they chose to hide content from a specific creator.

Therefore, we may assume that For You page videos are ranked based on the likelihood of a user's interest in a piece of content. That's why you need clarity on your audience and a great content strategy to get them hooked. More on content creation later. For now, let's address another ubiquitous question among new content creators.

Do I need thousands of followers to go viral on TikTok?

The good news is you don't. TikTok has confirmed you don't need to be a superstar to go viral on their platform. While a video will likely receive more views if posted by an account with a large follower base, it is not a prerequisite. TikTok stated, "Neither follower count nor whether the account has had previous high-performing videos are direct factors in the recommendation system."

Take a deep breath and celebrate your future success because, according to TikTok, you can still get attention if your content interests the target audience, even if you have zero followers. This is one of the reasons TikTok is pretty special. You might be on your first post and still have a chance of appearing on the For You page of potential followers!

Content Creation: What Can I Put Out?

Before you can put anything worth viewing on TikTok, you need to understand the interface. When you first open the app, you'll see two adjacent feeds. The first is called "For You," and this is where discovery and exploration usually happen. It's mysterious, and we all love it because showing up here can make or break your aspirations of becoming a TikTok superstar. Most users spend 75% of their time on the For You page. The For You page usually has content that is tailored to your interests. The more time you spend here, the more personalized this content will be. But you'll also find popular content that may soon go viral because the algorithm likes to test and see what you're more likely to engage with. Next to the For You Page is your "Following Feed." This is where you'll find all the content of the people you've chosen to follow. If you want to know the best content to put out, a great option is to follow brands in your niche that are not necessarily direct competitors.

The type of content you can post on TikTok continues to evolve. Although it started as a lip-syncing platform, there has been a significant expansion in various categories, making it easier for people with diverse passions and interests to succeed. Here are the main types of content that perform well on the site.

#1: Creating videos based on trending hashtags

You could search for trending hashtags on TikTok (we'll cover this a little more in the next chapter) and then create videos around the same theme. Instead of reinventing the wheel or figuring out what your ideal audience wants, you can copy what's already working. Make sure, however, that whatever you create is better quality and more enjoyable to your audience than existing videos. That will increase the probability of getting more views, shares, and new followers who enjoy the theme of the chosen hashtag.

#2: Cute Animals

Cute animals doing humorous or cool things will get you lots of followers. People are simply addicted to cats and dogs doing funny things or simply just looking cool. You can find plenty of cute animal accounts already succeeding on TikTok. So go ahead; if you're a cat lady or an animal lover, share that passion with the TikTok audience.

#3: Do the album cover challenge

This type of content is seriously growing as more and more content creators come up with humorous questions and convert them into videos. It works by first showing your question and then answering it by posing as a famous song's cover photo. The title of the song usually answers the question posed. Some TikTok users have taken this trend seriously, using costumes and elaborate makeup to resemble the album cover as closely as possible. The trick to getting this right is to be as specific as possible with the song choice. So, seriously consider the scenario and question you want to record. An example is a video I saw from @peytoncoffee, who created this content by posing the question her mom asks.

Mom: "What's the earliest you get off TikTok?"

If you watch the video, you see her recreating the album cover for Halsey's song "3 AM".

#4: Dance videos

Dance videos are super popular on TikTok. If you're an aspiring dancer, this is precisely what you need to put out as often as possible. I've seen many creators showcasing their talent and even doing group dance performances to attract attention on the platform.

But even if you're not a great dancer, you can use your personality and some creativity to entertain people, and you can still succeed at going viral with this type of content.

Go Live on TikTok!

TikTok Live has become increasingly popular for content creators who want a more intimate experience with their followers and those who want to start monetizing their brand. Unlike other social media platforms, going live on TikTok doesn't just happen. It would be best to meet specific criteria before that button can appear.

- You must have 1,000 followers in your account. It would be best if you had that to see the option of going live.
- It would be best if you were at least 16 years old. Although anyone age 13 can sign up, you can't access the live feature until 16. For those who would like to activate the part of receiving gifts from followers during live streaming, you must be at least 18 years old.

You can start live streaming on the app if you meet the above requirements. The mechanics of going live are pretty straightforward. What is less so is the content you will share on your broadcast. So before going "Live," invest some time outlining what you're going to share, the title of it, and a little description that will help people know what the video is about and what to expect. Whether it's a cooking class, dance-off, or just sharing your thoughts, you need to be thoughtful and strategic with your content creation so your audience can keep coming back for more.

To go live on Android and iOS, here's a simple step-by-step:

#1: Open the TikTok app and log in if necessary.

#2: Touch the +(plus) button at the bottom of the screen.

#3: Press the "Live" option under the record button.

#4: Title your livestream and add a description so viewers can get hooked and join.

#5: Click "Go Live" to begin.

#6: Tap the "X" button when you're done streaming to end your broadcast.

Why you should Go Live on TikTok

If you're still on the fence about using the Live stream feature, it might be helpful to learn of a survey conducted by Livestream.com in which 82% of the respondents shared that they prefer live video from a brand to social posts. 67% of viewers say the quality is the most important factor when watching a Livestream. So, going live will continue to be a massive trend across all social media, especially TikTok. It will help you gain more exposure and grow your brand authentically and rapidly.

Using It for Your Brand

TikTok is similar to Instagram for new brands coming into the platform with an existing product or service, except it's purely for videos. It can be a powerful branding tool when used appropriately, and yes, it can generate lots of business. The best part about TikTok is that it is easy to make creative, funny, entertaining, and inspirational videos for the TikTok community. And even if you suck at dancing, making a little effort on this platform will grab users' attention. Remember that TikTok is a moderate platform, so your content needs to be light-hearted, fun, and visually pleasing if you want your brand to thrive. Lots of big and small brands are doing well on TikTok. If you want inspiration, check out what brands like Pepsi, Nike, and Universal Pictures are doing.

How to leverage TikTok

Some of the best brand-promoting content I've seen is through the creation of "TikTok Challenge" campaigns. A brand creates a challenge and even provides new music clips for users to interact with. The winners get big prizes as a reward for their attention and participation. For example, fashion brand Guess partnered with TikTok on a campaign targeted at Millenials and Generation Z. In early September 2018, as TikTok users opened the app, TikTok directed them to the #InMyDenim challenge that urges them to post videos with hashtags. Although this challenge had no prizes, thousands of people still participated.

Another great example is Chipotle's #GuacDance challenge, which urged guacamole fans to show off dance moves dedicated to avocados. This Mexican Grill reported record results for this TikTok campaign with 250,000 video submissions and 430 million video starts during a six-day run. The promotion resulted in Chipotle's biggest guacamole day ever, with more than 800,000 sides of the condiment served. Avocado consumption jumped from 68% to 18,500% for National Avocado Day.

Both these examples demonstrate the viral power of TikTok. Challenging other TikTok users to participate in an activity is a crucial driver of viral growth. Every existing business serving the Millennial and Gen Z demographics would do well to leverage the platform in this way. For smaller brands without such massive marketing spend or brand recognition, create a challenge with enticing swag that these cool kids can get as a reward.

CHAPTER 4

Taking the First Steps

Now that you're acquainted with the TikTok platform's mechanics, it's time to get practical. The starting point should always be your account setup. In this chapter, we want to launch and establish your account correctly. We are starting with your profile.

Step One: Begin with Your Profile

Let no one tell you differently. First impressions do matter. On TikTok, your profile must match the users' psychology and the platform's nature. So, if you can slap your Twitter or Instagram profile there, think again. We need to approach the TikTok platform in a whole new way.

The main objective here is to create a profile that attracts viewers, grabs their attention, and entices them to follow your account. A few things you'll want to think about now include:

- The username you want to use.
- The profile photo.
- The word choice you use to describe yourself, your brand, and how you want to be perceived by the community.

Your profile bio is your big chance to introduce yourself to every potential follower because the short video format leaves little room for introductions. So, you have to make sure it's intentionally created.

The first thing you need to do is show your followers who you are and what you do. They might be able to guess a little about your brand and who you are based on your video content, but we want to ensure that the impression is accurate. The character limit on TikTok is super tiny (80 characters), so you must ensure you stay under that limit without compromising the message's quality.

I want you to fire up your Google document or a private journal and start writing sentences that boil down precisely what you want people to know before deciding if they wish to follow you. Use captivating, simple, and engaging language that conveys your brand's value and uniqueness.

Example of a good one-liner for TikTok: Fashion/Lifestyle & Beauty Blogger. AZ 🌵 Follow me on IG for daily looks.

Exercise: What sentence best describes your brand and your "Why"? I call this type of sentence a One-liner. Write variations touching on various aspects you might want to share on your

TikTok, then go for the one that feels right before moving on to the second step. You could even ask a few friends to vote for the best one.

The second thing is to add an emoji or two to your descriptive one-liner. Pick one that feels best from the sentences you wrote above and spruce it up with emojis. Why? Because TikTok is fun, casual, and entertaining. An emoji that helps you emphasize your brand's personality is a must-have. You can also use emojis to highlight your brand's actions without taking up much real estate space. For example, if you're an eCommerce brand selling clothing for teens, you might include a t-shirt 👕 emoji. Get creative with this and use emojis purposefully.

Exercise: What emojis can help you enhance your one-liner and give people an insight into your brand? Add it to your one-liner now before moving on to the next step.

The third thing to do with your profile is to add a good call to action in your bio. Tell new visitors and potential followers what you want them to do next or how you wish them to interact with you. For example, if you're a gamer on Twitch, let them know when they can join a live game. If you have a travel blog, include a CTA (call-to-action) to direct followers to a blog post link. If you have an eCommerce, add a link to your best-selling merchandise there.

If you're starting, feel free to send people outside TikTok. You can ask them to follow you on TikTok or send a message. The important thing is to train your new audience to receive actionable instructions from you.

Exercise: What CTA works best for you and your brand now? Please write it down and ensure the link is included to redirect people outside the platform.

The fourth thing is to decide on a handle name for your account. I don't want this to be the first step because it may evolve when you're done creating your one-liner and thinking about your niche. Now that you are closer to determining your place, which we'll get into shortly, you might already have some ideas of your handle name. That is the name that people will see and use to find you - @exampleaccount. It's essential to think through what you want to call your account because it should be an accessible name for your audience to recall and reflect your brand personality and purpose. If you still need to decide about your handle name, leave it until after you've settled on your niche, and then go with a name that matches what you want to be known for.

The last thing you will do is add a link to your bio. TikTok gives you space for a link on your bio, which is excellent for driving traffic to other pages you wish to promote. There are a few ways to ensure you're getting the most out of this valuable piece of real estate. First, you could send traffic to a single URL. This can be your most recent blog post, a landing page to download some free goodies, another social media profile you wish to boost, or any other page you want to promote. You could encourage multiple links through a link in the bio section. This is the best option if you opt for this because you can offer your followers numerous options when they click on your bio link. That enables you to share all necessary connections, including all the other social media platforms you're on and your online store if you have one. This service also lets you track traffic to see which links perform best with your audience. One of the reasons I like this method is that it saves the hassle of editing and creating new links whenever you want to promote a different product or service.

Please note, however, that it's okay if you cannot add a link to your bio. Some people (depending on the device) seem unable to access this capability. Suppose you're unable to add a link to your bio. In that case, I encourage you to access the TikTok Testers program, where you can receive instructions for accessing the various Beta versions of TikTok as they release them.

What's Your Niche?

TikTok operates a lot on "what's trending and cool," so it makes sense that you can start building an audience by copying the content that's going viral and gaining a lot of views. But there is another way to build your audience, and that is through a niche.

What is a niche audience?

A niche audience is a focused subgroup of a broader target market. It's a specific group of people with particular needs, and in your case, you'll want to go for a niche that you know you can serve well. Users across social media love discovering niche accounts because they know they'll get more specialized content that feels personalized to their needs. If you can pick the right niche and post valuable content, you can quickly become the go-to expert on TikTok. If you think about it, cooking is a target market, but it's pretty broad. Homemade Spanish cooking recipes are an example of a niche within cooking. People who love Spanish food will immediately resonate with your account. Such an account is more likely to gather like-minded people who share a passion for homemade Spanish food, leading to much interaction because it genuinely appeals to them.

So, if you start your new account specializing in Homemade Spanish dishes, TikTok will likely push your content to users who have expressed interest in cooking. Those most interested in Spanish recipes are likelier to click and watch your content on their For You page. The small group of individuals passionate about this cuisine will likely monitor the full video and click on your account profile to see if there are more Spanish recipes.

If they continue to find more and more on this niche topic, turning them into followers will be a natural byproduct. Whenever this user desires a homemade Spanish recipe, guess where they'll go first?

Examples of niche accounts on TikTok include:

drcody_dc uses his TikTok account to promote his chiropractic clinic. That's a niche audience. It's doing well for him as he shares small clips from his client sessions showcasing how he can help. That demonstrates his expertise in the field and does indirect marketing because anyone who needs a chiropractor will think of him first.

The best-performing niches on TikTok:

- **Lip-syncing**

The most popular niche on TikTok (the genre that launched its success online) is lip-synching. Most people use TikTok to make videos of themselves lip-synching to their favorite songs or scenes from their favorite movies. The key is to add a unique flair and twist to this competitive niche.

- **Dancing**

TikTok is all about music and dancing, so it makes sense that the most famous niche with a ready-built audience will be viewers who love to watch people dancing. You can be a professional or amateur dancer. You can even be doing dance-offs to famous songs with your grandma, and people will still love your content. There are many popular accounts of regular people "trying" to dance to their favorite tracks. It's hilarious, and viewers seem to enjoy the authenticity of such content.

- **Comedy**

This has to be my favorite part of TikTok. I enjoy catching Trevor Noah's comic rants about politics and our society. Kevin Hart spent his first several months creating content on TikTok, where he would say, "Let's do a TikTok video" to anyone around him. And he would comically shoot the entire 15-second video "trying to do a TikTok." Most of it was so funny. It didn't even matter that there was no substance to the content. Thousands of people still viewed and liked his videos. You can make clips of yourself either testing out jokes or doing something funny. You don't need to be famous or have a Netflix comedy special. If you can make people laugh, hit record and let the show begin.

- **Fashion**

Are you naturally great at putting outfits together? Are you currently in school studying fashion? There's an audience waiting for you on TikTok. People love seeing daily outfits and getting fashion advice. This is a niche if you like being a little edgy and creating "cool" looks that you would wear if you were part of a particular movie.

- **Cooking/baking**

If you enjoy cooking, this can be a great niche. You might already have a YouTube cooking channel, so this would be a great addition. Still, instead of long videos of preparing and cooking the entire meal, you make short segments and snap them together over some excellent music. Then, you link the recipes in your profile!

- **Arts and crafts**

This is another growing niche on TikTok. People enjoy watching videos of how to draw or craft something, mainly the process of getting to the final product. You can do it with painting, sketching, sculpting, pottery, or anything you're passionate about. Make it a montage or do a time-lapse of yourself drawing or making something and post it into your account. The creation process can be the entire content, which makes things feel more intimate and authentic. Then, you can send people to your shop or wherever you showcase the final products.

- **Fitness**

Although fitness is broad, we'll consider it a niche, and it is trending on TikTok. Share your tips on getting toned arms and sculpting a six-pack, or share your extreme sports passion with people, and you'll soon be amassing a loyal audience.

How to choose your niche:

- **Identify your skills and passions**

"I'm not good at anything. How do I choose a niche?" That is a common question, especially for young people who aspire to be influencers while still in school. It's easy for an existing brand or social media influencer to join TikTok and immediately identify their target audience. They need to look at their existing customer and follower database. But how do you approach this if you're starting and need to hone your hard skills? By creating where you are.

Where you are is the perfect place to begin. Start by identifying all the things you've been interested in since childhood. What do you enjoy doing most? What makes you skip lunch and forget to pee because of how engrossed you are in the activity?

Identifying everything you currently do just because you enjoy it and building an audience around it increases your odds of success. You're likely to keep creating content consistently, even without an audience.

Which comes first - the chicken or the egg?

On TikTok, the answer is that content comes first. If the chicken represents your audience metaphorically, and the egg represents the revenue, you need to produce a ton of content before any of that. There will be crickets; hardly anyone will see that content, but you must create it. Ultimately, that's the only way to attract the chicken and the egg. And since you already know that it has to be an ongoing effort of good quality content that your potential followers will find appealing, you need to go with something that you enjoy so you can have the enthusiasm and commitment that will produce excellent material.

Make a list of everything you feel passionate about or everything you wish to learn. There are skills you'd like to develop.

David is an excellent example of this. He hated school. Graduating from high school and getting into college was a burden, and the only reason he did it was that he didn't want to disappoint his single, hard-working mom, who had to take up two jobs to put him through school. When we started his TikTok account, he needed help to pick a niche. He had never excelled at anything before. To his mind, building an audience around a skill felt impossible. But David remembered that he enjoyed building his toy cars as a young boy from scrap metal. Throughout middle and high school, he spent his free time playing with magnets, making toy car models from recycled materials, and taking pictures of nature.

So, he first started posting content of what he was creating behind the scenes. He also took a free photography class and started documenting that journey on Instagram and TikTok. After a few months, he focused more on his toy cars from recycled materials for TikTok and his amateur photography tips on Instagram because his audience on TikTok seemed more responsive when he put out simple DIY videos of his toy cars.

It's only been a year since he started his daily posting, and his site has grown to 970,000 followers. David learned it's about something other than being an expert or having top skills. It's about finding and sharing something you enjoy doing with the world.

- **Begin by experimenting**

I always tell newbies that the best way to find a niche is to embark on a scientific experiment. Evaluate your passions, strengths, and what your audience will love to watch. A handful of these different categories should be the main themes for your content. Monitor the category with the most interactions as your TikTok account gains traction.

- **Narrow down based on audience feedback**

Once your account has grown and you have a decent-sized audience, consider narrowing it down to a specific category. Since your initial experiment started by going for themes that you naturally like, switching down to a single piece should be pretty easy at this point because you'll be working with content that you enjoy creating and your audience loves to watch. That is the ultimate sweet spot of picking a good niche.

Susan is a 14-year-old girl who cracked TikTok and landed influencer status almost accidentally. Or was it? Susan had a private account on TikTok for a year or so, just like all her school friends. When the lockdown hit, she created a public account, which she now uses to share sewing videos and tutorials under the nom de plume Fashionflip.

Within six months, the account had 127 videos, which attracted 37,500 followers and over 730,000 likes. Her fan base is between 7 years and nine years old. Before setting up the public account, Susan wasn't an avid sewer. She only acquired a sewing machine to help pass the time during the long pandemic, where she had to isolate herself from her friends. Her nanny taught her the logistical basics, like threading and running her machine. Adding her creativity and insights gained from watching YouTube videos, Susan was able to produce adorable stuff, which her audience loved. She said she just experimented and kept learning and iterating along the way. Her audience appears to be novice sewers who prefer Susan's more straightforward repurposing videos over complex multi-part sewing tutorials. Many of her followers started sewing after watching her videos, and they frequently tag Susan in their products, which Susan says is such a treat.

This is the power of TikTok. Users usually flock to the app and browse the "For You" page, which feeds them content similar to videos they've watched in the past. Because TikTok's algorithm focuses more on interest than anything else to determine what a user will see, sticking to a particular niche is crucial to one's success. Susan was smart enough to figure this out for herself. As a consumer, she would often watch videos from specific hashtags. Using the app first as a consumer, she identified that creators who use well-chosen tags in their videos tend to accrue more views, likes, and followers. That's precisely what she did when she launched her public account months ago. Susan shares that she will never post a sewing video on one day and a dance video on the next. That would confuse her audience and dilute their adoration of her account. "I make particular videos so that people who want to see them will find them. That's how you get followers."

Susan is spot on. So, while it may seem to be a chance or an accident that she's already an influencer, her simple strategy makes us aware of the critical ingredient you need before moving forward.

Is Having a Pro Account Necessary?

You know what TikTok is and the immense opportunities it can offer you and your brand, but have you heard of TikTok Pro? A TikTok pro account is an extension of the basic TikTok account. It's more of an analytical tool where you can better understand what your followers are looking for, what they are most interested in, and so on. If you're using TikTok for fun, then it's not necessary. But this tool will benefit you if you want to build a brand, influence, and monetize your efforts. The TikTok Pro will help you track down the number of views weekly and monthly so you can understand your best-performing content and traffic source in detail. This is a free feature, so if you already have an account, here's what to do.

Launch your TikTok application.

Select the "privacy and settings" tab on your profile page.

Tap on "Manage my account" > select "Switch to Pro Account" and follow the onscreen instructions.

Once you make the switch, you'll see a new "Analytics" button in the options. That's where you can analyze how to attract and retain audience attention and engagement.

Side note: If you currently have a private account, making this switch will make your account public. So, you may want to create a separate public account like Susan and use a pseudo name just like she does to get a pro account.

Creating Your First TikTok

Before publishing your first TikTok, you need to set up an account. Let's get that done first by setting up your TikTok account. You can skip over to the next part if you already have an account.

Download the app on your smartphone if you still need to, sign up with Facebook, Gmail, or Twitter, or create a new username and password. By default, TikTok assigns all users a unique username of random letters, so let's change that. Remember the handle name you were to think about? Here is where it comes into play. Set your new handle, and let's start exploring the app.

Once you're logged in, you'll be taken to the homepage. That is where you edit your profile with the information we created earlier and your profile pic. To edit, tap "Me" in the bottom right corner > "Edit Profile." Now, you can change your TikTok picture profile. This can be a static image or a video. Regarding a picture profile, the best practice is to use something that aligns with your handle name, the bio, and what your brand represents. The next thing to do is copy-paste the bio one-liner you came up with and the links you'd like to include on the account profile. You can also add your Instagram and YouTube accounts if you want. Once you're happy with the account setup, you can create your first TikTok. Let's go.

Filming your TikTok

Step one. Tap the + button icon at the bottom of the screen. As soon as it opens, it will be in selfie mode.

Step two. Choose video length and template. Under the record button, you have the options of 60s or 15s, depending on how long you want the content to be. The templates give you TikTok's premade video templates if you don't want to start from scratch. For those who will have the option to go live once they meet the criteria, this is also where the button will enable you to start a live broadcast.

Step three. Next to the record button, the "Effects" icon lets you access TikTok's built-in video effects. Tapping that will open up a long line of AR filters and other unique products that can augment your face or your surroundings. Please don't feel pressured to use any video effects, but I will tell you that these can make your video fun and appealing to a new audience. Let people see that fun side of your personality. Specific effects are usually trending on TikTok. I recommend spending some time daily on your "For You" page to see which ones look best. You can add an effect before or after you've filmed your video, but there are a few that you can only get before shooting. Play around with this to familiarize yourself.

Step four. TikTok is famous for its music library. Sound matters a lot on this app. Every trending or viral content has a great sound, so you need time to figure out your sounds. To do this, tap the "Sounds" icon to browse categories like trending top 40 and viral sounds.

Pro tip:

Instead of wasting time figuring out what sound to use, go to your For You page, find the sound you like, and tap "Add to Favorites" to save for later or "Use this Sound" immediately.

Step five. Film or upload your video

Now it's time to hit record or upload a previously recorded video. Make sure the content delivers value and that you're happy with it. Then, it's time to decide how you'll edit. Some content creators will use the features provided by TikTok, while others will use external editing tools. For in-app videos, there are several features to play with. All components are located on the right hand of the screen. Flip the camera to either be in a selfie or subject mode, change the speed of your video, film in slow motion or speed it up from 0.3x to 3x, turn on the "Beauty" filter to smoothen out skin and give a nice glow, select the timer option to turn on an auto-record countdown so you can film hands-free and on and on. There's quite a bit to play with here. Once you've chosen the desired settings, you can hit record.

If you'd like different scenes in each video or wish to record in sections, hold the record button for each segment, let go, and press again for your next shot.

For pre-recorded content, upload content by tapping the "Upload" button in the bottom right. You can repurpose specific content from your device, adjust your clips' length, or select multiple videos.

Kick-Off Your Content!

Before making your video live to the audience, you'll want to edit light and consider a few best practices. When you finish recording or uploading your segments, hit the checkmarks to switch to TikTok's video editor. That's where you can add text, adjust video clips, record voiceovers, and more. Some best practices here include:

- **Adding text**

Adding some text to your video provides additional context to your viewer. Tap the "Text" button on the bottom of the screen, where you can choose from various font colors and styles. You can also set text duration and use the sliding scale to decide when you want the text to appear or disappear on your video.

- **Record voiceover**

You can custom voice over your video by tapping the record button to record audio for your video. These are great if you're shooting a tutorial or educational content. Uncheck "Keep original sound" if you'd like the voiceover to be the only audio on your TikTok video.

- **Edit video clips and volume**

You can apply unique voice filters to your audio, for example, electronic or shake. You can also adjust the volume of your added and original sound by tapping the Volume button. This could be helpful if you needed to fix some parts of your audio.

- **Add sounds, stickers, effects, and filters**

Like on Instagram, you can add any filters, stickers, GIFs, and effects you like. It's your chance to share more of your brand personality. If you still need to add sounds, now is the time to pick a tune that will boost your video content. Once you're happy, click Next.

It's time to kick off your first TikTok video. Tap "Next" in the bottom right corner, and you'll be redirected to the final page, where you can add a caption, hashtags, and even tag others. Take advantage of this part because your marketing strategy depends on writing great captions and using the right hashtags.

The captions:

You can write up to 150 characters on TikTok, including any hashtags you want to add. Your captions should be compelling, short, and complimentary to your video. You can also include some key phrases or keywords that tell TikTok exactly whom to put your video in front of.

The hashtags:

We will talk more about hashtags in this book, but for now, I want you to realize that picking specific hashtags your ideal audience is searching for is the right approach. The more niched down, the more accessible people can discover your content. Make sure they relate to the content in the video.

The cover photo:

This is one of the last things you'll want to choose, but make sure it's done intentionally. The cover photo appears on your TikTok profile, so selecting something eye-catching is essential. You can add text to encourage your audience to click on the video.

Chapter 5

Getting More Views

On any social media platform, getting views on your content is significant. It shows social proof that you are someone of value and your brand has been accepted in that particular community. So, it should come as no surprise that TikTok and Twitch require some clever thinking for you to gather as many views on your videos as possible. If you've pushed out some content and are wondering how to increase video views, this chapter is for you.

Keep Your Friends Close

Once you start posting content, engaging in the community is the most important thing you can do. Posting a video is only half the job. The other is getting proactive and connecting with people in TikTok and other social media platforms where you have an existing audience. If you have zero followers online, focus on interacting with other accounts, creating great content, and leveraging your phone book and offline social circles. That includes friends, family, old schoolmates, and anyone you regularly connect with.

The more invested you can be in engaging your followers, the easier it will be to retain their attention and attract new people. Accounts where no one responds to comments struggle to have high engagement because other users see it as a sign that the owner doesn't care. The bottom line is that when it comes to audience engagement, people need to know you genuinely care about connecting with them and not just promoting your brand.

Here are a few tips on how to boost TikTok views:

#1: Find other brands to comment on and engage with.

This should be part of your daily routine if you're starting. The more you engage with existing users and their brands, the more known you become. Open up a Google sheet and research to find the top ten accounts that align with your brand and have a healthy audience engagement. Remember to choose a brand with a similar audience to the one you want to serve. Then, be generous with your time and insights. Comment on their content where relevant, ask questions, interact, and offer your ideas to other users to build more engagement for that account. As you do this in a non-promotional way, people will notice you and might be inclined to check out who you are.

#2: Use proper tags

When used correctly, hashtags can give incredible results for your TikTok viewership. You need to add a handful of relevant hashtags that tell more about your video genre. To do this, use the symbol "#" followed by a phrase or keyword related to the video. Whenever users search for or come across that keyword, they will be directed to your video content, thus increasing your video's visibility and views.

#3: Collaborate with friends

Getting existing influencers to collaborate with you will be challenging if you're starting. That will come with time and reputation. But you can always form collaborations with your friends. Even if both of you have small followings, you're still doubling your viewer list by creating content and posting it to each of your accounts. However, ensure your content is well thought out and beneficial for both audiences. Try to make it as interactive and exciting as possible.

#4: Post multiple times a day

Unlike most other social media platforms where posting more than once becomes spammy, these platforms promote you more when you actively post. Users on TikTok are accustomed to seeing lots of action from their content creators. By consistently posting at least twice a day, people will feel connected with your brand, leading to more engagement and viewing of your content. It shows you're serious about your work on the platform and sets you on the path of becoming a TikTok influencer.

#5: Create original and high-value videos.

This cannot be emphasized strongly enough. You need great content. It must be high quality and purposeful; otherwise, you'll drown in the ocean of TikTok videos. Instead of copy-pasting, stealing, or even mimicking other people, make authentic videos that mean something to you. That way, users can sense you have much more to offer when they come across it. That's how they'll keep coming back for more.

#6: Ask questions or make a quiz video

Creating interactive content is another way to get more views for your video. Most of the content on TikTok is passive, whereby the audience watches and gets entertained. You could spin your content differently by regularly creating quiz videos, polls, and even posing questions and inviting them to share their answers by commenting or shooting their video. It's an excellent way for users to voice their opinions and for you to land more views and followers. Just make sure the questions are relevant to your brand and the interests of your ideal audience.

Pro tip: Ask open-ended questions so that people feel engaged and loved. You can also ask questions about their interests or what they want to learn. That might also help you create better content in the future.

#7: Create challenges and participate as well.

People love participating in TikTok challenges. You can increase your videos' views by creating your challenge or participating in those already initiated by others. It helps launch you as an active member of the community and a creator in your own right.

Keep Your Enemies Even Closer

To complement audience engagement and your commitment to connect and build a connection with new and potential followers, we also need to discuss strategic ways to measure what's working so you save time on things that don't. That's where benchmarking comes in. Benchmarking is a tool that can be used to measure your performance. It's a tool you can use to figure out what's working, what you need to do more, and what you must stop doing. This process involves establishing best practices, evaluating your position within your niche and on the TikTok platform, and creating a strategy to ensure you stand out. So, that means you will need to dig into what your competitors are doing to ensure you're doing it even better. This should be distinct from competitor research.

While competitive analysis is excellent and mainly attempts to mirror what others are doing, it is, for the most part, a quick-fix attempt that some might even consider spying. However, benchmarking is continuous and essential if you want to maintain a competitive edge amongst your peers. It's about focusing on the audience you're serving and figuring out what they love best and what they need, not just copy-pasting everything your competitor does.

For example, suppose you realize your competitor is fast at creating videos and usually focuses on producing trending content to leverage that hashtag. Still, they also have evergreen content that does reasonably well. In that case, you don't just want to start copying their trending videos approach. Instead, you will dig deeper and observe the content that gets the most engagement and what the audience seems to enjoy more.

The trendy videos may get more views because of the hashtag, but you might realize that there are more comments with evergreen content. In that case, it would make more sense to invest time in creating high-value, evergreen content similar to the top performers because the audience clearly shows they want more of that stuff.

For you to set the right benchmarks, especially if you are new to social media, here are a few things you need to do:

- Create a process for yourself if you still need to create one. This will help you recognize gaps as you build your audience and post content.

- Develop a way to plan, monitor, and measure your content so that, down the line, you will have something to reference as you establish your new benchmarks.

- Write down benchmarking objectives and scope.

- Decide on the primary metrics you're going to monitor. What will you measure? How will you know you're growing? What does success look like for you?

- Identify research sources and initiate data gathering so you can have a different reference point that will enable you to spot the gaps in your growth.

If you're wondering how to find data that you can use for your process, don't worry; here's a benchmark report by Conviva that shares helpful insights on how top brands are utilizing the platform and what those efforts reap: (https://www.conviva.com/research/conviva-TikTok-guide/) The information is over thirty pages long. It delves deep into sports, television, and other big brands, but here's an overview that might inspire you.

#1: The top 20 sports media accounts average 1.6 million followers. They also average 61,231,565 likes. Each of these accounts has posted an average of 535 videos on TikTok, with an average of 109,162 likes per video.

#2: The top 20 television accounts average 1.5 million followers. They average 17,714 likes on average and have posted 222 videos on average as well. Their average likes per video are 135,610.

#3: The top 20 pro sports leagues account for an average of 1.2 million followers. They average 20,300,886 likes in total. These accounts have posted an average of 629 videos and 70,421 likes per video.

#4: The top 20 news and media accounts average 750,000 followers. They average 754 followers with a total of 12,301,922 likes on average. Each of these accounts has posted an average of 248 videos, with 49,181 likes per video.

Understanding what best practices are and how top brands are performing can help guide you on the kind of benchmarking objectives to have. If you're going after a smaller niche, get the top ten performers on TikTok and find the average total likes, the average number of videos, and the average number of likes for each video. That should get you started on the right path.

Trends on TikTok matter

Unlike any other social media, trends are a big deal. Both individuals and company brands should pay attention and participate whenever possible. It's an excellent opportunity to seamlessly end up on someone's feed, build that initial connection, and make your presence known without being too pushy. When you follow the latest trend on TikTok, it expands your brand's reach. Why? Because TikTok's algorithm gives preferences to trending videos. Besides, users enjoy exploring various interpretations of an ongoing trend. They'll often binge-watch video after video of new accounts and people they've never heard of just because they care about that particular trend. That can quickly lead to the discovery of your brand and new followers.

If you're not a fan of the term "trend," think of it as getting into the ongoing conversation. By participating, you tap into the algorithm. It gives you that credibility within the community that you are "one of them," and your account is relevant. In marketing speak, a top-of-funnel awareness is critical to growing a brand that ultimately drives revenue. While it's challenging to go sales through trends, it's much easier to drive awareness engagement and be crowned "the cool brand" when you ride trends on TikTok.

The most recommended trends on TikTok:

- Dances
- Sounds

- TikTok challenges
- Songs

TikTok Challenges

TikTok challenges can be organic or paid. They usually combine three elements: Text, sound, and movement (usually a choreographed dance). Anyone can start a TikTok challenge, but the most successful ones are often from individuals with many followers, influencers, or brands investing in TikTok advertising.

The key to an excellent TikTok challenge is the sound. There are many cool sounds on the platform, but you can also create and upload your own sound or find ones uploaded by influencers and other TikTokers. Most of the sounds on TikTok are pulled from movies, viral YouTube videos, and music, including chart-topping hits and indie songwriters.

Innovative businesses and aspiring influencers usually find prevalent existing TikTok challenges to jump into so they can ride that wave and gain new followers and potential customers. All they need to do is create a high-quality video based on a trending challenge.

Remember to think outside the box and get creative with your concept if you choose to do this. It needs to be entertaining to grab the audience's attention. If participating in an organic TikTok challenge, use the same audio clip as other challenge videos.

How to identify what's in and what's out:

#1: Spend time daily on the app

You need to be using the app to figure out the best trends. That first-hand experience is priceless and will enable you to participate in authentic things for your brand. Scroll through your feed, explore the For You page, and pay attention to everything you see and hear.

#2: Investigate causes or topics you like

Are you into sustainability or recycling? Then, do a quick search to see if there's a demand for that topic and whether something is trending that you could join. You should also check social and cultural events to see what's what. For example, there was a lot of content related to Black Lives Matter and the COVID-19 pandemic. Countless TikTok trends emerged from these social issues. If they resonate with your brand and you have something to share, that's your cue.

#3: Research the music

By this, I mean finding music playing a lot on the platform. The For You page is the best to help you identify which music is trending. If you hear the same song repeatedly, that's a signal you should pay attention to. See if you can create your interpretation or remix of the music or integrate it into your content. As long as it aligns, go ahead and do it.

#4: Explore someone else's TikTok

Since we know how specialized TikTok is, your For You page might become limiting because you will only see trends based on prior behavior. Get a friend's phone or a family member to share their For You page. You might be shocked to discover trends you'd never encountered.

Nothing Beats Consistency

Many content creators ask, "How often should I post to become successful on TikTok?" The answer is simple: Create high-quality content as often as you can. If you can only make one great content daily, then post one epic content daily. I recommend posting between 1 - 3 times daily if you can create more.

Here's the big secret, though. It would be best to be consistent with your content creation and posting. Sporadic, unpredictable posting will work against your efforts to become an influencer. People need to get accustomed to seeing new stuff from you daily or multiple times a day. This may sound too much, but you must realize that many of TikTok's millions of active monthly users also create content. That means you compete daily with users just as hungry for success as you are.

By picking a posting frequency and committing to it, you give your audience something consistent to look forward to. Think about your preference. Do you prefer following accounts that regularly publish fresh content? Have you ever followed someone you liked on social media who suddenly disappeared and stopped posting? If you're like me, that doesn't feel very pleasant, and it alters the authority you once gave that person. That's why you should be consistently posting on TikTok so that as new followers come, they get a daily reminder that you're a worthwhile and authoritative content creator. It keeps you top of mind with your already existing follower base.

When should you post?

It would be best if you experimented with this to identify what your niche audience prefers, but based on benchmarks and market surveys, we can assume the best times to start testing are Tuesdays at 9 a.m., Thursdays at noon, and Fridays at 5 a.m. If you're posting on Saturdays, consider doing it at 11 a.m., 7 p.m., or 8 p.m. On Sundays, the best times to post are 7 a.m. or 8 a.m. and 4 p.m.

Video content is interesting.

You need to earn that attention to stand out from the crowd and amass a large, engaged following. Your content will determine how people perceive you and how quickly you can rise to influencer status. Please do me a favor, head to your TikTok account right now, and search for Zach King, Will Smith, The Rock, or Gary Vee. Notice how different all these accounts are. But the one thing they all have in common is that they produce high-quality content rich with substance that their audiences find extremely interesting. These guys have teams helping them and enough of a marketing budget to go high-end with their production. But you can still create something your audience finds equally attractive.

First, you must decide that your account will not have useless posts. Never post something for the sake of maintaining consistency. Once you've committed, it's time to get serious about creating your content strategy so you always have ideas. For your audience to see your account as enjoyable, you must make fun, easy-to-interact videos tailored to your niche. In other words, only worry about being perfect if you are a professional magician launching your career. Don't worry about complex concepts. Instead, learn from many of these successful social influencers and the stories I already shared of regular individuals who passionately share their journey as they know and do silly, simple, fun activities.

Let's revisit one of the most successful TikTok challenges - Chipotle's #GuacDance Challenge. This brand did exceptionally well on a platform like TikTok, where hashtags and challenges dominate, and set new records with a simple campaign. The dance challenge involved the Guacamole Song from children's entertainer Dr. Jean. All people had to do was share a dance inspired by their favorite Avocado topping! How simple is that? And yet, it worked. Over 250,000 submissions!

The less severe you are on TikTok, the better. People want to see your personality and "humanness" rather than your status or pro skills. That's one of the things that makes this platform unique. Instead of trying to be perfect, think about your audience and what interests them, then align it with your brand values.

Some of the ways you can create exciting content:

- **Create content for your audience**

It doesn't matter how much you love a particular topic. If no one else is interested, you won't go very far because the marketplace will reject you. To increase the chances of showing up on the For You page and to continue attracting new followers, think about your audience. What would your ideal follower like to see and share with his friends? Once you have some followers, regularly create polls to help you learn what they are interested in watching.

- **Trigger emotions**

Social media is all about getting emotional and personal. When you can spark strong emotional reactions from your users, your content will likely perform better. Many studies show that emotions like happiness, sorrow, anger, and gratitude can engage people and make them share digital content. But use this technique wisely and ensure it aligns with your brand values.

- **Add a little humor**

Bring that to your content if you like being funny or enjoy adding humor to your life. Your brand is serious, but your content on TikTok doesn't have to be. Funny videos grab users' attention and promise you a fair portion of shares, so if this is your strength, lean into it some more.

Chapter 6

The Blue Check Mark

The coveted blue checkmark. Ah, searching for this symbol of social stardom and influence is glorious. It is an excellent boost for your brand and makes you appear more legit and authentic. But do you understand the psychology behind it? Sure, there's the fact that having a blue checkmark helps protect you from impersonators and people stealing your precious work. Besides, because of perceived value, everyone (who isn't a movie star, celebrity, pro athlete, or big brand) wants it. With this blue badge, people immediately assume you're some VIP, and everyone likes to hang around essential people. Psychologically, people are more inclined to follow you after watching one video if they see that checkmark.

How does one acquire such a holy symbol on TikTok, and why do they have it anyway?

Verified: What is it For?

According to TikTok, the account verification symbol is there for a simple purpose - they want to help users stay informed about who they are following, especially regarding celebrities, professional sports teams, artists, and official brand pages. They want people to know whether the account is real rather than fake or fan. The verification badge helps to confirm that an account belongs to the user it represents. Creating clarity within TikTok's community is essential to build trust among high-profile accounts and their followers. If you think about it, with the blue badge, it would be easier to tell whether the account you're following was JLo's fan club, an obsessed girl pretending to be JLo, or the honest Jenny from the block. You can usually spot it next to a TikTok's user account name in search and on the profile as the coveted blue checkmark.

How are badges given?

Several factors go into getting that blue checkmark. Before we talk about the best way to get one, let's talk about the scams and tactics you should avoid:

Scam #1: Do not buy a verification badge.

This is one of the worst ways to get this blue checkmark. Not only is it illegal to buy it, but most of the options are also shady and not guaranteed to work. You might spend your money (some people charge up to $10,000) and still need to get the badge.

Scam #2: Do not buy followers expecting to get verified

A large following doesn't automatically qualify you for a badge, especially when those followers are fake. You may have noticed that some accounts get verified despite having small followings or celebrity status. We'll talk about why that happens shortly, but the main point here is you cannot get away with fake followers on TikTok because the platform considers a lot more than just the number of followers you have.

The main factors that TikTok considers are whether the account is unique, active, notable, and, of course, that it adheres to their community guidelines and terms of service (make sure to read those when you join the platform). That being said, you may have spotted some verified accounts even though celebrities don't own them. Often, these are accounts belonging to individuals who migrated from musical.ly. If the person had a "crown" during their time as muscial.ly users, they would likely be rewarded with that blue checkmark now that they switched to TikTok. The platform also tends to give the blue badge to accounts likely to be copied to protect the account owners and their content.

TikTok wants to emphasize that having a badge isn't a form of endorsement. Although they only give checkmarks to public figures, big brands, celebrities, and publishers, there are certain things you can do to increase the likelihood of getting verified as the real deal. By the end of this chapter, you'll learn the six steps you can take starting today.

The 3 Main Benefits of Getting Verified

Why would you want to make the needed effort to get verified?

#1: It will increase your content exposure and video views

When people come across your account on the search and spot that blue tick, they are likelier to watch your content and even click on your account to learn more about you. It comes back to that paradigm of "celebrity status" and being the chosen one by TikTok. That symbol naturally causes people to assume you're worth watching. That increases your video views as more and more people share your content. Add to that that verified accounts have a priority of 1, whereas regular accounts have a priority of 0, and it's easy to see why your videos will show up more on feeds and the For You page.

#2: Generating a more significant following

The blue checkmark will generate interest from the general public with the probability of increasing followers. Why? Because that blue badge is a symbol of trustworthiness and celebrity status. It shows people that TikTok vetted you and approved you and the content you produce. This suggests to potential followers that they can expect high-quality content that is spam-free. The other aspect is that it increases your perceived value and importance. In other words, people assume you must be a "big deal" because you have that badge. Users are likelier to think you are worth following if you need to be more worthy to be verified.

#3: More visibility when it comes to searches.

If your username is typical, searching for you will be hard because many users may already have variations. But if you have the blue checkmark, you always appear at the top of the search result because you hold priority 1. As a result, you become easy to find whenever people search for your account. And sometimes, people will discover your budget as they search for someone with a similar handle just because your account ranks higher in the TikTok search.

Ultimately, growing this way will open up new monetization opportunities, as big brands might favor working with you instead of your competition. Getting that "Popular creator badge" or the "verified account" badge isn't easy as a content creator. Still, it will be worthwhile, especially if you plan on making money through this platform. Livestreaming is one of the ways your followers and growing fans can start supporting you with "gifts" and stickers. Establishing your affiliate marketing income stream is easy if you follow that monetization path. The more people perceive you as an authority, the easier it becomes to leverage that influence and monetize it.

6 Steps To Get That Check

#1: Create a good content strategy

Refrain from relying on moments of insight where great content ideas come to you. Although that's great when you get inspired to create something, you should always have a solid content plan running in the background to ensure abundant content from the moment you publish the first video. A great content strategy comes from understanding your niche, your audience's wants, the best trends to jump into, and identifying themes that help establish your brand credibility. Search for top-performing hashtags in your niche, join relevant challenges, and create content. Also, check out my list of best-performing video content for video ideas to help you get started.

#2: Be consistent with your posting

Consistency is the one thing that will demonstrate to your audience and the TikTok platform that you are noteworthy. Once you have a content strategy, producing and publishing content daily will be manageable, primarily if you use tools and software to stay organized. If you commit to publishing a TikTok daily, do it without fail. Stick to a schedule that works with your lifestyle. Ideally, you want to do it multiple times daily (shoot for three videos), but don't create meaningless content. To rise to the influencer level, you need each video to be valuable for your audience. As people get used to expecting your videos multiple times a day, they'll interact more with your account and increase your watch time, which is crucial for growth.

#3: Engage with other users

Equally as important as posting is actively engaging on the platform with other users and content creators. You do this by liking other people's content, leaving thoughtful comments, sharing their work, giving shout-outs, and tagging the people you talk about in your videos.

On your account, you need to make sure to respond to every comment. Make people feel valued and appreciated. You could also come up with challenges for your followers or invite them to do duets with you so you can interact more. This personal and high-level engagement will dramatically increase your account's engagement rate, and TikTok guys will take notice.

#4: Demonstrate consistent and steady growth

Suppose you want to increase your chances of receiving the blue checkmark. In that case, you need to make a lot of effort toward growing the number of people who follow you daily and the amount of time users spend on your videos. An excellent daily aim as a beginner should be around 500 new followers daily. That will get you on the right track to influencer states and the verification badge. Eventually, you can double that. The more people follow you and watch your videos, the more your channel will grow. If you start having views of close to a million per month in a few months, TikTok will notice you. It also increases the chances of going viral with some of your content. Viral content is the main bloodline of TikTok. It demonstrates that you can create videos that will go a long way in entertaining and holding other users' attention on the platform. That's ultimately what TikTok is after - to captivate and delight their users.

#5: Get media and PR coverage.

Consider creating some PR for yourself because I noticed that it's easier for your account to be verified if you're being featured in other well-known magazines, television, radio, etc. If you are on Forbes, CNBC, local TV, etc., it shows TikTok that you're a person of influence. That also gives them a reason to elevate your position on their platform. Please also consider participating in public projects or events that can help you get noticed by the media.

#6: Collaborate with others.

Round up your friends or find TikTok creators in your neighborhood and collaborate on some dances or challenges. Viewers love this type of content, especially if you find the right group and create something entertaining. It also increases your chances of going viral as your content gets more exposure.

Bonus Tip: You should also consider getting verified on other social media accounts. Whether it's Facebook, Instagram, or any other platform, being confirmed there seems to help you get verified on TikTok. Make sure these accounts are connected to your TikTok account.

There is no straight path to getting verified, and we all have little; we need more control over how it happens. Even if you know someone who works for TikTok (like I happen to), they will tell you it's not as black and white as many of us would like.

Therefore, while it is a great goal, please don't get hung up on it. Your brand's growth and success aren't directly tied to having the blue tick. Even without the blue checkmark, you can still become a prevalent and well-respected presence on TikTok. So, focus on producing fantastic content, engaging with your audience, and letting the rest take its natural course.

Chapter 7

Monetizing Your Content

Suppose you're new to social media, online, and passive income opportunities. In that case, you may need clarification about how posting content on social media can equal bills paid at the end of the month. A few years ago, the only way to pay the bills was to get a regular nine-to-five job. Add a second shift or work two different positions if you want extra income. Thanks to social media and platforms like YouTube and Facebook, people have new ways of earning extra cash and making their dreams come true. And I mean regular people! If you're wondering how this is all possible and how you jump in, this is the chapter for you.

We will focus on TikTok's monetization opportunities, which you should know are different from other social media platforms like YouTube. To make it work for you, a strong strategy is essential. Part of establishing a solid plan is to realize that TikTok doesn't work like Instagram, YouTube, or any other platform for monetization. Things are still like the Wild Wild West on the TikTok platform, so you need to approach it with some creativity.

There's No Ad Revenue?

TikTok doesn't have a creator ad monetization. But don't let that throw you off. Most of the money on this platform is made through the fan support you get while growing the account. The more people love you, the easier it becomes to receive donations/gifts and even open up opportunities for influencer marketing, which we'll discuss shortly.

The platform needs to be built explicitly around monetization and providing income streams to creators. However, it's still very commercial-friendly, and it continues to evolve. New opportunities for generating income are popping up each day. Unlike YouTube, this platform doesn't offer monetization of their videos through placement ads, but you can still make lots of money on this thing.

Suppose you want to get paid on TikTok. In that case, you must diversify your monetization sources and get TikTok brand deals. We will review how to monetize your account once you have a decent-sized following. The more followers you have on TikTok, the easier it is to generate income actively and passively. That includes getting brand sponsorships, live streaming, referral or affiliate links, and more. Now, there's also the opportunity to be part of the Creator Fund.

What is the creator fund? According to TikTok, it is a fund that content creators who meet specific criteria can apply to be part of, where they can earn money simply for producing excellent content. There are currently $70 million in funds available to thousands of creators across the European launch markets, i.e., the United Kingdom, Germany, Italy, France, and Spain.

TikTok is still raising funds to open this opportunity to more European countries and reward content creators for their hard work and creativity. Of course, this is only open to a few content creators in a particular part of the world, so let's not focus too much on this as a means to earn money. Instead, let's discuss the real moneymakers.

Getting Sponsorship from Brands

Sponsorship is when a brand pays you to promote and generate awareness around their products and services. It's part of influencer marketing, which I discuss in one of my other books. However, TikTok has no standard price since the app is relatively young. The influencers and the brands can only accurately predict the performance of content and the results that it can yield.

Therefore, although one can earn lots of money from this, it is still up for experimentation. Each creator has their way of approaching sponsored content. Take Bernath as an example. He charges a base price with an additional "X" dollars per million views. For someone like him (lots of his videos go viral on TikTok, and he also has a large audience on Instagram), this price structure seems reasonable to brands. Another TikToker (Skylar) charges $25 per 25,000 followers, which works for him.

Can you make a lot of money through sponsored content?

Loren Gray earned $2.6 million within a year with just over 45 million followers. It's safe to say - you can make a ton of money on TikTok. It's possible, but not everyone will.

If you've got a big following on TikTok with a growth trend of viral videos, brands will be eager to sponsor you. But there are a couple of things you should do first. It would be best to stop focusing on getting brand deals and making money and instead concentrate on your fans. Understand the nature of the platform. People are there to connect genuinely. It's supposed to be a "real" social app. That's why there is less editing and filtering of videos. So, if you want brands to notice you, get more REAL. Be proactive with your followers, interact with them, and show them that you care. You can start thinking about brand deals once you grow in follower count (at least 10,000).

You must also create a press kit to offer brands when you start reaching out. Let them know about the growth of your channel, how content performs, the follower count and demographics, a list of other brands you've worked with, any case studies you might have, the specific services you offer, and a little more about yourself and why you want to work with the brand. Be creative with this press kit, and make sure it rocks!

One more tip I want to share when it comes to getting the attention of brands is to create organic (non-sponsored) content about the brands you love. Demonstrate that you have the influence and the ability to drive sales. Likes and shares are great, but if you want them to knock, show them you can deliver. That's rather hard to do on TikTok because it still needs to be easily mapped out, like on Instagram, so I suggest creating content to prove that you can do it. Once you create content, upload the videos with a linked ObsessedWith.it page where your fans can shop for everything you recommend. Then, call out your links and encourage subscribers to buy. That will earn you commissions, and you can then use the sales records as proof to entice brands to sponsor you.

Utilizing the Ad Commerce Tool

This new tool that TikTok introduced first to the U.S. will continue to roll out elsewhere, so if you're reading this and need help finding the option available where you live, be patient. It's coming. But what is this ad commerce tool? It's a self-service advertising tool where users can add affiliate links to help with promoted content. You can use this tool to gain commissions from sales generated through your videos. There's also the added feature of showcasing goods during a Livestream so your viewers can shop in-app.

Gifts are Great! Virtual Gifts are Best!

One of the easiest ways to start generating money is through TikTok gifts. There are several types of in-app currencies (known as gifts), and to get some, your audience must purchase TikTok coins. There are different bundle options. The bigger the bundle, the better the discount will be. I encourage you to buy some TikTok coins to experience what your viewers will go through when they want to send you a virtual gift. Once purchased, the currencies can be exchanged for unique virtual gifts (Panda, Italian hand, Love Band, Sun Cream, Rainbow Puke, Concert, I'm Very Rich, Drama Queen).

If your viewers enjoy your content, they can support you by sending gifts. During a live stream, everyone watching the video and the person who created it will be able to see the username of the one giving the blessing and the type of gift they gave to the creator.

Once you receive the gift on TikTok, it is converted into a diamond on your profile. Diamonds measure a content creator's praise and popularity and cannot be bought with money. Hint. You need to collect as many diamonds as possible.

How this ultimately turns into cash:

Diamonds turn into cash once you reach a certain threshold. The minimum withdrawal is $100, and the maximum weekly withdrawal is $1,000. Payment is usually via PayPal or one of their preferred verified payment services.

Sharing Referral Links

For most people, TikTok is just an app for kids. And that's true, but there's more to this story than meets the eye. Let's do a little marketing math here. Around 40% of the TikTok audience is between 16 and 24. The app has approximately 800 million monthly active users spread across 155 countries. And in the United States alone, there are an estimated 80 million monthly active users. That means you have a potential audience of about 300 million (give or take a couple of hundred thousand who might be younger than 16) that can buy something from you. That's where affiliate marketing comes in. It is a gold mine if you're a savvy affiliate marketer who can match the right product with your niche. For example, if you plan to sell home loans or B2B services, this differs from your platform. But TikTok users are abundant if you're into gadgets and gizmos or fashion and beauty.

This is the best and easiest way to generate passive and active income. Depending on the range of products you set up, you could be making anywhere from a few thousand a month to tens of thousands each month. Talk about financial freedom!

What is affiliate marketing? It's selling a product you don't own for a commission or referral fee. Think about it like this: You buy a product you love and realize they usually pay a referral fee for anyone who sends the company some business. You create content for your 100,000 followers, share your experience with the product, and then tell them to try it themselves. Through the unique link you share with them, many of them head over to the company's eCommerce store and purchase. As agreed, the company (which tracked your unique link to know how many sales came through you) sends you a sweet little check at the end of 30 days or so for $10,000 as a thank you for sending over 250 new buying customers for their $50 product.

How to make money through affiliate marketing:

The most important thing is to have a big enough audience for the niche products you want to sell. You can either use organic or paid advertising. You can use the second option if you have a big advertising budget. For most people reading this, organic reach is the way to go. Let's see how to make that work.

With organic traffic, as long as you're pushing out great content and growing your following, you will see people clicking on your links. That's why you need to set up the following referral links:

- Add an affiliate link of the desired URL to your profile information.
- Promote a coupon code or URL in your video that sends them to the page you want people to visit.
- Add an affiliate URL to your content description.
- Redirect that TikTok traffic to another social media profile, e.g., YouTube, where you can lead them to your affiliate site.

#1: Adding an affiliate URL on your profile:

Remember, this only works if you have a business or pro account. If you want multiple referral links set up, consider using Linktree.com. It's free and allows you to add as many links as you need.

Pro tip: Don't add direct affiliate links. Experience has taught me that blog posts or any other kind of valuable content performs better. So, ensure the affiliate links are contained within the content you offer in the front end.

#2: Use Coupons and Promo codes:

Many affiliated products have discounts and promo codes that you can easily leverage to get your followers to shop through you. Using the coupon can be as simple as mentioning it in the video content or the description.

#3: Add a URL to your description:

You must copy and paste the link into your video content description so that it might feel monotonous. Still, I've seen many big influencers doing it, so it makes sense to add it as well. At the very least, it increases the chances that someone will not miss getting the link to your affiliate site.

#4: Redirect people to your desired social media platform:

This is more complex, but it works, especially if you follow the other social media platforms well. Suppose you have more content on the products you want people to buy. In that case, sending people to that YouTube or Instagram channel makes sense so they can move closer to making that purchase as they learn to trust your credibility. Adding a social media account is pretty simple. Just tap on the "Me" icon at the bottom of the screen on the app, then tap "Edit Profile" and add whichever profile you want.

Section 3

Dominating On Twitch

CHAPTER 8

What's Up with Twitch?

Twitch is the leading live streaming platform, and its growing popularity is a testament that people love watching videos, especially live videos (which is Twitch's specialty). Think YouTube, but in this case, purely live videos. Most people, however, don't know about Twitch, and that's okay. This platform is dominated by gamers who host and share eSports events and challenges.

What Do I Do Here?

If you're wondering why you should consider this platform to build your influence, then realize there are 15 million active users and growing. That means you can create a healthy audience size and gain much power. Combine this influence with TikTok; you can have any income and lifestyle you desire. But as with all social media platforms, strategy matters.

Now, if you're reading this and thinking, "I am not a gamer, this can't be for me!" That wouldn't be the first time I hear that statement, and I'm here to confirm that you don't need to be into games and sports to thrive on this platform. You can find all kinds of videos on Twitch. Recently (especially since the pandemic), more categories have started growing in popularity, especially music, cooking, creative arts, lifestyle, make-up, and DIY content.

The origins of Twitch:

Twitch started as a spin-off of Justin TV in 2011, and as it grew in subscribers, Amazon decided to purchase it around 2014 for $340 million. The platform is designed to help content creators demonstrate their skills, connect with their audience in real time, build niche communities, and make money doing something they love. On the platform, creators are known as "Streamers," so you'll see me use that term often in this section. There are many ways to make money on Twitch, but before we get to that, let's cover the basics of how it works and why you should join today.

From Hobbies to Social Experience

Are you not a fan of MMO-style games or any gaming adventures, for that matter? No problem; there's plenty of room for you to explore, share, and grow a tightly-knit community around your hobbies, especially if you love music, talk shows, travel, arts, and food. Are you a musician or starting a local teen band? Twitch can be great for enabling you to share your passion with the world. It would be best to have a little creativity and consider what your fans would like to see. You could Livestream band rehearsals, practice sessions, behind-the-scenes work in the studio, jams, and improv sessions with other artists, or you could do some live Q&A. If you're a DJ, consider live streaming during your mix-and-scratch practice. Think along the same lines if you're passionate about cooking, art, doing make-up, and so on.

A good rule of thumb is to approach live streaming as something you would do anyway but with the added benefit of sharing it with your niche tribe. Of course, as you Livestream, you must engage and interact with the audience, but we'll cover that shortly.

But Why Twitch?

The biggest reason Twitch live streaming is so appealing (aside from the obvious monetary opportunities that come with it) is that it enables you to have an immediate brand-to-audience engagement. In most other platforms, you will create content, but there's no real-time engagement, so in many ways, you're working with a monologue instead of a dialogue. When it comes to live streaming, however, the conversation is immediate. With every live-streaming effort, you make people show up, and they interact with you and give you instant feedback. It makes you feel that you are doing all this work for "real people," which is easy to forget on other social media platforms. Live chatting, commenting, and feedback are reassuring and motivating for a new content creator.

You also get the freedom to reach and build a real-time connection with anyone anywhere. Your location doesn't matter at all. You could be broadcasting from your tiny bedroom of your small town that none of us ever heard of, and yet we would all come to know and love you and your content. All you need is internet access. You can also create as much content as you like. Demand is always there for more videos. In fact, in the United States alone, the number of digital video viewers is expected to top 232 million over the next few years. Half a billion people are already watching videos on Facebook daily, and according to networking giant Cisco, live video will account for 13% of all video traffic by 2121.

How Do Algorithms Work?

Twitch holds an ocean of "live" content, which by default makes it more chaotic and challenging to sort out since everything happens in real-time. Still, compared to YouTube and Facebook, the algorithm seems straightforward. It may be too simple. There have been many complaints from streamers who felt the platform favors larger channels, making it hard for smaller ones to grow in audience and revenue. But things have shifted a lot recently.

Previously, it was only listed as the highest to lowest number of views. Now they're a bit more sophisticated on the platform with the "recommended for you" feature helping users find the streamers who are currently living that are like the people the audience already follows and watches regularly. I suppose it makes sense to have a different algorithm because it focuses on "live" content. So, the best thing to do is to show viewers the best options they have as soon as they log in. Their main aim is to help viewers stumble upon the right channel and community at the right moment when the streaming is going on.

To do this, Twitch uses machine learning that lets the machine determine what viewers are interested in. The system is directed toward certain "features" of streams we mentioned earlier in the book (audience chat and engagement, etc.) and uses it to determine the content's importance. The more people chat in the channel, the more the algorithm will push more people interested in the same category to join in and catch the live stream. The AI often categorizes a channel either as "chatty" or "not chatty" and determines which viewer to recommend which channel as soon as the user logs in. It also considers time lapse. If the streamer has been on for a while and you log in, you're likely to be recommended someone who is just starting their streaming or one who is just a few minutes in. In other words, it tries to match the timing of the viewer and the streamer.

Viewers versus Followings versus Subscriptions: There's A Difference

A viewer is a person who watches your Livestream. This person can be a first-time visitor, a follower, or a subscriber. A follower consciously chooses to support your channel by following you. A purple icon with a heart is at the top of your track whenever you stream content. If a viewer finds you, watches for a little while, and decides they like your stuff, they can show their support by clicking on that heart, turning them into followers.

If they want to show your support and take things to the next level, the follower can become a subscriber. Subscription is a much higher form of approval because it involves financial investment. Subscriptions are one of the ways streamers make money on Twitch. When people subscribe to your channel, they agree to make a monthly payment on Twitch, of which you will get a cut. In turn, the subscriber would receive unique benefits unavailable to channel followers. Your subscribers will have various options to choose from. Tier 1 is $4.99/month, Tier 2 is $9.99/month, and Tier 3 is $24.99/month.

CHAPTER 9

Setting Up Your Studio

Before starting streaming on Twitch, building an audience, and generating income, you must set up your Twitch account and studio. Streaming is straightforward, but the initial setup requires effort and careful planning. If you haven't done so already, head over to Twitch's official website, click the purple "Sign Up" icon in the upper-right corner, enter your desired login credentials, and hit the button at the bottom. Once that's done, you can click your username in the top-right corner for access. Before producing content, I recommend reading the Twitch community guidelines to familiarize yourself with acceptable conduct.

Streaming on Twitch is possible on several devices, including PC, Mac, Tablet, Xbox One, and PS4, among others. Let's take a look at the most recommended ones.

Which Device Should You Focus On?

- **Streaming from a PlayStation 4**

PS4 is one of the simplest devices to use for a Livestream. You don't need any external or additional software; you could even use a PlayStation camera as the microphone and "face cam" for all your broadcasts. That simplifies the number of equipment needed to set up your studio. Here's what to do:

First, you need to play a game. Open the game you plan on streaming before changing any broadcast settings. Once you've launched the game, press the "Share" button next to the touchpad on your PS4 controller to open up your broadcast settings.

Next, you should change settings to your preference and then start streaming! Select "Broadcast gameplay," and you'll see an option to stream via three different streaming services. Select Twitch, and the service will provide you with a streaming key. Then, go to Twitch.Tv/activate and enter the key. Your PS4 should be ready to start streaming in a few minutes.

From the "Broadcast Gameplay" menu, you can change your stream's title, adjust the quality, and choose whether to use your camera and microphone.

Note: If you have a PlayStation Camera and want to use it, ensure it's plugged in and check to ensure it hasn't been automatically muted from the quick menu on your console. Otherwise, you won't be able to use it once you start streaming.

If you're satisfied with the settings, press "Start broadcasting" and share your passion with the world.

Setting Up Your Studio

- **Streaming from Xbox One.**

This option is as easy as PS4, but you must address more technical issues. For instance, if you want a "face cam," legacy Xbox One owners can use the Xbox Kinect. It would be best if you had the Kinect because it's the one that is compatible with Xbox One's Twitch app. Once you have it, pair it with a headset to record your voice because Kinect's microphone is unreliable. It often cuts out intermittently during streaming, so plugging a separate headset in usually solves this problem.

The first thing to do is launch your game. Like with PS4, you must load up a game before starting the stream. Install and open the Twitch app and sign in with your credentials. You'll then receive a unique stream key to gain access. Activate this key at Twitch. TV/activate on either your mobile device or computer. Twitch immediately detects the game when it starts the stream, making it more discoverable for potential audience members.

The next step is to edit your stream's title and quality level before you go live. You can also move your Kinect's camera display to one of the corners of the screen. Finally, click on "Start Broadcast" to commence streaming. You'll see a display count at the bottom of your screen showing the number of viewers watching the game.

- **Streaming from PC or Mac**

Streaming from Windows or Mac OS is trickier than the first two options because most systems need built-in gaming software. If you have the budget, consider getting subscription-based products like XSplit, which helps you control every broadcast aspect. For beginners, however, downloading Open Broadcast Software (OBS) is the best starting place. It's free software that works with both Windows and Mac OS.

Another option for beginners, if you want to avoid a hassle with the setup, is to use the Twitch Studio app, which is currently only available on Windows. Assuming you want to settle for OBS, here's what to do.

The first step is to download OBS.

First, click on your username in the main Twitch interface and hit the "Creator Dashboard" link. Locate the three bars in the top left border of the screen to reveal a drop-down menu with a list of other options you can choose from. Look for the "Streaming Tools" option. That will take you to a page with several download links to streaming applications like OBS. Find OBS in the list and click down, or head to their main website, where you can choose the version you need to download.

The second step is to set up your streaming. Click the "Output" tab after clicking "Settings" in OBS and ensure your video bitrate is set to about 2,500. That should allow you to stream content at 720p, but you can increase this number if you want to broadcast at a higher resolution. You should set the audio bitrate at 128. If you're running a Nvidia graphics card that's a few years old, you can use the built-in NVENC encoder. Otherwise, you'll want to stick with OBS's default software x264 encoder. Once you're happy with the settings, click "Apply" to confirm and save changes.

The next thing to do is to enter your stream key.

You must return to the creator dashboard, click "Preferences," then select the "Channel" option from the drop-down menu. That will take you to a page with your Primary Stream Key and other options. Find the stream key area and then press the copy button next to it. If the stream key gets shared somewhere else unintentionally, you can always reset it here. Paste that stream key into OBS by clicking "Settings" in the bottom right, then "Stream." Once done, click "Apply" to save changes.

Now it's time to set up your game and plug in your microphone. Take a look at the Audio Mixer area in OBS. It should already have at least the volume bar set up for your desktop. In OBS, locate the "Settings" button in the bottom-right area of the application. That will open up a window where you can navigate to the Audio tab. This is where you can add or remove audio devices as needed. Ensure the Desktop Audio is set to the correct piece of hardware, and then locate the Mic/Aux audio options. Once that's done, open the game you want to stream and look at the Sources menu towards the bottom of OBS. Find the + button at the bottom, which should reveal a list of items when clicked. The easiest way to capture gameplay is to use the "Display Capture" option. That allows you to capture an entire desktop screen. To avoid sharing too much of your screen, consider selecting the "Game Capture" option.

Finally, you are ready to stream your game. Hit the "Start Streaming" button on the main OBS screen, and you'll instantly begin broadcasting from your Twitch account. When done, click on Stop Streaming.

Completing Your PC (For Those Who Need It)

Now that you know how to set up your live streaming on Twitch, let's talk about the options available if you'd like to do it through a PC but still need to own a good one. You see, when it comes to PC, you will need to invest in a high-quality one if you want a truly immersive gaming experience. If your budget allows, you could always buy one, but here's an affordable alternative for those who can't afford to spend money on something expensive. Build your PC.

The amount of money you spend on the computer parts will vary depending on your purpose and budget. You must match a store-bought desktop or laptop's performance to spend as little money as possible. If your primary goal is to get a high-performing beast without breaking the bank, you'll need the best possible performance in all your PC components. In that case, you should expect to spend a little more money, but the result will be a powerful PC.

If you're hesitant because you worry it might be too hard, don't worry. I've got you covered. Let's run through the necessary equipment and how to build a great PC without breaking.

What you need to build a PC:

- **Motherboard**

It is the first component to think about. The motherboard dictates your PC's build (physical form factor and size) and determines what other pieces of hardware your computer will need. Your motherboard's choice establishes the power of the processor it can handle, the memory technology (DDR4, DDR3, DDR2, etc.), and the number of modules that can be installed. It also determines the storage form factor (2.5-inch, mSATA, or m.2) and storage interface (SATA or PCIe).

- **Central Processing Unit (CPU)**

The CPU is the engine of your computer. It sets the performance expectation for the entire build—memory and storage fuel the processor, which controls every data transaction within the PC. When determining which CPU to install, pay attention to the gigahertz (GHz). The higher the GHz, the faster your processor. However, more GHz also means the CPU will consume more energy, leading to higher system temperatures that require better airflow or heat dissipation within the computer, so that's something you must consider.

- **Memory (RAM)**

The third important aspect is choosing your RAM. Adding memory is the easiest and fastest way to amplify your computer's performance. It gives your system more space to store data that's being used temporarily. Almost all computer operations rely on memory, including having several tabs open while streaming your content, typing and composing an email, multitasking between applications, and even moving your mouse cursor. To say that you need to pick the right RAM is an understatement. The more things you're doing with your PC, the more memory you need. Even background processes like system updates can draw from your RAM. Consider these two things: compatibility and how much RAM your system can support before choosing the best RAM.

You want to make sure you've identified the kind of module your system uses by specifying the form factor (the physical form of the module - generally, desktops use UDIMMs, laptops use SODIMMs), then figure out the memory technology (DDR4, DDR3, DDR2, etc.) that your system supports. When figuring out how much RAM your system can handle, think about the kind of system you're building. If you buy 64GB of RAM and your computer can only take 16GB, you're wasting 48GB because regardless of how big the RAM is, your computer will only utilize it by its limit. So, in other words, know your limits before choosing the memory.

- **Storage**

Your files and data are saved long-term on your storage drive. This data is either on a hard disk drive (HDD) or a solid-state drive (SDD). Hard drives generally offer more storage space, but solid-state drives are essentially the in-thing because they are faster and more energy-efficient. SSDs are, on average, six times faster and ninety times more energy efficient. Why? Because hard drives use mechanical moving parts and spinning platters, whereas SSDs use NAND flash technology.

- **Case, Fans, and Power Supply**

The materials you choose to use here will depend on the kind of computer you're building. If you're creating a high-powered performance workhorse, you'll need a robust power supply to make it run efficiently. You'll also need optimal internal airflow and fans to expel hot air that could damage the system. Buy some Zip ties to help manage the cables inside your rig and consolidate the wires, as that will improve airflow.

Tips for building your PC:

The exact process of setting up your PC will vary depending on the Owner's Manual, so I recommend following the instructions diligently. The installation is simple, but there is the potential for errors. That's why you must stick to the detailed step-by-step instructions. I also encourage you to wear an electrostatic discharge (ESD) wrist strap to protect your system's components from the static electricity that's naturally present in your body. Alternatively, you can ground yourself frequently by touching an unpainted metal surface. It's also helpful to keep a compressed air can to remove dust or acceptable debris from the interface as you install the processor, memory, and SSD.

- **Tips for installing the memory.**

The most straightforward hardware to install is the RAM. Locate the memory slots on the motherboard and hold the memory modules on the side to avoid touching the chips and gold pins. Then, align the notches on the module with the ridge in the slot and firmly press the module until it clicks.

- **Tips for installing the HDD or SSD**

A hard drive is probably your best option if you're looking for lots of memory at a lower cost. The kind of SSD you purchase may require a specific installation procedure, so reread the instruction manual. Still, in almost all cases, it involves attaching the drive to the storage interface and fitting it into the drive bay.

If you followed the instructions for installation from your provider perfectly, your system should be ready to launch in no time. Hit the power button and make sure the monitor and keyboard are connected to the PC. You should see a screen appear where you can enter the system BIOS. If you have a disc or flash drive with an operating system (OS), put it into the appropriate drive, boot up, and you can install the OS. Congratulations, you are now the proud owner of your new PC! Let the gaming sessions begin!

What's Gonna Be the Setup on Console?

You must know some things if you'd like to stream gameplay from your console. First, some consoles like Nintendo Switch don't have native streaming apps like the earlier mentioned Xbox and PlayStation, so the only way to do a Livestream is to use a capture card.

A capture card is a physical device that links your console with your PC and a TV, allowing you to stream your game into software like OBS, XSplit, or Elgato Game Capture. The software then broadcasts or records your gameplay and audio to Twitch.

You can choose from many capture cards, but the Elgato recommended is the most HD60S. It's cheap and works wonderfully. The installation is also fast and self-explanatory. It's also worth noting that some games on PlayStation can be blocked from streaming and recording. Many companies like Atlas (Persona 5) and Bandai Namco (Dragonball series) have included in-game functions that stop their titles from being streamed after a specific time. Unfortunately, you won't know when that happens until after. Since you cannot turn off this feature, finding a more sustainable solution for your streaming is best, especially if you want to make this a full-time career.

If you'd like to use your computer set up to stream on Twitch, there are some recommendations to consider.

- Your CPU Intel Core should be at least i5-4670
- Your memory should be a minimum of 8GB DDR3 SDRAM
- Your operating system should be Windows 7 Home Premium or newer

By going for the setup of a capture card, keep in mind you will also require the additional investment of a PC. The Elgato costs more than $100 at retail, and depending on whether you buy or build your PC, you could spend several hundred dollars (if not a few thousand) to set up your streaming.

The 3 Essential Gears To Invest In

In a world of countless live streams, you want to set yourself apart on Twitch because of the content you produce and the look and feel of the content. That's why you need to invest in these three must-have pieces of equipment:

#1: Video Camera

Twitch audiences enjoy watching both the game in session and the streamer playing the game, so investing in a good-quality webcam is necessary. Whether you're celebrating a victory, engaging with viewers, or throwing a full-blown rage fit, your growing audience will keep coming back for more when they can see you in high quality without interfering with the view of the game. Hook up a camera, and you can pull its feed into your chosen software and overlay the game stream.

Consider getting a Logitech Streamcam (1080p, 60FPS). It has autofocus abilities and a multitude of settings to make your studio set up top-notch. You can use it in both landscape and portrait mode. Mount it on a tripod or top of your monitor, and you're ready. An alternative to using a webcam would be getting a DSLR (e.g., Elgato Cam) or any other digital camera you fancy.

#2: Audio

It would be best to have a high-quality microphone and pre-amp set up for your streaming. Any streamer worth their salt needs a great mic to talk and engage with their audience while working their gaming magic. Your chosen mic should block out surrounding noises and focus on your voice. If you're into Elgato's lineup of products already, consider getting the Elgato Wave:3. It has an internal pop filter and an intelligent clip guard technology designed to stop your audio peaking even if you get a bit shouty while capturing audio.

The highlights of this microphone come when you pop it on a boom arm and dive into the Elgato Wave Link Software. This free software has a microphone and lets you do clever things with your audio. For instance, you can add audio sources, including Spotify, game audio, Discord chat, and more. That means you can customize the listening experience and easily monitor what your audience will hear when you go live on Twitch. The best part is that it's compatible with Elgato's Stream Deck, making it easy to tweak, monitor, and control audio on the fly.

Alternatively, if your budget allows, consider going for Shure SM7B. This studio-quality microphone is renowned for its capture capabilities, rich sound, and capable background removal. Unlike other standard microphones, this one doesn't have a USB connection, so you'll need a pre-amp and something to power and control the microphone (GoXLR). The Shure SM7B microphone combined with a Go XLR pre-amp gives you all the power you need to sound like a professional and excellent on-the-fly controls for adjusting the game, voice chat, and music audio levels while you stream.

The best part is you can block out irritating background noises like the buzz of your PC's fan, air conditioner, etc. Of course, the kind of microphone you choose should be based on your budget and the equipment you're using. Make sure you purchase something compatible with your devices.

#3: Deck Switcher

Although this is an additional cost to your investment budget, getting a deck switcher will help simplify your life as you stream content, and if you get the right one, it will help you add more flair to the gaming experience. A deck switcher is a control button switch that enables you to move seamlessly from one deck to another. The one that comes most recommended is the Elgato Stream Deck. This small control panel with 15 customizable physical buttons lets you control multiple things without leaving the game or messing around with commands elsewhere.

For example, you can press the easy-access button that disables your Webcam or mute your microphone if you need to gobble some food or talk to a family member who's just wandered into the room. You can even set a mute and deafen button for Discord to temporarily stop your friends from being heard while you talk to your audience. If you find that you're getting specific questions asked regularly, then you could craft a reply and send it to chat with the press of a button. This stream deck also gives you the ability to clip a stream, place a highlight marker for future editing, play an advert, delete the current chat, or change the current chat mode to follower-only, emote-only, or slow chat—all that and so much more at the touch of a button. Getting a deck switcher may not seem necessary, but trust me, you will never want to return after you've had one.

Outside the Four Walls

Would streaming from a mobile device be possible? Good news. With the Twitch app, you can easily do mobile broadcasting. All you need is some decent bandwidth and a commitment to providing a quality, entertaining, and informative gaming experience.

Streaming from a PC or gaming console will give you high-quality visuals during a broadcast, but you should still use mobile streaming abilities. Whether you're on the go or unable to invest in the equipment mentioned earlier, your Twitch influencer project can still progress if you have an Android device and an iPhone or iPad.

There are two ways to broadcast from a mobile device. You can install an app compatible with your operating system or install computer software that lets you cast the screen of the device you intend to use for streaming. The easiest option is, of course, to download the Twitch app. StreamLabs or Mobcrush can stream directly to Twitch from your mobile device.

If you choose StreamLabs, you must log in with your Twitch account. You'll see the Stream icon in the upper right corner of the window. Tap on it and wait for a dialog box to appear with the notification that everything displayed on the screen is being recorded. From there, tap on the "Start Now" option.

For Mobcrush streaming from your iPhone, you must enable the Screen Recording option in the Control Center menu. It would be best to ensure that the Access Within Apps option permits Mobcrush to record your activities as you play.

To start a broadcast on your Android, tap the broadcast icon and give your stream a title. Select the right category, e.g., IRL, Talk Shows, Creative, Music, Social Eating, then rotate your phone to landscape and start streaming!

CHAPTER 10

Make it Look Professional

Twitch is one of those unique platforms that allows you to watch content without an account, but if you want to get the most out of this platform, especially if you are starting your channel, the first step is to sign up and set up your channel.

Creating Your Profile

There are a few ways you can sign up, i.e., through Desktop or mobile. You can sign up for an account on your desktop by going to Twitch. Tv and select from the top-right side of your browser window the "Sign Up" option. That will open the opportunity to sign up for a new account where you can fill out the form by giving your preferred username and password and sharing legal information like your date of birth.

First, download the Twitch mobile app, launch it, and tap the "Sign Up" button. When signing up for an account on mobile, you can sign up using your mobile phone number or email address. Once you've completed the signup form, you'll get a six-digit code known as a one-time password (OTP) sent to your email or via SMS, depending on your chosen option.

Coming up with a username

It's imperative to seriously consider your username, as this will be what people see in Chat and how they will access your channel. Twitch is very strict about usernames and often shuts down accounts that violate their rules and guidelines. But it's more than just picking a name that isn't offensive. It's also about being creative and using this as a branding tool so people can remember your channel. The easier it is for people to remember you, the more likely they will search for you the next time they want to watch your content.

Another aspect of this is adding some key branding elements, like a good profile picture and a customized Twitch banner that helps viewers understand what your channel is about.

Once you're done following the instructions for signing up and verifying your account, you're, technically speaking, ready to launch your channel. Of course, at first, you will have no content. But even before you start streaming, you want to familiarize yourself with the dashboard and some of the platform's fundamental features.

Utilizing the Info Panels

A Twitch info panel or an info banner under your live stream is used as a call to action. It's a great way to provide more information about your stream or direct viewers to a specific page outside the platform. The recommended Twitch panel size is 320 by 160 Pixels. There are several different types of info panels that you can use to attract subscribers and followers, including:

- **Schedule Panel -** This Twitch panel shares your streaming schedule with viewers. That shows people you're serious and consistent about putting out fresh content and incentivizes them to follow you and show up at the mentioned time. Consistency is critical when you want to grow a large following and become successful on Twitch, so let everyone know when you will be live!

- **About Me Panel -** This graphic summarizes your channel and stream. Use it to introduce yourself to your first-time viewers.

- **Social Media Panels -** These are self-explanatory. They are great for cross-promoting your brand and getting users to follow you on other social platforms. Most viewers will have different accounts, including TikTok, Snapchat, Instagram, Facebook, Clubhouse, etc. You don't need to include every social media platform; use the most relevant social channels you frequently use.

- **Discord Channel Panel -** This is good to have only if you've got a Discord channel. It will help you build an engaged community of viewers and give you another way to interact with your fans outside of Twitch. We'll discuss Discord and how to set it up later in the book.

- **Donation Panel -** This panel allows you to create a donation button so that people can support your creative efforts. It will redirect people to an external website where they can "buy you a coffee."

- **Sponsored Panel -** Although this kind of panel will be valuable once you grow on this channel, it's still lovely to become aware of it. Sponsored panels are a great way to make money. These panels promote a brand or business that supports your channel. The panel sends people to the sponsor's website, and you get paid for driving traffic their way.

- **Stream Merchandise Panel** - This panel is used to sell and promote your products. It gives your merchandise greater visibility and drives direct sales, another excellent way to earn an income while streaming.

Best practices:

- Use your brand color when creating the graphics.

- Make sure the text is manageable. Keep things short, clear, and concise.

- Keep the image file size under 2.9 MB to meet Twitch's requirements.

- Maintain consistency and be relevant with the panel graphics that you use.

One of the main reasons Twitch panels are a must-have is that they help you customize your channel's branding, enabling you to stand out from everyone else in your niche. It also lets viewers know why they should tune in or follow your channel, ultimately attracting only the right audience.

Befriend OBS

In a previous chapter, we introduced OBS (Open broadcast software) as one of the more accessible options to stream on your Twitch channel. Still, given how new this terminology might be for beginners (which many reading this book will be), it best to invest a little more time in understanding and befriending the OBS. Please note that this information needs to be completed, and I don't claim to be a professional at any of these features or software. I am sharing what I've picked up over time as I continue growing my Twitch channel and brand.

So, what exactly is Open Broadcast Software? It's a production-level software that allows you to display multiple cameras and even desktop screens during a stream. You can control microphones, media, and so much more. You can do real-source and device capture, broadcasting, encoding, recording, and scene composition. In other words, it's the point where your inputs and outputs merge.

The best part is OBS is free to use and works with both Windows and Mac OS, and if you're feeling generous, you can always donate something to continue supporting the fantastic OBS Studio software. While OBS can feel pretty daunting for beginners, it can also be a great ally when you learn how to use it.

What does the OBS do?

It can help you mix real-time audio video and lets you choose per-source filters such as noise gate, noise suppression, and gain. With OBS, you can add screen recording between your videos or as part of your video by providing a small space on the same screen. During breaks, you can pause between your live sessions to display a pre-selected banner or video to our audience. You can also communicate screen recordings to your audience during live sessions, allowing you to share your screen.

How to set up OBS to stream on Twitch

The first step is to connect your OBS to Twitch by selecting it from the streaming services drop-down list. On your Twitch TV dashboard, choose Settings > Stream Key > Show Key and follow the instructions and prompts, then copy and paste the Stream Key into the Stream Key box in the broadcast settings menu in OBS. Then click Apply.

From here, you need to set up the layout of the stream. You can add a live webcam feed, lovely images, a banner around the edges of your stream, or even a social media handle for your favorite platform so viewers can follow you there. OBS has two windows: scenes and sources. Each set comprises multiple sources, from the game capture window to your live webcam input. You can create various game settings and load them up by selecting them from the scene menu. When starting, keep things simple and create a single set for all games. Once you've made your scene, you need to add sources. To add your game source:

a. Click the Plus icon in the Sources menu and select Game Capture.

b. Give your game capture a title to make it easy to recognize later.

c. Customize the capture settings. Be mindful of the mode you choose. You can set it up to automatically capture any full-screen application, capture the foreground window when a hotkey is pressed, or set it up to manually select which window should be captured. If you're using a game capture card, this is where you would select that. Once you're happy with the settings, click OK to save and add the source to your scene.

If you'd like to add some personality to your streaming, I recommend adding your Webcam to the live feed. To do this:

1. Click the plus icon in the Sources menu and select Video Capture Device.
2. Give your Video Capture Device a name, e.g., Webcam.
3. Select your Webcam from the Device drop-down and tweak any other settings if needed.
4. Click OK to add the Webcam to the scene. If you need to move your camera input or resize it, click on it and drag the corners to adjust accordingly.

You can also click and drag to adjust and move it from one side to the other.

For images (especially info banners), you can easily add them directly to your OBS by going to the Sources box and then clicking Add > Image. Name the source so you can locate it again next time. Click Browse on your computer to find and add it. Tweak the settings (you'll see various options) and click OK to add the image to the Livestream. Like the Webcam, you can move it around by dragging and dropping it wherever you want it viewed.

The process is similar if you also want to add text to your stream. Click the Plus icon in the Sources menu and select Text (GDI+). Enter a name for your text box (the name on the source, different from what people will see). You can customize the font, size, color, opacity, and more to get the desired effect in the text menu. Click OK to close and save the text. To adjust the text's position, choose "Edit Scene" and drag and drop the reader to the desired location.

It's time to go live once everything is set up and you're happy. In OBS, you need to click Start Streaming in the bottom right corner of the main OBS window, and that's it!

The difference between Streamlabs OBS and OBS

Streamlabs OBS and OBS are the most common and widely used broadcast software. They are both free and great for streaming, so which one should you go for? Let's look at the key differentiators:

- OBS is a high-performance software that delivers the ultimate user experience but lacks certain features and functionality. In other words, if you're into bells and whistles, you will only find them here if you develop them yourself.

- Streamlabs OBS is like the much-needed upgrade to OBS that certain streamers have sought. It is the same OBS code revamped with a better user experience. Unfortunately, it works best on Windows, so you're better off using the standard OBS if you have a Mac OS.

- Streamlabs OBS provides various themes and advanced features to create a unique experience for the streamer. There are dozens of themes to personalize your stream. It also includes alerts, widgets, built-in text-to-speech, layouts, and more. As you may have inferred, these are outside the standard OBS.

Make Sure You Are Heard!

When Twitch viewers tune in to watch your livestream, they expect to hear your voice, music, and sound effects from the game you're playing. They expect it to be a pleasant experience, implying you must ensure sound quality is on point. So, let's talk about how Twitch advises you to set up your audio and some additional tips.

When you launch Twitch Studio for the first time, you'll get the first-time setup prompts you need to follow. The first one is setting up your microphone. Your default microphone will be automatically selected, but you can change the mic at any time using a specific device. You can also change other settings by clicking on the personalize button.

Next, you want to navigate to the Twitch Studio screen, where you can see your Chat, Activity Feed, and Scenes. You'll see the bar for your microphone in the bottom left corner. Click the Audio Mixer icon with three lines to add an audio source. Then click the (+) Plus icon to add another available source if needed.

If you want to use a capture card to broadcast, add the device's output as a source for your Main Screen Share or any other Screen Share layer. Not all capture cards are compatible with Twitch Studio, so here are some of the most recommended ones by Twitch. You can use Elgato HD 60S, HD 60S Plus, HD 60 Pro, HD 4K Pro, and Screenlink for Windows. You can also use Razer Ripsaw and Ripsaw SD or Avermedia Live Gamer Extreme 2 (GC551), Live Gamer Ultra (GC553), Live Gamer Portable 2 Plus (GC513), Live Gamer Mini (GC311), Live Gamer HD 2 (GC570), and Live Gamer 4K (GC573A). For Mac, you can use Elgato HD 60S Plus and Screenlink or Avermedia Live Gamer Ultra (GC553), Live Gamer Portable 2 Plus (GC513), and Live Gamer Mini (GC311).

Besides getting these basics right, you must also consider the kind of mic you're using, the recording space, and your OBS settings. What do I mean?

Getting the right microphone doesn't need to be expensive, but you need to invest in something that will make you sound like a pro. You can get a condenser mic like Blue Yeti, which has a more extensive range and is more sensitive to loud noises, or a broadcast mic, which is often easier to work with. Regardless, you will need to position it correctly. The microphone's position will determine how you sound on the receiving end. Consider putting approximately 1-6 inches away from your mouth.

If you're using a headset, never place the mic directly in front of your mouth because most people don't want to hear you breathing. Instead, put it right around or under your chin.

You must also remember that every game differs, so you must test your audio levels before each session. To do this yourself, try settings before you start the actual Livestream by recording a preview of your stream and then playing it back so you can hear what viewers will listen to once you go live. Using your OBS, you can do this by clicking Start Recording. Let the game run for a few minutes, and talk into the mic a few times. Then, when you feel you have enough material, click Stop Recording. Find the recording by going to Settings > Broadcast Settings > File Path. That is where all recorded sessions will be saved. Play it back; you're good to go if it sounds fantastic.

Reach Out and Have Channel Moderators

When you're just starting, managing the live-streaming content and the work involved in engaging with your audience on the chat will be easy. However, as things evolve and your channel growth snowballs (assuming you follow and apply everything taught in this book), you'll get to a place where handling the chat activity will become overwhelming. And that is a good problem to have. How do we solve this issue? Simple. Reach out to the most active viewers (someone you resonate with) and invite them to be your channel moderator or mod, as often called in Twitch vocabulary.

A mod is someone who can help you monitor, clean up, and engage with your growing audience so that you can focus on doing what you do best - create epic entertainment. What should you look for when picking a mod?

- A good moderator is reliable and service-oriented.
- This person actively engages in the chat long before you ask them to be mods. They enjoy answering people's questions about your channel even before they know you and seem good at responding to comments.
- A good mod is trustworthy.

Not only should your moderator be reliable, but they should be trustworthy and believe in the same values you do, as that will make it easier for them to carry out the rules you give them on the general conduct of the channel. As they clean up comments, eliminate spam, and handle tough questions or criticism and comments regarding your brand, things will go smoothly if they believe and value the same things your brand stands for. So, make sure you pick someone you genuinely feel connected to.

How to make someone a mod:

There are two ways to make someone a moderator. First, you can type in the command /mod USERNAME in your chat while they are in your channel. That should automatically make that person a mod. The other option is to click on the person's name in the chat. You'll see the possibility of promoting them to mod. Click on it, and they instantly get the upgrade with the green sword icon next to their name.

Do you need to pay your mod, and how many do you need?

Mods are generally unpaid, but you could offer them perks or gifts during holiday seasons or work anniversaries. Gift cards, game codes, special stream perks, or other individual presents are commonly accepted.

When it comes to mods, there needs to be a standardized answer. Twitch recommends adding them as needed, which makes sense because the bigger your viewership, the more comments you'll get on your chat, and the more help you'll need. Twitch recommends five active mods for every 200 viewers once you see five messages per second. If you don't want to start with a human mod, you can always experiment with a stream chatbot that enables you to pre-customize specific rules so they can automatically delete things like hate speech, spam links, etc. With a chatbot, you can have hundreds of different replies. Some programs, such as Nightbot, offer dynamic replies, which is perfect if you only want an automated moderator while your channel gains momentum.

How to reach out to your audience:

If you're ready to bring in some human moderators, create a Google Form with a few questions to ensure you pick the right people. Post the link to the document in your Discord or profile and let people know you're looking for mods. If you've already spotted someone from your community that would be ideal, reach out directly and ask if they'd be interested in an interview. Do not just pick someone because they donate to your channel. Make sure it's someone who genuinely loves engaging with people. If you have real-life friends or relatives who enjoy socializing, it's worth asking them, too.

Make Your Streams Look Nice Using Overlays

All successful gamers on Twitch put a lot of effort into creating that customized look to imprint their brand on their audience. This is usually done through the use of overlays. An overlay is a graphic design consisting of varying graphics that appear along with your gameplay footage during a stream. Usually, the overlay is a transparent PNG image overlaid on top of the Livestream content. The graphics are positioned around the edges of the screen so that the center remains unobstructed. Still, depending on your brand image, you can always create one that suits your particular taste and the layout of the game you're playing.

You can include a unique color scheme, mascot logo, or stream information such as current music tracks, top donors, recent subscribers, and more on your overlay design.

Why do people invest in Twitch overlays?

It's the easiest way to stand out from the crowd of fellow streamers. It's also an excellent way to show off your personality and enhance the game's visual experience for your viewer.

How to make your overlay more attractive:

Choose designs that align with your brand and personality and the games you play. Choose brighter color schemes and creative design themes if you are colorful, playful, and energetic. Suppose you're playing genres such as MMORPGs, MOBAs, and so on that feature complicated User Interfaces. In that case, you're better off choosing hidden minimalist overlays to avoid obstructing critical in-game information. If you're playing First-Person-Shooters and Battle Royales, you can get more creative since you'll have more real estate to work with. So, before investing in an overlay, think about the games.

There are many accessible sources on the web to get some pre-made overlays, and if you're starting, that might be a good option. Once you've established yourself, however, I suggest getting a custom-made overlay, especially once you play around with a few and identify one that suits your channel. Consider visiting Nerd or Die, Twitch Overlay Maker Placeit, Ghost Rising, Zerging, WDFLAT, Haunted Twitch Overlay- visuals by impulse, and Own3D Club: Free Twitch Streamer Community. Just Google any of these names, and you'll gain access to the free overlays each platform offers.

Now, you're wondering how to get that overlay showing up on your stream. Streaming OBS or XSplit software on your PC or Mac would be best. Then, it's as simple as adding an image layer and selecting your files. Then, you can have it as a border around your Webcam or the whole 1080p experience, taking up the entire frame of your screen. While transparent PNG is the most common file type, you can also use GIFs and JPGs. Just note that JPGs will not be fine, and GIFs will not have the high-quality resolution that a PNG offers.

Chapter 11

And We Are LIVE!

At this point, you have ticked all the boxes on your checklist, and you should be feeling pretty excited because you can launch your live streaming and start growing your brand. But before you go live, you want to ensure that those details that could make you look unprofessional are well covered. Ensure you do a final check to ensure your channel branding is on point, your Twitch profile represents the brand image you're trying to create, and you've practiced with your streaming software.

Your First Live Stream

Besides the hardware and software, you must create a Twitch channel trailer, set up chatbots and alerts, decide on a schedule for your stream, and practice talking to chat. It would be best to plan some time to interact with other streamers with an audience. Use this opportunity to network, build relationships, and create opportunities for collaboration. Evidence supports that new streamers do better when they network with other broadcasters. Before doing your live stream, you must be active on at least five channels you can invite to come to support your first Livestream and cheer you on.

Before your live stream, you also want to ensure you've practiced the gameplay and developed sufficient techniques through study and practice. You need to be more sure if you can wing it and succeed on Twitch. You must understand the game well enough to be entertaining to watch while playing it. Game rehearsal is crucial before your first stream, and once you do start streaming, make sure you've planned it out well enough so you don't run out of entertaining content a few weeks down the road. Ideally, you want to ask yourself:

- What content will I stream?
- How long will each stream last?
- Who will be gaming with me, if at all?
- How often will I go live each week?
- What goals do I want to hit with each stream that I can track?

All these questions help you create a clear and measurable plan beforehand to stay focused, organized, and on purpose with your content.

The last quick check you need to make once you feel confident about doing your live stream is to make sure your design elements are on point. You need a profile picture, Twitch overlays,

And We Are LIVE!

Twitch banners, Twitch panels, Twitch emotes (if you plan on becoming an affiliate), and your overall profile design should be congruent with your brand image and ready to go. We've talked about these different aspects of your channels in previous chapters, so please go back and re-read them if you need help creating them.

Assuming you're ready, it's time to head over to your dashboard and let the magic begin. Always remember to title your stream in a way that will attract viewers to click through and watch your game. Remember to add tags and choose the language and game/category so that people can discover your content. The next thing is to go to settings to make sure you've selected archive broadcasts. That will automatically save your broadcasted streams to Twitch's "videos" tab. This is important because you want viewers to be able to watch VODs (videos on demand) whenever they miss your live stream. To limit commenting, click the "Followers-only" mode in your settings. Now you're ready to stream!

The step-by-step breakdown for newbies (recommended by experts):

#1: Restart your PC before streaming.

#2: Open your streaming software, e.g., OBS or Streamlabs.

#3: Prep the background music.

#4: Test audio for sound quality and your video to see how the lighting is.

#5: Open your Twitch chat, ready to go. If you have a mod or are using a bot, ensure they are prepped and ready.

#6: Grab some water-light snacks, and that you're sitting somewhere comfy.

#7: Hit the start streaming button and go live!

It's Not Just About Streaming Your Games

A question I get asked by new streamers is, "Can I stream without talking?" If you've been wondering the same, I'll take out the guesswork and tell you that you can stream without chatting on Twitch. There are specific scenarios where not talking is best. For example, speaking isn't recommended if you're doing a tournament and must be hyperfocused or streaming music. And by streaming music, I mean something intense like you playing the drums or piano. In this case, the viewers will get that you can't possibly play your instrument, make good music, and still read the chat. But on any other occasion, I discourage it because here's the thing. Twitch is more than just a place to play video games. It is, after all, a social platform. People come to Twitch to make friends with like-minded people.

So, if you want to grow your channel and attract more viewers, chatting is a big part of what you must be willing to do. Radio silence as you play your game will hurt your channel's growth and success because most people coming to view your game also care about interacting with you in some way. Many Twitch viewers value the community aspect because it's like a bonding session for them over a game they love or aspire to play.

How to best interact with your new viewers in chat:

You need to ensure your chat is set up so viewers can see it on the right-hand side of your stream. You can also integrate the discussion into your overlay to make it look more professional. There are widgets in Streamlabs OBS that can help you do this. Also, now is an excellent time to create a list of vulgar terms that you feed the AutoMod so that it can filter any spam or unwanted messages. Decide whether or not you want to add chat delays to give your mods time to filter out negative messages and whether users without verified email addresses are allowed to chat. All this is done in the settings area. If the preparation is done well, the rest will flow.

All you need is to have viewer questions ready to enable you to create dialogue and a script to help you welcome new viewers and followers. It will be up to you to maintain that high positive energy that will get people to understand what kind of streamer you are and how they should behave when interacting with your channel. This is especially true in the beginning when you're growing your audience. Set the tempo, be clear about your rules and guidelines, and constantly interact with your chat. Regarding topics for discussion, I strongly suggest avoiding politics, religion, or any sensitive issues that usually create too much heat and bad energy in the chat.

But what if you want to avoid talking?

You can do a few things when you don't want to talk, e.g., when you're sick or had a long day at work.

Announce on your title that you will not be talking on the stream. That way, people tuning in will immediately come with the right expectations, and you won't end up with complaints and nasty comments on your chat.

Let people know on the title that you won't be reading or actively responding to the chat. If you're fighting a cold, you could even make fun of that and let them know so they can understand why you're not actively engaging. If you're having microphone issues, you could also share that. Again, these ideas help you communicate beforehand so that people come in knowing what to expect.

Set the chat to followers only, sub only, or emotes only. That allows you to filter your discussion, so you get less spam and only talk to people who matter.

One thing I encourage my more introverted friends to do is to activate followers-only mode so they can adjust the chat to accommodate people who've been following them for a specific period. For example, you could open it up to people following you for at least two months. I will, however, insist that you train yourself to chat because it will be impossible to gain new viewers and followers if you never interact with the larger community.

How to deal with having no viewers:

When you start your live stream, you'll likely have viewers if you're fortunate enough to have friends and family who want to support your channel. So, what should you do when the chat is empty? Commenting on your gameplay is always a good idea, even if no one is watching. If someone were to pop into the livestream for the first time and find you adding commentary, goofing around, and making fun of yourself, they likely engage you and start some chat activity. Have you ever been to a social gathering and seen this person standing alone in the corner? Then you thought about saying hello but approached the group of guys laughing across the room. Why do we gravitate toward those who seem more open, friendly, and fun-loving? Because it's easier to join in and create a dialogue where one already exists. The same is going to be confirmed on Twitch. People will click on your Livestream, and if you come across as that aloof, silent kid on the corner who wants to be left alone, they will leave. And that will make it hard for you to grow your viewership, followers, subs, and account.

Learn The Etiquette

Twitch is a social platform based on sharing common interests, especially around gaming. It's up to you to establish the energy and behavior that will be acceptable and representative of your brand. How you interact with viewers and fellow streamers and the image you put out will determine how others treat and perceive you. Establish your own set of rules and guidelines that people should adhere to when interacting on your channel. When you visit other streamers, demonstrate the same etiquette level you want to see on your channel. So, if you don't like people coming to your stream to self-promote or spam your chat with links, make sure you never do that on another channel. It's also not a good idea to see fellow streamers as rivals or competitors you can steal content from. Don't steal or copy. Be your original streamer so that people can see what makes your channel unique.

You should invest time in the community by visiting other channels you enjoy to get inspired and motivated. And when you do network, do it because you genuinely want to be friends with that streamer. Do it because you want to surround yourself with successful, like-minded individuals who do what you want to be doing further down the line. Another good habit to get into is to reach out to channels like you in size and scope so you can support each other and grow together. Mutual respect for both streamers and viewers is essential to your success. Many people on Twitch want to feel like they belong to a specific community, so treat others as you wish to be treated and become an example. Then, your people will naturally gravitate toward you.

It's a Wrap!

Now that you're ready to stream and chat, let's ensure you also end with a bag. The end of your stream is an important part that requires a little thought because you want to ensure the viewers can continue interacting with you. You can do some shout-outs for your social media accounts or other fan pages that you may have where people can come to interact with you after the gameplay. If you were doing a collaboration or plan on doing one soon, give that a shout-out and let people know when they should attend that event. Let viewers know when the next stream will occur and any additional info you feel would be relevant. Encourage those who enjoyed watching you for the first time to follow and reach out with their questions or ideas. If you didn't have time to give shout-outs to new followers or subscribers and you'd like to do it, the end part of the stream can be a great way to praise and acknowledge all the new people who supported you during the stream. Be creative with this, have fun, and test out different endings to see which feels most natural to you.

5 Important Tips for Beginners

#1: Have a clear goal in mind.

Why do you want to stream? Is it just a hobby? Do you want to make this your full-time career? What exactly do you wish to get out of it? You need to identify goals to know whether you're making any progress because you're like a guy driving a car with no destination. Sure, he might be going west, but west to what destination exactly? Have the main goal subdivided into smaller ones that you can track. For example, if your main goal is to be a full-time gamer earning seven figures in the next ten years, you can break it down into smaller goals for the next year, leading to that long-term goal. That can include starting and growing your audience to X followers and subs in the next 12 months.

#2: Make the most of your social media.

Although it would be great to think that all you need to succeed is to buy the right gaming equipment, set up your Twitch channel, and start producing epic content, and the rest will fall into place. You must be more proactive with attracting an audience because that is the lifeblood of your gaming success. The best way to attract an audience is to leverage social media because that's where your potential fans hang out when they're not on Twitch.

Developing your social presence and building awareness about your brand on the channels you most enjoy is a must. You can be on some platforms, but I encourage you to consider YouTube, TikTok, Twitter, Instagram, and Facebook, as all these social platforms have large, engaged audiences who love gaming. TikTok is, of course, the most accessible place to grow an audience from scratch. Still, if you naturally enjoy being on any of the previously named networks, I suggest setting up an account there so you can have at least two active social media platforms. That gives you a place to let everyone know when you go live, which increases the chances of getting more viewers. It also allows you to communicate with your fans and fellow content creators. That will boost your credibility, build your identity, and establish your brand online. You can create compilations of funny moments or game highlights that you can share on these social networks.

#3: Collaborate with other broadcasters

The more social you are, the easier it will be to connect with and build relationships with fellow content creators. Then, you can cross-promote each other's content and even use dual streams to play a game while streaming. It is a great way to tap into each other's communities.

#4: Stick to your streaming schedule

It's essential to create a streaming schedule and train your viewers to expect to tune in and connect with you at a specific time each day or week, depending on how often you go live. Once you manage to create this pattern, you must stick to it. That makes a habit in the journey of your viewers and gives them something to look forward to. When getting started, try different slots throughout the day to see what is more comfortable for you and what yields more average viewers. Once you identify this pattern based on data, not guesswork, commit to streaming at that same time each week.

#5: Communicate, entertain, and engage your viewers

You have about ten seconds to grab someone's attention on Twitch, and if they don't like what they see and hear, they'll click away. People will come expecting to be entertained, so make sure you deliver. Communicate, be authentic,c and leverage your quirky traits. Talk about your strategy, your train of thought, and how you feeling throughout the game. Be verbal so people can feel immersed and engaged. That's how you'll grow the channel.

Chapter 12

Improving Your Stream and Getting More Viewers

Anyone can start a streaming channel on Twitch, but not everyone will succeed at turning that hobby into a lucrative full-time job. Those fortunate enough to do it have a couple of things in common. The main underlying is their commitment to creating the best possible stream each time they go live. How do you climb the ranks of the best streamers on Twitch? By adopting the same frame of mind, they have. That begins by ensuring that each stream is better than the last.

There's Always Some Space for Improvement

Regardless of how good your last stream was, make it a point to continuously up your game. There are many ways you can keep improving your stream from both a technical and quality perspective. The easiest is, of course, with your content. The more you learn and practice your gameplay, the better you'll get at streaming live. If you can get so good at playing your games, you might find innovative ways of approaching the game that your viewers will likely find enjoyable. That might involve taking a bit of a risk as you step outside the norm and establish your unique approach to the game. But as long as you're smart and you've practiced well enough, it could quickly help you stand out amongst other streamers, and it will train viewers to expect better content from you.

Regarding the technical bit, you should continue to educate yourself on how to tweak your OBS settings to get better quality and more optimization, depending on your PC and microphone. A few things you should know here include:

Streaming FPS or other fast-paced games is better in 900p@60fps than the standard recommendation (1920 X 1080@60fps). It will give your viewers better quality and less pixelation during fast movement.

To get a more efficient bitrate usage that will give you better overall stream quality, navigate to the OBS advanced settings and activate "Enable network optimizations."

Aside from the nerdy technical stuff, you can also improve your stream's appearance. First impressions matter, and you've got ten seconds to make a great impression. So, you want to tweak and upgrade your aesthetics continually. Here are some pointers when it comes to making things more appealing:

Use quality graphics and sounds and maintain a consistent look and feel. Even if at first you start with free or cheap pictures for your branding, be clear with the overall look and feel you want for your channel so that even when you begin investing in custom designs, people experience a manageable shock. Think of the overall color scheme, the sounds, and the style of your transitions, and then do your best to find free stuff that matches what you want to create. As you grow, you can always purchase or get someone to design something of higher quality. Still, if you correctly outlined the original brand personality, your viewers, followers, and subs would receive the upgrade very positively. If you want to purchase some excellent graphics on a budget, consider checking out Fiverr, which has creators who design exclusively for streamers and are likely to produce something epic that matches your budget.

Don't use over-the-top overlays. Tacky designs won't help your brand. Yes, lasers and flames are cool and theoretically sound like a good idea, but clean aesthetics make for a better viewer experience. Less is more in this case. You don't want things that take up 30% of your screen as that will disturb the eye, and most people will suffer from visual fatigue.

Use emotes and emote extensions such as FrankerFaceZ and BetterTTV to add flair and excitement. People love cool emotes. What exactly are emotes? These are Twitch's emoji glyphs that people can insert into their chat communications during a Twitch stream. They are an integral part of the Twitch streaming community's culture and identity-building process, so you want to use them to establish your brand's personality. Unlike standard emojis that you might find on WhatsApp or other social platforms, these emotes are diverse and have the power to add more expression. They can also be sent as standalone polyps without text to signify a particular moment during the stream. I also like to use them as a mini ad for my channel by encouraging my followers and mods to use my emotes. As other viewers see them circulating, they might feel enticed to join the community and subscribe. There are both free and custom-made emotes. To make custom emotes, you need to be a Twitch affiliate or Twitch partner.

You can also customize your alerts to have different follow and sub-alerts. Be subtle; don't overdo this, but consider creating an excellent tune for your special alerts so viewers who convert can see that you care. Your fans always appreciate a little celebration.

Plan Ahead of Time

If you want to succeed on Twitch or any other social media platform, there's one thing you must commit to - consistent content production. Proper planning and scheduling is the only way to be consistent, especially as your channel and responsibilities grow. I've heard of those rare beings who can produce lots of content without a plan. I don't buy it. It's never worked for me, so I cannot endorse it. What has worked thus far is having an organized content plan and a reliable scheduling system.

When should you schedule your streams?

From the moment you plan to go live for the first time. The younger and newer you are, the more you need to plan and schedule your stream. Streamers with thousands of viewers can get away with "on the fly" streaming, but if you're serious about growing your channel, a schedule is your best ally.

Think back to the days (if you're old enough) when you would have to tune in every Friday at the same to watch your favorite show. There was no binge-watching or on-demand entertainment, so if you missed it, you'd be bummed and have to wait another week. Okay, so nowadays, thanks to technology, that's not our entertainment experience. Whether you want to watch or listen to something, everything is on-demand. But still, the habit of wanting to know when a "fresh" episode goes live so we can tune in and catch it first lingers. That's why successful YouTubers, podcasters, and bloggers always announce when they'll release new content. And for streamers, reporting when you'll be going live makes it easier for people who like you enough to add you to their daily routine so they never miss tuning in. That is the perfect way to build a consistent following and to ensure maximum views. It also makes it easier to promote on other social media channels. If you like streaming in the afternoon, people will get used to watching you on your lunch break. Do you prefer evening streaming? Great. Let your people know so they can try to catch you at night before bed.

If you have a small community, especially in the first few months, consider sending direct messages as reminders so people get trained to show up at a specific time. For example, I like to stream in the evenings every Thursday, Friday, Saturday, and Sunday from 7:00 EST. Because I've set a specific schedule, I can send reminders about my upcoming stream on Twitter, TikTok, Snapchat, and Instagram. It also helps me plan. So, how would you go about doing this?

Option #1: Edit the stream schedule section on your creator dashboard.

Navigate to your channel to the section indicated as "schedule." This is what we are going to edit. Click "Edit schedule" and make whatever edits you desire. Once you're done picking your days, you should see them appear under your Twitch channel's schedule section.

Option #2: Create a Twitch panel (**we discussed panels earlier**) that includes your streaming schedule.

To edit your Twitch panels:

1. Go to the About Me section where the panels are located and turn the edit panels button on.
2. Create a panel that has your schedule on it, nothing fancy.
3. Just make sure it communicates the dates and times.

Pro tip: Consider putting your schedule on both the Twitch panel and your creator dashboard to maximize the effectiveness so everyone can see when you'll be live.

Don't Stop Engaging

Connecting with your audience should always continue when the Livestream ends. Engaging with your community should become a top priority at this point. Why? Because success on the platform hinges on having a healthy audience size. Twitch only monetizes if you create a highly engaged audience. That has to start at the beginning of your journey. I suggest the 80-20 rule whereby 80% of your time as a newbie should be invested in interacting with viewers, streamers, followers, and subscribers, and 20% goes into producing epic content. So, if you plan on releasing lots of content, consider that you'll need to make lots of time for community building to match all that content.

Contrary to what most gamers think, the gameplay is only half the equation of success. There are a thousand ways to do this. You can build up your social media and use Discord and any other suitable channel to ensure you're nurturing that relationship with your new fans and subscribers. Most gamers have found great success using Discord, and if you need to know what that is, I will walk you through how to set it up in the next section.

Making Use of Your Vod

Vod stands for Video On Demand, and it's a great way to ensure your viewers can rewatch that epic gameplay. It's also a great way to ensure your followers who may have missed the stream can still catch some of that action. However, before you can, it's essential to follow the instructions below to enable VOD for your channel.

#1: Click on your profile icon in the top right-hand corner of your Twitch and find "dashboard."

#2: Navigate to "settings" on the left-hand side and click "channel."

#3: You will see a list of headings under "Stream Key and Preferences" and a section titled "Store Past Broadcasts." Tick that small box to allow Twitch to store past broadcasts.

#4: Once you click the small box, a green check will appear, which confirms that you are allowing Twitch to save your past broadcasts, and just like that, your VOD is active and ready. If you ever want to turn it off, uncheck that small box again.

A few things you must remember, though, is that VODs have an expiration date. They are only saved for 14 days (two weeks) for regular streamers, but if you have Twitch Prime, Twitch Turbo, or are a Twitch partner, Twitch will save your broadcasts for 60 days (two months).

How to manually save your VODs.

If you'd like to have your VODs reused later or for a different purpose, you can download the VOD to your computer. They do take up a lot of space, so I recommend getting an external hard drive, which you can easily buy from Amazon, where you can store them.

If, however, you'd like to get creative and create a collection of your best moments so you can have that instead of the whole stream, you can create highlights that showcase portions of the live stream. How?

#1: From your dashboard, navigate to the screen's left side, scroll down until you see "videos," and click "video producer." A list of past broadcasts will appear.

#2: Locate the broadcast you want to highlight and click the "highlight" button next to it.

#3: A new tab will open up; here, you can begin highlighting different sections of your videos. Select the parts you want, click the "create highlights" button, and your highlights are complete.

When created properly, these little gems will provide an overview of your gameplay and show people what you do and what your channel is all about without you having to be online live streaming. It's incredible marketing and an excellent way to attract new viewers. Many people are casually scrolling through Twitch to look for new channels, and if they can land on your highlights, they are more likely to turn into real viewers, followers, and subs. Another reason you should consider creating highlights is that many of your subscribers may want to watch only some of the Livestream they missed, but they certainly would enjoy seeing your best moments. So, this works well as an update for your followers and subs. A good length to go for is 1-2minutes.

An Avenue for YouTube Content

Okay, so you have VODs downloaded to your computer, and you've been making epic highlights from your gameplay. Isn't there a way to repurpose this content? Yes, there is. None is better than repurposing your content on YouTube. There is a multitude of ways through which you can leverage YouTube to grow your Twitch channel. The most straightforward one is through the Twitch website. To do so, ensure you've linked the two accounts first (Twitch and Google).

Find the little arrow icon (on the Twitch dashboard) next to your name in the top right corner of the screen and click on Video Producer. That will take you to a list of all your Twitch videos, including your past streams. Click the three dots on the video you want to export to YouTube and click "Export." Remember to fill in the title, description, and tags for the video, which will determine the video's discoverability and ranking on YouTube. You can also decide whether you want YouTube to automatically split it into 15-minute segments. Hit "Start Export," and your video will be live on your YouTube channel shortly.

Should you upload your VODs directly to YouTube?

Given how long normal gameplay is, I suggest avoiding the shortcut of uploading a full Livestream. If you think about it, there are many "boring parts," ranging from bathroom breaks to time spent reading chats. These moments are fine for live viewers but can be a turn-off for people who tune in to watch the recording. On YouTube, especially, what I find works is uploading the highlights of your gameplay. That means creating highlights of your best moments as discussed earlier or, better still, editing the content like you would a regular video. It will ensure your YouTube viewers enjoy the content they find on your YouTube channel because it will be a different regurgitation of the Twitch Live stream experience. There are a few options here to consider:

The first and most recommended is to get video editing software and edit the downloaded VOD to make it more in-depth than a highlight reel. This might present some issues, mainly if you use a laptop or an older computer. You can handle lag time and slow downloads with a high-end gaming/streaming computer. Rendering is also another issue you might struggle with, so I recommend using special editing software that makes it easy to edit longer games. A common one that works for most gamers is Flixier. It runs in your browser and uses cloud servers to render video in 3 minutes or less. The best part is that it has a full Twitch integration, meaning you can link it to your account and import your VOD straight from the Twitch servers. Flixier also has YouTube integration capabilities, which means you can set it to publish your freshly edited content as soon as it's ready.

Chapter 13

Monetizing Your Content

Although you can make money through your TikTok channel, focusing on Twitch is easier and more fruitful in the long run. Some well-known gamers have found the formula to make good money. For example, Shroud makes about $100,000 a month from subs. And this is just one income stream. There are also sponsorships, tips, and other money-making techniques. Compared to TikTok and YouTube, the deal seems sweeter on Twitch when you consider that some platforms take as high as 50% commission on your total earnings. According to a poll conducted by gamer Sizzarz, Twitch viewers enjoy supporting their streamers through Gifting Subs (40.2%), Cheering Bits (28.9%), and Tipping (30.9%). So, in this chapter, we will walk through how you can start generating some or all of your income from the streaming platform.

Most people know affiliate marketing and establish affiliate marketing links on many of their social platforms. The standard affiliate marketing method is to sell something from Amazon that your audience might be interested in. Then, you get a small commission payment from all your sales. But that's different from being a Twitch affiliate, which I want to help you become. Aiming to become an affiliate is best once you gain momentum with your channel. It will take some work, but the fast-track route and its benefits are here.

Becoming an affiliate for Twitch unlocks the "subscribe" button, which viewers can use to access your custom emotes and show support through financial investment. As you can imagine, getting someone to subscribe is much more challenging than getting them to follow you since money is involved. Still, if you have great content and an addictive personality, your people will ultimately want to show their support by subscribing. Although it's not easy, it's easier than one might think.

Take, for example, the story of Cherry Horne, who says that she became hooked on watching Twitch streams during the pandemic season. Cherry watched seasoned dancers playing Just Dance, and since she'd purchased the game herself, she found watching these streamers quite motivational. She also learned a few moves. After a while, she grew fond of certain streamers and started "tipping" them as a token of her gratitude and ultimately subscribed to two of them. For Cherry, it's not just about getting exclusive content or "spending money" on the streamers but more about encouraging fellow creatives for the hard work they do. If she gets entertained and enjoys the streamer's content, she wants to tip to show her appreciation.

The bottom line is there are lots of people waiting to fall in love with your content and get entertained. Once your subscribe button is activated, your biggest fans will likely be more than happy to naturally upgrade into subscribers as long as you remain authentic and deliver epic content regardless of category.

Twitch requirements:

You must stream for at least 500 minutes per thirty-day period and have at least seven unique broadcast days. That means over 8hours of streaming a month. And you can't just stream one extended 8-hour gameplay. There have to be at least seven broadcasts within the thirty days. Then, it would be best to have an average of three or more viewers per thirty-day period and at least 50 followers on your channel. With such strict requirements,

Consider becoming a Twitch affiliate once you reach 100 followers. You can see your eligibility for the affiliate program by navigating to "Insights" > Achievements from your creator Dashboard. That's where Twitch will track your progress. Once eligible, you only need to click the button on your Path to Affiliate achievement. Twitch offers a complete guideline to read and follow once you qualify. Visit their Affiliate Onboarding Guide page and remember to read the terms of the agreement. So, the requirements aren't so impossible, but the question is, how do you get there? Here are a few pointers:

Be willing to put in the time.

In other words, you must commit to doing at least 500 minutes on seven separate days each month. This may sound like little if you're a teen with much more time, but this can be a lot for someone with a full-time job, family, and other obligations. Remember that just doing 500 minutes is the minimum Twitch wants from you, not the hours needed to build an active audience. When you're going from zero followers to the first one hundred, you'll need a lot more streaming and interaction time than a mere 500 hours.

Pro Tip: Some streamers are very strategic when hitting their monthly targets. Remember, you need the 500 hours done on seven separate days and an average of three viewers. Sometimes, streamers will turn off the stream without viewers because they don't want to risk missing the monthly requirement. So, if you don't have a large following yet with many active viewers, be strategic about when you stream so you can have the most significant number of viewers.

Pay attention to the ideal times for streaming.

Piggybacking on the last point, figuring out the best times to have your Livestream as early as possible in your journey is super important. That will enable you to create a schedule that makes it easier to create consistent content and for your viewers to show up on time. Nothing is more important than knowing what your audience loves and when they are usually available.

The other key aspect is finding creative ways to attract people to your stream. Given how many gamers play simultaneously, you can't just cross your fingers and hope someone will stop by to support your gameplay. It would be best if you had a plan, and in the last chapter, I will give it to you so you can finally learn how to attract suitable attention to your channel.

Leverage your offline social groups.

Since it will be essential to reach the average view target, a straightforward yet highly effective tactic is to convince (sometimes bribe) roommates, family members, friends, fiancé, and anyone else who can give you some time to watch your stream while you're live. Those views will still count toward your average monthly requirement, and it's likely to draw in new viewers because humans like to gravitate toward action. More often than not, action is dictated by how many viewers are on your stream. So, someone just casually browsing might come across two exact games simultaneously, and she is likely to click on the one with more viewers. It's just our human nature. Use this to your advantage.

Next Step: Partnership

The next level up when it comes to monetization is the Twitch partnership. That requires a sizeable audience to qualify for, but you should quickly scale up to a block if you're already successful with a Twitch affiliate. Here, you will earn revenue by accepting subscriptions from your viewers, which are $4.99, $9.99, $24.99, or the Prime Gaming free subscription. You can also unlock up to 50 channel emotes. Another way you can earn money is through Bits. Your viewers buy bits to cheer you on (tip you) without leaving the platform. You will, of course, share this revenue with Twitch, and you'll also get to customize your Cheermotes and Bit Badges. Lastly, as a partner, you can earn a share of the revenue generated from any ads played on your channel. You can determine the length and frequency of the mid-roll advertisements through your dashboard.

Twitch Partnership requirements:

To qualify for Twitch partnerships, you must complete the Path to Partner achievement or demonstrate a large, engaged viewership/following. Your content should conform to the platform's community guidelines, so you must read them as soon as you launch the channel. And if you think this is a one-time thing, please note that Twitch expects you to consistently maintain your channel status, meaning you need to keep your audience hyperactive monthly. So, this is the big league. You cannot just have this as a side hustle. The best-paid Twitch partners are doing it full-time.

How much can you expect to make as a Twitch partner?

Expert streamers earn between $ 3,000 and $5,000 monthly by putting in about a 40-hour workweek. This can become lucrative if you invest time and effort to grow a sizable audience. Add to that the extra revenue generated from ads ($250 for every 100 subscribers), and you can see how $10,000 becomes a realistic goal. So, it is an absolute possibility if you want to earn $10K a month playing video games. The path is logical. Many are doing it on Twitch already, so you can, too, once you develop the right work ethic.

There's More!

As mentioned earlier, we can generate revenue from Twitch in many ways. So far, we have discussed Twitch affiliates and partnerships. I also briefly touched on Twitch ads, which, according to CNBC, is $250 per 100 subscribers.

- **Twitch ads**

Twitch offers standard Interactive Advertising Bureau pre-roll and display ads. Streamers get paid based on the Cost Per Impression (CPM) model, which is every 1,000 views of your ads.

- **Paid Livestreams and Sponsorships**

Once you have a sizable audience, many opportunities become available on and off Twitch. One excellent option is getting sponsored by companies to market their products. That can include promoting their merch, discussing them during your live streams, and using their products on camera. For example, the famous Ninja usually enables DXRacer chairs, which he probably pays to display. Another form of sponsorship is a paid Livestream, where game developers will pay broadcasters to stream their game and get in front of a new audience, hoping that some will also purchase the game and play.

- **Affiliate marketing**

Affiliate or referral marketing is an excellent way for you to be able to make money on Twitch. Remember that this isn't the same as being a Twitch affiliate. With this method, you provide links to the specific products you want your audience to buy. Becoming an Amazon associate is the most common option for many streamers. Ass a Twitch affiliate, you can earn higher commission rates than standard referral accounts through Amazon Blacksmith (Twitch's built-in Amazon Associates tool).

Although most people only associate affiliate marketing with Amazon, you could establish relationships with the companies whose products you already use. For example, if you love the chair you're using, you might work out a deal with the company manufacturer and get a coupon code that you could share with your followers. Anytime someone uses your coupon code to buy the chair, the company cuts you some of their profit. The more your audience grows, the more your traffic to the products will increase, and if you're getting a fair commission, this can lead to a lot of money each month. If you've got a large following, affiliate relationships can be more profitable because you get paid a commission instead of the earlier option of a sponsorship, which is a fixed fee. I like affiliate marketing because you don't need to become a Twitch partner and go through all that hoopla. Money can start rolling in if you have a big enough audience that loves you.

Make Use of Your Channel Analytics

Understanding how your channel is performing is vital to your success. You must identify what's working and not working as early as possible. That requires tracking, measuring, and analyzing some data. Lucky for you, Twitch comes with built-in analytics to help you constantly improve your delivery and craft.

It would be best to learn how to read your channel analytics to increase your chances of getting affiliated and partnered with Twitch and ensure you continue to plan your streams better. Let's cover the channel insights on reading and using the data Twitch will provide you with over time.

Channel Insights

To access channel insights, go to Twitch. TV and select your icon on the top right. Find "Creator Dashboard" then "Insights" on the left sidebar. You will find the channel settings where all your data is stored here. There are three subsections:

- **Channel Analytics**

That will provide a holistic view of your channel. It gives information about average viewership, live views, follower gain, subscription gains, and revenue.

This section is excellent for keeping you accountable because you can see all of the streams you've done over a specific period, and it also shows you where your views are coming from, your top clips, and more. You can break down the data by date range, and I recommend a month-to-month comparison of how you're doing to stay calm and focused on the data.

An example of when to use channel analytics:

If you're considering switching game genres and want to determine whether or not it is a great idea, you can run some test streams. Then, use channel analytics to see how your average viewers and follower gains were affected. That will enable you to make an informed decision on how to proceed.

Another powerful way to use this tool is to check the streamers with a similar audience you could collaborate with. Find "Which channels have viewers in common with mine?" and start connecting with the people who you feel might make great partners so you can cross-pollinate and grow your communities together.

- **Stream Summary**

In the stream summary, you will see data from your previous streams. You can see stream duration, average viewers, max viewers, new follower count, total views, unique chatters, peak time, raids received, viewers by hour chat, tips, and opinions by source. This information is significant when growing your following to become an affiliate or partner. You can also use this data to figure out the best streaming times.

For example, you've been streaming from Tuesdays to Saturdays from 7:00 p.m. to 10:00 p.m. for the past three months. You now have ample data to help you figure out peak time. You might see in the stream summary that, on average, your peak time for concurrents falls at 9:00 p.m. You might also realize that at 8.30 pm, there's not much action, and yet by the time you're done streaming, you have double or triple the concurrents you had when you started. That data enables you to begin testing different alternatives. You could stream from 8:30 pm to 11:30 pm to see what (if any) changes would happen to your follower gain, concurrences, and overall reception.

Another thing you can do is to check your Views by Source box. This area shows where you are getting traffic to your channel. Track to see how effective you are at bringing people from your other social media accounts to Twitch. That is extremely helpful because you can learn whether your CTAs on Twitter, TikTok, and Instagram work.

- **Achievements**

As the name suggests, this tool enables you to stay accountable and keep track of your goals. If the Twitch partnership is a big goal, you'll want to monitor your achievements data. It also helps you track how many hours of streaming you have under your belt, how many average viewers you have over 30 days, and so on. It takes out the guesswork and the fatigue of manually figuring everything out. The best part is when you hit the desired goal of becoming a Twitch partner, that application form will open up for you automatically.

You can use Achievement in combination with Stream Summary and Channel Analytics to improve and change your content. Each of these subsections provides detailed information about specific items of your channel. Use them to see how your channel performed month by month, but remember, don't get lost or discouraged by what the data shows, especially when you're just starting.

Section 4

Growing Your Brand

Chapter 14

Engaging with the Community

The benefits of growing a successful brand on any social media channel, especially Twitch and TikTok, should now be obvious. There's a lot of success to be had on the Internet. But here's the thing. Everything hinges on growing a sizable audience. The more interactive and loyal your audience, the quicker you will succeed. Of course, that can only happen if you have the right mindset. What is the right attitude? Get into Twitch and TikTok to socialize and create connections with community members. You must take it as a social experience to reach your goals.

Some people desire fame and success on social media but hate the work needed. If that's you, then this won't be your right decision. You will only succeed if your community becomes essential in your eyes.

I understand it's a lot of hard work, and you already have a lot to take care of, but the fact remains - you need to engage with the community.

Instead of finding shortcuts, establish a routine that lets you have regular, personalized communications on all the platforms you enjoy socializing. More than one platform is advised because you can use that growing connection to drive traffic to your main account. For example, If you want to grow your Twitch career, having a Twitter and Instagram account is a fantastic investment because your fans will likely come to watch your live streams when you send out DMs since they already know, like, and connect with you.

It Goes Both Ways

Have you ever encountered an account with many responses from people (emojis or text comments) yet waiting for a response from the account owner? How did that make you feel? Would you feel inclined to connect with that person?

Keep that thought in mind as you grow your channel. Socializing is a two-way experience; you must invest time to interact with your audience, whether you have one response or one hundred. Sometimes, people expect the account owner to take the initiative, so I encourage you to visit the accounts you like, whether they belong to influencers or fans, and start a conversation with them. Make sure it's appropriate and positive. Avoid self-promotion as much as possible. Just be a generous and kind human genuinely interested in making a connection. A couple of things you can do to build genuine relationships on social media include:

- Asking for advice or recommendations.

- Pose a question to your community or an influencer's post to start a conversation. Just make sure it's relevant.
- Send special DMs with some value add, even if it's just a motivational message that will brighten their day.

Interactive content types to experiment with:

#1: Polls and Surveys

These are quick and easy to set up. As long as you craft something thoughtful, people will participate. You can use it to get feedback, audience preferences, and more.

#2: Contests

People on social media always love engaging in a contest, especially if great rewards are up for grabs. Not only will a contest grow your brand awareness and engage the masses on social media, but it may also help you with list-building efforts to grow an email list and build an internal fan base. A popular form of contest that you can try is the "enter-to-win" giveaway.

#3: Questions and Quizzes

You can create social quizzes and share the results on your social channels. It can be around the games you usually Livestream to add that touch of personalization and draw on people who already love what you do. Quizzes also allow you to capture data from the questions answered to gain insights about your audience. That will help you as you develop content and marketing ideas to grow your brand.

When creating interactive content to drive more engagement, utilizing all the free tools and resources available is most important. For example, create a free, fast, and easy poll if you have a Facebook account. Many social media platforms have features built that will enable you (with some creativity) to create opportunities for people to engage with you and vice versa.

Creating a Discord Server For Your Community

Discord is a social tool that gamers use to build their community within Twitch. It's free and offers voice chat channels and text, making it super convenient for streamers. Once you create your server, you can divide it into channels to separate whichever topics your community will engage in. The server can be public or private (private servers are for closed communities, and the public ones are for anyone, allowing larger groups to gather and share their interests, use custom emotes, and dedicate moderators to ban unwanted members).

A significant benefit of setting up your server is that it allows you to interact with your viewers off-stream, which will help you grow your channel faster. You can interact in real-time, form a genuine connection with your community, and have a dedicated space for your growing audience. Think about it this way. You can only be live on Twitch during a stream, but with Discord, you can be engaging and nurturing your audience 24/7. That's how brands are built on social media.

Many streamers use Discord for movie nights, off-stream game nights, and other events. It's also helpful when setting up both on and off-stream multiplayer games.

How to get started:

You can sign up for free on Discord by downloading the Discord app for Desktop or from your mobile device's app store and following the instructions. You can choose to use your username from Twitch or change it to something new, but since you're using this to grow your channel, I suggest keeping the same name and profile picture for branding purposes. Then, follow the steps below to create your first server.

One. Press the +Plus sign button on the left sidebar of the interface.

Two. Choose the "Create" option to go to a screen allowing you to enter your server's details.

Three. Select your region and a logo for the server.

Four. Name your server.

Five. After you create your server, go into your settings and set up the verification levels and notifications settings.

Pro tip: Set it to @mentions only so you only get notified when it's essential.

Once your server is live, you can add stream integrations as well. You can use bots like Nightbot, Muxy, or whatever else you prefer for your server to help you moderate the communications. You must open your Discord and click the User Settings icon next to your name. Select "Connections" and then click on the Twitch icon. If you're logged in to Twitch on your computer, it should auto-populate your account.

How Discord can help you grow your community and some best practices: Most people are looking for a place to hang out online with their favorite streamers and friends without having all their communication exposed on Google, and that's precisely what Discord will offer you and your fans. Because it's more controlled and private, this real-time chat nature of the platform makes the connection more intimate and genuine.

Another benefit is that by setting up your channel, you don't need a big following to be heard or build loyalty. It allows you to hang out with the people you want to hang out with and interact with them in any way you want, whether through voice, text, images, video, or whatever else. With Discord, you can set up an announcement channel to promote new products or anything else you'd like to share with your audience, and everyone will get the message. So, the more people value your ideas, the easier it becomes to create affiliate marketing sales. There's no reliance on algorithms, reach, or any of those technicalities with Discord because it's an independent third party that cares more about the community and the creators.

When you set up your first server, start with a welcome channel. Also, remember to be authentic and hold the right intention. Discord is not an advertising platform. It's a hang-out spot.

You should also pick one of the bots to integrate to track users' activity patterns and engagement. That will help you learn about peak hours, best-performing topics, etc. With this information, you can capitalize during the right time frame to do many activities ranging from basic conversations to tournaments. Just make sure to add only a few bots or moderators. If you already have enough followers, consider assigning some roles for your community members to help you run the server. The more users join, the more you'll need support from other members who can help with questions and concerns and keep the energy of the channels high. Use the same process you did with mods within Twitch by going for people who resonate with you and those who are highly engaged and active within the server.

Protecting Your Identity

Although we emphasize the importance of remaining authentic as you share your passion for gaming on social media, we must also insist on preserving your privacy. There are six things you should keep private.

#1: Your home address

The risk involved with disclosing where you live is not worth taking. And I don't just mean because of thieves and robbers who might use this to their advantage. I am talking about trolls and sometimes even crazy, obsessive fans who might make things uncomfortable for you and your family by stalking you. Besides, if someone has your full address, it's easy to search through different databases to acquire additional information like your phone number, employment history, and other sensitive information. And by the way, if someone has enough sensitive data, they can do crazy things like open up a credit card in your name or steal money from your accounts. Keep your location private.

#2: Clubs or other affiliation

The more information someone has about your interests and where you spend your leisure time, the easier it is to launch a successful phishing scam. It can be as easy as sending you an email that appears to be from an organization that you volunteer for.

#3: Pictures of your credit cards or driving license

This seems obvious, but it happens more often than you might think. The first time we get a credit card, or when the driving license finally arrives, that excitement can cause us to act without thinking. If you're tempted to share these with your social media fans, remember, anyone with access to your credit card number and expiry date can order anything they want online on your tab!

#4: The same goes for your bank information

Isn't it great to show social proof of the money you're making now that your accounts have started monetizing? While I agree it's motivating to show fellow creators that they can do it too, remember it's unwise to give people that much back-office access. Keep your financial statements to yourself if you want to attract hackers and ill-intentioned people.

#5: Insensitive rants ranging from politics to religion and so much more.

I will not dictate what you should and shouldn't discuss on social media, but I will warn you against off-color jokes, sexism, and religious and political debates. The world is already so divided when it comes to these heated topics. Do you need to be considered misogynistic or labeled harshly by people who would otherwise be helping you build a lucrative brand? A good rule of thumb is to apply your grandma's test. If you can confidently share that content with your grandma, it passes the test. Otherwise, please keep it to yourself.

#6: Sharing intimate information about your relationships

Before you post something about your parents, girlfriend, boyfriend, boss, or bank manager that made you angry earlier in the day, pause and think twice. While it might seem innocent at the time to bash the institutions you work with or work for or that it's cool to share selfies of you kissing your lover, remember someone can easily use all this sensitive information against you if they land in the wrong hands. Think of this scenario. Imagine tweeting a complaint to your bank and ranting about how horrible their service was and potentially even naming the manager who mistreated you. It's not a stretch to imagine that if someone wants to target you, they could use this information to contact you, pretending to be the bank and creating a whole scam around it.

Now, think of another scenario. Imagine sharing intimate details about your community about your girlfriend or boyfriend, how you surprised them at work, etc. By sharing all these details, someone can grab that information and contact them, luring them into a scam under the pretense that they know you. Some might say this scenario is unlikely, but it is possible, so try to limit what you share publicly, no matter how tempting. It's always a good idea to consciously consider what kind of information the post could give away and what the consequences of that might be. Not only does it protect your identity, but it also protects your loved ones.

Chapter 15

Connecting and Expanding

Now that you understand how both TikTok and Twitch work and how to launch yourself, it's time to utilize both these platforms simultaneously. Many gamers are experiencing great success in both viewership for their streams and attracting new followers and subs. The best part is that it's easier than you think.

Let's start with the fact that you already have content that can easily be edited and tweaked for the TikTok audience. Your live stream highlights can be easily edited as short clips with trendy TikTok music and published to that audience. That can act as an excellent teaser for your Twitch channel, and it draws in viewers and followers on TikTok who love gaming.

When publishing your highlight clips, the hashtags you use matter a lot. If you want to get discovered, you must add #FYP so that the platform can push your content to people likely to enjoy gaming. You should also add more relevant hashtags to the game you're promoting. For example, if you're highlighting your Pokémon game, it's best to go with hashtags related to that, including #pokemon #twitch #streamer #pokemongo #pok #gaming, etc. It would be best if you never attempted to be too general by going with trending hashtags that have nothing to do with your game.

What kind of strategy works best?

The correct answer is - the one you experiment with and see great results. Many gamers apply different strategies to drive traffic from their TikTok to Twitch. Try other things, be bold, and think outside the box. The content you publish on TikTok can be about something other than gaming. It can also be silly stuff that happens before or after your live-streaming. Twitch streamer OfficerStealth posted a video challenge on TikTok where he said that he would do one push-up for every like. That got the community engaged as they tried to see how many push-ups he could do. Although that has nothing to do with gaming, it's still calling him attention and new followers who can potentially convert to Twitch followers.

How to get more viewers to your Twitch broadcast using TikTok.

A new feature will become available once you've grown your TikTok to about one thousand followers. The Livestream version of the platform is similar to Instagram Live. You can broadcast directly from your smartphone, and when you're live, all your followers are usually alerted and invited to join the stream. This is the perfect time to interact with people and encourage them to join your Twitch stream. It's a simple strategy that works incredibly well, even for people with only a few thousand followers on TikTok. OfficerStealth likes to leverage this technique and usually begins a stream on TikTok before his Twitch broadcast starts to attract viewers. Then, he jumps over to Twitch and leaves the TikTok stream running while he streams his gameplay. The results have been pretty impressive as more and more people jump in and raid his Twitch from TikTok. If you will do this, here are a few things to remember. Make sure to start the TikTok stream before the gameplay on Twitch so you can interact with them.

Don't Stop with Just Two.

If you're feeling ambitious and serious about becoming a superstar on Twitch, this section of the book is for you. Chapter 11 of the book shared five tips for beginners, where I encouraged you to leverage social media to boost your growth and viewership on Twitch. Most people will opt for a maximum of two social media channels, but serious streamers often have more than two social networks. You will do that as you learn to make gaming your full-time, high-paying job.

We already mentioned that YouTube, Twitter, Instagram, and Facebook are great for connecting and building an audience that can convert into traffic, but how exactly would you do this?

First, you must set up profiles on these platforms, e.g., YouTube, Twitter, and Instagram. Then, follow best practices when posting content and growing an audience. Here are a few to consider.

#1: Cross-promote; don't cross-post.

That means you should never use the same content on any two channels because no social platforms are identical. People shift their psychology and preferences depending on the channel they're currently on. For example, the same viewer on Instagram might be more intrigued by your Instagram Stories highlights if you created the best moments of your last gameplay. They might follow your account if you usually post funny selfies of yourself before and after streaming. But on YouTube, they might want a more in-depth taste of the last gameplay and actual walkthrough of the game you specialize in. As you can see, this same viewer expects a different experience whenever he interacts with your content across various social networks, so repeatedly showing them the same content would only nauseate him.

A mistake I have seen with new gamers is that they will post a tweet that says, "I posted a new photo to Facebook," They will include a link that people should click. Does it ever work? Nope! You might want to save some time by taking the same content and mass distributing it, but if you're gaining new viewers and fans, you'll need to invest time and tailor your message to make sense to each particular audience.

#2: Use a customized URL to track when posting on social media.

Add trackable links to identify which social network offers the highest and best engagement is vital. If you need to know where the most traffic is coming from, invest your energy in the right place. For example, if you would like to be doing a live promo to get people to show up for your live stream, then half an hour or an hour before your Twitch stream begins, you will need to start prepping your audience on the other social platforms. Suppose you have no idea where the most traffic comes from, and you simply assume it's TikTok when it is, in fact, Instagram; then you might kill all your promo time on TikTok and ignore doing an Instagram Live, which would cost you more viewers on your Twitch stream. So take your time with this. Make sure each link on your social media accounts is tracked, and you invest your time and resources where you see the most traction.

#3: Use Twitter to Test Content Ideas.

If you're going to get a Twitter account, as most gamers do, consider using it to tap into potentially hot content ideas so you can produce more of what your potential viewers are likely to enjoy. Twitter is a great "content lab" for testing how well-received a piece of content is expected to be or gauging how much interest there is for a particular game. Even if you don't have a large following, you can learn much about what viewers want by following peers with bigger Twitter audiences, asking questions in their chats, and reading what others say. This is incredibly awesome when you're thinking about starting a new game.

#4: Use social media platforms to take followers behind the scenes.

Using Stories on Facebook and Instagram, you can easily create unique content that gives followers a different aspect of your life. Over 800 million people are engaged with Stories daily on Facebook and Instagram. What does that tell you? People love watching other people share their stories. It would be best if you leveraged this. Share as much or as little as you like about yourself, but I've found this "behind-the-scenes" content to be highly effective for attracting new people to my Instagram and, ultimately, my Twitch channel. I like to give people an inside peek at how I prep for my gameplays, choose what to play, and who I am. It creates a bond between the Instagrammers who show up for my Twitch streams and me.

Collaborate with other Content Creators

Some streamers see their peers as competition and hesitate to collaborate with existing content creators. That is very shallow thinking because only good can come when teaming with the right streamer. Your journey would be less lonely. You'd have an ally and someone you can grow with. So, if you're wondering whether collabs can help you achieve your results faster, the answer is yes. You must approach this relationship correctly and set clear intentions before reaching out. Working with the right kind of people can also help you create better content that will increase your exposure to a broader audience.

I also recognize that as gamers, we tend to be more introverted, so putting ourselves out there can be scary. Rejection is a big obstacle. If you need a little mindset work to help you become a better communicator and relationship builder, find resources online to help you do that. Once ready to reach potential collaborators, begin with the most appealing social networks. Here's how to go about this.

Consider looking for collaborations on TikTok, YouTube, Facebook Groups, Discord Channels, and through friends.

You can join popular Discord channels where you can start to network with fellow streamers and participate in their conversations so they can see you adding value and sharing your ideas.

When it comes to Discord, you can check out the StreamScheme Discord, Gaming Careers, Twitch Subreddit, and the Bait Squad. One of these Discord channels is bound to resonate with you. For Facebook Groups, you should check out Twitch.TV Streamers Community is active and allows you to network and promote your streams. Don't become spammy, though.

Contact them once you've researched and spotted a few people you like. Make sure you have clear criteria for the people you can collaborate with. It should be someone you feel naturally connected to so that you can leverage that chemistry while creating content. Viewers will be more attracted to good conversation and might be more engaged and interactive with your content. It would be best if you also worked with someone who compliments you. That means they have specific strengths that you lack. I like this approach because it enables both parties to create content and do things others struggle with together. That creates unique experiences for both and more value for the audience. The last thing I want to add is you need to find someone who resonates with your style of doing things and someone who is just as serious and committed to building their channel and community as you are. Stay away from partnerships with jokers because that will lead to disappointment.

There are different types of partnerships that you could get into. We'll talk about that shortly. But first, let's emphasize the importance of taking your time when initiating a partnership. Choosing suitable candidates is only the first step toward building a good partnership. Most people will not be the right fit for you, so take your time and thoroughly check before committing to something serious. You should both be willing to start slow. As with any relationship, dating is essential before marriage. Think of it the same way. So even when you reach out, start by building a friendship, commenting on their stuff, supporting them in any way possible, and building a relationship from there. As long as you remain authentic and sincere, your connection will grow, and collaboration opportunities will become a natural by-product.

Why partner with the so-called competition?

- **Mutual support.**

When you build a relationship and work with someone on the same journey, you will enjoy this process more. It also means you can get twice as much reach for less effort as you distribute and promote your content.

- **Reputation by proxy.**

As a newbie, you can grow your reputation by being associated with other high-authority figures in your niche. The more people see you with streamers they already know, like, and respect, the better they'll think of you.

- **Follower cross-pollination.**

The best part of collaborating with someone is that at least some of your followers will discover this person for the first time and vice versa. That means you get new viewers and followers who are more likely to become loyal fans and subscribers quickly.

Different types of partnerships to consider include:

#1: Commentary and discussion

This type of collaboration emphasizes engagement. Social media loves engagement, and when you and your peer can start a thread on your post or theirs and have a healthy discussion, even if you're not in agreement, it will attract more people and more conversations.

#2: True collaboration

This is when you come together to create content that you can share with your audience. It could be as simple as organizing dual gameplays or tournaments for your communities to participate in.

#3: Cross-promoting content

This type of partnership is relatively easy because all you do is agree to post each other's content and give each other shout-outs. For example, you could receive his latest gameplay highlight from your partner and publish it on your TikTok, then start a conversation around it to invite him and his followers to engage in your post. Your partner would then do the same for you.

The Power of Networks

Networking is vital to your Twitch success regardless of how much of a social animal you consider yourself to be. And if networking has a negative connotation, consider it relationship building. You don't have to spend all your time trying to reach out to everyone on Twitch, but you do need to have a scheduled time daily where you hang out on relevant Discord channels to find people who vibe with you. Connect with people who have a similar concurrent viewer count as yourself. Experts recommend a concurrent viewer count of 50% more than your own.

But don't limit yourself here. You can also connect with people who have a smaller audience. What matters is that you collaborate with people who have personalities that mesh with yours and people who bring fun and entertainment to the table. Think of it this way. If you stream for 12 hours a day, you have 12 hours where no one on Twitch knows about your channel and your fantastic work. Now imagine you've surrounded yourself with a strong team of fellow streamers, and you all support each other, mention each other's channels, and even talk about each other's games while streaming. In that case, even while you're not rushing, word about your brand and channel still circulates across Twitch, thanks to your team. That's the power of a good network.

Grow at Your Own Pace

While talking about big followership and earning thousands of dollars each month is exciting, I want to remind you that everyone's journey will be unique. Learn to embrace your journey and grow at the right pace for you. Even if you hear stories of people who went from zero to hero within six months and you look at your channel twelve months from now and realize you're still not there, don't let that discourage you. I know people who took five years to reach their goal. It took multiple years before my channel became as successful as I had envisioned. And I also know people who blew up within a matter of months. I am still determining how your story will play out, but I'm confident with the right mindset and that persistent attitude, you will hit your desired target.

Conclusion

You've reached the end, but this is only the beginning. We covered a lot in this book, and it might require a couple of reads on some of the earlier chapters to fully grasp all that was shared. By now, you can see the potential of both TikTok and Twitch and how they work together to help you realize your dreams. These platforms have grown significantly recently, and experts anticipate accelerated growth in the coming years.

The opportunities are endless if you are serious about creating an online business and passive income through both channels. You have a basic understanding of setting up each account and creating content that both people and the algorithm will love. You've received detailed strategies on how to grow your audience, where to go to build your network and collaborations, and how to start monetizing your account once you've got enough momentum. I walked you through a very detailed process of identifying your niche and finding gaps you can leverage so that people can learn to associate your brand with something specific that adds value. In all that technical education you've received, remember one thing. Nothing matters if you're unwilling to consistently create beneficial, entertaining, and valuable content for your target audience.

The main focus should never be on making money to become successful and wealthy. It must always remain on building and serving your audience. Most aspiring social media influencers fail because they need the right mindset and approach their online business from a self-focused perspective. Hopefully, this book has given you insights that enable you to see how serving the Twitch community and heavily investing in building yourself as an authentic brand is the best way to create the passive income and online success you desire. All of this is challenging. But if you can stick to it and follow the strategies and tactics outlined in this book, you will live beyond your wildest dreams sooner rather than later. Life on your terms, earning the kind of income your parents never thought possible, and, best of all, having the freedom to live, work, and play wherever and whenever you want. Isn't that why you picked up this book in the first place? That kind of freedom is outside your reach. It's time to take the next step and implement. Good luck, and may the Twitch and TikTok gods favor you on your journey to success online!

Book # 7

Blogging for Beginners

Unlocking Passive Income Streams and Making Money from Blogging

Introduction

There was a time when it was absurd to think one could earn a decent living outside a traditional corporate job. Entrepreneurship never used to be a fantastic title. Creativity and passion were not common qualities encouraged in any home or institution. I am so glad that the world no longer exists. Aren't you?

In today's digitally connected world, opportunities that our grandparents could never dream of are available to every one of us. The Internet has changed everything on this planet. I, for one, am grateful to be part of the generation that can enjoy this new way of life. However, only some know how to take advantage of these opportunities. Sure, you might own a smartphone and laptop, but are you using it, or are you being used by it?

Most people I've met have a desire to change their living conditions. They want to escape the rat race and feel more in control of their lives but have no idea how to do it. I sat next to such an individual on a plane recently. The guy was an insurance agent who had just lost his job and was struggling to figure out how to avoid falling into the pit of despair that awaited him. His car and mortgage payments. The new wife was expecting their first kid. His delayed dream of taking her on an unforgettable honeymoon would never happen. The reality of his loss was enough to stress any man. I wonder why he picked up a conversation with me. Speaking to a friendly stranger might have been out of sheer desperation.

Thankfully, choosing to speak with this stranger introduced him to a world of possibility far beyond anything he had imagined. Our two-hour flight passed by so fast. Ultimately, I encouraged him to reach out since we lived in the same city. He became one of my first students for a blogging program I had created but had yet to push into the market. After seeing how successful he became, I knew it was time to reach more people and help them take more control over their lives.

Something tells me you picked up this book in search of answers to help you achieve that same level of control and freedom. Whether you are just curious about the world of blogging or just lost your livelihood and want to find a different solution that will grant you more freedom and success, I can assure you this is the right book.

I have condensed all my best stuff from my blogging course into this book so that you can get step-by-step guidance on how to start a blog, monetize it, and create the lifestyle of your dreams.

Introduction

What This Book Can Do For You

I have successfully built blogs and online businesses since 2003. During that time, I've had some significant successes and failures. I have also seen the evolution of the blogging platforms and how content creation, distribution, and promotion have changed as people got used to consuming content online. The process of starting a successful can often seem overwhelming. More and more people are also jumping online to create blogs and online businesses, so competition is increasing daily. The good news I am here to give is that it doesn't matter how much competition or how many blogs exist today. Sure, in 2003, getting massive amounts of traffic on any content you posted was more straightforward, but you can still succeed today. The opportunity is still there, but you must have the right strategy.

That is what this book will do for you. I will outline and walk you through the fundamentals of doing it correctly. I'll also share the strategies to turn your blog into a money-making machine. This book is for you whether you think you're too old, too young, not qualified, or whatever other limitations you've put on yourself. You have what it takes to create a successful blog and online business. It takes little money to get started, and no - there is still time for you to join the party.

The Man Who Went From Sleeping On A Couch In His Mom's House To Running A Seven-Figure Business And Traveling The World

In the summer of 2009, while many of his peers were out catching some sun and sea, Grant was busy trying everything possible to ensure he passed his engineering exams. Going through this process proved harder than he had ever imagined. For some reason, Grant struggled to recall critical terms and important concepts that everyone needed to master before the final exam of this particular engineering course. He needed the win badly to land a better-paying job and leave his mom's house.

With the end of his course slowly approaching, Grant decided he would start a notebook and take notes to help him study excitingly. Instead of going the traditional route, he started a small blog. In it, he stored all the messages about this particular course. The blog started getting a lot of traffic as more and more people in a similar situation landed on his notes, looking for help. This encouraged him to keep adding and studying more. Months later, some of Grant's readers emailed asking if he could compile all his notes into an easy-to-read eBook, which he did. And the rest, as they say, is history.

Grant did a great job studying for his course, which enabled him to take the final exam, and he also helped many people in the process. The result led him to publish a simple eBook (more like a collection of his blogging efforts with other secrets on how to take the exam) that started earning him money the first month it was released. In his first month, Grant made $5,000. That was just the beginning. When we met at a blogging conference six years later, Grant ran a seven-figure business that grew from that single blog. He went from breaking, getting rejected from job positions at corporations and sleeping on his mom's couch to blogging full-time, selling products (his own and other people's products), and traveling the world. At some point, Grant had to hire a team to help with his rapid expansion. Since full-time employees weren't something

Grant wanted to have, he leveraged remote working. We'll talk more about this toward the end of the book. He also started getting invited to speak at conferences and teach workshops on how to succeed as a full-time blogger.

Grant isn't a particular case when it comes to blogging success. There are many stories of stay-at-home moms, unemployed people, and even teenagers who build an empire from a single blog. I want to share a simple, practical path you can follow if you desire the same level of freedom, success, and creativity bloggers have attained and continue to achieve as the digital economy booms. Are you ready for this? Buckle up because it's time for lift-off. The blogging adventure awaits.

Section I

Blogging Basics

Chapter 1

Introduction To Blogging

When I started blogging, I made a lot of mistakes. I didn't know what I was doing. Some of those mistakes came back to haunt me later on as the blogosphere matured. In writing this book, I want to ensure you benefit from the painful lessons I've learned so you avoid repeating the same mistakes. Back then, making mistakes was less taxing than today because few people even knew what a blog was. The search engines needed to be more sophisticated and as mature as they are today. The novelty of it all made readers more accepting of certain things. Today, it's a different story. To have a successful blog, you need to know the strategies that help you win with search engines and readers - otherwise, you'll drown in the deep ocean. To ensure your finished product is a winner, we must obey the order of life and begin with the basics. An excellent place to start is understanding what a blog is and what it is not.

What Is A Blog?

The most up-to-date explanation that makes sense to me comes from Hubspot, where they define it as a regularly updated website or web page that can be used for personal use or fulfill a business need. The blog was initially called "WEBLOG," we'll talk more about where blogging originated shortly. Before that, however, I want to mention that a blog is not a blog post. A blog is an entire website, whereas a blog post is an individual webpage that dives deeper into a particular topic contained within the blog. Blog posts are usually sub-topics that are mainly related to the central theme that the blog covers. In the Wild West of blogging, you would find a blog with all kinds of topics jammed into one blogging website. Today, however, as you will find out when we get into the technical aspects of successful blogging, the best blogs cover one topic comprehensively.

A blog should also be distinct from a website. You can have a blog without a website and a blog, but ideally, you should have both. The blog is a section of your website that regularly updates new, fresh content. As you know, a website has static pages, and the information generally stays the same. It's more like a business card. Your website communicates what you do and why, but your blog helps you interact and add value to your audience and potential customers. There are many types of blogs, which I will get into in the next chapter, as well as the benefits of starting your own. But aren't you even a little curious about the origin of blogging? If so, here's a brief history.

A Brief Blogging History

In 1994, Justin Hall created his site Links.net during his undergrad year to store exciting links to him while browsing the web. Many consider him the founding father of blogging, although it wasn't yet called that. At the time, they were more like personal pages or online diaries. Fast forward to 1997, and Jorn Barger coined the term weblog that I used earlier. Peter Merholz shortened the time to blog, and from 2001, there was a growing trend in blogging as more platforms emerged. 2002 marked a significant year for blogging as the first blog search engine, Technorati, was launched. WordPress, a more familiar platform for those reading this, was officially launched in 2003. It was also around the same time Typepad was born, and Meta blogs like ProBlogger.net started gaining significant traction as more people increased interest in blogging as a career.

As you can see, blogging has come a long way since the early '90s. For a long time, it was used more like a personal diary. Then, as the platforms evolved and demand increased, it morphed into an entire industry.

Today, blogging is still used to record personal information, but it goes beyond that. Businesses have joined the camp and are successfully using it to showcase their brands and connect with audiences in new ways. A blog adds a lot of value to any person or business entity.

Blogging Statistics You Should Know

Many statistics are proving the importance of blogging in today's digitally connected world. Here are some stats to be aware of.

- According to RyRob.com, 61% of Americans consume blog content three times more than emails.
- 90% of organizations use content in their marketing efforts, according to DemandMetric. Why? Because 70% of people report they would rather learn about a company through articles than a traditional advertisement.
- Blogs can result in a 434% increase in indexed pages and a 97% increase in indexed links. We are also told by the same DemandMetric report that companies with blogs produce an average of 67% more leads each month than companies that don't blog.
- 77% of all Internet users regularly read blog posts.
- 60% of people purchase a product after reading a blog post.
- 80% of searchers ignore sponsored posts in favor of organic content.
- Content marketing is 62% cheaper than traditional marketing.

With these stats alone, I hope you are getting excited to start on this adventure because, as you can see, both companies and individuals advocate the successful creation of a blog post. Close to 50% of marketers report that if they had to start over again, their main effort would be focused on blogging. With such vital facts backing up your decision to build a profitable blog, let's touch on the benefits of blogging.

Myths About Growing A Successful Blog, You Must Know

Before you can have a profitable blog that earns recurring monthly revenue so you can fire your boss and travel the world, we need to bust a couple of myths. If any of these linger in your mind, eliminate them now, as they will prevent you from achieving your dream lifestyle.

#1: Starting a successful and profitable blog is fast and easy.

If you read the 4-hour workweek and fell in love with doing less and earning more, blogging to grow a seven-figure business is not for you. There is no easy way to go from zero to seven figures with your blog. It will be challenging, and it will be a full-time job at first to get things moving. Blogging is a long-term gain that requires a lot of patience and consistency.

#2: Going viral is the easiest way for my blog to become successful.

Many bloggers obsess about writing a post that goes viral. Don't get me wrong. It's excellent when posts go viral or get into the hands of someone with millions of followers. You'll probably get a massive spike in traffic and even a surge of email subscribers. But all this is very short-lived and unlikely to get you long-term results. I've seen many cases where a blogger got thousands of shares on a post, but everything went back to quiet after that one incident. A viral hit is okay, but don't focus on it. Instead, I want you to invest your time working on creating valuable content consistently.

#3. Niching down on your blog will limit you.

Many newbie bloggers get turned off when I emphasize the importance of choosing a specific niche and blog topic to focus on. They feel it will limit their audience reach and ability to grow fast. That is not true. Blogs that are niche-focused perform better than blogs without. It is especially true if you're starting with limited funding or a team to help you manage tons of volume. Unless you want to be Business Insider or Huffington Post, I encourage you to focus on a specific niche. It will explode your possibilities instead of limiting them.

#4. You have to be a gifted writer to succeed in blogging.

Growing a successful blog that turns into a six or seven-figure business is not about being the JK Rowling or Lee Child. Inborn talent is different than what it takes to succeed as a blogger. Creativity, effort, commitment, a grand strategy, and the desire to share value with your community are what you need. Sure, it looks like blogging is about firing up your laptop, opening Google Docs, and typing away, but there's so much more to it. That is especially the case when you're looking to build a monetizable blog. Your blog is more like running a business. So, even if you need to improve your strengths, you will attract a good audience by setting up the right foundations and producing meaningful content. As your blog grows and you start making money, you can outsource by hiring a ghostwriter. Ghostwriters are an investment, and you'll need to have an allocated budget for that, but it's worth it when you consider the long-term ROI of having someone help you produce world-class content that is engaging.

#5. If you build it, they will come.

I've heard this one a lot! Even from famous, successful bloggers. What a bunch of BS. If you think like this, you won't go very far. Creating high-quality content and setting up a blog readers will love is critical, but your work continues. Content creation is only one half of the equation. The other half is marketing. Obscurity is your biggest enemy. Please read that again and let it sink in. Millions of blogs are active in the blogosphere, and everyone dreams of making it big with their blog. You might have the best message and content, but if your people need to learn you exist, you only have a poor person's blog because those bills won't pay themselves. It would be best if you had a strong marketing strategy. And it would be best if you prioritized the distribution and promotion of your blog as much as you prioritize content creation. I cannot say it enough. Try to create unique content and get it in front of your ideal audience.

Why You Should Start Your Blog Now

The benefits of blogging are too numerous to mention here. I'm going to summarize the ones that stand out for me.

- You'll have an outlet for expressing yourself and sharing your passions with the world.

- Blogging enables you to make money online and create passive income.

- Starting a blog will expand and build a new network. It will attract readers and open up new opportunities to connect with influencers in your industry.

- You can make a difference and help others through your content. If you're putting out great content, you will be helping someone on the web. You can educate, entertain, inform, and motivate like-minded people, which does make a difference in the world.

- Blogging is also a great way to control and build your online identity. Whether you are starting a personal or company blog, the information you put on that blog will help shape your identity so that when people search for you online, they get the right first impression.

- It can lead to new business opportunities—many of which we will mention throughout this book. For example, thanks to your blog, you can become a published author or get hired by a big brand or celebrity. It can also help you land an interview opportunity.

There's no end to the good that can come from you creating a platform representing who you are and making a positive contribution to the marketplace. That list is far from exhaustive, but I want us to move to the meat of this, so turn the chapter, and let's talk about how to start a blog.

Chapter 2

To Get Started with Blogging

Blogging can be overwhelming if you search online for how to get started right. So, I want to eliminate the overwhelm for you, especially if you're a beginner, by outlining simple steps.

Step #1: Determine the type of blog you want to start.

Step #2: Pick a good domain name.

Step #3: Pick a hosting provider.

Step #4: Find your passion, and from it, pick a theme.

Step#5: Start posting on your blog.

Step#6: List building

Step #7: Find traffic

Step #8: Set up income earners

Step #9: Rinse and Repeat.

Don't be fooled. It can be challenging because blogging is profitable, and many people have created lots of passive income. The blogosphere is a jungle where only the fittest survive. You need to get into the game with the right mindset, have the right tools, and put vast amounts of effort into this project before it can become a six-figure business. That simple outline above gives you an overview of the different areas we will dive into. It doesn't have to be complicated; it's not. But it will require your commitment and consistent effort. I will give you all the information necessary to make this a success; I ask that you take massive action.

The Most Popular Types Of Blogs You Can Build

Many different types of blogs cover a wide range of interests and topics on almost anything you can think of. Before dissecting the various steps for building your profitable blog, we should learn about the most popular ones.

- **Business blogs**

These blogs are more professional and often tied to a business entity or corporation. It's a great way to communicate with your customers if you have or plan to start a corporate brand. You can use the blog to educate, inspire, and inform your existing and potential customers about your products and services. Many B2B brands now own a blog, and they report it is a much cheaper and more rewarding investment in the long term.

- **Car blogs**

This is a favorite, although I don't own a car blog. I am an avid reader, and there are many like me out there who enjoy car blogs. Most of the content is around sports cars and luxury vehicles. You could cover many topics, including the latest car models, engineering, features, etc. You might also niche down even more and focus on vintage cars. Some bloggers partner up with local car dealerships to create win-win business opportunities. My favorite blog focuses on vintage vehicles, safety tips for driving, etc.

- **DIY blogs**

These types of blogs have a vast audience. It is a broad category type, so you should niche down and work with a subcategory like construction, woodwork, metalwork, arts and crafts, etc. Content from this type of blog is engaging and practical, promoting much communication.

- **Lifestyle blogs**

These are the most popular, number one, currently trending blog-type on the Internet. You can attract a variety of readers with a lifestyle blog. Readers come to these blogs looking for culture, arts, local news, and politics. So, this is a broad type of blog and can cover a wide range of topics. It isn't as niched as the other types, allowing much more room to play for your content planning and creativity.

- **Fashion blogs**

These are among the most popular types of blogs on the Internet. It's a huge industry, so you can niche almost anything you like if you are creative and have a keen eye for style and fashion.

- **Finance blogs**

Most of us need a lot of help when it comes to efficiently managing finances. That's where your passion or expertise can be of great value to your audience and enable you to build a profitable business. Readers from all walks of life, including young families trying to save for the future or seniors looking for investment advice, will be attracted to your blog if you provide real value.

- **Fitness blogs**

Interest in health and general fitness will increase tremendously as people worldwide seek advice on staying fit. This is an excellent opportunity to build something profitable online as a fitness instructor. It can be around diets, workouts, supplements, etc.

- **Food blogs**

These blogs are also among the top five of the most popular blogs. Many online readers are interested in food recipes, healthy eating, fine dining, etc. If you love food, this might be an excellent blog type.

- **Gaming blogs**

The gaming industry is booming. Many gamers scour the Internet daily, looking for information about the latest games, gaming hardware, game cheats, events they can attend, and so much more. If you're a gamer already, this is a no-brainer. But even if you're not addicted to gaming, you can still start a successful blog if you understand that world.

- **News blogs**

This type of blog is incredibly convenient for someone in journalism. It's a great way to build your authority. You can cover various topics or focus on a particular section. Make sure the type of content you create keeps your perspective and opinion the same because part of what makes a news blog successful is balancing news with your authoritative view. Topics include climate change, scientific innovations, technology, religion, etc.

- **Music blogs**

With a music blog, you can attract readers from all walks of life who share a passion for your music genre. Or you can teach music if you have that skill.

- **Movie blogs**

People passionate about or working in the movie industry often use this type of blog. The blogs contain news, reviews, the latest features of movies, and information about the film industry. Given how vast and wealthy Hollywood is, you don't need me to convince you of the exciting audience that awaits you. If you get good at growing your blog, you can easily get noticed by the right people and get invitations to watch premium shows before the public release of movies so you can help generate more buzz through your blog.

- **Parenting blogs**

New parents are always worried and searching the web for the latest information and best practices. This audience is also among the most engaged and passionate audiences you'll find on the blogosphere, as they are always willing to share and communicate their experiences. A more common niche, should you desire to segment even more, is starting a mom or dad blog. These blogs can include guidance on food, early home education, activities with kids, and more.

- **Personal blogs**

This type of blog has no limit to what it could be. Drawing off the original inspiration of how blogs started in the 90s, you can set up a personal blog to express your thoughts about life, share photos online if you're an artist, or even new concepts you're working on as an employee. A personal blog is excellent for both entrepreneurs and employees. For example, a chef could start a personal blog to share recipes. A photographer could document their startup journey, and a high school student can share their passion for poetry and short stories.

- **Pet blogs**

This type of blog is excellent for attracting pet owners, animal lovers, animal shelters, and people looking for pets. You can share tips on pet grooming, pet food, keeping pets healthy, etc. A great business opportunity here would be to partner up with a brand that deals with pet care products so that as more people discover and love your content, they can also purchase what they need for their pets.

- **Political blogs**

Are you passionate about politics? Good. Your readership will also be just as eager to read your content. This type of blog can be highly lucrative because many emotions are involved in political topics. Where there's emotion, selling is also effortless. You could cover news on politics, analyze political information, or even niche down to a particular political party.

- **Sports blogs**

Every country in the world has different sporting activities with its superstars. Sports blogging is, therefore, a genuine thing. In Italy, for example, where football is vast, there are many highly profitable blogs whereby a blogger gets paid to write content for Serie A (a big football league in the country.) It may also include getting paid by other organizations, such as ESPN in your state, to create content. But even if you're starting, you can start in a niche you love and share the latest events, team news, and more to attract sports lovers.

- **Travel blogs**

In recent years, traveling and digital nomads have become a real trend. Cheap air travel and Airbnb have made it easier for anyone who wants to explore the world to become a travel blogger. People are always looking for travel tips, advice, and destinations, so this might be a great topic if traveling is on your list.

Now that you understand the most popular blogs and the abundance of opportunities that await you to grow a readership and generate revenue, let's address a fundamental question: Which blog topic do I go for?

CHAPTER 3

Your Passion Will Lead to A Successful Blog

This fact will save you tons of wasted energy and resources. No matter what kind of marketing you do or how resourceful you are, you will only do well if you set up your blog correctly.

I'm not referring to the technical setup of your blog here. Instead, I'm talking about the proper foundation. And what does that entail? The niche and topic you choose to focus on and how you structure your content. This chapter ensures you get the blogging foundation properly, starting with the chosen niche and topic.

How To Pick A Profitable Niche

The best advice I can give you, especially if you are working with a tight budget, is to narrow your blog. Going too broad and trying to cover everything under the sun or to compete with big hitters like Business Insider and Huffington Post will lead to no results. It's easier to produce high quality and volume with a massive team consistently. On the flip side, I also want you to avoid niching down too much when starting your blog. If you pick a niche that barely gets organic volume on search, it will be hard to grow your traffic and monetize your blog. So, how do you find that sweet spot that can work for you?

An exercise for niche-picking

Consider what you enjoy, like, find interesting, or are already passionate about. Write down those topics on a Google document. Now, head over to Google Trends and type in each case one at a time. Wait for the results. You will use Google's data to determine what niche to go after. You want a niche that is big enough but not too big. What do I mean by this? Nutrition is too big. Digital marketing is small. Type in these two niches on Google and use them as your benchmark. Your topic should fall somewhere in between.

Deciding On Your Blog Topic

Once you find your niche, developing the central theme around your blog should be easy. But only for some. So, if you're still struggling with writing down blog themes or topics, don't worry; I have your back. At the end of this chapter, I have included a comprehensive exercise that'll walk you through identifying your passion. Why does that matter?

Because if you're not passionate about the blog topic, it doesn't matter how trendy it is. You will need to work longer to make the blog successful.

Blogging is highly competitive, and it takes a lot to stand out. It would be best to consistently create high-quality and large quantities to eventually rank high on search engines. That takes time, effort, and dedication. Without keen interest and passion, it will fail after a few months. So here are my tips for choosing the right blog topic

#1. Make sure it's something you're passionate about. Going for something that fires you up shows in your content, and readers can feel that energy. This, in turn, will help you build that readership and traffic. You're also unlikely to abandon your blog or run out of creative ideas.

#2. Make sure it's something your audience cares about. Nothing is more critical to your blogging success than knowing your audience and giving them what they want. We'll talk more about this later.

#3. Choose a topic that you enjoy researching already. To keep your blog fresh, meaningful, and reliable, you will need to put in some research work to back up your ideas. Becoming an expert on that topic would be best, which means continued education and research.

#4. Find a blog doing what you want to be doing and model their success. This doesn't mean you copy or steal their intellectual property. I am talking about mapping out what they are doing right and adapting it to suit your objectives. Listen, you're not going to reinvent the wheel in the blogosphere. Whatever you want to blog about already exists. If someone succeeds, you'll shave off a few months or years of trial and error by understanding and applying their strategy.

List ten blogs you admire that are either in your niche or completely different. Write down their best-performing article headlines and repurpose them based on your niche and audience. By going for their best-performing articles, you can create your own theme and blog topics similarly, making sure it's relevant to your niche and audience.

Do this with all ten blogs on your list, and you'll have a long list of article titles, blog topics, and a theme that will work. Again, do not steal actual content.

Only pick a niche or blog topic if people say there's money in it. You can monetize any blog as long as it's done right and offers value to people. The secret ingredient goes back to finding that sweet spot between what you care about and what your audience cares about, i.e., what's trending in the marketplace, and consistently producing fresh, meaningful content.

How To Identify Your Passion

I promised to give a practical exercise before moving to the next chapter if you're stuck on your passions. Take out that same Google document once again and answer these questions.

- What skills have you developed so far, either professionally or part-time, that you value?
- What types of classes did you enjoy in high school or college?
- What are your hobbies?
- What's one topic you could go on about for hours if your family or friends let you?
- What do you enjoy reading or learning about?
- If you could invest your time doing or writing about one thing for the rest of your life regardless of income, what would that be?

Chapter 4

How To Pick the Right Name Even as A Newbie

While it might seem easy to pick a name, many bloggers will tell you it's not. Several well-established bloggers had to painstakingly rebrand because their initial name choice proved inefficient in the long term. So, instead of dealing with the consequences of a lousy name three years from now, how about we help you pick a killer name for your blog? Something you'll be proud of for years to come. The best way to accomplish this is to break it into two phases. First, we shall consider the blog topics and the theme you settled on from our previous chapter. I am assuming you completed those exercises. Then, we shall move to phase two and vet potential blog names to see which one feels best.

Analyzing Blog Topics And Themes

Using Google Trends and tools such as BuzzSumo, I assume you now have a clear theme and a precise blog topic based on your passion and audience interests. For practicality, think you have settled on a food blog because you're a foodie. After going through all the exercises from the last chapter, your research may have led you to decide on organic cooking. By looking at the document and all the various article ideas that resulted from going through your top ten food and wellness blogs, perhaps you have words such as cooking, kitchen, organic food, natural, herbs, organic recipes, etc. Sit for a few minutes and brainstorm more words that help describe what you want to offer people when they visit your food blog.

Write down anything that comes up. It might include, "I want to share special ingredients and recipes. Cooking makes people feel good. Good food is what everyone deserves." Continue writing everything down, and once you feel entirely drained, move to the next step. Are there words or phrases on your page that make you feel excited and ready to create content? Circle or highlight these words. This is step one of phase one.

Step two of phase one is about finding your blog's tone of voice. Every piece of writing has a particular style. What tone do you want yours to be? Formal, humorous, casual, simple, approachable, sarcastic, serious, sassy? There's no wrong or correct answer. But I will encourage you to make the tone similar or exactly like your own personality, as that will create congruency when your fans meet and interact with you in the future. It will also help you come across as authentic.

What is your tone of voice?

Simple. Ask a few friends and family members to describe you in three adjectives. I also want you to ask yourself how you want your readers to relate to your blog. A good blog name will be congruent with your desired feeling and tone.

Step three of phase one shifts attention to your audience. As I have often said, blogging and business success will only exist with your audience. So, each step of our journey has to keep checking in with what we know the audience cares about and who they are. In this particular step, we want to lean more closely to who our target audience is. How well do you know your readership? If you answered "not very much," that's a fair answer. There's nothing wrong with not knowing. It takes years of constant blogging to genuinely know who your ideal audience is and what they want. You are starting out and probably need an audience built on any platform. That means you need benchmarks or data to help you accurately identify who your ideal audience is. That's okay; I've got your back.

How To Identify Your Target Audience When Starting Out

The best and fastest way to identify your audience is to create an audience persona of the reader you believe will benefit from your information. Your best readers are often similar to you because they share the same values and passions. So please open a new Google document and title it Target Audience Research. This is where you will brainstorm and record everything you can about your audience. Start with shared values. Answer the following questions.

- What are five commonly shared values between you and your ideal reader?
- What passions and interests do you suspect you might have in common? Going back to the example of the food blog, shared passions would be food, maybe wine or cheese, depending on what you want to focus on.
- What are some of the characteristics of your ideal target audience?

I want you to research the ten blogs you wrote down again. Please pay attention to the comments section; notice what they named their blog and their tone of voice. If they attract you, they will attract your desired audience, too. Learn as much as you can from them. That will let you know what your audience cares about and how to approach them.

With all this information, it's time to write down some blog names. The last step of this first phase is brain-dumping any words. Did a comment from a reader in your favorite blog stand out? Could you write it down? Go through the notes you've made so far and start paring words that feel right together. Don't worry about being perfect in the first round. Explore ideas and let your imagination run wild. Once you have made a list of names that stick, let it simmer for a day.

Come back after an afternoon or a day and look at that list again. Now, I want you to narrow it down through the lens of your main blog topic, the central theme, the tone of voice you will use, and what you think your audience will be attracted to. Only settle for the one you love. Give yourself enough time (even if that means sleeping on it) to find the one that sparks some energy and gets you excited. Please note that I have yet to ask your friend partner or focus group for their opinion. Bringing in people's views during a creative moment is bad for your self-confidence and the final product. Trust in your ideas and creativity.

Phase two is where we take our new name and vet it out. Now that we feel confident with the chosen term, we can test it and share it for feedback. The first place we do our vetting is to check if the domain name is available and whether there are any potential conflicts. If the domain name isn't unavailable, return to the drawing board. I encourage you to set up your blog on a .com because anything else is a disadvantage and could create conflict if the owner of the .com has trademarked the name. I will share a list of tools and resources you need to set up a profitable blog, but for this exercise of finding a word, I recommend that Namecheap.com vet your blog name.

The second step in phase two is to consider how the name looks as a domain name and whether the reader will misinterpret it for something you're not. For example, there's a site that carries the potential of an unfortunate misinterpretation (penisland.com). The site is Pen Island. But what did you first see? A lot of people need help seeing the pen at first. You don't want the same misunderstanding to occur. So make sure it looks good as a domain and reads as you intend unless you want to play dirty tricks. The other thing to think about is how relevant the name is.

If it's something other than what your audience can connect with, you're better off brainstorming a different name. You want your blog to remain TOM (top of mind) with your audience, and if you pick a name that they can't easily remember or connect with, it beats the purpose. It also doesn't make sense to start a blog called First-time Mom, Happy Mom to Lory, Young and Twenty-one, etc. These are all great, but they have no staying power. You will be twenty-one for a short time, and if you're planning to have more kids, it's probably not a good idea to have a blog with the name of your first child. Trendy words like YOLO might also sound terrific. Still, they will become irrelevant soon, and then your blog will appear outdated before you know it. I encourage you to focus on long-term relevancy and staying potential. Once you feel the name is vetted out properly, it's time to run it by a few people.

Please list people whose opinions you value and tell them in person or through a call and notice how you feel and how they respond. Consider if you feel awkward as you speak the words out loud. Use the feedback from trusted people who know you well (not your Facebook group) to make a final informed decision.

It did take a lot of effort to pick your killer blog name, but the reward is well worth it. Now, you will have a name you will be proud of further down the line. A word that aligns with your values, audience needs, and the topic you want to write about. If something doesn't feel right by the time you complete phase two, I'm sorry to say this, but you'll need to scratch that name and begin phase one again. Adjust this process as you see fit because no one size fits all exists. The process could take five minutes, five hours, or five days, depending on how you want to approach it. The critical thing is to pick a name intentionally that is relevant and has growth potential.

CHAPTER 5

Hosting Your New Blog and Tools of The Trade You Must Know

There are many options to choose from when it comes to blog hosting. Some are free; others require an annual investment. In this chapter, we talk about free and paid. I will also share the essential tools of the trade to set up your blog like a pro, even if you're a newbie and need more tech experience.

Free Blog Hosting

There are two big giants when it comes to free blog hosting. WordPress.com and Blogger. There's nothing wrong with a free blogging platform. Many successful bloggers, including myself, started with a free WordPress back in the day. Going big and monetizing a blog properly requires a paid hosting platform because self-hosted sites offer more flexibility and features. Whether you start with a self-hosted or free platform, you still have to experiment and go through the learning curve necessary. Depending on your situation, a free solution might be the best first step. There is no ultimate best platform. It would help if you went for the one that most fulfills your needs and budget. However, for the free platform, I want you to get something easy to use, has zero maintenance hassle, and offers as many perks as possible. Almost all free platforms will have limited customization, so if you already know what you want your blog to look like, you're better off skipping the rest of this because your needs will be fulfilled with a paid platform. Here are my top five recommendations as of the time of writing this book.

#1. WordPress.com

This is the giant when it comes to blogging platforms. Launched in 2005, WordPress.com is still going strong, with over four hundred and nine million people viewing over twenty-one billion pages belonging to this platform's network of blogs. According to WPbeginner, WordPress powers more than 30% of all websites on the Internet. In other words, it's prevalent among bloggers.

Almost any type of blogger will do well with WordPress.com. The platform offers many design options and way more customization than free platforms. If you start with WordPress.com, you can easily transition to a self-hosted WordPress later. Unfortunately, this platform isn't built for business, and there's a good chance WordPress Ad banners will appear next to your content.

#2. Blogger

Blogger is another free blogging service owned by the parent company Google. All you need is a Google account, and you're ready to get started. It is 100% free and easy to use, and you can manage it without technical skills. Unfortunately, as with many free platforms, you cannot customize your blog or add new features.

#3. Medium

This is great for anyone and everyone. I still have an active medium account because I use it to repurpose my content. More on that later. Since its launch in 2012, the platform has grown to a healthy community of writers, bloggers, journalists, and experts. Medium is minimalistic. It's a one-size-fits-all blogging platform, which is excellent if you don't care about design and customization.

What I love most about Medium is that it has a built-in audience of over sixty million unique readers and is growing. It's suitable for all blog types. Your blog will look super professional, and I find it more business-friendly than wordpress.com because you can monetize your blog with the Medium Partner Program. There's minimal tracking ability and almost no customization of the blog. It would be best if you also had the flexibility to use your domain name, so I recommend it as a secondary blog.

#4. Tumblr

I am including Tumblr on my list even though it's not a classic blogging platform because I've seen it work well for certain bloggers. It is a microblogging platform with social networking features such as sharing tools. I am a fan of this microblogging platform because it's free, easy to use, and you can even get a free subdomain. I also like that it comes with an integrated social media component, which means (unlike WordPress) you have a pre-existing community to tap into. That makes building up your readership a little easier. You can also add videos, images, audio formats, GIFs, etc. without a hassle. For bloggers who need more visual elements in their content, this is a great platform to consider. As with all free media, the main limitation is customization, and you can't add any new features to your blog. It's also challenging to import or move your existing Tumblr blog elsewhere once you feel ready to get a paid option. It's challenging but not impossible, so if you dig it, go for it.

Paid Blog Hosting

#1. Wix

Wix is a paid platform offering a 14-day free trial for you to test out. It is primarily a website builder that can also be used to start a fully functional blog. Many bloggers have successfully created blogs and monetized on this platform. It's an all-in-one drag-and-drop website builder that makes it fast, efficient, and easy to use. It's a great way to own your blog, even if you need to be tech-savvy, as long as you're happy paying the subscription fee. Wix has lots of beautiful-looking templates that you can customize. It also comes built-in with analytics, SEO features, and all the standard things you'd need, like commenting and social sharing options.

#2. Squarespace

Squarespace is another excellent paid option, especially if you plan on having an image-rich blog. This is a premium, fully managed, and hosted website builder. The platform has a limited range of templates and may need to be a better fit for every type of blogger, but it has incredible mobile-optimized templates. They've also integrated with Getty Images, Unsplash, and Google AMP, so you'll have plenty of images to choose from. The platform has a built-in analytics tool, and SEO features that can help your content rank. Squarespace supports audio files and sign-up forms, and you can add plugins or additional modules as needed.

#3. Wordpress.org

This self-hosting site turns your free WordPress.com into an autonomous blogging platform. Once you switch to the paid version of WordPress, you'll gain access to thousands of free and premium themes and plugins. You can also customize and monetize your site as you see fit.

#4. Weebly

Weebly is similar to Wix in that it's primarily a website builder you can use to build a blog. It has an easy-to-use interface with a drag-and-drop builder. There are several free themes; however, you need a paid plan option to customize or monetize your blog thoroughly.

Essential Tools Of The Trade

Starting a new blog can get overwhelming. Everyone tries to convince you of a new must-have or essential plugin that your blog needs—most of these shiny bells and whistles are just unnecessary expenses when you start. So, let's talk about the essentials your blog needs to succeed.

Domain Registrar.

Register your blog name, and make sure it points to your blog. Also, make sure you make it a private registration so that your details aren't shared freely whenever someone types your domain name into the Whois database—no need to overthink this part. As I said earlier, many solutions exist, but let me share my go-to domain registration platforms.

Recommended companies:

- Namecheap
- GoDaddy
- DreamHost
- HostGator
- Bluehost

Hosting Platform

A hosting platform is non-negotiable, especially if you want a blog that can turn into a six-figure business. Depending on your budget, you can find a hosting plan that suits you from reputable companies.

Recommended hosting platforms

- Bluehost.

- GreenGeeks.
- Dreamhost.
- A2 Hosting.
- Hostinger.

Themes

Many themes exist, especially if you set up your blog on WordPress. Only some themes are as good as they promise, so be vigilant to avoid falling for an awful theme choice. I need help recommending a specific theme because a fashion blogger will have different needs than an educational or health blogger. The best advice I can give is to test the free theme, and if you like it, only then should you invest in an upgrade. Alternatively, try to invest in a theme that is designed specifically for your niche market. Another good recommendation is to shop in marketplaces like ThemeForest and Studio Press. Both these marketplaces showcase high-quality themes from respected developers and are very trustworthy.

Email CRM

Start list-building from day one of launching your blog. This is yet another non-negotiable. There are many options, ranging from free to super expensive and complex. You can choose an email hosting service like Gsuite, mainly if you use their other Google services. Alternatively, you can get a CRM that helps you send newsletters and broadcasts.

Recommendations for email CRMs, both free and paid

- MailChimp.
- Aweber.
- ConvertKit.
- Getresponse.
- Drip.

Tracking And Analytics

From the moment you hit publish on your first post, make sure your tracking and analytics are all setup. Analytics helps you know how much traffic you're getting, where the traffic is coming from, and what content performs best. This is crucial to growing a readership and eventually monetizing your blog.

Recommendations for Analytics

- Google Analytics.
- Jetpack.
- Exact Metrics.
- Heap.

- Crazy Egg.

Site Performance

To help keep your site loading time efficient, I recommend keeping the number of plugins minimum. By getting a plugin like Jetpack, you can get almost everything you need in one plugin. However, you will need something to help you with your images and graphics, which also tend to slow down a site. **Consider getting one of the following tools for this.**

- Smush.it.
- BJ Lazy Load.
- Incapsula.

SECTION II

Copywriting, Content Creation Hacks, And SEO

Chapter 6

Content Creation Like A Pro

Now that you understand the technical aspects of starting your profitable blog, it's time to move on to the meat of this project. This is where most of your effort will go. The technical aspects should take up little time, and less is needed when starting. As long as you know your budget and you've decided on the look and feel of your blog, I encourage you to pick and choose the right tools and get the show on the road.

The real work begins when you sit down to create those high-value posts that will attract and retain new visitors. Blogging is not easy. Having topic ideas or a desire to share your insights with the world is one thing. Putting it down into words, audio, or video and formatting them in a way that is easy to digest is an entirely different game. That's why I am devoting the following two chapters to content creation. I want to give you the basics for creating unique blog content, how to be more organized, and where to find more inspiration when your writing well runs dry.

I will also name some valuable resources and blogs you can learn from to make your writing more impactful. We have much to cover in this book section, so let's jump in.

How To Create Blog Posts That Generate Traffic

Have you come across blogs crushing in producing high-quality content and engaging readers? You wouldn't still be reading this book if you didn't want to create a blog that performs at that same level. Want to know the secret to that magic?

It's not magic at all. To produce a top-performing blog, you need a process that helps you work efficiently. You need to create quality content, and yes, you need to understand the power of both content marketing and copywriting.

The difference between copywriting and content marketing

Most newbie bloggers need help with these two terms because they use them synonymously, which leads to half-baked results. Copywriting is putting words together to get a reader to take a specific action. That can be in written or spoken form. Most of the time, copywriting is done to drive a decisive action, such as a purchase, booking an appointment, or subscribing to your email list. On the other hand, content marketing involves creating valuable free content to attract prospects and convert them into repeat buyers. Both these terms are needed, and they can work together beautifully if you become intentional with your blogging. Your blog should be a combination of copywriting and content marketing. If you go through the trouble of setting up this blog and creating content for it, I encourage you to practice improving your copywriting skills so that more people can click on your post when they come across it.

Most bloggers (the ones who blog as a hobby and never earn a six-figure income) sit down to write content without a clear workflow and copywriting skills. They never educate themselves on copywriting because they assume it's only for marketers and salespeople. Copywriting is mainly sales letters and direct mail, but that's not all. Copywriting is also writing great headlines and enticing calls to action. You are grievously mistaken if you think that all it takes to have a successful blog is to write and post daily.

There are many moving parts when crafting high-value blog posts, but once you get the hang of it, you might be surprised how fast and easy it becomes. You can push out fantastic content in record time with time and much practice. But it all begins with getting the right strategy in place.

The Blogging Strategy

Your blogging strategy must include the following

- Content strategy
- Editorial calendar
- Blog post templates
- Blog writing process workflow
- A blog post checklist
- The plan for publishing, promoting, and repurposing your content.

You can easily download Most of these things on Google by searching for free templates, e.g., A content strategy template. You can then fill in the blanks to suit your needs. I want to focus on content creation and how to structure that first blog post, which will give you a basis for a blog post template.

How to write a great blog post in eight simple steps:

#1. Ideation

#2. Research

#3. Outline

#4. Headline

#5. Introduction

#6. Body

#7. Conclusion

#8. Visual content, Editing, and SEO

Elements Of A Great Blog Post

Before you can write a great post, knowing what elements go into a great post is essential. It would be best if you had a strong headline that grabs attention. It would be best to ensure the first opening lines are attention-grabbing and share critical insights that hook people. Next, you need to make sure there's a bold promise. Something that will entice your reader to stay and continue consuming your content.

Remember to start with an emotional connection as you get into the meat of your blog post, then dive deeper into more tactical or practical content. Depending on the length of your post, you can have multiple calls to action sprinkled throughout the page, but always remember to add a conclusion and a call to action at the end. Now that you know this, it's time to dissect each of the nine steps mentioned above so that you can hit the ground running as soon as this section is done.

#1. Ideation

This is the most natural step because you have just invested a lot of time in developing a theme, blog topic, etc. That means you probably already have a list of ideas you want to write about. Create an idea bank on a spreadsheet or Google sheet to have a backlog of views over the coming months. Some of the questions you want to ask yourself now include: What are the hot topics people discuss in your niche? Do you have any burning issues you feel are under-discussed?

#2. Research

Now that you have broad ideas on what you want to write about, it's time to research it to ensure we pick the right keywords. Why? Because we want to make sure the content is being searched and that we add the most appropriate keywords for SEO purposes. What we are looking for specifically is keyword volume and difficulty in ranking.

Ubersuggest is a great free tool that offers a lot of value. It can help you determine the best keywords, volume, difficulty in ranking, and the top-performing content covering the same topic.

Google Trends is yet another fantastic tool. I already mentioned this tool before when picking your blog topic. Use it to check for exciting trends under specific subtopics of your central blog theme and topic. Ahrefs is another top-rated keyword research tool that does far more than research. It also helps with your SEO and competitor analysis. This is a premium tool.

Now that you have the tools and the keywords for your blog idea, more is needed to stop there. Research is more than just keyword-picking. It's about gathering data that supports your claims. You need to back up your knowledge with reputable sources to link out for further reading and validation. It also helps to see what others have written about the topic. Don't plagiarize. Get inspired, quote them a statement or two that stands out, and work hard to create content that surpasses what they've created.

Thinking beyond Google with your research. Aside from Google, you can use research tools such as Wolfram Alpha. This tool works exceptionally well for food bloggers or bloggers dealing with data, numbers, etc. You can also research online archives like the national archives, archive.org, Google Books, Library of Congress, state libraries, historical archives, etc. Yes, research takes work and time commitment. If you want to become an authority on your topic, put in the effort.

#3. The post outline.

After devoting all that time to keyword and content research, it's time to start with the post's outline. The reason we outline first is that we want to organize your thoughts so that they make sense to the reader. Writing without a strategy is messy because it's like driving to a new destination without direction, and the result is often complex for the consumer. The post outline will save you a ton of time. Trust me on this. So here's a simple post-outline template for you to copy.

Your Blog Post Outline Template

Introduction

Main teaching 1

- •Expand on why that teaching is enjoyable.
- •Another reason this is interesting.
- •One more reason why this point is interesting.

Main teaching 2

- •Expand on why that teaching is enjoyable.
- •Another reason this is interesting.
- •One more reason why this point is interesting.

Main teaching 3

- •Expand on why that teaching is engaging.
- •Another reason this is interesting.
- •One more reason why this point is interesting.

Conclusion

Additional research and recommended reading

#4. The Headline

It would be best to have an attention-grabbing headline that would cause someone to click on your post. Without it, all your hard work goes to waste because it doesn't matter how great the content is; no one will ever read it.

The headline should capture your audience's attention and communicate the value they will receive. A great headline is usually punchy, delivers a clear benefit, and includes an action verb.

A free tool that can help you create awesome headlines for free is Headline Analyzer. Be patient and write about twenty headlines when coming up with a headline. They don't need to be clickbaity. Just focus on nailing the fundamentals.

#5. The Introduction

Although the introduction is essential to your blog post, please feel free to make it unforgettable immediately. When you sit to write it, allow yourself to be clunky. Let the introduction launch you into the writing spree. After you're done, you can return, revisit it, and add the appropriate hooks.

To make an introduction that entices people to keep reading, consider your unique angle for this post. Ensure the value you bring here aligns with the benefit you offered in the headline. A classic technique used by clever copywriters is WIIFM. It stands for - what's in it for me? Everyone who lands on your introduction consciously or unconsciously asks that, so make sure your introduction offers the kind of value they would find interesting. You could start with an interesting fact or a shocking statistic about your topic. Questions are also great to help the reader understand the answers covered throughout your blog post.

You can also use a story that intrigues or an anecdote that catches your readers' attention. However, ensure these tie in with the topic at some point. Example of Introduction: Coffee is incredible. It's considered humanity's best survival juice or the only morning hug your brain needs. What would Monday morning be without a strong coffee? Usually, every morning is made perfectly bearable by coffee... until it spills on your white shirt. And that almost always happens when you're either getting ready for an important event or meeting, running late, or both. But instead of ruining your day and the fabric, we have a few options for fixing it fast without covering up with an ugly borrowed sweater.

#6. The Body

Writing the blog post's body should flow naturally once you set the stage with your introduction. Keep the paragraphs simple, brief, and to the point. I recommend up to three sentences in a paragraph. That ensures your blog post is easy to read and skim through. Create sub-headlines wherever appropriate and add relevant points to support each header. In the template I shared above, consider each primary teaching a sub-headline. Support the sub-headline with facts and relevant information by adding two or three paragraphs for each bullet point. Whenever possible, add external and internal links to support your post further.

#7. The conclusion

Wrap it all up with a conclusion that recaps the main idea of your blog post. At the most basic level, you want to summarize what you said, resolve the problem, and suggest an action the reader can take.

Some bloggers write their introduction and conclusion first. Then, they jump into the main content. Others write it in order as detailed in the template. There's no right or wrong. Go for what feels natural to you.

#8. The visual elements, editing, and SEO

The last step you need to make before publishing and distributing your content is a combination of three things: First, you re-read and edit the draft you created. Sometimes, you should give yourself a break for a few hours to a day before you do the final edits. Fresh eyes will help you see any editing or grammar errors better. As you edit, you can also do an SEO check, which brings us to our second thing.

SEO check can be as simple or complex as your brain can handle. We will discuss SEO in the next chapter, but this is when you will do some SEO checks to help ensure your content ranks on search engines.

Lastly, we need the images, GIFs, and whatever else you want to add to your blog post. Now that you've edited and read through your post, it's easy to know which types of images to include in the blog post. You can hire a designer to help you create graphics, assuming your budget allows. Alternatively, you can do it yourself using free- or low-cost design tools.

If you work with a designer:

Designers are great because they seem to add magic to your post. I started hiring designers to help with my content once I started making some recurring income on my blog. So even though I talk about working with a designer, know that I started with zero budget doing all the graphics work myself. All the excellent tools I'm about to share with you didn't exist then, so it was a lot of manual labor! But I'm getting ahead of myself here. For the designer, you must give clear instructions on where you want the graphics to go and what you'd like. Include the exact copy and other information that they should know about. If you're working with a sound designer, they should be able to produce something extraordinary. If you want it to be a quote, illustration, or regular image, I suggest you let them know in the instructions to avoid miscommunication.

If you DIY (my preference)

This is where I started and where I recommend every severe blogger sharpen their craft. It's not that much of a headache to create professional-looking designs today. That includes people with no previous graphic design experience. Some new free or inexpensive ones include Canva (my favorite), Piktochart, and Venngage. These tools allow you to create amazing graphics quickly.

How many graphics should your blog post have?

Different experts offer different advice. Neil Patel, a famous long-time blogger and marketing influencer, says you should add an image every 350 words. Eric Hochnerger recommends as many as your content will justify. Both pieces of advice make sense to me. My opinion is as many as you need to make your content appealing and valuable. Now that we've walked through the creation of the blog post, it's time to turn our attention back to SEO.

Resources To Help Improve Your Copywriting And Content Creation

- Neil Patel's blog
- Copyblogger
- Wordstream
- Problogger

CHAPTER 7

SEO - Part I

Only two forms of traffic can find their way to your blog—Organic and Paid traffic. Anytime you have to pay for traffic to your blog in any way, shape, or form, that is considered paid traffic. Organic is when traffic flows into your ecosystem without paying for it. For all bloggers across various industries, organic traffic is significant to us. The longevity of our blogging business depends a lot on organic traffic, especially the one that comes from search engines. That is where the understanding of SEO becomes critical.

Search Engine Optimization (SEO) is a robust topic; it could take up an entire book. There are courses, training programs, and blogs focused on SEO. Bloggers can hire SEO experts for thousands of dollars a month because of how complex it can get, and sure, there are some benefits to hiring an expert. However, the return on investment will take a while to be experienced, so make sure you know what you're doing before hiring someone. I will do my best to give you basic SEO knowledge in this chapter and tips on making it work in your favor when starting a blog.

What Is SEO?

SEO is getting targeted traffic to your blog or website from a search engine like Google. You can rank high on a search engine in the unpaid (organic) section if done right. But Google isn't the only search engine. There's Bing, Yahoo, and even YouTube that all operate on search-based parameters. The purpose of creating SEO-friendly content is to help drive organic rankings to your blog, which means high-quality traffic you don't need to continue paying for, like in the case of paid ads, which we'll cover later in the book.

With SEO, there are three factors to consider: Your audience (the searcher), your brand, and the search engine. You must pay attention to these three to ensure your SEO efforts succeed. Most people know that SEO is about optimizing the blog post, but only some understand what needs to be optimized. Have you ever asked yourself that question? Is it the writing, design, or the links that need optimization? They all need optimization, and that's not all.

How Search Engines Work

It's good to understand how search engines like Google work so you can see the value of investing in SEO. Since Google owns the lion's share of search engine power, I will use it as the prime example, but know that the same principles apply to all search engines. When searching for something in Google, an algorithm works in real-time to bring you what the search engine considers the "best" results. Google will scan its index of hundreds of billions of pages in milliseconds to determine the best answer for your search. That content will naturally rank on the front page (your ultimate goal with SEO).

You might ask yourself, "How does Google decide the best result?" That's a good question. None of us know the complete answer. Google only shares bits of information here and there, but it's a best-kept secret for the most part. Here's what we know based on filed patents and statements from Google. They care about relevancy, i.e., the key phrase you put in has to be in the content they serve you. They also rely on authority, i.e., is your website trustworthy, how many other pages or sites are linking to your page, etc., and they focus on usefulness. That means they care about how user-friendly and valuable the content will be for the searcher. If the page is well organized, and people have an easier time interacting with it, Google will rank that page higher, even if it has less authority and links.

Why Is SEO Important For Your Blog?

The simple answer is that search is a massive source of website traffic. The current statistics on the number of blog posts published every second stand at 24. That's a considerable number. Think of how many blog posts will be issued after reading this chapter. On any given day, the term "SEO" gets a volume search of about 2.2 million on Google. You don't need me to tell you that SEO will be essential for your blogging strategy. With it, you can rank on the front page of Google and other search engines, which could mean the difference between your seven-figure blogging business and a failed blogging venture.

Imagine you have a food blog post on making Vegan Spanish Paella. You want the search engine (mainly Google) to like your content enough that it's willing to show your post as a top result to anyone who searches for the phrase "Vegan Spanish Paella." It would be best if you had the magic touch of search engine optimization to make this happen.

SEO runs very deep, as I said earlier. There is on-page SEO, off-page SEO, white hat and black hat SEO, etc. I will introduce these main terms within SEO and encourage you to continue your education as you grow your blog.

White Hat Vs. Black Hat SEO

There are two camps in the world of SEO, and you've got to pick which side you're on. Black hat SEO is a short-term strategy for those who want to make a quick buck. Instead of focusing on the formula I shared of your brand, audience, and search engine, this strategy focuses on tricks and gimmicks to get ranked even at the expense of being spammy. It includes stuffed keywords, invisible texts, duplicate content, cloaking or redirecting the user to another site or page, and links from sites with non-relevant content.

White hat SEO is the opposite. As you might have guessed, this is how to build a sustainable and profitable seven-figure blogging business. The strategy here requires you to create content that the searcher will enjoy, something that will make your brand, and, last but not least, optimized content that the search engines like to promote. Yes, this takes more time, effort, and dedication. Isn't everything worthwhile in life? White hat includes having well-labeled images, adding relevant links and references, and creating unique, relevant content with proper grammar and spelling. It also requires the standard recommended formatting and individual page titles.

I must mention that some bloggers have found a way to create a gray area where they operate with a mix of white and black strategies. Call this the gray hat SEO strategy whereby you're trying to rig the game and get a distinct advantage intentionally. Think about guest blogging. Depending on how you do it, that can easily fall into this gray area of SEO, significantly when your site suddenly spikes with traffic after guest posting for a vast place. Given how competitive blogging is, it's hard to say whether gray hat SEO is good or bad. I'll let you investigate further and conclude. SEO is constantly changing, and the game's rules often must be defined. It would be best to decide which path to take and educate yourself on the risks, downsides, and upsides of that choice to know what you're signing up for.

On-page SEO

On-page SEO is a tactic that ensures Google can find your blog posts so they can be indexed in the search results. It's also about having relevant, detailed, and helpful content that includes the search phrases you want to rank for. The Google algorithm will scan your blog post to see which terms show up over and over again. Google says, "This page must be about this repeated keyword!" So, we want to ensure that the chosen keyword or phrase is intentionally chosen and sprinkled throughout the post without overstuffing it.

Here is a simple formatting template to copy.

Headline Title Optimization - Make sure you use your primary keyword or key phrase in the title of your blog post. This is the first rule of on-page SEO. Your title tag should summarize what your blog post is all about and promise a benefit to the reader while telling Google what your page is about. For example, if you're writing about how to make Vegan Spanish Paella in record time, that headline should include the critical term "Vegan Spanish Paella."

Body Content Optimization - You'll want to sprinkle the keyword where appropriate throughout the blog post's body. Always think about the reader and how helpful the content will be. Do not overdo this. Google only needs to see it appearing a few times to realize that your page is focused on that topic. For example, I use or repeat my keyword 6 to 10 times on any post. My posts are usually over 3000 words long, so that's low density. But it's often enough for Google to get the gist and rank my content on page one.

Meta Description Optimization - Although Google officially announced that they don't pay much attention to the description, optimizing it is still essential. Your readers will use the report to determine whether to click the link. Adding the keyword to entice people to click the result is better. Another benefit of using the primary keyword in the description is that it will increase the chance you show up in the SERPs if someone searches for that exact term.

Synonyms and Variations - Use synonyms and variations of your target keyword through the blog post for further on-page optimization. This can also help your page rank for multiple keywords so you can end up on the front page of many searches. Find what's known as LSI keywords, which means closely related terms. You'll get suggestions by going to Google and

Bing and typing the keyword into the search bar. Use these suggestions within your content. For example, I just went on Google and typed the keyword "Vegan Spanish Paella." I got about 53,300 results in 0.70 seconds. That tells me we can rank for this term with a bit of work and creativity. At the bottom of the page, Google gave me more LSI terms that can go into our blog post, such as vegan paella brown rice, vegetable paella with chickpeas, vegetable paellas halloumi, vegan paella bosh, Spanish vegan recipes, etc. If you can use any or all of them, go ahead. These are some of the pro tips that the best marketers use to rank on the front page of Google, and now, you can enjoy the same thanks to your investment in this book.

Image Optimization - This is the next major component of on-page SEO. Search engines cannot read an image as quickly as text. We need to help them understand the file by adding an alt text to the image with the proper description and, if possible, the main keyword. If you have something like a fashion or food blog where lots of visuals and graphics are needed, this part is critical to your ranking. Always give your image a descriptive filename, add an image alt text, and finally, give the image a title. The alt text and image title can be the same.

The last thing I will mention before moving on is the user experience and the quality of the content. Always create rich, valuable content and be as detailed as possible. The more people get value from your blog post, the more they will share and keep reading your blogs. Famous bloggers like Neil Patel have become extremely popular online because their content is exceptionally high-value and user-friendly. Check out Neil Patel's blog to see what I mean. The web page is crisp and clean, with excellent user experience, and his content is always super detailed and well organized. No wonder he gets millions of viewers each month.

Off-page SEO

Off-page SEO is a little more complicated to control, but there are things you can do to help things work in your favor. One of the things you can start doing is establishing strong trust and authority with your blog. Try to get authoritative blogs and websites to link back to you, especially those that speak on your topic. We can talk later about how to build these types of relationships, but again, we want to do something other than get a link. Do it because you have created content that would benefit their readers. You can do things that will encourage mainstream media sites to feature you. This will take time because it means you need to create a lot of content and stand out in your niche, but hey, if you're thinking long-term, then this is doable.

Another thing you can do is manage your bounce rate. Bounce rate measures how many people view only one page on your site before leaving. The remedy for this is to entice readers to spend more time on-site. Do this by ensuring you have great content and creative ways of leading them down a rabbit hole where they can binge-read some more of your stuff. You can also test your current loading time to ensure it's taking less time, as that can be a turnoff. How user-friendly and beautiful is your blog experience? I mentioned this previously, but it's worth repeating here. If your user interface puts people off or needs to be better organized (for example, your HTML code needs to be in order or your blog post paragraphs need to be shorter), the eyes will wear out sooner rather than later, and you will lose a reader.

SEO - Part I

One last tip that can help your readers increase on-site time is incorporating videos into your blog posts. Buffer shares some excellent tips to get started with video. Find that link in the resource section of this book. People love watching videos; it can be the perfect way to keep people glued to your page.

Your brand identity is another component of off-page SEO to consider, although most bloggers skip over it. Brand building takes time and effort but will pay off in the long run. Think about it. If you need to buy new tires for your car, knowing how important your safety is, which link result are you more likely to click on? The one from an unknown blog or a company you recognize and trust? Branding helps build trust.

In the same way, you'd likely click on a company you already recognize; people will be more inclined to click on your link whenever your search result shows up if they become aware of your brand. Every effort to get your brand name out there through organic and paid means will pay off. Have a consistent brand identity; with time, people will recognize and associate your brand with the topic you cover. This will increase trust, demonstrate to Google that your domain has authority, and improve search traffic.

I want to mention one more category with off-page SEO that you can influence subtly. Consider the fact that all searchers see results relevant to the country they are in. Search engines interpret words differently based on location. Someone in the US searching for the keyword "comforter" will be served blankets for their bed. The exact keyword in the UK might produce pacifiers because that term is commonly used in that context. So, how can you use these subtle personal factors to your advantage? A couple of things you can do. First, make sure you make your keyword selection very conscious of the country you wish to target the most if you want to have a multilingual site and reach people outside your country. Just make sure to set up the infrastructure right.

However, expect that it will cost you to have an excellent multilingual site with accurate translations. Depending on how robust your blogging platform is, you can also set up geo-targeting. The second thing you can do is encourage socialization on the blog. Social media can help with your off-page SEO because Google serves more of your content to people who have engaged with other social platforms like Twitter, Facebook, YouTube, etc. The more people can interact with you on social media platforms, the better your blogs will perform, especially if they can share or comment—more on social media in an upcoming session.

Tools To Help With SEO

- Yoast SEO plugin.

This is a plugin that can help you optimize your site right off the bat. It makes setting up your blog posts, page titles, and description tags easy.

- Google Search Console.

This is where you go to verify your site so you can get access to an excellent tool that shows you all your traffic activity and indexing information.

- Google's Mobile-Friendly Test.

Google is now a mobile-first indexing engine, so you'll be in big trouble if your blog needs to be better optimized for mobile. Take the test with the tool and learn how and where to improve so crawlers can find all your best content faster.

- Woorank's SEO & Website Analysis Tool.

This Chrome extension gives you an overall SEO score and then shows you where your on-page and off-page SEO needs to improve.

- Can I Rank Keyword Tool?

CanIRank is a comprehensive keyword difficulty tool that tells you whether you can rank for that keyword. It also gives suggestions to help you rank for a specific term.

CHAPTER 8

SEO - Part II - Ten Tips for Getting Ranked in Google

Now that you understand search engine optimization, it's time to apply some of that knowledge. Remember, SEO is huge, and there's much more advanced ground to cover, such as technical SEO. You don't need to worry too much about that as a newbie. Grow your blog, put into practice the basics, and build from there. In this section, I want to ensure you have practical SEO tips that are current and proven to work, so here are my top ten SEO tips to help you rank in Google.

SEO Tip #1: Keep your blog centered on your audience.

That means you should create a blog that people enjoy. Search engines are designed to measure signals across the web-based on searchers' preferences at the end of the day. Their sole purpose is to give the people more of what they want. Make sure your blog is what your kind of people want. The more authentic and valuable your content, the more people will love and read your blog, which will, in turn, cause search engines to drive more traffic your way.

SEO Tip#2: Attract and retain the attention of your reader.

This is the second most important tip if you want to rank higher. First, as we said, is to create nothing short of fantastic, helpful, and well-organized content. Once the people land on your page and consume all that good stuff, you want to ensure they remain on-site as long as possible. The longer you can keep someone on-site, the more Google sees that as a sign that your content is worth staying at the top.

SEO Tip#3: Keyword placement should be spot on.

I mentioned this in the previous chapter, but want to ensure you get it. Do not do keyword stuffing on your blog post. Black hat SEO will only hurt your blog business. Adding keywords and having a keyword strategy is necessary, but we need to use them naturally. I already shared the different ways you can optimize your on-page SEO. Please read that part again because where you use your keywords is just as important as how many times. As I said, you want to ensure the keyword always appears in the title tag, the URL, and the first section of your blog post (usually between 100-200 words).

SEO Tip #4: Get creative with your longtail keywords search.

The best keywords to rank for when starting your blog are longtail keywords. What are longtail keywords, you ask? A simple illustration will help you understand it better. Let's go back to our earlier example of my food blog. I'm writing a blog post on Vegan Spanish Paella. Newbies will settle for short keywords such as Paella or, at most, Spanish Paella. Pro bloggers know that a better approach is to go longtail, i.e., using phrases that someone would search for.

A perfect example would be "Vegan Spanish Paella Recipe." Your chances of ranking significantly increase when you go longtail. The quality of the reader is also higher because someone who searches for that specific key phrase and then sees your link is likely to stay on-site longer and consume all your content, assuming it's great. Now that you understand longtail keywords, here's the secret tip. Don't just rely on Google when finding the suggested keywords. Use OTHER search engines such as Wikipedia, YouTube (yes, it's a search engine), and Bing.

SEO Tip #5: Consider publishing an industry study long-form post.

This will be a lot of work because you have to do a ton of research and use data, case studies, etc., but the long-term results will be incredible. Everyone in your niche will be linked to you because bloggers and journalists are thirsty for hard facts and proven data. Everyone will refer back to your blog even without asking, and Google will reward you more. This isn't something you can do in a week or even a month, so give yourself ample time to create something epic.

SEO Tip #6: Add multimedia files as much as possible and make sure they are keyword-rich in their title tags.

Visual content and multimedia files are great for attracting and retaining readership. People love beautiful images, infographics, GIFs, audio files, videos, and podcasts. Depending on what your resources and time can allow you to do, consider adding as much content variety to each post as possible. Podcasts and infographics are also great for generating backlinks and references. Remember to label these appropriately so that Google crawlers can know what they are.

SEO Tip #7: Create content closely related to your niche topic.

Marketers refer to these types of content as shoulder niche content pieces. They are not directly related to your niche but close enough so your ideal readership would benefit from reading the content. For example, I have a friend who is in home construction. There is nothing sexy about the technical aspects of remodeling a home. Instead, she created home construction shoulder niche content. These categories are closely related and are far more appealing and shareable, such as interior design, home improvement, etc. If you can find what topics are more attractive to your audience and create excellent content that people want to engage with and share, you'll start noticing a growth in traffic and SEO ranking

SEO Tip #8: Include "What are X" definitions in your blog content.

This is so simple, yet most people still need to do it. When a searcher goes to Google and types in a high-level term like "Spanish Paella," they typically want to understand what it is, i.e., the definition. If you notice the changes Google has made over time, they're seeking to define terms on the front page, so it helps when, in your blog post, you also include a definition. In the case of my Vegan Spanish Paella, it would be a wise move to have.."What is Paella?

SEO Tip #9: Add a Q&A section to your content.

Of course, this should only be used if appropriate for your blog content. I encourage you to do this because a large-scale study conducted by SEMrush revealed that Google SERPs tend to feature content with Q&A.

SEO Tip #10: Find pre-curated lists of top industry blogs in your niche.

This secret sauce will require effort but pays high dividends, especially when starting. Your blog is unknown and floating in the deep ocean of the blogosphere. You need people to know, like, and trust you. Google and other search engines must also like you and quickly see your brand as an authority so your dream of a six-figure business can materialize. How do you do this? Creating epic content, doing keyword research, optimizing the content, visuals, etc., is all part of the game, but you need more.

I encourage you to take the initiative and build relationships with strategic sites. By going on Google and typing in "best XYZ blogs," you'll tap into a potential gold mine of relationship and link-building opportunities that will skyrocket your rankings. For example, since I am looking to rank my food blog, I can type in the best nutrition blogs in a particular year or my city or country. The results I get will be a curated list of people who already built credibility. Now, I need to sift through each of those articles to find the perfect fit for someone I can partner with or develop another arrangement. When you carry out this tactic, make sure the chosen sites have high authority and that you have something to offer them.

In some cases, it could be a guest blogging opportunity. Using a tool like Ahrefs, you can tell how strong or weak a website is, how many backlinks the site has, and how long it's been around. As I said, this is going to take some work. Record all this data on a spreadsheet, and once you've got a couple of hundred sites, prioritize them in order of importance and start doing an outreach campaign.

CHAPTER 9

How To Write Blog Posts That Go Viral

This chapter is probably one of the main reasons you decided to buy this book. Creating a viral blog post is one of your goals if you're like most of us. Every blogger I know wants the secret sauce, especially when starting. It is not fun when you go through the effort of creating an epic post only to get crickets once you hit publish. We know publications like BuzzFeed Daily post content that spreads like a bushfire on the Internet. How do these guys do it? Is it sheer luck or the fact that they have a large team working behind the scenes?

There needs to be more luck involved. Whether or not you're a fan of BuzzFeed content, it would be nice to have people clicking and reading your tears, sweat, and blood. You deserve to have some reward and recognition for this commitment. It would be best to have the right strategy, a magical formula to apply to your unique content. The best part is you don't need to guess or invent anything; learn from people who are already crushing it and producing viral content. I will give you a high-level strategy that you can apply to increase your chances of virality as you build your blog. Follow this strategy, and you'll shave off months of errors and no growth.

Step One. Stop focusing on creating viral content.

Remember at the beginning of this book how much I warned you against creating content for the sake of fame and virality? I stand by my case. Each time I've encountered bloggers who only care about creating viral content, they only last for a while! Your profitable business of multiple figures needs more room for this goal. So scratch it off your list and, instead, add this goal: Create high-value content for my audience.

I want your main goal for starting this blog to be - creating and publishing the best possible content to educate, inspire, and entertain people about your chosen topic. So, it would be best to start thinking about who that ideal audience is and how you can achieve that goal of serving them at the highest level. Creating blog posts your ideal audience loves is the best way to build a sustainable blog and fulfill all your other business goals.

Step Two. Reverse engineer your competitor's blog posts.

Now that your head is in the suitable space and you're approaching this the right way, it's time to emulate success. To make your content stand out, you need to understand the kind of content your audience is already interested in and why. A good source of real-time answers is your direct competitor. Every blog has competition. If you have no match and no one is talking about your topic, it's probably not a good idea to invest the next few years in building that blog because there's no market demand. Competitors are great because they help validate that your topic is in need.

The other thing they help you with is learning through their mistakes and choosing only what works. So please find the best-performing content from your competitors, analyze it, and figure out the headlines and content pieces that received the most engagement. Do not copy the content that resonates with you. Instead, make it ten times better than what they created and introduce a new perspective or alternative. Make your content higher quality, more exciting, and thought-provoking.

Step Three. Walk a mile in the shoes of your ideal reader.

There's an old idiom that says before judging someone, you should walk a mile in their shoes. I want us to adopt that thinking to your blog writing, as it will help you produce content people want to engage with. Before writing your content, walk a mile in your reader's shoes.

You want to start a profitable blog and build a lifestyle business. And you want to accomplish that by creating content that can drive traffic and conversion. Well, your reader needs to learn about your goals and, frankly, doesn't care. They are going to trade five, ten, or twenty minutes and pay the high price of attention, and the only thing that matters for them is that they come out of that experience a little better than they were before. It would be best to start seeing your blog more from their perspective than yours. That is the secret sauce to creating content your audience wants. One way to begin walking in their shoes is by asking them what they want to read more about.

With every content you publish, ensure you get a sample size of people to read and tell you what they want more. You'd be amazed by how much people are willing to say to you. They'll even give you specific headline titles you can use. You can also use sites like BuzzSumo to uncover the most shared articles. For example, you can type your most shared article into BuzzSumo and see everyone who shared it and where. If you click on these people, you will also see other pieces they share, which tells you more about their interests.

Step Four. Experiment more with headline titles.

Every blogger knows the importance of a strong headline. No one will click to read your excellent post without a good headline title. The way to write good headlines is to practice writing lots of headlines. No book or article can help you. This comes with constant practice. Commit to writing at least 20 headline titles for each piece whenever you post. Trust me. This is the best way to write attractive headlines. Once you write an article, feel free to test and re-test the headline as much as possible because a tiny tweak could unleash the viral aspect, and the world will devour your masterpiece.

Step Five. Be generous with your visuals.

When writing long-form blog posts, which I highly recommend, visual aids are your allies. It would be best if you broke text with whitespace and captivating visuals. Posts with lots of visual imagery get 94% more views than those without. Images can more than double the number of shares for your articles. But don't just throw on pictures for the sake of it. The idea is supposed to complement what you're writing about. It should be visually appealing and relevant to your audience.

Step Six. Use the style of posts that works well for your audience.

Start testing different styles to see which one gets the most traction. List posts, tutorials, how-to, and checklists are all great to experiment with because people enjoy consuming them. Depending on your niche, one works better. Create more of what works.

Step Seven. Use data and keep working on your strategy.

The strategy works only if you work it. And you need data collected over a long enough period to figure out what's working best. Blogging is not guesswork. Data, not hope strategies, should back it. This is where meticulous research, gallons of coffee, and a spreadsheet are handy. First, gather data on your niche's best blog post length. Then, it would be best to determine which post styles perform best and how many images your competitor generally uses. After collecting all that data, you need to start tracking the performance of your content to see if the audience is responsive to your headlines, style, message, and quality. By using data to inform the creativity of the content you will produce and to track the content you push out into the blogosphere, you'll know exactly what works, and going viral will no longer be some random act.

So, in the end, while going viral is a great feeling and something every blogger dreams about, I encourage you to keep your eye on the actual price. That temporary spotlight that comes with going viral is only for a brief moment. But when you get good at producing well-researched, high-value content that resonates with your ideal audience, that creates something that lasts much longer than virality - loyalty. Your multiple-figure blogging business will thrive due to this approach, and with some luck, you'll also enjoy going viral occasionally.

How To Write An Epic Blog Post In Under 30 Minutes That Still Performs Well

If you need more time and you need to push out content that is high quality, you need a reliable methodology. Here comes one that can save you time and get your blog post ready for publication in less than half an hour.

You will need coffee (or tea if that's your thing), some post-it notes, a Google document open, and a lot of enthusiasm. First, ask yourself a simple question: What hot question or questions does my audience have about my blog topic? As you can see, we always start with the audience in mind. The blog post is always created to add value to the reader, whether a long industry case study or a weekly blog post. Decide on your hot-button questions and write them down in your Post-it notes in question-answer forms. These will constitute the body of your post.

The second thing is to determine the best way to convey the information you just noted down. Do you want it to be a numbered list, how-to, infographics with some texts, story-based, etc.? Keep your audience in mind when choosing this format, but also feel free to get creative. Once you've decided, it's time to use that Google document.

The third step is to brainstorm the introduction and conclusion. You have the body of it, so you know the central teaching. It would be best to engage people and draw them into the blog post so they can receive your value. The first few sentences and paragraphs should be designed with that intention. Consider sharing a relatable story or anecdote. Use statistics, graphics, or a shocking fact. Depending on your topic, start with a captivating quote and make the follow-up sentences even more enticing. Lead into the blog post's body so readers naturally fall into the rabbit hole before realizing it. In the conclusion, you'll want to summarize what you taught in the post. Make it digestible memorable, and call them to action.

The fourth thing to do is start working on your first few headlines. Looking at your sticky notes, the introduction, and the conclusion you now have, are you getting any ideas for the title? Don't overthink it at this point. Spend about 5 minutes writing down anything that comes to mind, no matter how awful. Attempting to create ten or more headlines within that period is a great start. Set those headlines aside, and let's start putting that article together.

The fifth step is two-fold. First, you need to determine the main overarching message that you want people to remember after reading your post. This is the main takeaway. If they remember nothing else, let this be the one thing. Write it down if you need to, or keep it in mind. The second part is transferring the content you placed on the Post-it notes to your Word document. Add it in the middle (between the introduction and conclusion) of the Google document. Don't worry about grammar or flow at this point. Just put everything on that one document in its raw version. That is your first fresh draft. Congratulations!

The sixth and final step is the actual creative process, where you begin from the introduction to the conclusion, fill the gaps, write your post, share the story, and teach your key takeaway. Only after this is complete do you run through grammar, edits, and finally take a whack at the headline. If more ideas have come by the time you get to the headline, write them down until you have about twenty. Then, head over to the tool I shared before (Headline Analyzer) and type in the ones that feel best for you until you find the highest-ranking one.

And there you have it. A completed blog post in record time. The best part is, with the SEO lessons you've learned in the last two chapters, it will be a breeze to incorporate those key phrases and terms into the blog post. You might realize you did it naturally by following this simple six-step process. So the next time you have less than an hour to get something created, no sweat. You have a simple, proven methodology to help you make an epic blog post. It's time to hit publish.

Section III

Publishing, Promotion, and Driving Traffic to Your Blog

Chapter 10

What To Do Once You've Hit Publish

At this point, you probably have mixed feelings. After putting in all that effort and long hours in getting that first blog perfect and ready, you might experience a combination of excitement, fear, confusion, and even despair. Writing your first blog and sharing your ideas with others is exciting. Knowing that the whole world will be reading your thoughts is a fantastic feeling, but can also stir up fear and insecurity in some. If you happen to have any of these mixed feelings, don't worry. You're not the first and won't be the last blogger to feel that way.

A more extensive and more pressing problem to deal with is what to do after you hit publish. Most bloggers invest a lot of time in setting up the blog and creating the perfect post. They must remember a crucial aspect of growing a successful blog - marketing. Even great content can drown in the blogosphere and go unnoticed if you don't take specific measures besides search engine optimization. I don't know if you know, but organic traffic is a long-term strategy. So, what can you do to help drive traffic and eyeballs to your fantastic content? That's what this chapter covers. We will run through an essential checklist of what you must do before and after publishing your post.

Your 6-step checklist:

#1. SEO

We've already covered SEO at length in previous chapters. You now understand how to beef up your content with relevant keywords and phrases your ideal audience is already looking up on Google. This will be the backbone of your traffic sources once you hit publish. The SEO work should ideally get done before hitting publish so crawlers can start working on your blog post immediately.

#2. Shorten URL

Most platforms do this for you by default, but if you want to share your link on a site or forum that doesn't automatically do this, I encourage you to manually shorten your blog post's URL. How? First, copy and paste the URL into a tool that offers link shorteners and analytics. Bit.ly is a great one to use. Once you use it, you can get click stats, geographic, and referring site data to know where your audience is coming from. You'll easily apply the tactics I share below with a shortened link.

#3. Syndication

Content syndication is the process by which third-party sites get access to your blog post and push it out on their end. It's a handy tactic for new bloggers as these sites can publish your articles and link back to your original post. Some are free; others require payment.

Do you have an RSS feed active? If not, it's time to activate it. RSS feed is one of the most basic forms of syndication. It allows you to automatically feed your blog's content to many different places, including social networking sites. Push notifications work when done right and only if you're producing great content, which I expect you to. Aside from the RSS feed, you can also use Quora, Slideshare, Mix, Reddit, Outbrain, Taboola, and Zergnet. Research these to see which is best for your blog post, depending on your niche and audience.

#4. Find and comment on other blogs

Part of being a successful blogger is engaging with people in the blogosphere. When you're new to the game and have yet to learn your brand, the most affordable and authentic way to build credibility is to seek other blogs in your industry and actively participate. Be a good community member. Don't spam and self-promote.

Instead, provide practical value as your comments. Wherever appropriate (especially if you've already covered the discussed topic), you may link to your post for further reference. That shortened URL will be handy in such cases. So add it to your daily or weekly schedule to carve out time for building relationships on other people's blogs.

#5. Blogger outreach campaign

Aside from scouring the blogosphere to find blogs where you can share your viewpoint, I encourage you to create an outreach campaign to fellow bloggers and social media influencers so they can help share your content. I learned this fantastic technique from Neil Patel, and it works amazingly well. The only caveat I must give is that it will take work. More than reaching out to ten, twenty, or even fifty bloggers will be required. It would be best to have the volume so that the numbers can work in your favor. Consider shortlisting about three hundred bloggers in a similar or complementary industry. If you feel your message will serve their audience and you like their brand, add them to your list. Now, you need to customize an outreach email that adds value in some way and ultimately asks for the share.

Build relationships with the people you choose to reach out to before asking them to share your stuff. Be willing to give something to them, too. You could offer something you know they will value. You can start commenting, sharing, and engaging with their content long before you ask to connect. Any effort you make to build genuine relationships with people serving the exact audience you want to serve will pay high dividends in the end. You can guest blog for them if they enjoy your content. Never make your outreach about getting. Focus on reciprocal relationships so you can have high-quality backlinks, more blog traffic, and subscribers as a natural consequence of your relationship.

#6. Social Media Marketing

In the next chapter, we will dive deeper into the benefits of a social media strategy for your blog. It's one of the best traffic sources, and in today's mobile-first world, where everyone is on social media, you want to take advantage of that traffic. Platforms like Twitter, Instagram,

Pinterest, Facebook, and even LinkedIn are incredible traffic sources, and you must use them strategically. Understand each platform's nature and subtle nuances so your content can attract more people. For example, many successful bloggers use Twitter to build followers and mini-chat communities. As a new blogger, you can set up a nice-looking Twitter account, grab your shortened URL, and head to their search bar for a phrase like "need help XYZ" (XYZ is whatever problem your post solves). As you scan the results, you'll find a handful of people reaching out for help in your area of expertise. Reply to these people by offering genuine advice tips and include that shortened URL for further reading. Do this often enough, and you'll quickly see your Twitter follower count growing and more readers to your blog post. These readers won't just visit your post. They are more likely to comment and share the post.

Tips For Driving Traffic To Your New Blog:

Getting more people to visit your blog and read your content is an art and science. As a newbie, you need as many hacks and tactics as possible to keep testing until you find what works for you. Let these tips help fill your toolbox so you always have activities to drive traffic back to your blog.

- **Work and rework your headlines.**

I mentioned this before, but your headline is critical when drawing people into your content. Don't just rely on the first headline that comes to mind. Work it. Tweak it some more. Use a headline analyzer to make sure it's scoring high. The more you invest in that headline, the higher your chances that people will click through to your post. You can use the following tools to help create better headlines. CoSchedule Headline Analyzer, EMV Headline Analyzer, or ShareThrough Headline Analyzer.

- **Increase the loading time for your blog.**

People have become so impatient. If your blog takes less time to load, you might lose a lot of traffic. As I mentioned, Google is now a mobile-first search engine, meaning your blog has to be fast and look good on desktops, laptops, and especially on mobile. The lowest hanging fruit when looking to increase loading speed is to reduce the number of plugins. Plugins tend to slow down a site, so unless you need them, less is more. You also need to make sure your images are compressed. Otherwise, they might take too long to load. Use magify.io to help you with this.

- **Join HARO and answer relevant queries.**

HARO (Help A Reporter Out) is a free publicity service that brings reporters and qualified sources together. If your niche aligns with this, sign up for free and briefly answer a HARO query. Done right, this can result in high-quality inbound links to your blog.

- **Add social sharing buttons.**

Much research has been conducted on the importance of having easy share buttons on each post. The winner is undisputed. If your blog posts have social sharing bottoms at the top and bottom for platforms like LinkedIn, Twitter, Pinterest, and other social networks, readers are more likely to spread the word.

- **Add a "click to tweet" widget.**

This sounds very simple, and it is. Yet it works like a charm if you're content is impressive. Please find a phrase or quote in your content that people can click to tweet. Add that short statement on the widget, and anyone can easily share it with their followers. Many tools help you set this up. Social Snap, ClickToTweeet.com, and Better Click To Tweet are great tools to help you do this fast.

- **Invite guest contributors.**

I know what you're thinking. Who would want to guest blog on your new blog? My experience has taught me that people are always willing to guest post, even if your blog is unique. It would be best if you dug deep to find the right people. The best part is that when others write for you, you don't have to register more to get ample monthly volume to meet your target. As a bonus, the guests who contribute get to share with their networks, opening up new readership avenues for you.

- **Add internal links.**

As you continue to create and publish content, make it a habit to link to previous content. Why? Because internal links help Google understand the context and relationship between different articles on your website. Then, it uses this information as ranking signals. Internal links are also great for helping increase time-on-site and reduce bounce rate, especially when strategically placed on the blog post.

- **Add videos to your articles.**

Videos are currently the most consumed type of content on the Internet. Users spend more time on blog posts that have a video than those with texts and images alone. Create a simple video, summarize the article, and upload it to YouTube. Then, embed it in your blog post. That way, you get double exposure because your content can also be found on YouTube, another search engine. Are you not a fan of being on camera? You don't have to be. Create slideshows with voice-over, use tools like Headliner to turn audio into video, or consider using animated videos.

- **Repost old content on your social media.**

Regarding platforms like Twitter, where everything disappears after a few seconds, you can bet very few people get to see your content. I encourage you to keep reposting old content on your social media platforms. Consider getting an automated software tool that can help you with this process. This way, you'll increase your visibility and keep your profiles active throughout the day. Tools like Buffer, Meet Edgar, and CoSchedule are all great for reposting content on social media.

- **Invest time in online communities.**

Online communities are great for generating traffic back to your blog, especially if you can find forums and chat rooms of small online communities where people are already discussing your central theme. YouTube also has a tremendous in-built community, which is worth exploring. You'll have to schedule this in your day because it takes time. Check out Facebook groups, LinkedIn groups, Reddit, etc., and find small discussions where people are engaged. Don't just start posting links to your articles. That would be poor etiquette. Instead, spend time answering questions, joining discussions, building relationships, and making a name for yourself. Only then share your blog if it's appropriate.

- **Interview an influential blogger.**

By interviewing an influential blogger, you get a different perspective on your topic and lots of creative inspiration. It also attracts more people to your blog. As a newbie, you can do written interviews or start a podcast. It's a great way to kickstart the relationship-building process; the influencer will probably share the conversation with their followers.

- **Invest in paid promotion.**

At the end of the day, if you want to grow your traffic and your blogging business fast, nothing beats paid advertising. In the next chapter, we dive deeper into this topic and how to start small. I want you to start warming up to the idea because it can boost your growth and help you reach your goals faster. Some platforms are costly; others are super affordable. Regardless of your budget, you can always find a venue that works for you. Another type of paid promotion you should look into is influencer marketing. If you have the funds and are good at building relationships, consider spending an influencer on social media to promote your content instead.

Chapter 11

Best Social Media Channels to Promote Your Blog

Social media is going to play an integral role in the success of your blog and business. Everyone is on social media nowadays, so your blog should also be there. This chapter will be your best resource if you want reliable and qualified social media traffic but need help determining where to begin. Read and implement everything we'll cover.

Why You Need To Integrate Social Media And Blogging

87% of bloggers say that social media helps them boost their exposure. That is especially true in the early days of blogging, when obscurity is one's biggest obstacle. The apparent reason, of course, is that social media will drive traffic back to your site. But I want us to look beyond the obvious. Consider that you wish to turn your blog into a highly profitable business. The only way to do that is to build a community or group of people who know, like, trust, and want to buy something from you. You will see that income soon if people will spend money on your offers.

There are two great ways to get people to trust and like you enough to buy. Email and social media marketing. These require two different strategies, and I encourage you to learn email marketing so that you can leverage it once your social media gains traction. For now, however, let's focus on going where the people are and giving them what they want. You've already done the homework, and you understand your audience. That also means you know where they will most likely hang out online. If you're in the food, beauty, or sports niche, you'd be right in thinking of Instagram and Pinterest. I encourage you to think outside the box because even if you're in a niche like photography, where you think Instagram is the only viable option, I'd like you to extend yourself and consider being active on platforms such as LinkedIn. Yes, it sounds so far-fetched, but here's the thing.

Your audience probably has five to ten social media apps installed on their smartphone. They will likely log into a handful of those platforms daily. So, even if you're dealing with photography, it's worthwhile being active on LinkedIn as long as you tweak your content to align with the nature of the platform. Each platform is unique and carries its vibe. If you add the proper context, the same visual on Instagram that got so many hits could only succeed on LinkedIn. Read that last part again because it's the difference between social media success and epic failure.

Know your audience and devise creative ways of speaking differently depending on where they interact with you. On Instagram or TikTok, you can be casual and even quirky. On Twitter, you need to be more authoritative; on LinkedIn, you must add professional or personal value. Many bloggers have a Twitter account because it's a great platform to chat, share quick tips, and join in the real-time conversation that Twitter offers.

Organic Vs. Paid Social Media

There are two main ways to leverage social media marketing to grow your blog. I recommend doing both simultaneously, but it's okay if you're working with a zero marketing budget. Organic social media is free social media. You set up your social profiles, post, and interact with others. After a while, people will start clicking on your stuff and eventually check out your post if relevant. As your followers, your ability to organically promote and send people to your post increases. This will take time, effort, and a strong strategy.

Paid traffic, on the other hand, is very straightforward. It involves paying for your content to be sponsored or shown to your chosen audience on a specific platform. Almost every central social platform has a paid option. Some are affordable, and anyone can get started with as little as $1 (Facebook); others are costly and require significant budgets (LinkedIn). The best part of paid ads is the fast results and increased traffic you will notice on your blog. Social media advertising does require a lot of knowledge, firm strategy, and clear goals. Let's take a look at each of the major social media platforms.

Twitter (Now X)

A tweet is short and sweet. It would be best to express something meaningful in 140 characters or less. With Twitter, you need to be proactive and creative. Make your tweet about the blog post original, and feel free to use the exact headline title. You can also include statistics or ask a question in your tweet. Although Twitter is more of a news and text-based social platform, images, GIFs, and other visually appealing creatives have become popular recently. Attach an excellent picture in your blog post tweet to attract more eyeballs.

Hashtags on Twitter are your allies. Use theme-specific hashtags when promoting a particular blog post; you can create your hashtag, like #myawesomeblog. But only do this once you have followers and some influence online. Otherwise, stick to post-related hashtags.

Retweets are great as your follower count grows. Ask your followers to retweet your update. Tweets that ask for an "RT" or "retweet" get twelve to twenty-three times as many shares, so don't be afraid to ask your people.

Twitter stands at 145 million monetizable daily active users, which is expected to grow. According to Twitter, they are the number one platform for discovery. 26% of people spend more time viewing ads on Twitter than on other leading media. So, if you have the budget and want to boost your tweets, you can do video ads, promoted tweet text, images, GIFs, polls, your entire account, cards, and so on. Visit their Twitter business site for complete details.

Instagram

A billion people use Instagram each month. Of that enormous number, 500 million are using Instagram stories daily. 63% of Instagram users report logging in to the app at least once a day, and over 200 million say they visit at least one business profile daily. Would you like your share of this incredible traffic volume to land on your blog?

Some organic ways to do this include creating Instagram Stories and adding a link to the relevant blog post. Since you are building from scratch, I encourage you to create a personalized welcome message for new followers. As they follow you, send them a warm welcome note, express gratitude, and direct them to one of your top-performing posts.

Another neat trick that works for me is adding a call to action that compels people to click on the link in my Instagram bio. I keep updating that link to match the posts I promote weekly. And I usually create Instagram posts that align with the blog post I want to encourage. This requires proper planning and a good content strategy, which we'll discuss shortly. Get creative with how you use Instagram Stories and the ever-increasing number of features they keep pushing out. Last but not least, let's talk about paid Instagram ads.

The paid ads option is one of my favorite content marketing options. The cost of Instagram Stories is still meager, among the best deals you will get in advertising. You can start with as little as $1 per day budget. I mean, come on! If you want a fast pass to drive more traffic from Instagram to your blog, this is a guaranteed way to reach more people. Clearly outline your objectives and develop a strong paid ads strategy to succeed. With paid ads, you can use videos, regular Instagram feed posts, or Instagram stories, which I strongly recommend. Be creative with this, and take the free Instagram course that Facebook (which owns Instagram) offers in the Blueprint Courses.

Facebook

Facebook is the king of the jungle on social media. Organic reach on Facebook is long dead, and only some can build something meaningful on organic reach within the platform. It would be best to turn to paid Facebook marketing options to see real traction with Facebook. You can also leverage the power of Facebook groups. Find a few groups that focus on your topic of expertise and become a regular participant so you can build relationships. Answer questions interact with members, and depending on the type of group, you can have a day to talk about your blog or even share a post.

With paid Facebook ads, you are spoiled for choice. You can boost a post or set up an account in your business manager and run video ads, stories, text and image ads, carousels, etc. You can even do list building right from the platform. The best part about Facebook is the vast database they work with. You can create a warm custom audience of highly targeted people who fit your audience persona and eventually grow your readership and blog simultaneously. Again, the education behind the Facebook ads platform requires much more than the introduction in this book. Sign up to Facebook Blueprint to learn how to start with Facebook advertising.

LinkedIn

Many may consider LinkedIn a professional cocktail party for official networking, but we've proven it can be a great source of traffic and revenue for bloggers. There are 675 million monthly users on the platform. 57% of them are men, and 43% are women. There are 30 million companies on LinkedIn, with the employees actively engaging on the platform. Play your cards right, and you can generate high-quality traffic on this platform. While the traffic volume may be lower than you'd get on more trafficked platforms like Instagram, the quality of the traffic tends to be better. Most of the users on the forum are college-educated and high-income earners. That means turning a blog reader into a loyal buyer is achievable when you leverage this platform, no matter how pricy your offer is. If you're going to sell high-ticket products or services, LinkedIn will serve you well.

The best part about this platform is that it's one of the few platforms where organic reach is still alive. Even if you're a complete newbie with no connections, your content can get traction and help you grow your followers. The most important thing is creating content these users want to see and share. On LinkedIn, that means educational, practical, or thought-provoking, but always from a professional point of view. The more career or business-focused it is, the better. So get creative here. Even if you're a food blogger, indeed, there is a way for your content to stand out and perform well on the platform.

For example, instead of just talking about food and how much you love cooking, create simple "one-pot" recipes that taste good for busy working moms. I bet many professional moms and single working parents will appreciate and engage with such content. Use LinkedIn updates to regularly push out written content, videos, and infographics. Grab your blog post, tweak it, and repurpose it on the LinkedIn publishing platform. I also encourage you to use hashtags wisely. Although hashtags are not as prominent on LinkedIn as on Instagram, they still work to get you some eyeballs if used strategically. Only a handful, and make sure they are relevant. One more organic tip I want to share is using LinkedIn groups. They may not be as big as Facebook, but it's a great way to connect with like-minded individuals and grow your connections. Ask to join groups within your niche or even a complimentary industry. Remember the best practices for all community interactions. Give more than you ask.

Although LinkedIn ads are among the more expensive ads you can get, they are considered cheaper than Google Adwords, and their reach is far more targeted. Your ability to get in front of a decision is high when you advertise on LinkedIn. Types of ads range from Sponsored Content (single image, video, and carousel) advertisements to Direct Sponsored Content. The difference between these ads is that Sponsored Content ads run as native news feed ads and Lead Gen Forms, whereas Direct Sponsored content is never published on your LinkedIn page feed. You can also do Sponsored InMail, which delivers targeted messages to LinkedIn-member inboxes, text ads, dynamic ads, or LinkedIn Audience Network.

Pinterest

Pinterest is now the third-largest social network in the U.S., right behind Facebook and Instagram. Of course, if you consider YouTube a social platform, it would fall back one position, but it's a big platform. Pinterest has 8.8 million monthly active users in the U.S. and is especially popular with moms. Women, in general, love the forum, so if your topic has an audience of women, especially moms, that is your go-to platform, as they are most likely hanging out there. The best part about this platform is that we know (according to Pew Research) that most Pinterest users are high-income earners with disposable income. So, if you've got a relevant blog with great offers, these people will buy from you.

As a newbie blogger, you should also be relieved to know that most users on Pinterest will interact with and Pin content from unknown and unbranded accounts. They enjoy discovering new products and ideas. Pinterest users enjoy shopping. 48% of users said they interact on the platform with a high intent to shop. Here's the thing. You need to ensure your content is visually appealing, as that is the main criterion on the platform for organic reach.

The first thing you need to do once your account is set up is create a board specifically for your blog articles. This makes it easy for your growing audience to find your blog posts and follow your blog board. Always choose your best blog posts with the best visuals to pin. Use compelling copy in the description and link directly to your blog article. Add the Pin It button to your blog post to encourage more sharing. I'm adding some extra reading material on the resource page to help you understand how to set your Pinterest profile and utilize it properly.

With paid ads, you can reach 169 million people. There are many types of Pinterest ads to choose from. You can run Promoted Pins, One-Tap Pins, Promoted Carousels, Promoted Video Pins, Promoted App Pins, Buyable Pins, and Story Pins. Getting started is very straightforward, but you must set up a Pinterest business account first.

Which Social Media Platform Should You Focus On?

Every new blogger wants a simple answer to this question. Unfortunately, there isn't a cookie-cutter answer. All platforms can work for you. The main thing to consider is why you pick one platform over another. An excellent social media strategy is essential regardless of which platform you choose.

It can seem overwhelming to determine whether your efforts should be focused on LinkedIn, Pinterest, Instagram, Facebook, Snapchat, Twitter, or all at once. So here is a simple process to help you make the first selection. I advise starting with up to three channels and expanding as your blog grows.

I want you to answer the first question: What is your social media strategy objective? This is important because your chosen social media channel should support attaining objectives. For example, if your main goal is to increase brand awareness, an excellent avenue to choose is one with a vast, engaged, growing audience.

Another thing to consider is that increasing brand awareness might happen faster if you add paid promotions. In that case, you'll also need to consider a platform that can give you a good ROI while respecting your budget. If working with a small budget for this, Facebook and Instagram become more appealing than LinkedIn because their advertising options are more pocket-friendly. So, think about the main objective. Is it lead generation, direct sales, or brand awareness?

The second question is: Where is your ideal audience most likely hanging out daily? After your social media goals have aligned with the proper channels, it's time to think about your audience's behavior. We know they are all on their mobile phones searching for things all day long on

Google. They are also scrolling through feeds, commenting, sending messages, tagging people, saving, and sharing ideas. Where is this taking place? Which app is your ideal reader most likely doing this?

Creating an audience persona is the best way to tap into this answer. Combine demographics and psychographics to have an idea of their reality. Your audience may be more active on Pinterest. Then, it would make more sense to invest the first several months of this blogging journey in Pinterest than Snapchat or TikTok. See what I mean? The more insight you have about their behavior, the easier it will be to focus on one or two channels and then expand. Please check out the Pew Research Center if you need help determining where to gather this data type. They have conducted an in-depth analysis that outlines key demographics for several social media platforms, primarily if you're serving the American market.

The third question you must answer is: Where is your competitor most active? Your blog topic is going to have several other bloggers who are already doing well. Although I don't necessarily consider them competition, for the sake of simplicity, let's view them as such. These competitors are active on specific channels. That should clue you in because where they are most active implies an engaged audience. Let this serve as a baseline that helps you determine what you should be doing. Remember, we've already researched content to see their top-performing blog posts, etc. Now, it's time to see which social channels they are actively using and the types of positions they are creating. Tools like Brandwatch Analytics can help you monitor your "competitors" across many social media platforms and even track any mentions of them across the Internet. The bigger your blog gets, the more beneficial some of these tools are, but you can do it the traditional way with a spreadsheet and your time.

How many channels can you manage without going insane? Gurus on the Internet will tell you to be on every platform and post at least 100 pieces of content daily. That sounds wonderful when you're amid their mesmerizing energy with your adrenaline shooting off the roof. But you and I know it's tough to make it happen alone. It would be best if you still had the supplies or human resources. Perhaps you're a one-man-show or a one-woman-show operating on a shoestring budget. Get honest with yourself instead of getting sucked into the world of online gurus and their intense, motivational tactics. Think about long-term consistency. Find what works for you, given your current situation. You can always upgrade a year from now when results start to show, but for now, I want you to avoid spreading yourself too thin. One excellent social media profile is better than five mediocre ones. So, how many can you honestly consistently handle on your own? Whatever that number is, stick with it until you see actual results.

Which of the top channels you're considering feel fun and aligned with your personality so far? This is important to answer because your blog won't do well if you hate being on social media. Your blog won't do well if posting and engaging with the community is a burden. Choosing a platform that aligns with your style, how you like to express yourself, and something that feels fun ensures you will stick to this social media marketing strategy. The more consistent you are, the better your results will be.

Once you've answered, all these questions, the channels that manage to tick all the boxes should be the ones you focus on. If only one channel is cut, then so be it! Next, I want to share some hacks for making your social media activities more manageable.

Tools For Automation To Simplify Social Media Marketing.

Automation is going to become your best friend as you grow your blog. Assuming you consistently publish high-quality content, interact with chosen social media communities, etc., you'll need help distributing your content in the coming months. That is where automation comes in. Every thriving blogger needs help. Automation is the key if you still need a team but want to produce content like an army is working for you. There are many tools to help you push out content daily into various social platforms. CoSchedule, Buffer, MeetEdgar, Loomly, Hootsuite, Tailwind, Sendible, Crowdfire, Later, and Everypost can help you schedule and publish your posts so you can focus on doing other important things like community engagement.

A Social Media Strategy Template For Your Blog

Writing things down on paper is essential to accomplishing that goal. Those who fail to plan plan to fail, as the saying goes. There's enough evidence to show that documenting your social media strategy increases your chances of success by 466%. Those odds look good to me. So, let me share a checklist and template you can copy that's proven to work.

Breakdown Of Social Media Strategy

- Describe the Strategy to be used.
- Choose all social networks you'd like to participate in now or in the future.
- What networks are most popular among your competition's followers? Write them down.
- List the social networks you believe you can consistently post and engage in. Set up those profiles now.
- Plan the content you'll share. What are your topics of expertise? Write them out here for both curated and created content. This is also where you write down the types of media you can create and the tools available—for example, Video content (iMovie) and Graphics Design (Canva Pro).
- The tone of voice. Write down three words that describe your approach to content creation.
- Block out the times you will monitor, listen, and engage within the platforms' communities—for example, Monday 12 pm-1230pm.
- Social media promotion plan. What is it you want to accomplish with social media? What is the number one reason for using social media right now? What metric will you use to measure that goal? How much of that metric do you want to receive weekly/monthly? Which tools will you use to measure that goal?

- How often will you share daily on the chosen social platforms? Write down each forum and the times you will post next to it.

- Outline your blog-sharing plan. This will be your approach to a single blog post on every social channel. Start with five rows that show when you will share, i.e., on the day of publishing, One day after the publishing date, three days after, a week later, and a month after publishing. For each of your chosen social media platforms, an activity must be on each selected day to help promote that blog post.

- Planning your budget. How much money can you allocate each month to paid social media promotion? Which networks will you experiment with? Write down the amount and social network names.

- Keep track of your boosted posts with Google Sheets. Ensure you track the date running, the channel being used, the budget per day, the target audience, the goal for boosting the post, and the results you're seeing. Update this daily or weekly.

SECTION IV

Blog Monetization

CHAPTER 12

Affiliate Marketing

There are many ways to monetize your blog and turn it into a profit-making machine. One of my favorites is affiliate marketing. That's what this chapter will help you set up if you want to start earning income fast.

What Is Affiliate Marketing?

The best definition I've found is by Pat Flynn from Smart Passive Income. He describes it as earning a commission by promoting other people's or a company's products. You see a product you like, promote it to others, and receive a profit for each sale you make. That serves the purpose of this book perfectly. However, as your blog grows, you should expand that knowledge base further because affiliate marketing can also be you getting affiliates to promote your product. But for now, you don't need to worry about that aspect of affiliate marketing. In this chapter, we focus on you as the affiliate.

How does affiliate marketing work?

Affiliate marketing can get quite technical. Fortunately, you don't need to know the mechanics running in the background. But if you're curious, here's an overview of what occurs behind the scenes.

- You join a chosen merchant program and receive your unique ID with a particular URL to use when promoting the product.
- This link will be used in your blog content and marketing efforts.
- A cookie identifying your affiliate ID is activated on their computer when a potential buyer clicks the link and visits the site. This cookie is vital because it ensures you get credited with the referral sale even if the purchase occurs days or weeks later. Once the purchase occurs, the merchant checks the sales record to identify the source of the referral.
- You are credited with the sale if the merchant finds a cookie with your affiliate ID. You will have access to the reports to see clicks and transactions.
- The merchant pays you the agreed-upon commission at the end of each payment period, i.e., revenue sharing.

The process is pretty straightforward once you get the hang of it, and it works the same regardless of the product you're promoting or how well-established you are as an affiliate marketer.

Before I show you how to set up your affiliate marketing funnel and monetize your blog, let's dispel a few misconceptions people have about blog monetization, especially when doing affiliate marketing.

These Lies Keep You From Monetizing Your Blog

You need a lot of traffic to make money.

Traffic is significant because you have an empty pipeline without it. However, you don't need as much traffic as most gurus claim, mainly if you sell high-ticket products. Traffic is less important than your ability to connect and convert your leads. Think about it. If you have 1000 people visiting your blog each week and would like to increase your income, doesn't it make more sense to focus on increasing the number of people who convert from that 1000 instead of looking for more traffic? That is precisely why I say this belief of getting lots of traffic is keeping bloggers broke. Please don't fall for it.

You have to wait a long time to make money with affiliate marketing.

How often have you heard a blogger say it took years before they started making money on their blog? It's a prevalent story, but more is needed to make it accurate. You can make money with affiliate marketing the same day you publish your blog post. What matters is the strategy you deploy and the quality of your traffic. By following all the steps outlined in this book, you'll avoid the pitfalls that stalled these bloggers who never make money. Knowing your audience, where they hang out online, what they care about, and offering them value around the product you want to affiliate with is a killer strategy. One that I am about to show you.

A Five-Step Process To Becoming An Online Affiliate Marketer

If you're a serious blogger and want to make severe income quickly, this next segment will give you everything needed to start seeing some money. The most important thing to remember is that you can only earn an income or get paid a commission when you give readers valuable insights on products or services they are already interested in buying. So, the more you can align your chosen products with things they are already buying, the easier it will be to get that sale.

Here's a simple outline of how you can start to take your journey as an affiliate marketer, even if your blog is entirely new.

Step One: Choose the product you want to promote as an affiliate.

The best way to choose a product is by doing extensive research. I don't mean reading about them online. You need to access and experiment with the product practically. That implies the best product to affiliate is either something you're already using that you love (assuming you can get their affiliate program) or something you can get easy access to by either buying it yourself or getting a free sample. Regardless of your approach, be prepared to invest time and money into this.

I recommend promoting products you already know and love. Why? Because you're already sold on the products. You have confidence in its use-value, and people can feel you authentically care about what you offer. This doesn't have to be a physical product; it can also be an event or service such as a course, mastermind, or coaching.

Exercise:

Take a self-inventory here. Make a list of all the products you already love and use. Which of these would you be thrilled to promote? Cross out the rest. Now, check online or call the company to find out if they have an affiliate program.

As a newbie blogger, this alone is enough to get you to make some money, but if you want more, explore the other suggestion I shared. Find products via an affiliate network. This approach requires a lot of time to ensure the product you promote is good enough for your brand. Do your due diligence to protect your reputation. The best and most reliable affiliate network sites include CJ Affiliate, Amazon Associates Program, eBay Partner Network, ClickBank, and ShareASale. Among these, Amazon products have become the easiest way to get started. You can start small and then scale to other types of more lucrative affiliate offers.

Step Two: Get set up as an affiliate.

Every affiliate program has a setup process. You must provide your personal and business details for tax and reporting purposes and your bank account where commissions will be sent. In exchange, the merchant will give you a unique affiliate link. This link is trackable; you must use it wherever you intend to promote the product. If it's a well-established company, you might also get marketing assets such as banners, graphics, webpage swipe copy, sample emails, etc. You might also receive a welcome guide with instructions on using their platform and other communications about promotions and new products. You'll get your link for each specific product you promote using a network like Amazon. Most merchants also offer support, educational materials, and even coaching to help you get set up, so be sure to check with your specific network for more information.

Step Three: Create high-quality content reviewing your chosen affiliate products.

The most straightforward products to sell to your readership are those that complement the topic you're blogging about. For example, if you blog about golf, you're better off selling golf-related products than baby-of-sale shoes. I found a great article on new ways to prepare peanut butter and jelly sandwiches from a food blog. The problem is the article was full of useless banners that ranged from online games to creating websites in under an hour.

Does that create trust or mistrust, in your opinion? That lack of congruency between the blog and the affiliate products hurts the owner.

That's why I recommend creating content that reviews the products you have on offer. Listen, slapping banners on your blog that link to affiliate products will not get you paid. It would be best if you did far more. At the very least, work with products that align with a topic you're already covering. If you're serious about making consistent income as an affiliate, here's what I suggest. Create a resource page on your blog to promote different products organized according to different types of readers and what they might need. Explain why those products would be helpful and how you use them to improve your life or business. The focus here is to keep it educational. The other thing you can do aside from writing product reviews is to create definitive content on a related topic. Make sure it's evergreen content that will be valuable for years. The focus here is to build trust and authority rather than to make a sales pitch.

One last tip for content is to create bonuses you can give your readers as an incentive. Make sure your affiliate agreement supports this, though. You won't be like other affiliates or bloggers in your niche. Examples of a bonus could be video demos or complimentary or discounted services such as coaching calls to help the buyer get the most value from their purchase.

Step Four: Start List Building.

I have found this next step to be a key ingredient to long-term success with affiliate marketing. Please invest ample time to learn and implement this step because when done right, you can make money while you sleep. While most affiliate marketing tends to rely on placing links and banners on the actual blog, that is very limiting and expensive because the only way to keep making sales is to drive new traffic to that page. The more traffic you pour in, the higher your chances of a transaction. That takes time and a lot of money. But imagine if you could find a different way of putting your offers in front of an audience you control. Done right, you can sell repeatedly because you have direct access. That's where list building comes into play.

List building, which involves email marketing, is, by far, my favorite method for affiliate marketing. Email is one of the best ways to market and make sales. Let no one tell you differently. Instead of wasting time telling you about it, let me show you three simple ways to start list-building immediately.

Add a call to action on top of your blog so that whenever someone lands on your blog posts, they always see that incentive at the top. Use a tool such as Hello Bar to do this in a few minutes. In the call to action, you can offer something valuable, tell them about a special offer they can't afford to miss, or invite them to a time-sensitive event. Once they click on the bar, you can redirect them to the page where they can enter their email in exchange for the goodies.

Add an exit gate to your content page. This popup will lay over the screen when the visitor is about to leave your website. It's triggered by the mouse action moving to the top area of the browser. With this, you need to be creative, not annoying! So, test different things such as asking for a Facebook messenger connection or like. You can also invite them to your Facebook group if you have a relevant one for your niche topic. You could tell them about a related case and encourage them to binge-read. Lastly, consider giving them a lead magnet related to the subject so they can dive deeper—all these lead to further interactions and acquiring their data, which is our objective.

Make sure you have a sidebar widget on every blog post. Instead of making your blog posts noisy and full of dynamic ads that constantly interrupt the flow when someone is reading, create a static sidebar widget. I only insist that you make it minimalistic. Make sure your sidebar is transparent, as I see with most bloggers. Less is more. If you give your readers 15 things to do, guess what? They won't take any action. I suggest picking one call to action in your sidebar. You can change it regularly to promote different things, but there should only be one offer at any given point. Whatever you offer should be valuable and relevant and require an email address exchange, at the very least.

Here's what I love about email marketing. Contrary to what you hear, most marketers say, you don't need a huge list to make sales and earn a good income. I have made 10K in sales with an email list of 500 subscribers. How? My list was hyper-targeted, and I built a strong relationship with them. I kept my audience engaged, provided much value each week, and built them up to know, love, and trust me and my ideas over time. When I presented the offer, it was a no-brainer. So again, remember, it's sometimes about the list size. Instead, it's about the relationship you have with your list.

Step Five: Comply with legal requirements and best practices.

In the U.S., the FTC requires every affiliate marketer to openly declare to the people that they are earning a commission. If you're outside America, check to see the laws and regulations. At a minimum, I encourage you to have a disclaimer and let your people know you earn commissions if they buy through you. That kind of transparency helps reinforce trust.

Many bloggers get slightly worried about being this open about their commissions because they wonder if people will be put off. The truth is that someone should know that you are getting paid to promote so they can decide whether or not to support your efforts. And again, it's a matter of adding value to them and genuinely demonstrating that you love what you're suggesting.

Chapter 13

Selling Your Products

Aside from using your blog to sell other people's products for a commission, you can also monetize your blog with your products. This chapter will cover how to start selling your products and some things you should know before going down this route.

Where most bloggers start when it comes to monetization

Most bloggers generate income from advertising networks such as AdSense or opt for affiliate revenue sharing with programs like Amazon. These options are plentiful and will produce a steady income if done right. But having read this far into the book, I want to give you something that will take things to a new level. What am I talking about? Creating and marketing your product.

The Two Types Of Products You Can Create And Sell

There are two main categories here for creating and selling a product. It can be a physical product or a digital product. Please note that I'm not including services in this chapter because that would require a different strategy since you'd have to trade in time to deliver the service. Since I want to help your blog generate high income without your direct investment of time proving a service, we will only focus on physical and digital products you can create and sell independently. As you gear up, you'll want to read this chapter several times in the coming months.

What are the best physical and digital products to create and sell as a beginner? Many bloggers often want a straight answer when choosing a physical or digital product to sell online. Which one works best? The simple answer is both. You can quickly grow a six-figure business that runs on autopilot, selling a physical or a digital product. Instead of telling you what to sell, let me share some pros and cons for each so you can decide for yourself.

Physical products

Physical products are what most people are accustomed to, so selling them or demonstrating value is relatively straightforward. Examples of physical products include books, clothes, toys, household equipment, art, baseball cards, etc. A significant benefit of selling physical products is that you can clearly explain their purpose, and most people perceive physical effects to be of higher value because they are tangible. The transaction aspect is also very straightforward, and once you map out your buyer's journey, you'll know precisely how many follow-ups are needed to get you the sale.

Of course, with physical products comes the additional work of handling shipping, delivery, and packaging costs. That is one of the main disadvantages of physical products. There's also the question of storage, inventory, and staff to manage and track the products. The good news is that with the introduction of drop shipping, which is booming in the e-commerce world, you may have an easier time organizing this aspect. To learn more about this, check out Shopify's blog and learn how they simplify this process.

Physical products will be more complex to scale and time-consuming because you must consider much more than just getting people to the checkout page. So, if you want to get started immediately and with the least stress, feel the second category of products.

Digital products

A digital product is something that your buyer can get instant access to as soon as they complete the online purchase. Examples include eBooks, online courses, software, etc. This is the holy grail of passive income once you set things up correctly. It will give you much freedom because you can sell from anywhere to anywhere, and automating this process is relatively simple. The profit margins you get with digital products are also insane. Consider the story I shared at this beginning, where a simple eBook results in thousands of dollars.

What's great about digital products is that they carry the least risk because you don't need to worry about storage costs or inventory. There's also no time lag between purchase completion and delivery. I also like that you can scale this faster than physical products without needed overhead costs.

The considerable downside I've experienced with a digital product is that it takes more work to demonstrate value. Hence, it would be best if you did much more planning, explaining, and convincing to get people into that point of purchase. Most people still don't view digital products as "real" because they are intangible. As a result, they often have a lower perceived value.

Getting a high-quality digital product ready is serious work. Unlike affiliate marketing, creating digital or physical products requires much planning, testing, and iteration. So don't expect to profit from your development as quickly as an affiliate product because you need time to develop and perfect it. Both categories will earn a healthy income, especially if you create high-quality products and sell them well. The best part is you don't have to trade your time for money, and as the product owner, you get to keep 100% of the profits. That is why selling your product is a lucrative way of building a profitable business.

Profitable products you can sell online

- Hard copy and paperback books.
- Printable coloring book pages.
- Comics.
- •Printable journals.
- Printable calendars.
- •eBooks.
- Recipes.
- Cookbooks.
- Magazines.

- Travel guides.
- Songs.
- Sound effects.
- Ringtones.
- Instrumental tracks.
- Stock video.
- Video tutorials (DIY at home).
- Wallpapers.
- Posters.
- Stock photos.
- Apps.
- Browser plugins.
- Games.
- Courses of all kinds.
- Meal-prep plans.
- Nutritional plans.
- Workout plans.
- Sewing patterns.
- Board game printouts.
- Worksheets.
- Study guides for all educational levels.
- Essays.
- Contracts and policies.
- Templates.
- Illustrations.
- Graphics design.

How To Create And Sell Your First Product

If you know what kind of products you want to sell, you already know whether you're going the digital or physical route. Consider your niche marketing and what your readership and audience are more likely to purchase. For example, if your audience demographics are people who enjoy something tangible because you're blogging about your favorite football team, you may want to create a physical product. The next thing is to consider your risk tolerance. Can you handle dealing with inventory, delivery, etc.? Are you willing to buy your list upfront, or do you prefer to wait to invest until a customer makes a purchase? How automated do you want this business to be? Bloggers who sell digital products can fully automate the entire sales process and never even need to make live contact with the customer. But if you have to package, ship, and deliver an item, you must be more hands-on in case of returns, replacements, etc. While I encourage you to start with one, understand that you can always sell physical and digital products on your blog.

The creation process of your product will depend on the type of product you wish to create. Ultimately, whether it's a physical or digital product, you can build it or get someone else to create it. For example, you can make a homemade beauty soap, sew together that bowtie collection, or write that cookbook yourself. Alternatively, you can outsource the beauty soap from a company, order handmade bowties from a manufacturing company in China, or hire an expert ghostwriter to help you write, edit, proofread, and design the cookbook.

Since you're in the early stages of building your blogging business, I will assume you need more funds to invest in outside help. So, gather your knowledge, experience, and resources and DIY this first product. Once you make a few sales, get feedback, and iterate it, you can always hire an expert to improve it. If it's a digital product, you can use the following platforms to create it:

- Blurb and Aerio both help you create eBooks to sell online.
- The creative market is excellent for getting eBooks and other digital asset templates.
- Thinkific and Teachable are great for creating online courses.
- Kajabi is an all-in-one platform that can help you create and deliver almost any digital asset and online course.

How To Sell On Your Blog

Understand that you can create a fully customizable e-commerce store to sell your products and integrate them with your blog. Check out sites such as Shopify, Amazon, and Etsy to see what I mean. These platforms allow you to set up shop so that all you have to do is drive people from your blog to your online store. This is the fastest and most streamlined way to sell your products.

You'll need a way to create your store to distribute the products and handle the payments. Gumroad, SendOwl, and Easy Digital Downloads are the top recommended distribution platforms. You can check out their links on the resource page at the end of this book. These three work best when you are running a WordPress blog.

A personal recommendation when selling your products on your blog is to use Easy Digital Downloads. It's how I sell my digital products; as mentioned above, it's one of the top recommended solutions. Easy Digital Download operates exclusively with WordPress, so all its features and functionalities are optimized for WordPress users. This is a premium product, so you'll have to be ready to pay the price, but I assure you it more than pays back that investment.

The bottom line is when it comes to choosing a product category, creating, distributing, and selling it, you need to get creative. Think about the resources available to you, the most favorable platforms, and your niche market values. Combine that with your objectives, meaning, are you creating this blog to become a six-figure business that enables you to travel all over the world while generating passive income? Then, starting with a digital product that's valuable to your audience and can be fully automated is the best step. Please consider all the advantages and disadvantages, and remember, the sky is the limit when selling online.

CHAPTER 14

Online Advertising to Market Your Blog And Sell On Overdrive

I decided to add this final chapter to this book because online advertising is one of the fastest and best ways for a blogger to scale a business. Only some bloggers do it right, so I want to ensure you have the tools and strategy to make the most of it. First, you must set aside a monthly budget for online advertising. Everything we've talked about to help drive organic and social media traffic is still valid. However, if you want to see more significant results faster, this is the secret fuel to ignite that fire. Online advertising is fuel for your blog. It will enable you to reach your ideal audience sooner rather than later. That, in turn, leads to a growing audience and more prospects for your products. Even if you only affiliate products on your blog, I encourage you to run some paid ads campaigns. Here are a few tactics to experiment with.

#1. Amplify your blog posts with some Google Ads and Bing Ads.

If you have an ample budget, consider creating Google Ads or Bing Ads so your blog post can appear at the top of the page. This involves A learning curve, so I recommend taking the company's Google Ads training to familiarize yourself with the platform. And if you're starting this blog on a shoestring and can only afford to spend under five dollars a day for this, fret not; the following solution will work just as well.

#2. Use Facebook ads to boost your posts.

Facebook provides a tremendous opportunity for a blogger to promote content directly to their ideal audience. They have a vast audience network and Instagram; you can start with as little as $1. Consider creating short video versions of your blog post and running those on Instagram Stories and Facebook stories. Then, have a call to action that drives people to your main blog. If you're new to the Facebook advertising world, I encourage you to take their Facebook Blueprint Course for free.

#3. Promote your blog posts with recommended content advertising platforms.

Sites such as Taboola, Zemanta, and Outbrain allow you to promote your blog post for a small fee. They then suggest your content to their readers, which can give you great exposure if you are sure your readership is under their radar.

#4. Influencer marketing to amplify your post.

I have yet to see many people talk about this, but I've been testing it, and it works. The gist is that you build a relationship with a social media influencer who has the audience you want to read. Then, you trade a little exposure for some cash, which is entirely negotiable. Some of them might even give you exposure if you give them free products. There's no rigid rule here. I recommend working with someone who has a healthy email list so that they can promote your blog post on both their social media feed and their email list to ensure you get as much exposure as possible. When done right, you can start growing your readership pretty quickly, and if you choose the right social media influencer, it can be more effective than regular paid ads.

Remember, this method can be expensive if you need to know what you're doing. The best way to avoid messing it up is to find the cheapest form of paid traffic available and where you believe your audience hangs out. Given how big Facebook is, you can start with Facebook ads. When you start paying for traffic to your site, ensure you're collecting emails on that blog page and that your content is actionable so that people can remember you and subscribe.

Conclusion

You have now discovered how to start a blog from scratch, grow it, market it, and turn it into an income-producing machine that helps you achieve financial freedom. All through blogging about what you're passionate about. Finally, you don't have to toil away at a job you hate with a boss you can't stand. Instead, you get to design and live life on your terms.

In this book, I've outlined the foundation for choosing a blog that will be in demand for years. You also have all the tools, resources, and strategies needed to take it from an average blog to a six-figure business.

Each section of this book walks you through the different aspects that you will need to make your blog successful. You are ready to create high-value content that attracts, engages, and converts your audience into buying customers. Whether you opt for affiliate marketing first or create your product, I am confident you will generate income with your blog relatively quickly.

In this era, where information and the digital economy are booming, you can start a simple blog and make millions. Stay aware of all the shiny objects online marketers like to show off. Stay focused on what you're doing, read this book, and follow each step as outlined. Before long, you will be building your passion-based business, making a difference in the world, and enjoying financial freedom. Congratulations on taking the first step toward your new lifestyle. Now, start building wealth and creating your passive income through blogging.

Thank You

You could have picked from hundreds of other books, but you bought mine, and I appreciate it. Thank you so much for purchasing my book.

Not that you enjoyed (I hope) my book, can I ask you for a tiny favor? Can you please post a review on the platform? Posting a review is the best way to support the work of independent authors like me.

Your feedback will help me keep writing the books that will help you get the desired results. It means a lot to me to hear from you.

I am happy for anyone to reach out to me for help, comments, collaboration ideas, or feedback at

brian@brianscottfitzgerald.com

Visit my author page with this link or Scan this QR code

https://www.amazon.com/author/brianscottfitzgerald.

Printed in Great Britain
by Amazon